This is the first scholarly biography in English of one of France's foremost political leaders of the late nineteenth and early twentieth centuries.

In a career which ran from the 1880s to the 1930s, one of the most formative periods of modern French history, Poincaré held the principal offices of state. He played crucial roles in France's entry into the First World War, the organisation of the war effort, the peace settlement, the reparations question, the occupation of the Ruhr and the reorganisation of French finances in the 1920s. His life and work is surrounded by controversy and myth, from 'Poincaré-la-guerre' to 'Poincaré-le-franc', which this book dissects. Using a host of new archival material ranging from ministry of finance sources to private diaries, Professor Keiger explores the historiography of the president.

Raymond Poincaré is a subtle and fascinating portrait of one of the Third Republic's most prominent, yet most elusive, leaders – a politician who, somewhat surprisingly, held animal rights and feminism to be as important as party politics and public finance.

Raymond Poincaré

Raymond Poincaré

J. F. V. Keiger

University of Salford

Published by the Press Syndicate of the University of Cambridge
The Pitt Building, Trumpington Street, Cambridge CB2 1RP
40 West 20th Street, New York, NY 10011–4211, USA
10 Stamford Road, Oakleigh, Melbourne 3166, Australia

First published 1997

Printed in Great Britain at the University Press, Cambridge

A catalogue record for this book is available from the British Library

Library of Congress cataloguing in publication data
Keiger, John F. V.
Raymond Poincaré / J. F. V. Keiger.
    p.   cm.
Includes bibliographical references.
ISBN 0 521 57387 4 (hardcover)
1. Poincaré, Raymond, 1860–1934.
2. Presidents – France – Biography.
3. France – Politics and government – 1870–1940.
I. Title.
DC385.K45   1997   944.081'092 – dc20   [B]   96–26316   CIP

ISBN 0 521 57387 4 hardback

CE

For Victoria, Emma, Laura and Edward

Contents

Acknowledgements

I am glad to acknowledge the kindness, advice, help and encouragement of many friends and colleagues during the researching and writing of this book. After working for so long on a biography, one develops an unfortunate tendency to identify many people with characteristics of the subject of the study. Suffice it to say here that most people who knew him closely acknowledged that, for all his faults, Raymond Poincaré was erudite and kind. Dr Robert Tombs made most valuable, and amusing, comments on several versions of the typescript, particularly where Poincaré was at his most priggish or sentimental. Professor Angus Easson, who shares a love of cats with the subject of this book, was very kind and helpful in providing information and insights into the feline world. Professors Peter Morris and Roy Bridge rescued the text from numerous solecisms and suggested useful amendments. Professor Christopher Andrew gave help and encouragement, as he has done for many years. Stella Walker, Elaine Murphy and Heather Lally have been patient and helpful with numerous word-processing problems demanding instant solutions.

I am grateful to The British Academy, the Leverhulme Trust and Salford University's Christopher Hale Memorial Fund and European Studies Research Institute for generous financial assistance. Grateful acknowledgement is also made to the following archives for permission to quote material: Archives Nationales, Bibliothèque Nationale, Bibliothèque de l'Institut de France, the Ministère des Affaires Etrangères, the Public Record Office London, and finally the Bibliothèque de l'Ordre des Avocats, Paris where Monsieur Ozanam offered unfailing assistance.

This is a pleasant opportunity to renew an overwhelming debt of gratitude to my parents for their unstinting support. Finally, four people have come to live as closely with Raymond as myself: Victoria, Emma, Laura and recently Edward, all of whom I thank for their support and forbearance and to whom I dedicate this book. Its shortcomings and imperfections are mine alone.

Introduction

Raymond Poincaré is the only political figure to have exercised as decisive an influence on the first half of the Third Republic as the second. In a political career which ran from 1887 to 1929 he held most of the major offices of state both before and after the First World War. He played crucial roles in France's entry into the war, the organisation of the war effort, the peace settlement, the reparations question, the occupation of the Ruhr and the reorganisation of French finances in the 1920s. Yet as the novelist and essayist Emmanuel Berl wrote in his obituary in October 1934, 'France never experienced for Poincaré either the flights of love it felt for Gambetta, for Jaurès, or the flights of admiration it felt for Clemenceau'.[1] To this day he remains a controversial figure. As 'Poincaré-la-guerre' and 'Poincaré-le-franc' he has provoked opprobrium and praise. His role in the outbreak of the First World War and the sealing of 'union sacrée' has cast him alternately as warmonger and saviour; his management of the occupation of the Ruhr in 1923 has been depicted as either a courageous effort to ensure German execution of the Versailles Treaty or as evidence of visceral Germanophobia; his role in bringing order to French finances in the 1920s has led him to be portrayed as an austere deflationist or as one of France's twentieth-century financial wizards. His identification with a certain number of values which posterity has tended to view as unfashionable – order, dignity, politeness, honesty, thrift – and his association with the middle class, which claimed to incarnate those values and which historiography has not found exciting or treated kindly, has left Raymond Poincaré if not one of the unsung heroes of French history, then one whose political stature has not received the recognition it deserves.

This lack of recognition is reflected in the small number of modern studies on Poincaré either in English or French. This is partly to do with the decline of political history in France from the 1930s until the 1970s and the academic profession's desire to eschew the study of politically unfashionable subjects, especially those associated with the Right, in order to concentrate on worthier issues such as social history, the Left or the labour movement. It is also partly to do with the domination of the Annales school of history since the 1930s and of its perception of biography as an unscientific historical form for the emphasis it puts on the action of the individual as opposed to more profound historical forces.[2]

There is no full-length biography of Poincaré in English and only two in French, the first published by Jacques Chastenet in 1948, and the second by Pierre Miquel in 1961.[3] Despite their merits, neither provides the full apparatus of scholarship, nor did their authors have access to Poincaré's private papers which since the 1970s have come into the public domain. Indeed, Miquel began his preface with the unfortunate statement that Poincaré destroyed all his private papers used to write his memoirs and that most other papers would be closed to the public until 1990. More surprising still, following the presidency of Valéry Giscard d'Estaing and the premiership of Raymond Barre, when there had been public interest in the antecedents of their liberal economic policies (and hence in Poincaré), Miquel's biography was reprinted in 1984 with the same erroneous statements about Poincaré's private papers.[4] The value of those papers in reassessing Poincaré's place in French history is of particular importance.

In its obituary of Poincaré in 1934, the Viennese *Reichspost* remarked that to retrace his political career with its consequences, its honours, its triumphs, was to write the history of France over the previous forty years and that of Europe over the previous twenty.[5] Any biography must attempt to silhouette the man against the background of his times. Failure to do so condemns one to become what the eminent French historians Jacques Le Goff and Pierre Nora referred to unforgivingly as 'those low-level vulgarisers, those anecdote hacks'.[6] Setting Poincaré's life in its times could involve charting his position in relation to all but six years of the Third Republic's existence – a monumental task. By way of economy, this study will look at the whole of Poincaré's life, but through the prism of the myths associated with his name from 'Poincaré-la-guerre' to 'Poincaré-le-franc'. Not surprisingly, such an account cannot help raising the question of how a particular perception of a politician develops. Poincaré, in particular, seems to have been at the receiving end of both a Whiggish interpretation of his destiny to greatness and an a posteriori rewriting of his earlier actions in the light of later ones motivated by political considerations. In attempting to demystify him, like John Buchan's preface to his biography of Oliver Cromwell, 'I hope I may claim that at any rate I have not attempted to constrain a great man in a formula'.[7]

1   The private man

Poincaré is a statesman whose geographical family origins in Lorraine have been both a help and a hindrance. All of the character traits evoked when a crude geographical determinism is applied to that region have been attributed to Poincaré-le-Lorrain. For admirers, robust Lorraine characteristics of order, steadfastness and resolve destined him for high office; for critics, a native coldness instilled by the harsh climate of the eastern marches rendered him calculating and heartless. Even the uneffusive Waldeck-Rousseau was said to have remarked of him, 'He has a stone for a heart'.[1] More specifically, admirers have seen in his Lorraine origins a guarantee of patriotism following the German annexation of most of Alsace and Lorraine in 1871, when he was ten years old. For his enemies, in France and abroad, the amputation of much of his homeland ingrained in him a rabid anti-Germanism, a ceaseless longing for 'revanche', an intemperate desire to restore the 'lost provinces' to France by any means, even war. Similarly his solidly middle-class background has cast him either as a symbol of the middle-class principles which established the greatness of at least the first half of the Third Republic or, as his critics would have it, the narrow-minded, priggish defender of privilege and the status quo. Myth and counter-myth have drawn on his origins for fuel, mining deeply differing preconceived perceptions of the man, when in reality those formative years were less clearly traced and far more ambiguous.

Family life

Raymond Nicolas Landry Poincaré was born at Bar-le-Duc in western Lorraine on 20 August 1860. As with all but the most incompetent politicians, myth would have it that from birth he was predestined to politics: that day the bells were ringing for a legislative election and the obstetrician was said to have exclaimed: 'Here is a future *député*!'[2] Mild controversy and not a little family conceit surrounded the etymology of the name 'Poincaré'. This centred on whether the first syllable derived

3

from the words 'pont' (bridge), 'point' (point) or 'poing' (fist). Raymond preferred the latter derivation for its obvious robust connotations. He was much pleased to see this confirmed following his election to the presidency in 1913 by a member of the French Institute. Antoine Thomas showed that the name Poincaré could be traced back to the early fifteenth century and a student at the University of Paris whose Latin name was Petrus Pogniquadrati. In 1418 the secretary to Queen Isabelle of Bavaria and the Duke of Burgundy had been called Jehen Poingquerré. He was further flattered to discover a reference to a medieval verse-chronicle which described the heroic Duke Thibaud as having, 'Les bras ot lons et les poings bien quarrez'. In the context of his elevation to the Elysée, the relevance of this information did not escape him, as his secret diary shows: 'Ingenious etymology, which merely proves how much the country needs *poings carrés*.'[3] As if to emphasise this connection, he was said to favour the spelling of his name with two r's, even though his family used only one. Following his election to parliament in 1887, for over two months the *Journal Officiel* recorded him as Poincarré, though why that ceased is unclear.[4]

The Poincaré family had been established in Lorraine since at least the end of the seventeenth century. The paternal side, characterised by the forename 'Nicolas', was of lowly bourgeois status until the beginning of the nineteenth century. From then onwards medicine, science and public service prevailed. Raymond's grandfather, Jacques Nicolas, set up a pharmacy in Nancy in 1817. He had two sons: Léon (father of the famous mathematician and professor at the Collège de France, Henri Poincaré) became professor and dean of the faculty of medicine at the University of Nancy; Antoine, known as Antoni, Raymond's father, was born on 13 February 1825 in Nancy and went on to study at the Ecole Polytechnique and the Ecole des Ponts et Chaussées, from where he graduated as a civil engineer. State-employed, Antoni was first posted to the Sarthe and then to the Mayenne in the north-west of France, but finally returned to his native province as chief engineer in Bar-le-Duc until 1880, when promotion moved the family to Paris. He was a republican, a *laïque* and president of the Société des Lettres, Sciences et Arts of Bar-le-Duc, which he founded in 1870 and ran with his wife's great-uncle the Legitimist, Paulin Gillon. He died on 21 June 1911. Raymond's younger brother, Lucien, would attend the prestigious Ecole Normale Supérieure and eventually become director of secondary education at the ministry of public instruction and vice-rector of the University of Paris.[5] In short, the Poincaré family typifies the ascension of the French middle class since the Revolution, benefiting from 'careers open to talent' in public service, steeped in Science and Reason rather than religious obscurantism, believing in the values of the Revolution which had ensured its elevation and bonded to the Republic which sought to perpetuate those values.

Raymond Poincaré's maternal Lorraine ancestors were singularly different. The Gillons were from the upper bourgeoisie and would distinguish themselves as politicians and judges. Jean Nicolas was a *député* killed by the Prussians during the Revolutionary Wars; his brother Jacques was *député* for the Marne during Napoleon's Hundred Days. The former produced a son, a farmer, mayor of Nubécourt village and member of the conseil d'arrondissement for twenty-five years, who distinguished himself for having returned to local *émigré* gentry the lands he had bought at the time of the Revolution. He had five children of whom two sons, Raymond Poincaré's great-grandfather and great-granduncle respectively: Jean Landry (1788-1856) and Paulin (1796-1878).[6]

Jean Landry, barrister then *procureur général* in Amiens, was made *avocat général* at the Cour de cassation in 1839 and then *conseiller* at the same court in 1840 until his death in 1856. At the same time he held public office as president of the *conseil général* of the Meuse (like his great-grandson seventy years later), was re-elected *député* for Bar-le-Duc for the duration of the July Monarchy, under which he was a member of the governmental majority.[7]

His younger brother, Paulin, was also a barrister with initially the same liberal Orleanist views. In 1830 he was made secretary general of the Prefecture of the Meuse, member of the *conseil général* and *bâtonnier de l'ordre des avocats* of Bar-le-Duc. Mayor of Bar-le-Duc from 1840, at the time of the 1848 Revolution he was elected *député* for the Meuse and re-elected in 1849. Then began his drift to the right. He voted to elect Louis-Napoleon as president of the Second Republic. Though he refused to support the *coup d'état* in December 1851, his opposition could not have been strong for he was included on the list of *députés* able to continue exercising their mandate. He returned to the Bar. Increasingly fervent in his Catholic faith, he came to believe that it would only be through a return to a legitimate monarchy that France would find stability. The events of 1871 reinforced this. He was elected Legitimist *député* for the Meuse in the Assemblée Nationale in 1871, voted consistently with the conservative majority and voted against the constitutional laws of 1875 which established the Third Republic and by virtue of which his great-grand-nephew would be elected president of the Republic. Defeated in the 1876 legislative elections, he died when Raymond Poincaré was eighteen.[8]

Raymond's grandmother, Nanine-Marie Gillon, daughter of Jean

Landry Gillon, was a fervent monarchist, who even under the Second Empire kept a diary about the exiled Orleanist family.[9] She married a successful wood-merchant by the name of Ficatier and their daughter, Raymond's mother, was born in 1838. It was Raymond Poincaré's request that on his death he be buried in the maternal family plot at Nubécourt, thirty-four kilometres from Bar-le-Duc, alongside his maternal ancestors and father. The Gillons then were characterised by monarchism, Catholicism, the law and politics.

Raymond Poincaré was born of two distinct family traditions. Seemingly the only point in common was that both families had suffered losses during the Revolutionary wars fighting Prussians. Since their marriage, Antoni Poincaré and Nanine Ficatier-Gillon, thirteen years his junior, had moved into the maternal grandparents' spacious town house at 35 rue des Tanneurs (now rue Dr Nève) in the centre of Bar-le-Duc. The Poincaré family, consisting of Raymond, his brother Lucien – two years his junior – his parents and their two maids, lived on the ground floor, the Ficatiers above.

There was little that was remarkable in what seems to have been a happy early childhood. What is noticeable is that, notwithstanding the family unity, a cheerful co-existence of differing political and religious outlooks existed within the extended family. Here may lie the clue to an understanding of the adult Raymond's behaviour. It is a commonplace that an unhappy childhood can be the root of certain personality traits later in life. A happy childhood is more often than not ignored. With Raymond Poincaré those idyllic years might explain the ambivalence and tolerance which characterised his later life; an ambivalence which mirrored the differing beliefs which characterised the maternal and paternal sides of his family. His Christian names, Nicolas from his father's scientific ancestors, Landry from his mother's legal and political side, almost symbolised the divided loyalties he felt to his parents. It is tempting to see in the debt of gratitude he believed he owed them, that he should try and repay it by making them happy through success in his own life and, perhaps more subconsciously, by adopting some of the characteristics, behaviour and beliefs of his parents, however contradictory.

Within the extended family on his mother's side were other conservative and Catholic figures such as the Bompards, the Plauschs and the Dreschs, with whom the Poincarés regularly socialised. His maternal grandparents with whom he spent so much of his youth were thus Orleanist and, his grandmother at least, a devout practising Catholic. She lived surrounded by cats and dogs, as would Raymond. Throughout his life he maintained a deep affection for her. His mother, who was particularly close to her parents, was described by Raymond as 'a very tolerant believer'. His father, on the other hand, was a 'very liberal free-thinker' and a Republican. Raymond was very close to his mother and spent most of his time with her. He described her as 'very beautiful yet simplicity itself, the most natural and amusing mind, the most dependable heart ... a most caring and devoted wife ... an incomparable mother'. She loved animals but confided to the young Raymond that she could never keep any for fear of seeing them die. His father, he noted, was 'a character of an unbending honesty', an animal-lover and tamer of wild birds: 'I could also compare him to a bird, to an owl, that wise bird which only shows itself at night'.[10] Here were the first signs of ambiguity which characterised the adult Raymond. His infamous rigid, cold exterior came from the father; his shy, tender, caring side – rarely displayed – was a maternal trait. Poincaré was very conscious of what he referred to as the 'profound difference in outlook' between his parents:

My father was an ardent *laïque*; he never set foot in Church. But very tolerant, he allowed my mother to go whenever she wished and there was no service she did not attend. My father's beliefs extended to his whole family, to his brother Léon, doctor of medicine and professor at Nancy University [father of Henri Poincaré]. My mother's feelings were shared by all her relations, the Bompards, the Plauschs, the Dreschs, so that in Bar-le-Duc, where they all lived or stayed, they made up a conservative, closed society, whose doors were not open to everyone.[11]

His mother was responsible for initiating him into the Catholic faith, for taking him and his brother to church every Sunday. He was certainly devout by the age of ten. His childhood diaries, already written in that tight, regular, but virtually undecipherable handwriting that was a lifelong trait,[12] reveal the importance of religion in his younger years. Rising at quarter to seven every morning he began with his prayers, occasionally attending morning mass or vespers and finishing with his bedtime prayers at eight o'clock. 1871 was the year of his first communion and he spent days revising the catechism. When on 16 July that day arrived he was awake well before 6 a.m. with excitement: 'I was to take Communion, – what a wonderful day – !!! On what other day could one be happier! What a memorable day!!!'[13] His mother probably also organised his schooling at age four with a very devout old lady by the name of Mlle Maré who taught him to read and write. From there he went on to a local independent school where he was in Father Forget's class before going to the *lycée* in Bar-le-Duc at nine years old.

A strict religious upbringing might, on the face of things, appear to conflict with his future public image as Poincaré-le-*laïque*. Yet having an indifferent father in religious matters and a pious mother was not uncommon under the early Third Republic, and often led to a certain anticlericalism in the politician.[14] But despite the cooling of his religious convictions from his student days and his conversion to *laïcité*, Poincaré was not anticlerical. He was too tolerant for that. As will be seen, his *laïcité* was that of the positivists, like Jules Ferry, who recognised that Catholicism was the religion of a majority of the French and therefore deserved respect, while believing that clerical influence over civil society should be progressively reduced. This explains an apparent ambivalence towards religion. It certainly throws light on Poincaré's future stance on the separation of church and state and the treatment of religious congregations which was far more tolerant than myth would have it. Indeed when first chosen as a parliamentary candidate it was reported that in his first ever political speech on 17 July 1887 his only clear statement of policy was that he was against the separation of church and state.[15] This positivist approach to *laïcité* calculated that separation would only be 'opportune' once the hearts and minds of the majority of the French were ready for it. Like Jules Ferry, he may have undergone the separation in his own heart, but he did not believe that it should be imposed on others, especially his own family. His ambivalence to *laïcité* was demonstrated in the tribute he paid to his mother on 5 May 1913, following her death on 11 April. In a service performed by Mgr Baudrillart, his old school-friend from Louis-le-Grand, Poincaré and his wife, already married in civil law since 1904, were married in a secret religious ceremony in his mother's Paris flat at 10 rue Babylone. He claimed this to have been 'the best deed of my life'.[16] This was not without considerable political risk for a proclaimed *laïque* president of the Republic. But his motives were clear as he later told Mgr Baudrillart: 'It is out of respect for the memory of my mother. It is also out of consideration for my family and my wife's family: all our relations are Catholic and many are very religious.' And he added, surprisingly for someone ostensibly committed to *laïcité*: 'But there is another reason: the head of a Catholic state owes this example to his country.'[17] Was this remarkable last statement the tip of an underlying faith or, in the manner of Henri IV, a personal sacrifice in the interests of national unity? After all, despite the *laïcité* of the Republicans a large majority of the French were still practising Catholics and Jules Ferry's civil marriage in 1875 had at the time caused a sensation. In the last days of his life, ill, and possibly encouraged by his devout wife, Poincaré may have been torn from his agnosticism; though it is more likely that he agreed to a religious side to his funeral out of consideration for his wife. His funeral service was characterised by parallel civil and religious ceremonies maintaining the ambivalence of his *laïcité* to the end. On his death, mass was celebrated in Notre Dame, and the bishop of Verdun blessed the coffin and read the final prayers in Nubecourt cemetery.[18]

If the tolerance in his attitude to religion could be said to have evolved naturally from the opposing influences in his family life, so too could his political outlook. Poincaré's republicanism, like that of many of his generation, was of the moderate variety developed by Gambetta and Ferry and best summarised in the maxim, 'neither revolution nor reaction'. He was a parliamentary liberal. Of this too there was a foretaste in his family. The close relationship with his Orleanist maternal grandparents, and the example of the parliamentary liberalism of the Gillons, may explain this atavistic trait. But though an admirer of the English constitutional monarchy, he was not a monarchist, accepting the republican constitutional framework, as did the paternal side of his family, the Poincarés. It is no surprise that the foremost expert of the French Right, René Rémond, should place Poincaré in the Orleanist centre-right tradition of the three rights: 'the political expression of bourgeois France born of the Revolution; beyond the founders of the Opportunist Republic, it is linked to the militant Orleanism of 1830, as vigilant about protecting itself from the right as from the left'.[19]

Nowhere was Poincaré's dedication and commitment to his parents more clearly in evidence than in his secret diaries. On 20 August 1919 on his fifty-ninth birthday in one of his melancholic moods, he mourned the absence of his parents, his father having died in 1911 and his mother in 1913: 'Ah! my dear parents! They loved me so much and they were so good to me.' His thoughts on his parents revealed how long after their death they continued to have a prominent place in his thoughts.

When my father died he wanted to be buried next to my mother in our family cemetery at Nubécourt. They were sleeping there when the Germans came in with a few of their own dead whom they laid out next to ours. I dreamed, that day, that my father said to me: 'Do not get annoyed, leave them alone. Unfortunately they will not wake us.'[20]

The former political director of the French foreign ministry, Jules Laroche, explained how in September 1923, at a meeting with the normally impassive Poincaré, he had apologised for having to attend his father-in-law's funeral the next morning: 'I saw his face darken, and he said to me in an emotional voice: "What, Mme Laroche has lost her father? That is a horrible thing. I have never come to terms with the loss of mine. Please convey all my sympathy to her." '[21] Strongly influenced then by a profound love for his parents, Raymond Poincaré's own life could be divided into two halves – one devoted to the Ficatier-Gillons, the other to the Poincarés.

Legend, again, has pointed to Raymond Poincaré's school-days as particularly studious and brilliant. In the knowledge that in later life Poincaré would rise to the top in everything that he did, it is often believed that as a schoolchild he came top in everything. He was only nine when he entered the *lycée* at Bar-le-Duc. As a member of the privileged middle class, secondary education was a natural progression. Fewer than 5 per cent of children of secondary school age (10-19) were in secondary education at that time, with no girls until 1881.[22] Though hardworking, he was no prig and was often admonished for chatting and teasing other pupils. Neither was he always top in everything. His school reports show his capacity for hard work, but that was not always to his benefit, as his Latin master remarked: 'Perhaps he has worked too hard in the course of the year: now one can sense the tiredness in all his work'. In mathematics he was described as an excellent pupil 'but does not know how to make the best of himself, needs practice at the front of the class' (a besoin de s'habituer au tableau). That year, Raymond Poincaré came third out of eighteen.[23] A clever but playful child, even at the age of ten he felt the urge to push himself further. On 26 September 1871, after mass he appealed to God, 'Let him light up my intelligence and shine on me. Let me do well in class. That is all I ask of him.'[24] As a child he enjoyed listening to adult conversations. He also took particular pleasure in impressing his young friends by doing complicated multiplication and division exercises which his father taught him.[25] His early tendency for displaying intellectual superiority remained an unendearing characteristic into later life. Jules Laroche noted that in rare moments of relaxation he would talk about art and literature 'with that omniscience which evoked admiration, and sometimes a little irritation'.[26] It went hand in hand with a fear of being underestimated. This made him touchy and sharp-tongued and led him into many a school fight.[27]

Home-life in Bar-le-Duc was typically middle class, characterised by calm, order and regularity. Summer holidays were spent in his mother's nearby village of Nubécourt, where the various branches of the extended family would come together, and occasionally at his maternal grand-father's hunting lodge at Courcelles aux Bois. This fostered a deep love of country walks. But despite his grandfather's passion for hunting wild boar and even wolves, Raymond would maintain a strong distaste for blood sports. He would retain from his childhood a great love of animals. As a child he had a little white dog called Pompon, several budgerigars and some squirrels.[28] Later, when married, he and his wife Henriette would keep a cat, Gris-gris ('lucky charm'), on which Poincaré would lavish the deepest affection, not having any children of his own. In the last days of March 1929 he was heartbroken at the sixteen-year-old Gris gris's death. Since its birth it had shared his domestic life with his wife Henriette and they had treated it like a child. His moving account in his diaries of the half paralysed Gris-gris's last hours laid bare a side of Poincaré that virtually no one saw: 'I carried him to the bed and he stretched out, with his child-like movement, on Henriette's chest, as he had done so often.' The cat's death was a deep bereavement, and it received an appropriate funeral: 'As the mouth remained open, we shut it with a small cloth, we closed his eyelids. I could not stop myself bursting into tears.' On returning from the Senate that afternoon he took the cat in the small coffin his wife had had made for it and dug a grave himself. One senses in this love for his cat, even at sixty-eight years of age, a desire to recreate the domestic happiness which had characterised his childhood and which his late marriage at the age of forty-four had not allowed him and his wife to recreate. Once again his parents were ever present: 'I saw Gris-gris again at father's feet, on mother's knees on Lucien's! He had known all my family. It is a piece of them which is going for the second time. In the midst of public sadness, this private pain breaks my heart, like the loss of a companion and a friend.'[29]

Animals

Animals were more than just a distraction for Poincaré; he referred to them as 'mysterious creatures which are in no way inferior to us'. This was only partly to do with his not having any children. When the noted political figure Queen Marie of Romania gave as her excuse for not attending a dinner party the fact that her dog had just died, he praised her action, stating that 'even women who have children can be very attached to what men stupidly call beasts' (ce que les hommes appellent bêtement les bêtes).[30] He and Henriette lavished affection on a host of domestic animals. Siamese cats were Poincaré's favourite, in particular Gris-gris, who was a constant companion in his study. The couple's first dogs were collies and later large sheepdogs with names such as 'Scott', 'Nino' and 'Miette'. He certainly overcame his shyness in their presence and attributed to them special powers:

The instinct which guides them, but which is not the only one, I am convinced, to guide them, is it not, on the contrary superior, in many instances, to our most scientific and subtle reasoning? I discover in them a sense of logic differently profound from that which one witnesses in many human beings, and a refinement of sensitivity of which many of us seem to me to be quite incapable.[31]

His love for all creatures went as far as a political commitment to animal welfare which led him to support organisations for the protection of animals and animal rights. He was party to, or instrumental in organising, protests against vivisection.

As president of the Republic he refused to take part in hunting parties at his official country residence at Rambouillet. During his presidential visit to Spain in 1913, the diplomatic community noted his refusal to attend a bullfight with the king.[32] During the war, when Paris was being bombed, he would be a good deal less preoccupied with his own safety than that of his dog and cat whose transport to the safety of the cellars he personally supervised. And when in 1915 his presidential role led him to be present at unsuccessful French poison gas trials, he was as preoccupied with the suffering of the sheep and rabbits, which 'watch us with stunned and mournful eyes', as the failure of French technology.[33] In 1926 the death of his dog, like that of his cat, three years later, provoked heart-rending outpourings of grief. On the death of his dog, Nino, he wrote to his old friend Gerald Nobel, 'When one sees friends leaving you without understanding why, how can one not appreciate more and more such faithful affection? There was more feeling in the heart of this good dog than brains in the head of many a person.'[34] The older he grew, outliving the small nucleus of family and friends, the more he came to rely on the company of his wife and their domestic animals.

But Poincaré's love of animals and championing of their rights needs to be set in a wider political context. By the second half of the nineteenth century, scientific discoveries in the natural sciences harnessed to the earlier evolutionist theories of Lamarck and then Charles Darwin reduced the hitherto apparent gap between the human and animal kingdoms; the publication in 1859 of the *Origin of Species* demonstrated their shared origins. The perception of animals began to change, first in Britain and later in France. The animal experiments of the French philosopher and physiologist Claude Bernard caused a stir on both sides of the Channel. The reliance of certain scientific discoveries on vivisection stressed the commonality of human and animal functions and reactions. Paradoxically, the rationale for vivisection that animals feel pain like human beings produced the logical justification for opposing it. In both countries anti-vivisection movements had been set up in the latter part of the century, but in neither Britain nor France were animal rights campaigners a marginal group of eccentrics. In Britain the celebrated anti-slavery campaigner William Wilberforce was recruited in 1822 to help MP Richard Martin pilot a bill through parliament recognising the rights of cattle, which in turn paved the way for more extensive legislation against cruelty to animals.[35] Wilberforce's anti-slavery counterpart in France, Victor Schoelcher, teamed up with the well-known republican historian Jules Michelet to support the Grammont Law of 1850, the first French legislation on the protection of domestic animals.[36]

Thus Poincaré's respect for animals was far from eccentric and reflected a general liberal intellectual and political movement in favour of the 'emancipation' of so-called 'inferior beings', whether 'savages' or animals, which was well under way in Great Britain and gathering pace in France. As far back as 1835, in Britain the Society for the Prevention of Cruelty to Animals had had a royal patron, Princess Victoria, who, three years after acceding to the throne, would in 1840 dignify it with its royal prefix. Significantly, republican France chose as the honorary president of the Société française contre la vivisection, founded in 1882, the school-boy hero of all Republicans, Victor Hugo.[37]

The RSPCA's official journal *Animal World* of 1873 stated what would be Poincaré's philosophy: 'We are reminded that not only are the lower animals capable of experiencing the same physical pain and suffering with ourselves, but also that they are in possession of the same kind of reasoning faculties.'[38] Poincaré's refusal to attend a bullfight when on a state visit to Spain in 1913, though a reflection of his strongly held views on animal rights, had additional French political overtones. Maurice Agulhon has described the political movement against bullfighting which characterised Parisian left-wing republican and intellectual circles in the latter part of the nineteenth century. Apart from the moral belief that persecution of animals ran counter to the emancipatory ideals of the Enlightenment, their opposition was further exercised on the grounds that the 'autocratic' Napoleon III had been instrumental in introducing it to the south of France.[39] The Third Republic was even said to have attempted to make love of animals one of the commandments to instil into children, passing its own legislation to curb cruelty to animals in 1898.[40] It was in that year that Poincaré, approached by his friend the author and orientalist Pierre Loti, rallied the support of eminent political figures for a petition to prevent the massacre of dogs in Constantinople. It was one thing to protest about practices outside one's country, but Poincaré's sensitivities on the question of animal rights were so acute as to lead him to take part in anti-vivisection protests in France. He sent an indignant telegram to a Professor Richet protesting about his vivisection experiments. Poincaré's love of animals seemed to stem from an almost pantheistic philosophy. An author who sent him his latest book on animal rights received a warm and fulsome letter of praise carrying the mystical comment that it was much the pity that there were not in France organisations to protect trees as there were said to be in Spain.[41]

What gave the animal rights philosophy in France added political appeal for the *laïque* Poincaré and other moderate republicans was its secularist undertones. Animal liberation philosophy consciously broke with the anthropocentrism of Catholic teachings and fitted a more *laïque* and materialistic interpretation of Creation in which the new secular man would have a general respect for life in line with the Enlightenment, hitherto restricted by the church to his own species. It also seems that Poincaré believed, in common with a number in Britain, in the immortality of animals and the existence of their souls. This – in conjunction with a typical sentimentality – helps explain the ritualistic burial ceremonies which he and his wife performed at the death of their pets.[42] Animal rights was thus one of the few areas where Poincaré's public persona betrayed his private sentiments.

Because few ever saw his sensitive side, Poincaré was remembered quite wrongly as a man of few emotions. Jules Laroche gave a typical account of how he was viewed by those who worked with him: 'He neglected . . . all personal charm, and his politeness, perfect, but without warmth, led one to believe that he was more imbued with the notion of duty than sensitive to considerations of pure humanity.'[43] His apparent coolness became almost legendary when his character was transparently fictionalised as the cold, callous Rebendart by Jean Giraudoux in the romantic novel *Bella* published in 1926.[44] The problem was that his austerity was mistaken for insensitivity. In reality this shy man was, in private, deeply affectionate and sentimental. His life-long friend and colleague, Gabriel Hanotaux, described this as a power of love: 'This power, therefore, he hid right inside himself because it belonged to his heart. It was a magnificent faculty for affection: he loved. He loved with total commitment.'[45]

Experience of war

At barely ten years old Raymond Poincaré was uprooted from the order and calm of his home surroundings to be plunged into a world of chaos and fear. The defeat of the French Imperial army brought Prussian troops into Lorraine. On 13 August 1871, a week before his birthday, the decision had been taken to evacuate the family to Dieppe while Raymond's father remained in Bar-le-Duc. During the following two-and-a-half months, in which the family moved from hotel to hotel in France then Belgium, his home town was occupied. At serious risk to himself, his father maintained contact with the new republican Government of National Defence.

Four years later, Raymond recorded his impressions of his evacuation to Normandy and Belgium based on a contemporary account kept day by day. One senses from the lyrical and rhetorical style, the quotations in Latin, that his observations are not those of a ten year old child, but of an adolescent who has since taken in comments from his adult surroundings.[46] It is an attempt to begin creative writing, something that he would enjoy during his student days. 'I have never written ... How shall I begin? What should I say first? What shall I say next? Really I do not know at all. Yet I would truly like to recount the journey I made in 1870, at the time of the war with Prussia.' His ability to write is clear, but his retrospective comments on the war are of greatest interest, albeit rather tainted by his desire for lyrical flourishes: 'Despite the fact that in reality we were emigrating, we were not completely sad. We were stricken by France's fate, not by this little enforced trip. As we were always waiting for the hour of *revanche*, the moment of reprisals, we experienced moments of happiness.' On describing the fall of Sedan on 2 September 1870 he revealed his unsympathetic view of the Second Empire, though he stated that he would keep his promise not to talk politics. In October mother, boys and maid Cécile, returned to Bar-le-Duc, still under Prussian occupation. However much the 'emigration' may have seemed an adventure, their return was laden with sadness. 'If we did not leave France in order to rediscover her defeated, one cannot judge what we felt on crossing the frontier. We painfully contemplated the battle-fields where lay rotting horse carcasses, bags and swords ... What a return! God! when I think about it again!'[47]

Raymond's bedroom was occupied by a Prussian officer and the family was forced to move upstairs for the duration of the occupation, which lasted another three years.

Disgusting soldiers are in the house. One paints a skull and crossbones on our sideboard, the other spits, like a Cossack, in our stew. At every moment we see ourselves watched. We know our words are weighed, our gestures noted ... How wonderful was that day when the bells pealed out to announce that the last soldier had left the Town, that day when all the flags flew from joyful houses.[48]

Once again the fourteen-year-old Raymond's retrospective description is more revealing of a certain literary licence and a quest for stylistic accomplishment than it is about how he really felt at the time. In his contemporary diary for this period there is little trace of animosity towards the Germans. Even in the rewritten version of his diary, as distinct from his 'travel story', he remarked on 19 June 1871, 'Today we had the very pleasurable visit of six soldiers who had come to be billeted.' And he was pleased to play with the little water mill they built in the garden and which his great-grand-uncle Paulin Gillon had mended.[49]

The apparently contradictory attitude to the German occupation, which Poincaré's two sets of diaries display, is in fact fully representative of the state of French public opinion in Lorraine at this time. From 21 August 1870, the Prussians had created a Gouvernement général de Lorraine whose headquarters were in Nancy and which administered *départements* such as Meurthe-et-Moselle and the Meuse. That administration attempted to show goodwill to the local population, and thus the occupation was not always perceived negatively. In Lorraine reaction against the invasion was muted until mid-December 1870. Poincaré lived in 'French' Lorraine where there was a brief moment of resistance, then resignation, eventually to be followed by repulsion. With the Prussians occupying one-third of French soil hostility surfaced, particularly in the Eastern provinces. A fundamental transformation of the image of the German took place which the Third Republic would strengthen and codify. This would itself play a part in crystallising and reinforcing France's national sentiment.[50]

Raymond Poincaré's reaction to his first-hand experience of defeat and occupation mirrored that of the local population. By 1874, when he was rewriting his diaries, his perception of the Germans had changed. For his entry dated 25 October 1871 he talked in heroic terms of his desire to learn German: 'I must get down to it, however: because if ever ... and I hope so ... I go to fight in Prussia ... do not worry I will not get myself killed. If ever, say I, I fight the Germans in their country, I must be able to say to them: "You are my prisoner!" '[51]

Too much, however, has been made of his Lorraine origins and the war as being the foundations of a pathological desire for *revanche* to restore the 'lost provinces' to France. Certainly this period ingrained in him a serious mistrust of Germany and an ardent patriotism. But this was tempered by the disorder, destruction and sadness of war, experienced at first hand, and which he referred to as 'the tragic events which we have just suffered'.[52] If anything it made him aware of the need to avoid war, particularly as any future conflict with Germany would most likely have his native Lorraine as a battleground. In 1874 he could already write that 'France, everyone knows, imprudently declared war on Prussia'.[53] His boyhood experience would, in his later political life, lead him to ensure that France be always prepared, diplomatically and militarily, for any eventuality. Many years later he wrote to the historian Ernest Lavisse, 'These long months have, more than the lessons of my first teachers, steeled my soul, and accustomed my mind to reflection. I still have in my mind's eye those German troops marching in the streets and public squares of my native town.'[54]

But back in 1871 the young Raymond's principal preoccupations were his first communion, his class results and ranking. His contemporary diaries testify that although he received the first prize for catechism he was by no means first in all other subjects, fluctuating between first and sixth. Indeed, that explains why he was given private lessons during the school holidays. His diaries display a later well-known trait – attention to detail. It comes across in everything from the lateness of the train to the meticulous list of presents he received for his communion. Poor health was also something which dogged the young Raymond. During 1871 and 1872 he was often ill; nothing serious, but he was a sickly child, who often noted being given a glass of beer for medicinal purposes. But he adjusted to his illnesses with fortitude, remarking on 15 December 1871, 'I have a few chilblains which do not make me as comfortable as I might wish, but pah! ... I'll see worse, it's nothing ... and when I'm a soldier, it will probably hurt much more to have a bullet in the thigh or elsewhere.'[55] If he was worried at all it was that his sickness would upset his schoolwork: 'I am so tired that I will get such a bad mark that I won't even dare to mention it.'[56] His childhood ill-health would have its sequel in adult life, notably in 1885, when he would contract diphtheria. This, and perhaps a thirst for self-discipline, explain why as an adult he was careful to take exercise, in particular long walks, and what he called his 'swedish gymnastics', which comprised a three quarters of an hour 'work-out' every two days with a physical training instructor followed by a fifteen-minute massage. In this he was no different to several politicians from Gambetta to Barthou and Clemenceau. All were doubtless influenced by the Third Republic's taste for physical exercise, sport and patriotic pursuits which became fashionable as a result of the regime's preoccupation with the causes of national decline.[57]

Above all Poincaré's diaries are testimony to a single-minded struggle to be top. He details the errors made by a candidate sitting his public oral examination for the *baccalauréat* during a trip to Nancy. 1875 sees the close-run contest with his class-mate Rouiller, to get the *prix d'excellence*: 'Let us fight with passion, let us believe in God and don't let us forget that, if we make the effort that is expected of us, reward will follow work.'[58] On 19 March he did come top with the general proficiency prize and nine subject prizes for 1875, including Latin, Greek and Natural History, beating the previous year's seven prizes.

Raymond's parents, in best middle-class tradition, did their utmost to ensure that their son received a well-rounded education. At the end of 1871 he had been taken to Paris to the Assemblée Nationale where he had seen Thiers, Trochu, Pouyer-Quertier, the Duc d'Aumale, Grévy, but his interests did not seem to lie with politics. He questioned his diary to know whether he should talk of the 'Republic of Monsieur Thiers'. But no, 'for as far as I am concerned I don't understand a thing, other than that the French are weathercocks (girouettes)'.[59] He maintained the same cynicism in 1874 after seeing Henri Wallon, the minister of education, make a speech at the Sorbonne.[60]

If as yet politics were not to his liking, literature, poetry and even drawing were, as the little sketches in his diaries testify. He was taken to Paris to the theatre where he particularly enjoyed the Greek tragedies. Like most young men of his day and background he took fencing lessons, where he showed a certain prowess, and dancing lessons where he was less accomplished. He regretted in particular not being able to have a female dancing partner. With the self-consciousness of adolescence, he also regretted his small stature; he was therefore overjoyed when by chance he met a former teacher who commented on how much he had grown – and he noted it in capital letters in his diary. Self-consciousness about his diminutive stature stayed with him for the rest of his life; the statue erected in his memory in Sampigny shows him wearing stack heels.[61] Thus working hard at school, keeping a diary, beginning to write his first literary accounts of his journeys, which now included Savoy, Switzerland and even the notorious German spa town of Ems, he was a busy young man, who still found time to enjoy the local countryside and to play like a child. Everything he undertook he completed, displaying the perseverance, pride and a certain vanity which were to be lifelong traits. On one occasion, bored with his diary and finding nothing to put in it, he contemplated abandoning it. Characteristically he never did. But the order, warmth, affection and security of those youthful days were soon to be over.

Having successfully passed the first stage of his *baccalauréat*, which since the reform of 1874 was in two parts, it was decided that he should complete the second part in Paris. His father, like most graduates of Polytechnique, had hoped that his son would follow in his footsteps. It was perhaps evidence of his tolerance that he should respect Raymond's literary tastes and not impose a scientific training on him. In 1876 he was sent to Paris to continue his schooling. Of course the capital had always been a magnet for the French provincial middle class, though it was said that the real motive was his father's reluctance to see his son continue to be taught by a clerical philosophy teacher. There is also a suggestion that the choice of Paris may have been connected with a desire on the part of his parents to distance him from a rather precocious local love affair. On 1 October 1876, with much sadness, he entered the prestigious *lycée* Louis-le-Grand.

Growing up

No one could have been less suited to boarding school than Raymond Poincaré. An idyllic family life, a passionate attachment to his parents, a deep feeling for his home town and native Lorraine was not appropriate preparation for a boy barely sixteen to begin a new life in a cold dormitory surrounded by 108 students in a distant Paris. Contemporaries remember the repressive regime of boarders in the Paris *lycées*:

> Those who were to be pitied were the full boarders [*internes*]. Fortunately they were few; boys without a home in Paris, or whose home was no fit place for them. With the callousness of adolescence, we gave no thought to their loneliness and secret tragedies. They were derelicts, 'interned', incarcerated, and we took it for granted that they had deserved their fate. In return they protected themselves with an armour of rudeness. In six years I do not believe I exchanged one friendly word with an *interne*.[62]

Leaving his mother, whose warmth and tenderness he most missed, was particularly hard that first day. But already armed with self-discipline, choking back the tears, he set himself the task of reading several pages of the *De Officiis* every evening as consolation. But the intensely competitive spirit of the Parisian *lycées*, with their myriad *concours* and prizes, did suit Poincaré. As for Ferry or Waldeck-Rousseau, the dash to be top, the work ethic and the adrenalin of competition became almost obsessional. Poincaré threw himself into his work, and by Easter had overtaken such able classmates as the future ambassador Maurice Paléologue and future archbishop Baudrillart, collecting prizes in a variety of subjects. This was not sufficient to overcome his homesickness which was clearly evident in his letter of 10 April 1877 to his old school-friend Pol Brouchot back home: 'Last night at 9 o'clock, the heavy door of my prison closed behind me, last night, I returned to my narrow, hard bed, my vast and freezing dormitory; last night, instead of friends, I only saw around me more or less indifferent classmates.'[63] Small wonder that he referred to his *lycée* as his 'pedagogic barracks' and sought to relieve his loneliness in a rejection of 'odious leisure'.[64]

Counting the days to his next return home he told of how three things kept him going – 'imagination, memories, hope'. Thanks to them 'I live another life, I inhabit a house which gives me greater pleasure: I see parents, a brother, friends, I tread with them a beloved soil, far from this accursed Paris.'[65] That nostalgia for Bar-le-Duc, his beloved Lorraine and his family had not vanished two years later – nor would it ever; rather he had found more intellectual activities to occupy his mind. He wrote letters in Latin and German, composed portraits of his schoolfellows in the style of La Bruyère and other seventeenth-century writers;

he sketched, took piano lessons and even tried his hand as an art critic. He confided his thoughts to his 'cahier rouge' entitled, in that dry, ironic humour characteristic of him, 'Thoughts philosophical, vulgar, banal, soporific and others by Raymond Poincaré'. He found it difficult to make real friends, not because he was not liked, although rather bossy, but because of his middle-class upbringing: 'I should not like to be associated with a young man who had never known my parents, whose family I had never seen and who only knew my real friends by name.' But his religion was still with him, and he continued to attend mass regularly, though his intellectual activities were taking their toll of his faith. Later he would comment, 'I did not voluntarily free myself from the Catholic faith; I did not distance myself from it out of indifference. I was brutally and painfully torn from it by my studies.'[66]

At the end of June 1877 he had become prey to severe headaches; the doctor counselled rest and his headmaster finally persuaded the ailing Raymond, the most hard-working pupil of his career, to return home temporarily. Even there he continued to work for the final part of his arts baccalauréat and was rewarded with brilliant results. The bright young elite of Louis-le-Grand wondered to what heights he would not rise and attributed to him ambitious Superintendent Fouquet's motto: Quo non ascendam. Of course, obtaining the baccalauréat was nothing exceptional for someone of Poincaré's social background, but it consecrated his entry to the country's elite; as late as 1909 the annual total of new bacheliers was merely 7,000 for a population of some 39 million.[67]

Now he was faced with a choice. For a time he seems to have returned to the idea of preparing for Polytechnique, or even the Ecole Normale Supérieure. At least he had seemed clear in March 1877 that he did not want to study law, by far the most widely studied subject in French universities in the second half of the nineteenth century. But it was probably the idea of having to return to Louis-le-Grand to prepare for these institutions which finally deterred him. He wanted to be free and independent, if only to impose on himself a more rigorous self-discipline – baring again the contradictory nature of his character. As Fernand Payen, his semi-official biographer, put it, 'How strange yet engaging, this serious-minded and caring boy, authoritarian and timid – cold looks, passionate thoughts – who could not stand any external constraints and yet who imposed on himself the most rigorous discipline in affairs of the heart and mind!'[68] During the 1877 summer holidays he weighed up the pros and cons and, guided by his mother's practical mind, decided to study law in Paris. In the meantime he had worked for his science baccalauréat as a safety-net, and passed it in November 1877.[69]

Student days

Back then to Paris, but this time to a small room on the fourth floor of a small hotel on the Boulevard St Michel next door to his cousin, Henri Poincaré. Henri had just graduated from Polytechnique and was now a student at the Ecole des Mines, while Poincaré attended the law faculty. Though for a time still homesick, here he was able to give lease to his imagination and stretch his intellectual wings, though not in the realm of the law. Law studies at this time concentrated on Roman Law and the Napoleonic Civil Code, viewed as an 'intangible expression of justice', and only briefly addressed criminal, commercial and administrative law. Stress was laid on rote learning of the Civil Code and how to apply it to a given case. This legal training made for a cold and precise juridical mentality which was said to characterise the future generation of lawyer–politicians like Waldeck-Rousseau, Millerand and Poincaré, whose summations were characterised by a meticulously prepared, tight argumentation and a cold and mechanical delivery devoid of sentiment: 'As legislators they tended to regard an institution as founded, or a reform accomplished, when inscribed in a rigorous legal text.'[70] Poincaré found his law studies dry and sterile and decided to study in parallel for an arts degree, something common to this day in France. His self-imposed workload was astounding, but he still found time to keep up his personal correspondence, in particular with his close friend Pol Brouchot. Here the two young men roamed with youthful freedom from Philosophy to the Classics, Poincaré displaying a naïve, vaporous and wistful romanticism constantly struggling to break free from material life:

Does it never happen to you, my dear Pol, when in the evening you find yourself alone in your room, surrounded by scholarly works, your head weighed down with some dull question, don't you ever let go of the reins of your imagination and allow yourself to be transported, on the wings of daydreams, to the most wonderful days of our childhood?

When, after ten or twenty minutes, I feel repelled by my arid studies, when the subtlety of our lawyers revolts and irritates me, when I am overtaken by disdain for a futile and purely human science, I open my window, go onto my balcony and there, melancholically leaning on the railings, breathing in deeply the almost pure air of the fourth floor, I lift, with joyous pain, the veil of the past. I see us both, working together in my little bedroom, wrestling with the difficulties of some Latin or Greek sentence, from time to time forgetting our homework, and carving out some naïve, fresh and childish conversation, like the dawn of a beautiful day. False prediction, because the day is laden with sadness and the sky grey. How sweet it is to sleep in the morning of one's life and to know nothing of it.[71]

In Paris under the influence of Henri Poincaré, six years his elder, he was initiated to student life – cheap meals at the 'pension Laveur' in the rue Serpente in the Latin Quarter, and interminable political, philosophical and religious discussions, punctuated by banter and paradox. It was the positivist Henri who appears to have most steered his younger cousin away from his faith. On 8 May 1877 Raymond wrote, 'A reasonable positivism is the system which I consider the most plausible.' However, positivism – which sought to explain everything through science – and Catholicism were by no means mutually incompatible at this time.[72] Though Poincaré's natural romanticism and youthful idealism had not evaporated, he was, like many of his generation, being converted to a moderate positivism which would condition his political outlook.

Poincaré's was not the clichéd bohemian and licentious student existence of Paris, but the more sober, ardent life of the future administrative and political elite. His friends at this time would also become political or legal colleagues, like Gabriel Hanotaux or fellow students from the law faculty such as Alexandre Millerand, Maurice Bernard, Paul Revoil or Georges Payelle. He also mixed with figures already established in the political world, such as his close friend five years his senior, Henri Lavertujon (*chef de cabinet* to a sous-secrétaire d'état), and the *député* for Bar-le-Duc, Jules Develle (the friend of the family who would provide the opening for Poincaré's political career). He struck up a particularly warm friendship with Alexandre Millerand. They *tutoied* each other, a mark of familiarity which Poincaré studiously avoided throughout his life other than for his closest friends; they playfully called each other *maître*, the formal term of address for a lawyer. Poincaré even wrote to Millerand for advice on his disappointingly slow progress in an *affaire de cœur*; the future ninth president of the Republic would also dedicate poems to the future eleventh president of the Republic.[73]

Politics was an inescapable topic of conversation for this group in the early days of the Third Republic. The regime was tottering between republicanism and monarchism. 1875 had seen the voting of the constitutional laws of the Third Republic, 1877 the so-called '*coup d'état* of 16 May' – a royalist attempt to reverse the republicans' electoral successes. Poincaré's entourage was republican, though he continued to eschew any clear political stance. It was at this time, according to Gabriel Hanotaux, that his friends nicknamed him 'Prudence Lorraine'.[74] What most played on his mind was the defeat of 1870, and French political leaders' inability to deal with it – a sign of his growing republicanism. Certainly at this time the notion of *revanche* was characteristic of the Left, the reflex action of wounded nationalism.[75] The Bonapartist Right of the Second Empire was blamed for the defeat, the monarchist Right, now in power, was criticised for pursuing a foreign policy of national humiliation in the face of Bismarck. Poincaré's diaries had already testified to his belief that the Second Empire was at fault. But by 1878 he believed that the time for recriminations was over. What was needed was a policy of *juste milieu*: 'Have we not pushed reaction too far? Between bravado and cowardice, between chauvinism and indifference there are *justes milieux* called prudence and patriotism.'[76] This appeal to moderation and consensus would be a characteristic Poincaré trait. His concept of French foreign policy was already traced: 'It was not that we fear war, we hate it. But our love of peace, however natural and praiseworthy it be, should not seem to anyone to be marked by weakness.'[77] Thus he advocated not military *revanche*, but a prudent patriotic policy – neither chauvinism nor submission.

Poincaré had no trouble passing his first law exam in August 1878 and returned home to his parents. Here he prepared his *licence ès lettres* which he passed in November at the University of Nancy with *mention très bien* and then returned to Paris to his second year of law. This was followed in 1879 with a year's voluntary military service with the twenty-sixth infantry regiment in his beloved Lorraine at Nancy. That decision was not necessarily inspired by patriotism. By volunteering, paying 1,500 francs and passing an exam, one's military obligation was reduced from five years to one. He found his tasks easy and congenial as his letters show.[78] With his usual application he was soon promoted to corporal and eventually sergeant, at the same time managing to complete his final year of law. In August 1880 he was awarded his degree. A few months later he completed his military service and was made a sub-lieutenant reserve officer in the *chasseurs à pied*.

Again came the question of what to do next. For a time he had thought of an academic career in law. Yet despite future comments about him being made for the law, he had found the subject neither interesting nor challenging. His passion was poetry and literature. From 1877 to 1881 Poincaré had already written four novels, one of which had been serialised in the *Echo de l'Est* from January to February 1880 under the title *La correspondance d'un avocat*. This he signed pseudonymously Juliette Landry, which though unsurprising for bearing one of his forenames, was remarkable for its gender and the fact that women were debarred from the law. Poincaré's first literary efforts were sugary, idealised stories about romance, heavy with symbolism and sentimentality, and his poetry, accounts of star-crossed love. In his unfinished short story about Pierre Dupic and Marthe Récourt, Marthe is a

fourteen-year-old boarder in a convent in Nancy who falls in love with
Pierre Dupic, a law student. Marthe is sent away to Paris and Pierre later
follows, then volunteers for military service with a regiment in Nancy.
One day he sees Marthe in the street, now married. The notes are
unfinished.[79]

Very little is known of Poincaré's sentimental life about which he was
scrupulously secretive. But his literary works, mostly unpublished and
some unfinished, are almost voluntarily transparent. The story of Pierre
Dupic seems remarkably autobiographical. Does it point to an unhappy
adolescent love affair with a girl from Lorraine which was interrupted by
his despatch to Paris ostensibly to complete his *baccalauréat*?[80]

Feminism

Given Poincaré's conservative, strait-laced image, his championing of
animal rights and 'feminism' appear eccentric. Yet such interests were,
to an extent, characteristic of a certain intellectual left-wing Republicanism under the Third Republic. His writings clearly displayed an
interest in women. He spent by far the greatest part of his childhood in
his mother's and grandmother's company, his father often absent, or
working in his office – though that was not exceptional for any child at
this time. He readily sought women's company for their perceived
qualities of intelligence, intuition and warmth, whether for romance or
friendship, occasionally incurring the jealousy of male friends such as
Gabriel Hanotaux.[81] His writings showed an idealisation of all the
feminine clichés. Pierre Dupic's mother's resemblance to his own was
more than fictional: 'Everything in that woman was maternal and good
... She was conciliation incarnate, a personification of kindness,
obligingness made woman.'[82] But nor was this exceptional for the time.
Women personified 'the graces, beauty, and love' and were 'sublime in
their maternity', while men were expected to embody the qualities of
'force, resolution, and work'.[83] Nevertheless his choice of women's
names for pseudonyms was striking in its originality, running counter to
the prevailing trend in nineteenth-century European literature where the
reverse was more often the case.

At this time all women were denied the rights of citizenship: they had
no vote in parliamentary or local elections. Certainly according to
French law women were inferior beings who needed to be treated as
minors. The Civil Code required of wives obedience to their husbands,
and placed responsibility for the management of the couple's property in
the husband's hands. The subjects Poincaré proposed for debate for the
junior barristers' conference in 1883 concerned women's legal rights.

Though it was not until 1907 that wives were given the right to dispose freely of their own property and earnings, nearly a quarter of a century earlier Poincaré set the question, 'In the event of the husband's refusal, can the courts authorise a woman to publish a literary work or to produce a dramatic work of which she is the author?'[84] When in 1883 he began writing legal articles for the newspaper *Le Voltaire*, he would occasionally write on women's fashion under the pseudonym Sergine. As a *député* in November 1898 he would be one of the originators, with René Viviani, of the bill to enable women to become lawyers. Though his championing of that cause was successful on 1 December 1900, a mere 0.29 per cent of the profession was female by 1910. Poincaré understood the extent to which this was due to discrimination and unequal educational opportunities. The 1880 Sée Law may have introduced state secondary schools for girls, but the curricula of these establishments did not prepare for the *baccalauréat*, which was the key to higher education and the professions. Though at the time there was little parliamentary support for enhancing female education, as minister of education in 1893, at the opening of a girls' *lycée*, he exhorted women to play a full role as educators in the home and to teach the last 'adepts of the past to turn progressively towards the modern world'.[85]

France had its own feminist movement, though it never exerted the influence or pressure of the English suffragettes. More moderate in tone, the French movement comprised the Conseil national des femmes françaises and the Union française pour le suffrage féminin, founded respectively in 1900 and 1909; by 1914 the former had 100,000 members, the latter 12,000. The leadership of the movement was composed largely of well-to-do women, often linked to the male republican elite. Their approach was moderate, legalistic and gradualist and would have appealed to Poincaré on these grounds alone. They did have a certain impact on public opinion through their own newspapers and by 1914 through the columns of large-selling Parisian dailies such as *Le Journal*. Though they promoted the suffrage issue, they were particularly active in contesting traditional assumptions about female roles and in so doing often introduced a 'feminine' dimension to the great national questions of the day, from depopulation to social affairs. But opposition to women's suffrage spanned a range of political views: the church wished women to preserve the Catholic faith in an increasingly secular world; the Right worried about the undermining of male authority and the family; moderate republicans feared that women's suffrage would mean a return to clericalism and threaten the very existence of the regime; socialists and syndicalists denounced the exploitation of women workers – probably with an eye to the threat they posed to male bastions of labour – and called for the right to domestic bliss for the working-class family.[86]

Poincaré was a supporter of the feminist movement in its moderate guise. As an advocate of marriage and the family, he was sensitive to the belief that it was precisely because they were primarily wives and mothers, and therefore in a position of relative power within the family, that women should have a clearer say in the running of society. On 17 July, at Le Puy for the opening of a girls' *lycée*, the theme was women's education in which he criticised the opponents of women's secondary education and exhorted women to go on and teach republican values: 'You will teach everyone tolerance and mutual respect ... To the rich the notions of sacrifice and generosity, to the poor the secret of persevering work, of thrift, of providence, to all the spirit of solidarity ... And above all you will instil in citizens the feeling of duty to their country.'[87]

It is not clear what his own wife's views were on the subject; Henriette Poincaré, an obviously independent woman and divorced – though still a Catholic – had long mixed in intellectual and artistic circles and been involved in charity work which was a common route to feminism. Of course, there was a Catholic feminist movement organised by Marie Maugeret before the war which had a significant following in the provinces. Whatever support Henriette may have given to such movements, she was always a strong influence on her husband. To a certain extent he acknowledged that in tangible ways. As president of the Republic, he was instrumental in giving to the wife of the president the modern features of the 'First Lady' by calling on her to deputise for him at certain official functions, to a certain extent infringing the tradition of sending the president's private secretary as his official envoy. Thus Henriette would visit the devastated regions of France in the aftermath of the War on behalf of her husband and attend the *Te Deum* at Notre Dame to mark the end of hostilities in 1918.

In January 1921 Poincaré was made a member of the *comité d'honneur* of the Ligue française pour le droit des femmes, comprising 'the most eminent personalities in favour of feminism'.[88] At the time he shocked the literary establishment by declaring that he saw no reason why women should not become members of the Académie française – something which would be resisted until 1980. In an interview he gave to the monthly review *Le Droit des Femmes* to celebrate the fiftieth anniversary of the founding of the Ligue française pour le droit des femmes, he declared proudly, 'You know very well that I am a feminist.' And he went on to declare that French women should immediately be given the vote: 'Is it not rather humiliating for France to see little by little all countries giving women the vote, when nothing has been done here in that direction.' All the more so, he remarked, as women had done their duty during the Great War, when they were the equal of men. This was also his theme on 3 December 1921 in a speech at a gala to honour Belgian women, organised by the Ligue française pour le droit des femmes. The journal *Le Droit des Femmes* described the speech as marking a great victory in the history of 'French Feminism'.[89] Such hyperbole can be explained by the scoop of having got no less a politician than the former president of the Republic to endorse women's suffrage. This was all the more significant as Poincaré's 'feminist' stance just after the war was by no means general. Though the war years had clearly advanced the participation of women in the labour force to over 40 per cent of industrial employment, by 1921, after demobilisation, fewer women worked in industry than in 1906, even if greater numbers were employed in the more modern industries and the tertiary sector. Men had reclaimed their former positions. Nor had attitudes to feminism improved as a result of wartime experience. The effects of the war on France's demography, and potentially her great power status, strengthened the pro-natalist lobby and weakened the campaign for women's suffrage. A bill to give women the vote got through the Chamber of Deputies in 1919 but was rejected by the Senate in 1922 due to the hostility of the anti-clerical Radicals and the old fear that it would give succour to the clerical enemies of the regime. French women's suffrage would be blocked on at least another four occasions by the Senate denying them the vote until 1944.[90]

It would be wrong to see Poincaré's 'feminism' in a modern guise. He believed in equality of the sexes, but much less in the interchangeability of traditional gender roles. It was the kind of feminism advocated by the contemporary Academician and playwright, Ernest Legouvé, who was a co-member with Poincaré of an exclusive intellectual dining circle, 'Bixio'. Legouvé's feminism was for 'difference in equality', which won approval from male and female feminists alike, as well as moral and financial support from the republican parliamentary establishment.[91] However, where Poincaré was more radical was in his championing of female equality in the work-place. Though the Republican regime had fostered women's education with the development of state secondary schools for girls following the Sée Law of 1880, republican educators made it clear that this did not mean occupational equality.[92] In general though, his liberal, even progressive, attitude towards women can be explained in terms of a wider desire for tolerance and freedom, and also as one current of left-wing republican thought.

The law

A literary career was where Poincaré's heart lay. But when he submitted some of his work to the writer André Theuriet, he was advised to make a position for himself in another area. This tallied with the wishes of his mother, who believed that a profession was needed to provide the material support for his literary indulgences.

On 20 December 1880, at twenty years of age, Poincaré became the youngest barrister in France. At the same time, his father was promoted to the post of Inspecteur général de l'hydraulique agricole in Paris. The Poincaré family was reunited with its sons, as the younger brother was studying at the Ecole Normale Supérieure. At 4, carrefour de l'Odéon, the new family home in the Latin Quarter, Raymond had his room and office. Three courses of action were open to law graduates: a third prepared for a doctorate; others spent two years in a law firm; most enrolled on the three-year-long Bar exam course. Poincaré did all three. His doctoral subject was particularly dry, though again betraying a 'feminist' interest: 'On the possession of chattels in Roman Law'. At the same time he gave evening classes at the Union de la jeunesse républicaine, (the moderate parapolitical youth movement which subsequently slid to the far Left), as Millerand did and Louis Barthou would do.[93] He and his close friend Millerand attended diction classes given by the actor Talbot from the Comédie française.[94] This was not uncommon among Third Republican politicians, though in Poincaré's case it was largely motivated by a certain self-consciousness at his thin, nasal voice. He continued to find time to write his poetry, sentimental as ever, and still on the theme of lost love.

As always Poincaré had his sights set on the top of the legal profession. He hoped to become a member of the ordre des avocats of the Paris Court, which would give him the right to practice in the Paris Court of Appeal. But that required completion of three years probation. The probationers, known as *stagiaires*, were members of a body called the Conférence de l'ordre des avocats, which provided a weekly seminar. There were some two to three hundred probationers who had the opportunity of competing for twelve prestigious positions as *secrétaire* of the Conférence du stage by defending or prosecuting a case. In February 1882 Poincaré became a candidate in this near hundred-year-old highly competitive debating contest which produced the aristocracy of the profession. The title of *ancien secrétaire* guaranteed professional success and election to the Conseil de l'ordre des avocats, the profession's twelve- to fifteen-member governing body, within twenty years, and to which Poincaré would be appointed in 1911.[95]

Public speaking had never been Poincaré's strength, for he was shy. His performance, like his first political speeches five years later, was at first tentative, but he gained confidence to become authoritative and impressive. Whereas others might cut a dash with pure oratory, Poincaré could convince by mastery of his subject and a forensic eloquence which Maître Barboux of the Académie française compared to that of a Spartan magistrate.[96] On 26 July 1882 he came top, beating his friend Millerand into seventh place, and earning the prestigious title of first secretary of the Conference. This gave him the prerogative of choosing the following year's subject for debate. He chose the law and women's rights, and the issue of literary property – an area in which he would specialise later in his legal career. Tradition also required the first secretary of the Conference to prepare a eulogy of a former great barrister. Poincaré chose Jules Dufaure, former *président du conseil*, *bâtonnier de l'ordre des avocats* and member of the Académie française – all offices which Poincaré would hold. His choice was the more illuminating for the nature of Dufaure – a prudent and not very glamorous liberal politician who had served both the July Monarchy and the Republic and who was a colleague and friend of the Gillon family. In pronouncing his eulogy on 23 November 1883, Poincaré described the qualities which would be his own hallmark – moderation, patience, seriousness, honesty, modesty, hardwork, adding that 'He knew how to get himself appreciated little by little, without noise or scandal, and to take his place without drama.'[97] Thus would Poincaré spend his first three years as a *député* observing before seriously entering the political fray. Dufaure's watchwords had been 'national independence' and 'liberty': Poincaré's would be no different.

Winning the Conférence du stage was to have much bearing on Poincaré's subsequent choice of political collaborators. Whereas on the whole the radical leader Joseph Caillaux would select his from the *Inspection des finances* from whence he came, and the moderate Paul Deschanel from graduates of the Ecole des Sciences Politiques, Millerand and Poincaré would choose theirs from the former *secrétaires* of the Conference. Thus Poincaré would become the patron of a network of lawyer–politicians contributing to the characterisation of the period as the 'république des avocats'.

Meanwhile he had to make his living in the law. He joined the practice of a successful commercial lawyer by the name of Du Buit, where he learnt his craft, meticulously and patiently, among the dry rules of the Civil Code, while Millerand made a more theatrical debut defending the miners of Monceau-les-Mines. 'Juridicism' was the one thing which later was seen to characterise Poincaré. He was said to suit the law and the law to suit him – or deserve him, in the view of his critics. His adversaries later found his legalism a convenient peg on which to hang all criticism of him: 'He remained a man attached to one idea, one period, one system, one class ... Is it as a result of the original laws from which he benefited that he owes his indelible juridical imprint? And should one explain by that his desire to squeeze into structures which are not always appropriate phenomena, events, life?'[98] His arch-rival Clemenceau was more forthright: 'One should never put in charge of a country someone whose heart is stuffed with files. It is too dangerous.'[99]

Though Poincaré was undeniably legalistically minded, the caricature was overdrawn, ignoring in particular his artistic side. Writing was still his passion. He had already begun to contribute to a Paris newspaper, even if in November 1881 he had written to Millerand to complain that he 'merely copied and put together stupid sentences'. This was the period of great press expansion and there was ample opportunity for young hopefuls to place their copy with the fifty or so dailies published in Paris alone. Dining one evening with a number of Gambetta supporters, including the secretary of the editorial board of the Gambettist newspaper *Le Voltaire*, he was offered the job of legal chronicler. For two years from 1882 'Maître Aubertin' wrote his daily column. Even then law seemed a means to an artistic end because his column included at every conceivable juncture references to the arts and literature. Articles on literature also appeared in such diverse publications as the *Revue Politique et Littéraire*, the Radical *Le XIXe Siècle*, the *Revue Libérale*. An article in the latter on 'physiologist literature' (better understood today as 'naturalist') earned him letters of congratulation from established literary figures such as Alphonse Daudet and Jules Claretie, and the sincere plaudits of Emile Zola, the naturalist movement's leading light, who even made enquiries about 'such maturity' in a young man of only twenty-two.[100]

He had been working for Maître Du Buit for three years and was earning a decent living, with his writing providing some extra pocket-money. Though not shy of the laborious, anonymous work Du Buit's practice demanded of him, he was beginning to feel the desire for greater independence; all the more so for many of his friends and colleagues at the Bar were turning their hands to politics. In France, as in Britain, the Bar was the antechamber of parliament. Millerand had become a radical *député* for Paris at twenty-six years old, Gabriel Hanotaux had moved from the academic world to the Foreign Ministry, Paul Revoil and Georges Payelle had joined ministers' private offices. As yet Poincaré demonstrated no particular interest in politics, and certainly less than friends such as Millerand, who in the spring of 1883 had become a freemason as befitted his Radical views.[101] Poincaré frequently stated that politics should not be looked upon as a profession.[102] But when an opportunity arose he took up the challenge.

At twenty-six years of age much of Poincaré's personality was already cast. From his devoted family upbringing he had acquired a caring nature which was a lifelong trait. But he felt no desire to wear it on his sleeve, nor to distribute it superficially. Nevertheless he was capable of the most effusive displays of emotion. His family and relations apart, the only beneficiaries were a handful of school, university and legal friends to whom he would remain loyal all his life – Pol Brouchot, Maurice Bernard, Félix Decori. His emotional reserve came across either as a sentimental gaucheness or more often as heartlessness. From his child-hood came also a dry sardonic humour which allowed some to detect the more playful side of his nature. Fundamentally shy, he soon learnt at school that this could be a handicap to success where oral prowess was called for. He compensated for it by calling on other qualities he had in abundance – intelligence, clarity of thought, rigour and a prodigious memory. That memory was a legend in his own life-time. It is well known how during Poincaré's presidency the King of Spain attempted to put it to the test. While Poincaré was speaking at a gala dinner at the Elysée without any notes as usual, the king observed a deviation from the prepared text of the speech. The speech over, the king eagerly pointed out to his host this flaw in the president's 'infallible' memory. Poincaré reached into his pocket and pulled out two versions of his speech, the second showing a last minute alteration he had made to the first text which the king had been following.[103] By committing his speeches to memory before speaking, Poincaré overcame a certain oral inferiority. His interventions seemed impressive, but at the cost of spontaneity, heightening the impression he gave of seriousness and provoking Clemenceau's barbed pun, 'il devrait être moins carré' ('he shouldn't be so square').

His cultured middle-class family background, in which seriously differing opinions were firmly held but generously tolerated, gave him from an early age a broad political and philosophical outlook. He appears to have picked freely and unashamedly from liberal Orleanism and Opportunist republicanism, from Catholicism and secular free-thinking. The framework for his intellectual outlook was moderate positivism, and the guiding themes already dominating by the time he embarked on a political career were tolerance and liberty. They would remain his watchwords throughout his life and career, making Poincaré first and foremost a parliamentary liberal. The political personalities he knew best were on his mother's side. Essentially liberal monarchists, they had served under successive regimes; but what characterised them was their belief in service to the state. On his father's side, though of a different political outlook, public service was also a credo. Raymond Poincaré would adhere to that principle, always putting devotion to the state above party politics. In ending his pleading to the Conférence du stage he encapsulated two lifelong traits of romanticism and duty: 'There are only two beautiful things in the universe: the sky above our heads and the sense of duty in our hearts.'[104] But it was not out of a particular desire to serve the Republican regime that Poincaré would take up politics. As yet he did not even think of it as a career. His move into politics had more to do with accident than design at a time when he had no clear sense of direction. Subconsciously that move may have been influenced by the longstanding involvement in politics among his mother's relatives and a sense of service to the state, that of the functionary, on his father's side. Poincaré was almost in spite of himself, the inheritor of a family tradition. Certainly his social ascension was typical of a scion of the upper middle class of this time, the family playing a crucial role in determining the future social position of the son through the transmission of culture, financial security and the personal introductions necessary to a career.

In sum, Poincaré's upbringing was quintessentially that of the French bourgeoisie, the cornerstone of French nineteenth-century society which Stanley Hoffmann has described as being the product of three influences. First, its peasant origins which determined the nature and role of the family and the bourgeois conception of work, thrift, providence and individualism. Second, the bourgeoisie's pre-revolutionary paths to progress by either money or, through intellectual careers, prestige. Third, the feudal atavism which meant that traditional Catholic doctrines, especially that which denounced the cult of money, profoundly affected the French bourgeoisie's behaviour and mentality. That atavism was also responsible for the bourgeoisie's imitation of the aristocracy, part of which was the code of service to the sovereign who was then the State. The French bourgeoisie identified itself with society and was the model and the matrix of the rest of society, promoting values which were thought broadly acceptable to all social groups – stability, harmony and permanence: in short, consensus.[105] At the moment he entered politics Poincaré was fully primed with values developed since the eighteenth century, apparent under Louis-Philippe, and which would fast become the collective morality of French society under the Third Republic.

Poincaré was not a natural politician. He had shown no enthusiasm for the subject other than as a fertile source of academic debate like any other during his student days. He was probably, in those early years of the embryonic Third Republic, ill-suited to politics. The 1870s were passionate years when politicians of the Right and Left held deeply conflicting opinions about the political course France should set. By upbringing and temperament Poincaré was the opposite of passionate and doctrinaire. Young, liberal, tolerant and cautious, he was far more in tune with the settled and relatively well-established Third Republic of the 1880s. What the regime appeared to need in its second decade was not so much idealists as realists, not so much innovators as administrators, more managers than politicians *per se*. Republican lawyers fitted the bill perfectly. They wished to build democracy into a framework of precise legal texts based on the great tenets of 1789: individual freedom, civil equality and national sovereignty. The great Republican laws on the press, education and religious associations would be expressions of this. Almost effortlessly Poincaré could glide into the political establishment and along with the political trends of the first half of the Third Republic which marked France's apprenticeship of political democracy. He even fitted the statistical profile of the early Third Republican government member in coming from the north-east of France, which, contrary to received opinion, was the chief purveyor of ministers and not the south-west, whose day would come under the so-called 'Radical Republic'.[1]

Posterity has surrounded Poincaré with epithets such as 'Poincaré the Republican', 'Poincaré the *laïque*', suggesting that he came to politics with a vocation if not an ambition, like his close friend Millerand. Not so. He went hesitantly because a family friend recently promoted to agriculture minister needed someone to run his private office in January 1886. Jules Develle, *député* for Poincaré's native Meuse, and like him a former *premier secrétaire de la Conférence des avocats*, was a moderate republican, intelligent and charming, but no hard worker. Poincaré's first reaction to this invitation was one of caution. At that time, holding the official position of *chef de cabinet* and being a member of the Bar was deemed morally incompatible and would have meant abandoning the law temporarily. This he was reluctant to do, all the more so as political office was renowned for its instability under the early Third Republic. He consulted his superiors at the Paris Bar. They granted him a dispensation so long as he agreed not to plead during the tenure of his political appointment. This as well as family pressure and the example of his friends would have contributed to converting him to the idea of a job in politics.

Hindsight shows us that this was the beginning of Poincaré's political career. But this was by no means evident to Raymond Poincaré himself. He held a rather jaundiced view of the fickle nature of politics since his youth, and had no strong loyalty to the Republican regime. At that time the *cabinet du ministre* did not have the importance it would assume under the Fourth Republic. For the moment the *cabinets* were made up of a handful of mostly a mixture of journalists, friends of the minister, or civil servants usually at the beginning of their political or administrative careers. They were intended to act as links between Paris and the minister's constituency and political apparatus, rather than play an active role in the running of the ministry. At that time the minister usually dealt directly with the *directeurs* of the ministry, whose stability of office and influence increased substantially under the 'Republic of the Republicans' from the early 1880s.[2]

The advantage for Poincaré was that Jules Develle was not hard working, leaving scope for his *chef de cabinet*, who was. During his eighteen months as *chef de cabinet* Poincaré entered the political world only tentatively. He was happy managing the minister's activities, preparing dossiers on all aspects of agriculture, drawing up the budget, familiarising himself with political institutions and dealing with the minister's correspondence. His impersonal efficiency was already in evidence from the pro forma letters he had printed to reply to the numerous grace and favour requests addressed to the minister, and which so annoyed him.[3] He found local politics true to his vision of politics in general, rather lowly and dominated by factional interest.

As with his début in many things, Poincaré came to politics almost in spite of himself. The law had not interested him and yet he became a lawyer; so it was that he became a politician: 'Never even since I became a member of a *cabinet ministériel* did it cross my mind to seek political office. I felt in no way attracted to parliamentary debate.'[4] When the moderate republican *conseiller général* for the Pierrefitte-sur-Aire ward in Poincaré's home department was promoted to a post incompatible with a political mandate, a new candidate had to be found for the forthcoming local elections. But the choice was a delicate one. Notwithstanding the much criticised example of the Second Empire's partiality during elections, under the Third Republic a candidate whom the governmental majority viewed with a favourable eye would receive every support from the local organs of the state, beginning with the *préfecture*. The local *sous-préfet* doubted whether a republican candidate would be able to hold the seat, because in the previous year's legislative elections the conservative–monarchist list of candidates had gained the majority. He warned, 'Everything will hang on the choice of candidate and on the kind of campaign he will have fought.'[5] Jules Develle was approached and declined. He suggested his *chef de cabinet*. Poincaré seemed an ideal candidate in that he could appear all things to all men: a moderate republican, but also the descendant of the monarchist Gillon family. The *sous-préfet* of Commercy reported:

Raymond Poincaré will enter the fight with a clear chance of success: his family has around Pierrefitte very useful contacts, his present functions [Jules Develle's *chef de cabinet*] and the hope of obtaining governmental favours will not leave many voters indifferent. Moreover M. Poincaré is very intelligent, a pleasant speaker, who has a real desire to please and to get on.[6]

Or as Jules Develle told him, 'Your name is known, you benefit from the veneration for your father, your ancestors.'[7]

The *conseil général* was responsible amongst other things for the maintenance of roads, streets, sewers, hospital services and railway routes across the department. Being a councillor was not an onerous task; there were only two sessions a year each lasting from two to three days. Poincaré claimed to have agreed unenthusiastically. His patron, Develle, set about organising the twenty-six-year-old's campaign by using his political relations in the area and the local press under his control, especially the republican *Indépendance de l'Est*, of which he was a founder. On 18 July 1886 the *Indépendance de l'Est* announced the candidate Poincaré as being 'the great-grandson of Landry Gillon, *député* in 1830–1848'.[8]

Poincaré's 'profession de foi', while stressing his local roots, was no less inclined to evoke his monarchist ancestor: 'Born of an old family of the Meuse which gave to our department one of its most faithful servants, my great-grandfather Landry Gillon, I have for a long time been attached to the Pierrefitte *canton* by old family relations ...'[9] The republican *Indépendance de l'Est* could unashamedly proclaim, 'We wonder whether our opponents will dare fight the great-grandson of Landry Gillon'.[10] Supporters of his monarchist opponent, Count Nettancourt-Vaubecourt, replied, 'Poincaré is wrong to recommend himself on the strength of his great-grandfather Landry Gillon, because M. Gillon was a fervent monarchist, and would be much saddened to see his great-grandson in the opportunist party.'[11] Poincaré's public response showed his apparently apolitical nature: 'I am and will remain the enemy of adventurous and vain political agitation, which has no other effect than to block the quiet and thoughtful study of affairs.'[12] He may have been adhering strictly to the forgotten law of 1871 which forbade overtly political stances in the deliberations of the *conseil général*. More likely, it suited the republican cause that their candidate should appear apolitical in these elections. But there was also the fact that what mattered most for the young Poincaré, now and later, was practical politics rather than ideology. After his election to the *conseil général* of the Meuse in the first round of voting on 1 August 1886, he made this quite clear. Though elected as a member of the moderate republican 'Union des Gauches', he refused to take a party line on issues but judge them purely on merit. This caused many raised eyebrows amongst his political friends and the *préfet*, notably when he refused to renew a longstanding agricultural subsidy with electoral implications on the grounds that it was not legal.[13] Even at this early age, Poincaré's honesty and respect for the law would not allow him to accept the practice whereby prefects under the early Third Republic were expected to favour elected republicans by giving them privileged access to the local state administration in order to benefit their constituents.[14]

During his period as *conseiller général*, not an onerous task, he continued to live in Paris and act as *chef de cabinet* for Jules Develle. But in May 1887, following the fall of the Goblet ministry, Develle lost his agriculture portfolio and Poincaré his post as *chef de cabinet*. He returned to the Bar, to writing for the *Voltaire* and to playing a greater role in the *conseil général*.

Despite his stated reluctance to embark on a political career, Poincaré increasingly had the profile of an early Third Republican politician and was certainly involved in all the right things to become one; journalism, the law and local politics. The osmosis between politics and the press under the Third Republic meant that most senior politicians understood the importance of having a regular newspaper column, just as the press understood the need for politician–journalists when so much copy was devoted to parliamentary life and politics. Like 70 per cent of *députés* between 1871 and 1898 Poincaré had been through higher education, and like 45 per cent of those elected to the Chamber in 1881 he had a degree in law. The typical parliamentarian was changing, with the traditional elites giving way to the middle to upper middle classes drawn principally from the liberal professions; moderate Gambettist politicians like Poincaré came increasingly from the law and journalism. The *conseil général* was on its way to becoming a useful stepping-stone to a political career and, given the weakness of the parties, a precious local power base for a parliamentarian, as Jules Ferry and René Goblet's careers testified. Though Poincaré would not have known, the *conseil général*, renewed by half every three years, was to be a barometer of French public opinion at large on major issues such as hostility to Boulangism in 1889 or income tax in 1896, and support for the establishment of the Republic and the separation of church and state.[15] He would continue to play an important role in the *conseil général* of the Meuse until shortly before his death nearly half a century later. For the moment, there was a hint of disingenuousness in his protestations about wishing to begin a political career, the kind of feigned reluctance he would display before embarking on any major undertaking; Poincaré was ambitious and driven by an ingrained competitive spirit that pushed him to be top in all that he undertook. Louis Barthou, someone with whom Poincaré had made friends at the law faculty and whose career would follow an almost identical path to his own, was later to write about his step from local to national politics:

When one is clever, attentive, approachable, open, eager, obliging, dedicated, you quickly earn both popularity and a clientele. You are the instrument, the intermediary, the voter's commissioner to the administration. You make yourself known to the sub-prefect, the prefect, the city engineer, the comptroller, the school inspector. You make things happen, while making news. Little by little you secure control of the situation, and make yourself indispensable.[16]

Poincaré seems to have been no different.

Député

In 1887 the death of the *député* for the Meuse led Jules Develle and his political friends to encourage Poincaré to stand in the by-election. They were beginning to understand his need for reassurance in public life and his fear of failure. He agreed, again with an impression of reluctance. It should be said that this was a common refrain from new candidates, who invariably maintained that it was only at the insistence of friends that they had decided to sacrifice a quiet life for one of duty, when in reality they had been working towards a political career by seeking the patronage of a political figure and doing their apprenticeship in the *conseil général*.[17] But first he had to face selection before the local Republican committee. With Jules Develle as his political patron, this was a mere formality. His speech on 17 July 1887, which was timid, hesitant and largely apolitical, did make one clear political statement: he was opposed to a separation of church and state on the basis that an independent clergy would be too powerful. He was selected, but Poincaré's political reserve led the *Courrier de Verdun* to remark correctly, 'Monsieur Poincaré shows a white paw to the conservatives and a red paw to the "radicaux de gauche".'[18] This was a charge made against him throughout his political career and reflected a temperamental centrism.

He went on the stump, making academic and dry speeches which praised the Opportunists' policies and drew the fire of local radicals. The opposition press drew attention to his 'puppet voice which has an effect on the nerves similar to a high-pitched grating sound and which is analagous to a wildly out-of-tune clarinet'.[19] He had close-cropped hair, small stature, dark tailed coat and a grave air, and he looked young despite attempts to camouflage it with an adolescent moustache. He had already adopted his characteristic rounded goatee beard, sported by his father and moderate republicans like Jules Develle, in contrast to the thick full beards of the extreme Left typified by Camille Pelletan or Jean Jaurès. Campaigning was good training for him, especially having to deal with hecklers. He gained in confidence from it, though he never really learnt how to accept criticism. As a child he had always liked the last word. Now he learnt how to ridicule his opponents through sarcasm.

Nothing is known of how his campaign was financed, though the support he got from Jules Develle would have reduced his costs. One could expect it to have cost less than 20,000 francs, which was the average for even a modest campaign at that time, the state making no contribution for either posters or ballot papers. This was a considerable amount of money given that the annual parliamentary salary was then set at 9,000 francs. Tradition dictated that much expenditure should go on bar bills during election rallies. Poincaré would have saved money – but lost votes – on this item, given his abstemiousness. But as a governmental candidate, he would have received the unofficial support of the resources of the state for his campaign. This by-election was to be one of the last to take place under the list system of proportional representation which had been introduced for the 1885 general elections. Despite the fact that single-member two-round majority voting every four years would be used for all other legislative elections between 1876 and 1914, Poincaré would later express a preference for proportional representation. Intimidation of voters and corruption were not unknown, especially in rural areas. The voter brought his own ballot paper, and it was not until the laws of 1913 and 1914 that polling booths, envelopes for ballot papers and the right of the voter to place his ballot in the urn himself were institutionalised.[20]

Poincaré was elected to the fourth legislature of the Third Republic with 74 per cent of the vote on 31 July 1887. This was to be the beginning of a forty-two-year parliamentary career marred by no electoral defeats. He would continue to represent the Meuse constituency as a *député* until 1903 and then as a senator until 1929, broken only by a seven year interlude as president of the Republic.

Poincaré was the youngest member of parliament at twenty-six. This was well below the average age of forty-two for *députés* first elected to the Chamber under the Moderate Republic, even though this was lowering and careers were getting longer.[21] Most of his colleagues lived in the 'political ghettos' of the capital in the vicinity of the Chamber and ministries between Etoile, Invalides and the Latin Quarter. So too did he. But whereas they could expect to pay rent in the order of 2,000 francs a year, he continued to live with his parents in the Latin Quarter, leaving more of his income to cover the *député*'s numerous expenses from campaign funds to travel costs. In this, as in other ways, Poincaré was representative of Jules Ferry's followers within the Republican movement, as opposed to those of Gambetta. Though politically similar, social differences separated them. Whereas the latter were of more humble origins, had 'come up the hard way' and now met and mixed socially, the former were generally from a background of *notables*, had attended university and were now members of the liberal professions. Ferry's followers tended to live in family surroundings and were more independent of the activities of the average professional politician. The Gambettists tended to live by, and thus for, politics. This social independence, with which some might reproach Poincaré, also allowed him to keep his distance from political life and thus remain at important moments aloof from scandal or sufficiently detached to criticise the political system and its mores.[22] For the moment, as a protégé of the moderate governing Opportunists in the Chamber, he merely followed their line, claiming that it was not his responsibility to take an independent line.

Poincaré entered the Chamber as the era of the founding fathers of the regime was drawing to a close, following the fall of Jules Ferry in March 1885. Economic and social problems were beginning to tarnish the image of the parliamentary liberal Republic for the urban masses, who were beginning to turn to ideas more in tune with their interests: nationalism and socialism. These phenomena would come together under Boulangism, bringing about a crisis of the regime. The 1885 general elections had seen a decline in the fortunes of the moderate republicans to the benefit of the Right. The former had held power from 1881 to 1885 but had been dogged by the Radical republicans led by

Clemenceau, *tombeur des ministères*, who sided with the conservatives to bring down government after government. Parliamentary instability, economic depression dating from 1882, the continuing international isolation of France by Bismarck and the concerted electoral strategy of the Union of the Right, increased the Right's electoral score, though insufficiently to oust the moderate republicans. They clung to power by including Radical ministers in their governments to secure a majority. One of those Radicals was the new minister of war, General Boulanger. He quickly made himself popular by reforms within the army and by sounding the patriotic chord, notably on the question of 'revanche'. The general's displays of international bravado towards Germany during the Schnaebelé Affair in April 1887, when a senior French police officer was detained in Alsace by the Germans, worried moderate republicans like Jules Ferry who were in favour of a more conciliatory attitude towards Berlin, given France's military weakness and absence of allies. The Opportunists agreed to overturn the Goblet ministry. Its successor, led by Maurice Rouvier at the end of May 1887, excluded Boulanger. This left the latter free to garner support among the many discontented from urban working class to bourgeoisie, and from socialists to monarchists. Of the Left, although anti-parliamentary and favouring a strong plebiscitary executive, Boulanger rallied tremendous popular support. Boulangism was born and by September 1887 represented a formidable opposition force to the Republican regime.

Poincaré was elected in this political atmosphere, though his by-election had been an uneventful affair, largely unnoticed in the national press. The Chamber to which he was elected contained on the Right 201 *députés*, twice as many as in 1881, made up of Bonapartists, monarchists and 'conservatives', and on the Left 383 republicans. But the latter were divided into several different tendencies which could be roughly grouped under the radical and moderate labels.[23] Poincaré took his place among the moderates or Opportunists. Their political philosophy took its cue from the older, more moderate Gambetta, and Jules Ferry whose republicanism was practical and cautious and whose reforms were mainly political in character. They shared the belief that France had had more than her share of political violence and turmoil since the Revolution. The Republic now in place was the regime which was, in the words of Thiers, the veteran Orleanist who became its first president, 'the government which divides us least', provided it remained conservative.[24] They were satisfied with the present political institutions of the Republic – Chamber, Senate, presidency – which favoured political moderation. On the religious question, firmly rooted in French politics since the Revolution, their stance was militantly secularist encapsulated in the term *laïcité*. They were influenced by positivism and the republican tradition of anti-clericalism, that believed that religion was destined to wither away, but that in the meantime the Catholic Church, a pillar of obscurantism and political reaction, should have its influence reduced. But no attempt should as yet be made to disestablish the church, and religious conviction should be tolerated respectfully, for, as Jules Ferry realised, 'our electors go on pilgrimages'. Nevertheless in this 'republic of lawyers', imbued with a reverence for the written text, the legal mind jarred at the still privileged status of the church which ran contrary to the great Revolutionary principle of freedom of conscience. Bringing the church into line was as much to do with legal tidiness as justice. Poincaré would most certainly not have disagreed with the lawyer–politician Waldeck-Rousseau, father of the 1901 Law on Associations, when he commented 'that an institution is founded, a reform accomplished only when written down in a rigorous and unassailable text'.[25]

In as much as Poincaré already had any serious political convictions, they could certainly blend with Opportunism, or Progressism as it would soon be called. As yet he was not even registered as belonging to any parliamentary political group. During the next two years he would make no speech in the Chamber, nor be active behind the scenes, apart from writing a couple of short parliamentary reports. He bided his time, getting to know the workings and traditions of a rather inhospitable Chamber, and probably attempting to overcome the embarrassment of his voice and a lack of self-confidence. He himself admitted that the idea of making a speech in parliament 'frightened him terribly'.[26] As a member of the ruling majority there was no need for him to do so. This unhurried, risk-free strategy would later pay dividends. His method was in tune with his ideas: empirical, cautious, adapted to the times and in step with public opinion. Poincaré the public and private man would have been at ease with Gambetta's 1877 statement 'One should only commit oneself wholeheartedly to a question when one is sure of the support of a majority of the country ... When the country is reticent, whatever my passion, I resist.'[27]

In the meantime Boulangist agitation continued its noisy growth. 'Le brave général', as a contemporary popular song referred to him, began to represent a serious threat to the regime through the 'Comité du parti national' and its programme for constitutional revision in favour of a more authoritarian and socially committed regime. Political scandal fuelled the movement. Daniel Wilson, son-in-law of the president of the Republic Jules Grévy, had been discovered trafficking in Legion of Honour decorations. Anti-parliamentary feeling soared. On 2 December

1887 the president resigned, raising the major question of whether Jules Ferry, detested by nationalists and the extreme Left, should succeed him. The scandal helped crystallise Boulanger's support in Paris and create the threat of widespread public disorder. Grévy was eventually replaced by Sadi Carnot, but Boulanger's political ascension continued apace following his compulsory retirement from the army for political activity in March 1888. Having been successful in a series of by-elections across the country in 1888 when multiple candidatures were possible under the *scrutin de liste* electoral system, he went on to be elected in Paris on 27 January 1889 with noted success in a number of working-class districts, hitherto bastions of the extreme Left Blanquists. Some hoped that Boulanger would march on the Elysée, but he refused, preferring to put his faith in the 1889 general elections. Some believed, after the event, that a Boulangist *coup d'état* might have succeeded. But as at other moments in the history of the Third Republic a threat of this nature galvanised republican forces. The proportional representation system, with its department-wide constituencies and plebiscitary multiple candidatures, was changed back to the *scrutin d'arrondissement* majority system. Members of the Boulangist committees were charged with treasonable activities. Boulanger was threatened with prosecution for subversive activities by the Senate in its role as supreme court. On 1 April 1889 the valiant general took fright and fled to Belgium and the arms of his tantalisingly named mistress, Mme de Bonnemain. The general elections of September, while demonstrating the hold Boulangism had over the urban electorate, were far from a victory for the movement. The general would soon commit suicide on his mistress's tomb in Brussels. As for the discontented popular electorate which had supported him, it now turned to socialism. At the same time, patriotic and *revanchard* nationalism metamorphosed into an anti-parliamentarian and authoritarian variant. Radicalism, hitherto urban and revisionist, lost Paris and began its implantation in the French countryside. A further consequence of Boulangism was to discredit revision and reform of the state, apart from that of the Senate, as well as any step towards a more authoritarian form of democracy. Though the army was not implicated in the Boulangist crisis, in the longer term it would suffer in republican memory from having had one of its leaders as the driving force of the movement.[28] Though Poincaré took no part in the crisis, the legacy of Boulangism stigmatised and handicapped a number of constitutional reforms he later deemed necessary to improve politics under the Third Republic.

In this first serious test of the Republican regime, Poincaré remained a mere spectator despite encouragement from friends like the Radical

Millerand and the moderate Hanotaux. Throughout 1888 and 1889 he took no part in any parliamentary debate, though his vote was regularly recorded. Thus he voted for the abolition of the short-lived *scrutin de liste* system in an effort to curb the success of demagogues such as Boulanger though, like certain other republicans, he remained committed to it over single-member majority voting. His action was purely administrative, as his role as *rapporteur* for a number of petitions to parliament covering anything from winegrowers' grievances to wrongful imprisonment proved.[29] Here was a foretaste of what some of his friends would later refer to as his lack of moral courage. His native prudence would not allow him to assume a vocal role until he had fully learnt his parliamentary role. But his silence was no different from that of the large majority of *députés* who never spoke and whose only proof of existence in the Chamber was their vote, albeit often cast in their absence.

But getting on in politics in the early Third Republic was by no means restricted to making speeches in the Chamber or a parliamentary commission; an ability to speak in a salon could be more beneficial. Among Opportunist republicans in particular there was a tradition of intimate political dinners where careers could take off more effectively than in the Palais Bourbon. Poincaré was a member of several dining circles (which, like 'La Bombe', were not always political in nature) with his legal friends, 'Les esclaves de la morale' (The slaves of morality), or 'Le roulement' comprising only Lorrainers, where politics, the arts and frivolity mingled.[30] He had a reputation for enjoying ladies' company, but was always most discreet. Romantically he maintained a certain distance in his relationships, which gossip columns would interpret as confirmation of his bachelor status. He had by now left his parents' flat in Paris for one of his own at 29, rue de Bourgogne.[31]

Back in the Meuse his constituents were disappointed with his performance nationally and locally. The 1889 changes to the electoral law were unlikely to benefit him, as the smaller single-member constituencies favoured committed local candidates, which he did not appear to be. In the 1887 by-election he had been unopposed; but in the 1889 general election he was faced with a conservative and a Radical with Boulangist convictions, the Radicals having split over support for Boulangism. He threw himself into an extremely polemical and bitter campaign. Even before campaigning had officially opened Poincaré had become embroiled in a dispute with the Radical candidate Tugny, a former primary school teacher turned journalist on the Boulangist newspaper *Le Républicain de l'Est* and *conseiller général* for Commercy. In the *conseil général* Poincaré refused to sign a document bearing Tugny's name on the grounds that he was a demagogue. Tugny took offence.

Poincaré refused to withdraw his remarks and threatened, 'If my remark displeases him it is something to be settled outside this sitting, if he agrees.'[32] A duel by pistols was arranged. Poincaré's seconds were a *député* and a senator. Each of the duellists fired a shot, but neither was wounded. Though illegal, duels among politicians were not infrequent under the Third Republic. It has been calculated that between 1875 and 1900 some 200 duels a year were fought, with up to 300 in years marked by political crises such as during the Boulanger and Dreyfus affairs, even if there was less than a 2 per cent chance of fatality. But pistols – used by Poincaré in this case – were more dangerous, which explains why they were used in only 10 per cent of French duels. Of the hundred or so political duels which took place during the 1880s there were no deaths and only eleven serious woundings.[33] Duels were so established in the Third Republic's masculine code of honour that newspapers regularly carried notices of them, redolent of births, deaths and marriages. Poincaré appears to have fought only this one, another in 1894 being settled before reaching the duelling ground, as was the case for one third of all French duels. Clemenceau is credited with twenty-two virtually bloodless episodes; his technique, doubtless not unique, was to fire wide. The French bourgeoisie's desire to ape aristocratic codes and identify with a French chivalry stretching back to Charlemagne might explain such theatrics, though 'honour' should not be underestimated as an important moral component of the Third Republic.[34] Duelling probably appealed to Poincaré's romantic nature, notwithstanding the calculation that a dash of courage would enhance an otherwise unheroic image in the forthcoming elections. Many writers and politicians felt it a point of honour to have fought at least one duel in their careers.[35]

The 1889 election campaign was particularly acrimonious, reflecting the general political atmosphere of Boulangism's populism, nationalism, anti-semitism and anti-parliamentarianism. Tugny attacked Poincaré's bourgeois, Jewish candidature. Poincaré was by comparison almost politically colourless. His *profession de foi* written on 10 September 1889 stated non-committally, 'I am a republican without a label, I am the enemy of controversy which blocks decisions'. But he did denounce the unholy and impossible alliance between the extreme Right, represented by the monarchists, and the extreme Left, mainly the Blanquists: 'You can see monarchists and the agents of social upheaval arm in arm. Both share as an aim destruction and as a means slander; today in agreement on overthrow, tomorrow they would be unable to agree on reconstruction.' It was a characteristic denunciation of reaction and revolution, and an implicit appeal to moderation. His final flourish was so moderate as to border on the banal: he simply reminded the voters that this was the year of the centenary of the 1789 Revolution 'which created modern society'.[36]

Poincaré emerged from the first round on 22 September with 8,033 votes, ahead of the conservative with 5,288 and the Radical Tugny's 3,273 – a good score which gave him 46 per cent of the vote, just short of the absolute majority which would have ensured his election on the first round. For the second round the Radical withdrew in favour of the conservative, putting Poincaré in a weak position. Poincaré intensified his campaign, increasing the number of speeches and public meetings, ignoring or countering the most vicious and notably anti-semitic attacks. It paid dividends. In the second round Poincaré was elected with 55 per cent of the vote.

If any single event contributed to making politics a career for Poincaré it was this election campaign. For the previous two years he had merely observed the political scene, devoid of any strong political convictions other than a moderate republicanism. His impressions could not have been good. Certainly for the moment the Republican regime appeared the most appropriate in the absence of anything better; public opinion appeared to accept it, albeit without enthusiasm, and it provided a framework for moderation. But it had shown itself corrupt in the Wilson scandal and inefficient by its instability. The election he had just fought for the Meuse/Commercy constituency was a microcosm of French national politics – the moderate pitted first against the Right and Left and then against both together. His moderate, middle-of-the-road campaign had triumphed over the violent invective of the Boulangist/conservative onslaught. As he himself remarked,

never before in our constituency had the enemies of the Republic acted with such offense, such calumny, never before had they so openly made such a shameful alliance, nor employed such guilty machinations. Their efforts here as in the rest of the country have only rendered their failure more complete. You have valiantly resisted the assault of that coalition, with many of you, in the second round, sickened, disillusioned, voluntarily coming over to swell the number of my votes.[37]

The lesson of these elections was two-fold: it confirmed Poincaré in his view that the moderate Republican regime was what France needed; it showed him that he could be of political service to the country. As the local *préfet* noted in his report of 20 December 1889, 'He is a man of action and of will-power on whom the Republic can count on all occasions'.[38] Greater self-confidence now led him to wish to reinforce the Republic and improve its organisation and workings. This he intended to do not by rhetoric and starry-eyed nostrums pontificated in the Chamber, but by something which came more naturally: hard work and gradual reform.

Le service de la France

In France the notion of service to the state, as opposed to one's country, is stronger among politicians and civil servants than it is in most other countries. It carries with it a sense of honour and loyalty that followed the transfer of sovereignty from the monarch to the nation at the time of the Revolution. Poincaré, in common with other lawyers of the Third Republic such as Gambetta and Ferry, was steeped in the Roman conception of public power and confidence in the virtues of reason applied to serving the general interest through autonomous action by the state. As Pierre Avril has written,

With the Republic, the State gave itself an objective above party politics (the general interest) which it pursued with the aid of a privileged instrument (public service) in terms of a set of values laid down by the Declaration of the Rights of Man. It thus possessed a body of principles enabling it to regulate itself, quite independently of any political pressure. The machine could function on its own and take the necessary initiatives.[39]

Poincaré's conception of public service derived from his family ancestry, his training in law and a strong personal sense of honesty, probity and duty. It is not surprising that in later years when he came to publish his ten volumes of political memoirs he should entitle them *Au service de la France*.

Poincaré's future reputation as one of the most honest politicians of the Third Republic would be admired by some, despised by others, or merely thought of as too good to be true. Like Robespierre he earned the nickname of 'La Blanche Hermine'. His whiter than white image began to take shape shortly after his election to the *conseil général* when he had refused to sanction a politically motivated subsidy, to the astonishment of his political colleagues and annoyance of the *préfet*. It would assume a more positive and practical nature on his return to the Chamber after the 1889 election. The composition of the new Chamber offered moderates such as Poincaré many opportunities; Radical influence was greatly reduced. The conservative republicans (the term Opportunist was no longer current) might not have a majority over Right and Radicals combined, but they were not far from it. They only needed to detach a few Radical deputies, which was not difficult given the absence of disciplined political parties, to form a majority; it was even less of a problem given the absence of any clear divide between conservative republicans and moderate Radicals. Thus the period from 1889 to 1896 would be characterised by shifting majorities and governmental instability which provided middle-of-the-road characters like Poincaré with ministerial openings. The period would be all the more amenable for moderates because important political issues were largely ignored in parliamentary manoeuvrings; that the French parliament was settling into one of its most quiescent periods was a further blessing.[40]

Buoyant from his electoral success, Poincaré's period of observation was over. He set about ensuring his nomination to a parliamentary commission. Under the Third Republic the constitutional and practical dominance of the Chambers made them masters of parliamentary business and legislation. A government bill could only be discussed after a report had been prepared by a parliamentary commission nominated by the eleven *bureaux* comprising all *députés*. The army and budget commissions, though officially *ad hoc*, had in reality become permanent since the beginning of the regime.[41] The priority of restoring national credit after the Franco-Prussian war had conferred particular prestige on the thirty-three man budget commission. Membership also conferred privilege in that commissioners were not expected to vote in the Chamber on delicate issues. Consequently, according to former premier Jules Simon, nomination involved 'shameless haggling'.[42] Friends in high places must have secured a place for Poincaré in the commission, given his youth, his newness to parliament, the absence of a parliamentary speech and the fact that by his own admission he had no knowledge of, nor affinity for, financial matters. His only asset would have been his identification with the politics of the moderate governing republicans. Jules Develle had recommended he specialise in finance, and probably ensured his appointment to the commission.[43] In this Poincaré was well counselled; the number of financial specialists in the Chamber was limited, and even then was predominantly composed of the old generation, including Méline, Peytral, Ribot or Rouvier.[44] His patron was certainly in a position to exercise influence; he had returned to government as agriculture minister from March 1890 until January 1893, and thence as foreign minister until the end of that year. Poincaré's first ministerial appearance in 1893 coincided with his political patron's holding of a major office of state.

As ever, application, thoroughness and sheer hard work quickly brought Poincaré to an understanding of the intricacies of the commission in its scrutinising of every aspect of the finances of the state. He soon came to the attention of the chairman, the influential Casimir Périer, who decided to entrust him with preparing a report on the finance ministry and the administration of the state mint (Monnaies et

Médailles), often considered as a stepping-stone to the office of reporter-general for the budget commission.[45] Only twenty-nine years old and his brief was to examine in detail the workings of a strategic department of state, Poincaré could not have had a better start, nor been better suited. The finance ministry was the crossover point between serving the state and politics. Though it was the purse for every department of state, the strings were held by parliament via the budget discussions and the voting of the finance bill. When Poincaré did not understand a problem he took out books or sought advice until he had mastered it. But it took no feat of erudition to understand that economic liberalism and strict financial orthodoxy formed the canon of early Third Republic economics, as it had since the July Monarchy. State intervention in economic life was minimal. Individual private property, the virtues of thrift, profit and a healthy return on savings kept taxes on property or income at bay and underlined the inexpediency of state expenditure. As one economic historian has remarked of this period, 'The tradition of Colbertism, though by no means dead, was never less potent than at this time.'[46] Poincaré would certainly have no difficulty identifying with the reigning economic orthodoxy. It is safe to assume that as a law student he had been as much an admirer of the political and economic liberalism of John Stuart Mill and Herbert Spencer as was his close friend Millerand.[47] But whereas Millerand had moved to more radical politics, Poincaré had not deviated. As far as state expenditure was concerned the orthodox principle, though not the practice, was a Gladstonian respect for balanced budgets.

By October 1890 Poincaré was sufficiently confident to take part in the budget discussions in the Chamber. A few months before, he had been given the chance of a practice run on the question of the conversion of a state loan. On this typically dry and technical subject he had spoken before the Chamber, of which he was still one of the youngest members, with clarity, crispness and authority. He himself remarked, 'On that day I jumped into the water and realised that I was swimming without too much effort'.[48] Reports in the press were flattering, apart from noting that a stronger voice and a little more height would have improved his performance. Poincaré's oratorical style resembled that of his friend Millerand. Both had assimilated the demonstrative method of their legal profession, both had taken diction lessons with the same actor from the Comédie française. Millerand's eloquence was said to be 'cold and correct'. One contemporary admirer noted, 'Listening to Millerand, one is struck by the total absence of warmth and by the icy indifference in every sentence – almost every word.' Another compared Millerand's delivery with that of his contemporaries and noted that Jaurès poured forth, Clemenceau rejoined, Alexandre Ribot advised, Briand seduced, while Millerand tried to convince. Millerand enunciated each syllable and proceeded with calm, sobriety, clarity and order.[49] This typified Poincaré's performances, together with an unfortunate nasal and high-pitched tone.

On 24 October 1890 he made his real début in the budget discussions volunteering to speak in defence of the budget. The Chamber appreciated the calm, clear, precise quality of his speech. He also impressed on substance. His theme was almost that of his unnoticed by-election manifesto for the Meuse constituency in 1887. Though defending the present budget he criticised French budgets in general for the lack of coherence and homogeneity in their accounting. He criticised the long-established system of 'creative accounting' whereby supplementary credits and accounts masked extra-budgetary expenditure, whether it be in the ministry of war or the tobacco and matches monopoly, all of which distorted the general accounts and which he castigated as 'parasitical budgets which live off the resources of loans'. In stating that the cause was historical he spread the blame across all regimes, but he claimed that it was time to bring order to this confusion by unifying the budget to enable politicians to keep a firm control of the accounts. Only then would it be possible truly to balance the accounts and redeem the national debt, not as now by subterfuge and financial expediency, but by voting the necessary taxes. And he concluded with a reference to the liberal economist Léon Say's remark that there were three types of courage, 'military courage, civil courage and fiscal courage' which led him to remark, 'For my part, I believe that fiscal courage is merely a form of civil courage'.[50] The speech was punctuated with applause from benches on the Left and Right, which testified to its even-handedness, and was greeted with widespread press praise. Poincaré modestly commented, 'Here I am raised to the status of financial expert without, however, knowing much about public finance'.[51] The speech was noteworthy for its non-partisan approach. It had apportioned blame for the state of the nation's accounts to all regimes; it implied criticism of the Right in attacking the supplementary credits and excessive expenditure of the ministry of war without wishing to threaten the nation's defences; it harried the Left by calling for administrative reforms which would flush out costly overmanning in the civil service. Apart from the occasional jibe at the Right, it was as balanced as the accounts he sought for the country. It was as skilful a piece of financial management as it was of politics. The *rapporteur*'s task was to investigate and criticise; in so doing Poincaré put state interests above party politics. Financial stringency and a balanced unified budget would become synonymous with 'Poincarism', even if in reality budget deficits were not eradicated under his stewardship. But his criticism of the budget had been carefully directed to fall within the bounds of tolerance of the governing moderates, thereby maintaining his political capital with the Opportunists.

The success of this first major intervention boosted his confidence considerably. Contrary to the account given by Payen and repeated by Miquel, this initial success was not followed by seventeen months' silence. Instead, barely five weeks later, while still *rapporteur* for the ministry of finance's budget, he was engaging in amusing repartee with his audience in the Chamber and relishing playing to the gallery. When a *député* criticised the diabolical nature of the finance commission Poincaré retorted, 'I cannot let pass without a short protest the comparison which our honourable colleague made between hell and the commission where I had the pleasure of collaborating with the bishop of Angers [laughter].'[52] His new self-confidence was demonstrated on three other occasions when through a mixture of rhetorical flourishes, sardonic humour and a bank of statistics he was able to win the plaudits of the Chamber while taking on such formidable parliamentarians as Camille Pelletan.[53]

He still found time to continue his own legal work and that of M^e Du Buit. This can be explained by his unwillingness to abandon anything he had begun. As a child, despite not having much to write in his diary he had refused to put it aside. So it was with the law and his other interest, writing. His native caution made him doubt that politics, like writing, could ever be a steady career. It was said of him that, while representing his constituents to the best of his ability, he liked to feel that his life rested upon a solid basis and was disciplined by regular work.[54] He would later write of this period, 'At a time when I had already gained a degree of notoriety in politics and the semblance of a reputation, I was willingly doing junior work in the law courts convinced that only long experience could help me exercise the profession of barrister.'[55]

Of course, political life under the Third Republic afforded ample opportunity for pursuing other interests. Parliament sat for seven to eight months a year, only three days a week and then usually from 2.15 in the afternoon. Absenteeism was common, particularly on the Right, facilitated by proxy voting, something which the British House of Commons did not allow. A *député*'s most laborious task was dealing with his mail. This was largely made up of requests from constituents for protection or mediation in their dealings with the cumbersome and often tyrannical administration. Something which Poincaré, and others, could not abide was the constant stream of 'recommendations' for jobs or favours which he would later attack vigorously as a sign of the weakness of the regime.[56] Poincaré's capacity for hard and efficient work enabled him to devote time to his other activities.

He kept up his writing by regularly contributing political articles under his own name to *La République Française* and *Le Siècle*. He wrote a foreign policy column for *Le Lyon Républicain*, which he signed 'un diplomate', and which he had taken over from Gabriel Hanotaux in 1889 when the latter had moved from parliament to the foreign ministry.[57]

In the political arena Poincaré could only have been appalled by disclosures concerning the politico-financial Panama scandal. The soaring costs incurred as a result of technical difficulties involved in cutting a waterway through the isthmus of Panama forced the Panama Canal Company to rely more and more heavily on floating loans to bail out its finances. The French parliament authorised this in 1888; but this did not stop the company going into liquidation in January 1889. In May 1891 legal proceedings were begun against the directors. Questions were asked about the ease with which parliament had sanctioned the loans, given that many members of parliament had financial interests in the company. Following the sudden death in November 1891 of the company's financial advisor, Baron Jacques Reinach, uncle and father-in-law of the leading Gambettist politician, Joseph Reinach, a parliamentary commission of enquiry was established. Governments began to topple as revelations were made about collusion between high financiers and parliamentarians. On 16 December 1891 two directors (the illustrious canal-builder and chairman of the Panama Company Ferdinand de Lesseps, and a former *député*) were arrested, while the lifting of parliamentary immunity for five *députés* (among whom was the former finance minister Rouvier), was called for by the head of the government, Alexandre Ribot. On 22 December 1892 twenty parliamentarians were charged with having taken bribes from the Panama Company in exchange for their votes, while another 104 names, including several ministers, were under suspicion. In February and March 1893 de Lesseps was tried for corruption, together with the parliamentarians. The latter were acquitted, apart from the former minister Baihaut who had made the unfortunate mistake of confessing. As the Panama affair took shape as one of the great scandals of the Third Republic politicians and governments toppled; the affair gained an international dimension as the Russian ambassador in Paris was implicated at the height of Franco-Russian *rapprochement*, to the delight of Germany. Although few members of parliament were actually found guilty of receiving bribes from the Panama Company at the trial in March 1893, all those who figured on a list of some one hundred suspected parliamentarians were discredited. Georges Clemenceau was forced to abandon, temporarily, his political career after defeat in subsequent elections. Many Opportunists and Radicals were for some time to become discredited in political life and the scandal precipitated a regrouping of the republican Left. A new generation of politicians emerged of whom Poincaré was one.

For someone as committed to duty to the state and incorruptibility as Poincaré, the Panama episode was unpalatable. It could only have reinforced his belief that the Republican regime should be renovated and a new political morality be installed. Gabriel Hanotaux rightly characterised Poincaré's political career as intended 'to provide France with a good administration of the public sphere' (la chose publique).[58] This could begin with proper financial accountancy in the French administration, keeping within budgetary limits specified by parliament and doing away with supplementary estimates. It was to this theme that he returned as *rapporteur* for the finance ministry's budget on 28 March 1892. He attacked departments which overspent. Recalling Baron Haussmann's quip about the cynical process behind budgetary overspending, 'Let's begin with the superfluous, useful expenditure will always be made', he ridiculed the ministry of the interior for asking for supplementary credits for the harsh winter of 1890–1 which had occasioned, on inspection, not only increased expenditure on heating, but also on furniture, vehicles and postage-stamps. He criticised the ministry of war for overspending under the cloak of patriotism and national defence, when in truth prudent spending was in the military interests of the country.[59] It was a courageous speech for, though couched in impersonal terms, it implicitly attacked the minister of war, Charles Freycinet, who was also premier and a leading Opportunist. This it was not intended to do, but principle not politics saw to that. It pleased the Left because it attacked the 'reactionary' ministry of war. This it also was not intended to do either, circumstance not politics had it that way. Ironically then, on the principle of financial stringency, which in the 1920s cast Poincaré as a politician of the Right, he disappointed the centre and pleased the Left. But again his performance was sufficiently skilful to balance carrying out the functions of *rapporteur* properly and overstepping the bounds of tolerance of the governing moderates. Certainly Freycinet would not harbour any grudge against him, later supporting Poincaré's candidature for the Académie française. One aspect of his parliamentary career was already clearly in evidence: an ability to evoke a united response from both sides of the Chamber on two issues which would be the mainstays of his reputation – namely financial rigour and patriotism.

By November 1892 he had been promoted from *rapporteur* for the ministry of finance to *rapporteur général* for the budget as a whole. Thus at the height of the Panama scandal he struggled to contain public expenditure. Though reasonably successful in tightening up the budget, when the finance bill reached the Senate, the upper chamber adopted a method of procedure frequently followed since and 'disjoined' it, which meant that reforms were not rejected but adjourned. The budget commission refused to accept this and referred the budget back to the Senate. Poincaré and the head of the government, Alexandre Ribot, disagreed with the commission's action, seeing in it the potential for an open conflict between the two assemblies. Caught between two evils, the Senate's profligacy and the commission's risky action, Poincaré resigned as *rapporteur général*. His successor upheld the commission's point of view and the conflict foreseen by him arose, for the reforms in question were not incorporated in the budget. But the incident proved the soundness of his judgement as well as demonstrating his moderation and practical common sense, all of which enhanced his parliamentary reputation. Thus when the second Ribot cabinet fell on 30 March 1893 and Jules Méline was called upon to form a new government, Poincaré was offered the ministry of finance. His hesitation and then refusal terminated Méline's attempts to form a government. The president of the Republic, Sadi Carnot, called on Charles Dupuy to try his hand. Dupuy was a new man to the premiership, an example of the post-Panama political class. He also offered the finance portfolio to Poincaré, who refused, but agreed to accept the ministry of *instruction publique, beaux-arts et cultes*. Poincaré probably turned down the finance portfolio out of caution, preferring to try his hand at a lesser ministry before a major department of state – at thirty-two he was said to be the youngest-ever minister in the Republic's history. Nevertheless, education was considered vital to the wider acceptability of the Republic and thus an important portfolio. The first Dupuy government was installed on 4 April 1893 and Poincaré took his place alongside his old protector Jules Develle at foreign affairs.

Poincaré's precocious elevation could be attributed to his membership of a new generation of moderate politicians untainted by scandal or the wear of office which included Louis Barthou and Théophile Delcassé, the latter of whom joined the new government. Added to this was the sturdy reputation he had acquired for technical competence, rigour and principle, while his cultivation of centrist politics did him no harm. And then there was his growing reputation for duty to the state which transcended narrow political commitments and even forms of regime. This he had demonstrated during the 1893 budget debate in responding to the question of expenditure incurred by previous regimes: 'When a pension is recorded in the ledger of public debt, it is not the Republic or the Empire, or the Restoration, or the July Monarchy which has signed. It is the State, it is France, and all parties should repect that.'[60]

At a more anecdotal level his tolerance and commitment to the substance rather than the form of things was demonstrated at the moment Charles Dupuy had sent for him to join the cabinet. Poincaré had been at Chantilly as a guest of the duc d'Aumale, son of former King Louis-Philippe. This had shocked the other members of the embryonic cabinet, but Poincaré refused to make excuses no matter how suspicious his Republican colleagues might be. He merely listed the other guests at the gathering which revealed its literary nature.[61] The duc d'Aumale was a recognised intellectual figure and a member of the Académie française. To a large extent the arts were an ideologically neutral terrain which allowed people of different political outlooks to frequent each other with equanimity. But here, as in the future, when choosing friends or company Poincaré would ignore labels and appearances and act freely. Such independence of mind would occasionally expose him to criticism; for some it was an endearing characteristic, for others it betrayed a lack of political judgement.

Minister

On hearing of Poincaré's appointment to the education ministry his mother was said to have remarked, 'Minister, that is not a career for a young man'. Still youthful in appearance, despite efforts to camouflage it, when he arrived at his ministry he was mistaken for the president of the students' union. He was soon installed with his old school-friend Payelle as *chef de cabinet*. When the latter took to referring to his former classmate as 'Monsieur le Ministre', Poincaré stood up, searched under the furniture and with a smile said, 'Nobody is here, I assure you ... No Monsieur le Ministre'.[62] Poincaré's realistic assessment of the longevity of ministerial life and his desire for independence were reflected in his declining to live in the official ministerial apartment: 'I'll soon be sacked ... I don't want to have it recorded that I haven't even scratched the furniture.'[63] He was not far wrong; the government lasted only six months. But he was particularly proud to have in his charge French universities which he held dear, having at one time thought of an academic career.

Contrary to received opinion, it was not easy to become a cabinet minister under the Third Republic. There were far fewer portfolios than today; only ten in Dupuy's government, which was about average.

Despite the legendary instability of French cabinets, the maxim 'instability of ministries, stability of ministers' accurately described how successive ministers tended to be drawn from the same small pool of personalities. Poincaré was a perfect example of the cabinet minister of his day. Like 36 per cent of ministers between 1877 and 1899 he was a lawyer.[64] Between 1871 and 1914 38 per cent of fathers of ministers, the largest proportion, were, like his own, from the *bourgeoisie diplomée et de fonction*. Like him, three-quarters of ministers were from the middle classes; 60 per cent were, like him, from small rural towns of between 2,000 and 20,000 inhabitants, reflecting the decline, since the Commune of Paris, as purveyor of the French governing class. The latter trend increased as the Republic evolved, leading to a substantial over-representation in French politics of the already dominant conservative countryside. Like two-thirds of ministers under the Moderate Republic up to 1900 Poincaré continued to hold local office as *conseiller municipal* or *général*, thus like most ministers he continued to be imbued with the values of the provincial bourgeoisie.[65]

Selection for ministerial office could depend on a host of factors from the influence of a political 'patron' to the power, particularly in republican circles, of masonic lodges. Poincaré benefited from the former but was not a mason. In the early Third Republic Lorrainers, Vosgiens and later southerners had a higher than average success rate; under the Moderate Republic from 1877 to 1899 nearly one-quarter of ministers were, like Poincaré, from the east of France. It was a region of peasant proprietors with a long democratic tradition, which had not been won over to Napoleon III, though it was Catholic and rejected radicalism in the 1900s. The patriotism generated by the region's proximity to the German frontier gave it an affinity with the new patriotic appeal of the twentieth-century Right. Ferry, Méline and Poincaré were characteristic politicians of the east, which became a bastion of Progressist or moderate republican ideas. This modern democratic form of conservatism in this region subsequently helped rejuvenate the French Right and facilitated its adaptation to democratic conditions. The east was part and parcel of Poincaré's political career. He had followed what would become a classic career path: a short apprenticeship in the Chamber, a first contact with the affairs of state through a parliamentary commission – ideally finance – and a good solid speech on a technical subject, and the trajectory was drawn. Of course wives, mistresses (often drawn from the Comédie française, or that other nursery of 'ministresses', as they were referred to at the time, the *corps de ballet* of the Opéra), or the need for the obligatory moderate to balance the edifice, could also do the trick.[66]

Becoming a minister also meant a change in life-style. The salary increased to some 32,000 francs, between thirty and forty times the starting salary of a primary school teacher.[67] Apartments and numerous servants gilded the promotion. But Poincaré forswore the baubles and chose to live in his own flat out of a desire for independence and a certain simplicity of life-style which his middle-class background had ingrained in him.

As a minister he preferred to concentrate on the technical and administrative nature of the work as opposed to the politics. His enormous capacity for work, his ability to digest mounds of information and immediately winnow out the essential, quickly impressed the members of his private office. Many reforms were in the pipeline, notably the question of assembling the various disparate higher education faculties into a homogeneous integrated system of universities individually blessed with a certain autonomy. A bill to this effect had been laid before parliament in 1890. But in March 1892 the Senate blocked it after serious differences, notably on the question of which faculties in the provinces should become universities; those not possessing all four faculties of medicine, law, science and arts were unlikely to be given the status of university, thereby putting local interests at stake. The question of reforming the archaic curriculum of the law faculties also awaited action, as did a reform of medical studies. As all of these questions were on his desk when he arrived at the ministry there was no need to innovate – it was difficult enough just to carry through serious reform given the transitory nature of ministerial life under the Third Republic. Poincaré merely took his position in the line of ministerial pass-the-parcel, other than expediting matters faster and more efficiently than most. It was not until his second stint with the education portfolio that a law would be passed in 1896 creating a modern French university system.

Poincaré took the opportunity of his ministerial appointment to go out into the country and in his own words get across 'without pretension a few sane and simple ideas, make the Republic loved in the world of arts and letters, and above all stimulate everywhere patriotic feelings'.[68] More opportunistically, it was also a chance to get his own name known. Nevertheless, it was becoming evident that Poincaré's confidence in Republicanism was growing. The Republican regime was now nearly a quarter of a century old and had lasted longer than any other regime since 1789. It was proving its worth in bringing, if not ministerial stability to France, at least social and institutional stability. Since his re-election to parliament in 1889 Poincaré had joined the Progressist parliamentary group in the Chamber. This group hoped to give a new style to discredited Opportunism. It was initiated by Paul Deschanel at the beginning of the new parliamentary session in a speech which called for a 'progressist' policy to save France from the dangers of revolutionary socialism.[69] The renewal of parliamentary personnel amongst Opportunists and Radicals in the elections of 1889 and 1893 following the Boulanger and Panama episodes provoked a realignment of political forces which suited both Poincaré's temperament and political outlook. The new men who would play a dominant role in French politics right through to the early 1930s were the radical Léon Bourgeois and the moderates Paul Deschanel, Charles Jonnart, Georges Leygues, Louis Barthou and Poincaré. The pioneering political scientist, André Siegfried, who attended the parliamentary dinner parties thrown by his politician father, described these men as 'another generation, distinct from its republican ancestors and which, born into the regime, had not had to suffer in its founding'.[70] They brought a new style to discredited Opportunism by imposing the notion of 'progressivism'. Its substance had been set out in an innovatory speech by Paul Deschanel, which had called for 'progressivism' to protect France from the evils of revolutionary socialism. It sought to shift republican politics back to the centre away from the traditional reliance on majorities based on the Radicals through the idea of a 'liberal Republic', 'open to all men of good will'. The watchword was tolerance, particularly on the religious question. But already some moderates were looking to the Right for support with the likelihood that the cohesion of the governmental majority would be weakened.[71]

As minister for education and the arts, already with the lifelong trait of a keen eye for publicity, Poincaré embarked on a series of peripatetic speeches intended to promote both the arts and himself. Thus far his reputation extended only to the political elite of the country. As parliamentary and governmental life had an artistic and literary dimension in the first half of the Third Republic, showing oneself to be a dynamic and sympathetic minister for the arts could enhance political standing by giving a human dimension to an otherwise dry and technical silhouette.[72] The arts also appealed to Poincaré for their ideological neutrality. And then, of the three strings to his bow, law, politics and writing, the latter was particularly dear to him. Most arts ministers, when solicited by hundreds of associations to speak at myriad functions, would delegate the task to subordinates. Poincaré accepted invitations with enthusiasm. Only two days after the government was in place he was presiding over the opening session of the Congrès des sociétés savantes. His speeches were never superficial and always meticulously prepared. He was on his way to becoming an impressive speaker and his political convictions were about to become more publicly known.

Liberal republican

Raymond Poincaré has probably accumulated more hackneyed epithets than any other political figure of the Third Republic: Poincaré the Lorrainer, the bourgeois, the republican, the *laïque*, the patriot, the warmonger, defender of the franc, man of the Right, not to mention some of the more eulogistic or condemnatory labels. These labels have been a source of confusion in understanding the man, and no more so than in the political sphere. That Poincaré was of the political centre by temperament was clear by the 1890s. That he was ready to promote reform legislation on occasions is not in question. But some modern scholarship has questioned the motives of such moderate reformers and suggest that they were no more than clever counter-revolutionaries attempting to defer wholesale reform and preserve the social order and the interests of the middle class. In a recent thoughtful and sensitive biography of Louis Barthou – probably the Third Republican politician with the most similar career to Poincaré – Robert Young has asked how one is to characterise the practitioners of such reform, 'as liberals who promote change in order to preserve the social order, or as conservatives who have submitted to it for the same reason?'[73] This is reminiscent of that old debate as to whether the reforms of the Paris Commune were objectively or subjectively socialist. Of course, terms such as 'social order' and 'conservative' or, for that matter, 'opportunist', beg the question as to whether in the early Third Republic they had the same negative connotations they have since acquired. It would be reductionist to suggest that the moderate political leaders of this time were motivated wholly by class interest or that their policies did not hold to any more altruistic political philosophy. They worked within the confines of a philosophical framework broadly contained within the term 'Republic'. Certainly within this framework questions can be raised as to the uncomfortable position and motivations of centrists, as they are for centrists on any scale. Robert Young raises the important point that 'in contrast to the brittle rhetoric of revolutionaries or reactionaries, these are the centrists who are compelled to ponder every issue'.[74] Though people such as Barthou and Poincaré might subscribe to the goal of the 'Republic', the means to that end were constantly under review. This is axiomatic if they subscribe to a philosophy of positivism in which political and social progress is sought through empirical and evolutionist reform. Young's analysis of Barthou is as relevant for Poincaré:

Barthou was among those who would not exchange reflection for certainty. Sometimes he endorsed reform legislation, sometimes not. Sometimes his opinion seemed to alter with circumstance, as his weight shifted from one centrist parliamentary group to another. Of surface constancy there was little; and thus his critics made him out to be the sort who trimmed his sail to the prevailing breeze, not for any destination but only for the sake of keeping afloat. This view of him was widespread, a sacred belief among his enemies, a nagging doubt even among some friends.[75]

Centrists such as Barthou and Poincaré have not been helped by being grouped under the flag of Opportunism, which subsequently acquired its pejorative connotation. But what was the nature of Poincaré's politics? Central to any answer must be the description of him as 'Poincaré-the-republican' – the most elastic of epithets.

Certainly in his student days and first years at the Bar Poincaré showed no serious commitment to republicanism, which varied from the conservative version of Thiers to the radical version of Clemenceau. When starting out tentatively in politics, Poincaré gave no impression of having any particular enthusiasm for the Republic. It was almost an acceptance of the regime 'faute de mieux'. Temperamentally cautious, he would doubtless have preferred to see the Republic prove its worth before making any serious commitment to it. In this he was no different to certain Orleanist liberals and conservatives, examples of whom were to be found on his mother's side, who were beginning to discover in the 1880s, as the positivists Auguste Comte and Emile Littré had earlier explained, that the Republic was the only regime capable of 'pacifying' the French. What would have further attracted Poincaré to republicanism was the increasing evidence that this regime could also, in the best positivist tradition, combine Order with Progress.[76] By the time Poincaré had become minister of education in 1893 the Third Republic had outlived any other since the Revolution and had proved its worth. But what was Poincaré's conception of that shifting term 'Republic'?

Two conceptions of the Republic crystallised from 1875 to 1885: that of the 'républicains de gouvernement', the term dear to Jules Ferry; and that of the Radicals. That division, whether the 'républicains de gouvernement' be known as Opportunists or later in the Chamber officially as 'progressists', would be a running theme of the Third Republic. The republican form of government, established in 1875 by what one specialist has called a 'semantic surprise', would be electorally conquered in 1879 and thoroughly republicanised between 1880 and 1884 through the wave of legislation on laïcité, constitutional reform, municipalities, freedom of association and of the press. It would then be administered, and according to some exploited, by the 'Opportunists' until the 'Bloc des gauches' in 1902.[77]

The term Opportunist was, however, like much French political terminology, misleading. The leading lights of the movement, including Gambetta and Jules Ferry, were far from being men of few principles. On the contrary, they proudly proclaimed a carefully constructed and coherent 'doctrine', as well as a philosophy of action derived from the positivism of Auguste Comte. For moderate positivist disciples like the republican lexicographer and political philosopher, Emile Littré, who so influenced the founding fathers of the Third Republic, the aim of the Republic should eventually be to bring about a fusion of the two wings of French society: the monarchist and clerical elite and the leaders of revolutionary socialism. And the reason why, according to Littré in 1873, the Republic was the only regime capable of resolving this dichotomy was because it was based on 'apprenticeship': it was both the subject and object of a constant learning process which repeated elections tested and corrected – what Gambetta called 'the education of universal suffrage'. Because of this need for flexibility and evolutionism, the followers of Littré could not agree with Radical republicanism which wished to set in stone a regime which did not necessarily coincide with public opinion and material realities. Speaking of the moderate and constitutional Republic in place since 1875, Littré defined it in terms of order, time, opportunity and compromise, and added,

Such is the spirit which drives the present Republic, which reconciles many radicals and conservatives to it and, to name the two extremes of radicalism and conservatism, many workers and peasants. It is called the conservative republic; so be it: I do not object to such a title; because conservative signifies a guarantee of order, and republic a guarantee of progress.[78]

Thus, according to Littré, the 'conservative republic' was most likely to realise the inseparable virtues of the positivist formula of Order and Progress. Already in 1873 he had noted, 'Because it is necessary to stop both counter-revolution and revolution, a conservative policy is necessary'. That 'conservative republic' should guarantee freedom of all religious, philosophical, political and social opinions. Thus for a republican to be conservative meant above all 'conserving for oneself public opinion' by remaining 'rigorously and everywhere within the bounds of the law'.[79] The emphasis should be on gradual reform able to carry with it public opinion. This was also the definition of Gambetta and Ferry's 'conservative republic' to which Poincaré would fully subscribe: it did not rule out major reforms, but insisted that they be conditioned by the art of the possible, or as Ferry put it a 'policy of results'. Thus positivism was the mother of Opportunism; and Poincaré was a firm positivist. In 1896 the militantly positivist *Revue Occidentale* published Poincaré's name alongside the names of politicians whom it considered to be the greatest supporters of its cause.[80]

On the essential issue of *laïcité*, moderate republicans from Gambetta to Ferry and Waldeck-Rousseau again followed Littré's line in making an important distinction between Catholicism, the religion of the majority of the French, and Ultramontain clericalism. The former, 'catholicism according to universal suffrage', in Littré's words (which so annoyed Clemenceau and the Radicals), was regarded as acceptable for having in the past elected republicans when necessary. *Laïcité* for positivists and most republicans, involved a rejection of clericalism (in other words all claims by the church to intervene in civil society). What it did not seek was either to deny God or attack religion. Many of the new generation of positivists were agnostic rather than atheist. *Laïcité* was therefore intended to 'declare God to be in the private domain, and not in the public domain', largely because many republicans, like Poincaré, were confronted within their own families with the piety of women. The gradual withering away of religious belief would come eventually with education, which explains the emphasis laid on women's education since Victor Duruy. Thus, as Littré stated in 1875, tolerance had to be at the heart of *laïcité*.[81]

Poincaré was naturally suited to these moderate political and intellectual ideas. One can understand why he and other positivists between 1889 and 1893 chose Jules Ferry as their spiritual mentor, whose ideas Claude Nicolet has summarised as 'Order, Progress, reforms and conservation, weight of experience and continuity, refusal of apriorisms, of over-ambitious programmes' and a commitment to associate peasant and worker with the Republic.[82]

Just as Claude Nicolet says that it would be reductionist to attribute all of Ferry's and Gambetta's ideas to positivism, so it would be in Poincaré's case. Poincaré's republicanism, again like that of Gambetta and Ferry, incorporated a tradition which fell outside positivism. That tradition, which positivists even stigmatised as 'retrograde dogma', was an attachment to the mystique of the French Revolution and its establishment of the rights and institutions fundamental to republican France. As with Ferry, a further characteristic of Poincaré's republicanism was the notion of national unity which refused to overlook the contributions made to French greatness by those other than republicans. Thus national unity, that holy grail of French history, was more important to him than the unity of the 'republican family' itself. Notwithstanding Poincaré's desire to unite the 'republican party', the differences between Poincaré and the Radicals now became apparent. Given Poincaré's ambivalent relationship with the Radicals throughout his political career, it is important to see what set him apart from their ideas.[83]

For all republicans the Republic was the continuation and completion of the agenda set by the French Revolution. But like the moderate republicans, and unlike the Radicals, Poincaré instinctively recoiled from the excesses which followed 1793. Thus he could not accept Clemenceau's famous remark that 'the Revolution is a bloc'. What he retained from the Revolution was above all the 1789 Declaration of the Rights of Man, as he stated in a speech on 23 August 1896. And he listed what he considered to be the agenda set by the French Revolution:

Sovereignty of civil society; inviolable freedom of conscience; respect for private property, by State and citizens alike; equality of all before the law, before appointments, before social burdens; consent to pay taxes according to the capacity of the tax-payer; active fraternity and efficacious solidarity: it is on this synthesis of dominant ideas, it is on these clear and luminous summits that our gaze should be fixed, as if on the still distant goal of the struggle for democracy.[84]

Here was quintessential opportunism. Poincaré neither sought to add to that programme, nor to accelerate the time-scale for its execution, which was firmly lodged in the pragmatism of the positivists and which further set him apart from the Radicals, whose aim was to carry out the Revolution's agenda in all haste:

the building whose foundations were established by the French Revolution is still unfinished, and not for a long time will it be crowned. Before the gigantic enterprise which our fathers conceived and began is finished, generation will have succeeded generation. Let us avoid either falling asleep in reprehensible repose or becoming intoxicated with fanciful ambitions. We are the workers of one moment bent on an age-old task.[85]

There was no difference here from Poincaré's first *profession de foi* of 1887 which, in the mould of the moderate republicans, had stated that he was the 'enemy of reaction and backward steps' and called for 'matured reforms, wisely worked out and not hasty and foolhardy reforms',[86] the banality of which was only matched by its tautology. Such beliefs were shared by the large majority of French politicians and were the basis for the consensus at the heart of the Republican regime. These centrist ideas also placed Poincaré at the heart of the 'républicains de gouvernement' who, under successive labels of 'opportunist', 'progressist' and 'moderate' composed, with the Radicals, the vast majority of governments throughout the Third Republic.

Differences with the Radicals went further than mere questions on the nature of the Revolution and a time-scale for the application of its principles. The stress placed on anti-clericalism by the Radicals contrasted with Poincaré's more tolerant *laïcité*, characterised by a rejection of anti-religionism. Finally the Radicals' republicanism distinguished itself from the moderate variant by the emphasis it placed on the notion of 'solidarism', whereby the state should intervene to help those in need, as opposed to the insistence on self-help and the fostering of mutualist societies proposed by moderate Republicans. Such differences between Radicals and moderates provoked the cynical Radical quip that whereas Thiers had insisted that France should have 'the Republic without the Republicans', under the Opportunists France had 'the Republicans without the Republic'.

The Republican regime established on 4 September 1870 and defined by the constitutional laws of 1875 was a constitutional compromise. The Third Republic needed to be, in Thiers's words, 'conservative' and had survived for that reason. Poincaré had observed it develop under the moderate republican governments of the Opportunists and found that he could identify with it. Though fundamentally attached to parliamentary democracy, he would not have denied its mixed ancestry from the Revolution, the July Monarchy and the positivism of the Opportunists. Like the moderate republicans he was happy with the parliamentary institutions as they stood, unlike the Radicals who were officially in favour of a single chamber. But he could not overlook the fact that the republican institutions were not yet working as efficiently as they might, as governmental instability demonstrated. As time passed and the Republican regime proved itself to be the natural form of government for the French, Poincaré began to think of improving it by increasing the powers of the executive. But even here he was taking his cue from his spiritual mentor Jules Ferry, who at the time of the 1884 constitutional amendment rejected a proposal to limit further the president of the Republic's powers by abrogating his right to dissolve the Chamber. Poincaré would not have dissented from Ferry's 1889 speech praising the right of dissolution for being 'the only serious, efficacious, practical way of appealing to the people'. He could agree with Ferry that the Republic's future must not be undermined by a *'régime d'assemblée* which haunts the republicans'.[87] Poincaré shared Ferry's conception of the right of dissolution as being important for the establishment of an 'open' Republic in which two great political parties or coalitions would alternate on the British model. In this way national unity, forsaken for a century, could be rediscovered. He would also share Ferry's hope that the republican movement should stretch to the outer reaches of the nation. This was calculated to produce a large consensus around a centre Left which eventually would eradicate, through a mixture of firmness, concessions and careful 'progressism', the two opposing extremes of Left and Right. Here he was drawn closer to the Radicals. The legitimacy of the Republic lay in its ability to convert all the French, even its opponents, but without alienating the Radicals.[88] This explains Poincaré's constant striving from the beginning to the end of his political life to work with the Radicals, to serve in governments led by them and to include them in governments led by him. To a certain extent, he would have liked the same to apply to the other end of the political spectrum with the Right, but here his action was constrained by the ideology of the Republicans for whom an 'invisible line' existed at the frontiers of militant Catholicism, which could not be crossed. It followed that if the Republic was to be legitimate and universal along the lines drawn by Gambetta and Ferry, the notion of class struggle and class itself had to be outlawed. But to ensure that the universal principle of the Republic should not be diluted, it was obliged to exclude heretics until they underwent a conversion.[89] This was how Poincaré would view socialists, communists and the Catholic Right.

As a positivist republican, Poincaré was a believer in the science of organisation and of giving order to progress. This encompassed improving the efficiency of the republican institutions. For the moment his only tangible idea for improving the Republic's efficiency was by financial stringency designed to reduce state expenditure. His conception of the role of the state distinguished him from the Radicals and, even more so, the socialists. Of course, he recognised the need for the state to pursue social legislation, but more out of a need to maintain social peace than to promote equality. Like all liberals he was wary of what he saw as the state's tendency to usurp or thwart individual initiative, which he considered a fundamental value of the Republic. Such beliefs also motivated his *laissez-faire* conception of economics. This had been clear in his budget speeches of 1891. Like most centrists, he rejected certain aspects of the Napoleonic administration which had been grafted onto the Republic and which increased state intervention. He wished to reduce state bureaucracy, preferred private initiative in the form of co-operatives or mutualist insurance, supported the idea of arbitrational tribunals to settle industrial disputes and profit-sharing contracts for workers in private industry. It is not surprising that he voted against Clemenceau's ministerial recommendation for the nationalisation of the Western Railway in July 1908.[90]

In short, Poincaré was a liberal in political philosophy, in his conception of the state and parliamentary institutions, in his belief in private property and market economics and in his subscription to pragmatic reform. In as much as he considered that the Republic now provided the least unworkable framework for serving the French state through liberalism, Poincaré was a republican.

Poincaré's classification as a 'laïque' has misleadingly become synonymous with anti-clericalism. The liberalism he espoused elsewhere did not stop at religion, which he considered a private matter. *Laïque* he might be, but, like Ferry, 'antireligieux jamais'.[91] Thus the state's attitude to religion should be one of strict neutrality, which is how he conceived *laïcité*. It is likely that the individual freedom and tolerance of his upbringing had some bearing on his thinking. It was only fair that the state should observe strict neutrality regarding spiritual beliefs, notably in French schools, out of respect for those like his mother who wished to believe and those like his father who did not. Until his student days he too had been a devout Catholic. On the schools question, he told the socialist Jean Jaurès in December 1895, 'We want complete, sincere neutrality based not on negations but on impartiality; and we do not expect the schoolteacher to profess, in school, on human life, on the world or on society, philosophical or religious doctrines likely to contradict the religious or philosophical doctrines of his neighbour. That is true liberty; that is true neutrality.'[92] As with Jules Ferry there was no trace of anti-religion or anti-clericalism in this policy. What children thought or were taught in their homes or at church was their own, or their parents', choosing. But in state schools, to avoid divisions and maintain a consensus, a strict neutrality should be observed. In keeping with Ferry's speech to the Congrès pédagogique on 19 April 1881,[93] Poincaré believed that teachers should maintain complete political neutrality. They should remain aloof from the great passionate and divisive debates of the moment and especially those of party politics, in order to teach only what did not divide. For that reason he was opposed to examining primary school children on moral questions, favouring, himself, subjects which would allow them to express their personal feelings. The only moral teaching admissible in his eyes 'rests on personal conscience, with natural notions of good and bad ... It lies in the methodical cultivation of conscience, in the trial of will-power, in the affirmation of duty and responsibility, and also in the salutary lessons of work, that is to say in respect for property ...' His tolerance was also apparent from his belief that strict neutrality in state schools did not imply avoiding all religious references. On the contrary it involved borrowing from 'all systems the eternal maxims which make up the common and substantive part; let us borrow from ancient wisdom, from the Decalogue, from the Gospel, from the books of the moralists of all ages, those few essential precepts accepted by all religious denominations and consecrated by tradition and ratified by human reason'.[94] For the rest of his life Poincaré would champion *laïcité* as meaning essentially religious and political neutrality in state institutions, and the avoidance of anything likely to jeopardise consensus. Thus he would vote against the Law on Associations of 1901. And he was able, following his election to the Senate on 22 February 1903, to avoid taking part in the debate on that other great piece of anti-clerical legislation of the Third Republic, the separation of church and state in 1905. Others, such as the Radicals, had a more fundamentalist conception of *laïcité*. They conceived of it as an anti-clerical, even atheistic, crusade to establish a monopoly of secular education by doing away with religious schools altogether as a step towards the ending of Catholic influence, which would become the Radical party's official policy at the Marseille congress in 1903. Poincaré campaigned for his moderate *laïcité* through *laïque* organisations such as the Ligue de l'Enseignement, one of the pillars of the republican movement. And it is along these moderate lines that Poincaré's celebrated retort to a conservative Senator, Charles Benoist, conscious of the common political ground between himself and Poincaré and surprised at the absence of a *rapprochement*, should be interpreted: 'But between us there is the whole span of the religious question'. Though most moderate republicans shared his views on the religious question, his ideas erred more on the side of tolerance than other like-minded moderate republican politicians with whom his name was so often linked, such as Barthou.[95]

Fundamental to all of Poincaré's politics was thus the cautious liberalism of positivist and moderate republicanism. He would surely have agreed with his contemporary Emile Durkheim's assessment of the principles of 1789, in a book review of 1890, as being 'social factors with which all our national development for a century shows solidarity' and his quoting of the notion that, 'the strict duty of contemporaries will still be to gather piously from the Revolution's heritage those priceless treasures of patriotic faith, of devotion to the public good, of national solidarity, which our fathers laid down as examples for their descendants'.[96] Here was the agenda of Poincaré's whole political career – patriotism, service to the republican state and national unity.

His many speeches as minister of education echo those republican principles, as well as evoking values with which his name would be closely associated throughout his life. First there was evidence of his lifelong suspicion of party politics for its tendency to divide the nation, as well as his deep respect for public service. At the inauguration of the statue of the physicist François Arago he noted, 'Let us give thanks to François Arago for not having got mixed up in party intrigues, but let us congratulate him for not having been uninterested in the state.'[97] On

18 June 1893 at Château-Thierry for the celebrations in honour of La
Fontaine, he pleaded the cause of moderation: 'La Fontaine denounced
without ostentation or exaggeration the evils which he observed. He
never mistook high-sounding words for good logic; he had too much
delicacy, too much moderation to fall into mere declamation. What is
the good of noisy indignation and irritated gestures?'[98] On 1 July at the
Salon des Artistes français the theme was 'Art and freedom'. On 31 July
in Paris for the national prize-giving of the concours général he
underlined the importance of discipline and obedience for democratic
institutions and for the life of the nation: 'The exercise of discipline is a
great manifestation of patriotism', without which democracy and social
order would turn to anarchy. He praised the idea of pragmatic and
progressive reform:

There is still injustice to correct, pain to heal, misery to console. You will not
have the pretension to cure all of them. Try anyway, like those who preceded
you, to lessen at least some. Others will follow you to take up and continue the
task. And it is from these partial efforts, these successive pushes and in spite of
momentary stops and apparent reversals, that the uninterrupted progress of
humanity is made.

At Bar-le-Duc on 2 August during the *lycée*'s prize-giving he philoso-
phised, 'it is in the intrinsic and distinctive nature of man, of the free and
responsible thinking being, that we discover the basis of our duties, the
thirst for beauty, the love of good, sociability, the notion of universal
order'.[99]

By the time the general election took place on 20 August 1893 – his
birthday – the beliefs of Poincaré the politician had been made clear to a
far wider audience. He presented himself to his electorate in the
undemagogic terms in which he saw his political role. 'You do not like
any more than me election promises ... You know that I have never
made any ... You know that I will always consult your legitimate desires
and that I will loyally fulfil my mandate ... You know that, like you, I
want an honest and industrious Republic, a united, strong and respected
France.'[100] Here again was the positivist belief in progress conditional
on the consent of public opinion. Here also was his suspicion of the
demagogy of some republican politics and his censure of the inefficiencies of excessively ideological French party politics. Nevertheless he
would remain profoundly attached to the notion of opposing parties as a
necessary feature in the political life of a healthy democracy and as a
prerequisite for representative government: 'There must be parties and
parties which oppose one another, and which strive for precedence,
waging war upon one another in the process. This is the price of

progress. An idea deserves to live and to become an accomplished fact only after being ripened by the defeat of a party and tested by its final victory.'[101] Here was evidence of Poincaré's moderate position in the republican camp, because it hinted at the possible establishment within the Republic of an alternation between a 'radical' party and 'conservative' one on British lines, with which many left-wing republicans would not agree, believing fundamentally in the need for a left-leaning partiality to the Republic. Odile Rudelle has suggested that this 'radicalisation' of French republicans and their 'ideological' tint was characteristic of the political class but not of the voters, and is at the heart of the crises in French political history such as Boulangism and the Dreyfus Affair. Thus the Chamber, through its parties and majorities, would always divide on the principle of republican 'legitimacy', making compromise impossible despite there being in the 1880s a 'centrist' majority amongst the electorate.[102] This is a problem which Poincaré had detected by the 1890s, when he would attempt to steer republican politics towards its liberal ancestry and greater consensus, albeit unsuccessfully. He was not happy with the 'ideological' nature of 'legitimacy' for hampering the smooth functioning of parliamentary government, for the way it excluded some from participation in government, and most of all for the way it weakened national unity. It was this ideological 'exclusiveness' which would tend, in the end, to exclude him and cast him to the right of republicanism in the eyes of Radicals such as Clemenceau. It was brought to the fore during his candidacy for the presidency in 1913, when he ignored the 'republican party', or Left's, designation of the 'legitimate' republican candidate, and stayed in the running.[103] A further consequence of this republican sectarianism was that the absence of consensus in parliament forced it to coalesce elsewhere to enable the system to function. It did so in public administration, which, despite its partisan nature, was characterised by notions of 'public service' and the 'general interest'[104] in which Poincaré by temperament, training and political belief could sublimate his republicanism. It is not surprising that he believed the Republic's finest hour to be August 1914 when this 'ideological' sectarianism was overcome and national unity sealed.

The patriot

A central element of republican thinking under the Third Republic was *la patrie*. Despite the fact that after Boulangism nationalism became the rallying cry of the anti-republican Right, for republicans it was still a celebration of the messianic, but benevolent, nationalism of the French Revolution. It was fast becoming a central element in Poincaré's political universe as a centripetal force able to counter the centrifugal tendency of French political culture. It was an important weapon in the quest for that other republican goal: national unity. Thus patriotism was as worthy of being taught as *laïcité*. As Poincaré told Jaurès in December 1895, 'There is another pillar of morality which we teach our children – the notion of *patrie*. It is the axiom, the essence, the soul of our education.'[105]

Like an illustrious successor half a century later, Poincaré had a certain idea of France, which he expounded on 24 September 1893 at Vaucouleurs in Lorraine on the subject of Joan of Arc: '*La Patrie* is not an agglomeration of faithful subjects: it is a free association of interdependent citizens ... Joan soars above parties. She is the prisoner of no sect, no group, no school. To embroil her in a political struggle would be to diminish and misconstrue her memory.'[106] For years Joan of Arc had been merely a cipher of generations of royalist historians, but in the 1840s she was rediscovered as a popular nationalist heroine by the Left for having been 'betrayed by the king and burnt by the Church'. From the 1860s the church had adopted a similar view of Joan as popular heroine, the symbol of a rival Catholic nationalism. By the 1880s the struggle between the two views of Joan mirrored the wider conflict between the 'two Frances', only to be followed by a more centrist trend. This focussed on the Catholics of the *ralliement* who, according to Gerd Krumeich, were 'close to those 'national' centrist republicans who were defenders of 'order''. The bishop of Verdun, Mgr Pagis, expressed this very clearly during the Joan of Arc celebrations at Orléans in 1898: 'Since France wants the Republic, let's have the Republic! Let us keep the tricolour flag.' This chimed in with Poincaré's great hope for national unity through patriotism, symbolised by the heroine of his native Lorraine, Joan of Arc: 'Joan can unite all the French people through all the fundamental values of patriotism, above party considerations, because she represents the passionate desire for the independence and greatness of the nation.'[107]

Here then was an essential element in Poincaré's politics, *la patrie*, capable in his view of drawing together Left and Right, clerical and anti-clerical. As he would often stress, the notion of *patrie* transcended politics itself. For someone who strived for consensus, national unity and *patrie* were the supreme goals. Anything likely to produce divisions in French society was to be eschewed. Thus the Republic, which as Thiers said 'divided the French least', and *laïcité*, which Poincaré liked to see as neutral for shunning religious and philosophical antagonism, were mere props to the ultimate goal of national harmony. *La patrie* was far more positive in actually fostering national solidarity. For that reason he believed, like other moderate republicans, that it needed to be taught in French schools. This idea would continue to grow in him. In a lecture given on 16 March 1910 to inaugurate the new building of the Ligue de l'Enseignement, and published under the title *L'idée de patrie*, he noted, 'More than ever, indeed, school should strengthen patriotic education'. He attacked 'our antipatriots', pacifists, internationalists and extreme socialists who would only fight for the class struggle.[108]

For republican positivists true political action involved intellectual or moral action through education.[109] Certainly Poincaré was temperamentally better suited to this kind of cerebral political action than what he would always regard as the rather vulgar politicking of party politics. He was more at ease educating for the republican cause than fighting for it. Heeding his own call for patriotic proselytising among the young, in 1912 he published a textbook for children about to leave school. It set out their civic duties and responsibilities and stressed how they were foundations of patriotism. Written in a light and breezy style, *Ce que demande la cité* is a clear and concise exposition of elementary French political science. The work reveals much about Poincaré's conception of French society and the functioning of her political institutions. The section devoted to *la patrie* offers a sympathetic definition of patriotism inspired by Ernest Renan and Maurice Barrès:

France is the country where you were born, where you grew up, where your relations lived, where your ancestors died. These are all memories which can be summarised in that beautiful word of *patrie*. Patriotism does not contradict our duty to humanity; on the contrary it is a necessary condition of it. The best way to love mankind, is first of all to love that portion of humanity which is near to us, which surrounds us and which we know best. Instead of scattering our affections and wasting our energies let us concentrate and use them productively in that corner of soil where nature rooted us.

And he went on:

La patrie is therefore the material heritage which our ancestors have bequeathed to us and which we must, in turn, pass on to our descendants. It is not simply our land, it is also our national soul, that is to say our common hopes or sadnesses, our glories and our tribulations, our literature and arts, our scientific discoveries, all of the attendant ideas and feelings evoked in us by the name of France.[110]

It was quite unlike the xenophobic nationalism of this time; it was also apolitical – neither obviously republican nor obviously nationalist. It was instead a form of social bonding intended to overcome the internal divisions of French society without decrying the virtues of other nations. To combat still further those divisions, the textbook outlined the rights of the citizen while stressing duties. It depicted the state as a purveyor of help and financial aid, but only as a last resort, when self-help had failed. 'Self-help first, my friends. Then the State, which is not heaven, will help you, if it can.'[111]

Ce que demande la cité is a lesson in how to avoid or overcome the divisive tendencies of French society. Thus the 'illustrious' Adolphe Thiers, founder of the conservative Republic, is depicted as a national hero 'who denounced in advance the folly of war ... who attempted to reconcile France with the fleeting sympathies of Europe'.[112] He portrays the majority voting system as divisive. It enabled voters to get to know their representative, 'however, it has the serious disadvantage of enslaving the elected representative to local influences and of allowing him to perceive only in a fragmentary way the country's interests'. Proportional representation, on the other hand, in having larger constituencies had in his eyes 'the advantage of favouring wide currents of opinion'.[113]

This work is a manifesto for overcoming the divisive forces in French society. Measures designed to overcome the divisiveness of the régime d'assemblée and the dominance of the legislative by reinforcing the executive are clearly favoured. Parliamentary questions to ministers, so often responsible for bringing down governments, needed to be limited. Likewise, parliamentary inquiries tended to abuse their power and usurp the role of the judiciary: 'Politics and the spirit of party do not always sit well with the serenity of justice.'[114] Of particular note in *Ce que demande la cité* is the idea which Poincaré was already developing in the 1890s and which was to dog his period as president of the Republic – the weakness of the executive. He believed that the 1875 constitution already contained enough provisions to limit the role of the legislature, in particular by the president of the Republic's right to dissolve the Chamber – a prerogative which had fallen into disuse as a result of the monarchist President MacMahon's discrediting of it in the so-called 'coup d'état du 16 mai': 'The use to which the government of 16 May put this right of dissolution in 1877 has since cast a shadow and discredit on this part of the Constitution. It does not deserve, however, the unpopularity with which events have surrounded it.'[115] By the 1890s, Poincaré was coming round to the idea that greater use should be made of presidential power to combat the endemic instability which he saw as producing the divisions which were the French state's greatest weakness. By the 1890s a programme for overcoming the divisions in French society was clear in his mind: the republican system which divided the French least, *laïque* schools which avoided subjects likely to produce divisions, the development of the notion of *patrie* intended to bond together French society and a more efficient application of the constitution of the Third Republic. It was reflected in the type of governments Poincaré chose to serve in: those claiming to be governments of national union. Thus he would refuse to serve in cabinets which he regarded as too partisan, whether of the Left or Right. The cabinets he would lead strived self-consciously to be governments of national union. Meanwhile, his efforts would be channelled into endowing the existing Republican regime with greater technical efficiency.

3   Poincaré the Opportunist

In the space of six years in politics Poincaré had gone from local councillor to minister, had carved himself a sturdy reputation for probity and competence and had the grand tenets of his political ideas in place. He was recognised as one of the 'bright young men' of French politics, though some saw him as one of the four musketeers along with Barthou, Jonnart and Deschanel – men with knives.[1]

Clean records and moderate politics posed a threat to the old republican guard in the wake of Panama. The August 1893 general elections returned him to a more moderate Chamber of Deputies, cleansed not only of the Boulangist elements but also those associated with Panama. The monarchists had been reduced from 166 to 84, of whom 35 accepted the Republic. The moderates, on the other hand, composed mainly of progressists, Poincaré among them, now formed a centre grouping of 311 deputies. On the left the Radicals had seen their numbers drop from 122 to 100 largely to the benefit of the socialists in the towns whose numbers had increased from 18 to 50 deputies. Even though these political groupings had none of the discipline and organisation of the British party system since the 1867 electoral reform, especially in the centre, it seemed that acceptance of the regime and moderation were spreading. This impression was further helped by the so-called 'ralliement' of the Catholic Church to the Republic at the behest of Pope Leo XIII in 1891. Most Catholics now accepted that religious practice was no longer incompatible with republican institutions. This could only have pleased Poincaré for whom institutional consensus and national unity were pre-eminent. The republican institutions seemed on the face of things to be coming into their own – the traditional violently pugilistic multi-party politics appeared to be giving way to more sober parliamentary activity in which the extremes were diminishing. Perhaps Poincaré could see the glimmers of a more bipartisan political system on the British model in which the moderates and progressists would be the Tory party, the radicals and socialists the Liberal party, as so many moderate French statesmen since the

Restoration had hoped. If so, the functioning of the republican institutions needed to be improved by a more serious and honest administration, less dominated by *clientèlisme* and short-term party politics. This was more likely with 190 new *députés* in the Chamber and the new generation of politician born into the republican regime and more committed to its efficient management rather than its establishment, like Léon Bourgeois for the Radicals, Paul Deschanel, Charles Jonnart, Georges Leygues and Poincaré for the moderates. Many would remain prominent until the end of the 1920s.

Poincaré's spell at the ministry of education had lasted eight months until Dupuy's resignation in November 1893. It had got his name and ideas known and had given him experience of ministerial office. Since then he had been happy to return to his legal activities. But that was not to be for long. On 30 May 1894 Charles Dupuy formed his second government; his cabinet contained three members of the new generation of politicians, Gabriel Hanotaux at foreign affairs, Louis Barthou at public works and Poincaré at the finance ministry.

During his first tenure of the ministry of finance Poincaré would be preoccupied with measures to finance an incipient welfare economy. He attempted to do so in two ways: promoting laws to establish structures to finance welfare and ensuring that state expenditure did not outstrip income. Of course the two were inextricably linked. France's economic and social development, and in particular urbanisation's tendency to break down the old rural forms of social support, were making welfare protection indispensable, particularly as France lagged behind other developed nations. Though a wide-ranging bill on this issue had been drafted in 1881, its passage would be delayed until 1898.[2] Pressure for reform was reflected in the increasing militancy of the trade union movement and the progress of the socialist party in the recent elections. As a member of the new Progressists dedicated to stealing revolutionary socialism's thunder by greater social reform, and as a member of a moderate government committed to maintaining social stability, Poincaré felt that action had to be taken to avoid social unrest. But as a believer in liberal economics he was opposed to the idea that the state should, or could, finance all of the social reform necessary. He, like many among the governing class in the latter part of the nineteenth century, whether of the Right or Left, was a believer in the idea of a 'social economy', by which reform, integrated into the purely political economy, could moderate the excesses of liberal capitalism and state socialism.[3] The instrument of this policy was the specifically French system of the *secours mutuel*, a half-way house between the British and American system of private provident and friendly societies, and the

German and Austrian models of compulsory insurance. At the international congress on mutuality in 1900 the president of the Republic Emile
Loubet described the philosophy of the movement as:

To ensure that fraternity is not meaningless; to realise in the material world a
progress that our fathers had only glimpsed; to stimulate and encourage, as a
first condition of this progress, individual initiative, helped as generously as
possible by the State and local authorities; to proclaim the greatness of that
rejuvenated formula: 'Help yourself, and humanity will help you!'; to teach some
the necessity of self sacrifice and others that of thrift and association; finally, to
prepare and maintain social peace, which French democracy, faithful to its
historic mission, has the duty to offer as an example to humanity: these are the
general features of the mutualist programme.[4]

The mutualist movement with its two million members became an
instrument of republican values espoused by Poincaré and other senior
moderate Republicans such as Deschanel, Barthou and Ribot. It dove-
tailed so closely with Poincaré's Progressist philosophy that he became
president of a mutualist society.[5] In theory, protection involved some
state control but no interference beyond this. The advantage to the state
was that it provided the mechanism for the financing of welfare measures
without incurring the full financial or administrative costs. For a minister
of finance this was attractive. Poincaré was quick to pass mutualist
enabling legislation: the law of 29 June 1894 established a form of social
insurance through a mutual fund for miners' welfare and retirement;
that of 5 November 1894 established the Crédit Agricole mutualist
savings bank for farmers; the law of the 30 November set out the role of
the state-owned Caisse des dépôts in the construction and management
of subsidised housing.[6]

This legislation also met Poincaré's second target as finance minister –
to continue his earlier work of bringing greater rigour to the state's
finances by a tighter control of expenditure. Linked to this issue in 1894
was the question of instituting a national income tax, strongly supported
by the Radicals but opposed by the moderates. As with the most
developed powers at the end of the nineteenth century, French national
expenditure was increasing rapidly to pay for new systems of education
and burgeoning social and military costs. France's reliance predominantly on indirect taxation was not raising sufficient revenue – budget
deficits were growing and the fiscal burden was falling more and more
unfairly on those least able to pay. It was time for fiscal reform. But
Poincaré was no radical reformer. He preferred a more cautious
evolutionary approach, as well as being instinctively suspicious of
measures likely in his view to erode individual liberty, namely income
tax declaration forms. He would be careful to skirt around the

potentially divisive question of income tax. His compromise involved refusing to tax total income, but favoured taxing its various sources ('revenus'). Similarly he was opposed to any declaration of an individual's total income which the socialists favoured, but which to his mind would only lead to the honest citizen being penalised in relation to his dishonest counterpart. He believed that official investigations into a citizen's private financial affairs ran counter to French tradition and respect for private property.[7]

How did Poincaré propose to redress the nation's finances? His period as *rapporteur du budget* had revealed areas where state expenditure was either unnecessary or inefficient. He wished to divest the state of some of its functions and return them to the private sector by encouraging private initiatives, especially in areas such as colonies, or replacing state social protection by private insurance. His idea was to reverse what he saw as the recent creeping tendency to turn too readily to the state: 'We must limit the apparently irresistible movement which tends to concentrate the resources of a country under State control; we must attempt to awaken private initiative and stimulate individual freedom. It is much more a question of politics and social behaviour than a financial question.'[8] He called on parliament to assist governments in curbing state spending by acting more responsibly when voting amendments to bills with serious financial implications for the Exchequer. For the moment Poincaré believed – erroneously – that, a few fluctuations aside, rising national prosperity would ensure a sufficient increase in revenue for the Exchequer. In his budget speech on 4 December 1894 he announced a progressive inheritance tax which avoided the vexed question of a general income tax, but which instituted the radical idea of progressivity in taxation. It was his usual bid for consensus:

I am told that tax should be proportional to the taxpayer's ability to pay. It is certainly not I who would contest that. But I have already said, and it needs to be repeated, that this doctrine, which is my own, which is also the Government's, the Revolution's, the republican majority's, I could almost say this Chamber's unanimously, apart from a very advanced guard, this doctrine of progressivity has unfortunately remained theoretical.[9]

He insisted that his fiscal policy was strictly compatible with the government's general policy which was not revolutionary but motivated by order, progress and social improvement. He rejected criticism from the Right that such a tax would frighten the French bourgeoisie. He insisted that the latter had complete confidence in the governments of the Republic and that to give any other impression was false. The bourgeoisie, with which Poincaré was so firmly associated, was in his own words 'liberal, it is generous, it is progressive, it will carry out its duties to democracy without wavering'. The majority applauded and a well-known moderate shouted, 'I resign myself to being a socialist with M. Poincaré'.[10]

Poincaré's speech was a perfect example of the new progressist policies and was received rapturously in the Chamber with the supreme accolade, *l'affichage* – the posting up of his speech around the country. Contrary to a traditional view of him as an unaccomplished speaker, he had overcome his earlier oratorical inabilities and become a polished debater, whose performances were by no means dull and earnest. His speech demonstrated competence, confidence and clever debating skills, mixing irony and humour to mock his opponents. His sarcasm was too much for weaker opponents whose only recourse was to heckling. The socialist Rouanet's interruptions led Poincaré to challenge him to a duel from the tribune on 26 November. Though his seconds were despatched nothing appears to have come of it.[11]

During the budgetary discussions which lasted for most of December 1894, an incident had come to occupy the headlines from 19 December – Captain Alfred Dreyfus's court martial for spying for Germany. Poincaré, like other cabinet ministers, had learned of Dreyfus's arrest through the newspapers on 1 November. At the emergency cabinet meeting Poincaré's friend, foreign minister Gabriel Hanotaux, voiced objections to the arrest for the damage it could do to relations with Germany. But the minister of war, General Mercier, produced 'evidence' of Dreyfus's guilt and had little difficulty convincing the ministers, who preferred to be rid of the affair as quickly as possible. The decision to begin judicial proceedings was unanimous. At the time this had no direct political effect on the government of which Poincaré was a member, nor on him, in what seemed a purely judicial matter. With no counterfactual evidence, the whole government was committed to Dreyfus's prosecution.[12]

Disillusionment

No matter how much Poincaré might decry, and attempt to rectify, the weaknesses of the Third Republic's institutions, he was still a prisoner of them, especially governmental instability. Though the new Chamber appeared more coherent with its moderate majority, the first two years of the legislature were marked by acute ministerial instability. The third Dupuy government ended on 14 January 1895, only to be followed the next day by a presidential crisis resulting from the resignation of Casimir Périer after a left-wing campaign against him. The new president of the

Republic was the moderate Félix Faure and from 26 January 1895 the new premier was the conservative republican, Alexandre Ribot, who formed a 'cabinet of republican union'. Though Poincaré could have retained the finance portfolio he insisted that in order to keep a tighter rein on the state's finances the premier should cumulate the two functions. As Ribot was opposed to the notion of progressive taxation this would mean the end of Poincaré's projected tax reforms. Poincaré was happier to leave this political minefield and return to the ministry of *instruction publique, beaux-arts et cultes* where he could continue the reforms he had begun a year earlier.

At the education ministry, Poincaré passed a series of laws, the most important of which in January 1896 created the modern French university system and revitalised provincial universities which had suffered from the centralising tendencies of the Empire. By a decree of 30 April 1895 he also reformed and modernised both undergraduate and doctoral law studies. This was partly a result of his own experience of the archaic undergraduate syllabus, which was now broadened, and partly a result of the success of the more practical training of the increasingly prestigious Ecole Libre des Sciences Politiques, founded in 1872. He also established an improved system of scholarships for secondary school children based on merit, improved teachers' pay, reorganised the Bibliothèque Nationale and, in line with his belief in private initiatives taking over from the state, instituted a scheme enabling the major museums and art galleries to receive and administer gifts and legacies. All of this was punctuated by a tireless stream of erudite speeches to various literary and academic institutions and salons, which made him a popular minister of education. As literature and the arts remained his passion this was true enjoyment for him.

But his ministerial office also brought him into a venomous debate in the Chamber on the question of taxing religious orders introduced by the Ribot government. This insignificant tax law sparked off the religious debate nationally. It showed Poincaré at his most combative and revealed more on the nature of his *laïcité*. The Assumptionist newspaper *La Croix* led a campaign of resistance against the tax with the clerical Right claiming that such 'persecution' demonstrated the futility of the 'ralliement'; this in turn provoked the Left to call for the separation of church and state.

It was not easy being a republican *ministre des cultes*; Briand encapsulated it well with the quip that 'a Minister of Religious Affairs is like a hen sitting on duck's eggs'.[13] Poincaré preferred to take refuge in a strict application of the law. In his capacity as *ministre des cultes* he punished priests who broke the law by criticising the government from the pulpit, and stopped payment of their stipend under the terms of the 1801 Concordat. On 11 July 1895, during a debate on a motion by the Left calling for a separation of church and state, he was confronted with calls from a monarchist *député* for all Catholics to begin a counter-revolution against their persecution. Poincaré replied angrily that 'the republican party had never been disrespectful of religious beliefs, had never thought of hampering religious services or the freedom to carry out religious devotion'. And he delighted in his centrist position: 'I was told a short while ago, almost at the same time, from both sides of the Chamber: from one side, that I was Satan in person; and from the other side, that I was a cleric. I'll take the average (Laughter).' He criticised the radical–socialist René Goblet for wanting separation of church and state immediately. He justified punishing members of the clergy out of respect for the law enshrined in the Concordat, which was being flouted by extremist priests. He ridiculed the church with a forensic dissection of its opposition to the laws of the land and with examples of how even the July Monarchy had been obliged to cut off the pensions of priests unwilling to obey the law. And he ended, 'The Government is not making and does not want to make threats; that would be unworthy of it and of the clergy; but it is determined that the Concordat be applied strictly by those who benefit from it as well as those who foot the bill. (Very good! very good!)' Seven motions were tabled ranging from a call to support resistance to the Republic – 'instrument of the Jews and Free-Masons' – for its persecution of Catholics, to a call for separation of church and state. To applause from the centre and Left, Poincaré called on those in favour of a separation of church and state to vote for it, adding, 'But the Government has not hidden the fact that that is not its policy. Its policy is that of the pure and simple, and strict, application of the Concordat. (Very good, very good, on the same benches.)' It was a skilful performance.[14] The episode revealed two things about him: his scrupulousness in wishing to see religious laws, like all others, applied to the letter, and the extent to which his *laïcité* was in line with that of the moderate majority of republicans. In theory anti-clericals looked forward to the abrogation of the Concordat and the separation of church and state; in practice it was a subject for hope not action.[15]

As Poincaré continued with his ministerial duties, so his disillusionment with the political system increased. He made speeches criticising the too often sterile debate of party politics and called for patriotism to overcome a divided society. He was as much a victim of the parliamentary waltz of ministries as anyone. On 28 October 1895, a mere nine months after taking office – the average life-span of a government of the Third Republic – the Ribot government was brought down. French political life was beginning to take its toll of Poincaré's patience. On leaving the education ministry he made clear in a press interview his intention not to accept another ministerial post for ten years and to concentrate on his legal career. When on 3 November 1895 his friend, the historian Ernest Lavisse, asked him to write a few political articles for the *Revue de Paris* he declined, but accepted two days later an offer by the same journal to write on literature and the arts. Close political friends such as Millerand, who was not of the same political persuasion, and Revoil, who was, encouraged him not to give up politics altogether. There was talk of him not standing in the 1898 general elections. Revoil in particular insisted on how much he was needed by the centre. 'You owe it to the ideas you represent. It is only to your call that they will rally. If the centre remains mute and inactive they will blame you for its weakness.'[16] Given that Poincaré rarely abandoned anything he had started, it is unlikely that he would have relinquished politics altogether. But he was determined to distance himself from governmental power, if not politics. As a concession to his political friends he did agree to stand in January 1896 as one of the four vice-presidents of the Chamber of Deputies to signal that he was not withdrawing completely from politics, a post he was repeatedly re-elected to until the end of 1898. Ironically the machinations surrounding his election, to which the Radicals and socialists were hostile, could only have increased his disappointment with French political life. Though he would continue to shine on occasions in the Chamber his main efforts would be concentrated on his work at the Bar which began to take off. So began his ten year passage in the political wilderness.

What caused this disillusionment and what did he suggest to remedy it? As a moderate republican politician he was happy with the political system, but not its inefficiencies or the low standards of conduct of French political life. He had never been an ideological politician, but he was a fundamentalist as far as institutional and political practice were concerned. He criticised 'the absence of all governmental method' and the 'deviations suffered by the parliamentary regime'. This was the start of his dissident action within the Progressists. The latter's anti-Dreyfusard stance and right-ward drift would lead to left-wing centrists, like Poincaré, setting up the Union démocratique in June 1899 and its inheritor the Alliance républicaine et démocratique in 1901.

During the summer holidays of 1896 he discussed in great detail with Louis Barthou, who shared his views, the obstacles to a proper functioning of French parliamentary institutions: ministers whose day to day departmental business was disrupted by a constant string of parliamentary amendments from political adversaries merely intent on scoring political points; political parties devoid of organisation and discipline, comprising moderates, who were too conservative, and radicals, who were all talk and slogans and incapable of serious reform. He was particularly disillusioned with his own party, the Progressists. He and Barthou were agreed that 'Our party has neither programme, leaders, nor discipline, nor method. What would we do without our adversaries? They do us the favour of confirming our existence. We only succeed in having a few ideas as a result of opportunities which they give us for opposing theirs.' He and Barthou were worried about the effect which this spectacle of immobilism and disorganisation had on public opinion: 'The country watches on, indifferent and sceptical. Like you, I am scared of this scepticism and I fear that it might presage a new period of disillusionment and revolt, one of those mad moments when, drawn to some glorious name or adventurous soldier, the Nation surrenders itself, preferring anything to what exists.' This fear encouraged Poincaré to embark on a political crusade around the country to warn of the dangers threatening the parliamentary regime and to try to 'restore civic energy'. From August 1896 until the end of 1898 the crusade comprised speeches, lectures and articles. It was agreed, however, that he should not reveal too much of the pessimism which he, Barthou and now Hanotaux felt, and that his action should concentrate on solutions to the problem.[17]

The backdrop to Poincaré's concern was the beginning of the modernisation of French political parties in which the moderates were slow to get off the mark. Despite the moderates' relatively good showing in the 1893 election this did not lead to improved governmental efficiency. Four governments fell between November 1893 and April 1896. Meanwhile, the radical and socialist Left continued to strengthen its position: in the 1896 spring municipal elections the socialists took control of some thirteen large towns and industrial centres, announcing the prospect of municipal socialism. Buoyed by these results their different factions met at Saint Mandé in Paris at the behest of Poincaré's old friend Millerand to set out a common programme for a reformist socialism with, as its aim, 'the necessary and progressive substitution of social property for capitalist property'. Though the programme attempted to reassure the lower middle classes, it was profoundly worrying to the French bourgeoisie. It presaged the uniting of the socialist movement. Meanwhile, the Radicals had embarked on their own reorganisation around departmental federations and committees which had led in November 1895 to a united and dynamic organisation entitled Comité d'action pour les réformes républicaines. This heralded the birth of the modern Radical party in 1901.[18] Modernisation and revitalisation of the moderates' political rivals stimulated Poincaré into doing something similar for the moderate camp, which lacked modern party organisation, especially at local level.

Poincaré reserved his harshest criticism for the Chamber of Deputies, whose abuse of parliamentary procedure and lack of discipline he blamed for rendering the system powerless – too many parliamentary questions, amendments and interruptions. Worst of all, the Chamber's belief in its sole and infallible personification of national sovereignty encouraged it to usurp all competing powers whether of government, Senate, civil service or the courts. The result was the unbelievable confusion 'we have arrived at under the guise of a parliamentary regime', when no one knows whether responsibility rests with the legislative or the executive.[19]

Given Poincaré's political prominence, his campaign did not go unnoticed in parliament or the press. On the Right and in the centre it found favour, though not – a few exceptions apart – on the Left, where he, Barthou and Deschanel were referred to as 'the future consuls'. With the general public, however, his warnings made not a stir. A certain naïveté and arrogance had led him to believe that a grass roots movement might bring about change. He was disappointed and criticised the 'sort of blind casualness, moral torpor and sloth' of the average Frenchman.[20]

During 1896 and 1897 his campaign took the form of articles and speeches. The political, social and financial remedies he suggested made up a sort of manifesto for the 'Républicains de Gouvernement'. The underlying theme was the restoration of governmental authority: 'there must be a government to carry out the will [of the people], to block individual and collective egoism'. Of necessity the government had to be strong: 'To be a government, is to know what one wants and to want strongly what one can achieve; it is said that government is foresight, I think it more correct to say that government is determination.' Of course, that government had to make clear its commitment to be republican, laïque and democratic:

In political or religious matters, any indulgence towards the enemies of the Republic would be treason; no one amongst us can think of reducing, for the benefit of reactionary and clerical influence, the necessary privileges of civil society and we are firmly resolved to protect from all attack not only the institutions which ensure popular sovereignty, but also the democratic and republican spirit.

Another pillar of this moderates' charter was private property, which led him strongly to reject burgeoning socialism. Private property 'is one of the material guarantees of freedom and one of the most efficacious stimuli of human activity; there is between these three terms: private property, liberty, progress, intimate and solid links.' Socialism, he believed, might seduce temporarily by its vague idealistic slogans but eventually the people would see through it. He rejected collectivism as contrary to historical experience; an all-powerful state would be a backward step because, he argued Whiggishly, the development of civilised societies had always benefited individual freedom: 'progress should derive from the persevering action of individual freedom at the service of the general interest, which it should not overturn, but improve progressively'. By no means did Poincaré's rejection of socialism imply a slavish adherence to free-market principles. As has been shown, he, like many moderate republicans, was a believer in the social market economy through mutual friendly societies. The chief intellectual exponent of these ideas was the economist Charles Gide, whose ideas he much admired. Rather than turning to the state, which was already weighed down by excessive administration and expenditure, free associations of individuals should correct the imperfections of the market by aiding the weakest elements in society. The state's role should be to foster the development of these organisations, not to run them.[21]

On taxation Poincaré emphasised his unerring belief in the need for balanced French budgets. Improvements had already been made by careful and progressive reform; others were necessary but they should always be guided by the all-important principles of justice, equality and individual freedom. The latter principle placed Poincaré in the camp of the opponents of income tax, which was thought to threaten individual liberties because of the administrative controls its application imposed.[22]

Poincaré's intellectual energies were accompanied by more tangible attempts to stimulate the moderates into modernising themselves. In April 1897 the Comité national républicain du commerce et de l'industrie was established with Poincaré, Deschanel, Waldeck-Rousseau and Jules Siegfried as its patrons. This pressure group was designed to elicit the support of the commercial bourgeoisie. Its support for the protectionist Méline government tended to push the moderates themselves towards protectionism. But in reality it did little to reorganise the moderates. A more promising step was taken in 1898 with the creation by the founder of the *Revue politique et parlementaire*, the intellectual organ of moderate republicanism, of the *Grand Cercle républicain*, which was intended to be the headquarters of the moderate republicans. It was opened on 22 March by Waldeck-Rousseau whose speech encapsulated the movement's, and Poincaré's, beliefs. Waldeck praised the principles of the French Revolution and criticised those of socialism. He called for the defence of these principles 'against all the counter-revolutions, mon-archical counter-revolutions which are ending, socialist counter-revolutions which are beginning', and he warned his audience not to 'conceive of progress outside liberty'.[23] But even this organisation met with little success in galvanising the moderates into establishing a more coherent programme or organisation. It fell well short of Gambetta, Waldeck and Poincaré's grand desire for, in Waldeck's words, a 'great compact, homogeneous party with superior and constant principles'.[24]

There was nothing very exciting or even new in Poincaré's manifesto, which was firmly rooted in the ideals of Ferry and Gambetta. He, like them, was confronted with the fundamental problem of the nature of the moderate movement which had little taste for organisation. There was also the problem, which he knew from experience, of moderate republicans in local constituencies not wishing to cut themselves off from the perceived party of progress on the Left when confronted with attacks from the reactionary Right.[25] Though he, in the manner of the Opportunists, might summarise his beliefs as 'neither revolution nor reaction', the latter remained a dirtier word than the former. Though his efforts in the end met with little success in modernising moderate Republicanism, they did confirm Poincaré as one of the unofficial leaders of the movement. This was demonstrated in April 1898 when the *Revue de Paris* called on the best qualified member of each of the four main political groupings to give his views on the state of the country: Léon Bourgeois for the Radicals, Denys Cochin for the conservatives, Jean Jaurès for the socialists and Poincaré for the moderates.

What was becoming apparent as Poincaré's political stature grew was that he was increasingly being seen, at only thirty-eight years old and with only eleven years of political experience, as one of the few politicians capable of uniting the disparate elements which held the ground between reactionary monarchism and revolutionary socialism. His brand of conservatism and reformism was designed to realise the Gambettist vision of a major centrist party which could draw together moderate republicans and radicals. But his lack of success led him to stand back from further political action. When the progressist republicans called on him to lead their parliamentary group in 1898 he declined; when the moderates called on him to stand as president of the Chamber he refused. Was this remarkable diffidence part of a strategy? He told his colleagues, 'I would be a candidate if it were a question of duty but I see no duty'.[26] Was it partly conceit which led him to believe that he could wait in the wings for the moment when the country would call on him to realise his great dream of uniting the French? More modestly it was also evidence of his tendency to shift his allegiance in the centre ground according to the direction and force of threats to the moderate Republic. The perceived threat since the 1898 elections came increasingly from the clerical right and would become more so as anti-Dreyfusism reared its head. He believed that progressism was not responding sufficiently to that challenge; for that reason he preferred to avoid governmental office and concentrate on his legal practice.

The law remained a surrogate family for Poincaré to which he could always return. There is little doubt that his ministerial experience enhanced his legal career. But by the standards of the time he was scrupulous; at no point did he use his political position directly to benefit his practice. On the contrary, in February 1896 when the press announced that he was to become the ministry of finance's legal counsel with a salary of 15,000 francs per year he withdrew his acceptance for fear that his appointment would give the impression that his independence had been bought, even though he had accepted on the strict agreement that he should not be remunerated at all while he remained a *député*.[27] His well-known sympathies for the art and literary worlds quickly earned him briefs, notably as legal counsel for the Société des Auteurs dramatiques and for the French press association. His already successful legal practice rapidly took off. He expanded it physically, taking on more and more partners, amongst whom was his future official biographer, Fernand Payen, and four others who were themselves to become ministers. The work methods he fostered with his associates at the spacious and sombre practice in the rue des Mathurins on the edge of the eighth and ninth *arrondissements* were mostly those he imposed on himself – independence and personal initiative in preparing briefs and dealing with clients. His partners were largely chosen from the conférence du stage. He invariably became their role model, with a number following in his own political footsteps often with a hand up from their mentor into a *cabinet ministériel*. This produced a Poincaré stable to compete with those of Millerand, Caillaux and Deschanel. The most successful of Poincaré's men were André Paisant, who became a junior minister, Maurice Colrat and Léon Bérard who became ministers of justice, while Charles Reibel and Bérard followed more closely in the footsteps of the master by adding membership of the Académie française to ministerial office.

Poincaré's cases were mainly in the area of commercial law, but in May 1897 a large literary brief was given to him concerning the contesting of the will of the celebrated writer Edmond de Goncourt. He agreed to act on behalf of ten writers to whom Goncourt had left his estate in order to form the Goncourt Academy, but on the sole condition that he received no remuneration. On 8 July 1897 the case came to court. Despite difficulties Poincaré triumphed, making him a celebrity and the instant toast of the literary world. Alphonse Daudet remarked, 'Our dear friend Goncourt founded the Academy, but Poincaré has breathed life into it!'[28] He also acted on behalf of the Society of Musical Composers and championed a celebrated actress in a case against the Comédie française. His reputation was made. Henceforth he would continue to act in famous drama and literary cases, though always without a fee. This was done out of a love for the arts, but he was well aware of the kudos this earned him.

Literature and the arts remained his true passion. At the same time as he expanded his legal practice, he continued to produce articles for literary magazines and to preface books as well as keep up private correspondence with many of the great literary names of the day. His reputation as a writer was growing. In 1898 the *Revue des Revues* invited some thirty writers including Poincaré to give their impressions of what constituted 'L'Esprit français'. Though he protested that he did not merit such a title, he sent in an impressive contribution all the same. He continued to mix with writers, artists and musicians, many of whom would later vote for his election to the Académie française in 1909, despite many of them holding differing political views to his own. Though at first appearance his presence in this milieu might seem out of place given his reputation for coldness, severity, even austerity, he was something of a favourite in literary salons and dining clubs with a reputation for wit, repartee, even occasional frivolity. In reality this merely revealed a side of his character that was not often shared with others. As he himself publicly remarked some years later, on the characteristics of the Lorrainer:

We do not like either theatrical gestures or high-sounding phrases. We do not parade our feelings at the despatch box or at dessert time at the end of some copious banquet. We are thought to be cold and uncommunicative and it is possible that we do not wear our hearts on our sleeves, but if we do not distribute our warmth lightly, it is because we prefer to condense it in order to use it without fuss for our true affections and essential works.[29]

The literary world and his family apart, Poincaré found his greatest relaxation working in his office with his books, his dog and cat. His early love of dogs would later become a passion for cats. He exchanged amusing letters on the nature of cats with his colleague Robert Mitchell, who would supply him with the Siamese cat which would be the ancestor of a whole line in the Poincaré household[30] and which he was said to have had baptised in solemn fashion in the presence of political colleagues and friends.

His reserve and a jealously guarded privacy apart, another trait of Poincaré's character was his patience and caution. His description of Lorrainers in 1921 is very much a self-portrait: 'We plough our fields patiently before seeding. We study our problems thoroughly before solving them.'[31] That character trait had paid dividends until now. But in 1898, as the Dreyfus Affair reached its apogee, Poincaré's caution would seem to some to smack more of indecision, even cowardice. To be an important political figure and to wish to remain aloof from the violent debate which broke out in 1898 was fantasy, though many did try, including Waldeck-Rousseau.

The Dreyfus Affair

The image of the Dreyfus Affair as the great *cause célèbre* which nationwide pitted Frenchman against Frenchman has long been revised. Those most concerned by the Affair were the Parisian and urban middle classes. Nevertheless the divisions here, especially among the political class, were bitter and deep and extended well beyond the comparatively insignificant question of the guilt or innocence of an unknown French army captain.[32]

Ever since his sentence by court martial to life imprisonment on Devil's Island in 1894 for espionage and treason, there had been little reason to believe in the innocence of the Alsatian Jew Alfred Dreyfus. Only his family and a few friends attempted to have the case reopened. Across the entire political spectrum from Left to Right Dreyfus was assumed to be guilty. In 1898 Dreyfusard newspapers accounted for less than 10 per cent of the press and were restricted largely to Paris.[33] For a lawyer such as Poincaré with an unbending respect for the law and its application there was no reason to suppose a miscarriage of justice.

It was only in 1896, when the new director of the French counter-intelligence service, Colonel Picquart, discovered that the German military attaché was in correspondence with a raffish French officer by the name of Esterhazy, that things took a new turn. Esterhazy's writing was remarkably similar to that of the docket relating the military secrets which had sealed Dreyfus's conviction. By August 1896 Picquart had proof that he was the real traitor. But Picquart's superiors at the war ministry would hear nothing of it, and organised his dispatch to Tunisia in November 1896. However, Picquart had passed his evidence to his lawyer, who alerted the Alsatian vice-president of the Senate, Scheurer-Kestner, who had already been contacted by the Dreyfus family. Rumours of Dreyfus's innocence began to circulate, encouraging the Army and counter-espionage section to attempt to reinforce the case against Dreyfus by forgery and take action against Picquart. He would later, in July 1898, be arrested and punished with sixty days' imprisonment. For the moment, with the vast majority of the press still anti-Dreyfusard there was no question of a retrial. The nationalists and their press insisted that, apart from the docket, there existed further proof of Dreyfus's guilt which the members of the government in 1894 had seen.

According to Poincaré's partner in his law practice, Ferdinand Payen, this is when Poincaré became suspicious. As minister of finance in 1894, like his colleagues in the cabinet, he had only learnt of the Dreyfus incident from the newspapers two weeks after Dreyfus's arrest. He remembered that at an emergency meeting of the cabinet the minister of war, General Mercier, had cited only the docket as incriminating Dreyfus. Payen suggests that in 1898 Poincaré contacted General Mercier, who privately tried to reassure him by revealing the existence of a secret file which had been communicated exclusively – therefore illegally – to the prosecution and which proved Dreyfus's guilt. Payen describes Poincaré as shocked and upset by this news – shocked as a lawyer and upset at the possibility that the evidence in the secret file might not be incontrovertible. Henceforth, like many other belated Dreyfusards, he was of the conviction that the case should go before France's supreme court, the Cour de Cassation, to test the legality of the judgement and, if necessary, to go to a retrial.[34]

Though Poincaré made no secret of this point of view among friends and in the salons he frequented, he refrained from speaking out in the Chamber. In this he was very much a bell-wether of the time, for there was far more activism in the world of letters and the salons than in politics. Bredin has explained that in 1897, even 1898, from a political point of view, Méline was right – there was no Dreyfus Affair. Nearly the whole of the political world was anti-Dreyfusard – 'by instinct, prudence, or ignorance'. It was only slowly through the year 1898 that professional politicians began to choose their camp. Poincaré's centrists, who rejected the Dreyfus Affair, would themselves be forced to choose, leading to their break-up at the end of 1898.[35] For a politician of Poincaré's caution, there was little chance that he would break with the general trend. He could justify his inertia on two grounds. First, the existing government was moderate and its leader, Jules Méline, a long-time leading light of the moderate republicans, appeared to be restoring a semblance of stability to French government with his eighteen-month old cabinet. He, and his government, were convinced of Dreyfus's guilt and refused a retrial. It was the unfortunate Méline who, on 4 December 1897, notoriously declared to the Chamber, 'There is no Dreyfus Affair'. Second, and of greater importance to Poincaré, was that many of the Dreyfusards were now attacking the Army as a whole, which he found intolerable.[36] But at root was Poincaré's habitual circumspection, which some called moral cowardice. For the moment, in his view, there was still insufficient evidence to make any serious impact on events. A number of his friends were anti-Dreyfusard: Lavertujon, 'with many ministerial and anti-semitic friends', begged him not to speak out; the Academicians André Theuriet and Pierre Loti; and his friend the interior minister, Louis Barthou, was all for measures against the revisionists.[37] Of course, other friends were in the opposite camp. Even within his family there were divisions, with his mother an anti-Dreyfusard. It was the kind of issue of principle guaranteed to send Poincaré into the worst crises of doubt, hesitation and procrastination. Events seemed to lend a hand in providing pretexts for hesitation. Inertia was further justified by the decision to bring Esterhazy before a court martial – much to the chagrin of the anti-Dreyfusard camp. Poincaré could calculate that if he were found guilty Dreyfus's innocence would be axiomatic. However, on 10 January 1898 Esterhazy was acquitted on the grounds that the docket he was supposed to have written was a fake.

Whatever Méline might say, the Dreyfus case was becoming the Dreyfus Affair. What completed the metamorphosis was the publication on 13 January 1898 of Emile Zola's famous letter 'J'accuse' in Georges Clemenceau's newspaper L'Aurore. He accused the French General Staff of having shown the secret file to the prosecution and of having faked evidence to prove Dreyfus's guilt. His many accusations were important because they ideologised the 'Affaire'. There was uproar. Two camps began to crystallise which would mirror the 'two Frances', one democratic and republican, the other reactionary. The Dreyfusards insisted that the innocence of an individual had been sacrificed to protect a right-wing military establishment, thus imperilling the ideals of the French Revolution and making the Republic no better than the Ancien Régime. The anti-Dreyfusards, many of them anti-semites and nationalists, were indignant at Zola's letter and pointed to a plot to undermine the guarantors of stability in French society – the army and the church. At first Méline was opposed to prosecuting Zola, but pressure from the anti-Dreyfusards changed his mind. Though Zola, who had fled to England, was found guilty of slander, the court case in February 1898 brought to light the existence of the secret file. Though passions were violently unchained and the press and intellectuals chose their respective camps, parliament refused to debate the issue seriously as the rest of Europe looked on. The general elections were due in May 1898, but by all accounts the majority of the population was not interested in the Affair.

Poincaré continued to refrain from taking a public stance, though his private utterances were beginning to worry some of his moderate political colleagues, who feared that his intervention might overturn the government.[38] He did attempt, however, to see the members of the cabinet individually to get them to examine the case closely. He begged Méline, 'Look at the file, look for the truth and rid us of this nightmare'. His efforts were to no avail. He himself stated, 'For several months I lived through the most painful convulsions'.[39] But in his election campaign, which he virtually conducted from Paris, Poincaré made no reference to the Affair and was re-elected unopposed in the first round on 8 May 1898. In his silence he was no different from most candidates, as the Dreyfus Affair was not yet a party political issue. In many ways it cut across traditional party lines. When it came down to it, according to Léon Blum in his *Souvenirs sur l'Affaire*, it was the liberals, the men of the centre, those committed to respect for the law and liberty who were Dreyfusard.[40] Poincaré might be all of these, but for the moment he was at best only privately a Dreyfusard.

The elections had been dominated by the Radical campaign against the 'clerical' Méline. The Progressists had faired well, at least in terms of seats, with 250 deputies, while the Radicals had gained and the Right had lost ground. The two parliamentarians who had nailed their colours to the mast in favour of Dreyfus, Jean Jaurès and Joseph Reinach, lost their seats. But those elected from the centre, such as Poincaré, had been alarmed during the election campaign by the rise of a violent, clerical Right, reminiscent of the worst days of Boulangism. Fear that the 'republican spirit' was threatened by those newly elected, or by their supporters, pushed the likes of Poincaré, Barthou and Leygues towards the Radicals. Though sincerely republican, they had been satisfied with a conservative Right; henceforth they would look towards a moderate Left.[41]

Méline believed that he could continue to govern with the support of the Right against the Radicals. But a number of Progressists, like Poincaré, would not accept that, and on 15 June Méline was defeated. The new premier, the Radical Henri Brisson, offered Poincaré a place in his predominantly Radical government. He refused on grounds of illness, which some newspapers described as a diplomatic malady.[42] All the same, he had participated in what would be a decisive reclassification of political forces.

The Radicals were still uncommitted to revision in the Dreyfus Affair. The new minister of war was the model republican and Radical, Godefroy Cavaignac, widely respected as a man of honour, justice and patriotism. Poincaré hoped that now at last he would be rid of this 'nightmare'.[43] But Cavaignac decided to demonstrate Dreyfus's guilt by reading to the Chamber the secret – and faked – 'Henry' document, forged by the head of the French counter-espionage service. His acclaimed speech of 7 July 1898 was unanimously voted the honour of publication on every official notice-board in France – alongside the 'Henry' forgery. The next day the press displayed near unanimous satisfaction. Poincaré's friend, Alexandre Millerand, wrote in *La Lanterne* of 9 July that the minister of war 'had relieved the public conscience'.[44] Poincaré continued to harbour doubts. He had a private meeting with Cavaignac in July 1898 in which he explained his suspicions about the letter (the 'faux Henry'). He told him 'at least, thanks to you we are emerging from mystery and we will be able to discuss things based on documents'.[45]

At the end of August, Colonel Henry of the French counter-intelligence service committed suicide after confessing to having faked the letter Cavaignac had read. This turned the tide in favour of the Dreyfusards and a retrial. Nevertheless, Cavaignac refused to agree to a retrial and resigned on 3 September. He would be succeeded by two ministers of war before the end of the month. Violent clashes took place between Dreyfusards and anti-Dreyfusards. The atmosphere recalled that of the height of Boulangist agitation, with the threat of a *coup d'état* from the increasingly powerful extra-parliamentary Right. The Republic was threatened, strikes had broken out, and the Fashoda crisis with Britain was at hand. According to Payen, Poincaré decided to speak out.[46] Then Brisson decided on a retrial, which Poincaré saw as another reason to wait. On 25 October, the third minister of war to resign in a month went, shortly followed by the whole government, defeated by the centre and the likes of Barthou and Poincaré. Charles Dupuy was called by the president of the Republic, Félix Faure, to form a new government. He had led the 1894 government in which Poincaré had served and which the nationalist newspapers continued to claim had seen further evidence of Dreyfus's guilt. Dupuy approached Poincaré to offer him either the ministry of war or justice. But, according to Payen, in the space of a short conversation Poincaré realised that Dupuy was not ready to deny the rumours that the 1894 government had seen the secret 'evidence' against Dreyfus. He turned down the offer. Continuing privately to urge Dupuy to speak out, he kept his own silence.[47]

A year had passed since the Dreyfus case had swollen to such dimensions. For much of that time Poincaré had a good idea that a miscarriage of justice had taken place, but he refused to speak out. Yet one senses that he was ill at ease with his conscience. His friend the historian Ernest Lavisse receiving him into the Académie française in

1909 put this down to his acute critical faculties, remarking ironically, 'It is clear that you are not a quick tempered soul'.[48] Like Hamlet, he spent so much time weighing the pros and cons of an action that he rendered himself inactive. He was particularly decisive when working with legal texts; he was the opposite when faced with the complexity of men and events. For someone who had always known success, he was worried about failure and what might be thought of him. As Payen noted, 'He neither liked to provoke nor go against public opinion. He hoped that union would take place over all the great questions and over his own actions. He would have liked to have been approved, even by his opponents.'[49] For that reason, throughout public life, press praise was an obsession, as his personal diaries testify. And without popular approval he was loath to act. His old friend Millerand remarked, 'What Poincaré lacks most is moral courage'.[50] But it was Clemenceau who was the most perceptive about his future adversary, in an article entitled 'Le Poincarisme': 'Fine calculator, he excels at drawing up for himself and his ideas accounts showing liabilities and assets, balanced according to the state of the art. It is there that he looks, in vain, for the components of determination because his energy is spent calculating the advantage of what is good or bad over what might be.'[51]

Poincaré's predicament over the Dreyfus Affair was helped by his having friends, and indeed family, in both camps. General Lyautey had expressed to him a view that reflected his own: 'I am in much turmoil between the certainty of an injustice and anxiousness at the conse-quences for the Army.' The Dreyfusard camp exerted even greater pressure on him. As early as 1897 Ernest Lavisse had written to urge him on: 'I am beginning to feel extremely worried. Of course, everyone who has something to say must speak out, and very candidly, if only to relieve their conscience.' His legal colleagues and associates such as Félix Décori, Maurice Bernard and Millerand called on him to take a stance by pricking his legal conscience. The parliamentarian Joseph Reinach, who had championed Dreyfus's innocence from the start, had challenged his hesitancy in a letter: 'You know my feelings of friendship for you, but you know our differences ... You will tell me one day what kind of political injustice you need before you boil over ... ' His conscience was cruelly tortured and he was said to be dreadfully unhappy.[52]

Poincaré was deluged with letters from political colleagues and friends shocked at his continuing silence:

Are we to witness the collapse of the republican party for want of a politician whose conscience is publicly outraged? ... I cannot understand how you can keep silent. Are you not convinced that Picquart dishonoured means France dishonoured? The whole world is watching us and will judge us on that ...

It is no longer just a judicial error, it is a crime of military jesuitism ... Even if we accept that Picquart revealed evidence, broke the rules, etc. .... It is still the case that he is the man who sacrificed himself to save an innocent man and his country. And the country wants to show its recognition by allowing the General Staff to take its revenge of him?

Is it only socialists who are moved by these things? You and your friends stand idly by, are you so sure that this act will not be carried out? Excuse me for being so moved by it that I am unable to keep quiet ...

Poincaré wrote to one of his closest friends, 'It is a terrible and painful conflict between two duties. Let us wait and have confidence.' Back came the cutting reply:

'Oh how I would love to be certain that your reply even satisfies yourself. Please the heavens that it be one of those grave, one of those terrible conflicts of two justices, of two duties, of two respectable authorities ... Then, we could, as you say, wait and be confident. But think for a moment of the way in which all that will appear unequivocally for history, before too long.[53]

In November 1898, the investigatory commission of the criminal section of the Cour de Cassation was preparing, against all manner of obstacles, to recommend a retrial. However, charges were being pressed against Picquart, who by 13 November had spent 122 days in prison; he was to appear before a court martial on 12 December accused of forgery and the communication of secret documents to an unauthorised person. It was far from certain that there would be a revision of the Dreyfus judgement. Protests broke out in both camps. Deputies and senators put down motions for debate in parliament. The Left wanted the government to adjourn Picquart's court martial, as the law allowed.[54]

Racked by his conscience, Poincaré at last decided to speak out. But cautious as ever, he chose to do so on concrete issues; in other words, legal ones – Picquart's arrest and the right of the government to call on the Cour de Cassation to review the judgement. On 28 November 1898, well over a year since the Dreyfus case became 'the Affair', he seized on a reference to his name in a speech in the Chamber as an excuse to take the floor. It is most likely, however, that he had prepared himself well in advance.

His speech was a *mea culpa* and an indictment of the handling of the Dreyfus case. He began by stating, 'I am convinced that at the moment the silence of a few of us would be true cowardice. (Very good, very good.)' He claimed that for two years he had wanted to know the truth of these 'painful incidents'. But he had hesitated because he deplored the outrageous campaign against 'our army' and believed that 'a judicial decision should not be undone by devious, illegal and almost revolutionary means'. With characteristic respect for the law he refused to mention directly the Picquart trial, which was *sub judice*, or to criticise 'the honourable officers' called upon to judge Picquart. But he chided the military authorities for what he called their double standards in persecuting Picquart while other more serious misdemeanours 'benefit from a scandalous impunity'. Prefacing each of his accusations with 'what I know and what I have the right to say', he catalogued the failings of the ministry of war. The speech was extremely carefully orchestrated, demonstrating a fine understanding of the mood of the Chamber. Eliciting questions from the floor, which took him to the point he wished to make, he confessed that those who were in power in 1894 had an obligation to see that the truth was revealed. Back came the question as to why he had not made enquiries in 1894. With relish, and to immense applause from the Left and centre, he explained how his colleagues in 1894 had learnt of Dreyfus's arrest from the newspapers two weeks later. Then came a series of questions as to why he had not spoken earlier – something he had clearly expected. He explained that he and his colleagues had been given no other evidence of Dreyfus's guilt than the docket, and certainly no secret or diplomatic file. Clearly aware of the protests his words were provoking from numerous interruptions, he was at pains not to criticise the army and, as usual, struck the patriotic chord to justify his action and restore unity.

By making these statements here, I might find myself in disagreement with some of my friends, but I have the feeling of accomplishing an act of enlightened patriotism.
Yes, Gentlemen, an act of patriotism, because patriotism would mean for us, in time of war, fighting alongside officers of the professional army. The army is not a cast within the nation, it is the whole nation. (Applause) But, in peacetime, what would patriotism be if it did not reside in the respect of our national traditions of justice and freedom? (More applause)
I can see that by breaking today a silence which burdened me ...
From the right: It's too late!
Poincaré: ... I expose myself to attack, to insults, to calumny. I do not care, and I am happy to have chosen, at this tribune, the opportunity too long awaited to free my conscience. (Loud applause on a large number of benches on the left and centre)[55]

His intervention was skilfully crafted, giving the impression of self-sacrifice, yet putting him publicly on the right side of the turning tide. His 'confession' had a considerable impact on the Chamber.[56] But there was little that was new in what he had said. At a personal level it probably was cathartic, it was so typical of Poincaré in coming at the end of a long period of hesitation and soul-searching. It was also typical in that it was by now to a large extent risk free. The effect it had on the

Dreyfus Affair at this late stage was probably small. Poincaré had publicly sat on the fence for far too long. Even he realised that he had to come down or be knocked off. But its impact did become apparent following a similar intervention by the very distinguished republican civil lawyer, Waldeck-Rousseau, in the Senate three days later. Thereafter the belated Dreyfusards and famous lawyers Millerand, Poincaré and Waldeck-Rousseau, soon joined by Barthou, consulted with each other. As Bredin notes, 'Neither the parliament nor the press could fail to see what was happening. The rallying of these men, who cultivated their careers with utmost care, was a sign of the future.'[57]

Characteristically, Poincaré felt it necessary to justify himself by spending the evening of his intervention until well past his normal bedtime scribbling letters to all those political colleagues and friends whom he believed he had offended. His former pupil-master, Du Buit, an ardent nationalist, was high on the list. As with so many of his actions, it was not so much that Poincaré wished to be liked as that his rationale be understood; he had a strong need to convince and was hurt when he failed. Finally, his action brought him into line with the paternal and republican side of his family. It must however, have distressed his mother, whose name was significantly absent from the letter he wrote to his brother that evening. 'I knew only too well, my dear Lucien, that by speaking out I would please Marie-Andrée and you, as well as father. And that thought was not absent from my decision.'[58]

His devout mother's attitude, given the Catholic Church's anti-Dreyfusard position, had doubtless prolonged his anguish and delayed his publicly taking a stand. Not surprisingly, the Dreyfusards reproached him his tardy intervention. One letter in his post-bag remarked bitterly, 'It was up to you to liberate your conscience a few years or a few months earlier'. Some congratulated him while others, not just in the nationalist camp but also among the Radicals and moderates, castigated him for the prejudice he had caused the government. He was said to have broken with the spirit of the 'ralliement'. The very Dreyfusard Ligue des Droits de l'Homme had ordered his speech to be posted up all over France the next day. Back in the Meuse, which like most of the north-eastern frontier was nationalist, his speech was badly received – he was said to be 'in the pay of Jews'.[59]

Opposition to revision had grown explosive. By February 1899, in order to quieten nationalist agitation, the moderate government led by Charles Dupuy attempted to pass a bill framed to relieve the central Criminal Court of jurisdiction over a re-trial of Dreyfus in favour of the fully constituted Cour de Cassation. This seriously worried the Dreyfusards as the Criminal Court was believed to be pro-Dreyfus.

When the Chamber passed the bill, Poincaré, who had voted against it, signed a petition which brought together dissident progressists, radicals and socialists placing him on the same side as his old friend and political opponent, the socialist Millerand. The law contravened the fundamental principle of the non-retroactive nature of legislation and was therefore anathema to Poincaré and his liberal cohort whose views were encapsulated in the title: 'Perish the Republic rather than Principles'.[60]

Poincaré's action was increasingly leading him away from the governmental majority which he had long supported. But this was happening across the whole political spectrum. The traditional party frontiers were being redrawn. Many of the Radicals, traditionally hostile to the church and suspicious of the professional army, found themselves in the anti-Dreyfusard camp, while some moderates were Dreyfusard. As Léon Blum noted, the political parties emptied and refilled themselves to their mutual benefit or disadvantage.[61] Overall, French politics shifted to the Left as the Dreyfus Affair progressively discredited the Right, the church, the army and large tracts of the centre. The socialists, however, when at last they rallied behind Jaurès from August 1898, had increased their credibility. Poincaré was not slow to recognise the change. He noted that because of the Affair 'and as a result of the regrettable abstention of the moderates, the axis of republican politics is increasingly being displaced. The revolutionaries are winning hands down; the national spirit is under threat and our military institutions are likely sooner or later to be undermined.'[62] Given Poincaré's disillusionment with party politics, notably that of the moderates, whose behaviour during the Affair had further disappointed him, he was ready for change. If ever he was to realise his great aim of uniting the centre parties in a large republican union he would have to move with the tide to the Left.

On 9 February 1899 Poincaré was one of the founder members of a new parliamentary group, the 'Républicains de gauche'. On 10 May he sent a letter announcing his withdrawal from the 'Républicains progressistes' to Jules Méline. The reason he quoted was his dissatisfaction with the group's stance during the Affair and its drift towards the nationalist Right. As he told Méline, he had been invited to form a new group several months before. When the Affair was over a number of lessons would have to be learnt, in particular the administration of the army should be brought under tighter civilian control,

to defend this army both from clerical manoeuvring and from attacks from the militarists. And in order to do that, to rebuild at equal distance from the extremes a republican party rid of all reactionary behaviour and protected from all collectivist influence.

That is the task which tomorrow we will have to carry out. I would have been happy to work with you on it, but you only fear the revolutionary danger at a time when the reactionary peril seems to me more threatening than ever.[63]

Here was quintessential 'Poincarism'. It was also characteristic of moderate republicans such as Waldeck-Rousseau. It was not that Poincaré wished to shift to the Left, but that the centre was splitting again and Poincaré refused to be on the Right of the divide.

Domestic politics indeed looked menacing. The death of the president of the Republic, Félix Faure, in amorous circumstances at the Elysée Palace on 16 February 1899 was attributed by the anti-Dreyfusards to a conspiracy and gave rise to a comic-opera attempt at a *coup d'état* at his funeral on 23 February by the nationalist Paul Déroulède. But on 31 May Déroulède was acquitted by a pro-nationalist jury – an event that greatly alarmed Republicans. On 1 June a nationalist reception was prepared for Commandant Marchand – of Fashoda fame – hailed as a hero. Four days later the nationalist Baron Christiani struck the new left-leaning president of the Republic, Emile Loubet, at Auteuil races. The following Sunday, a massive demonstration of 100,000 was organised in defence of the Republic. The Dupuy government gave the impression of being powerless to control events; it was voted down on 12 June. Loubet called on Poincaré to form a new government.[64] He made a vain attempt to pull together a Republican centre bloc, which excluded on the Right all those tainted with clericalism and on the Left all those linked with socialism. But the Radicals refused to have Barthou in the cabinet and the socialists, led by Millerand, insisted on a portfolio for one of their number, Viviani. Poincaré abandoned his attempt and suggested Waldeck-Rousseau instead.

Four and a half years previously Poincaré had taken a personal vow not to return to power for ten years except to come to the country's aid in its hour of need. It was an error to have tried to form a centrist cabinet during this troubled period. He told a friend, 'Passions are rampant ... One cannot govern at the moment. The republicans only want to fight.'[65] What was needed was a politician willing to deploy original, even radical means to overcome the Dreyfus trauma. That involved taking risks, which were not part of Poincaré's make-up. Loubet called on René Waldeck-Rousseau. With difficulty he put together a cabinet which excluded Poincaré and his small group of friends, who were considered too ambitious and too complicated.[66]

It is not clear whether Poincaré would have wished to serve in Waldeck's cabinet for he was beginning to withdraw from active politics. In his eyes French politics were in a worrying state of flux. The moderate party had been split by the Dreyfus Affair, whereas the Radicals were beginning their reorganisation which in 1901 would transform them into the more disciplined 'parti républicain radical et radical-socialiste'; the socialists had for the first time a place in the government and were in the ascendancy. Poincaré was faced with the dilemma of the centrist politician: he wished to occupy the middle ground, but since Dreyfus he was on bad terms with many of the moderates, while remaining suspicious of the Left. He looked to the Left on the religious question, but sympathised with the Right on the social question. He voted for Waldeck's government for its proclaimed *laïque* stance, but had doubts about other policies. He was opposed to its inclusion of a socialist, albeit his friend Millerand – something, ironically, with which the 1904 Amsterdam Socialist International Congress would concur when it condemned the presence of a socialist in a 'bourgeois' government.

Disillusionment and withdrawal soon gained him a reputation for abstaining in parliamentary votes. When seen rushing from the law courts to the Palais Bourbon, a legal colleague remarked wryly, 'He's running to abstain'.[67] He was often absent from the Chamber during important debates, giving as excuses sickness, legal commitments or simply holidays abroad. Colleagues mocked his diplomatic absences. Others attempted to persuade him to prepare to lead a new ministry by appealing to his sense of duty and vanity. But he continued to shy from any clear political action. Was it in order not to jeopardise his chances of leading a government in the future? His friend and colleague Gabriel Hanotaux, criticised him for not possessing 'more fixed political principles, a firmer political mind'.[68] A more severe critic, Waldeck-Rousseau, reproached him his 'lack of character', as did others, such as Clemenceau. The ambassador Paul Cambon, who would cross swords with him in 1912, expressed this more crudely: 'what M. Poincaré lacks most is guts'.[69] Yet Cambon himself put his finger on the essential contradictions of the man when he noted, 'there is something Napoleonic in Poincaré's manner'.[70] Clemenceau unwittingly revealed this ambiguity in his quip, 'No character, Poincaré; he has the worst character I have ever known'.[71] If Poincaré lacked character, how could that be squared with the criticism often made of him that he was stubborn and dictatorial? Administratively he was efficient and crisp to the point of bluntness. His problem was reaching a decision when in his own eyes the issue was not clear. Then would come hesitation and tergiversation. His admirers might call it patience and waiting for more favourable circumstances; his critics, procrastination and opportunism. This admirer of Gambetta must have cherished the master's words of 1877 which were as relevant to Poincaré's political instinct as to his conscience: 'one should not invest oneself totally in a question until one is sure to have the support of the majority ... When the country is reluctant to accept a measure no matter what enthusiasm drives me, I resist.'[72] This was classed as a quality in the master; with the disciple it was perceived as a failing. Poincaré's caution was shot through with the self-doubt that was his Achilles' heel. Small wonder then that his longstanding friend Alexandre Millerand could state that 'moral courage was never the characteristic of Poincaré, he had to a degree which I have rarely witnessed, a phobia of responsibility'.[73] This exposed him to manipulation. Paul Cambon pointed this out to his brother: 'Fear of responsibility is the best means of action against him. One should never omit repeating to him: "Here is what you asked me to do, I obeyed your orders".'[74]

Poincaré's predicament during the Waldeck government was created by his undecided course of action and lack of political will. He remained disillusioned with French political life and the squabbling republican centre for which he had had such high hopes as the core of a national patriotic force to unite France. He was thinking of resigning from politics altogether. In 1899 Lavisse had pleaded with him, 'I don't have to tell you how much you are missed, is it true we will miss you for long? ... Rumour of the voluntary retirement of someone such as you is very worrying. If it is true it is an ugly sign of the times.'[75]

Things were not improved by the policies of the Waldeck government. On the religious question, in particular, the extremism of its legislation clashed with Poincaré's personal conviction of tolerance. He refused to vote for the 1901 law which regulated freedom of association as a means of controlling religious associations, or the rather dubious legal means used. He saw no reason why the right of association should be refused to certain categories of Frenchmen. He applied the same logic to the laws designed to limit the freedom to teach and to establish a state monopoly on teaching, which he condemned as 'usurping the rights of the father of the family, useless bullying, a dangerous attempt at unification, whereas diversity of attitudes is a source of dynamism, of wealth and power for a nation'.[76] For reasons of tolerance, equality among Frenchmen and to avoid measures which increased internal divisions, he voted with the Right against much of Waldeck's anti-clerical legislation. In the name of French interests abroad, he unsuccessfully opposed measures debarring French missionary associations – whose propaganda benefits to France were considerable – from having seminaries in France. Like his mentor Gambetta, he believed that anti-clericalism was not for export. In the eyes of many he began to be cast as a man of the Right, when in reality he was defending principles which he had always defended. It was not that he had moved to the Right but that the centre of gravity of French

politics had lurched to the Left as part of that general movement which
François Goguel has described as 'sinistrisme'.[77]

In May 1901 the Alliance républicaine démocratique party was born
from the parliamentary group of the Union démocratique. It was largely
a collection of personalities of whom Poincaré and other dissident
Progressists, such as Barthou, were members. It was the left-wing half of
the former Progressists, whose right-wing made up the Fédération
républicaine. The former's programme was avowedly 'anti-collectivist
but concerned with social progress', 'anti-nationalist, but a jealous
guardian of the power and honour of *la patrie*', 'anti-clerical but not anti-
religious'. It was organised around simple themes common to Opportunism of twenty years earlier, with as its objective a liberal Republic. Its
first president, Adolphe Carnot, described the movement as intended to
'bring together the two factions of the great republican party', something
dear to Poincaré's heart.[78] Although a member of the new group, he did
not attempt to take up a leading position. Following his election to the
Senate for the Meuse in 1903, he set out the party's programme:

Our party does not include, will never include, reactionaries, nor supporters,
however disguised, of clerical influence in public affairs. It includes in its
programme the defence of *laïque* society; but it will not oppress consciences. It
will not open its doors either to quasi-philosophers or to those fanatics who
believe it possible to impose a sole model for all human intelligence. The
separation of Church and State will be liberal or will not be.[79]

Voting with the Right on occasions did not protect him from attacks
from the increasingly active nationalist Right. As the 1902 election
approached, in his own constituency he was accused of defending Jews.
Those local attacks increasingly focussed on himself or his family. His
disillusionment increased and with it his holidays abroad and around
France. His friends tried to overcome his reluctance to stand again for
election in the Meuse. But he did stand, though the election was no
foregone conclusion. Some moderates could not forgive him for having
tarred himself during the Dreyfus Affair with the revisionist and anti-
militarist brush. They put up their own candidate. On the Right was a
royalist candidate. Ironically Poincaré now found himself cast to the
Left. Lorraine at the turn of the century had begun its slow drift towards
the Right but remained sufficiently republican to ensure his re-election
on the first round with the support of his erstwhile opponents, the local
Radical Socialists.[80]

Nationally, the drift towards the Left was confirmed in a poll in which
a remarkable 80 per cent of the electorate turned out. The religious
question and the attendant 1901 Law on Associations motivated the

voters. The left-wing majority of the 'Bloc' obtained approximately 350 seats to the opposition's 250. The Radicals were the main victors with more than 200 seats: Waldeck's followers, with whom Poincaré sat officially, though increasingly uncomfortably on certain issues, numbered fewer than 100.[81] Whereas until Dreyfus the great questions which had racked the Third Republic were 'for or against the Republic' and the social question, in the wake of the Affair, given the church's stance, what now separated Left from Right was the religious question.

This issue would totally dominate French politics until it culminated in the separation of church and state in 1905. The government of the radical anti-clerical Emile Combes replaced Waldeck after the latter's sudden resignation on grounds of ill health in 1902. Combes's cabinet would be carried along by the 'Bloc des gauches', which provided the momentum for an anti-clerical crusade. Using the 1901 Law on Associations, which he applied with rancorous inflexibility, Combes began a witch-hunt against the remaining religious orders, that even provoked the hostility of Waldeck-Rousseau in May 1903. When the latter approached Poincaré in November with a request that he should denounce this policy, Poincaré fell back on his recurrent abstentionism. Once again, in his perception of things there was no clear dividing line between the issues at stake. On the one hand his liberalism and belief in the secular state would not allow him to defend outright the privileges of the church, whose action since Dreyfus he roundly condemned; on the other he was not fundamentally anti-clerical. On a more practical level, the government's policy had substantial support in the Chamber which he could not hope to turn back, organised as it was into the *délégation des gauches*, which exercised a veritable dictatorship over the Bloc's majority. Furthermore, political passions in the Chamber were riding high in both camps, and it had always been Poincaré's instinct to allow the dust to settle before saying his piece. But those such as Waldeck and Millerand, increasingly spoke out. For many, his continued inaction smacked of weakness, if not cowardice.

His poor health provided extenuating circumstances, or a convenient excuse. During the summer of 1902 he contracted pneumonia and retired to the south of France to convalesce with his friend and legal colleague, Maurice Bernard. On his return to Paris he took up temporary residence in the verdant western suburb of Ville d'Avray, which was also a spiritual pilgrimage for having been Gambetta's home until his death in 1882. Here he was overcome with melancholia, in which all action seemed futile. Even when that had retreated he was left with his longstanding dilemma of a legal versus a political career: 'Why prefer politics to the Bar? and why the Bar rather than *le jardin de*

Candide? The object of the activity matters little.'[82] In the law and politics he had almost reached the top. He was the legal counsel, still unpaid, for the Société des Auteurs dramatiques, the Société des Auteurs et Compositeurs de Musique, for the Syndicat de la Presse parisienne, the Société des Artistes français and the Œuvre des Trente ans de Théâtre. His considerable reputation as a persuasive, eloquent and versatile barrister brought him large commercial clients as well as the custom of the rich and powerful. In politics he had long been considered something of a 'boy wonder' who had quickly attained high office and even been offered the task of forming a government. He was consulted on most issues. Yet he still had the feeling of being unfulfilled. His disillusionment with party politics had not evaporated. He decided to seek election to the Senate, following the death of the local Meuse senator in 1903. The senatorial election system of electoral colleges of delegates of municipal councils favoured candidates from republican country towns of a socially conservative and *laïque* persuasion.[83] Poincaré was elected effortlessly on 22 February. Now he was able to escape the rancorous politics of the Chamber and devote more of his time to the *conseil général* of the Meuse, whose vice-president he became. Though he remained the target of local politicians and journalists, notably from *La Croix Meusienne* in 1904, who questioned his liberalism in the face of Combes's attacks on freedom of education and religion, he was able to devote his attention to more personal and pleasurable pastimes.

Marriage

Poincaré was highly secretive about his private life. Little is known of his sentimental liaisons, though he was said to be often in 'charming company'. Caillaux tells of a holiday he and Poincaré spent in Italy with their respective mistresses. But Caillaux recalled Poincaré's natural discretion: 'mine I displayed, his he kept hidden'.[84] Small in stature, not particularly handsome with his receding hair-line, goatee beard and austere, unimaginative dress, he was none the less an eligible bachelor. What he lacked in physical attributes he more than made up for in intellectual qualities and celebrity and, despite an austere public persona, charm. Cultured, entertaining and a witty conversationalist with a sardonic humour, he was much sought after in the Paris salons where many a hostess might think it a personal triumph to match a leading politician with a charming table companion.

Henriette Benucci was an attractive and elegant woman of Italian origin born into a modest family in Passy, Paris on 8 May 1858. Two years older than Poincaré, she had already been married twice: first to an apparently irresponsible spendthrift American or Irish extraction. The marriage had ended in divorce in 1890 with Henriette continuing to eke out an existence from private Italian lessons she gave in Paris. Her second marriage to a wealthy, but considerably older, lawyer at the Paris Bar, named Bazire ended as swiftly as it had followed on from the first.[85] In 1892 she was a widow. Her financial position, though not greatly improved, allowed her to devote more of her time to charitable works. Part of that work involved looking after an old lady for whom she sought a good nursing home. On asking a friend for advice, the reply, given that Poincaré apparently had no expertise in this, smacked more of matchmaking than information: 'We will have to ask little Poin ... You don't know little Poin? ... I'll organise it for you to have dinner with him.'[86] Thus Poincaré met Madame Bazire at a dinner hosted by Madame Cael, wife of the director of the General Post Office for the Department of the Seine. By all accounts, Poincaré was immediately won over by her. They met again at other dinner parties. Poincaré obtained seats for her at the Chamber of Deputies, sent her flowers and according to Payen gave the tell-tale sign of lending her his books.

It has been written of Joseph Caillaux, Poincaré's erstwhile friend and later political rival, that as long as his parents were alive he never felt the need to marry.[87] Poincaré's parents and family seemed to provide all the affection he needed, while his professional activities absorbed most of his days. But by the turn of the century the latter no longer monopolised his time, which, in keeping with the European upper middle classes of the day, was increasingly devoted to cultural trips in the aristocratic style of the grand tour. Henriette accompanied him on many of these excursions, often serving as an interpreter in Italian, English and German. On 17 August 1904, three days before his forty-fourth birthday, they were married in a strictly civil and private ceremony in the town hall of the seventeenth *arrondissement* of Paris. Many of Poincaré's colleagues and friends only learnt of his marriage, to their irritation, from the newspapers. But this too was typical of his secretive nature.

Though members of the upper middle class married on average later than today, Poincaré was well beyond the average marrying age of even a cabinet minister, which was between thirty-three and thirty-four years; but he would have been inconspicuous among the 20 per cent who chose matrimony when they were past forty. Henriette did not fit the average age for ministers' brides, which was more likely to be between twenty-three and twenty-five.[88] Poincaré, who in most respects was typical of middle-class mores, did not conform in his choice of bride, which seems to have been made according to personal, rather than financial or social criteria. His marriage appears very much to have been for love or friendship and not convenience. The courtship with Henriette may have been long; his natural prudence would probably have led him to hesitate before marrying someone two years his senior and unable to bear children. There seems little reason to doubt that he would have wanted children given his own happy childhood. His brother had two daughters 'whom the President treats like daughters'.[89] They were unmistakably surrogate children to their uncle. This is apparent, in particular, from the almost weekly correspondence he maintained from 1908 until his death with the elder niece, Lysie Lannes, for whom he appears to have had a particular affection. During the war she would become the wife of Poincaré's future private secretary at the reparations commission in 1920, François Guionic. Here again the deeply emotional and tender side of his nature contrasted with the cold outward image attributed to him. He began his letters to her, 'My dear little Lysie (because that is the spelling I prefer to give to your name, like your father)' and ended them with, 'Au revoir, ma chérie, I kiss you with all my heart' and the signature 'Roncle'.[90] Despite his massive work-load he always found time to devote to his nieces, playing croquet with them or extensively annotating Lysie's homework, from sophisticated mathematics to explanations about the significance of Molière's plays. Indeed, Lysie seems to have lived with Raymond and Henriette when attending the *lycée* Molière in Paris, as they both signed her *livret scolaire* in place of her parents.[91] This devotion, especially to Lysie, attained such proportions that the correspondence he carried on with her through the years was eventually destroyed by Henriette in 1915. That action, for whatever motive, caused him considerable grief, as his diaries show: 'Private sadness. Henriette, in my absence, opened the drawers of my desk and read the letters from Lysie. Despite the purity of this correspondence, she has informed Lucien [his brother] and Marie-Andrée [his sister-in-law] . . . I won't have my little ray of sunshine in my prison any more . . . '[92] His parents, who were still alive at the time of his marriage, would probably have loved him to provide them with grand-children. In the end, his choice of a wife was motivated by affection and the marriage seems to have been a very happy one for the rest of his life.

The couple began by moving to an apartment in the rue du Commandant Marchand in the sixteenth *arrondissement*. With the attraction of Poincaré's Lorraine growing stronger and his commitment to Paris weaker since his transfer to the Senate, work began shortly after the wedding on building a large house as a country retreat at Sampigny near Bar-le-Duc and which was baptised 'Le Clos'. It was here, walking in the large gardens, that he would feel truly at home.

The marriage modified his behaviour, which, though still outwardly severe and reserved, became more relaxed. Their home was thrown open to more guests, often from the world of the arts and literature, which Henriette also enjoyed. Surprisingly, though ordered and efficient in his public life, Poincaré's management of his own finances had been chaotic. Money had never interested him and he had habitually tossed fees from clients into an old drawer. Henriette, acting in general as a personal secretary, soon brought order to his personal life, using her languages, classifying his documents or correcting proofs. When separated from her he would always write, sometimes up to three times a day, and even leave little notes when forced to depart early for work.[93] This was a reflection both of his remarkable epistolary reflex which led him to reply even to letters of thanks, and his sentimental nature. His old school-friend, fellow *député* since 1889 and senator since 1900, Henri Lavertujon, was correct in calling him 'a real sentimentalist'. That devotion, like that to his mother, caused him to agree to the marriage being solemnised religiously in 1913 after it was discovered that Henriette's first husband had died in 1909.

At the time of his wedding the state of French politics gave Poincaré no reason to intervene more actively in political life. On 28 October 1904 the 'affaire des fiches' became public. Civil servants, and especially army officers who attended mass, had been kept under surveillance and secret files prepared on them with the connivance of republican masonic lodges which were then used to hamper or ruin their careers. Though Poincaré was distressed by this activity, as were several members of the governmental majority, he refused to criticise publicly what many saw as a witch-hunt redolent of the Terror. He and others feared that criticism of such a policy would brand them as clericals. He also had doubts about voting against Combes's republican governmental majority for fear of playing into the hands of the increasingly influential socialists. The centre-left Alliance républicaine et démocratique party, formed in 1901 from dissident progressists who had followed Waldeck,[94] and of which Poincaré was an executive committee member, was tied to the Combes government by the presence of one of its number, Maurice Rouvier, at the finance ministry. Thus Poincaré conveniently abstained on the issue of the 'affaire des fiches'. Once again there was a contradiction between his cherished principles of personal liberty and tolerance and his refusal to intervene in a case where those principles were being flouted. Moral cowardice and a fear of tarnishing his republican credentials, and with that the future possibility of stepping forward to 'save' the country in its eventual hour of need, would also have contributed to his inaction.

More charitably, Poincaré's attitude to the religious question accurately mirrored the contradictions at the centre of the 'parti républicain' which championed on the one hand respect for religion out of liberal tolerance, and on the other defence of the state against clericalism.

The Combes government finally resigned on 19 January 1905 after an indirect vote of no confidence over the election of the anti-governmental candidate for the presidency of the Chamber of Deputies, Paul Doumer. The time was ripe for a drift back to more centrist politics. There was talk of President Loubet calling Poincaré to form a government, but in the end the offer went to the Gambettist Rouvier, who offered Poincaré the education portfolio. At first he accepted, but soon turned it down because in his own words he was 'sickened by parliamentary appetites and squabbling groups'.[95] As one of only two representatives of the Alliance démocratique in the incipient cabinet, he claimed that his freedom of manoeuvre would be restricted, though one senses his desire to bide his time before returning to government life.

He returned to the law and to compiling an edition of the speeches he had given from 1896 to 1897 criticising parliamentary practice and mores entitled *Idées contemporaines*. The volume reflected his continuing disillusionment with contemporary politics and his disappointment at not being able to organise a coherent and disciplined centre grouping. Though it was not reflected in his book, Poincaré should have been heartened by the success which the Alliance démocratique appeared to be having, less in terms of party organisation than influence among the republican political, administrative, financial and business elite. In the moderate press such as *Le Petit Journal*, *Le Matin*, *Le Petit Parisien* and, increasingly, *Le Temps*, its ideas and personalities prevailed, as they did in the Academies and the Senate. The Alliance démocratique formed a pool of experienced republican politicians from which all aspiring *présidents du conseil* had to select at least some members in order to have any chance of forming a coherent government. Its programme continued the old Opportunist theme of 'neither revolution nor reaction'. It was anti-collectivist, but concerned with social progress; it was anti-nationalist, but a jealous guardian of the power and honour of *la patrie*; it claimed to be anti-clerical, but not anti-religious; in the face of the clericals and nationalists, the Alliance wanted to bring together the two factions of the great Republican party; in other words not to break with the Radicals. The *Alliance* competed for the centre ground in French politics with the more rightward leaning Fédération républicaine, but the former refused any association with the clericals and anything likely to dilute their own commitment to *laïcité*. The fault line which kept the two centres apart at decisive moments, to Poincaré's private frustration, was perfectly encapsulated in his famous retort to Charles Benoît, 'Between us there is the whole span of the religious question'.[96] In many ways, though less coherently organised than its *frère-ennemi*, the newly organised Radical party, the Alliance démocratique, was an all-pervading force with a considerable influence on all governments up to 1914 and whose strength under the Third Republic may have been underestimated in the face of the more visible Radical party.[97]

Poincaré's position on the religious question had not been a comfortable one. The balancing act he tried to perform was as unsatisfactory to himself as it was to many of his political colleagues, friends and adversaries. Abstentionism and distancing himself from the heat of events did not even relieve his own conscience. The brutal and divisive manner in which Combes had set in motion the movement towards separation of church and state had again led him to think of abandoning politics. Fellow parliamentarian from the east, Albert Lebrun, noted, 'I found him very discouraged, I was even going to say sickened ... He told me of his sadness in seeing the Republic moving away from its own ideal. He was even contemplating giving up his seat.'[98]

He might attempt to remain aloof from the divisions which the religious question in Combes's hands had provoked but he understood that separation of church and state was now a foregone conclusion. All the same, he was not happy to have his name associated directly with the legislation on the separation which the Rouvier government was committed to passing. This had been a further reason for turning down a place in the government. Once the Chamber had debated the separation in spring 1905 he hoped that it would be possible to return to normality and get on with other more concrete matters, as he told a meeting of the Alliance démocratique on 19 June 1905: 'Thanks to the cohesion of our friends in the Alliance démocratique, it is now to be hoped that the Separation will be free. Let us hope that it clears the way for the efficient study of financial and social questions.' Again he was disappointed. The Separation Law of 9 December 1905 was a predictable culmination to the anti-clerical policies followed since Waldeck-Rousseau. Though the Republic was legally bound to guar-antee freedom of worship it ceased to recognise or subsidise any form of worship whatever its nature, while church revenues and assets were to be handed over to a new organisation of *associations cultuelles*. But it was the application of the more material clauses of the Law, especially those requiring the preparation of an inventory of church property to facilitate its transfer, which in March 1906 provoked serious and occasionally bloody disturbances in parts of France for its seemingly sacrilegious nature. For some the divisions were as great as at the time of Dreyfus. The Rouvier cabinet, defeated on a vote after many of its right-wing supporters abandoned it, resigned on 9 March 1906.

On 18 February 1906 the president of the Senate, Armand Fallières, became president of the Republic. A reshuffle of posts in the Senate led to Antonin Dubost becoming its president and Poincaré *rapporteur général* of the finance commission. Because of his relatively neutral stance on the religious question he was called upon to form a goverment. He refused on the grounds that having disapproved of the parliamentary majority's recent actions he could hardly now lead it. Furthermore, not having 'a radical–socialist state of mind' he could not accept that party imposing its line and its members on his government. Nevertheless, possibly sensing that the religious question had passed its worst and that a return to order needed promoting, he agreed to serve in a government that endeavoured to put the religious question behind it. In the end, the mild, colourless, Radical Sarrien – 'the man with a calf's head' (l'homme à la tête de veau) as Caillaux referred to him – was able to form a government on 13 March. The Radicals supported it because it included the Radical Clemenceau at the interior ministry, though his inclusion was strongly opposed by Poincaré on the grounds of his anti-clericalism.[99] The Radical Léon Bourgeois was given foreign affairs and Gaston Doumergue colonies, while the independent socialist, Aristide Briand, was given education, arts and *cultes* to apply the Separation Law.

The result was a well-balanced government of Radicals and moderate republicans who had opposed Combes, like Poincaré and Barthou. Poincaré's pious mother was displeased at his serving in a cabinet with such anti-clerical members, as was his old friend Henri Lavertujon, who wrote to him, 'I haven't the courage to congratulate you ... Tell your wife that I dreamt of something other than a portfolio in a Clemenceau Cabinet for her husband.'[100] But a desire to promote reconciliation and turn the government to more 'mundane' financial and social issues motivated his action. The moderate Méline congratulated him on 15 March 1906 for his 'act of courage', stating, 'We are rounding a very difficult cape and we need skilful pilots'.[101] This would not be the last time that Poincaré would be regarded as having made a sacrifice by agreeing to work with Clemenceau in the wider interest of the nation. Neither was it the first or last time that he would wish to concentrate on bringing order to French finances which had been sorely neglected during the recent turmoil.

'The country's finances', wrote *Le Cri de Paris*, 'are now in the hands of an honest man.'[102] Economies and balancing the budget were what Poincaré wanted. But the Radicals had their own desiderata with which the liberal Poincaré disagreed: an income tax, around which he had already skirted in 1894, and the nationalisation of the western railway network. His tax proposal was for a reorganisation of the old *contributions directes* (such as window and shop taxes), increased duty on postage stamps and a tax on bottled mineral water which, as a virtual teetotaller, he consumed in large quantities. It was also at this time, on 18 April, that he announced to cabinet the successful conclusion of negotiations for the official quotation of a new Russian loan, apparently unopposed by once Russophobe Radical members such as Clemenceau.[103]

The general elections of 6 and 20 May 1906 had a turn-out of almost 80 per cent, the highest since 1877, and were a resounding victory for the Left despite the 'Affaire des fiches' and the disestablishment battle. As in 1902 it was a Left bloc versus Right bloc fight in which the right-wing opposition scored some 43 per cent of the votes. Of the 591 members, the amalgam of conservatives, nationalists and progressists obtained about 176 seats while the Bloc des gauches government party now held some 411, an increase of about 60. The losers were the progressists, while the real victors in numbers and power were the Radicals who would no longer need to rely on the socialists for a majority in the Chamber.[104] This was the view of the former foreign minister, Delcassé, who so informed the British embassy. He believed that the election results demonstrated the electorate's support for the work accomplished in the last legislature, from the anti-clerical measures to the reduction in military service from three to two years.[105] Ironically, the apparent leftward drift of the electorate paved the way for a shift towards the centre in the Chamber and perhaps also in government. This would certainly have pleased Poincaré, who still cherished the idea of a great centre party. It did not escape others of similar beliefs either. At a banquet on 31 May 1906 given by Poincaré's party, the Alliance démocratique, in honour of its five cabinet members which included Poincaré, Adolphe Carnot, president of the Alliance, pointed out that the majority which supported the government numbered 352 deputies including the independent socialists but excluding the 53 unified socialists. This, he noted, was the first occasion on which the Republican party had formed a compact majority in the Chamber.[106]

As finance minister, Poincaré was as ever intent on establishing a balanced budget. One week after the elections he made a forthright speech to deputies from the Meuse and neighbouring departments on the country's financial position. Now that victory had been assured for the parties of the Left it was necessary, he stated, to begin re-establishing a balanced budget. The outlook for 1907 was gloomy. Expenditure forecasts showed formidable increases which would have to be curbed even if it meant applying unpopular measures. But, he insisted, income tax could not be a solution as its aim was fairer wealth distribution not revenue generation.

This firmness on government expenditure appeared to pay off in the short term; the press announced at the beginning of June that the projected deficit would be reduced from 260 to 180 million francs. But in the budget commission Radical pressure continued to press for an income tax.[107] Poincaré had proposed a limited version of an income tax with differential rates for earned and unearned income. This merely opened him to attacks from Left and Right which he relished. It was typical of Poincaré's mastery of the art of, in Albert Thibaudet's words, reassuring 'interests which tend to the right and mysticism which is on the left'.[108] But in cabinet he clashed increasingly with colleagues, especially his old friend Barthou, over issues ranging from profligacy to the repeated interference of deputies in the running of the country's affairs for electoral or petty local reasons. In June 1906, in a divided cabinet, he threatened resignation if Barthou's expensive proposal for railway workers' pensions was accepted. In July he drafted his resignation. But Sarrien and President Fallières convinced him to stay on until the new session of parliament in October when the leader of the government, who supported him, would himself resign on grounds of ill-health.

On 23 October, Clemenceau replaced Sarrien in a new government which did not include Poincaré.[109] The former minister of finance's well-publicised differences with members of the government on spending and his subsequent resignation reinforced his reputation as an upholder of financial stringency. The British embassy in its 1906 report on French politicians noted of him, 'He is a Moderate Republican who works with the Radicals. His great abilities and his personality generally seem to mark him out for the highest offices in the State.'[110] Over the next six years he repeatedly turned down offers of portfolios in July 1909, November 1910 and March and June 1911.[111] He was clearly intent on an attitude of contemplation in politics and placing himself once more 'en réserve de la République'.

Poincaré's first twenty years in politics are very much the history of his political life. They are marked by an apparent ambiguity: on the one hand the left-wing moderate consistently committed to republicanism, laïcité, opposed to militant xenophobic nationalism and willing to work with the Radicals; on the other the centre-right moderate committed to the social order, wary of state intervention in economics and social reform. Poincaré's position is seen to zig-zag between the two political positions, earning him the label of opportunist in the pejorative sense.

Yet that is to ignore the threats which he and others genuinely perceived as haunting the Third Republic alternately from Right and Left, whether from monarchism, clericalism, nationalism or socialism. To a large extent Poincaré's political positioning, like that of Barthou, appears more consistent over the longer term if it is viewed as constantly shifting to counterbalance whichever force of the moment appeared most hostile to a liberal–democratic Republic. For that reason both men believed that nimble footwork and a movable political centre were honourable and important positions to occupy. This helps make sense of why he shifted rightwards with progressism after the 1893 elections pointed to the rise of socialism, then leftwards when the 1898 elections and anti-Dreyfusism signalled the return of reaction and clericalism, and once again rightwards once socialism appeared the enemy after Waldeck. Without this explanation, self-serving opportunism cannot adequately explain why he so often refused office or resigned from it.[112] More often than not he was acting in defence of the Republic. Poincaré's political stances were the weather-vane of perceived threats to the 'liberal' Republic, even if lack of moral courage and an eye for self-enhancement occasionally helped tilt that weather-vane in a particular direction.

4   Poincaré en réserve de la République

At about the time that Poincaré decided to step up to the Senate and back from ministerial life, significant changes were taking place in the nature of the French parliament and in the role of the *député* in particular. Though only in his mid-forties and still young in relation to the average age of parliamentarians at the turn of the century, Poincaré's conservatism, upper-middle-class values and fifteen or so years' parliamentary experience did not dispose him favourably to those changes. The first of these was the democratisation of the *député*. Until the 1902 elections they had been recruited from the middle and upper middle classes, the *notables*. With the beginning of the so-called 'Radical Republic' increasing numbers came from the lower middle class, even below. With a greater dependency on their parliamentary salary, re-election became more important and professionalisation of the *député*'s role increased. As Robert de Jouvenel put it in his classic *La République des camarades* in 1914, 'whether one is moderate, radical or revolutionary, one is above all a *député*'.[1] With this came a certain *esprit de corps* symbolised by the increasing use of the informal 'tu' form of address among *députés*, especially after 1910, and which the very formal Poincaré never took to. Absence of a private income or an alternative profession soon led *députés* to seek a rise in their parliamentary salary which leapt from 9,000 francs a year – the same as in 1848 – to 15,000 following a vote on 22 November 1906. This made them, by a still greater margin than before, the best paid legislators in Europe.[2] Poincaré would not have approved of such profligacy, nor the bad example the people's representatives were setting. Public opinion was not pleased. Anti-parliamentarianism resurfaced to chants of 'Down with the *quinze milles*'. As the pressure on *députés* to be re-elected increased so too did the need to do favours and 'pull strings' for constituents, leading to an increase, amongst other things, of appeals to ministers for dispensations, promotions or appointments. This *clientèlisme*, which Poincaré had for so long abhorred on moral and efficiency grounds for the way it burdened and distracted the minister's political life, let alone its contravention of the republican principle of equality before the state, confirmed him in the need for proportional representation to loosen the *député*'s ties to his constituents. A change which he doubtless approved of for the greater coherence and stability it could bring to French political life was the greater tendency for *députés* to operate in political groups and parties.[3]

The changes taking place in the Chamber of Deputies were matched by the increasing authority of the Senate. Its ability to overturn governments was real. Three of the longest serving governments of the Third Republic in the decade 1899 to 1909 – those of Waldeck, Combes and Clemenceau – were led by senators. Ever since Loubet in 1899, a tradition had been established whereby presidents of the Senate moved up to the presidency of the Republic. This signposted the powerful role of the Senate in the inter-war years.[4] Poincaré would have to have been blessed with unusual foresight to anticipate this. But his flair for sensing where power lay and his patience in waiting for it to come to him made the Senate the right place to be. Furthermore, the upper chamber was increasingly perceived as a bastion of moderate republicanism, where the excesses of the lower chamber were tempered. Finally, a place in the Senate seemed a natural step for someone of his instinctive yearning to be top and which his school-friends had already identified: *Quo non ascendam*.

The Academy and the Bar Council

1906 was a good time for Poincaré to take stock of changes taking place in French politics and to await developments from the vantage point of the Senate. He often said that he never thought of politics as a 'métier', more a service one performed for one's country, perhaps a duty in its hour of need.[5] In the meantime he had his law practice which he had grown to love and which had acquired a considerable reputation in the commercial and artistic worlds. Though his literary output had not increased since the sugary contributions of his youth, like many politicians of the Third Republic his journalistic output was considerable. In a country where, according to Raymond Aron, politics has always had a literary flavour,[6] he was no different to many politicians. But at the turn of the century most writers scorned politicians whom they regarded as vulgar, philistine provincials without serious convictions.[7] Poincaré had written only three books by this time, which was below the average of five for cabinet ministers,[8] none of which was either substantial or recognised as of particular merit. More importantly, he had carefully cultivated his reputation as a lover of the arts by attending many literary salons and dinners (even when that was not to his political advantage), by his unpaid legal defence of authors, artists, playwrights and their representative bodies, and finally by his enthusiastic patronage of the arts as minister of public instruction and *beaux-arts*. The Academy was an ambitious step for most politicians. It was a natural one for the ever-ascending Poincaré. At that time it had greater prestige than today, when it was perceived as a meeting place for the different elites of the time: the *beau monde*, the arts and politics. Selection as one of the forty 'immortals' conferred added prestige on a politician in the eyes of his colleagues as well as public opinion.

Poincaré had been talked of as a potential Academician well before a letter arrived on 4 August 1906 suggesting that his name be put forward. The Academician André Theuriet, a friend of the Poincaré family, explained that Poincaré could count on the support of the dramatists, together with the parliamentary Academicians, Berthelot, Mézières and Ribot, as well as four of the Lorraine contingent in the Academy. That would give him the certainty of between sixteen and seventeen votes with the serious prospect of others following to secure his election.[9] Poincaré's influence over a number of Academicians had already been demonstrated in 1905 when he had successfully proposed Maurice Barrès. Now it was his own turn, as his old friend and Academician Gabriel Hanotaux told him. However, another two candidates came forward, a lawyer, Barboux, and the Marquis de Ségur. The political nature of the contest and the machinations involved soon became apparent. In the end, fear of upsetting relations with the eminent lawyer led him to withhold his candidature. Was he already thinking of another coveted position, that of *bâtonnier* of the Bar Council, for which the benediction of the former holder of that office, Barboux, would be important? Barboux was delighted by this gesture. As Poincaré had withheld his own name he was not considered to have been a candidate, something which was important to him as he never liked to lose. Poincaré's friends, though disappointed, made it clear that his election was only a matter of time. He had put down a marker in keeping with tradition. He bided his time until circumstances were right, allowing his cousin, the mathematician Henri Poincaré, to precede him.

Keeping at arm's length from ministerial office, he continued his legal labours. He cut back on political commitments at national level, giving up his long-held position as *rapporteur* of the budget commission of the Senate. But he maintained his local power base, becoming president of the *conseil général* of the Meuse on 26 September 1910 – a position to which he would be regularly re-elected until his death. Two years previously he had demonstrated his attachment to his local roots by having his second home outside the little village of Sampigny, some twenty miles from Bar-le-Duc, completely rebuilt by the Nancy architect Bourgon for 300,000 francs. Despite the flourishing at this time of Ecole de Nancy *art nouveau*, his new home reflected nothing of this.[10] It was very much in the traditional heavy style of many Third Republican constructions; a large chateau-like construction in red brick, with mullion windows and mansarded roof, redolent of a railway station or a *mairie*. This was where he was most at home and to where he retreated by train from Paris at every opportunity. He called it his 'petit paradis meusien'. In September 1914 as the invading German army swarmed across Lorraine, the house was struck by some fifty German shells which devastated the garden and gutted the house. After the war he refused any compensation for the damage caused and paid for the reconstruction out of proceeds from the sale of a property belonging to his wife. Before the war he had been comfortably off from his successful legal work and from a substantial inheritance from his father, which brought Raymond's personal fortune to between two and a half and three million francs in 1913. Yet during the war, as calls on his generosity increased, he dilapidated that fortune by overspending to the tune of 600,000 to 700,000 francs a year on his presidential expenses. By the end of the war he had barely enough money to purchase a modest Parisian apartment, rue Marbeau.[11] But it was the 'Clos Sampigny', austere, solid and alone in the Lorraine countryside which was the most fitting retreat for its owner.

The years devoted to his legal work after 1906 were interspersed with frequent cultural trips to Italy and Spain. He continued to act as legal counsel for artists and writers without payment. Even when he acted for the best-selling Jules Verne he refused a fee. This added to his reputation as a patron of the arts, as well as increasing his chances of election to the Academy. Nevertheless he remained particularly selective in his choice of legal cases. Unlike the English tradition of the law, in which acceptance of a brief has no relation to a barrister's personal opinions, Poincaré had to believe in the rightfulness of each case; he also hated to lose. His position as a *député* also made him refuse any case involving the French administration for fear of restricting his independence in parliament. He held his independence dear, whether in politics, the law, or the arts. He cultivated his reputation for honesty; he sent back fees when he had reached an out-of-court settlement; he held back his brother Lucien's promotion in the education ministry for fear of it being misconstrued as nepotism, telling him at each time he returned to power, 'Again you must bide your time'.[12] Anecdotes abound of his probity: his attempt to punish a member of his private office for using his official title to secure a minor favour from the dean of a law faculty, or his instructions to his *chef de cabinet* to be sure that a private letter to his publisher should not go by ministerial courier. He systematically refused all gifts, whether to himself or his wife, no matter how small or insignificant.[13] This integrity verged on the obsessive. As always with Poincaré, it is difficult to separate ethics from image. Apart from the desire to keep a clear conscience, he did not overlook its wider benefits, as he told a young *député*: 'If you always do, strictly, meticulously, what at each occasion is the most commendable you will please yourself. And then ... others will end up knowing it.'[14] This image contrasted markedly with the general low esteem in which parliamentary morality was held at the turn of the century. Daniel Halévy commented, 'Poincaré is not only the statesman, he is also the man of integrity – an amazing integrity which he carried to the point of perfection ... Even having served the State, he never serves himself.' And it paid dividends. In the courts he was referred to as 'la blanche Hermine', in parliament as 'le Chevalier Bayard'. As the writer Emmanuel Berl put it, 'he was without doubt since Robespierre the man whose incorruptibility was most believed by his contemporaries. This explains the respect he inspired on the Left for whom corruption remained the essential mark and the most repulsive aspect of capitalism.'[15]

This helped bring him the glittering prizes he coveted so much. In 1907 his fellow barristers elected him to the ordre des avocats. He was delighted. As he told his legal colleagues (in somewhat *risqué* fashion for him), he had grown to love the law, and all the more so for his ministerial absences from it: 'I am like those husbands who are unfaithful to their wives but who love them all the more they are unfaithful to them.'[16] He would be re-elected to the Council eleven times from 1907 to 1911 and from 1921 to his death. But it was not until much later than he had hoped, in June 1931, that he received the supreme legal accolade, president of the Bar Council, and which his illness the following October would force him to relinquish. He described his nomination as 'an incomparable emotion of my life'.[17] But neither the law nor ministerial office was enough. He set about ensuring his election to the Académie française.

1907 and 1908 saw Poincaré increase his literary output by speeches, lectures, articles and membership of committees. He wrote on a range of subjects from Joan of Arc to the art of judging, from patriotism to Belgian literature. He became a member of the Council of the University of Paris, the board of the Pasteur Institute and he had a hand in founding the review *La Renaissance*. In 1907 he published a well-received collection of political articles entitled *Questions et figures politiques* to complement his *Idées contemporaines* of the previous year. He began to gather material for a major study of Adolphe Thiers, with whom he bore some remarkable similarities: small stature, thin voice, clarity of style, intelligence, hard work, wide knowledge, pragmatism, liberalism, order, patriotism and – as Gambetta once said of Thiers – the middle classes' 'most typical representative'.[18] It was a work he would never complete but never abandon either, continuing his researches until as late as 1927, though no trace remains.

By the time that three Academicians had died in quick succession in 1908, Poincaré's standing as a potential 'immortal' had been embellished. He had not, however, gone to the extremes to which his friend and colleague Barthou would later go to get into the Academy, of publishing fourteen works between 1913 and 1919.[19] But 'immortality' could never be left to chance. Poincaré's campaign was orchestrated by the Academician, Paul Hervieu, whom Poincaré had decorated when minister for the arts. Whoever Hervieu asked him to buttonhole, to write to, to entertain, from the Orleanist Albert de Mun to Cardinal Mathieu, Poincaré obliged. Hervieu even suggested to him that he ask his ministerial colleague, Gaston Doumergue, whether the *légion d'Honneur*, coveted by a particular Academician, would be awarded in order to apprise him of it and win his vote. When Poincaré wanted something, as Payen discreetly put it, 'The art of pleasing was not unknown to him'. Hervieu's tactics paid off. Poincaré was elected on the first round with twenty of the thirty-one votes cast. When asked by journalists for his reaction, in his measured manner he remarked, 'They were grateful to me for having waited'. Modesty apart, he was only forty-eight in an institution not known for its youth. Once again that old tactic of not being in too much of a hurry had paid off. As Payen comments, 'He arrived as he arrived everywhere with an even, measured, prudent step careful not to overturn any barriers, paying attention not to upset anybody'.[20]

His investiture took place on 9 December 1909. Flanked by his two proposers, the Lorraine Senator Alfred Mézières and Paul Hervieu (who would also propose Barthou in 1919), he pronounced the traditional eulogy of his predecessor, the historian of the Italian Renaissance, Emile Gébhart. Ernest Lavisse agreed after initial hesitation to give the welcoming address, identifying Poincaré as 'a very wise Lorrainer', whom he characterised perfectly: 'You have sometimes been reproached for a certain coldness. It is true that being born on the banks of the Meuse, a river which flows not into the Mediterranean, nor the Gulf of Gascony, but into the North Sea, your words do not precede your thoughts and you wait until you are moved before becoming emotional.'[21]

For twenty-five years Poincaré took his duties at the Academy with typical seriousness and diligence, even introducing the word 'mirabellier' (a species of plum tree) to the Academy's dictionary. He would himself be the proposer of other parliamentary colleagues of both Left and Right, from the Radical Léon Bourgeois to the militant Catholic Denys Cochin, as well as the writers Le Goffic and André Hallays. Though disqualified from voting during his term as premier, he had a serious hand in supporting the candidature of the great colonial general, Lyautey, in 1912, as well as convincing Anatole France to stand in 1916.[22]

Reflections: politics, proportional representation, patriotism

Poincaré's voluntary absence from ministerial office since the end of 1906 enabled him to secure a number of prestigious appointments; more importantly it was a time to reflect on the state of French politics and society. It could be said that Waldeck-Rousseau's stewardship of the country had concentrated on politics, that Combes had sacrificed everything to anti-clericalism and that Rouvier had cultivated inaction. Social issues had not had their day. Yet from the beginning of the century many Frenchmen were increasingly preoccupied with the need to overhaul social legislation. From 1906, pressure for social change exerted itself forcefully.

Since the 1890s, syndicalist organisations, heavily tinged with anarchism, were in the ascendant. At the October 1906 Amiens Congress of the Confédération Générale du Travail (CGT), they won a notable victory over the moderates, carrying a resolution, which became the famous Amiens Charter, rejecting any association with political parties and advocating the general strike as the principal weapon to expropriate the capitalist class. Despite a background of economic expansion and an increase in real wages from 1900 to 1910, industrial unrest brimmed over. Militancy and violence were largely a consequence of economic growth and modernisation, which led to efforts by employers to increase productivity and modernise working practices. The Sarrien cabinet, which included Poincaré, made the long-demanded concession of establishing a ministry of work. But workers clamoured for further qualitative improvements such as an eight-hour day, better working conditions and retirement pensions.[23] The Clemenceau governments which followed from 1906 to 1909, in which Poincaré did not serve, were dogged by widespread strikes and disturbances from Marseille to Dunkirk, organised by electricians, dockers, navvies, workers in the building and food industries, as well as by violent clashes with wine-growers in the south hit by over-production and a fall in prices. 1909 saw the most threatening strikes from the government's point of view: first the post-office workers and then a call from the CGT for a general strike, albeit unsuccessful. Moreover, the nature of the strikes was changing. They were longer in duration, and occurring in smaller and smaller companies,[24] bringing their effect home to the middle classes, who increasingly called for protection. Poincaré could only deplore these syndicalist activities which, apart from having a strong anti-militarist streak, also posed a threat to the state itself.

Clemenceau's readiness to take on the strikers, often with troops, became increasingly distasteful to his old allies the parliamentary socialists whose champion, the eloquent Jean Jaurès, inveighed against him in parliament. Had he not been so pained by these bitter political divisions, Poincaré might have relished the sight of Clemenceau, 'tombeur des ministères', who typified the Radical distrust of strong governments, adopting such an authoritarian posture and being forced to rely increasingly on the support of his old enemies the Progressists. But it did help bring home to Poincaré the Tiger's strong will and sense of purpose in times of crisis.

With the fall of Clemenceau's cabinet in July 1909, on a relatively trivial issue, a period of political instability was reopened and with it anti-parliamentarianism. This instability resulted from the progressive dislocation of the Bloc des gauches and the Socialists' slide into opposition. The Radical party, which held the balance, was itself divided between its pro-socialist and centrist wings. It had been thought that the nimble tactician and smooth-talking Aristide Briand might salvage much of the Bloc. Though once an ardent socialist and advocate of the general strike, he headed two governments which adopted Clemenceau's repressive measures to put down a new wave of strikes such as that of the railway-workers in October 1910, further reducing the support of the socialists and radical–socialists. The last of his governments resigned on 27 February 1911, giving way to two more cabinets before the end of the year.

The slow drift of governments towards the political centre was helped by the elections of 24 April and 8 May 1910. The winding down of political tension was both cause and effect of the fact that, for the first time since 1898, the elections were not contested on a bloc to bloc basis, which probably accounts for the high abstention rate of 22.5 per cent. The elections brought 235 new *députés* to the Chamber, many of whom were moderates, despite their opportunistic adoption of the vote-winning Radical label. The new Chamber was further to the centre than its predecessor.[25]

A novelty in the new Chamber was the obligation on *députés* from

1910 to join a single parliamentary group, whereas previously multi-membership was common. The group's membership was then published in the *Journal Officiel*. Groups now also appointed the members of the parliamentary commissions. This should have brought greater coherence to French parliamentary life by reducing the individualism of *députés* and producing a semblance of party discipline; but parliamentary groups did not match political parties outside parliament, except in the case of the socialists. The 1910 Chamber was the one with which Poincaré would have to work in 1912. The parliamentary groups were constituted from left to right as follows: the socialists of the Section Française de l'Internationale Ouvrière (SFIO) had 75 *députés*, the républicains socialistes 30, the républicains radicaux–socialistes 150, the Gauche radicale 113, the Gauche démocratique 72, the républicains progres-sistes 75, Action libérale 34, the Right group 19 (royalist tradition), the Independents 20 (comprising nationalists like Maurice Barrès, as well as unaffiliated *députés*).[26]

Observing to a certain extent from the political sidelines, Poincaré was alarmed by the social divisions and disturbances which appeared to threaten the state, while being pleased at the drift back towards centrist politics. The period was marked by a call for constitutional reform from several quarters; some wanted constitutional revision, others merely a reform of parliamentary practice to bring it back into line with the 1875 constitution. Poincaré was among the latter. He was ever more convinced of the view he had first expressed in the 1890s that in order to combat the divisions of French society it was first necessary to correct the defects of the parliamentary system and mores. In 1908, responding to a survey in the *Revue* on this issue, he called for proportional representation and a reduction in the number of *députés* to ensure that parliament be 'the image and not the caricature of the nation'.[27] He wished to break the habit of *députés* pandering to petty local demands or the sectional interests of parliamentary groups – what Briand would refer to as bringing a purifying breeze to the 'little stagnant ponds'. *Interpellation*, the questioning of ministers on the floor of the Chamber followed by a vote, was becoming more than ever a self-seeking ploy of *députés* more interested in preserving local interests and their parliamentary seats; this weakened governments and delayed legislation. The increase in parliamentary standing committees from seventeen to twenty in 1902, plus the proliferation of *ad hoc* committees, had similar deleterious effects. The dissolving action of these myriad committees, groups and individuals earned the political system the title of 'Republic of Committees' in which the centralised state structure seemed to be crumbling along with national interests.[28]

This helps explain the revival of anti-parliamentarianism. Revolutionary syndicalists and the neo-monarchist Action française found common cause in wishing to sweep away the parliamentary system. Centrist republicans such as Poincaré and Barthou merely wished to overhaul the machine of government by strengthening the executive and limiting the legislative. Poincaré identified the constitutional problems at about this time in his small work of civic instruction for schoolchildren, *Ce que demande la cité*, which appeared in 1912. Attempting to redress the popular image in many parts of France of the minister as a 'donkey', he attributed much of the blame for this view to parliamentarians seeking to exercise patronage over administrative posts on behalf of their electors, or to purely sectarian interests. Thus, he explained, much of the minister's working day was taken up with 'an unending procession of supplicants', *députés* and senators 'who have adopted the annoying habit of recommending candidates for all posts'. Without considerable hard work and mental agility a minister merely became 'the plaything of parliament or the instrument of its *bureaux*'.[29] Where that agility was most needed was in dealing with the constant stream of interpellations. By repeated recourse to a vote after the interpellation ministers and governments could all too easily be brought down. France, Poincaré recommended, should adopt the British system of fewer questions and fewer votes. He also blamed the parliamentary commissions who arrogated to themselves greater and greater powers to interfere in the administration, and even take on a quasi-judicial role.[30]

To overcome *députés'* tendency to be guided by predominantly local interests, Poincaré made clear his commitment to proportional representation. The desire for a change away from the single-member majority system in place in France since 1889, for which he had voted, was by 1910 sponsored by the conservatives, the progressists, the Alliance démocratique and the socialists, who wished to relinquish their electoral pacts with the Radicals, who were the big winners from the existing system. While recognising that the single-member majority system allowed the voter to get to know his parliamentary representative, Poincaré explained that the proportional system was what Gambetta supported because it promoted broader currents of opinion through larger multi-member constituencies.[31] Like many he saw electoral reform as a panacea. In an article in the *Revue de Paris* of 15 April 1910, he explained that proportional representation would lead to, 'after order in parliament, after order in the administration, order in Justice: after restoring legislative power, after consolidating the executive, the reconstitution of the judiciary'.[32] Electoral reform would be put to the vote under Poincaré's premiership in 1912 but, though the Chamber approved it, the Radicals, whose party organisation was based on the *scrutin d'arrondissement*, rejected it in the Senate and the elections of 1914 were held under the old system.

Poincaré also favoured strengthening the role of the president of the Republic. *Ce que demande la cité* called for the effective restoration of the presidential power of dissolution of the Chamber, which had not been used since 1877. He also outlined the 'crucial role' which the president of the Republic still possessed in the area of international relations, and which he would later exploit to the full. He eschewed any formal change in the president's powers, because this was a demand of the authoritarian Right; the republican nationalists such as Déroulède and the *rallié* Catholic Action libérale populaire were clamouring for direct presidential elections or a wider electoral college. Besides, Poincaré was the wrong kind of politician to introduce constitutional reform, even had he desired revision. He did not have the strength of character for such an undertaking, which would have meant confronting sizeable parliamentary and press opposition, which he always tried to avoid, and confronting the deep-seated republican political fear of 'Caesarism' since the Second Empire. By temperament an administrator rather than an innovator and with a lawyer's belief in the sanctity of legal texts, he was not someone to take the risks involved in constitutional reform. Hence his remark in 1908 on parliamentary powerlessness: 'From the clumsiness of the mechanics we should not conclude too quickly that the machinery is faulty.'[33] Better then, like so many moderate republicans, to settle for tinkering with the electoral system to improve the system.

Reconciliation around old themes of national unity, nationhood and national identity was another area on which he had reflected deeply, making clear his ideas publicly in the 1890s. Like many republicans he believed in patriotism as a means of uniting the French. Given the clear social divisions in the first decade of the twentieth century, it seemed an appropriate moment to emphasise the virtues of patriotism, all the more so as international tension with Germany increased after 1905. He was also reflecting a strand of the broad movement known as the 'nationalist revival'. But Poincaré's was not the nationalism of the 'authoritarian nationalists' like Déroulède, though he might share certain ideas on patriotism with their leading intellectual exponent, Maurice Barrès. Their particularist and racialist brand of nationalism was by definition divisive; it was turned inwards to force out the alien elements in French thinking and society. Poincaré's nationalism, by contrast, was ecumenical.

The republican and *laïque* Ligue de l'Enseignement was a vehicle for patriotism enjoying much success at this time. It was committed to developing popular education with a view to establishing the Republic and its ideals firmly in the minds of all Frenchmen. Poincaré was chosen to give a lecture on 'L'idée de patrie' at the Ligue's new Paris home in rue Récamier on 16 March 1910; it was an opportunity to reiterate his beliefs. He began by attacking those who labelled patriotism as bad. On the contrary, 'let us not tire of showing that this feeling, said to be contrary to nature, is the necessary product of nature, that it is not only legitimised, but ordered by history and that to interrupt or slow down the "training" of this instinctive tendency would be to betray the cause of humanity itself'. Distancing himself from the authoritarian nationalists, he quoted Lavisse to show that patriotism needed to be cultivated, otherwise, left to its own devices, it could assume an unfortunate chauvinistic character, leading to 'a frivolous vanity' and scorn for the foreigner. This, he stated, had contributed to France's defeat in 1870 only to be followed by a self-deprecating admiration for the conquering foreigner, resignation in the face of the indignities inflicted and a renunciation of any idea of national dignity. More than ever, schools should promote patriotic education and the state ensure that it is carried out. Out of duty writers and military officers should teach young Frenchmen to 'breathe at all moments the healthy air of la patrie'. He criticised those 'anti-patriots' who dissected the idea of patrie until it no longer existed. France had her own distinctiveness of temperament, even though it may not always be to the liking of foreigners. And he quoted Schopenhauer's remark, 'Other parts of the world have monkeys, Europe has the French', to which Poincaré remarked, 'We are insulted therefore we exist!' But 'patrie' was more than this, 'More still than a geographical being, or than an ethnic being, or than a linguistic being, la patrie is an historical being'. And he traced the origins of the word back in French history to the Ancien Régime, revealing his belief in the continuity of French history, even though 'The Revolution clarified in the eyes of all the French the notion of national unity'. This was the essence of Poincaré's concept of the nation: the unity of all Frenchmen in time and space. Thus he stated that 'la patrie is not only a de facto necessity, and patriotism not only an inexorable duty imposed by circumstance. La patrie is, if I might say, a human necessity and patriotism the most accessible form, the most certain, the truest, of our duties to humanity.' For that reason he criticised the internationalists, extreme socialists and pacifists for weakening and dividing France. Referring to Durkheim's belief, expressed in L'education morale, that national sentiment blended with the human conscience, Poincaré concluded on the universalist and humanising nature of patriotism: 'The idea of the family helps us to conceive of the idea of *la patrie*; the idea of *la patrie* helps us to conceive of the idea of humanity.'[34]

Poincaré's brand of republican patriotism, reminiscent of Michelet, set him apart from the xenophobic integral nationalism of the Action française, the revolutionary patriotism of the 'authoritarian republicans' and the more Catholic and Orleanist inspired nationalism of the 'ordinary nationalists' devoted to the French army and represented by the *Echo de Paris* newspaper and Count Albert de Mun.[35] Though the moderate Left comprising Jaurès, his colleagues in the SFIO and a portion of the Radicals did not reject patriotism – Jaurès even remarked that patriotism was attached 'by its very roots ... to man's physiology'[36] – theirs was too bound up with internationalism to square with Poincaré's patriotism. The latter's was a republican and 'defensive' patriotism which exalted national qualities, was not chauvinistic, but which rejected anti-militarism, pacifism and also bellicosity and which wished to see France's foreign policy strong and in a position to defend her national interests.

Foreign affairs

Poincaré's voluntary absence from ministerial office took place against a backdrop of increasing tension in international relations since the First Moroccan Crisis of March 1905. Irritated at Foreign Minister Delcassé's reluctance to consult Germany on the future of Morocco over which she had treaty rights, Kaiser Wilhelm II delivered a powerful speech in Tangiers calling for an international settlement of the Moroccan question. Delcassé was forced to resign, disavowed by a frightened Rouvier cabinet for refusing to agree to the German proposal for an international conference. That conference held the following year at Algeçiras gave little satisfaction to Germany as well as reinforcing the recent Entente Cordiale with Britain. The whole episode conjured up once more the spectre of the German threat. Though officially a *détente* in Franco-German relations followed, symbolised by a joint economic convention on Morocco in February 1909, this was gradually undermined by nationalist and Germanophobe French permanent officials in the Quai d'Orsay and on the ground in Morocco, and whose actions contributed to the Second Moroccan Crisis at Agadir in 1911 and Poincaré's return to power.[37]

A rebellion against the Sultan in May 1911 provided the French with a pretext for intervening militarily at Fez and Meknès. This effectively placed central Morocco under their control. Germany saw this as an attempt by France to secure a *de facto* protectorate over Morocco which flouted the 1906 and 1909 agreements. On 1 July 1911 the German gun-boat, Panther, anchored off the southern Moroccan port of Agadir. The German authorities warned that her recall would depend on suitable French compensation. That soon turned out to mean France swapping freedom of action in Morocco for German control of the Congo. The French cabinet was split between premier Joseph Caillaux, who favoured a conciliatory attitude, and the inexperienced foreign minister, Justin de Selves, under the sway of nationalist officials at the Quai d'Orsay. After long and difficult negotiations, in which Caillaux resorted to secret and unofficial contacts with the Germans to circumvent the foreign minister and his officials, a new Franco-German treaty was signed on 4 November 1911. France was given a free hand in Morocco and Germany a large share of the French Congo.[38]

Whatever the merits of this agreement, in France at least, it was not widely perceived as being to France's advantage. From 14 November in the Chamber the treaty was attacked by the conservative and nationalist Right for ceding so much territory to Germany. Though ratified on 20 December by 393 votes to 36, 141 *députés* abstained, with no one from Lorraine voting for it. But it was in the Senate that it faced greatest opposition.

On 28 December 1911 Poincaré was unanimously appointed *rapporteur* of the Senate commission called to examine the treaty. Not known for having any experience of foreign affairs, other than his former foreign policy column in the *Lyon Républicain*, he was nevertheless clearly recognised as a patriot and a symbol of republican unity. He approved of the treaty despite the opposition of *députés* from the east of France. He understood the necessity of working with Germany: 'In all the ministries to which I belonged, whether from 1893 to 1895 or 1906, I approved the specific ententes concluded with Germany. I never thought that loyalty to our memories dictated, in relation to our neighbours, a sort of chronic animosity and prohibited us, them as much as us, on all points of the globe from the hope of specific agreements.'[39] The desire to have a working relationship with Germany would characterise his foreign policy in the pre-war and post-war periods.

For the moment Poincaré had reservations about the secret negotiations with Germany that premier Caillaux had engaged in behind his foreign minister's back, and told him so. The two men were, however, on friendly terms at this time; Poincaré had been one of Caillaux's second wife's witnesses at their recent wedding on 21 October 1911.[40] He now advised Caillaux on what he should say in his defence. Clemenceau, another commission member, had misgivings about both the treaty's content and how it was negotiated. When on 9 January 1912

Caillaux stated to the Senate commission that no unofficial negotiations had taken place with Germany, Clemenceau turned to the foreign minister for confirmation. That was not forthcoming. De Selves resigned on the grounds that he could not take responsibility for a foreign policy with which he did not agree. Caillaux tried to patch up his cabinet by offering the ministry of foreign affairs and navy to Delcassé and Poincaré respectively. Both refused.[41] Poincaré could see that Caillaux's tottering government had no future. He doubtless believed that the moment had arrived when he could step forward and play a great role. He was encouraged in that thought by a chorus of letters from political colleagues like the Radical Théodore Steeg: 'Co-ordinate the republican majority yourself, give it momentum, take power ...' Others repeated the message: 'An experienced pilot is needed, with a clear eye, a calm spirit. You are him ...' Or: 'Help this resourceful and willing people to rediscover confidence in its Government. You will have done for our great Country, without bearings, unrecognised, discouraged, uncrowned, the most notable service.'[42] It was not the first time that he had received such appeals, nor did he underestimate their hyperbole. But he was always susceptible to praise, while feigning not to be. Most of all, he appears to have understood the potency of an area like foreign affairs, where he had little expertise, but which seemed capable of uniting the country.

When Caillaux tendered his resignation on 11 January 1912 the crisis, at national and international levels, was flagrant. France was without a government and unable to ratify a treaty whose rejection could mean war. The Bonapartist Ernest Judet wrote gleefully in *L'Eclair*, 'It is the débâcle and with it that of the 'bloc', of the whole system, of the regime.' *La Liberté* echoed him: 'A national crisis. M. Fallières [the president] should beware: today he is going to play one of the last cards of the Republic.'[43] The press called for a personality with experience of public affairs, authority and integrity. Poincaré seemed a natural choice. On 13 January 1912, President Fallières called on him to form a new government. Because of the confidence he inspired, the seriousness of the situation and a personal desire to set the pace of things to come, he established what was to be a record for the swiftest forming of a government under the Third Republic.[44] Called to the Elysée at 10 a.m., his cabinet was complete twelve hours later.

In his fifty-second year Poincaré formed the fifty-second government of the Third Republic, a coincidence which might be thought to capture the tidy, precise nature of his personality and his foreign policy. In many ways the new government was no different from the average ministry of the Third Republic before the First World War. With twelve ministers it was in line with the usual eleven to twelve since the turn of the century; twelve had been the number in Ferry's second cabinet and Gambetta's government. Four *sous-secrétaires d'état,* a common number, was a standard means of garnering more parliamentary support and distributing the work-load of the larger departments. Like all governments of the Third Republic it contained ministers from the previous cabinet – in this case, five. As no prime-ministerial office existed – the office of *président du conseil* was not even mentioned in the constitutional laws of 1875 – it was customary for the head of the government to take on a ministerial portfolio. It would not be until 1936 that the *président du conseil* would become a self-standing office. As a symbol of the importance that foreign affairs would play, Poincaré broke with the recent custom of reserving for the premier the portfolios of either Interior or Justice and took on the foreign ministry. As he had stated in *Ce que demande la cité* the year before, the foreign minister 'is, if you like, the minister of Honour and of Peace'.[45] Although the thirteenth premier to combine his office with that of foreign minister, Poincaré gave impetus to what would become accepted practice: from 1871 to 1918, 28 per cent of premiers were also foreign ministers (though mostly from Poincaré onwards); between 1919 and 1939, 53 per cent held the two offices simultaneously.[46]

The new government shifted politics further towards the centre. But Poincaré was at pains to give it the image of a union of *républicains de gauche* by excluding the progressists and the Catholic Right. His old friend the former socialist Alexandre Millerand became minister of war, a post Poincaré had recently described as 'the organiser of national defence. He ensures ... that we are ready in advance for any eventuality'.[47] Another ex-socialist, Briand, was given the ministry of justice, Delcassé navy, Albert Lebrun colonies. Public works was reserved for Senator Jean Dupuy of the Alliance démocratique, owner of the *Petit Parisien* newspaper and president of the *Syndicat de la Presse parisienne,* whose legal counsel was Poincaré. Though the very moderate *Alliance démocratique* was the mainstay of the government, Poincaré was eager to rally the support of the Radicals by including Théodore Steeg at interior, Léon Bourgeois at the ministry of labour and Jules Pams at agriculture. That the new cabinet should have its detractors in both the Left- and Right-wing press was a measure of its centrist character. Moderate newspapers such as *Le Temps* welcomed it. Similarly *La République Française* hoped that the new government would be able to avert disaster by renouncing 'the policy of groups' and by forging a union of all republicans. The government's programme reflected this desire: on the domestic front with a commitment to proportional representation, defence of the laws on *laïcité*, and social reform; externally by a policy of peace and a desire to work with Germany.

The British Foreign Office was particularly interested in Poincaré's new government. It had been worried by Caillaux's negotiations with Germany during the Agadir crisis, which it perceived as a possible attempt to establish a Paris–Berlin axis likely to undermine the Entente Cordiale. Sir Francis Bertie, the ambassador and shrewd observer of French political life, described Poincaré as having a 'considerable personal position outside political cliques' and as being credited with 'great versatility' and with being 'equally at home in art, science, literature and politics', though he was 'said to be impulsive in character'. Bertie explained that he had become in recent years 'the mentor of contemporary politics' displaying 'interesting and original views on current events from a standpoint which was not that of the regular party politician. He has given the impression of late that he was ploughing his own furrow.' This, explained Bertie, is why public opinion viewed him as no ordinary politician. Having remained aloof from scandal and recent political controversies, he was now blessed with a 'considerable amount of prestige'. But Bertie felt that he was 'too moderate to be entirely a *persona grata* with the radical-socialist majority in the Chamber'. He warned in particular that Poincaré had no particular aptitude for foreign affairs and concluded, 'In view of the enormous demands made on the energy and time of the head of the Government in France, it is likely that any one holding that post will be very dependent on the officials under him at the Quai d'Orsay.' Bertie concluded that Fallières's aim in entrusting the formation of the new cabinet to Poincaré had been to ensure a government composed of eminent men who could command respect and neutralise the attacks against the republican regime itself, and he noted how Poincaré's government was being compared with Gambetta's 'grand ministère' of 1881 and Waldeck-Rousseau's ministry of 'republican concentration' formed in 1898 to terminate the Dreyfus affair. The difference was, Bertie concluded, that Poincaré's ministry had been assembled for reasons connected with foreign affairs and the situation that had arisen out of the manner of conducting them.[48]

The other power with an interest in Poincaré and his government was Germany. Though German public opinion showed scant interest in French domestic politics – scandals and upheavals apart – German diplomats were another matter. Former foreign minister and now ambassador in Paris, Baron von Schoen, another acute observer of the French political scene, reported after his first audience, 'He gives me the impression of a man whose thinking is in strictly legal terms. He is a man who defends his convictions with remarkable energy and whose political objectives are shouldered by great will-power.'[49] In Germany, Poincaré's new government was favourably received; the influential *Berliner Tageblatt* noted that 'The Poincaré Cabinet can only be favourably welcomed in Germany'.[50]

At this time Poincaré seemed to combine what Raoul Girardet has described as the necessary components to be acknowledged as the 'guide' or 'saviour' who has so often emerged in French history: 'gravitas', 'firmness in adversity, experience, prudence, sang-froid, measure and moderation'; he had undergone a period of waiting and had at last received the call.[51] How would he fair? Ironically, the politician best known for his capabilities in domestic politics was about to make his mark in foreign policy.

5　Poincaré the diplomat

If ever there was a chance for Poincaré to make his mark it was after the Agadir crisis. A new mood reigned in the Chamber. The international threats were well understood. There was widespread agreement on the need for a strong government that could rise above petty party squabbling. The new cabinet was well received generally. Poincaré's great goal of achieving national unity seemed distinctly attainable. But he understood how ephemeral the present consensus could prove to be. In his inaugural government statement of 16 January, for the first time in decades he chose to focus a government's policy on foreign affairs. He made clear his intention to defend the 1911 Franco-German treaty on Morocco which would allow France to work with Germany: 'Equally it will allow us to maintain between a great neighbouring nation and France, in a sincerely pacific spirit, courteous and frank relations, inspired by a mutual respect of interests and dignity.'[1] He called for a strengthening of France's international position by cultivating her system of alliances; at the same time he stressed the need to strengthen national defence in view of the alarming events of recent months: 'Although our country is profoundly pacific, she is not the master of all eventualities and intends to respect all her obligations. We shall devote careful attention to our army and navy which, like you gentlemen, we regard as the sacred pillars of the Republic and *la patrie.*'[2]

In order to achieve this objective he called for a moratorium on divisive domestic issues, claiming that it was parliament's duty to 'follow the example of the country' and to gear its conduct to the public interest. To that end he moved to calm the stormy religious question that had for so long dominated domestic politics by an even-handed statement of commitment to secular state schools, but at the same time to a guarantee of freedom of conscience. Thus he remained true to *laïcité* while rejecting intolerance. It was the application of long-held beliefs. So too was his reaffirmation of the salutary nature of the *scrutin de liste* as opposed to the *scrutin d'arrondissement* (for which he had voted in February 1889) and which he now proposed to introduce in conjunction with proportional representation. This was the only potentially divisive aspect of his general policy statement. But its importance to Poincaré lay in the need to strengthen the powers of the executive and release it from the shifting sands of unstable parliamentary majorities over-reliant on the parochial interests of the *députés*. Political cartoonists would not fail to notice when the electoral reform bill came before the Chamber in July 1912 that *Représentation Proportionelle* and Raymond Poincaré had from the start certain things in common. By 446 to 140 the Chamber voted confidence in the government. Poincaré's policy of national unity was supported by the centre and the nationalistic Right, while the radical Left endorsed at least the foreign policy. Throughout 1912, virtually no opposition was voiced by left-wing republicans against Poincaré's doctrine of strength and energy in international relations and unity at home. Not even the socialists offered much resistance until 1913, when the Three Years' Conscription Law aroused major controversy.[3]

In 1912 Poincaré worked hard to maintain the political balance he had achieved with his first cabinet. At one point, however, during discussion of the bill on electoral reform, in uncharacteristic manner he nearly reopened old wounds by a quip made to a right-wing senator which subsequently achieved almost legendary status. When the latter, addressing himself to Poincaré, remarked that 'from you to me there is hardly any difference', the premier immediately retorted, 'There is the whole of the religious question.' In press and parliament there was a chorus of either protest or assent depending on political stance. Poincaré explained his remark in an interview with the journalist Marcel Hutin. When asked whether he had been trying to suggest that Catholics should be excluded from the Republic, the measured reply he gave was a far more accurate picture of his views on *laïcité*:

I am not so stupid as to have such a narrow and such a lowly conception of the Republic. But unfortunately the manner in which the religious question is conceived, I mean the means of regulating relations between the Church and the State, is not the same for all Frenchmen ... All left-wing republicans consider – it's a fact – that religion is an individual thing, that it should be kept out of politics and that it should not command any of the organs of civil society.

He ended by turning the discussion around to the essence of his government's policy, by affirming that in all questions to do with foreign policy and national interest 'this difference is easily erased by the unanimity of patriotic feeling'.[4] Though for the moment he had dampened the embers of a resurgence of the religious question, the remark would live on to caricature him erroneously as anti-clerical, even though that was not always to his political disadvantage.

The political centre can be an uncomfortable position to occupy. At the time of the Dreyfus Affair, Poincaré had clashed with the Right thereby moving to the Left; the Left was now beginning to engage him in combat on domestic issues, giving the impression that he was moving to the Right. The balancing act he was forced to maintain in domestic politics had its counterpart in foreign affairs, the central plank of his government's policy.

Foreign policy

French politicians traditionally showed little interest in foreign affairs and Poincaré was no exception. This was not surprising given the magnitude of the domestic agenda drawn up since the beginning of the Third Republic and the controversy it provoked. Foreign policy was generally left to the specialist ministers or the professional diplomats and bureaucrats.

Poincaré's only early experience of foreign affairs had been as a journalist writing for *Le Lyon Républicain*. In the last six months of 1911, however, he had gained a knowledge of the foreign ministry while preparing a detailed study of its workings for the Senate finance commission and, more recently, as *rapporteur* for the Senate commission called to examine the proposed 1911 Franco-German treaty. In the former he had denounced the 'unbelievable administrative disorder' at the Quai d'Orsay and had called for its reorganisation; in the latter he had spoken of his 'pitiful impression of this ministry'.[5] If foreign affairs were to be the central plank of his government's policy, Poincaré felt the need to reform the ministry to make it an effective instrument for implementing his diplomatic programme. Poincaré's six-year absence from power after 1906 virtually coincided with the evolution of French diplomatic strategy towards a policy of *détente* and conciliation towards Germany, which he believed had failed. Called to restore France's prestige and security in the face of what was widely perceived as German intimidation, Poincaré believed that a return to where Delcassé had been forced to leave off in 1905 could improve things. It was a policy which required no innovation, simply good management, clarity and authority. Maintaining the European balance of power implied little more than abiding by the letters which Delcassé had exchanged with his Russian counterpart in 1899 and which stated the maintenance of that balance to be an aim of the Franco-Russian treaty. Poincaré, with his juridical precision, wanted the balance of power observed to the letter – a total separation of the two blocs. His policy towards Triple Alliance members would however be one of peaceful coexistence.

Poincaré probably disapproved of the foreign ministry's personnel as much as he did of its organisation. It began with a fundamental incompatibility of character and outlook. The foreign ministry had developed a tradition of independence from parliamentary interference; it was perceived as a bastion of social and political tradition rooted in the aristocracy, despite various republican purges. Since Foreign Minister Delcassé's forced departure at Germany's behest in 1905, policy was formulated and executed as part of a triangular struggle in which the young nationalistic officials in the *bureaux* of the Quai vied with independent-minded and powerful ambassadors all to the detriment of their political master, the minister, nominally at the apex. Poincaré was not alone in believing that such disorganisation, by allowing reckless decisions to be taken by politically irresponsible permanent officials, had contributed to Agadir and the confused negotiations surrounding the settlement of the crisis.[6]

Poincaré's plan for reorganising foreign policy was quickly drawn up and implemented. First, he selected an inner cabinet of loyal and efficient permanent officials to work in conjunction with the minister on major issues, among whom was included his old school-friend Maurice Paléologue, who became political director. Second, on 23 July 1912 he reorganised the central administration to concentrate decision-making nearer the top and away from the 'bothersome and meddling *bureaux*'. Concentrating virtually all power in his own hands at the same time as running the government demanded considerable industry. But his capacity for work was extraordinary. Gabriel Hanotaux, his friend for fifty years and a hard worker himself, recorded that Poincaré had 'a passion for work, a persistency in toil which I have never seen surpassed or even attained by anyone else'. He was said to rise at six or six-thirty and begin his day by reading a page of the four or five languages he knew.[7] He was at his desk by eight o'clock demanding to see everything personally, replying in his own hand to ambassadors, minuting all files, seeing to all his post and demanding comprehensive written notes from all his collaborators before coming to a decision. Meals were expedited in a few minutes accompanied only by water. When dining out he always made it a rule to return home by 11 p.m. Administrative decisions were dispatched with ferocious speed in sharp memoranda which irritated many. Paul Cambon, ambassador in London since 1898, was ruffled by Poincaré's attention to detail and affinity for work, claiming, 'He ends up losing himself in his telegrams, his proposals and his paper-work'.[8] This was untrue, as Cambon well knew, for only three weeks before he had told his brother, the ambassador to Berlin, 'Poincaré has his dossiers organised like a barrister'.[9] The policy was proving successful. Even the intriguer Philippe Berthelot, assistant director for Asia, noticed the difference two months after Poincaré had taken over: 'The department is calm: the *bureaux* are kept out of things.'[10]

Ambassadors and permanent officials were treated in the same imperious manner. It was said that the longest-serving French ambassador, Camille Barrère in Rome, who, like the Cambon brothers, was a staunch republican and a household name, 'was sent the text of the communications he was to make to the Italian government, and he was ordered not to change one comma'.[11] There was a particular reason for treating Barrère in this fashion which was at the heart of the problem that confronted Poincaré in 1912. Ambassadors had grown unaccustomed to taking orders from foreign ministers whose ignorance of international relations they scorned and whose transitoriness they considered their greatest quality. For that reason ambassadors often developed their own policies towards the countries to which they were accredited and which their political masters were often unable to control. As Paul Cambon told his brother on the subject of ambassadors, 'If the gentleman is nothing himself, he is sacrificed. If he is somebody and represents a policy, he is untouchable. Your retirement or mine would be political events which would create a definite fuss for our government whichever it might be.'[12] Barrère had developed a policy intended eventually to draw Italy into the Triple Entente from the Triple Alliance where, with Austria–Hungary, she was Germany's ally. In Vienna, the ambassador, Philippe Crozier, was pursuing a similar policy towards Austria–Hungary. In Berlin Jules Cambon had been pursuing a policy of *détente*, which in some eyes looked more like a *rapprochement* and which could upset Russia and Britain, France's partners in the Triple Entente. Paul Cambon had long sought an alliance with Britain. Aspects of these policies were undoubtedly in France's interest; but they could also be contradictory and very dangerous. Poincaré was aware of that. Many of them clashed with his conception of international relations at this time which refused any interpenetration of the two alliance blocs of Triple Alliance and Triple Entente. As Poincaré later stated, his philosophy was perfectly encapsulated in the words of the British foreign secretary, Sir Edward Grey:

We wanted the Entente and Germany's Triple Alliance to live side by side in amity. That was the best that was practicable. If we intrigued to break up the Triple Alliance, our contention that the Entente was defensive and was not directed against Germany would cease to be true. Disturbance and possible war, it was clear, would be the consequence.[13]

Thus Poincaré viewed any attempt at upsetting the alliance systems as examples of ambassadorial insubordination and as strategic errors. Although Germany had in 1905 attempted to dislocate the Triple Entente, if France acted in the same way Germany's fears of encirclement would be heightened and with it her aggressiveness and the danger of war. Naturally, Poincaré did not intend to leave Germany unchecked, which he also believed might lead to war. He wished to steer a course between these twin dangers. As he had already made clear, this did not rule out strengthening the Triple Entente in order to contain the Triple Alliance. In short, the essence of his policy, as with so many European politicians at this time, was for a balance of power to act as guarantor of peace.

Poincaré's policy was first exercised in regard to Italy.[14] In 1900, Barrère, in conjunction with Delcassé, had succeeded in obtaining an exchange of letters with Italy which guaranteed Italian disinterestedness in Morocco in exchange for French disinterestedness in Tripoli. It was also stated that if any political or territorial adjustment was to take place in Morocco then Italy reserved the right to develop her influence in Tripolitania-Cyrenaica, which approximates to present-day Libya. This agreement was enhanced by a further exchange of letters equivalent to a non-aggression pact between the two countries concluded on 30 June 1902, but post-dated to 1 November. To a certain extent this negated Italy's commitment to the Triple Alliance, at least in respect of France. The Germans were quick to learn of the agreements and tried to put a brave face on it by talking of wives waltzing with partners other than their husbands and yet remaining faithful. But no one was more aware than Chancellor von Bülow that Italian flirtations could have more serious consequences, for his wife was an Italian lady who had eloped with him when she was still the wife of the German ambassador in Rome and von Bülow was on his staff.[15] Franco-Italian relations stayed at that level for several years, despite Barrère's attempts to take them to their logical conclusion – the extraction of Italy from the Triple Alliance. In 1911, as a result of the Agadir settlement which virtually made a French protectorate out of Morocco, Italy decided to activate the 1900 agreement with France. On the pretext of Turkish persecution of Christians in Tripoli, the Italians attacked the Turks with the intention of annexing Tripolitania. Their hopes for an early victory were thwarted and Italy cast around for scapegoats. France was accused, without justification, of allowing arms to reach the Turks from the French protectorate of Tunisia. Barrère believed that if France were to curb this trade and show good will to Italy a general Mediterranean agreement could be reached with France likely to undermine Italian membership of the

Triple Alliance. It was at this point that Poincaré took over at the Quai.

Barrère believed that, as Italy was receiving no diplomatic support from her Triple Alliance partners in her war against Turkey, there was an opportunity to be seized by France. But in the face of French reluctance to offer diplomatic support, Italy turned to Russia. The two powers had signed an agreement at Racconigi in 1909, according to which Italy agreed to acquiesce in Russian designs on the Dardanelles Straits in exchange for Russian benevolence over Italian ambitions in Tripoli. This was unlikely to please Poincaré, intent as he was on reinforcing bonds between Triple Entente members, because it could certainly cause trouble between Britain and Russia. There were already problems with Franco-Russian relations – the cornerstone of French security – which had been allowed to deteriorate. Italy's overtures to St Petersburg risked damaging them further, while increasing the possibility of tempting Russia into a strike for the Turkish-controlled Straits and the danger of a general conflict.

Two days after Poincaré came to power, the Italians seized the French postal ship *Carthage* in the Mediterranean, which they suspected of carrying an aeroplane to the Turks. On 18 January another French vessel, the *Manouba*, was seized. Whereas Barrère and the Rome embassy called for France to indulge the Italians, Poincaré made a powerful speech to the Chamber of Deputies on 22 January calling for the release of the vessels. From this point onwards, relations between the two men were soured. The situation was worsened by the fact that the cabinet noir, the French deciphering department at the Quai d'Orsay, was intercepting Italian diplomatic communications between Rome and the Italian embassy in Paris. These showed that the Rome embassy had been misrepresenting orders from Paris calling for firmness in dealing with Italy. Poincaré would come to rely increasingly on these intercepts to determine his policy towards Italy, thereby marginalising the 'italophile' Rome embassy.[16] The *Carthage* and *Manouba* affair was finally resolved in the International Court of Justice at the Hague in France's favour. But it confirmed Poincaré's prejudices about Italy's untrustworthy nature as well as those about French ambassadors. He continued to keep both at arm's length.

Poincaré had similar problems with the French ambassador to Austria–Hungary 'going native'. Ambassador Philippe Crozier believed that Austria–Hungary could be enticed from the Triple Alliance by granting her access to the lucrative Paris capital markets. Russia, Vienna's traditional adversary in the Balkans, had been opposing loans of this nature for several years, insisting that they would be used to finance defence expenditure. When Crozier persisted in these 'loony dreams', Poincaré had him replaced, claiming that nothing 'was more likely to irritate Emperor William II, if he got to know of it'.[17]

Franco-German rivalry was the root of the two opposing alliance blocs; Paris and Berlin were the two poles which had attracted the members of the Triple Alliance and Triple Entente. Yet France and Germany had not always been implacable enemies since 1871. Until 1904, Britain had periodically occupied the position of hereditary enemy. Of course the Treaty of Frankfurt, by which Germany annexed Alsace–Lorraine, remained the barrier to a normalisation of relations, but between 1871 and 1914 Franco-German relations fluctuated according to who was in power in France and Germany. From a threatening posture in the four years following the peace treaty of 1871, Bismarck moved to a more conciliatory attitude, enthusiastically welcomed by the moderate republicans until Boulangism ended the *détente* in 1887. Good relations were not fully resumed until 1894, coinciding with the governments in which Poincaré served. Seven years of animosity under Delcassé were followed by seven years of *détente* under pressure from ambassador Jules Cambon in particular. This was where Poincaré came in.[18]

Both Jules Cambon and the Germans were optimistic about the new incumbent of the Quai d'Orsay. The Kaiser and Chancellor had expressed a desire to see someone of authority at the helm in France to assume responsibility for a policy of *détente* with Berlin. Excuses were made for Agadir. As Cambon explained to Poincaré in March 1912, the time was ripe for *détente*. The Kaiser's recent request to dine at the French embassy in Berlin showed his 'persistent tendency for a *rapprochement* with us'.[19] Unofficial German overtures to the Berlin embassy continued. But when Poincaré heard of them he ordered they be discouraged, fearing a trap in which the German government 'seems to be pursuing with tireless obstinacy a *rapprochement* which only a complete break with the past would allow'. He believed that the consequences would be dire: 'we would fall out with England, and with Russia, we would lose all the benefits of a policy that France has been following for many years, we would obtain for Alsace only illusory satisfactions and we would find ourselves the following day isolated, diminished and disqualified'.[20]

By October 1912 changes on the international scene led Jules Cambon to broach the subject of a Franco-German *rapprochement* once more. Italy's victory over Turkey signalled to the Balkan states an opportunity to liberate themselves completely from the weakened Ottoman Empire by declaring war on Turkey; on 18 October the first

Balkan War began. Jules Cambon stressed to Poincaré the common interests of France and Germany in this area, in particular a commitment to the integrity of the Ottoman Empire which was now under threat. Whereas Cambon pressed for a joint Franco-German proposal for mediation, Poincaré, ever suspicious of plots to drive a wedge between France's Entente partners, rejected any move which did not include Russia and Britain. A row broke out between the Berlin ambassador and Poincaré, in which Paul Cambon in London took sides against his brother to point out how difficult a policy of improved relations with Germany was to implement: 'opinion in France at the moment does not want to hear talk of an entente with Germany . . . you would like to see a policy carried out which no one in France is able to conduct'.[21]

However, the ambassadorial conference which opened in London in December 1912 to settle the Balkan conflict saw a transformation of Poincaré's ideas on Germany. He began to realise the importance of safeguarding French interests in the Ottoman Empire. There was a likelihood that disaffection in the Empire might spread, lead to an intervention of the great powers, an internationalisation of the area and subsequently a decline in France's traditional influence in the Levant. Already Italy was challenging France's religious and cultural predominance in Syria and the Lebanon, and Britain her economic influence in the area. In response to this threat, Poincaré developed a Syrian strategy which would gradually draw him closer to Jules Cambon's ideas and closer to Germany.[22]

The problems Poincaré encountered with Triple Alliance members were not wholly absent from relations with those of the Triple Entente. When Poincaré came to power France's relations with her Entente partners were not as secure as he wished. Just as Franco-German relations were not always bad, so Franco-Russian relations were not always good. What little time was devoted to foreign affairs was not guaranteed to strengthen those links. Governments since 1905 were dependent on the support of the Radicals who, though having overcome their repugnance for the autocratic Russian Empire, were never enthusiastic about Franco-Russian relations. There was no talk of abandoning this pillar of French security, but little thought was given to tightening links with Russia; Joseph Caillaux had even been sceptical about the need to continue supporting Russian finances, which had been at the heart of the Dual Alliance since its inception.

Since the conclusion of the original political entente of 1891, reinforced by the military convention of 1893–4, the Dual Alliance had been the cornerstone of French security. The Franco-Russian exchange of letters in August 1899 reaffirmed the Alliance and extended its scope from merely shadowing the Triple Alliance and maintaining peace, to preserving the European balance of power. But during the Bosnian crisis of 1908–9, France had refused to support Russian opposition to the Austro-Hungarian annexation of Bosnia-Herzogovina. Smarting from this perceived betrayal, Russia had subsequently committed certain infidelities to her ally by two nominally secret agreements: first with Italy in 1909 over the Balkans, and second with Germany in 1910 over Persia and the Baghdad railway. At the height of the Agadir crisis, Russia repaid France in kind for her lack of support in 1909. Finally, at the end of 1911, in an attempt to satisfy her age-old desire of controlling the Dardanelles Straits and thereby allow her Black Sea fleet unrestricted access to the Mediterranean, Russia increasingly supported Italy diplomatically in her war against Turkey. France disliked this for two important reasons: first, a Turkish defeat could lead to a collapse of the Ottoman Empire and with it France's interests in the Levant; and, second, Russia might act imprudently and provoke Austria–Hungary and then Germany, with the serious prospect of dragging France into a war in which she had no direct interest. By January 1912 Russia was soliciting French support in the event of the Straits question coming up for discussion; at the same time, several of France's ambassadors were warning of the Russian foreign minister's dangerous action 'careless of the repercussions his policy could have on France'.[23]

Poincaré was of the generation of politicians who best understood the importance of the Russian Alliance; he had been part of the cabinet which had negotiated it and brought it to fruition in the early 1890s. He was anxious at the state of the Alliance in 1912. His solution lay in a middle-of-the-road policy: to restrain Russian actions without jeopardising her good will, let alone the Alliance itself. But that policy would be difficult to implement, as Poincaré would quickly discover, because of the unreliable and conspiratorial Russian ambassador in Paris, Isvolsky, and the old, ailing and inefficient French ambassador in St Petersburg, Georges Louis.

One of Poincaré's first moves as foreign minister was to issue instructions to the French ambassador in Russia to discover exactly what Russia's intentions were in the Near East. Meanwhile, reports continued to reach Poincaré of Russia's *rapprochement* with Italy and of the possibility of similar overtures to Austria–Hungary, following the appointment of a new foreign minister in Vienna. There was talk of a resurrection of the old *Dreikaiserbund* between Russia, Austria–Hungary and Germany. French intelligence reports showing a build-up of Russian troops along the Turkish border prompted Poincaré to summon the Russian ambassador in Paris and make clear to him that the Franco-Russian Alliance obliged Russia to refrain from any important initiative in the Near East without first consulting France. He warned Isvolsky, 'it is not enough that you inform us, it is necessary that we should concert beforehand'.[24]

Poincaré had now received warnings about Russia from five of the eight French embassies in Europe. The Dual Alliance was arguably at its shakiest since its formation. Georges Louis was recalled for discussions. Poincaré was particularly annoyed at Russian Foreign Minister Sazonov's evasiveness and Louis's inability to pin him down.

Poincaré's struggles with his ambassadors were numerous; that with Louis received the most publicity and assumed the most serious proportions. After the First World War, the 'Georges Louis affair' became a focal point in the debate on responsibility for the outbreak of the First World War, with revisionists claiming that the sacking in 1913 of the 'peaceable' Louis was proof of Poincaré's 'warmongering'. The stakes in the debate were high. If Germany could show that responsibility for the war did not rest solely with her, she could contest article 231 of the Versailles Treaty which justified reparations on the basis of Germany's war guilt. At the same time, the new Bolshevik regime in the Soviet Union was more than pleased to pour further discredit on its tsarist predecessor in order to reinforce its own legitimacy. It was delighted to present the tsar's ambassador in Paris, Isvolsky, and the 'bourgeois' Poincaré as conniving in Louis's replacement and working for war. Meanwhile in France itself the Left, intent on blocking Poincaré's return to power, gave credence to these claims in post-war election campaigns. These revisionist interpretations thrived in the post-war world, where a substantial current of opinion, disgusted by the horrors of war, sought to apportion blame to all the powers in the belief that war would be outlawed forever as a means of settling international differences. Thus for diplomatic, political and moral reasons, the question of war guilt became clouded and the question of Poincaré's relations with Louis lost all touch with reality.

Today it is clear that Poincaré was quite justified in replacing Louis. Contrary to received opinion, Poincaré did not pander to all Russia's demands and give her *carte blanche* in the face of Louis's protests; rather he attempted to restrain her where Louis was so dismally failing. The cause of Louis's lack of resolve was his serious ill-health. Poincaré's opponents have always contested that fact; yet letters from Georges Louis to his brother, the writer Pierre Loüys, prove he was suffering from chronic bronchitis, dreaded the cold Russian winters and was carrying out very few diplomatic duties; and he even confessed that on occasions he was near to death. By the end of January 1912 he had lost his sight and was unable to write.[25] Moreover, he had already reached the official retirement age of sixty-five. It is quite clear that Louis was unable to fulfil the role that Poincaré's new energetic diplomacy called for: to maintain constant vigilance of Sazonov and Russian governing circles in order to monitor the direction of Russian diplomacy; to report diplomatic conversations meticulously; and to pin down the wily Sazonov to Alliance commitments. He no longer had the physical stamina to be able to attend the numerous court and social functions which were the essence of diplomatic duties in St Petersburg. Given the presence in Paris of the intriguer Isvolsky, and the inability of the cabinet noir to break the Russian cipher, Poincaré decided that a commonality of views and action could only be restored if he visited Russia himself. By 20 March 1912 arrangements for an August visit were in train.

At the end of March Poincaré received news of the recently concluded secret, and ostensibly anti-Austrian, Serbo-Bulgarian mutual assistance pact. Poincaré was infuriated that Russia could have acted without first consulting France. He sent instructions that Sazonov be warned that 'on such serious questions, we [France] could not be content with a posteriori information'.[26] This strong rebuke was to be backed up by a series of measures intended to bring Sazonov back into line, from a refusal to float a Bulgarian loan on the Paris market, to a meeting between Louis and the tsar.

By mid-April Poincaré had had quite enough of Russian flirtations with Italy in her war against Turkey: 'What does this double game mean? What is the Russian government looking for? We are carrying out the Russian Alliance with scrupulous loyalty, would it be too much to ask her to do the same?'[27] By 16 April he had discovered, probably from Italian intercepts, that Isvolsky had encouraged Italy to occupy the Aegean islands to pursue her war against Turkey. Russia was encouraging the conflict to spread. On 18 April Italy bombarded the Dardanelles and Turkey reacted by closing the Straits to foreign navigation, cutting off vital Russian trade from the Mediterranean. There was now a serious risk of Russian involvement. By May Louis had still not obtained an audience with the tsar to protest about Russian policy. On 8 May a letter was dispatched to him calling for his resignation. However, the instigator was not Poincaré, but Isvolsky, who had presented a request from his government for Louis's recall in early May on the grounds that the ambassador was not properly fulfilling his political and social duties. Leaks to the press about his dismissal soon ensured that the well-connected Louis held on to his post.[28]

Poincaré was doubtless relieved to embark on his trip to Russia in August 1912. Official visits of this kind were as yet unusual for *présidents du conseil* and it drew much attention. The press were particularly amused by Poincaré's original head-gear – somewhat akin to a chauffeur's cap – which would become famous during his numerous visits to the front during the war. Though Franco-Russian diplomatic relations left a lot to be desired, at a military level the joint military staffs had worked out plans in July for co-ordinated action in the event of war. The notes made by Poincaré during his official visit demonstrate, by the nature of the subjects discussed, his conception of Franco-Russian relations: cohesion and restraint. Only by closer ties could Russia be restrained and the strength of the Triple Entente be demonstrated. But he had been shocked when Sazonov had shown him a copy of the Serbo-Bulgarian treaty and exclaimed, 'But it's an agreement for war!' He made plain his disapproval. However, he considered his visit a success, principally because the Tsar had reaffirmed his faith in the Alliance. The visit seemed to have done the trick, for he now heard from several French diplomats that Russia appeared to be co-operating more loyally with French demands. Nevertheless, as Paul Cambon pointed out, there remained a basic incompatibility of interests between the two powers in the Near East. If war broke out in the Balkans, France might be forced to choose between sacrificing her interests in the Ottoman Empire and the Russian Alliance. But Poincaré was determined to maintain the fine balance needed to avoid having to choose one way or the other. That became particularly difficult following the outbreak of the first Balkan War in October 1912; Poincaré continued to claim that the only way for Britain and France to restrain Russia was to keep 'clinging on to her, because it is the only way to maintain her within the bounds of reason or to stop her from carrying out a settlement with others'.[29]

By December 1912 an armistice had been concluded between the Balkan states and Turkey, and the ambassadors of the great powers were meeting in London to supervise the drawing up of a peace treaty. Poincaré's policy towards Russia appeared to have survived despite being handicapped by Louis and Isvolsky. By this time he was looking to the presidency of the Republic as the next goal in his ever-ascending career, confident that his policy of the separation of the two alliance blocs and the strengthening of the Triple Entente had bolstered France's diplomatic position.

For the Triple Entente to be truly reinforced it was necessary to improve relations with Britain. This proved easier than with Russia, but a number of problems still had to be resolved. Caillaux's attempted deals with Germany had caused a cooling of relations with London. Poincaré wished to reassure Britain of France's friendship and perhaps get the Liberal government to overturn Britain's traditional policy of refusing any continental alliances. This would not be easy. Mutual suspicion characterised Franco-British relations, particularly in the colonial field where both powers arguably had better relations with Germany than with each other. Since the Entente Cordiale, Franco-British relations had been consolidated in 1905 by the secret conversations between the two countries' military staffs. However, as the British foreign secretary ceaselessly pointed out to the French, who thought differently, these talks in no way bound either country to come to the other's assistance in the event of war.

Paul Cambon, ambassador in London, was over-confident about Britain's commitment to France and would pass on that unfortunate misunderstanding to Poincaré; and the two men's inability to get on together further compounded the problem of Franco-British relations. Cambon underestimated the seriousness of British attempts to come to an agreement with Germany on a reduction of naval expenditure from February 1912 in what became known as the Haldane Mission. Only when the British ambassador in Paris made a point of warning Poincaré of the dangerous nature of the talks was he able to upbraid his ambassador. Poincaré was pleased with him, by contrast, when Cambon succeeded in building on the Anglo-French military talks and reaching a naval agreement with Britain. This stipulated that France would concentrate her fleet in the Mediterranean and protect British interests there, in exchange for Britain's concentrating hers in the Channel and along the North Atlantic seaboard and agreeing to protect French interests. The result was an exchange of letters between Grey and Cambon on 22 and 23 November 1912. These acknowledged the continuing military conversations between the two countries and the agreement on the disposition of their respective fleets. But the letters stressed that these agreements in no way restricted the freedom of either government to decide whether or not to assist the other in the event of a conflict. What pleased the French most was the understanding that if either party had reason to expect an unprovoked attack by a third power or a threat to the general peace, then both governments would concert on possible joint action and, if agreed, activate the plans of the joint general staffs.

Whereas the British prime minister viewed the agreement as a 'platitude', for such action would have taken place anyway, Poincaré noted 'their great value'.[30] In fact, Poincaré, largely as a result of Cambon's excessive confidence in the idea that Britain had virtually committed herself to come to her aid, over-estimated the value of the documents. At any rate, in the last days of July 1914, France and Poincaré would discover from London's hesitation about entering the war the extent to which the British believed freedom to choose had not been limited.

From the beginning of 1912, Poincaré had set out clearly his diplomatic programme for France, and by the end of the year, through dogged persistence and industry, he had improved France's diplomatic standing. He was perhaps the first *président du conseil* to have devoted so much of his political programme and efforts to foreign affairs since Jules Ferry in the 1880s, and with more success. That success could be measured not only by France's enhanced diplomatic position, but also through the consensus which his policy had generated at home around that old component of republicanism – *la patrie*. His political achievements led the extremely competitive Poincaré to look, as ever, even higher, this time to the supreme office of president of the Republic.

Poincaré's grand design for France was unity; that unity was seen as the key to the greatness which he, and others before and after him, believed to be France's destiny.[1] Unity had seemed within reach when he had formed his broadly based government in 1912. He believed he was furthering it when in July he had ensured the vote of the law on electoral reform in the Chamber of Deputies in the belief that it would usher in a new political morality and strengthen the executive, something he considered a *sine qua non* of domestic unity. In the military field, reforms had been undertaken to arrest the decline of public esteem for the army since Dreyfus, and to enhance the army's own strength and unity by tightened military discipline and a higher public profile. Public military tattoos, banished since the Dreyfus affair, had been resurrected and had restored some public pride in the army, countering the anti-militarism and pacifism of the revolutionary syndicalists and extreme Left.[2] Poincaré certainly believed that his concentration on foreign affairs had strengthened France's international position and united a majority of the political class and the country, as he made clear on his return from Russia in the autumn of 1912:

The Republic has upheld France's position in the world by a policy of wisdom, sang-froid and dignity. Only our material and moral strength can give value to our friendship and maintain our position above persistent circumstances. Let us therefore endeavour to preserve and enhance the vital energy of our country, and I am referring not only to her military and naval strength but above all to this political confidence and this unity of national feeling which endows a people with grandeur, glory and immortality.[3]

Armand Fallières's seven-year mandate as president of the Republic was due to end in January 1913. According to Payen, though friends encouraged Poincaré to stand from September 1912, he refused on the grounds that the elder statesman of the Radical party, Léon Bourgeois, was more likely to be a unifying candidate. But when approached by Poincaré he refused on health grounds. It was only in the evening of 26 December 1912, following a visit to his flat in the rue du Commandant

Marchand from his old friends and colleagues, Millerand and Maurice Bernard, who had 'begged' him to announce his candidature, that he agreed to stand. Thus, up until a mere three weeks prior to the election, Poincaré had declared that he would vote for either of the moderates, Ribot or Deschanel, even though neither had announced their candidature.[4] Whatever the circumstances surrounding his desire to stand, the presidency of the Republic would have been hard to resist for the extremely competitive Poincaré. It might seem a logical one, too, for his quest to unite the French, but only if the office had any power.

The 'crisis of 16 May' 1877 had been formative for the nascent Third Republic. Henceforth presidents of the Republic were expected to be feeble creatures. But just as Poincaré believed that opposition to the army had gone too far after Dreyfus, so he believed that the curtailing of presidential power had been overdone after MacMahon's so-called *coup d'état* of 1877. In his book on political science, *Ce que demande la cité*, intended for schools and published in 1912, he had made clear his belief in an increase in presidential power to temper the excesses of a *régime d'assemblée*.

Political tradition may have dictated that presidents of the Republic should be mere figureheads, but the constitution had never been altered to reflect that; and Poincaré was nothing if not a lawyer with an overarching belief in the sanctity of legal texts. The three constitutional laws of 1875 endowed the president with considerable powers, even if most required a ministerial counter-signature. It was in the realm of international affairs that these powers were greatest. Officially, the president commanded the armed forces, appointed to all military and civil posts (including ambassadors); foreign envoys and ambassadors were accredited to him; he negotiated and ratified treaties and informed parliament of them only when the interests and security of the state permitted. It was in the area of foreign policy that Poincaré wished above all to ensure continuity. But the president also maintained an important role within the executive by his prerogative to choose the premier, to influence the latter's choice of foreign and war ministers, and his right to chair cabinet meetings and, since 1912, the conseil supérieur de la guerre. For a politician committed to strengthening the executive as a means of increasing national unity, the presidency was the key. It was also to be prized for offering that rare commodity in Third Republican political life – a seven-year mandate of stability and continuity. Poincaré's subsequent protestations that he agreed only reluctantly to stand need to be treated with the same caution as his repeated feigned hesitations witnessed during his early political career. In his secret diaries he quoted Millerand's remarks to a journalist from the *Echo de Paris* without contradicting them: 'Poincaré has always been a candidate. He was yesterday. He is even more so today if that is possible.'[5]

Poincaré's own justification for becoming a candidate was to watch over foreign policy. As he informed the National Assembly following his election, 'I shall remain the faithful guardian of the constitution and the law. I shall keep the interests of our national defence far from any attack and in agreement with the responsible ministers I shall look after the unity of our foreign policy.'[6] More importantly, in his memoirs he justified a more political role for the president on the grounds that the moral authority of the office overrode the constitutional duty to remain above party politics and direct political action.[7]

The election was to take place on 17 January. But there was by no means unanimity around Poincaré's candidacy. Paul Deschanel, president of the Chamber of Deputies, and Antonin Dubost, his counterpart in the Senate, were serious contenders, while Jules Pams, minister of agriculture in Poincaré's own government, had the support of the Radicals. The latter were opposed to Poincaré for having voted in proportional representation and for having steered what they considered to be an anti-radical course in domestic politics in 1912. In particular he was accused of having garnered support from anti-republican groups, thereby betraying the Republican party.[8] But at no point between 1912 and 1914 did the left-wing Radicals ever accuse him of being a warmonger, let alone oppose his candidature on those grounds. It was only later that they claimed that his election had been opposed because his foreign policy was a threat to peace. The Radicals' spokesman, Clemenceau, no stranger to hyperbole, attacked Poincaré on purely domestic issues as a neo-Boulangist who dreamed of imposing by 'force and dissolution his arrogant infallibility and his regal scorn for the constitution'.[9] In an attempt to discredit Poincaré and scupper potential support from the Catholic Right, certain Radical newspapers emphasised the fact that Madame Poincaré was a divorcée and only married to Poincaré by a civil ceremony; others strained credibility in claiming that she had worked the cabaret scene and even been a circus dancer.[10] Newspapers such as L'Œuvre and L'Eclair raised the question as to the suitability of a divorcée to become France's First Lady and whether Catholic députés had the right to vote for a candidate who was not even 'properly' married. This was the continuation of a whispering campaign begun by the Radicals to dissuade Poincaré from standing and which he had already commented upon in his diary: 'The radicals are carrying out an abominable campaign in the corridors against Henriette and think they can discourage me with their slander.'[11] But Poincaré's ambition could not be blunted so easily: 'This slander torments, but it forces me to remain a candidate whatever happens.'[12] This bitter atmosphere, and Clemenceau's vitriolic attacks against him, would lead to a serious row on election day, with Poincaré challenging his adversary to a duel.[13] Nevertheless, the campaign against Henriette continued to run for several years. Ironically, playing to the religious gallery in presidential elections would return to haunt the atheist Clemenceau seven years later when his own candidature was said to have been rejected by Catholic *députés* fearful of the prospect of having to hold a secular state funeral.[14]

In the pre-election 'primary' of the left-wing republicans on 15 and 16 January, which Poincaré described as being buffeted by a 'wind of calumny and hatred', after three ballots Pams was marginally ahead of Poincaré. But Poincaré knew he could count on the votes of the moderate republicans and refused to stand down, even in the face of Clemenceau's heated insistence that this ran contrary to 'republican discipline'. Poincaré countered by insisting that he was no less republican than Pams and that several left-wing republicans were insisting that he maintain his candidature. The animosity between Clemenceau and Poincaré was exacerbated by this incident.[15]

On Friday 17 January, the day of the election, Poincaré felt assured of success. The 'socialistes unifiés', he reflected, were not opposed to his candidature because of proportional representation, some Progressists were committed to voting for him, and the Right too. Poincaré's diary entry on this last issue is worth quoting at length for the information it gives on the deal which some polemicists subsequently suggested he made with the Right to secure his election:

I have never solicited, nor have I had solicited, any member of the right, but de Mun came to tell me spontaneously that he and his friends will vote for me 'out of patriotism' despite what separates them from me politically. I did not conceal the fact that Henriette was divorced, that we did not know what had happened to her former husband, and that we were only married in civil law. He thought for a moment and replied: 'Well, never mind, the country first'. He asked for no undertaking from me, I gave none, and the approach of this very gallant man, entirely inspired by what he considers, rightly or wrongly, the national interest, touched me to the bottom of my soul.

So I go to Versailles, free in relation to everyone, having promised nothing to anybody, having asked nothing of anyone.[16]

Poincaré travelled to Versailles with his friend Barthou, basking in the acclamation of the crowds along the route. The electoral college of senators and deputies got underway at 1.15 p.m. Henriette and Poincaré's mother, brother and sister-in-law waited at home in the rue du Commandant Marchand for news by telephone. After two ballots at

6.45 p.m. the result was officially announced: Poincaré was elected by 483 votes to Pams 296 to brisk applause from a large number of benches on the Left, centre and Right. Poincaré recorded proudly in his diary that his 483 votes 'undeniably contain the republican majority' whereas Pams did not. And in that rather juvenile competitive spirit that often characterised him, he noted that he had obtained more votes than his predecessors Casimir Périer, Félix Faure and Armand Fallières. Nevertheless his 'adversaries appear ill disposed to accept the *fait accompli*', with Clemenceau in particular leaving, as Poincaré put it, 'pale and enraged'.[17] Poincaré's observation was corroborated by the moderate Charles Benoist, who on remarking to Clemenceau that it was all over and done with now, received from his 'incensed' interlocutor the reply, 'Ah! you think it's over! No! It's just beginning!'[18] It was the first time since 1879 that a president of the Republic had been elected against Clemenceau's wishes.[19] Poincaré recorded in his diary how, following Casimir Périer's example after his election, the new president had burst into tears: 'I easily contain my emotion, but I feel the weight of this solemn occasion on my soul'. In his speech he vowed, 'I shall easily forget the struggles of yesterday, even the insults. Be convinced that everywhere and always I shall be an impartial arbiter.' He also promised to become the 'faithful guardian of the constitution and laws', to maintain inviolate 'the interest of our national defence' and to 'watch over, in agreement with the responsible ministers, the unity of our foreign policy'. He ended by stating that they could count on his 'absolute devotion to the Republic and to *la patrie*'.[20]

Tradition had been broken in two respects: first, the self-styled 'republican' candidate had not been elected; second, the president-elect was a prominent serving *président du conseil*.[21] Poincaré's election had been secured, as he himself explained, by the fact that the socialists had refused to support the Radical candidate and had fielded their own. They saw no reason on the grounds of either foreign policy, which they and their leaders such as Edouard Vaillant viewed as peaceful, or domestic politics, to block Poincaré's election and play the Radicals' game. The leaders of the républicains-socialistes and their press, generally to the left of the radicaux-socialistes, believed that Poincaré had worked for peace in 1912 and called on their followers to vote for him as a guarantee for peace and national dignity.[22] He was further aided by the division in the republican majority, which meant that the anti-republican and nationalist Right held the casting votes. Much has been made of this to show that Poincaré was the 'chosen one of the Right', but recent research has shown that during 1912 he made few serious concessions to the Right in domestic policy or in exchange for support of his candidature. The Right supported Poincaré because objectively they agreed with his foreign policy, as did the socialists in broad terms, such were the deep impressions left by the shame of Agadir. The basis of his political action was a commitment to establishing a stable political majority based on a patriotic and liberal political ideology. It would be churlish to refuse the Right's support if that was going to contribute to the realisation of that goal.[23]

'Prisoner of the Elysée'?

Poincaré's election as president of the Republic met with press approval in France and abroad. The way he dwelt in his diaries on his 'notices', particularly from the foreign press, reflected his usual mixture of vanity and search for reassurance. He was particularly pleased with comments in the German press which, contrary to received opinion, generally applauded his election along the lines of the democratic *Berliner Tageblatt*'s description of his attitude to Germany as 'reserved, courteous and pacific'. The *Lokal Anzeiger* congratulated the French for having chosen 'such an eminent man', while the *Vossische Zeitung* spoke of him as 'reflective and moderate'.[24] Following Poincaré's election, Jules Cambon, who had never liked Poincaré, noted that the German press 'puts a brave face on it, but they are not happy with a choice which brings to the presidency this vain, stubborn and discourteous Lorrainer'. But there was no mention of aggressiveness, and he admitted to his brother that, as far as German statesmen were concerned, few knew much about the new president. Even the Kaiser had shown no hostility towards Poincaré or his election, and had merely commented to Jules Cambon that Pams was 'too unknown, too much a newcomer . . . As for M. Poincaré, I cannot say: I do not know him.'[25] Jules's own view of Poincaré was fairly accurate when he told his brother that he had 'many qualities, but one above all others is always to think of showing himself in the best light'.[26] Others reckoned his election to be the most popular of any president since Thiers.[27] There was a general expectation that he would be a strong president. A more sentimental measure of his popularity was the substantial increase in the number of babies christened 'Raymond'. Despite this, the day after his election Poincaré appeared to harbour doubts as to the extent of his power. According to his old school-friend Maurice Paléologue, the new president had reflected all night on the question and feared that 'the principle of constitutional irresponsibility will divest me of all initiative and condemn me for seven years to silence and inaction'.[28] There was a certain amount of disingenuousness in Poincaré's analysis. Though conscious of the limitations of his office, he had more than likely decided already to use the presidential powers to their constitutional limit. It was an example of his characteristic self-doubt and need to be reassured before any serious undertaking. Certainly the circumstances of his election coaxed him in the direction of a strong presidential role – not only was he the youngest ever president of the Republic, he was also the first example in the history of the Republic of an elected candidate being a serving head of government. For someone of Poincaré's energy and prestige it would be hard not to wish to activate the presidential powers that lay dormant. Continuity was almost encouraged by the fact that between the date of his election and his official inauguration on 18 February 1913 constitutionally he was expected to expedite current business. The continuity in foreign and domestic policy which he sought could also be maintained by the president's constitutional right to choose the prime minister, as well as by the less formal influence he had over the appointment of the foreign and war ministers. He made clear his intent to use his presidential powers to the full and to maintain his foreign policy in his inaugural address to the two chambers on 20 February, claiming that 'a reduction in the powers of the executive is neither the will of the Chamber nor that of the country' and adding that 'it is only possible for a people to be pacific if they are always ready for war. A diminished France, a France exposed by its own fault, to challenges, to humiliation, would no longer be France.'[29] Consequently, after 1912 the main tenets of French foreign policy were maintained: a strengthening of France's diplomatic and military posture through a further tightening of the Triple Entente. But at the same time, following the expulsion of Turkey from Europe in the first Balkan War, the French, under Poincaré's leadership, would increasingly turn their attention to protecting and consolidating their position in Syria and the Lebanon.[30]

Though Poincaré resigned the premiership the day after his election, he negotiated with President Fallières, as interim president, for Aristide Briand, the interior minister, to lead the government.[31] Briand did so until 18 February when he symbolically resigned to form a new government. With Charles Jonnart as foreign minister, Poincaré could keep a tight rein on foreign affairs.[32] Jonnart could be relied upon to support France's new drive in Syria and the Lebanon. It was an added bonus for Poincaré that, apart from the governor generalship of Algeria (largely an administrative post), Jonnart had very little knowledge of foreign affairs. He admitted quite openly that he would have to rely on Poincaré for guidance. This was what the Austrian ambassador in Paris had confirmed following a conversation before the election in which Poincaré had assured him that after his election 'I will see to it that a man is put in my place who will follow my policy. It will be as if I were still at the Quai d'Orsay.'[33] It was certainly what Poincaré confided to his secret diary: 'I still command Jonnart, I go to the Quai d'Orsay every morning.'[34] Poincaré even extended open invitations to foreign ambassadors in Paris to deal with him directly at the Elysée whenever they saw fit. Though much was made of this in relation to Isvolsky for polemical reasons after the war, it applied equally to his German counterpart, even if he was initially startled by the offer. Poincaré's personal diaries up to the war, punctuated with *in extenso* quotations from diplomatic dispatches, bear witness to his continuing control of foreign policy, as do the comments of France's ambassadors. This was particularly apparent during negotiations to settle the Balkan imbroglio where French interests conflicted with those of her Entente partners, and coincided with Germany's. Jules Cambon, informed by his brother that Poincaré 'is still running the Quai d'Orsay', commented that Poincaré's attitude to Germany had undergone a revolution. He claimed that his former anti-German stance had been an election ploy, 'how benign he has become since his election'. Poincaré, he remarked, 'had flung the motors of an anti-German policy into reverse'.[35]

A more benign policy towards Germany did not mean France dropped her guard against her potential enemy. A tenet of Poincaré's policy since 1912, reiterated in his presidential address, was to strengthen the armed forces. That policy seemed justified by the German army bills under discussion in the Reichstag in early 1913, which threatened to increase the size of the German army and render impracticable the French military strategy of the offensive currently in gestation, and soon to be enshrined in Plan XVII. After much discussion between politicians and generals, the solution was deemed to be an increase in the length of French military service from two to three years. Poincaré was brought into these discussions for the first time on 15 February by the minister of war, Etienne, who informed him of the need to increase France's military strength in order to keep up with Germany. Poincaré chaired the meeting of the Conseil supérieur de la guerre which agreed on this course of action on 4 March.[36]

The project for a Three Years' Law was a political bombshell. Reducing the length of military service in 1905 had been a major goal of the Republic and was perceived as one of the few tangible consequences of the victory over the army in the Dreyfus case. The new bill met with substantial opposition from the socialists and a growing number of Radicals. Much controversy surrounds the motives for the bill, which post-war revisionists pointed to as proof of France's new nationalistic and aggressive stance under Poincaré. This was pure polemic. In truth France was confronted by the stark reality of an inferior military position in relation to Germany at the beginning of 1913. The British military attaché in Paris was certainly of this opinion and perfectly summarised the position in his annual report for 1912:

When it is remembered that the population of Germany amounts to close on 70,000,000 inhabitants whilst that of France is only about 39,000,000, it can be understood that whereas Germany can command a sufficiency of men for her first line troops without having to call to any extent on her reserves to complete them to war strength, France would have to call up probably six classes of reservists; this is a still more important matter as regards the 'troupes de couverture', those of Germany being kept practically on a mobilised footing in peace time. In accordance with two successive laws dated the 27th March, 1911, and the 21st May, 1912, the peace effective of the German army was augmented, and amounts at the present time to about 655,000 men, whilst the strength of the French army actually in France (excluding Algeria, Tunis, and Morocco) is only 500,000 – say a difference of 150,000 men – since also the German army on mobilisation would attain a strength of 4,300,000 as against France's 3,878,000, it is evident that France is at a great disadvantage as compared with Germany both in her peace strength and on mobilisation, a serious matter, and one which would be still more so were Germany at any time to deal with France single-handed.[37]

The problem for Poincaré was that there seemed to be no way round the proposed legislation. It could not be a matter of indifference to France that Germany had gained a serious margin of superiority over her. The only other course of action would have been a reorientation of French foreign policy in the direction of a *rapprochement* with Germany. That was both risky, in that it would lead to a break-up of the Triple Entente when Germany's real intentions were as yet unclear, and probably impossible in the wake of Agadir. Thus Poincaré supported the bill. On reading of mounting opposition in the press he noted in his diary, 'It will be necessary to fight'.[38] The bill's foremost opponent was Jean Jaurès, the leader of the French Socialist party, brilliant orator and author of an impressive work calling for the 'New Army'. He held to the radical republican view that a truly republican army should consist only of the 'nation at arms', in other words a citizens' militia. A heated debate in the Chamber of Deputies was underway by the first week of June. But the bill was finally adopted on 7 August 1913 with a reasonable majority, despite opposition from the socialists and many Radicals. This was by no means the end of the matter. The Law was unpopular: some troops revolted when they learnt that they would have to serve for an extra year; some of the middle classes believed that it would produce a shortage of labour and increase the cost of living, while the peasantry opposed it for taking away their sons, often their only source of labour. The Radical party chose to make opposition to the Law a prominent feature of its political platform. At the party conference at Pau from 16 to 21 October 1913 it chose as its leader Joseph Caillaux, who was to lead the campaign in favour of a return to two years' service.[39] This put Poincaré, already the Radicals' declared adversary since his election to the presidency, squarely in the firing line. The Three Years' Law would remain the running sore of French political life until the war, making Poincaré's active role as president particularly difficult.

Life at the Elysée

It was soon evident that Poincaré's term as president would be of a different nature to that of his predecessors. Despite certain misgivings about the ambiguity of his role, which he referred to as his 'bat' status, presumably for its ambiguous half-mouse, half-bird status,[40] Poincaré was intent on using to the full his constitutional powers. His work rate in no way relaxed. He fulfilled all of his representational and protocol functions – what Clemenceau would refer to as 'opening flower shows'. At the same time he received all diplomats, politicians, journalists, artists and writers who requested an audience of him. He paid particular attention to state visits, going to Spain and Russia in the first two years of his presidency at a time when such journeys had become less common. He was given access to virtually all diplomatic correspondence, he read military reports, the *Journal Officiel* and digested the national and international press with alacrity. He sustained his passion for the arts, attending the theatre and concerts, and recording critical appraisals in his diaries, or in a voluminous correspondence with friends, colleagues, even strangers. He even found time to collaborate in 1913 with Paul Bourget, René Bazin and Francis Charmes on a book dealing with 'contemporary materialism'.

The vigour and tone he gave to the outward presence of the presidential office was matched by the example of discipline he wished to set. He agreed reluctantly to Briand's cabinet proposal of 30 January for an armistice bill for minor offences which traditionally greeted the election of a new president, and which survives to this day; he was more successful in opposing another bill calling for 18 February to be declared a public holiday.[41] Ever suspicious of taking advantage of an official position, he ordered the director of the Paris police to inform his officers not to make special traffic arrangements for his car when he was travelling privately around Paris and for no special privileges to be granted to any other cars from the Elysée.[42] However, motor cars played an important part in his attempt to enhance the prestige of the presidential office, with official tours of central and southern France being carried out in cars. 'To pay tribute to the army' he re-established the military secretariat at the Elysée, which Fallières had suppressed; he appointed as his civilian secretary general the former deputy director of his private office at the Quai d'Orsay, Adolphe Pichon. On the day of his inauguration, 18 February, he made what would be an often repeated gesture during his presidency of donating money for distribution to the poor of Paris, in this instance 20,000 francs.[43] Whether this was a personal gift from his own purse or that of the presidency is not clear, though by the end of his presidential mandate he had dilapidated most of his personal fortune.[44]

On 19 February Poincaré and his wife left their apartment in the rue du Commandant Marchand to move into the Elysée palace. One senses the influence of Henriette on the presidency. She counterbalanced his natural tendency towards austerity and set about transforming the domestic organisation of the Elysée, doing away with the tradition of having food prepared in outside restaurants, and appointing a chef. Receptions at the Elysée were given a new sparkle. It was decided that the president should socialise more, and he began by breaking with the habit of his predecessors of not dining at foreign embassies. On 20 January 1914 he dined at the German embassy – the first time the head of state had done so since 1870.

The higher profile he gave to the representational role of the office probably also had to do with his desire to court press and public esteem. Gabriel Hanotaux characterised it thus: 'He serves opinion and uses opinion; it is his strength but he cannot do without it.'[45] If any theme runs through his secret diaries – so secret that he would not take them with him on state visits, requiring them to be locked in the Elysée safe – it is that of an obsession with popularity. It was common practice at this time in France for ministries such as the interior, foreign affairs and seemingly the Elysée, euphemistically, 'to subsidise' the press from their secret funds. Despite his pristine image, Poincaré was no exception, as his diaries and correspondence prove. Letters from the parliamentary journalist Hippolyte Hamard, in 1913 show Poincaré's direct intervention to ensure that the journal *La Politique Etrangère* received a subsidy from the foreign ministry's secret funds.[46] But such arrangements could only be palliative. As Poincaré's popularity began to wane and the opposition of the Radicals and socialists increased, so his confidence to act dwindled and with it his executive role.

Franco-German *détente*

Up to the war Poincaré saw to it that the main tenets of his foreign and domestic policy were applied. He did so by a judicious selection of *présidents du conseil*, which was his privilege, and by strongly recommending the appointment of certain foreign ministers, about whom he was allowed to advise. When the Briand ministry fell on 18 March following a vote in the Senate on proportional representation, Poincaré first appealed to the Radical Léon Bourgeois, and following his rejection on grounds of health, to the moderate Louis Barthou. Poincaré and Barthou, the 'boy wonders' of politics in the 1890s, though 'young crocodiles' for Jules Cambon, were both members of the Comité de l'Orient, and could be expected to maintain the prominence of foreign affairs in the new cabinet. They agreed on the appointment of the former ex-president of the Comité de l'Orient, Stephen Pichon, as foreign minister. It was hoped that he would be able to arrest the decline of France's presence in the Levant, undermined by developments in the Balkans and the risk that the Ottoman Empire would disintegrate. Because the First World War began in Europe, hindsight has led us to believe that before its outbreak politicians' minds were solely fixed on the European arena. In reality France was as much concerned with the Levant, and the 'Syrian' strategy cut across her traditional alliances, giving her more in common with Germany than Russia over a number of issues.[47] Though during Pichon's term at the Quai d'Orsay Poincaré kept a lower profile in foreign affairs, it was he who engineered the temporary shift of French diplomatic priorities to the Levant. As Jules Cambon told his brother, 'Pichon has dropped Clemenceau and has become completely "poincariste"'.[48] The most notable effect of this policy was a continued improvement in relations with Germany and a growing incompatibility of French and Russian policies in the Ottoman Empire.

Poincaré's willingness to negotiate with Germany was probably given added impetus by the mood of confidence that affected the French government and High Command at the end of 1912.[49] It was sustained by the victory of the French-trained and armed Balkan states over German-trained and armed Turkey, which some saw as a dummy run for a future European war. Confidence and perceived military parity after the passing of the Three Years' Law inspired negotiation, even conciliation. When negotiations began in earnest with Germany over the financing of the Baghdad railway and the future of Asia Minor, Jules Cambon told the German chancellor that the hostile elements of 1911 'would this time be with us and that an entente on Asia Minor would be welcomed'. And he confirmed that Poincaré was personally 'in the best of frames of mind'.[50]

The Liman von Sanders affair put this policy of *détente* with Germany to the test. Shortly after it became known on 27 November 1913 that the Turkish government had appointed as inspector-general of the Ottoman army and commander of the first Ottoman army corps in Constantinople the German general, Liman von Sanders, Russia protested strongly at the prospect of a German controlling the Bosphorous garrison and called on France to support her. At a cabinet meeting of the newly formed Doumergue government, Poincaré recommended forcefully that Russia be turned down.[51] His action refutes two long-held beliefs: that he unfailingly acquiesced to Russian demands and that he was unconditionally opposed to Germany.

The von Sanders affair was finally settled on 15 January 1914 when Germany agreed to a compromise whereby von Sanders kept his rank of inspector-general of the Turkish army but relinquished direct command of the Constantinople army corps. At the end of 1913 Franco-German relations were more promising than for many years. Even the Russian prime minister was able to report to the Tsar on 13 December 1913, 'All French statesmen want quiet and peace. They are willing to work with Germany and are much more peaceful than two years ago.'[52] In instigating such a policy Poincaré was by no means compromising his position on the separation of the alliance systems. That separation applied to the European and not the imperial arena where France and Germany could work together for their mutual benefit. That benefit was soon apparent. Negotiations with Berlin resumed on 15 January 1914, five days later Poincaré dined at the German embassy in Paris and within a month, on 15 February, a Franco-German agreement was signed on the financing of the Baghdad railway and spheres of influence in Asiatic Turkey. This was the first step towards the partition of Asia Minor. It was consolidated by the French agreement with Turkey on 9 April which cemented France's economic and religious presence in the area and promised to make her, as Jules Cambon predicted, 'the definite master of Syria'.[53] If the Syrian strategy had paid off it was due in no small part to Poincaré's willingness to work with Germany. It was followed by further Franco-German talks over spheres of influence in Central Africa. The German secretary of state, von Jagow, told Jules Cambon that if France, Britain and Germany could agree on respective interests in Central Africa 'all chance of war would be averted for many long years'.[54] This never went further than unofficial discussions. It was to be the last move in favour of Franco-German *détente*. Colonial questions, where Paris and Berlin could agree, were soon to be displaced

by infinitely more serious problems in Europe where interests were not
so easily shared. War, instead of being 'averted for many long years' was
just around the corner.

Waning popularity

The bitterness that certain Radicals had felt at Poincaré's election took a
few months to be orchestrated into a campaign against him. Poincaré's
vulnerability was increased in a number of ways. The first was connected
with his private life. The Radical press campaign against Henriette
Poincaré had made public her marital history with the intention of
smearing Poincaré in the eyes of the Right and the public. The secret
religious solemnisation of his marriage in May 1913 could, if it leaked
out, undermine his *laïque* credentials with the Left. Despite Mgr
Baudrillart obtaining dispensations from the cardinal-archbishop of
Paris to avoid a public record of the ceremony, the secret was not well
kept. The culprit was neither his brother, nor the two witnesses,
Maurice Bernard and the lawyer Gibou, who were all sworn to secrecy,
but Poincaré himself. He summoned Albert de Mun to the Elysée to tell
him the good news, obviously with the hope of garnering the support of
this key figure of the Right at a time when their votes would be at a
premium in parliament. But the immediate effect was not to Poincaré's
advantage. De Mun wrote to Cardinal Vannutelli to inform the Pope.[55]
It was something of a *coup* for the Vatican to hold information that the
president of the *laïque* French Republic had been married religiously
while in office. Leaks inevitably occurred, providing the Radicals with a
weapon against him.

A further hostage to fortune concerned French relations with the
Vatican, broken off following the separation of church and state in 1905.
The imminent death of ailing Pope Pius X in April 1913, provoked
Paléologue, as political director of the Quai d'Orsay, into encouraging
Pichon and Poincaré to urge French cardinals to elect a francophile
Pope. It was hoped that this might redress France's influence over her
religious protectorates in the Middle East. But Poincaré was fearful of
the risks he was taking, particularly if it reached Clemenceau's ears. On
30 April Armand Nisard, France's former ambassador to the Vatican,
was ordered to make contact with the French cardinals. However, the
cryptographic services of the *Sûreté* at the interior ministry deciphered
three telegrams from the Italian ambassador in Paris to Rome which
revealed the secret negotiations which Poincaré and Pichon were
developing with the Vatican.[56] On 6 May 1913 Klotz, minister of the
interior, produced the telegrams at the cabinet meeting. There was

uproar, with Pichon threatening to resign if the ministry of the interior continued to intercept communications. Though interceptions by the *Sûreté* were suspended, it was too late to stop such incriminating information from damaging Poincaré's reputation. Poincaré's fear of the Radicals was now so acute that he was said to be trying to patch up differences with their leaders and even to have offered Clemenceau the London embassy either as a gesture of goodwill, or in an attempt to rid himself of this tiresome adversary.[57] Seeing the Radicals' campaign against the Three Years' Law to be 'the continuation of the struggle against himself',[58] Poincaré began to adopt a lower profile as president.

Barthou's ministry was brought down by the Radicals over fiscal reform in December 1913. Their influence was now so strong that moderates such as Deschanel, Ribot and Dupuy were unwilling to form a government and Poincaré was obliged to resort to the Radical Gaston Doumergue. The political centre of gravity was shifting to the Left. But Poincaré was able to extract conditions from the new premier. As a former colonial minister, member of several colonial movements and a past-president of the *Mission Laïque*, whose aim was the expansion of French secular education, particularly in the Middle East, it was believed that Doumergue would continue to execute the main lines of Poincaré's foreign policy, with which the Radicals were not in disagreement. Poincaré had been careful to put this condition to him, as well as that of the maintenance of the Three Years' Law.[59] Finally it was at Poincaré's insistence that Doumergue took on the foreign affairs portfolio – because of his admitted inexperience in this area.

Some of the advantages Poincaré had hoped to gain from appointing Doumergue appeared neutralised by the latter's inclusion of Joseph Caillaux at finance. Though the Radicals' stated aim was a return to two years' military service, the new government stated that it would 'loyally apply the Three Years' Law'. The Radicals' popularity continued to grow. To counter this, before the parliamentary elections of April–May 1914, some of the most able parliamentarians who supported the Law united under Briand's leadership to form the Fédération des gauches. The battle lines were drawn for the elections.

Poincaré's direct control of policy was on the wane. He considered the last ministerial crisis sufficiently serious to contemplate resignation. Admittedly, thoughts of resignation were the *leitmotiv* of his seven-year mandate, but he now felt under attack and no longer able to intervene in general policy. Paul Cambon, no friend of the president, confirmed that 'those two adventurers who are after him, Clemenceau and Caillaux, do not hide their aim of slitting his throat'.[60] Doumergue, under the protective wing of the Radicals, was not turning out to be the docile creature Poincaré had hoped. Apparently in an attempt to disprove the belief that the Radicals were not supporters of the Franco-Russian Alliance, he appeared to be pandering to the Russians, first over the Liman von Sanders Affair, and second in acceding to Russian desires for a state visit from the French president. Furthermore, as Poincaré lamented, foreign affairs were no longer discussed in such detail in cabinet, which reduced his influence over them. On 16 January, aware of his impotence, Poincaré reflected nostalgically on the enthusiasm which had surrounded his election a year before: 'A year has passed! My good mother is no longer here, the last ministerial crisis has broken the charm and smashed the national movement; a large part of those wonderful hopes has already withered and the constitution imposes on me the cruel duty of not interfering.'[61] By March, political colleagues were even encouraging him to take the constitutional, yet politically explosive, step of intervening by a presidential note in the Chamber debate on the reorganisation of the officer corps, considered vital to France's defences but which looked like being rejected by the Chamber. Typically he hesitated for several days: 'The present cabinet has taken away much of my popularity. I was elected to act. I cannot be a President like Fallières and Loubet.'[62] But he came down on the side of caution and did nothing.

During the lull in international relations since the ending of the second Balkan War, domestic scandals began to surface. A tawdry and prolonged financial scandal dating back to 1911, the Affaire Rochette, risked tarnishing the image of certain ministers, notably Caillaux. The conservative press, especially *Le Figaro*, began using this in a campaign against him. Caillaux learnt that the editor of *Le Figaro*, Gaston Calmette, had in his possession potentially politically damaging letters from Caillaux to his first wife, as well as an incriminating note from the Public Prosecutor concerning obstruction of justice by Caillaux during the Rochette trial when he was finance minister. Caillaux called on his erstwhile friend Poincaré to intercede. According to Poincaré's diaries of 16 March, Caillaux poured out to the president how he was being 'hounded as had no other politician'. Claiming that he could not accept this, he told Poincaré, 'If these letters are published, I shall kill Calmette'. Poincaré agreed to speak to his friend Maurice Bernard, who knew Calmette, to stop publication of the letters. Later that day he did so. But that evening Poincaré learnt that Madame Caillaux had entered Calmette's office and shot him six times. His diary notes his sadness, but the same night while dining at the Italian embassy, where ironically Poincaré was supposed to have been seated next to Madame Caillaux, he joked with his new neighbour, Madame Stephen Pichon, about when she and Henriette would both go and kill Clemenceau. Contrary to claims by Caillaux in his memoirs, Poincaré appears to have had no hand in encouraging Calmette to wage his campaign against Caillaux. He noted in his diary that Calmette had been cruelly wrong in his campaign, though he did wonder whether Calmette had acted in the belief that it was in Poincaré's interest:

I don't have the right to forget what he was for me and for Henriette before and after the presidential election. Last summer, dining at the Elysée, he spoke of me to Henriette with a sort of religious fervour. I had lifted the prestige of France, I was necessary for the country; Henriette should watch over me, care for me, keep me ... Who knows? Perhaps he thought he was doing me a service and defending me against the enemy.[63]

Poincaré believed that Barthou and Briand were behind Calmette's campaign against Caillaux. Nevertheless, Caillaux's resignation from the cabinet after the incident was a blessing for Poincaré. The two men would not be reconciled thereafter.

A further dimension was soon added to the scandal. Rumours began to circulate about two deciphered German telegrams in Caillaux's possession, which revealed Caillaux's secret negotiations with Germany during the Agadir crisis. The German ambassador learnt of these rumours and called at the Quai d'Orsay to protest. It was serious enough that the French had intercepted German communications, but if the affair became public, continued the German ambassador threateningly, 'a bomb would explode'.[64] This seemed likely at Madame Caillaux's trial which was set to open on 20 July. Of particular concern for Poincaré was Caillaux's threat to divulge Italian intercepts in his possession which might make public Poincaré's negotiations with the Vatican. Thus the prospect of a diplomatic crisis involving two Triple Alliance powers seriously preoccupied French political leaders in the spring and summer of 1914. In the end, the French government issued an official denial of the existence of the German intercepts, getting both them and Caillaux off the hook. Caillaux's blackmail had paid off. His good fortune was complete when on 28 July 1914 his wife was acquitted of murder after what Poincaré described as a disgustingly run trial.[65]

Though his freedom of manoeuvre in domestic affairs was reduced a large degree of consensus remained on foreign affairs. He seized the opportunity of basking in the publicity of King George V's state visit to France in late April; he encouraged the reluctant British foreign secretary, who accompanied the king, to begin talks with Russia on an Anglo-Russian naval agreement intended to please St Petersburg and further cement the Triple Entente. Little wonder then that, following the king's visit, Paul Cambon should remark of Poincaré, 'it is he, and he alone, who is the minister of Foreign Affairs'.[66] With Caillaux out of the cabinet Poincaré did enjoy greater initiative in some areas.

The received wisdom has been that the 1914 general elections were a repudiation of Poincaré's 'nationalist' policies. This perception was coloured by the politically motivated Poincaré-la-guerre myth of the inter-war years, according to which Poincaré, in the two and a half years before the outbreak of the Great War, had developed a nationalistic foreign policy intent on, or unperturbed by, a war with Germany. This myth demonstrated the inevitable march to war of 'Poincarist' policies, brushing aside growing opposition from left-wing parties and public opinion. Yet, as has been shown, Poincaré's foreign policy, whether in 1912 or subsequently, was more supported than opposed by a majority of left-wing political parties, none of whom saw it as bellicose. Opposition to Poincaré was over domestic not foreign policy, as was the case with the Three Years' Law. Though contemporary analyses of the 1914 elections described them as being determined by opposition to the Three Years' Law, modern scholarship has shown this not to have been the case.[67]

Analysis of election manifestos shows that only two political parties had clear views on the Law: the socialists and the Fédération des gauches against. Other movements were a good deal more ambiguous, with the Radical party's manifesto neither upholding nor rejecting the 1913 party conference's decision to oppose the Law. The ambiguity was apparently intentional. Substantial opposition to the Law was not evident from the 2,451 candidates: only 51 per cent were opposed and 44 per cent in favour. However, in the first round of voting candidates in favour polled 55 per cent of the national vote while those opposed obtained 43 per cent. Of those candidates elected to the Chamber, the division was approximately half and half. In reality these elections signalled no major change in public opinion. It would seem that the country as a whole was resigned to the Law, even if the majority in favour was beginning to shrink.[68]

Following the elections, supporters of the Law approached Poincaré to engineer Doumergue's resignation so that a more forceful defence of the Law could be mounted. René Viviani, the former socialist, was suggested as an alternative head of government. Typically, Poincaré hesitated, fearing that he might be overstepping his constitutional role. In the end the decision was made for him when Doumergue resigned on 2 June. There followed a two week long crisis during which Poincaré worked to ensure that any new government would agree to maintain the Law. Meanwhile, the Radicals stepped up their campaign to discredit

Poincaré. He heard that two emissaries had been sent at Caillaux's behest to the United States to trace Henriette's first husband, hitherto presumed dead, and that a letter had been sent to the queen of England about France's First Lady being a bigamist.

Viviani's laborious attempts to form a government failed on 8 June. Rather optimistically, given the predominance of the Left in the new Chamber, Poincaré called on the old man of the centre-right, Alexandre Ribot. Four days later his government was still-born, voted down by the Chamber. In desperation he called on Viviani again, knowing that he was one of the few capable of gaining a majority and keeping the Law. Poincaré was now seriously contemplating resignation should Viviani fail, claiming that he would not be a party to the repeal of the Law. He believed that repeal would leave 'the way clear for the opponents of the Russian Alliance and the perfidious artisans of a Franco-German *rapprochement*'. Though Viviani had formed his cabinet by June 12, taking on the premiership and foreign ministry, Poincaré was pessimistic about his own position: 'My constitutional powerlessness will bring me new attacks, my declining popularity will disappear altogether, unpopularity will triumph, but I will have made the effort right until the end to save the country.'[69] The fact that the government won a majority shows that the Three Years' Law was not the divisive and overriding issue once claimed. The government made a commitment to uphold the Law, a large majority of its members actually having voted for it the year before. Despite Poincaré's anxiety about his popularity, his ideas and policies had triumphed as they had now done for two and a half years.

The July crisis

Assessments of Poincaré's role in the so-called July crisis have become a good deal more muted since the polemical days of the 1920s and 1930s. Far from believing any more that France played a crucial role in the events which led to war, recent scholarship suggests that she was the most passive of the great powers, following events rather than creating them. The July crisis was not perceived as a grave crisis at the time, either in the chancelleries of the Triple Entente or amongst public opinion at large, until only a few days before the outbreak of hostilities.[70] Despite the assassination of the heir to the Austro-Hungarian throne by Bosnian Serb nationalists on 28 June 1914, in France the only sense of crisis and theatre for almost the next month concerned the Caillaux trial which resulted from a quite different assassination. Even as late as three days before French general mobilisation, the trial had more coverage than the European crisis in France's most respected newspapers. Diplomatic events did not figure any more prominently in cabinet meetings in the three weeks after the Sarajevo incident than before it. With the inexperienced Viviani at foreign affairs, Poincaré was at his most influential, yet his papers and diaries show little preoccupation with Austro-Serbian affairs. News of the Sarajevo assassination was passed to him as he was attending the races at Longchamps with members of the diplomatic corps. The Austrian ambassador withdrew but Poincaré and the others remained to watch the grand prix. On Tuesday 30 June at the first cabinet meeting following the assassination, the incident was hardly mentioned. Poincaré continued to follow a heavy schedule of social functions from artists' dinners to the cycling grand prix at Vincennes. His sole preoccupation was with the machinations surrounding the Caillaux trial and the plots against him by the Radicals, still intent on forcing his resignation by further scurrilous revelations about his wife. He believed Caillaux was trying to force him into putting pressure on the judges to acquit Madame Caillaux by threatening to produce witnesses at the trial to testify that the president had backed Calmette's campaign.[71] Meanwhile, an assortment of politicians and journalists continued to appeal to him to halt the decline in his popularity by intervening more. The Caillaux trial and its ramifications apart, the most serious issue to preoccupy Poincaré in the first half of July was the parliamentary uproar surrounding a recently published Senate report highly critical of what it considered France's inferiority in armaments to Germany. The Senate appeared intent on withholding approval for the government's military budget. Fearful of this, Poincaré envisaged cancelling his forthcoming state visit to Russia and Scandinavia, something the Sarajevo incident had never led him to contemplate. Approval of the budget was finally secured after a marathon Senate debate, held quite exceptionally on Bastille Day, after the government agreed to a parliamentary enquiry into the state of French armaments.

The French decision for war in the summer of 1914 must be set against a background of two vital issues: the state visit to Russia and Britain's position. The French state visit to Russia and Scandinavia during crucial moments of the international diplomatic crisis in late July meant that France's principal decision makers were, to a large extent, isolated from the diplomacy of the time. Consequently France was less well informed of events, less able to communicate with other powers and was reacting to events far more than other great powers. Second, when Poincaré did return to French soil on 29 July, a mere three days before French general mobilisation and only five days before war was declared on her, his overriding aim in managing the crisis was to ensure that the country would enter the conflict united and with British support. Every decision was weighed to ensure that France did not put a foot wrong domestically with her civilian population, and externally in the eyes of international public opinion and especially British opinion. If the French decision for war could be presented as defensive then that aim, it was calculated, would be fulfilled. This automatically implied exercising restraint over France's closest ally, Russia; imprudent action by her could threaten that strategy.

Poincaré was relieved to embark on his trip to Russia, Sweden, Denmark and Norway, organised six months previously, and to escape for a time the tribulations of domestic politics.[72] With him went Viviani and the political director of the Quai d'Orsay, a Poincaré appointee named de Margerie. They sailed from Dunkirk in the early hours of Thursday 16 July, leaving France without its senior political and foreign policy decision makers. The decision to embark on a voyage timed to last until 31 July was an indication that the French were unaware of serious trouble on the international scene. Back in Paris the minister of justice was deputising at the Quai d'Orsay, while the newly appointed sous-secrétaire d'état for foreign affairs had confessed to being ignorant of all things diplomatic.[73] All this was at a time when radio cabling was in its infancy and there was little expectation of being able to keep in constant contact with the presidential party. Should the question of France's responsibility in the outbreak of the Great War still be an issue, in the words of one historian: 'It is hard to imagine the leaders of the country indulging in the joys of tourism ... having plotted the outbreak of a European war'.[74] Furthermore, the forceful ultimatum which Austria was preparing to issue to Serbia was only communicated to her on 23 July once Berlin and Vienna were sure that Poincaré and his party had set sail from Russia for stage two of the tour. In this way it was calculated that France and Russia would not be able to co-ordinate a response to the Austrian note. Thus as a result of a combination of accident and design, on the eve of the Great War French leaders were literally and metaphorically at sea. Until the party finally cut short its trip and returned to Dunkirk on 29 July, French leaders were less well informed of events, less able to communicate with other powers and in short, less able to influence the course of events than any of their counterparts. By the time they returned to French soil it was probably too late to stop the outbreak of war. To a large extent, then, France's action could only be reactive not preventive. This was the picture painted by the Bavarian minister in Paris, von Ritter, who on 26 July wrote to the king,

The French government, the French press, and public opinion have been inconceivably surprised by the sending of the Austrian note to the Serb government. After the heated debates on income tax, deputies and senators had turned their backs on the capital and since Paris has become almost dead ... All the ambassadors, except M. de Schoen, are absent from Paris. The Italian Ambassador, M. Tittoni, is in Ireland[?]. The running of the ministry for Foreign Affairs is in the hands of the minister of justice, Bienvenu-Martin, who is unfamiliar with foreign matters ...[75]

The question remains as to what Poincaré did discuss during his stay in Russia. His diaries tell us that he spent the four-day voyage to Kronstadt giving foreign affairs lessons to Viviani, whose ignorance in such matters he found worrying. He thought it useful to brief him on 'details about the alliance, about various subjects dealt with at St Petersburg in 1912, about the Chinese consortium, Franco-Russian military conversations; Anglo-Russian negotiations on the proposed naval convention; relations with Germany'. He insisted on the necessity of maintaining the Three Years' Law and explained how he 'had never had any serious difficulties with Germany because I have always used great firmness with her'.[76] Viviani was more worried about the potentially explosive consequences of the Caillaux trial, and the where-abouts of his unfaithful mistress from the Comédie française. Poincaré noted in his diary, 'How sad to see from a distance France's attention concentrated on questions of this nature'.[77] Poincaré's only sign of discomfiture during the whole voyage was when a 'catastrophe' was narrowly averted as the French cruiser on which he was travelling crashed into a Russian tug in the fog.[78]

Early in the afternoon of Monday 20 July, Poincaré was greeted by Tsar Nicholas II aboard the imperial yacht *Alexandria* with Sazonov, the Russian foreign minister, Isvolsky, the Russian ambassador in Paris, and Paléologue, the French ambassador in St Petersburg, and together they sailed for Peterhof. That evening, before the banquet at the Palace, Poincaré and the tsar, and Viviani and Sazonov, began their diplomatic conversations. Telegrams between Paris and St Petersburg during the visit deal only with domestic issues.[79] But Poincaré's personal diaries do record the gist of some of those talks, much of which is omitted from both his published memoirs and the volume he later published entitled *Comment fut déclarée la guerre de 1914*. On 20 July the tsar expressed a hope that the Three Years' Law would be maintained, to which Poincaré replied that, in recently voting by a majority of 150 to fund its application, the new Chamber had demonstrated its true will. The tsar informed him that Caillaux had been in touch with the Russian Count Witte, the advocate of an alliance between France, Russia and Germany.

The next day talks continued on Anglo-Russian relations and the Russian desire to see a naval agreement with London. The Balkans were discussed, with the emperor expressing his concern about Austria and Bulgaria. Yet Poincaré's otherwise extremely candid diaries do not contain any signs of anxiety about Austro-Serbian relations whether on his part or that of his Russian hosts. Russia had taken no steps to recall her holidaying ambassadors to their posts in Paris, Berlin, Vienna and Belgrade, or for that matter the Russian General Staff's leading expert on mobilisation.[80] This is not surprising as Russia, like other Triple Entente powers, was still unclear about what was afoot in Central Europe. A sign of the tsar's peace of mind was his request to reciprocate Poincaré's state visit with a similar one to France in the summer of 1915.

Signs of trouble on the horizon were revealed, however, during a reception with the diplomatic corps in the Winter Palace on Tuesday 21 July. The British ambassador, Sir George Buchanan, expressed the fear that Austria would address a stiff note to Belgrade. This was confirmed personally to Poincaré by the Austrian ambassador, who stated that Vienna was about to take steps against Serbia, whereupon Poincaré warned that Serbia had friends. Later that evening, at a dinner at the French embassy for the Russian government, foreign ministry officials and a few military chiefs, Poincaré and Viviani were informed of a telegram from the usually cautious Jules Cambon in Berlin, forwarded from Paris. In it he warned that Germany would support Austria in her *démarche* at Belgrade. In talks with Poincaré and Viviani, Sazonov now seemed more worried, confessing that should things deteriorate, Russia would have great difficulty mobilising as the peasants were still harvesting.[81] Most of the other entries in Poincaré's diaries concentrate on the serious and embarrassing attack of 'neurasthenia' which afflicted Viviani following further worrying developments in the Caillaux trial cabled to him on 22 July. Viviani's illness, for which a doctor was summoned, meant Poincaré taking over full control of conversations with the Russian authorities for the rest of the visit.

There is no evidence that during his visit to Russia Poincaré did anything other than reaffirm the Franco-Russian alliance. He did not offer *carte blanche* in the event of a Balkan war. At that time there was no certainty of such a conflict, two Balkan wars having recently been settled peacefully; only hindsight lends that interpretation to events. But given the growing rumours of impending Austrian action against Serbia, Poincaré, Viviani, Paléologue and Sazonov did discuss the Balkan question and agreed on joint action. What had been agreed in those talks was explained to the British ambassador by Sazonov and Paléologue on

24 July, after the Austrian ultimatum had been presented. Buchanan was told that the French and Russian governments had stated that: first, they were in full accord on the various problems concerning the maintenance of peace and the European balance of power, particularly in the Orient; second, they would inform Vienna that she should refrain from any action which could be considered an attack on Serbia's sovereignty and independence (this point was no longer valid given that the ultimatum had now been presented); third, they agreed to accept the obligations imposed on them by the alliance (this was merely a reaffirmation of the alliance).[82] Given that a potential international problem had arisen which concerned at least one of the two allies, it was natural, indeed essential, that the two allies should consult. Even then Poincaré did not proffer unrestrained support; it was not in France's interest to do so and would have run counter to the general thrust of his foreign policy over the previous two and a half years, during which he had worked to avoid Russia dragging France into a Balkan war. It is likely, however, that Poincaré did counsel firmness to Russia in her dealings with Austria, for that was how he had always conducted affairs with the central powers, believing that the clarity of such an approach was what the Germans, at least, best understood. This explains Sazonov's telegram late that evening to the Russian *chargé d'affaires* in Vienna instructing him to inform the Austrian foreign minister, 'in a friendly, but firm manner', of the dangers of any action that was incompatible with the dignity of Serbia. He added that, 'From my conversations with the French foreign minister, it is apparent that France is also worried about any change which might take place in Austro-Serbian relations, and that she is not disposed to allow an unjustified humiliation of Serbia'. Sazonov explained that this was also Britain's view, who together with France would also be counselling moderation. He ended with the hope that warnings given by the great powers in good time would keep Austria from taking 'irrevocable measures'.[83] Much of this telegram bears Poincaré's mark, either indirectly through his influence over Viviani or directly through his conversations with the Russian foreign minister. The 'firmness' which he had counselled to Viviani in his dealings with Germany during the voyage to Russia was now being applied.

23 July had been the last day of the visit. A farewell dinner was given on board the *France* for the imperial family and court. After what Poincaré considered a mediocre meal, the French cruiser weighed anchor and set sail for Sweden. The timing of Poincaré's departure had been crucial for the *dénouement* of subsequent events. On it hung the dispatch of the Austrian ultimatum to Serbia, as the numerous intercepted telegrams between the Austrian foreign ministry and its

embassy in Paris, later deciphered by the French cryptographic service, show.[84] The Germans advised the Austrians to delay delivering the ultimatum until 6 p.m. central European time on 23 July to avoid it becoming known in St Petersburg before Poincaré's timed departure of 11 p.m. local time. This was indeed what happened, as Poincaré later explained to the socialist Albert Thomas.[85]

On learning of the ultimatum the British foreign secretary described it as 'the most formidable document I have ever seen addressed by one state to another that was independent'. As intended, Poincaré learnt of it at sea through a series of garbled radio messages on 24 July. Though he, Viviani and de Margerie concerted, it seems that Poincaré's ideas dominated. Their plan of action was remarkably restrained. Viviani telegraphed to St Petersburg, for relay to Paris and London, that Serbia should accept as many of the Austrian conditions as honour would allow, that an extension of the deadline to forty-eight hours be sought and that an international inquest on the assassination should be substituted for the Austro-Serbian one.[86]

The state party reached Stockholm on Saturday 25 July. Poincaré was still calm and able to enjoy the beauty of the Swedish coastline, though he was lapsing into one of his periods of self-doubt, this time on the pros and cons of halting the voyage and returning to Paris. News arrived that the German ambassador in Paris had told the acting foreign minister that Germany supported the Austrian note and had insisted that the affair be localised to avoid the alliances being activated with incalculable consequences. For Viviani, de Margerie and Poincaré this demonstrated that Germany had abandoned the Concert of Europe as the means of settling international disputes similar to those of 1912 and 1913.

Hesitation about returning to Paris resurfaced. Inertia triumphed: interrupting the tour would only excite French public opinion and give the impression that somehow France was mixed up in the events; anyway, what more could be done in Paris? As proof of this, and to ensure that Bienvenu-Martin was not left in charge, Poincaré asked Viviani to inform the Havas news agency, via its director, M. Pognon, who was in their party, that the French foreign minister was assuming control of foreign policy. This effectively put decision-making in Poincaré's hands, as the head of government and foreign minister was again overcome with neurasthenia. Already Poincaré's diaries showed that every decision taken by Viviani was preceded by 'on my advice'.

The king of Sweden informed Poincaré that at 6 p.m. on 25 July the Austrian ultimatum had expired and that the Austrian envoy had left Belgrade. Poincaré confessed to feeling powerless. On 27 July, as the state party was sailing for Denmark, the government in Paris telegraphed to request their return home. The visit to Denmark and Norway was aborted and the *France* set a course for Dunkirk. That day a telegram informed Poincaré that Sir Edward Grey had stated that if war broke out in the Balkans no nation could remain disinterested.[87] That spurred the French president into action which he recorded in his diary:

I point to this firmness as an example to Viviani, who is more and more troubled and anxious and turns over the most contradictory ideas.
I get him to keep contact with St Petersburg and to tell the Russian government that, in the interests of peace, France will second her action.
I had beforehand advised de Margerie to prepare a telegram to that effect. Viviani, after more hesitation, makes up his mind to send it . . .[88]

Interestingly, Luigi Albertini, relatively unsympathetic to Poincaré in his monumental study of the origins of the First World War, was unaware that Poincaré had written the telegram, and remarked that it was 'timely, unexceptionable in tone and indicative of a level-headed, pacific attitude on the part of Viviani'.[89] Poincaré's strategy in offering such support was consistent with his policy since 1912: to bring home to Russia the loyalty of France as an ally in order to keep control of her actions. This he conceived as the best way of maintaining what was the cornerstone of French security. To give Russia the impression that France might abandon her would diminish Russia's interest in the alliance. He already knew that Sazonov's position was not secure and that if he fell from power his replacement could come from the strong pro-German faction at the court and in the army. The prospect of revolution, evident in the strikes which Poincaré had recently witnessed, could lead the Russian government to turn to Germany for support in the hope of bolstering her monarchical institutions through a renewed St Petersburg–Berlin axis. Poincaré was in a delicate position in relation to Russia. Fortunately, only two days before, he had received a telegram from Paléologue explaining that Sazonov was acting peacefully in asking Serbia not to counter if she were attacked. This was the kind of restraint which Poincaré believed should be reinforced.[90]

When on the evening of 27 July Poincaré received news of the Austrian mobilisation, again his watchword was 'firmness'. Learning that Bienvenu-Martin had had several visits from the German ambassador, Poincaré noted in his diary, 'So long as Bienvenu-Martin in his desire to maintain peace did not appear too weak!' Again Poincaré explained to Viviani that it was necessary to be firm with Germany and to remain calm. Both Poincaré and de Margerie were increasingly anxious about Viviani's state of mind: 'He is nervous, agitated, never stops pronouncing imprudent words or sentences which show a complete ignorance of foreign affairs.' And Poincaré added dismissively that Viviani was only relaxed when talking about socialist conferences, Jean Jaurès and Edouard Vaillant.[91]

When Poincaré landed on French soil on Wednesday 29 July, the period of his greatest presidential power began. The decline in his popularity was reversed. The crowds which greeted him filled him with a strong sense of mission: 'It was no longer to a person that these acclamations were addressed; it was to the representative of France vis-à-vis the world.' This gave him the confidence he needed to put aside his self-doubt and overstep his constitutional role. Persuading himself that Viviani would be 'hesitant and pusillanimous', he noted, 'I am determined to take over myself responsibility for Viviani's action'. He ordered cabinet meetings, which the president chaired, to be held every morning.[92] He firmly took control of the affairs of state. But he soon came to the conclusion that there was little that he could do to stop the course of events now in train. Two weeks had passed in which the diplomatic and political masters of France had been absent from the hub of events and, to a large extent, intentionally isolated from what has come to be known as the July crisis. Berlin had even sent instructions to its radio transmission service at Metz to jam all Franco-Russian radio communications and those between the battle-cruiser France and Paris, as the instructions in the service log for 27 and 28 July show.[93] Poincaré could merely familiarise himself with the communications and the recent news of which he had been deprived since his departure from Russia five days earlier. His reading of those documents gave him the impression that the situation was far more serious than he had at first believed. Certainly within the next forty-eight hours, if not already, he would come to the conclusion that war was inevitable. For that reason, and because of his long-held belief that France's salvation rested with her unity, his strategy henceforth would be to ensure that the country entered the war united. That meant taking every precaution to ensure that any war appeared defensive in the eyes of the world, and especially in those of his fellow citizens. That would be no mean feat; the most cursory glance at back copies of the left-wing press showed a widespread hostility to war which ranged from a reiteration of the CGT trades union's official policy of a general strike in the event of war being declared, to the Socialist party's appeal for international action against war. Rhetoric apart, there had been a substantial demonstration against war in Paris on 27 July and a host of others were organised for the capital and provinces for 30 and 31 July.[94] Observers who were more independent, such as the British ambassador in Paris, Sir Francis Bertie, also believed that French public opinion was against going to war over

Serbia.[95] Hence the importance of ensuring that a French decision for war should be perceived as defensive. Like many other republicans, Poincaré had not forgotten the disastrous French diplomacy surrounding the outbreak of the Franco-Prussian War of 1870–1, when the French foreign minister, the duc de Gramont, had fallen into the trap laid by Bismarck in the form of the 'Ems telegram' to goad France into declaring war on Prussia, thereby forfeiting international support. Henceforth, France's domestic, foreign and defence strategies became one: a marketing strategy to present any French decision for war as defensive.

An essential element conditioning France's management of the international crisis was Russia. While Poincaré had been cruising the Gulf of Finland, important events had been taking place in St Petersburg. Sazonov had learnt of the content of the Austrian note on the morning of 24 July and had immediately requested consent from the government and tsar to partial mobilisation against Austria, which was, however, only to become operational should Austria actually move against Serbia. The Russians had then begun to press Britain to make a clear statement to Germany of her intention to support France and Russia, if necessary militarily, in a war against the central powers. This the British refused to do. France, by contrast, was not free to act as she wished. The alliance limited her freedom of action. This explains why Poincaré was constantly at pains to maintain the fine balance between too much, or too little, support for France's ally, either of which could have dire consequences.[96] The question of the role of the French ambassador in St Petersburg, Maurice Paléologue, in his dealings with Russia during the crisis, allegedly proffering unauthorised support to the Russians, supposedly in Poincaré's name, has been the subject of much polemic. Much has been made of Poincaré's friendship with Paléologue as a sign that the ambassador spoke in the president's name. This is in fact without foundation. In reality Poincaré was well aware of Paléologue's tendency towards exaggeration and had even attempted to deny him the St Petersburg embassy, having already found his predecessor, Delcassé, too Russophile.[97] However, new evidence about his role, which will be discussed below, must lead to a less censorious view of his activities.

Whatever Paléologue's attitude in the crisis, Russia continued to give the impression of remaining peaceful, as both the Austrian and German ambassadors in St Petersburg were prepared to state, at least in private. Moreover, on 29 July – the day after Austria had declared war on Serbia – the Germans continued to believe that France was 'setting all levers in motion at St Petersburg to exercise a moderating influence there'.[98]

Even the socialist leader Jean Jaurès now believed that French activity was pacificatory, as his speech to the International Socialist meeting in Brussels on 29 July showed:

We [French socialists], do not have to impose a policy of peace on our government. It is carrying one out. I who have never hesitated to take head on the hatred of our chauvinists by my stubborn desire, which will never weaken, for a Franco-German *rapprochement*, I have the right to say that at this moment the French government is the best ally for peace of this admirable English government, which has taken the initiative toward conciliation.[99]

By now most powers were in the preparatory stages of mobilisation.[100] Already on 26 July the French minister of war, Adolphe Messimy, had recalled French officers from leave and taken steps to protect the railways as a response to similar German measures in Alsace. A potential problem for decision makers in Paris was Russian action during this period of tension. Intemperate moves by France's ally risked undermining her strategy of ensuring that any decision for war should be perceived as defensive by French domestic and foreign opinion. As if France's principal decision makers had not been obstructed enough by their inability to communicate with other powers during their Baltic cruise, they were now to be faced with inadequate information about the activities of their principal ally. Traditionally historians have placed the blame for this on the French ambassador in St Petersburg, Paléologue, who supposedly wished to keep Paris in the dark about the advanced state of Russian war preparations for fear that the decision makers in France would require Russia to act with more restraint, which was indeed the case. However, new evidence produced by Jean Stengers relieves Paléologue of much of the blame by showing that the French ambassador was himself handicapped by poor information.[101] As Paléologue's position in the management of the crisis has hitherto been considered important, it is necessary to reconsider his role.

Evidence of a less conspiratorial role on the part of Paléologue is to be found in the diary of the wife of the French military attaché at the St Petersburg embassy, the marquise de Laguiche. Just after 10 p.m. in the evening of 29 July the French military attaché, General Pierre de Laguiche, was told by the Russian military authorities that a general mobilisation had been ordered. The marquise de Laguiche notes, 'Pierre is asked to inform Paris, but not to speak to Paléologue until midnight, his lack of discretion being known!'[102] Despite Russian attempts to keep the news from Paléologue, he learnt of the general mobilisation order at 11 p.m., not from Laguiche but Basily, the deputy-director of the Chancery at the Russian foreign ministry.[103] Paléologue immediately ordered the first secretary at the French embassy, Chambrun, to take a telegram to the Russian foreign ministry for dispatch to Paris explaining that the Russian government had decided on two things: first, to order that night the mobilisation of thirteen army corps for use against Austria; second, secretly to begin general mobilisation. The reason why the telegram was taken to the foreign ministry was that it was feared that the French embassy cipher might not be secure.[104] When Chambrun reached the Russian foreign ministry he met Laguiche who had been summoned to the ministry to be informed by the foreign minister's *chef de cabinet*, Schilling, that the tsar had rescinded the general mobilisation order. Schiller insisted to Laguiche that this news should remain secret: 'I confide this to you alone in the whole world, not a word to the Embassy staff, neither Basily nor anyone else knows about it.'[105] As the marquise de Laguiche remarked, this put her husband in an invidious position *vis-à-vis* Paléologue. Laguiche ordered Chambrun to suppress the last sentence of the telegram for dispatch to Paris which stated that the Russian government had decided 'secretly to begin general mobilisa-tion'.[106] According to the marquise, the next morning Paléologue was furious with both her husband and Chambrun.[107] Thus it would seem that Paléologue did not intentionally keep Paris in the dark about the shortlived Russian general mobilisation order and its abrogation, rather it was he who was obstructed by others.[108] Indeed, Paléologue appeared particularly anxious that news of the Russian general mobilisation should reach Paris as soon as possible. At midnight on the 29 July, before he had learnt of the tsar's counter-order, he had telegraphed (no. 306) to Paris: 'Please collect from the Russian Embassy *as a matter of extreme urgency*, my telegram no. 304'.[109]

As yet, the poor quality of information being sent to Paris had not had a serious effect on the French management of the crisis, which was predicated on the notion of restraining Russia to avoid giving Germany a pretext for war. The French desire to restrain their ally was made clear on the night of the 29–30 July following an urgent message conveyed to Viviani by the Russian *chargé d'affaires* in Paris, Sevastopoulo. It was in the form of a telegram from Sazonov to Isvolsky warning that Russia was about to ignore German threats and begin mobilising because Austria had already mobilised and because war was imminent. More worrying still it instructed Isvolsky to thank the French government 'for the declaration which has been made to me officially in its name by the French Ambassador that we can entirely count upon the allied support of France. In the present circumstances, this declaration is particularly precious to us.'[110] Viviani was so disturbed by this message that he called on the minister of war and together they hurried to the Elysée to wake the president just before two o'clock in the morning. A telegram was drafted and dispatched at 7 a.m. on the 30th with Poincaré's approval, which stated quite clearly that Russia 'should not immediately proceed to any measure which might offer Germany a pretext for a total or partial mobilisation of her forces'.[111] Though the telegram did not arrive in St Petersburg until after Russian partial mobilisation had been declared, clearly Poincaré and Viviani were attempting to exercise a restraining influence on Russia, whose forward policy was in danger of undermining their strategy for managing the crisis.[112] That strategy was designed to allow Germany to incur the blame for the conflict in the eyes of French domestic and international public opinion. The initiative for such a policy clearly came from Poincaré who, as usual, chaired the cabinet meeting on the morning of the 30th and whose way of thinking pervaded the business at hand. Abel Ferry, *sous-secrétaire d'état* for foreign affairs, recorded in his notes of that meeting:

Impressive cabinet. Solemn men.
1 For the sake of public opinion, let the Germans put themselves in the wrong (Laisser vis à vis de l'opinion les torts du côté allemand)
2 Do not stop Russian mobilisation
Mobilise but do not concentrate
Cabinet calm, serious, orderly.[113]

Ferry's second point suggests that Russian partial mobilisation was discussed with a view to asking Russia to rescind it for the reasons already main plain to her earlier that morning. But at that time, because of the inadequate communications from the St Petersburg embassy, the French cabinet was quite unaware of how close to general mobilisation Russia was, and the decision to do nothing was carried.

Where the question of information from the St Petersburg embassy did have an impact on the French management of the crisis was following the Russian decision to 'proceed secretly with the first measures of general mobilisation', of which Paléologue informed Paris in his telegram at 7.50 p.m. on 30 July.[114] Paléologue was by now very worried about the safety of the French embassy cipher and the possibility that French communications were being intercepted by Germany. For that reason he had informed the Quai, apparently via the very circuitous Scandinavian route for safety, for the telegram took more than twenty-four hours to arrive, that he was changing the embassy cipher. In the end he felt that even this was insufficient and decided to use the Scandinavian route to inform Paris of the Russian general mobilisation, which the Russians were so insistent upon keeping secret. This was the route which his Belgian colleague also used that day.[115] This explains the notorious delay over Paléologue's telegram no. 318 to Paris of 31 July marked 'extrême urgence' announcing the general mobilisation of the Russian Army and minuted at 8.30 a.m.[116] His wire took nearly twelve hours to reach the Quai d'Orsay, with another half hour for deciphering. By then Viviani had left for home, from where he went on to a cabinet meeting.[117] As a result French decision makers were again less well informed than their counterparts. At this time they had received from neither Isvolsky nor Paléologue official notification of Russian general mobilisation. This explains Viviani's anxious telegram to Paléologue on the evening of 31 July, minuted 9 p.m. and 9.20 p.m., informing him that the German government was insisting that the Russians had ordered '*total*' mobilisation and that, if they did not demobilise, Germany would herself mobilise. Viviani was forced to tell von Schoen that he had not been informed of Russian total mobilisation. Thus, when asked by the German ambassador what France's attitude would be in the event of a Russo-German conflict, Viviani told Paléologue that he had not replied. He ordered Paléologue, rather crisply, to tell Sazonov of all this and to inform Viviani urgently as to the facts of the 'so-called' Russian general mobilisation. He ended with the remark, 'As I have already informed you, I have no doubt that the Imperial government, in the greater interest of peace, will avoid, for its part, anything which could begin the crisis.'[118] It is hard, therefore, to disagree with Poincaré: 'However useless these instructions, they proved once more not only that France had remained ignorant of Russian mobilisation but that she continued to regret this measure and to find it precipitate.'[119]

Paléologue replied with a distressed telegram on the morning of 1 August enquiring as to whether Viviani had received his telegram announcing general mobilisation.[120] He then drafted a memorandum detailing the reasons for the delay in his telegram no. 318, announcing Russian general mobilisation, reaching the Quai d'Orsay. In the light of the new evidence unearthed by Stengers suggesting that the French ambassador's role was more innocent than has hitherto been suggested, it now seems fair to give more credence to Paléologue's own explanation for the delay in the receipt of telegram no. 318, particularly in view of the Russian authorities' desire to keep this secret.[121]

Paléologue states that he learnt of the Russian general mobilisation at 6 a.m. on 31 July. He asked his second military attaché to check with the Russian General Staff as to whether the order had been posted up across the empire. He then discussed the situation with his first secretary. Following the return of the second attaché he wrote telegram 318 (announcing the general mobilisation of the Russian army). At 8.30 a.m. this was taken urgently to the telegraph office which was at a distance of three and a half kilometres from the embassy. The bearer of the telegram returned at 9.30 a.m. explaining that the telegraph office had been particularly agitated since the military authorities had requisitioned it. Paléologue then adds that he saw another reason for the delay. As the normal route for telegrams from Petersburg to Paris via Berlin was no longer secure he had used the route specified by the French and Russian general staff in the event of war, which he explained to be via the Scandinavian and British wires. But in order to do this, he further explained, it was necessary to inform all the intermediary posts, which he lists as 'Helsingfors, New Biggin, Londres et la variante Copenhague, Esbjerg, Calais ...' This would, Paléologue claims, have amounted to a delay, of three to four hours according to specialists. Thus he calculated that his telegram should have reached Paris at about 6 p.m. He concludes his memorandum by stating that he did not understand why at 9.30 p.m. Viviani should have sent him a telegram stating that he did not know of the Russian general mobilisation.[122] Choosing such a circuitous route was nothing exceptional, as the Belgian ambassador's action proves. On 1 August Paléologue took a similar precaution when he telegraphed to Paris via 'Odessa and Fredericia' the news that the German ambassador had informed Sazonov of his country's declaration of war against Russia.[123] Thus it would seem that the French ambassador did not act so conspiratorially in informing Paris of the Russian general mobilisation. More importantly, the criticism that Russian general mobilisation was approved in Paris appears to be flatly contradicted by the evidence, as well as being in conflict with Poincaré's overall strategy for managing the crisis, which was to let Germany put herself in the wrong.

Though France was reacting to events more than creating them, she nevertheless appeared to have a clear strategy, namely of ensuring that any French decision for war should be seen as defensive at home and abroad. The French government was not deflected from that aim by problems such as poor communications with its principal ally, Russia. But on the evening of 31 July one event looked like undermining the whole strategy for a domestic united front: the socialist leader, Jean Jaurès, was assassinated by a half-witted fanatic driven to action by the vituperative attacks in the nationalist press against the 'pro-German Socialist traitor'. Poincaré, who had often crossed swords with Jaurès in parliament, believed that he was far from being a traitor: 'Jaurès had over the last eight days expiated many faults. He had helped the government in its diplomacy and, if war breaks out, he would have been amongst those who would have known how to do their duty.' And he noted emotionally at the end of his diary entry, 'What an abominable and stupid crime!'[124] Though his outrage at the assassination was heartfelt, it was partly motivated by the fear of a reaction in the labour and trade union movements which could have devastating consequences for national unity as France stood on the brink of war. Former minister Etienne Clémentel's private diary echoes that fear: 'It is a stupid crime and could have grave consequences on the eve of mobilisation. The crime is all the more absurd because the socialists have an excellent attitude and because Jaurès's articles since the start of the crisis have been irreproachable.'[125] The fear that the assassination could have a destabilising effect was heightened by the fact that the trade union movement had repeatedly stressed an implacable opposition to war, with certain elements well known to the police threatening insurrection or a general strike to combat mobilisation.[126] To defuse the situation the otherwise moderate government immediately sought to associate itself with the Socialist party's mourning. Poincaré wrote messages of condolence to Jean's brother, Admiral Jaurès, and Mme Jaurès, probably with the intention that they be published, in which L'Humanité duly obliged. The letter to Jaurès's widow displayed a mixture of genuine sympathy, political expediency and a clear understanding of the press as an instrument of policy. It spoke of 'a moment when national union is more necessary than ever' and was intended to head off the possibility of demonstrations of sympathy combining with the strong anti-war feeling on the Left to paralyse France at such a critical moment. The prefect of police, Hennion, warned the cabinet that disturbances were very likely. The cabinet agreed to retain in Paris two regiments of cavalry scheduled to depart for the eastern frontier; they also ordered a notice to be posted up immediately across the country linking the government with the mourning and appealing for 'union': 'In the grave circumstances through which la Patrie is passing, the government counts on the patriotism of the working class, of the whole population, to remain calm and not to add to public emotion by agitation which would bring disorder to the capital.'[127] Assurances were immediately sought and obtained from the socialists that they would help maintain calm. This was facilitated by the arrest of the murderer the same night. Meanwhile, Poincaré's friend, the nationalist Maurice Barrès, wrote a public letter of condolence, probably at Poincaré's behest, to Mme Jaurès, disassociating the nationalist Right from the crime.[128] Even the nationalist press, such as the Action Française, which had hitherto pilloried the socialist leader, joined in the chorus of condemnations. By 1 August the labour movement was rapidly abandoning opposition to war in favour of that old republican reflex of duty to defend la patrie en danger. The headlines in La Guerre Sociale of 1 August perfectly illustrated the transition: 'National Defence above all! They have assassinated Jaurès! We will not assassinate France!'[129] The government's skilful handling of the assassination proved more successful than could have been hoped. Paradoxically, national union was forged around one of the foremost opponents of war; it was only a small step from there to *union sacrée*.

The question of British participation on France's side in the event of war also conditioned Poincaré's management of the crisis. Like Sazonov, many French diplomats were convinced that the preservation of peace lay in Britain's hands: if she declared her willingness to come to France's assistance in the event of her being attacked then there was a chance that conflict could be avoided. Poincaré certainly believed this. But despite pressing appeals by the French ambassador, Paul Cambon, to Sir Edward Grey, this was not forthcoming. Tired of Grey's tergiversations, Poincaré, backed by the government, made a direct appeal by letter to King George V on 31 July. It was to no avail. Nevertheless, Poincaré remained optimistic: 'I do not despair; the Foreign Office is very well disposed towards us; Asquith also; the English are slow to decide, methodical, reflective, but they know where they are going.'[130] Of course, Britain's assistance was not valued in merely military terms. Poincaré would not have disagreed with Clémentel's assessment of a British refusal to come to France's assistance: 'It would be a serious complication which would lead to the diminution of moral force by the reduction in confidence.'[131]

Despite the gravity of the situation, Poincaré's diaries show him to be remarkably calm. He noted on 1 August that Russia had ordered general mobilisation on the grounds that Germany had begun her mobilisation; Germany had then immediately called on Russia to suspend those measures: 'it is almost inevitable war'. At the same time he revealed a degree of frustration: 'Germany clearly does not wish us to negotiate on an equal footing; she claims to agree to talk; but she does not want Russia and us to be able to defend ourselves in the talks.'[132]

Poincaré's diaries show that he was, by 1 August, convinced of the inevitability of war. Without precluding further negotiations for a peaceful settlement, his strategy did not waver from ensuring that France should appear the injured party to unite the country in a defensive war and to ensure that she obtained the necessary diplomatic and military support from countries such as Britain and Italy. Indeed, good news on this front arrived on the evening of 31 July with Italy announcing that she considered the attack on Serbia to be an act of aggression which released her from the obligations under the terms of the Triple Alliance and allowed her to declare herself neutral.

In the meantime France had taken certain military precautions whose moderation was specifically designed to convey to domestic and international opinion the fundamentally defensive nature of French action. Following discussions between Poincaré, Viviani, Messimy (the war minister) and General Joffre (chief of the General Staff), in which Poincaré played a prominent role, it was decided to put to the French cabinet a set of proposals, which were duly accepted in the morning of 30 July.[133] These stipulated that, without beginning general mobilisation, covering troops should be ordered to take up positions along a line from Luxemburg to the Vosges mountains, but on the express condition that they get no closer than ten kilometres to the frontier. The proposals were, the cabinet agreed, designed to avoid giving German patrols a pretext for war and to convince British public opinion of France's reasonableness, and also to have a positive effect on French domestic opinion. It was certainly a remarkable gesture of restraint, the like of which there can be few cases in the history of warfare.

The propaganda value of such action to the French can be measured in terms of the military risks which such restraint incurred at a time when France's principal decision makers believed in the inevitability of war. General Joffre, for one, was not happy with the decision, given that Germany was proceeding with military preparations. Apart from the fact that the withdrawal formed no part of France's Plan XVII, Joffre had calculated precisely what France was sacrificing. The following day on 31 July he informed the war minister and the cabinet that every twenty-four hours' delay in mobilising the eastern army corps was equivalent to a fifteen to twenty kilometre loss of French territory.[134] But the cabinet was convinced of the moral value of such a measure, as the minister of war subsequently commented: 'Nothing made such an impression on British opinion (all accounts are agreed on that point), nothing was better proof of our pacific intentions than this decision to keep troops at a slight distance from the frontier.'[135] The immediacy with which the British government was informed of the measures and the degree of sacrifice involved merely confirm the extent to which French decision-making was conditioned by the need to secure the support of Britain. Though Joffre bowed to his political masters, at 8 a.m. on 1 August, following news that Germany had begun serious mobilisation measures, the chief of General Staff was threatening the minister of war with resignation if the mobilisation order was not issued.[136] It was calculated that France was already two days behind German mobilisation.[137] Again revealing where decision-making really lay, an hour later Messimy had marched the general off to the Elysée. Poincaré agreed to Joffre's appearing before the cabinet that day. The cabinet agreed that mobilisation notices should be issued that afternoon, Saturday 1 August, at

4 p.m., with effect from the following day, but that the ten kilometre withdrawal from the frontier be maintained.[138] The reason for the demarcation zone and the seriousness with which he wished it to be respected were revealed in a telegram dispatched at 10.30 p.m. on 1 August from the minister of war to the High Command:

The ministry of War insists again, on behalf of the President of the Republic, and for serious diplomatic reasons, on the necessity of not crossing the demarcation line indicated by the telegram of 30 July and reiterated in a telegram of today. This prohibition applies as much to the cavalry as to other units. No patrol, no reconnaissance, no post, no element whatsoever, must go east of the said line. Whoever crosses it will be liable to court martial and it is only in the event of a full-scale attack that it will be possible to transgress this order, which will be communicated to all troops.[139]

Poincaré revealed the extent to which this was for propaganda purposes. Though in his published record of events he attributed to the cabinet of 1 August the initiative for issuing the public proclamation explaining the mobilisation measures, its motive and true source were clear from his secret diary: 'In order to maintain, to the end, the pacific character of the measures we are taking, I have proposed that a proclamation by the government to the country be posted up throughout France. It seemed to me to be necessary that I sign it myself and have it countersigned by all Ministers.' Viviani then pointed out, correctly according to Poincaré, that two or three ministers – in particular the minister of work and social affairs, Senator Couyba – had privately criticised the decision to mobilise immediately. But Poincaré noted of Viviani, 'In truth, he has hesitated more than the others and is not annoyed to be covered by all'. That meant that a quarter to a third of the twelve strong cabinet had doubts about the decision to mobilise. But the imperative was to hold up the government's unity as an example to the country, as Poincaré confided to his diary: 'the idea that everyone sign is, in any case, a means of proving government solidarity. At my request, Viviani then drew up rapidly in the cabinet a proposed statement.' Poincaré then made alterations which were adopted.[140] The two-page proclamation was a clear appeal to unity which presaged Poincaré's call for a *union sacrée*. Stating that 'mobilisation is not war' it ended:

Strong in the ardent desire to reach a pacific solution of the crisis, the government, protected by the necessary precautions, will continue its diplomatic efforts and still hopes to succeed.

It counts on the composure of this noble nation not to allow itself to indulge in unjustified emotion. It counts on the patriotism of all Frenchmen and knows that there is not one of them who is not ready to do his duty.

In this hour, there are no parties. There is *la France éternelle*, peaceful and resolute France. There is the *patrie* of right and justice, completely united in calm, vigilance and dignity.

As Poincaré remarked, 'The cabinet has itself, therefore, in preparing this statement, given the example of unity which it recommends to the country'. He was particularly pleased that when the minister of the interior revealed the proclamation to waiting journalists it was greeted with cries of 'Vive la France'.[141]

At seven o'clock on 31 July, the German ambassador had called at the Quai d'Orsay to learn of France's intentions should war break out between Russia and Germany. Would France remain neutral? Poincaré and Viviani had already discussed this problem and had agreed that a clear reply should be avoided. On getting this response von Schoen replied that he would return for an answer early the following afternoon. He returned on 1 August at 11 a.m.; but Berlin was now insisting that even if France promised to remain neutral, she would still have to surrender her principal fortresses along her eastern frontier as a guarantee of 'sincerity'. Viviani, after consulting Poincaré, replied that France would act in accordance with her interests.[142]

Further evidence of the importance to Poincaré of the need to engineer the most favourable circumstances to rally all sections of public opinion to the defence of the nation was revealed in his diary for the night of 1 to 2 August. At 11.30 p.m. he received a visit from Isvolsky who had come to learn of France's attitude following Germany's declaration of war on Russia earlier that day. Poincaré explained that France would respect the alliance,

but that we had an interest, Russia and us, that mobilisation should be taken as far as possible before war was declared. I added that it would be better that we should not be obliged to declare war ourselves and that it be declared on us. That was necessary for both military and domestic political reasons: a defensive war would raise the whole country; a declaration of war by us could leave some doubts about the alliance, amongst part of public opinion.

The Russian ambassador, in sombre mood, acquiesced. Poincaré immediately called a cabinet meeting which lasted from midnight until four in the morning, at which his response to Isvolsky was unanimously endorsed. Only one member of the cabinet was not present, Senator Couyba, who according to Poincaré's published account could not be contacted, but who in the diaries was rumoured to be going around 'repeating that we are leading France into war'.[143]

News of the German declaration of war on Russia and of German troop incursions into France across her eastern borders, about which France formally protested in writing,[144] led General Joffre to request that the ten kilometre withdrawal be lifted. The cabinet hesitated, then agreed to lift the order at 2 p.m. on 2 August. The note which Joffre dispatched at 5.30 p.m. to the army commanders, after agreement with Viviani and doubtless Poincaré, again revealed the French obsession with ensuring that Germany appear the guilty party for reasons of diplomacy and national unity:

For national reasons of a moral nature and for imperious reasons of a diplomatic kind, it is indispensable that the Germans be left with full responsibility for hostilities. Consequently, and until further notice, covering troops will restrict themselves to expelling across the frontier any assault troops without giving chase any further and without encroaching on opposing territory.[145]

On that Sunday, 2 August, attempts were made to reshuffle the cabinet to bring in Briand and Delcassé, possibly in an attempt to weed out the waverers. Though the socialists blocked the move, Poincaré still described their mood as 'excellent'. On the morning of 2 August a meeting of the Socialist party in Paris made known its intention to defend France in the event of war. With the question of national unity firmly on his mind Poincaré noted, 'Excellent attitude of the socialists, even of the revolutionaries and of the CGT'. It seemed, therefore, that it would be unnecessary to take repressive measures to guard against opposition to war breaking out. 'We have not arrested any of the individuals registered in the Carnet B – apart from a few rare exceptions, when the *Préfets* believed themselves confronted with dangerous anarchists.'[146] The decision not to arrest trade-unionists, pacifists, anti-militarists and suspected spies named in the blacklist compiled by the authorities and known as the 'Carnet B', helped rally support to the cause of national defence as the impending struggle came increasingly to be presented by the press and the government as a case of *la patrie en danger*, the great rallying cry of the Republic since the Revolution.[147] The government was helped in this by Germany's invasion of Luxemburg that same day and reports of German violations of the French border. The German declaration of war against Russia on 1 August confirmed her guilt in Poincaré's eyes: 'Thus Germany assumes full responsibility for a horrific war'.[148]

The conditions for a *ralliement* of the whole of France were now fulfilled. This was apparent following news from London on 2 August that the British Labour party was about to organise a public demonstration against British participation in a conflict. Viviani was immediately able to get the influential socialist Marcel Sembat to write to Ramsay Macdonald, the Labour party leader, to ask for the party's support in favour of British intervention.[149]

But the need for calm, dignity and patience was still a priority in Poincaré's mind as the French dutifully awaited the British decision. This explains Poincaré's distress at the anti-German demonstrations which were breaking out in Paris, and which targeted supposedly German-owned companies such as Maggi, in reality a Swiss food manufacturer. In other large towns, most German-sounding individuals who were accosted turned out to be Poles, or Alsace–Lorrainers. Poincaré was appalled:

Yesterday Paris gave a sad spectacle which contrasts with the sang-froid of these last days and with the sang-froid of the whole of France. There were many incidents of pillaging of shops. The dairies of the Maggi company were widely plundered; it is true that the cause of this violence is competition between this company and small milk suppliers. But, added to this, German and Austrian shops were looted; and the police stood passively by these scenes of disorder: officers even watched them with a certain complicity. I instructed Malvy [minister of the interior] to ask Hennion [prefect of police] to be merciless and to maintain public order at all cost. The fomenters will appear before a war tribunal.[150]

The calm, order and unity which Poincaré had worked for nationally needed to be reflected in the cabinet. The minister of the Navy, Gauthier, had shown incompetence, even negligence, and was replaced on 3 August on 'health grounds'. Viviani was a unifying figure for the Left in parliament, but gave the impression of not understanding foreign affairs. It was the confused Viviani who, in Poincaré's words, was 'extraordinarily ignorant of foreign affairs' and who 'was not able, even once, when reading a telegram from Vienna to speak of the Ballhausplatz without saying the Boliplatz or the Baloplatz'. Given his continuing neurasthenic state, on 3 August he was at last persuaded to relinquish the foreign affairs portfolio in favour of Gaston Doumergue, much to the relief of senior diplomats at the Quai d'Orsay and of Poincaré in particular.[151]

Other measures designed to seal national unity had been taken in cabinet on the afternoon of 2 August. These bear Poincaré's imprint: suspension of the recent decree ordering the closure of various religious establishments and an amnesty for revolutionaries condemned for violation of the press laws. Poincaré noted, 'No; there are no more parties'. He was particularly gratified by a letter from Prince Roland Bonaparte, one of the Pretenders to the French throne, offering to serve the government of the Republic. Though such service was forbidden by the law of 1886, the prince was allowed to place his home at the country's disposal for use as a hospital.[152] This seemed to symbolise to Poincaré the degree of national unity which had been achieved in those few days since his return to France. A few days later he would suggest to cabinet, without success, that the law of 1886 be repealed following further similar offers from other Pretenders and their relatives.[153]

What is extraordinary about these days preceding the German declaration of war against France is the extent to which Poincaré was managing events. And he had every opportunity to do so. Cabinet meetings, which the president of the Republic chaired, were now taking place several times a day, on his orders. This was one constitutional prerogative which he used to the full. Although there was no such thing as cabinet minutes, it is apparent that Poincaré was trying to keep the cabinet in almost permanent session and that the president was making decisions on questions of minor importance which in the British system were taken by individual ministers. Since Poincaré's return to France, the decision-making process gave the distinct impression of being one long conseil des ministres. Despite what he recorded in his published memoirs and his book on how war came about, which expressly state that his constitutional role precluded him from taking a lead in decision-making, Poincaré's unpublished diaries give a quite different picture. However, those diaries show no evidence whatsoever for the idea that Poincaré either wanted, or was instrumental in bringing about, war. On the contrary, many of the decisions he took or initiated have since been wrongly attributed to people such as Viviani, whose peaceful image was never tarnished. Poincaré never sought to correct that impression because it might lay him open to the charge of overstepping his constitutional position, to which he was acutely sensitive. Such a charge in the hands of his worst critics after the war, including the Germans, was more than likely to be used to implicate him eventually in the war guilt debate. But his diaries do show him attempting to square the circle between bringing to bear on events his considerable organisational skills and sense of perspective, and a lawyer's respect for the constitution.[154]

It now looked as though the first condition for a French decision for war had been met: national unity. The second was still in doubt: Britain's participation alongside France. All France's efforts were now channelled in that direction.

On Sunday 2 August Poincaré had signed the proclamation of a state of emergency. The constitution demanded that parliament be recalled from recess within forty-eight hours. Once again the extent to which French policy remained conditioned by Britain's actions was demonstrated by the French cabinet's decision to delay calling parliament until Tuesday 4 August precisely because it was hoped that by then there would be a British reply. On the Sunday evening the British cabinet learned of the German invasion of Luxemburg and, the following morning, of the German ultimatum demanding free passage through Belgium. The importance of Belgian neutrality to Britain was something Poincaré well understood. In 1912 he had turned down Joffre's request to develop an offensive strategy based on a French violation of that neutrality as a means of countering a German strike before it reached France. Now he reflected on the value of that decision and how its benefits should not be squandered:

We are expecting, of course, a German attack through Belgium, as our High Command has always predicted. We have constantly recommended to General Joffre not to permit any crossing of the Belgian frontier nor over-flying of Belgium until further notice. On that depends the support of England and the attitude of Belgium. When King Albert came to Paris, he promised that Belgium would defend herself against Germany. Let us do nothing which could discourage that good will.[155]

King Albert and the Belgian government rejected the German demand on the morning of 4 August. As yet the French had heard nothing from the German ambassador in Paris. Poincaré remained cynical about his activities in Paris: 'He ostentatiously goes to dine at the Palais d'Orsay and appears to be seeking to be insulted so as to provoke an incident'. But at 6.30 p.m. on 3 August, on the false pretext that French aeroplanes had bombed Nuremberg – which Poincaré described as 'an audacious invention' – Germany declared war on France. Again, serious precautions were taken to see that the German ambassador was not the subject of demonstrations: 'all measures have been taken to ensure that he is not insulted by the crowd. For the last two days we have dreaded demonstrations against him and his embassy.' At the cabinet meeting that evening the whole of Poincaré's strategy since his return to France, and thus the strategy of the government, appeared vindicated:

It was for all the members of the cabinet a real relief. Never before had a declaration of war been welcomed with such satisfaction. France having done all that was incumbent upon her to maintain peace and war having never the less become inevitable, it was a hundred times better that we should not have been led, even by repeated violations of our frontiers, to declare it ourselves. It was indispensable that Germany, who was entirely responsible for the aggression, should be led into publicly confessing her intentions. If we had had to declare war ourselves, the Russian alliance would have been contested, national unanimity would have been smashed, it would probably have meant Italy would have been forced by the clauses of the Triple Alliance to side against us ...[156]

Naturally, such words, innocent as they were, never saw the light of day in the published version of his memoirs. Taken out of context they could have been used with explosive impact by Poincaré's adversaries.

Poincaré's obsession with national unity was also reflected in the sympathy he felt for Sir Edward Grey's attempts to maintain the British cabinet's unity and carry public opinion. Whereas Viviani continued to fluctuate between blind optimism and telling journalists that England was betraying France, Poincaré more than anyone understood Grey's predicament: 'Grey is evidently having some difficulty in obtaining the unanimity of the cabinet for energetic resolutions. Burns, Morley, Harcourt, are creating difficulties for him; but his tenacity will overcome their resistance.' This probably explains why the previous day the president's own tenacity had been in evidence when he had announced to the conseil des ministres that he would expect the resignation of any ministers unable to maintain secrecy, clearly in the hope of silencing any internal opposition and thus avoiding Grey's problems. The way he spoke about the British question to the new foreign minister showed his calm and how he was now seeking to extend his influence over Doumergue: 'I demonstrate to him that England always proceeds step by step and promises, in general, less than she gives'.[157] An hour after writing those words Poincaré learnt that on the afternoon of Monday 3 August Grey had spoken in the Commons in favour of British intervention on the side of France.

If British actions had been of the utmost importance in determining Poincaré's moves, and thus those of France, Grey's thinking and method of proceeding continued to have a considerable influence on him. Both men were sharply focussed on the necessity of preserving and maintaining the unity of their respective nations, so essential to success. Poincaré described Grey's speech to the Commons on Monday 3 August as 'of supreme skill'. 'English public opinion, quietly led by Grey to where he wished to take it, is now completely in favour of France.' It was not only that Grey had carried British opinion in favour of supporting France, but also Grey's ability to unite the House of Commons, and through it the nation, which most impressed Poincaré. Grey's speech provided the model for Poincaré's own famous message to the French parliament on 4 August. He had already written and read a first draft to the conseil on 2 August. But that first draft contained a passage which other ministers rightly believed could have been mis-construed:

I had spoken of the [illegible] of things and added that at last we could release the cry, until now smothered in our breasts: Vive l'Alsace–Lorraine. Thomson and Augagneur rightly pointed out to me that it would be better, *vis-à-vis* foreign countries and even *vis-à-vis* part of French public opinion, to say nothing which could detract from the strictly defensive nature of the war. I bowed to their observations.[158]

The reference to Alsace and Lorraine was excluded and the speech was redrafted in the light of Grey's performance in the Commons.

Poincaré's famous *union sacrée* speech was never in fact spoken by him. Constitutionally the president of the Republic had no right to address the Chambers directly. Thus at three o'clock on the afternoon of 4 August the presidential message was read by the minister of justice to the Senate and by the prime minister to the Chamber of Deputies. It encapsulated all that Poincaré believed he had worked for since 1912. It emphasised the peacefulness of France for the last forty years, even since the Austrian ultimatum; he placed the blame for war squarely on the German Empire, which would have to bear, 'before History, overwhelming responsibility'. Describing the president of the Republic as 'the interpreter of unanimity', the speech stressed the unity of the nation and its 'sang-froid since the beginning of the crisis'. Supported by Russia and Britain, and with the sympathy of the civilised world, it noted that France once more represented liberty, justice and reason and would have on her side right and moral strength. His speech ended by emphasising that elusive quality which throughout his political life he, and others, had worked to instil in the nation: unity. The most famous phrase declared, 'She will be heroically defended by all her sons, whose sacred union will never be shattered in the face of the enemy' (dont rien ne brisera devant l'ennemi l'union sacrée). Most rewarding to him was that his strategy for managing the crisis had paid off and unity had been achieved: 'In the Chamber, the reception was enthusiastic and absolutely unanimous. The socialists were as ardent as the others. The ministers returned to the Elysée, totally moved by this grandiose occasion. In the Senate, the same unanimity and the same patriotic fervour.'[159] For someone of Poincaré's thirst for public acclamation this was a moment of triumph and a vindication of his policies since 1912.

On the morning of 4 August 1914, treating their guarantee of Belgian neutrality enshrined in the 1839 treaty as a 'scrap of paper', German troops crossed into Belgium. A British ultimatum demanding their withdrawal was disregarded and as Big Ben struck midnight Britain became France's ally in the war with Germany.

For the third time in a century France was faced with a German invasion. But, unlike 1814 and 1870, she was not alone. The country which had annexed Alsace and Lorraine and had appeared to threaten France in 1875, 1887, 1905 and 1911 was perceived once more as the aggressor. The *union sacrée* was not, however, the result of a nationalist revival since 1905 with Germany as the focal point. Most Frenchmen did not believe that war was inevitable, nor did they want it. Opposition to the war was much greater than has often been thought, whether in

France or elsewhere, until about a week before it broke out. However, the opposition had been divided on tactics for thwarting it, whether in the trades unions – federated in the CGT – or the Socialist Party. At its general congress from 14 to 16 July, half of the party had supported the idea of a general strike against war with reservations, the other half had opposed it. The CGT should have been the motor of opposition because its stance against war had seemed unambiguous. In the end, even its comité confédéral abandoned the idea of a general strike and was converted to the patriotic cause in the final hour, like the British Trades Union Congress. Like Poincaré, French decision makers understood the latent dangers in the domestic scene. Hence their desire first and foremost to unite the country. The mystery and rapidity of international events, as well as the disconcerting assassination of Jaurès, skilfully defused by the government, confused people into last-minute patriotism and support for the war. The idea that they were fighting a just war for values common to most Frenchmen, indeed to most civilised nations, prevented what had always been Poincaré's great fear, a divided France. This is what had inspired Poincaré's every move since his return to French soil and which he later summarised:

I have always believed, of course, that the French did not want to declare war for Serbia. I even believed that France would not rise up united to keep the promises of the alliance with Russia and that, if we had been led into declaring war, the country would be cruelly divided. But I had never had doubts about France in the event of her being attacked, even if it was over Serbia.[160]

The success of this policy was reflected more objectively by the Bavarian minister in Paris, who on 4 August, before leaving French soil, wrote to the king: 'I had until the last moment the impression that the French government wanted to avoid war at any cost.'[161]

The army General Staff had expected that up to 10 per cent of French conscripts might disobey the mobilisation order. In the event, the national average was only 1.5 per cent,[162] a remarkable achievement given the state of anti-militarism and the opposition to war which had characterised the French labour movement and its political representatives as late as the third week of July. Though Poincaré could not have known it at the time, the *union sacrée* was merely a political truce for the duration of hostilities in order to win the war. In reality there was no abandoning of convictions on either side. The war was all things to all men: the Left were fighting in defence of the rights of man and democracy; the Right to defend its own conception of France. Of course the *union sacrée* was the more solid for having been conceived at a time when most of Europe believed this would be a short war, which would be over by Christmas at the latest. Thus the *union sacrée* was not a myth created by Poincaré or the government, nor was it the climax of nationalist feeling. Nationalism was not in evidence after mobilisation was decreed, *revanche* was hardly evoked, Alsace-Lorraine even less. Once war began it was another matter. Indeed it would have been unthinkable for the French, more so their political leaders, not to have as a war aim the return of the 'lost provinces'. At last, in memory of Gambetta's old dictum, the French could both think of Alsace–Lorraine and speak of its recovery, as Poincaré had shown in drafting his message to parliament.[163]

France entered the war united behind the man who had been her effective leader from January 1912. Poincaré's diplomatic efforts to strengthen the bonds of the Triple Entente in order to protect against future German aggression, and his efforts to maintain national unity, survived the final test of fire. During the July crisis Poincaré remained the principal decision maker. However, because of his isolation from events during the trip to Russia, he, more than any other European statesman, was reacting to events rather than controlling them. A major preoccupation remained Russia. Speculation has always surrounded his three-day visit to Russia and whether he encouraged her into intransigence. At the time the Austrian ultimatum had not been delivered. The Serbian crisis was discussed, as one would expect between major allies. But it seems unlikely that, though Poincaré might have encouraged firmness, he should have made any clear commitment to Russia, come what may. The Russian military did not think so; they were still uncertain of French support. Five days after the visit, the Russian military attaché in Paris even asked General Joffre whether, according to the Franco-Russian agreement, in the event of Germany mobilising part of her forces against Russia, France would mobilise. Pierre Renouvin has seen this as proof that Poincaré in his talks in St Petersburg did not go any further than a simple statement of fidelity to the alliance.[164]

When looked at against the general thrust of Poincaré's policy towards Russia since 1912, unconditional support for her would have been an illogicality. For two and a half years he had perfected a balancing act in his dealings with Russia which he has well summarised:

not to break up an alliance on which French policy has been based for a quarter of a century and the break-up of which would leave us in isolation at the mercy of our rivals; and never the less to do what lay in our power to induce our ally to exercise moderation in matters in which we are much less directly concerned than herself.[165]

This was all part of a foreign policy predicated on the belief that peace was best safeguarded by a policy of deterrence inherent in the balance of power which lay at the heart of the rigid separation of the two alliance systems. Poincaré conceived of no alternative international order. In the wake of war such views would be criticised. In retrospect, the rigidity with which he applied the notion of the strict separation of the two alliance systems inevitably built into it the inflexibility which was its greatest failing in times of crisis. In this way, Poincaré's foreign policy could be seen as contributing to further crystallisation of the two blocs. Thus, in the words of a leading revisionist historian, whereas in 1907 Triple Alliance and Triple Entente 'had stood side by side; in 1914 they stood face to face'.[166]

A last comment on Poincaré's position in the war guilt debate might be the way in which commentators and historians have treated him in particular. It seems clear that during the July crisis he was the principal decision maker. Viviani was considered by a number of professional diplomats to be a liability; he had never really wanted to take on foreign affairs in the first place and was not unhappy to relinquish them on 3 August. His forte was domestic politics, and he seemed quite happy to follow the cool, methodical, experienced Poincaré, even to the point of signing dispatches and documents drafted by the president. Yet historians such as Luigi Albertini and Jules Isaac praise Viviani's consistency, correctness and moderating influence on Russia, while attributing to Poincaré the worst motives when, more often than not, he was the instigator of that policy.[167]

However, the principal fact about 1914 was that Poincaré, like Sir Edward Grey, was finally constrained by events into taking his country into war – a defensive war. His freedom to choose a different course of action was severely limited. Failure to honour the Franco-Russian alliance would have condemned Russia to certain defeat, thus ever more gravely jeopardising France's security. Even if the final decision had not been made for her by Germany's declaration of war on France, she would have felt compelled to fight alongside Russia. In the end France, like Britain, entered the war for negative reasons – because not to have done so would have been a threat to her national security in the short and long term. Thus just as Britain's decision for war was not solely to uphold the 1839 treaty of guarantee of Belgian neutrality, but because she feared the consequences of German domination of the continent, so France did not go to war simply to honour the Franco-Russian alliance, but because she was not willing to live again in the shadow of an all-powerful Germany. These strategic reasons apart, both Grey and Poincaré believed that they were fighting a just war against German aggression; but whereas Grey made plain his hatred of war, his fear of it, and was for many reasons ill-suited to deal with it,[168] Poincaré, because he acted with firmness, resolve and confidence, gave the impression that he accepted it without regret. This was not true. On 3 August he reflected deeply on the toll in human lives war would bring.[169] But Poincaré was a victim of his own success. In peacetime he had prepared relentlessly for any eventuality and had worked for national unity. War was now a reality, the nation was united, determined to fight and supported by strong allies. The crisis had been well managed. Critics and historians would not forgive a Lorrainer this coincidence.

Raymond Poincaré remained president of the Republic for the duration of the war. It is with the war that his name is the most closely associated: in a positive way, for his establishment of *union sacrée*, for his unbending commitment to its pursuit and for his careful management of the war effort; in a negative way as the subject of what would become a powerful myth in the post-war period – 'Poincaré-la-guerre'. According to that myth, Poincaré actively sought war before 1914 in order to regain the lost provinces of Alsace–Lorraine. The idea gained currency at the end of the war as part of the 'war guilt' debate surrounding the war's origins and was then applied retrospectively to interpretations of Poincaré's and, by extension, France's responsibility in the outbreak of the war. Such teleology – already demonstrated in Poincaré's supposed pre-war Germanophobe policies and the supposed left-wing opposition to his foreign policy – was in part motivated by international politics and Germany's determination to shift more of the blame onto France, and in part by French domestic politics and the Left's desire in the post-war years to discredit Poincaré in the hope of thwarting his return to power. To get a clearer picture of Poincaré during the war years and subsequently, it is necessary to understand the nature of the Poincaré-la-guerre myth and its genesis.

The Poincaré-la-guerre myth

The Versailles Peace Treaty took the unprecedented step of including an article, 231, which lay sole responsibility for the outbreak of the war with Germany – the so-called 'war guilt clause'. This clause, first proposed by the French, became the justification for the massive war reparations Germany was to pay in the post-war period, principally to France. It followed that if Germany could show that she was not solely to blame for the war she could challenge the validity of article 231 and with it the payment of the reparations. This she set out to do.

The other great power with an acute interest in the war guilt debate was the new Soviet regime. For ideological reasons she wished to heap discredit on her tsarist predecessor in order to increase her own legitimacy and popularity both internally and externally. If she could show that the tsarist regime in collaboration with the 'bourgeois' Poincaré were together responsible through the Franco-Russian alliance for the outbreak of the Great War, she could kill two birds with one stone: discredit tsarist Russia and partly justify not repaying to France the massive pre-war loans.

The stakes in the *kriegsschuldfrage* were extremely high. France made a most credible scapegoat on to whom the blame could be shifted given the loss of the provinces of Alsace–Lorraine to Germany in 1871 and the fact that France's effective leader in the two years preceding the war had followed resolute policies intent on strengthening France's links with her allies, especially Russia, and was a Lorrainer to boot. It was suggested that Poincaré had plotted a war of *revanche* against Germany. The war guilt debate became all the more impassioned for the fact that in the post-war period Poincaré was still in power and pursuing a strict application of the Versailles Treaty and the payment of reparations. Germany began a campaign to promote such views. A special office was created in the German foreign office to deal with this issue – the War Guilt Section. It organised, financed and directed two other units: the Working Committee of German Associations for Combating Lies concerning War Responsibility which provided the 'right' literature and information to organisations such as trade unions and various clubs; its stable-mate was the Centre for the Study of the Causes of the War, created in 1921 and which from 1923 published the influential monthly journal *Die Kriegsschuldfrage*, edited by the historian Alfred von Wegerer. This is where the 'serious' historical work was done to demonstrate the inaccuracy of article 231 by 'sponsoring' journalists, editors, publicists and academics in the 'cause of patriotic self-censorship'. The work of these units provided much of the impetus for the 'revisionist school', which in the 1920s dominated historical writing on war origins from Europe to the USA, successfully displacing much of the blame from Germany.[1]

What was lifted from Germany's shoulders now fell more heavily on France and, in particular, Poincaré's shoulders. Attempts to smear Poincaré's pristine image had a long pedigree dating back to his candidature for the presidency in December 1912, as has been shown. Emanating from the Left and the Radicals in particular, such rumours were intended for domestic political reasons to undermine his popularity and eventually his capacity to hold political office. Centred largely on the marital past of his wife, they met with moderate success in the pre-war years. But barely a month after the outbreak of war rumours began to circulate about Poincaré being responsible for the conflict. Some were said to be encouraged by his political opponents, despite the political truce of the *union sacrée*. There is strong evidence to show that these rumours were financed by Germany, either by 'subsidies' to the French press, whose venality was well known when it came to foreign monies, or through chosen individuals. German documents captured by the allies in 1945 from the German foreign ministry and published in 1962 and 1966 show the degree of subversion of foreign powers developed by Germany intended to foment troubles within enemy borders in order to force separate peace agreements.[2] That activity focussed not on revolutionary groups but established figures, whom it was calculated might be able to reverse official government policies. In France the link-man was Poincaré's long-standing critic, Ernest Judet, editor of the influential Paris daily *L'Eclair*, later accused of receiving money from Germany and tried in 1920 for consorting with the enemy.[3] He had been contacted as early as Autumn 1913 by individuals from the German legation in Berne, the hub of German international propaganda; so too had the unscrupulous financier, Paul Bolo, whose intention was to return Caillaux to power. German documents reveal that by the time of the outbreak of hostilities a number of Radical deputies such as René Besnard, a minister in Poincaré's 1912 cabinet and again during the war (eventually ambassador to Rome in 1924), Paul Meunier and Léon Turmel (arrested in October 1917)[4] were in contact with the head of the German legation in Berne, Romberg. With German support these politicians sought to establish, through Masonic lodges and parliamentary contacts, a network dedicated to undermining the Anglo-French alliance, deemed responsible for the outbreak of the war.

Poincaré was a focus of the attacks. Their impact was partly in evidence from the menacing and insulting letters in the presidential post-bag blaming him for the war, and partly from the Poincaré-la-guerre rumours whose eponymous subject was seriously worried by their effect and noted them in his secret diaries from September 1914 to December 1915. On 13 September 1914 a left-wing *député* criticised him for allowing war to come when France was not ready, to which he retorted in his diary, 'As if I hadn't done the impossible to maintain peace!'[5] On 23 October Viviani read to the cabinet a telegram, apparently based on a secret service report, that Germans in Barcelona were preparing to assassinate Poincaré.[6] On 18 December he was informed that Deschanel had said that Poincaré was personally responsible for the war, while in the Senate Milliès-Lacroix had made a similar remark.[7] On 15 January 1915 Poincaré showed his indignation at similar remarks by Deschanel and Leygues, noting, 'Not one of these two slanderous idiots has seen his [illegible] profaned, his house destroyed, his country devastated. And it is I who is supposed to have allowed such disasters to strike down my country ... ' By 27 January he was receiving threatening letters: 'They seem inspired by German agents.' Clandestine publications blamed him for the outbreak of war and he attributed them to a campaign inspired by the enemy: 'but it does not pass without causing insult; and sometimes a stray bullet'. His wife informed him that on the trams and in the metro she had often heard people saying, 'After the war we will demolish Poincaré, we have had enough of him, we'll dump him, we'll blow him up.' On 5 March he was told of an 'energetic and absurd' campaign against him. In July there was talk in the corridors of the Chamber that war could have been avoided and that the men in power in 1914 'will leave in history names as detested as those of Emile Ollivier and de Gramont', to which Poincaré noted in the margin of his diary, 'Thus having done everything to avoid war, having sacrificed one's leisure, one's tastes [?], one's happiness for one's country ... And to be so idiotically accused.'[8] On 10 September his hairdresser told him of the feeling among the southern population that he was responsible for war, to which he retorted: 'Clearly there is a German campaign, encouraged by the intrigues of Deschanel and the political opposition, and which eventually hits the target.' Five days later he was warned of possible threats on his life, and that the pacifists were blaming him for war.[9] On 13 December he heard rumours that his desire to continue the war was leading the Germans and socialists to wish to get him out of power, while the next day he learnt that the radical–socialists were blaming him for the war. Two weeks later it was the turn of a delegate at the socialist congress who claimed that Poincaré had encouraged the Tsar to be 'firm' during his visit to Russia in 1914 and that consequently he was partly responsible for war.[10]

Of course, such rumours were partly the result of the frustration which French politicians and the population were beginning to feel at the course of the war which, far from being over by Christmas 1914, had become static trench warfare with massive casualties and no end in sight. In many ways Poincaré was becoming the focus for that frustration: from the Left which wanted to see its men in power; from the Right which wanted the president of the Republic to assume greater executive control and diminish the power of the Chamber; and generally in the country at large where there was also a belief that the president was, and should be, all-powerful and thus more active in saving the country. Criticism of him was made public through stinging articles such as that by his long-standing adversary, Clemenceau, which criticised premier

Briand, the High Command and Poincaré for the present military strategy. All of this was fertile ground on which the Poincaré-la-guerre myth could germinate.

Rumours of Poincaré's responsibility in the origins of the war assumed a more tangible form by 1916 when doubts as to Germany's total blame were expressed in the French pacifist organisation, Société d'études documentaires et critiques de la guerre. Its aim was to unite the diverse internationalist and pacifist forces springing up and to encourage and prepare for a negotiated peace. It brought together a broad group of individuals including the liberal economist Charles Gide, whose work Poincaré had long admired. Other members were Mathias Morhardt and Victor Basch from the Ligue des Droits de l'Homme, trade unionists such as Merrheim and Rosmer, the pacifist Jacques Mesnil and, for a short time, the historian Charles Seignobos. The secretary of the movement was the philosopher Alexandre. Perhaps more revealingly, another important member was the radical–socialist *député* Alphonse Accambray who, according to German documents, was in the pay of the Germans and working to undermine the French war effort, as is shown below. Poincaré was the target of much of their work. He was even more the subject of bitter attacks from the anarchists, in particular Lecoin, and the pacifists such as Brizon, who unreservedly laid the blame for the war at Poincaré's feet. By the time of the mutinies in 1917, despite censorship, the press was using the term 'Poincaré-la-guerre'. Meanwhile, a socialist organisation entitled Comité pour la reprise des relations internationales also insisted that the Franco-Russian alliance was responsible for the war and that France had capitulated to Russian interests.[11]

This was the context for the Poincaré-la-guerre myth. But then one would expect Poincaré to blame Germany for rumours which he found unpalatable. Nevertheless, there is strong evidence to show that Germany was actively nurturing such rumours and beliefs. German documents reveal that at this time Germany had as co-ordinator for the French campaign against the Anglo-French alliance a certain 'Herr 32', who was none other than the radical–socialist *député* Léon Accambray. He had set about rallying opposition through Masonic lodges and parliamentary contacts.[12] His interventions in the Chamber show him to have been extremely critical of the military command from 1915 to 1917 and later of Poincaré's foreign policy in 1922 and his financial policy in 1926.[13] In 1916, during the Battle of Verdun, contacts were established with important individuals who received funds from Germany to finance their campaign in France. Premier Briand noted in cabinet in September 1916 that 'piles of money are put at the disposal of pacifists by

Germany'.[14] In 1917, during the strikes and mutinies, the German government did not turn to the revolutionaries to demoralise France further, but to 'Herr 32' who encouraged a pacifist campaign in favour of a separate peace between France and Germany in exchange for German renunciation of Alsace and Lorraine.

'Herr 32' seems to have been the key to a vast strategy devised by the German chancellor, Bethmann Hollweg, to get France out of the war. In 1917 Bethmann was convinced that a number of important French individuals were in favour, one way or the other, of ending the struggle.[15] Poincaré was seen as the principal obstacle to this, and thus the man to target in a campaign to discredit him by stressing his responsibility in the origins of the war. As has been shown, in the pre-war period there had been no suggestion that Poincaré's foreign policy was in the least bellicose. On the contrary, it had been praised on the socialist Left. Criticism of Poincaré had centred solely on issues of domestic policy, such as the adoption of proportional representation or his reluctance to introduce an income tax. Indeed, during the July crisis Poincaré's role was viewed by the socialists and their leader Jaurès, in particular, as pacific and defensive, which was a major reason why the French entered the war united in the *union sacrée*. It was only in retrospect that the Left would reinterpret the pre-war period to give the impression that they had always opposed his foreign policy as bellicose.

The desire to discredit Poincaré by tarring him with responsibility for the war was also motivated by French domestic concerns in the post-war years when the Left wished to thwart or destabilise his return to power which, notwithstanding this opposition, took place from 1922 to 1924 and from 1926 to 1929. By then Poincaré was perceived by certain elements of the Left as being of the centre-right. Though the Radicals would broadly support his firm line against Germany over reparations and vote for it in parliament, they were not averse to exploiting the 'Poincaré-la-guerre' myth when politically expedient, like during the 1924 general election campaign. The far Left, especially the communists, were, on the other hand, unswervingly critical of his policy and already in favour of resuming the pre-war policy of seeking improved relations with Germany as the solution to what was becoming the German 'question'. In the 1920s, all Poincaré's political opponents were able to draw on the potent myth of 'Poincaré-la-guerre' to defeat him, and did so quite unscrupulously.

The myth was fuelled in the post-war period by a mixture of revisionist literature and polemical pamphleteering. It developed in an international intellectual and moral climate which, as a result of the horrors and carnage of the war, tended towards pacifism and anti-militarism and looked to the newly formed League of Nations for the settlement of international disputes. In 1920 the militant socialist Gouttenoire de Toury's pamphlet entitled *Poincaré a-t-il voulu la guerre?* was published by the communist Éditions Clarté accusing Poincaré of having been in the pocket of the warmongering pre-war Russian ambassador in Paris, Isvolsky.[16] In similar vein, in 1921 an open letter by Mathias Morhardt to the Ligue des Droits de l'Homme entitled 'Les origines de la guerre' blamed Poincaré for placing pre-war France in Russian hands. In 1924 Morhardt published a book, *Les preuves,* which purported to demonstrate Poincaré's responsibility in the origins of the war. Written at the time of the French occupation of the Ruhr, it attempted to demonstrate the continuity of Poincaré's anti-German policies which were described as 'narrow, full of violence and hatred'. In the same year the former diplomat and prolific writer, Alfred Fabre-Luce, published *La victoire* which laid the guilt at the door of the Triple Entente and in particular the Franco-Russian alliance and Poincaré. Similar works appeared in 1926 when novelist Victor Margueritte produced *Les criminels* alongside Georges Demartial's *L'évangile du Quai d'Orsay.* Poincaré was the object of these attacks which continued into the early 1930s with, for instance, René Gérin's *Comment fut provoquée la guerre de 1914?* and Félicien Challaye's direct incrimination of Poincaré for preparing a war of *revanche,* which appeared in 1933 as *Les origines de la guerre mondiale. Les responsabilités russes et françaises.* Like the numerous pamphlets by Gustave Dupin on Poincaré's responsibility, such as his *M. Poincaré et la guerre de 1914. (Etude sur les responsabilités)* published in 1931, the titles were an accurate guide to their absence of impartiality. They were almost always polemical works by journalists, largely inspired by the Left, extreme Left, pacifist organisations or agents of German propaganda. They were often given credence by their proximity to a Marxist interpretation – of particular credibility given the sympathy for the Soviet Union, notably on the part of the newly formed French Communist party – of the causes of the war in which the representative of the bourgeoisie and big business, Poincaré, had pressed for war to further their class interests. Furthermore, these views received very wide circulation. The only credible counter to them was the research by Pierre Renouvin, notably his *Les origines immédiates de la guerre* of 1925. But this kind of serious scholarly study was more suited to the academic community than the more sensational world of the press where the 'revisionist' line prevailed. At least Renouvin's work prompted Poincaré in 1928 to commission him to publish the series of French diplomatic documents on the origins of the war. This was intended to counter the biased forty-volume German collection, *Die Grosse Politik,* whose publication from 1922 to 1927 gave Berlin the dual advantage of portraying the German government as wishing to hide nothing, while being the only extensive official collection of documents on which scholars could work. Even so, the delay in publishing the French documents, which eventually appeared between 1929 and 1958, with the important volume on 1914 not appearing until 1936, was partly to blame for the inability to correct what had become an incipient orthodoxy resulting from nearly two decades of rumour and revisionist literature.[17] The publication of the *Documents diplomatiques français* certainly had little effect in balancing the picture during Poincaré's lifetime. Much of the mud had stuck and the popular pre-war figure's image was severely tarnished in the eyes of many by the time of his death in 1934. Indeed, it is noteworthy that following his death most of the polemical works attributing direct responsibility to him stopped as the possibility of him returning to power disappeared. Little matter that the question of war responsibility had been so closely linked to French domestic politics, in the collective memory of many French people Poincaré was now perceived as the right-wing, middle-class, Germano-phobe warmonger from Lorraine who had taken France into war. Such views were reinforced abroad by historians who proceeded with greater subtlety and erudition to implicate Poincaré, especially in the United States where H. E. Barnes's *The genesis of the World War* (published in 1926) and Sidney Bradshaw Fay's *The origins of the World War* (published in 1928) set the trend for the international domination of the revisionist interpretation.[18]

Much of this view of Poincaré and France's role continued even after World War Two, despite the fact that that war made many historians look again at German responsibility for its predecessor. The problem was that there was no new proof. It was necessary to wait for the various national archives to be opened to the public. But again Germany appeared to lead the way because of the capture of her archives by the Allies at the end of the war. Then came Britain, followed by France in the early 1970s. Work on these archives has only emerged in published form for France in the 1980s and is already assigning a more passive role to France and to Poincaré in the origins of the Great War. In the most recent historiographical survey of the war origins debate, it is estimated that over 25,000 books and articles have been generated by the controversy; and it would seem that the majority have been influenced by the revisionist thesis of the 1920s and 1930s. Indeed, the same survey suggests that in American classrooms and textbooks even today the origins of the war are those of the classical revisionist position, as though the debates of the last quarter of a century have been reserved for

specialists.[19] This may explain why for nearly three-quarters of a century
the notion of French, and in particular Poincaré's, responsibility in the
origins of the First World War survived in France and abroad.

Maintaining national unity

Poincaré would be dogged by suspicion and rumour associated with the
war for the rest of his political career. For the moment, the war
threatened the very survival of the liberal republican regime. It placed
Poincaré at the junction of fundamental questions many of which had
dogged French politics since the Revolution: the ability of the republican
regime to maintain its unity when confronted with a lengthy war
threatening the nation itself; the distribution of power between civil and
military authority at issue since Napoleon; the balance of power between
executive and legislature and the ability of the republican institutions to
operate quickly and effectively.

At the start of the war Poincaré was at his most popular in incarnating
the *union sacrée*. He appeared the guide and saviour of the French
people, a position he had always coveted; elusive national unity appeared
sealed in France's finest hour in defence of *la patrie* against the
aggression of the authoritarian central powers. Yet the tremendous
moral authority invested in him at the outset of war was also his greatest
weakness; it placed on his shoulders a burden which the constitution did
not allow him to carry effectively. His constitutional position as
president of the Republic had a built-in inability to deliver what the
public and many of his political supporters would demand of him: to
lead and co-ordinate the war effort to the same degree as he had been
perceived as doing in the first few days of August. Apart from bathing in,
at most, a month of public manifestations of *union sacrée*, including his
own with Clemenceau, his popularity suffered progressively from his
constitutional inability to act.

Somewhat surprisingly for a nation with a predilection for constitutional legislation, no particular organisation of government had been
foreseen in the event of war other than the emergency powers common
to most states. On 2 August a state of emergency was declared. On the
4th the Chamber voted without discussion a number of bills for rigorous
diplomatic, military and political censorship, war credits, an increase in
the Bank of France's right to print bills, allowances for mobilised
families, a moratorium on payments. On 3 September Poincaré signed
the decree closing the emergency session of parliament. For nearly four
months the executive was able to govern as a quasi-dictatorship.[20] In the
short term this benefited Poincaré, who assumed full control of events.

Cabinet or war cabinet meetings, both of which he chaired, took place every day.[21] On 5 August he noted, 'Viviani, Doumergue, Malvy, Messimy, Augagneur, are almost permanently at the Elysée'. Thus the prime minister, the foreign, interior, war and navy ministers were in constant contact with him and likely to come under the sway of his arguments and encyclopaedic knowledge of the detail of policy. Thus Poincaré made clear on 5 August that the principal war aim must be the recovery of Alsace and Lorraine. When Russia proposed seducing neutral Italy to the allied side by offering her Trentina and Vallona, Poincaré called on Viviani, now the first *président du conseil* under the Third Republic without a portfolio, and Doumergue, foreign minister since 3 August, to make clear to Russia 'that we will first have our national claims staked, that is to say Alsace–Lorraine'. What followed was an example of Poincaré's method of overcoming his theoretical constitutional powerlessness: 'I have some trouble convincing Doumergue, who is seduced by the idea of first detaching Italy. He ends up coming round to my opinion.'[22] The next day a similar incident of even greater importance demonstrated Poincaré's domination of events.

I am warned, in Viviani and Doumergue's presence, that the United States' ambassador wants to see me. 'That must be', I say, 'for an offer of mediation'. Viviani's face lights up. 'It would be', I add immediately, 'the greatest misfortune which could befall us, if mediation were to be accepted today by Germany. Doubtless the immediate war would not take place; but, as we are not victorious, the peace would not be in our favour, Germany would remain as powerful and we would be exposed, before long, to new threats'. Doumergue backs me up, and also Augagneur, and even Malvy. Messimy energetically supports me. In short, it is agreed that, if it is an offer of mediation which is brought to me, I shall reply:
1 that not being the aggressors, we cannot accept mediation;
2 that we cannot ever do anything other than with the agreement of Russia and England;
3 that there can be no question of mediation after the invasion of a neutral territory.
Herrick brings me his little piece of paper, which is not a firm proposal, but a platonic declaration, and he tells me himself that he thinks, for the present moment, all mediation impossible.[23]

The other reason for refusing mediation, which Poincaré omitted to mention to the American ambassador, was the return of Alsace and Lorraine, because of the wrong impression that might convey to a neutral foreign power. This had not been the reason for going to war, but now that war had been declared on France he was determined that the opportunity be seized to reunite the 'lost provinces' under the French flag.[24] The episode also demonstrated Poincaré's initial optimism for victory. The former minister, Etienne Clémentel of the Gauche radicale, was certainly impressed with Poincaré's management of events and general demeanour when he saw him on 6 August: 'He is still remarkably composed, calm and lucid. He directs our action with the serenity of a man who imagines he is ill.'[25]

Poincaré's general mood of optimism which flowed from the *union sacrée* was enhanced by his reconciliation with Clemenceau on 6 August – a political truce of a similar nature. Following an uncommonly flattering article by Clemenceau on his *union sacrée* speech, Poincaré noted in his diary, 'In the present circumstances, I considered that after this article, I had the duty to call in Clemenceau. He came today. He was less brittle and less inscrutable than a few months ago. We spoke of the war and he became so emotional as to break into tears on pronouncing the word Alsace.'[26] The two met three days later with Poincaré describing Clemenceau as 'more and more friendly'. But the limits of this reconciliation were soon made clear to him: 'Clemenceau told Jean Dupuy that I shouldn't imagine that he was ready to disarm against me. It is a truce, it is not peace. What does it matter?'[27] In a curiously similar way personal relations between the two erstwhile adversaries would mirror the vagaries of national *union sacrée*.

Poincaré's executive control of events also saw its first challenges. 'I must pay this tribute to Doumergue that he never decides anything without referring to me, but he is now very full of himself, usurps, in discussions, the role of *président du conseil* and truly believes himself a great diplomat'. What Poincaré disagreed with in particular was the foreign minister's desire to delay going to war against Austria–Hungary, who was not yet officially at war with France or Britain. Though he agreed that France should not declare war on her, he noted in an argument used in relation to Germany a few days earlier, 'In my opinion, everything must be done to ensure that it is declared on us as soon as possible', as Austria–Hungary represented a military threat to France, notably her fleet.[28] For the moment, Poincaré was also perceived by foreign governments and their envoys as being in control, as the steady references to him in foreign diplomatic correspondence testify.[29]

The optimism of those early days in August 1914 was warranted by French military success. The first French victories were an extremely emotional moment for Poincaré, albeit in private. On the evening of 17 August the colours of a German regiment captured by the tenth Batallion of *chasseurs à pied* from Saint Dié, in his native Lorraine, were brought to the Elysée. 'With Maurice Bernard and Henriette we stared for a long time at this witness of our first victories. I was overcome with a sort of emotion – [illegible]. Do I deserve this favour and this honour? To be at the Elysée, the day we at last take hold of a German flag.'[30] Such emotional patriotism did not, however, destroy his fundamental level-headedness. Following a further visit from Clemenceau to complain that the press was exaggerating the victories and avoiding mentioning defeats, Poincaré was inclined to agree with him, 'but the ministry of war hardly informs me any better than it does the public'.[31]

If Poincaré had had a foretaste of the limits on his constitutional power, he was soon to glimpse the fragility of *union sacrée*. On 2 August the minister of the interior had ordered prefects to suspend measures under the 1901 and 1904 laws against religious congregations as a gesture in favour of national unity. Poincaré fully supported that kind of initiative and was therefore disappointed to see the religious question and party politicking resurface in cabinet: 'For a few days now, several ministers have been moaning about reactionary intrigues; the parochial attitude is awakening in them.' The issue concerned the Red Cross, which Messimy criticised in cabinet for being a clerical organisation, while Viviani threatened to withdraw army chaplains (reinstated for the duration of the war) to punish the Red Cross. Poincaré, who had asked the navy minister to authorise the presence of one chaplain on each battleship, noted in his diary that if Viviani carried out his threat 'the unfortunate soldiers who wished to receive the last rites on the battlefield would be the victims of a fit of pique'.[32] Ignoring such small-minded secularism, on the death of Pope Pius X on 20 August it was Poincaré who pushed the government to secure a French candidate for the papacy,[33] who might not be so hostile as his predecessor to agreements with the French state. The French Catholic Church had itself rallied perfectly to *union sacrée* and was running its own propaganda section under the direction of Mgr Baudrillart[34], Rector of the Institut Catholique, who had officiated at Poincaré's religious marriage just over a year before.

By 22 August France began to experience a number of military set backs as Plan XVII had failed to foresee the magnitude of the German invasion through Belgium. With Lunéville being shelled Poincaré could only bemoan: 'My Lorraine, my Lorraine.' As the enemy's troops advanced across his homeland his thoughts revealed both a heartfelt patriotism and an increasing lament for a waning *union sacrée*:

Where are our hopes of days past? ... Poor Lorraine ... Will this country have the strength to be patient? Salvation is in duration. Will it understand? Will it wish to?

Unfortunately, we are paying the high cost of politics: a relaxing of military discipline, sectarianism overriding the national spirit, humanitarian dreaming.

Today trade unionists, pacifists, almost all see clearly and some like Jouhaux, like Hervé are leading an admirable patriotic campaign. But one cannot restore to a country, in one day, its soul.[35]

This would be the *leitmotiv* of Poincaré's presidency for the war years. And though he exercised to the full his constitutional right to advise and encourage the government and military, his frustration would continue to grow, despite the remarkable energy he employed in trying to 'appease these lamentable differences'. These divisions, political and military, surfaced on 24 August in the war cabinet following the invasion of northern France, the threat to Lille and the evacuation of recaptured Alsace. They turned to virtual defeatism in Poincaré's eyes: 'We are anticipating the eventuality of defeat, the invasion of Paris, the necessity for the government to withdraw to Bordeaux. I protest against this idea.' The military position was desperate: 'It is failure all along the line. Many troops lacked cohesion, the liaison between the armies was bad, subaltern command was mediocre.'[36]

As the military position deteriorated, Poincaré prevailed on a reluctant Viviani to reshuffle his government and broaden its support; it was virtually the same cabinet as had been in place since the Left's victory in June 1914, apart from a minor reshuffle on 3 August to bring in a few radical–socialists. Poincaré did not oppose Viviani's invitation to Clemenceau, who all the same refused, while Briand hesitated. The ensuing confusion saddened Poincaré: 'Who can one have faith in? On whom can one rely? Poor France, "be wary of individuals".'[37] Then there was talk of a Clemenceau cabinet – the Tiger having made it clear that he would only accept the post of *président du conseil*.[38] Poincaré had his doubts on that front, and noted prophetically, 'Clemenceau is certainly on the up with public opinion which believes him to be energetic and which is demanding a firm hand. But, if he were head of the government, he would certainly claim to direct military operations personally and we could be led a merry dance.'[39]

A new government, the second of the seven of the war period, was finally in place by 26 August. It was more in tune with Poincaré's outlook. Viviani stayed as premier while Delcassé became foreign minister. Poincaré's old friend and minister of war in his 1912 cabinet, Millerand, returned to his old post, to which he seemed particularly suited given his closeness to the High Command. Briand came in at justice and Ribot at finance. These were men of the centre who had opposed the Left in the 1914 elections. Nevertheless, no-one came in from the conservative or Catholic Right, much to Poincaré's disappointment, even though for the first time a member of the SFIO joined the government, in the shape of Jules Guesde, all flowing hair and bushy beard who had greeted the president of the Republic with a democratic 'Hi, there!'[40] Marcel Sembat, director of *L'Humanité*, was the second socialist, who on 18 May 1915 would be followed by a third, Albert Thomas. It was not truly a national government, given the absence of the conservative Right.[41] This failure to embrace the Right was against Poincaré's wishes.

The government reshuffle encouraged Poincaré to believe that the halcyon days of early August could begin anew. His first thought seems to have been for another reconciliation with Clemenceau, despite the latter's reversion to his traditional hostility. Though Poincaré believed that with his 'incoherences' Clemenceau would be 'extremely dangerous' as *président du conseil*, he was more complimentary about his potential as a minister: 'He would have been a useful minister, on the condition of never having an administration under his direct orders and of sticking to giving advice, that one could freely discuss, and follow or not.' For that reason and 'As he has however, at the moment, a certain credit with public opinion and as I have decided to put to one side all personal questions', Poincaré asked him to come and see him. Poincaré was obviously struggling against a deep-seated antipathy to the politician who had constantly attacked him so personally for nearly a decade; but this demonstrated his desire to put the country's interests first, and in so doing perhaps set an example to the many other politicians who seemed unable to overcome their petty rivalries. This second olive branch was, in Poincaré's eyes, trampled upon by Clemenceau. The latter began by criticising Poincaré on a number of issues. 'In short he spoke to me, for a few minutes, with virulent hatred. Poor man, who judges others by his own standards. Had I been free to act and to speak, I would have slapped his face or thrown him out of the room.' Clemenceau's habit of expressing himself in long and passionate diatribes against Poincaré to his face was unlikely to meet with the latter's approval. Unable to control himself any longer, 'I looked at him stupefied, I let him go on a few minutes, he got up, fidgeted and left saying: "It is a relief for me to go". I simply barked out this sentence: "You are mad, mad, mad, mad ... ".' And Poincaré scribbled in his diary: 'Poor man, envious, hateful, [illegible], great intelligence, lowly and soiled soul'.[42] Thus ended the attempted second reconciliation. The composed, moderate, reasoning and articulate lawyer confronted with the passionate, fiery, candid and cantankerous seventy-three year old politician. Indeed, it is difficult to imagine how two such opposing temperaments and personalities could ever be reconciled. It was a tribute to Poincaré's patriotism that he would be able to put those differences to one side in 1917, when he finally called Clemenceau to lead the government. Even then, like the *union sacrée*, it was merely a truce and not peace between the two men.

Civil–military relations

The concentration of so much of France's vital productive activity in the north-east of the country was, by the first months of the war, a serious blow to the French war effort. The area affected by the invading German armies accounted for approximately two-thirds of French manufactured iron and steel production, three-quarters of coal and coke production, four-fifths of pig-iron and woollen production, and over 90 per cent of the output of linen goods and copper.[43] Worse still, by 29 August Paris itself was under threat from the German advance. The cabinet decided that if Paris were to fall the government should withdraw to Bordeaux. The triple error of 1870 lived on in politicians' minds: the splitting of the executive into two, the switching of the provincial half first to Tours then to Bordeaux, the isolation of the head of government and foreign minister in a besieged Paris. On 30 August in the first aerial bombardment of the capital, a German plane dropped three bombs killing one person. Poincaré told the newly appointed war minister, Millerand, of his desire to remain in the capital until the last moment. Millerand, with no less sense of history, could not agree.[44] Poincaré was hostile to abandoning the capital to the kind of despair and revolution which had given rise to the Paris Commune. His anxiety was heightened for, as in 1870, most of the middle-class population had fled the capital, leaving it largely a workers' city.[45] As the Germans continued to advance, forcing the French into a general retreat, the capital came in effect under martial law, which was not to Poincaré's liking. He was particularly critical of the chief of the General Staff, Joffre, and wished the executive to maintain overall control of the general conduct of the war and for the General Staff to conform to it. On 2 September, the day the official communiqué was signed for the government's departure to Bordeaux, another German plane flew over the Elysée, leaving Poincaré more upset by the frightened sparrow which had sought refuge in his library than by fears for his own safety. As the Elysée's works of art were removed to safety, he reflected in typical mawkish manner on his departure: 'To leave this time is to die completely. Leaving this courageous population which showed me so much affection. Alas! having the courage to seem cowardly ... Henriette is devastated and sobs despairingly on departing.' She left the Elysée that evening at 10.25; Poincaré left fifteen minutes later for the station where ministers were waiting to leave by the same train.[46] Not only was the whole political class transferred to Bordeaux, it was followed by the capital's major commercial banks and newspapers. Though the move naturally provoked disorder, it was nothing compared to what took place twenty-six years later in 1940.[47]

Poincaré was installed in the préfecture of the Gironde, while Viviani's residence became the town hall. He was pleased to note the acclamation of the local people of Bordeaux: 'its cheers warm my heart'.[48] But the move to Bordeaux would compound Poincaré's problems of powerlessness. As parliament had not been in session since 3 September, its members settled into a mood of frustration, which quickly turned to intrigue and rumour-mongering. The High Command, out of arm's reach of the civil authorities, began to act independently.

In the first days of September, the military position was dire as the right wing of German troops under von Kluck veered south-east towards the Marne to encircle the French armies. General Galliéni, recently appointed military governor of Paris, set about massing troops into an army under General Maunory, unbeknown to the enemy. This allowed for a counter-attack against the German flank. The ensuing Battle of the Marne from 6 to 9 September forced a German retreat to the river Aisne. Poincaré was informed from deciphered German radio intercepts that the enemy was showing signs of fatigue and even division.[49] These encouraged him to ignore news from the French ambassador in Washington of a German desire for mediation, which, Poincaré believed, could lead to divisions in French opinion. Meanwhile, he was distressed by news of a more personal nature concerning fighting in his home village of Nubécourt, where his family were buried: 'My sweet memories! My dear graves!'[50] This would have strengthened his resolve to resist any cessation of hostilities until at least the return of the lost provinces was assured. At an even more personal level both he and his wife were deeply affected by the news that his house in Sampigny had been intentionally shelled by the Germans.[51]

French losses up to and including the 'miracle of the Marne' stood at 250,000. Though press censorship would have ensured that such figures did not reach the home front, the war was beginning to excite the kind of opposition which German subversion could manipulate and sponsor, in particular the Poincaré-la-guerre myth. Genuinely moved by the suffering of the French people, but also sensitive to his public image, Poincaré attempted to show that he was not out of touch with their fate. On Sunday 13 September he was out visiting hospitals in the Bordeaux area where from the 25th his wife worked as a nurse. On the 18th he again asked to visit troops at the front, which hitherto had been declined by both Messimy and Millerand. It would be unduly cynical to attribute Poincaré's motivation merely to wishing to rebuild his popularity; he was deeply affected by France's suffering. But he understood the importance of maintaining a good image of the president of the Republic as an active symbol of France's unity. As he told his friend Maurice Bernard when complaining about Millerand, 'he has a taste for unpopularity and he does not understand that, under a public opinion regime, one must use public opinion to maintain courage and the spirit of sacrifice in the country'.[52] On 18 September he insisted to cabinet that if he were not given official permission to visit the front 'I would end up taking this step without authorisation'.[53] That permission was finally granted on 9 October. Visiting troops near Epernay, he slept in a bed which had recently been occupied by the commander of the German Second Army, General von Bülow, which led him to comment rather priggishly, 'if I had known in advance, I would have refused such distressing hospitality'.[54]

Poincaré's choice of outfit for his visits to the front would become legendary, resembling a chauffeur's uniform in navy blue, buttoned to the neck and complete with black leggings and peaked cap. One wonders whether this otherwise extremely conventional dresser had not developed an eye for the publicity generated by such an eccentric outfit, even though he might tell his niece that the peaked cap enabled him to give the military salute to the French flag.[55] His outfits did seem to have been selected more for their political, rather than sartorial, impact. When reproached for not wearing the uniform of a captain of the chasseurs alpins, to which he was entitled as a reserve officer, he replied 'personally I would be happy to wear it, but as the representative of civil power I have never wanted, in relation to the chambers, to seem to be abandoning civilian clothes'.[56] Whatever benefits he might derive from an understanding of the interconnection between media and politics, much was lost at the level of his personal contact with the troops. This often appeared as a mixture of formality and awkwardness. Though he was profoundly moved by the soldiers' plight, this most formal and shy of men was incapable of relaxing in public or displaying affection.

Poincaré's frustration and irritation with the conduct of the war increased. As usual, he was critical of ministers such as Viviani, whom he described as 'as always, absorbed, absent-minded, silent, directing nothing, reaching no conclusions', or Delcassé, 'confused, obscure, mumbling, reading his telegrams with difficulty and appearing to learn of their content in cabinet'. Though he praised Millerand as 'precise, methodical, categorical, absolute', he was critical of his refusal to communicate. Lack of information was among Poincaré's greatest complaints.[57] Unsurprisingly, he felt he was neither sufficiently informed nor consulted. With his remarkable ability to process mounds of documents and files, information in Poincaré's hands truly was power. Ministers or civil servants may not have intentionally deprived him of the information he craved, but probably did not fully realise his ability to absorb it in such quantities. This at the service of a remarkable memory made his arguments difficult for an ordinary minister to contradict. Clemenceau ridiculed it when he remarked acidly that Briand knew nothing but understood everything which was the opposite of Poincaré. Nor did Poincaré's ubiquitous interest in events spare military operations. He was unhappy with the division of the country into military and civil zones, which he saw as breaking the sacrosanct unity of the country. The rich irony was that he was increasingly finding himself in agreement with many of Clemenceau's criticisms, not least that Viviani's second government was stocked with 'mediocrities', and that the High Command was too independent. Saddened by Briand's preoccupation with his personal affairs, he noted, 'I end up understanding and excusing Clemenceau, who assimilates me with so many mediocrities'.[58]

With hostilities stabilised on the western front, Poincaré was increasingly preoccupied with his and the government's return to Paris, believing their absence to be a public relations error. In cabinet on 22 October he insisted on returning to Paris. But Doumergue was adamant about the need to protect the 'Queen Bee', to which Poincaré could only retort with a mixture of indignation and courage: 'if there is a risk in returning, that is another reason for not delaying further'. And when Millerand suggested that it would be necessary to return to Paris by 15 November, Poincaré remarked defiantly, 'I declare that personally I will not wait for that date to go to Paris and that my intention is, whatever happens, to spend a few days there next week.'[59] There were members of the cabinet such as Albert Sarraut, minister of public instruction, who actively encouraged his independence and greater personal power. Though wary of overstretching his constitutional role he casuistically justified to himself the need to be more active: 'Without indulging in personal power, I certainly have the duty, in the best interests of the republican regime, not to appear to be self-effacing.'[60] His reasons as usual were logical: 'From all quarters, it has come back to me that intrigues are brewing in Paris against the government and me and that our remoteness encourages these machinations.'[61] In the end, a mixture of encouragement and self-justification led him to take a firmer line on his return to Paris, which ended in a sharp row with Briand in cabinet. There was a quick reconciliation, with Poincaré feeling that a spirit of self-sacrifice was necessary in the circumstances: 'in the present hour, everything must be forgotten, one must forget oneself, and it costs nothing to overlook it'.[62] He was no doubt sincere, but such an effort came so much more easily once Briand had withdrawn the offending remarks. All the same, Poincaré had already given instructions for his wife, domestic animals and servants to leave Bordeaux on 24 November for the Elysée, although he would return briefly to Bordeaux after a visit to the armies in the east.

Poincaré genuinely believed that a spirit of sacrifice was vital to maintaining *union sacrée*, the key to victory. This, combined with his natural asceticism, made him contemptuous of what he viewed as the deplorable politicking and the sordid escapades of politicians and their hangers-on in Bordeaux. He was annoyed by the high life of the *demi-monde* which had decamped to the country's temporary capital. He was dismayed at news that the minister of the interior, Malvy, was allowing his mistress to use his ministerial car around Bordeaux. The egotism and absence of governmental solidarity contrasted sharply with his descriptions of the suffering and sacrifice of ordinary people. Perhaps because he and Henriette had no children, they were profoundly moved by those who lost them in the war. The death of his friend Louis Barthou's son affected them deeply: 'Henriette and I are much aggrieved, it reminds me of the little Max as a child and I see Henriette so saddened. I cried and I thought of all the mothers who are already in mourning.'[63]

He seized every opportunity to go to Paris and to the front to galvanise his public image and to escape the vitiated air of Bordeaux. He was particularly pleased to meet King George V in northern France on 1 December and to be able to tour local villages: 'The population recognises me next to the king, the crowds gather and cheer us: politicians' intrigues and the Parisian salons do not extend to here.' He was happy to learn how the king had supported war against Germany in the event of it being declared on France first. The problem had been with British public opinion, a problem with which Poincaré sympathised given his desire to carry French opinion united against Germany. He was reassured to hear the king tell of his words to Sir Edward Grey, 'It's up to you to prepare public opinion, you must succeed; and he did succeed.'[64] His visits to the battlefields of northern France and to the wounded evoked the same emotive language: 'They are happy and proud. Tears come to my eyes. Ah what good people!'[65] A further restriction on his movements in Alsace led to another outpouring in his diary in which vanity and the interests of the country appeared conterminous:

There is however an interest for the Republic and France herself in allowing the President to make a few gestures which could restore his lost popularity.

I put up with the consequences of a war which I did everything to avoid, a departure which I did everything to stop, a series of clumsy moves which were committed in spite of me.

It would bother me little if I alone was to blame. But I was a new force for the country and for the regime, and stupid jealousies are conspiring to destroy that force.[66]

His wistfulness continued the following day when he sat down with Maurice Bernard to analyse the reasons for his loss of popularity, much of which was put down to the departure from Paris being perceived as cowardice and as an abandoning of the capital. A further cause stemmed from the hope invested in Poincaré at the outset of the war: 'The French people, sentimental, enthusiastic, evidently expect from a President in wartime, acts which the constitution would not allow and gestures which ministers and the military have stopped me carrying out.' What had been wanted from Poincaré was 'both punch and panache', whereas

I simply attended to all the governmental and administrative work; I presided and directed cabinet meetings; I egged ministers on; I co-ordinated their action.

But, other than that all happened in the shadows and in silence, they evidently wanted something else . . .

And that something else, each time I tried to do it, to the extent that the constitution would allow it, they chained me up.[67]

A certain martyrdom apart, this was a reasonably accurate picture of Poincaré's role in the first four months of the war, the reason why he, in particular, bore the brunt of so much criticism and, in the end, why things were unlikely to change given his legal respect for the constitution.

By 8 December 1914 the war front had been sufficiently stabilised north of Paris to allow the government to return to the capital. Poincaré's insistence on the need to return had triumphed and his commuting could end. On 22 December an extraordinary parliamentary session marked the return to political normality and gave Poincaré new reasons for hope. Even Viviani, according to Poincaré, spoke with energy of the need to 'weld to France forever the lost provinces'.[68] This was timely given Viviani's recent comments to Millerand that France might be satisfied if Germany returned Alsace without Lorraine, which had caused Poincaré to declare that if such remarks were repeated then he would call for his resignation. Poincaré believed that Germany should understand France's resolve not to seek an early peace.[69] He was therefore particularly pleased with the chambers' 'unanimous adherence to the government's declaration on outright war, and that is the essential'.[70]

Thus France settled down to the idea of a long war. Ironically, the year ended with relations between the two men most able to speed victory, Clemenceau and Poincaré, at their lowest ebb. The further irony was that, in spite of themselves, these two energetic, but temperamentally opposing figures, did see eye to eye on a number of issues. The final irony was that both felt restricted in their freedom to act: Poincaré described himself on 6 December as 'shackled' (enchaîné), while Clemenceau in the first week of October changed the title of his newspaper, *L'Homme Libre*, to *L'Homme Enchaîné*.[71] Relations were at their nadir following an article by 'The Tiger' criticising Poincaré for allegedly having asked Millerand to recall troops from the front to provide him with a personal escort for the New Year celebrations and for having increased his expenses while others were dying of hunger. Clemenceau was clutching at straws in his desire to malign Poincaré, whom he continued to accuse quite wrongly of lack of energy. Whatever his faults, he could not be accused of grandness or money-grubbing. Poincaré immediately wrote a vitriolic letter to Clemenceau refuting this 'double calumny'. He explained how he had specifically asked for no military escort and had already proposed a cut in his presidential expenses. He went on,

I remain stupefied at the facility which you have for believing the most absurd rumours when they echo your prejudices. What you told me at our meeting already proved to me what strange errors of psychology you make when labelling someone unworthy. But all the same, you could say to yourself, that apart from being a coward and demented, a man who has the responsibility and the honour to perform certain tasks should be, by the invincible nature of things, morally and physically incapable of giving in to self-interest, in circumstances such as these. If you really do not understand, I pity you for having in your soul such a blind power of hatred and disdain.

Poincaré noted in his diary that this letter would probably remain unanswered 'and this nasty man will continue, in the face of the enemy, to attack the official representative of France. Crazed pride? Nastiness? Who knows?'[72] But Clemenceau repeated his attacks in the following days, leaving Poincaré to explain in his diary how following his trip to Russia he had returned 75,000 francs to the Treasury and following his trip to Britain 57,000 francs, all of which he was authorised to keep, 'and I am falsely accused of asking for a rise! Let them ask the poor of Paris and the suburbs; they'll see if I'm tight-fisted'.[73] He was certainly generous to the poor. He and Henriette were constantly distributing money to the civilian population – along with pipes in his effigy to the troops – most of which came from his own pocket, so that he was overspending on his presidential expenses to the tune of six to seven hundred thousand francs a year. It is for this reason that his not inconsiderable personal fortune of two and a half to three million francs had been decimated by the end of the war.[74]

The president was a prime target for Clemenceau's *L'Homme Libre*. The newspaper was constantly at war with the censors and yet often at peace with the German authorities. It was one of the few newspapers which the Germans allowed to be distributed to French prisoners of war, and it was the source of articles for the French language German newspaper distributed in the occupied territories under the title *Gazette des Ardennes*.[75] For the next two years Poincaré was forced to put up with Clemenceau's sniping, unable to defend himself publicly given his presidential role.

By the beginning of 1915, Poincaré was discovering a new role for himself, in which he made greater use of his constitutional position instead of fulminating against it. He gradually made a virtue out of what he had hitherto viewed as a vice in his presidential role: that of arbiter between the civil and military powers and stimulator of the nation's energies. Such a role emerged as parliament, after an interlude of six months, resumed its normal sitting on 15 January 1915 and took up its customary role of controlling the executive.

Poincaré the arbiter

Poincaré's control of events since the outbreak of war had never been as feeble as he claimed. He might describe himself as the 'prisoner of the Elysée', but he had continued to make that claim since his election in 1913. For the moment, arguably he continued to influence policy more than any other president since the beginning of the Third Republic. The director of Millerand's *cabinet civil* at the war ministry, Raoul Persil, in his war diary, referred to Poincaré in the same sentence on 5 November 1914 as both 'the arbiter' and 'the despot'.[76] Poincaré's belief that he was powerless derived from a number of causes: the first was relative and had to do with the difference between his experience of the office in the one-and-a-half years before the outbreak of war, notably in foreign affairs, and his experience of it after the outbreak of war. In reality, the period of adjustment to France's new war role which gave the executive quasi-dictatorial powers allowed a dynamic and experienced president considerable scope for action. He was the only politician to whom an overview of events was granted by virtue of his constitutional position, let alone his personal mastery of the myriad problems. For the first month he was working with a government which he had grown used to influencing in the pre-war period, though this would be less and less the case as war progressed. Finally France, like all of the major powers, gradually settled down to the realisation that war would not be of short duration. In becoming the norm, by definition war lost the exceptional character which had initially given Poincaré the opportunity tö ìñtervene. As parliament reasserted its authority so Poincaré's would decline, unless he could adapt his role to the new circumstances. The crucial issue in French politics until Clemenceau's accession in November 1917 concerned relations between the civil and military authorities.

Article 3 of the constitutional law of 27 February 1875 stipulated that 'the armed forces are at the disposal' of the President of the Republic. On 24 August 1914 Poincaré had reminded General Joffre of his constitutional subservience to the government and the fact that it was the latter's role to determine the

general, political, financial, economic, diplomatic conditions for pursuing the war. From that moment it is indispensable that the General Headquarters does not isolate itself in an ivory tower and evade all control. Without doubt it would be a dangerous absurdity to allow the government to intervene in the conduct of military operation, but it must be better informed than it has been up to now.[77]

Poincaré was well placed to exercise the important, but difficult, role of arbiter in this political struggle which increasingly resembled trench warfare.

In many ways French domestic politics mirrored the international picture. The enthusiastic opening offensives of all the major powers and the counter-attacks which followed soon led to the war's most distinctive feature, stalemate. For the next three and a half years a continuous line of trenches stretched from Switzerland to Flanders. The stalemate on land was replicated at sea, where no clash of battlefleets occurred and where neither the Allied blockade nor German submarine warfare produced quick results. In diplomacy, too, stalemate characterised events, despite occasional peace initiatives and the posturing over war aims.[78]

Thus Poincaré settled down to arbitrating between the increasingly entrenched positions of the military and civil authorities. By now Germany occupied almost all of Belgium as well as the industrial areas of the Nord and Lorraine. But French offensives on the western front during 1915 failed to make any significant progress, despite their horrendous cost. Ironically, though Poincaré constantly remonstrated with Clemenceau for his irascibility and readiness to espouse the cause of all critics of the executive's performance, he was to be found behaving in similar fashion. His door was open to the complaints of generals and parliamentarians, whose views he then related to cabinet in his usual formal and unforgiving manner. These were then followed, more often than not, by long, legalistic, closely argued, and tightly written manuscript letters to individual ministers detailing what their course of action should be. Georges Wormser, a member of Clemenceau's personal secretariat when the Tiger was *président du conseil*, has well described the almost sublimatory function of Poincaré's letters:

In one go, with no crossing out, they are an accumulation of occasionally acerbic remarks and always strongly presented arguments. Once he has exhaled his worries and put across his thoughts he disregards the repercussions and often even what follows. There is no request for a reply. He has expressed himself, that is his need, and often he is satisfied with that. Has he merely written for History, as Clemenceau will later reproach him bluntly? That is not correct, because he has neither misrepresented nor altered anything, it is all as it is, spontaneous.[79]

The consequence of this behaviour was that, by nature sparing in praise, Poincaré came to be seen by certain ministers as something of a negative force. For all his incitement to action in others, some saw Poincaré as justifying his own inaction in other matters on the grounds of constitutional irresponsibility. This was not how he saw things. On the second anniversary of his accession to the presidency he reflected on his constitutional passivity and almost accepted the confining of his role to that of arbiter and advisor: 'If they want to involve me in criticism and in parliamentary debates, then give me the means to act and proper rights. But, not as long as I am unable to act without ministerial counter-signatures, so long as I can give no orders to anyone, so long as they leave me with my role, somewhat diminished of arbiter and advisor.' However, he already seemed to be preparing his return to more active politics in the post-war era: 'Be patient, good gentlemen. When I leave the Elysée, I shall tell all and, age permitting, I shall act.' For the moment, he was disappointed by what he saw as the dissipation of national unity, which he believed he had done so much to foster:

18 February! Two years ago, Paris was celebrating, crowds in the streets, enthusiastic cheers as I passed. Courageous people, what wonderful things we could have done with their support, without the intrigues of Clemenceau and of Caillaux, without the little dirty tricks of the Barthous and the Pichons, without the blinkers which the constitution imposes on me ... the great national movement was an irresistible force for liberty, for progress and for victory, if only the envious had not strived to slow it down and stop it.[80]

In the meantime confining himself to his constitutional role of advisor and arbiter, on 14 March he wrote to Millerand calling for 'merciless sanctions' against any delays in munitions production. Barely a month after the start of the war, France's shortage of munitions, predicted by a Senate report in July 1914, was apparent. Poincaré deluged Millerand with detailed requests for information of a highly technical nature concerning munitions production. Poincaré's ability to grasp such

complex issues was revealed in the minutes he appended to the replies.
Though seconded at the Elysée by his military staff, which since the
opening of hostilities comprised retired military personnel, there was no
doubt that Poincaré fully grasped the technicalities of such issues.[81]
Examples of his harrying of ministers are to be found in his letters to the
foreign minister, whom Poincaré continued to monitor very closely. He
did so through regular reading of intercepted and deciphered foreign
diplomatic dispatches, for which he had a predilection since 1912, and
which provided an alternative picture of events. On 21 March he was
insisting adamantly to a recalcitrant Joffre that he comply with the
government's request for troops to be sent to Italy.[82] Even so, a mixture
of vanity and a professed powerlessness continued to characterise his
diary entries. At a reception for wounded soldiers he was sorely hurt by
the absence of applause when he left the room: 'Where are the
ceremonies when my entrance and exit were the signal for formidable
ovations? Today I don't count anymore. What is a civil President in wartime. It is soldiers who now represent *la patrie*. In a moment of exaltation
such as this, I leave them cold, they ignore me.' And he ended with
typical self-pity: 'As I cannot give my life for my country, the least that I
can give it – or rather return to it – is my popularity'.[83]

The reputation of the Viviani government continued to slide in line
with French military results in 1915. Troop morale was low with reports
of surrendering to the enemy and summary executions of deserters.
Poincaré increased his criticism of Millerand, whom he accused in
cabinet on 27 May of accepting Joffre's orders too readily and of
'ceaselessly abdicating the rights of civilian power'.[84] The failure of
offensives directed by the High Command in Artois and Champagne
resulted in considerable French losses. Frustration over France's plight
manifested itself in a number of ways. It was reflected in the increase in
rumours of Poincaré having caused the war, of letters of insult, threats
on his life, even vicious gossip that Henriette Poincaré was the mistress
of the head of the president's military staff, General Beaudemoulin.[85]
Not surprisingly the general atmosphere in the country gave him cause
for serious concern: 'what worries me, is the state of mind revealed by
this correspondence: a spreading malaise which, by gnawing away at
French powers of patience, can bring disaster'.[86] Increasingly, delegations of politicians of all persuasions approached Poincaré with requests
to put pressure on the government to act more firmly or to get the High
Command to bow to tighter political control. In early July 1915 the
powerful Army commission of the Senate under Charles Freycinet, and
with Clemenceau as a member, wished to speed the implementation of
major reforms in the organisation of the war effort by appealing directly

to the president of the Republic to implement them in his capacity as supreme commander of the armed forces. Poincaré refused on the constitutional nicety that his actions had to be countersigned by a minister and that, by the same token, the government was responsible and not him: 'All these people are looking for a king; but none of them thinks of giving me real powers and, if I had them, they would revolt against me'.[87] Was his refusal a sign of his fear of responsibility, as some suggested, or, more likely, a desire to see that the government's power was not further usurped by parliament?

Ever since the return from Bordeaux to Paris, parliament had sought an increase in its control of the war. Socialist deputies had secured parliament's right to be in permanent session. Parliamentary commissions were exercising tighter control over government action. Memories of the Revolution revived hopes and fears of committees of public safety dispatching commissars to control the military. By the end of July tension between parliament and army was giving rise to talk of a *coup d'état*. The lessons of French history which haunted French politicians, chief among them Poincaré, pointed to the hydra-headed monster of *coup d'état* and revolution emerging after French military defeat. Hostility between parliament and the government was a particular source of anxiety. In the end Poincaré was happy with a compromise which clearly separated civil and military tasks: the General Staff kept responsibility for the conduct of military operations; the civil authorities looked after the home front, supplies, production, morale and the general conduct of war from diplomacy to Allied relations. Poincaré would endeavour to maintain this distinction and avoid the friction it generated. It would not be an easy task and civil–military relations deteriorated further with calls for Joffre's replacement. An uncomfortable stalemate had been reached and public dissatisfaction turned on the government and Poincaré. A general mood of despair reigned.

For the moment Poincaré was opposed to a ministerial reshuffle, fearing that it could open a political crisis. He told the cabinet on 27 July that 'if a ministerial crisis is prolonged, parliament, which is already very unpopular, would become even more so and everything is to be feared, a revolution, a military dictatorship, and all that in the face of the enemy'.[88] Though the time might not yet be right, this did confirm Poincaré in the belief that a new, more robust government was necessary. He would begin sounding out potential candidates for a cabinet reshuffle. Millerand, the war minister, was increasingly unpopular with the Senate army commission, which held him responsible for the failings of French artillery, for allowing the General Staff too much independence, for his authoritarian manner and for his opposition to parliamentary missions of inquiry into the conduct of the war. To limit Millerand's independence, four under-secretaries of state with particular responsibility for issues such as artillery and procurement were created.

By August, Poincaré was describing Viviani as 'flaccid as a rag'. The *Président du conseil* had been to tell him that he could no longer continue in office. Certainly he had been in poor health for some years, but whether the cause was that suggested by Poincaré's secretary general of the Elysée, Félix Décori, is not clear: 'Décori asserts that according to a reliable source Piérat [Comédie française actress] gave Viviani syphilis which her husband, Guirand de Scevola [French painter and organiser of the camouflage section in the Great War], brought back from America.'[89] Certainly Viviani's psychological symptoms, as described by Poincaré since 1914, correspond to the tertiary stages of syphilis with a general weakening of the intellectual faculties, loss of memory and capacity for work, deliriousness, incoherence and melancholia. Of course syphilis was a common disease at this time, affecting at least 10 per cent of the French bourgeoisie, with politicians by no means exempt, as Gambetta would have testified.[90]

The Bulgarian decision to enter the war on the side of the central powers on 22 September was a further blow to the cabinet and principally to its foreign minister, Delcassé. By October 1915 Poincaré was branding nearly every important minister involved directly in the management of the war with sloth. Of course, measured by his own colossal capacity for work almost all mortals seemed listless, but such a yardstick also justified his own intervention. His letter to Millerand of 2 October revealed much about his active involvement in affairs:

I would be obliged if, in the future, you could automatically communicate to me, as happens with the Quai d'Orsay, telegrams you send to our military attachés, their replies and all instructions given to the expeditionary corps. Immediate knowledge of these documents is indispensable, all the more so as I may be forced to contact other ministers and because, in agreement with the *Pt du Conseil*, I must establish the necessary harmony between the different services.

Of course technically the constitution gave him the right to be informed, but Poincaré often went beyond that as the cabinet, and individual ministers, lost momentum. Thus Delcassé's feebleness was such that 'I decide to take up my pen and to write, in collaboration with the members of the government, several telegrams which I believe necessary to send before midday to London, Athens and Sofia'.[91]

The irony was that Poincaré continued to beat his breast in feigned constitutional inertia: 'Ah! if I were still *président du conseil*! If I had the right and the means to act! If I could give orders!'[92] However, when a tearful Delcassé offered his resignation on health grounds on 11 October (related to fears that his officer son was now a German prisoner and might be mistreated given his name), Poincaré insisted to Viviani that it should be refused to avoid giving 'a deplorable impression to Russia and Britain'. Delcassé reluctantly agreed to stay, but on 13 October Viviani took over fully as foreign minister. Viviani had to be persuaded by Poincaré of the logic of this, despite the latter's noting almost in the same paragraph of his diary that Viviani 'is decidedly quite impervious to foreign policy questions'. This was exactly what Poincaré had remarked when he had put Viviani in charge of foreign affairs before the war. In effect this all resulted in power being passed to Poincaré, as in 1914. Poincaré seemed to concede this when trying to console Viviani: 'I try to cheer him up, but those that Clemenceau calls my "employees" give me a lot of trouble'.[93] Things turned out much as Poincaré must have expected, for on his first day as interim foreign minister, Viviani came to see Poincaré four times, in the course of which the president altered French foreign policy.[94] Rumours were rife that Poincaré had his own office at the Quai d'Orsay. An exaggeration perhaps, but he was none the less the éminence grise. And though he might protest in a letter to Delcassé that 'I have never given any order to an agent of the ministry and it is always to you that I have made known my opinions', the truth was a good deal more subtle than that.[95] Poincaré influenced decisions fundamentally, without having to give direct orders, by virtue of his mastery of the details of a problem and his barrage of letters suggesting solutions. The more power Poincaré assumed during the death throes of the cabinet, the more he was asked to assume. Some, like the left-wing professor and leading member of the Ligue des droits de l'homme Victor Basch, supported by the moderate député Georges Leygues, suggested he should take on the premiership: 'Is there some subterfuge which would allow you to be both Président du conseil and Pt de la République? I reply that I would willingly abandon the latter for the former'.[96] They came up with the idea of the president of the Senate taking over the presidency and Poincaré the premiership. But despite the socialist Sembat's approval, Poincaré let the idea pass.[97]

A move of that nature would probably have been popular across the country and in the army. The French population with its intermittent appeals to an all-powerful guide in its hours of need, seemed ripe for someone with a reputation for firmness like Poincaré. He himself seemed to understand the need for more authoritarian control when he noted tiredly, 'We talk, we discuss, each gives his opinion ... How much better it would be, in wartime, to have a single will!'[98] The military also already believed that Poincaré was the real political power, with Joffre constantly being summoned to the Elysée for consultation. The Quai d'Orsay and most foreign envoys understood Poincaré's crucial role in French politics. One might ask why he did not look at the option of moving to the premiership more seriously. Was it a further example of his fear of responsibility? Or did he feel that a new government could still reverse France's beleaguered position?

Viviani's cabinet limped on, after barely managing a vote of confidence (with numerous abstentions) on 12 October. But Poincaré insisted to him that there was a need for a 'widening and a reinforcing of the cabinet', and began soundings for his replacement. He approached Freycinet, who refused, but suggested Bourgeois or Clemenceau. Poincaré agreed that the former be included in a reshuffle; as to the latter he repeated that he had no personal objection, but did not believe he would make either a good premier or minister of war.[99] By the 29th, Viviani felt he no longer had the confidence of the Chamber and resigned.

Poincaré had already begun preparing his replacement with the eloquent Aristide Briand, the man with a 'violin for a voice', who on 29 October also took over the Quai d'Orsay. Briand offered Clemenceau a portfolio. He refused for the same old reason, as well as claiming that Poincaré would continue to run the foreign and war ministries.[100] Viviani was switched to the ministry of justice and Millerand was gently replaced by Genéral Galliéni, viewed as the real victor of the Marne.[101] At the technical level Poincaré boosted co-ordination of foreign affairs by creating the post of secretary general of the foreign ministry, which in 1912 he had opposed, and appointed to it Jules Cambon, with whom he was now on good terms. He also took the opportunity to widen the political scope of the government further, in the interests of *union sacrée*, by bringing in the man of the clerical Right, Denys Cochin, together with the recently befriended Emile Combes, and other experienced men of the old guard, Freycinet, Jules Méline and Léon Bourgeois. The only omission was Clemenceau, but then he had already made it clear that he would accept nothing less than the premiership. When Clemenceau's name had been suggested to him as a potential premier in July, without ruling out such a possibility Poincaré had remarked, 'I shall never allow myself to be deflected from my duty by objections of a personal nature, but Clemenceau, very intelligent, very talented, is impulsive and incoherent'.[102]

For the first time five ministers in the new government were given the prestigious title of 'ministre d'état'. These included such political opposites as Denys Cochin and Jules Guesde to symbolise *union sacrée*. Most significantly, this was the first occasion since the 'Republic of the

Republicans' at the beginning of the 1880s that a representative of the Catholic Right had become a member of a government. More surprising still, Cochin was not of the Right which had rallied to the Republic, but of the parliamentary Orleanists faithful to the heir to the French throne, the comte de Paris.[103] Ever since the outbreak of war Poincaré had pushed for Cochin's entry to the cabinet, along with that of Albert de Mun, and had repeated it when the socialist Albert Thomas had been made *sous-secrétaire d'état* in May. Poincaré had opposed the latter's appointment on the grounds, so dear to him, that it would upset the balance of political forces in the cabinet necessary for the maintenance of *union sacrée*. At the time he had taken his cue from the British cabinet, which according to Asquith was about to widen its political base by including members of the opposition.[104]

Poincaré had been the driving force in putting together what was the most widely representative and balanced government of the Third Republic. Its authority was enhanced by including six former *présidents du conseil*. It was more than just the consecration of *union sacrée*, it was for Poincaré the realisation of that most elusive of goals, French political unity. The premium on unity was further demonstrated by the establishment of a Comité de défense nationale to co-ordinate diplomatic and military issues and which would be composed of ministers and military commanders under the chairmanship of the president of the Republic. In this way Poincaré hoped that the running sore of the war years, civil–military relations, would find their own *union sacrée*. By the winter of 1915 Poincaré seemed to have regained some of the power he had lost during the course of the year. By ensuring that all important decisions were taken in his presence in cabinet, he had managed to keep a firm grasp on government. But with a new cabinet and a new organisation of the war effort had he really consolidated his control of events?

Life under Briand

It was unlikely that the new Briand cabinet, which he had played such an important part in putting together, would afford Poincaré the same degree of influence. As Poincaré well understood, his influence as president was greatest when a power vacuum existed, which was no longer the case. Though he continued to influence events by his Herculean capacity for work, the number of cabinet meetings was reduced to three per week from the daily schedule which Poincaré had encouraged. Not surprisingly he disapproved: 'So, here is all the authority they are leaving me: three cabinets a week, three cabinets where I have one voice in fifteen or sixteen ... And during this time, all the good people of France write to me: you who are the master, you who can do everything.'[105] Nevertheless, Poincaré was not shy of standing his ground in cabinet. As Ribot explained, 'the *Président de la République* used to intervene and engage in dialogue with the *Président du Conseil* which, more than once, degenerated now and then into violent language'.[106] Even though Poincaré might claim that his role was becoming decorative, that had certain advantages. His vanity was momentarily soothed by a French war cabinet meeting attended by Asquith, Grey, Balfour and Lloyd George on 17 November: 'Great new event in history, a Franco-English council deliberating under the Chairmanship of the *Président de la République*'.[107]

By the end of the year his own position was again under attack from yet another campaign led by Clemenceau. Following an article by the Tiger attacking Briand, the High Command and the president of the Republic, Poincaré fulminated against his old adversary:

And he accuses me of personal power! Me! Is he sincere? Is he mad? Is he blinded by hatred and envy? Does he or does he not know, that all my hours, all my minutes, I spend them working to the best of my ability for the country, trying to co-ordinate ministers' action, pointing out and rectifying errors I discover, spurring people on in a post where I not only have no power, but no means of acting personally?

And he went on:

The whole of Clemenceau's game today is to attribute to me unlimited personal power and, subsequently, responsibility for everything. The other day, he wrote: 'The Good Lord, I mean M. Poincaré ...' He knows very well that he is not telling the truth, that the constitution leaves me no rights and that I am too scrupulous to break out of the tight circle in which it locks me. But he also knows that the people are unaware of my fetters and believe me to be all powerful. The naïve and touching letters which I receive every day demonstrate that everywhere I am thought to be an absolute power ... That common misconception naturally favours Clemenceau's campaign and the moment will come, doubtless, when speculating on public disenchantment and violating the constitution, he will succeed in making me responsible for everything. What would it matter if the country was saved? But, if Clemenceau triumphs, if he seizes power, how many incoherences, reproaches [?], treacheries [?] will one have to fear![108]

When criticised by the Clemenceau supporter, senator Henry Cheron, for being opposed to Clemenceau on personal grounds, Poincaré could still tell him, '1) that I have done everything to bridge differences; 2) that if a Clemenceau ministry was signalled by the deliberations of the Chambers or even by events, I would carry out my constitutional duty by calling Clemenceau'. But he added that he still believed such a contingency to be worrying, given the man's impulsiveness and instability, and confirmed that for the moment he would give the present ministry his full support.[109]

Meanwhile Poincaré's control of events continued to slip away under Briand as disagreements in the Chamber gave him cause to doubt the future of *union sacrée*: 'In all this, I don't see Briand. He doesn't speak to me, he doesn't consult me on anything. My influence is limited to discussions in cabinet.'[110] As 1915 drew to a close, Poincaré was looking tired and confessed to feeling ten years older. This was partly due to the colossal work-load he imposed on himself and partly to his disappointment at being distanced from the heart of decision-making. He noted with obvious disappointment and a certain sadness how Briand appeared to wish to act independently: 'After the formation of his cabinet, Briand came to see me for a couple of days for a few moments chat before cabinet meetings. Then he stopped his visits completely. I only see him in cabinet meetings. Then he is very amiable, but he is obviously trying to arrange his complete independence.' Thus, on Christmas Day Poincaré noted melancholically in his diary, 'Christmas, sad Christmas . . .'

That sadness was probably aggravated by the loss some two months earlier of one of his few real friends, Félix Décori, a former legal colleague and, until his death, secretary general of the Elysée.[111] This increased his sense of isolation. Nevertheless it was clear that Poincaré was not going to be side-lined easily. An entry in his diary for 26 December 1915 was typical of the self-justificatory process he went through in his own mind before finding reason to intervene in policy-making. He simply decided that a particular individual was incapable of the task before him, thereby rendering his own intervention both constitutional and necessary: 'But Briand is he really, as he once said, an achiever? He increasingly has a nonchalant, careless air . . . He looks like an oriental, a levantine, wraps himself in the smoke of his cigarettes, dreams, and hardly seems to act.'[112]

Differences between the two men widened. Briand's lackadaisical and informal manner, which led him to have meetings with those such as the war minister 'in pyjamas, a cigarette in the corner of his mouth', belied a determination to be his own man. This was not to Poincaré's liking.[113] He was increasingly of the impression that Briand was less committed to fighting the war to the last than negotiating some diplomatic deal to end it. This was at a time when the unsuccessful French offensives of 1915 were taking their toll of military and civilian morale and requests for a negotiated settlement were gathering momentum. Poincaré had all along made clear that he was opposed to anything but the signing of a victor's peace.

In the meantime the question of civil control of the military continued to be a source of friction and tension that called for Poincaré to mediate. It was an area in which he was even more well informed than usual, thanks to the summaries of military events presented to him daily by one of the General Staff liaison officers.[114] Moreover, as president of the Republic he was aided in military affairs by the Elysée's personal military staff of seven officers.[115]

At first the minister of war, Galliéni, attempted to collaborate with the parliamentary commissions. In this he received little support from Briand, who regarded parliamentary commissions as an unjustified interference. Galliéni's relations with Joffre were no better and his assessment of Poincaré particularly severe, claiming that in cabinet he was 'hair-splitting, spiteful, suspicious of everyone, jealous, and eager to take part in affairs, but without responsibility'.[116]

Poincaré's shying from responsibility was not new, but his problem was that he had the unenviable task of arbitrating between so many strong personalities and so many organisations. To the Senate army commission had been added a foreign affairs commission in February 1915, both of which Clemenceau had presided over since 4 November 1915. In the meantime, on 21 February 1916 began the protracted siege of Verdun, a crucial offensive designed by the German commander, von Falkenhayn, to bleed the French army white and force France, and inevitably Britain, to the peace table. The battle raged fiercely until July 1916, after which in the months of October and December the French regained much of the lost ground. But the Battle of Verdun was to cost the French 270,000 lives and the Germans 230,000.

When the siege of Verdun began, national morale seemed to tighten. But Galliéni soon fell ill with what seemed to be a common complaint of Third Republican politicians, including Clemenceau and Poincaré: prostate infection. He resigned in March. His replacement, General Roques, was a good deal more self-effacing, thereby allowing the High Command to recapture some of the independence they had been forced to relinquish. This did not please Poincaré. Given the gravity of the military situation Poincaré allowed the military temporarily to have their own rein. But as the struggle for Verdun continued, national morale sank and an air of defeatism surfaced which Poincaré actively sought to combat. He made this plain in a speech at Nancy in May in which he reaffirmed the pledge that France would impose her own peace conditions on the enemy. But he remained preoccupied by the numerous letters in his post-bag calling for a peace settlement.

The continuing siege of Verdun and flagging national morale produced further calls from the Chamber of Deputies for tighter parliamentary control over the military in the form of secret committees in which the chambers would deliberate in camera, but with no account of the proceedings in the *Journal Officiel*. Poincaré was initially opposed to such enquiries as too restrictive for the executive, but also divisive in this hour of need: 'The edifice is slowly falling apart, one can feel it ... The unease increases the anarchy every day. And I have no right, no means of acting!'[117] But the pressure was such that Briand was obliged to accept the institution of the secret committees. The Chamber's first meeting discussed Verdun on 16 June 1916. Briand also had to bow to parliamentary inspections of the army and to live with mounting pressure to revoke his decision of 2 December 1915 to create a 'generalissimo', in the person of Joffre, charged with establishing 'unity of direction' in the conduct of the war.[118]

The power of these committees was demonstrated on 7 December 1916. Following a vote, the Chamber committee blamed Joffre for the carnage at Verdun and forced Briand to relieve him of the supreme command and appoint him technical advisor to the government, at the same time obliging the premier to reshuffle his cabinet. Then there were the Senate secret committees, two of which sat in 1916 and two more in 1917, and which also applied considerable pressure to the executive and the military over the conduct of the war. Following an article by Joseph Reinach suggesting that Poincaré should take greater control of events, Poincaré replied with a letter on 11 December 1916 again on the theme of presidential powerlessness:

The constitution says: Article 1. The President has all rights. Article 2. He exercises none of them without cabinet authorisation etc. etc.

There remains what the government is willing to leave him: in peacetime, a decorative role and a very weak general influence; in wartime, the possibility of advising, which can be listened to or not, a right to oversee which is not easy for him to exercise, sometimes the opportunity and the faculty to stimulate energies, sometimes the painful feeling of being scorned. In the end, it is not a reason for imitating Casimir Périer, especially in the face of the enemy ...[119]

One can, at least, sympathise with Poincaré's growing frustration at the multiplication of organisations wishing to participate in policy-making, decision-making, and appealing to him as constitutional arbiter to support their claims. But this was the nature of the office, which demanded impartiality not participation in affairs of state. Poincaré could not easily reconcile himself to that fact.

On 12 December 1916 Briand formed a new government, his sixth. He abandoned the notion of 'ministres d'état', all of whom left the cabinet except for Cochin, who became *sous-secretaire d'état* for the blockade. The number of ministers of cabinet rank was reduced from seventeen to ten. With the departure of Guesde and Sembat, only one socialist remained, Albert Thomas, who took over the ministry of armaments. General Lyautey became minister of war. Unlike its predecessor, the new cabinet placed a greater premium on technical competence than notoriety. The following day the army command was split between the commander of the north and north-eastern armies under Nivelle and commander of the army of the Orient under Sarrail. Shortly afterwards Joffre was awarded his marshal's baton and relinquished his role as technical advisor to the government. Poincaré supported Joffre's replacement for a number of reasons. The High Command was increasingly blamed in parliament for the losses at Verdun and for the muted success of the diversionary offensive on the Somme. Public opinion and the press, like Tardieu in *Le Temps*, now favoured commanders with a more defensive strategy which reduced loss of life, such as Pétain at Verdun. Joffre's apparent seclusion in his headquarters at Chantilly gave the impression of imperviousness to the control of the civil authorities. The problem for Poincaré was to find a way of disposing of him without sending signals to the Allies and enemy alike that France was in disarray. The president summoned Joffre to smooth his departure. Joffre's analysis in his memoirs of Poincaré's motives seems reasonably fair, except for the omission that by now Poincaré also believed in a more defensive strategy, which Joffre was unlikely to deliver:

The President of the Republic, who dominated this sorry debate, was as intelligent as M. Briand and his experience of affairs gave him a great ability for understanding a question rapidly, but he was worried about public opinion and impressed by the opposition which he felt to be growing in parliament. The attacks on him by his political adversaries visibly preoccupied him and I regretted that this honest man and this great patriot was not able to find in the conscience of his duties, which he accomplished passionately, the strength to defy these attacks.[120]

One of the first requests the president made of Joffre's successor, Nivelle, was that he transfer his headquarters from Chantilly to Paris. Meanwhile, the idea of unity of direction in the conduct of the war was switched from the now defunct 'generalissimo' to a war cabinet, though its decisions, unlike those of its British counterpart, still had to be sanctioned by the full cabinet.[121] Thus by 1917, after an initial period of independence, the French military were more effectively controlled by the politicians than their British counterparts,[122] partly as a result of Poincaré's action.

Poincaré supported the maintenance of Briand as *président du conseil* despite Clemenceau's vehement opposition. Poincaré had attempted another reconciliation on 12 December 1916 in inviting his adversary to the Elysée to discuss a new peace initiative by the enemy. This had emerged following the central powers' recent victory over Romania. At least Poincaré knew that whatever else they might disagree on continuation of the war was not one of them.[123] Though Clemenceau accepted the invitation, this pretext for a truce between the two men was again rejected. The Tiger continued to excoriate Poincaré in his newspaper for allowing Briand to continue in office. Though he attempted a *rapprochement* partly to defuse Clemenceau's systematic opposition to the executive, Poincaré should nevertheless be given credit for initiating reconciliation.

Clemenceau could at least take pleasure from the failure of Briand's second cabinet, which resigned over the issue which had dogged the French war effort, civil–military relations. Like his predecessors, the minister of war came into conflict with the Chamber and refused to reveal technical details in a debate. In the face of fierce protests from left-wing *députés*, he resigned on the spot on 14 March 1917, to be followed by the whole government four days later. Lyautey would be the last general to occupy the war ministry during the war. Poincaré did not approve of the war minister's attitude and supported the decision to discontinue the idea of a general with that portfolio.[124] Thus ended the period of Briand's premiership, during which Poincaré's opportunity to influence events had dwindled. The rest of the year would see his influence decline further in what would be, according to volume nine of Poincaré's memoirs, 'L'année trouble'.

1917: a difficult year

The year 1917 was fateful for government and country alike. Two and a half years of war was beginning seriously to wear down nearly all the belligerents. As Jean-Jacques Becker has shown, until the end of 1916 the attitude of the French had been reasonably constant: refusing to accept the idea of a long, drawn-out war, but hoping with every six month period that the conflict would end. With 1917 the light at the end of a series of tunnels disappeared. Consequently *union sacrée*, which was merely a truce for the duration of hostilities, began to fall apart.[125] Political and social divisions were exposed, with very serious consequences. Poincaré believed that the political class had not been setting a good enough example for some time. But the war governments had each lasted some fourteen months until Briand's second cabinet, no mean feat given the legendary transitoriness of Third Republican ministries. They now slipped into a period of instability which did nothing to bolster flagging morale.

The experienced head of the Progressists, Alexandre Ribot, was chosen to replace Briand, after the refusal of the other moderate, Paul Deschanel. Poincaré had entertained good relations with Ribot over a number of years, as well as having had a chance to admire his prudent management of the country's finances during the war years. More importantly, Ribot was known to be a supporter of all-out war. In his cabinet of 20 March he took on the foreign affairs portfolio, with the science professor Paul Painlevé at the war ministry. Maginot, *député* for Bar-le-Duc, a war invalid, was given colonies. The finance ministry was given to another Progressist, Thierry, who would introduce the long-delayed income tax.

Despite Ribot's known hostility to a negotiated peace, he and Poincaré began with a disagreement following the *Président du conseil's* announcement in his ministerial declaration that France 'intended to continue hostilities until a victory which included the return of Alsace–Lorraine, but that she harboured no spirit of conquest'. Poincaré was not happy with the draft of the speech, feeling that it could bind a future government on any territorial gains that might be needed to ensure France's security. He suggested amending Ribot's sentence to read, 'a victory which ensures the restitution of our provinces, with the necessary reparations and guarantees'. Ribot refused, leaving Poincaré anxious.[126]

Poincaré may have bemoaned the reduced number of cabinet meetings under Briand, but under Ribot there would be further reductions. Poincaré must have winced at the new premier's announcement in his first cabinet: only two cabinet and two war cabinet meetings a week. Furthermore, their duration would be reduced from four to two hours and the president of the Republic would no longer be allowed to speak longer than the premier.[127] The president should, however, have expected Ribot to assert his independence given previous comments to Poincaré. Louis Loucheur, *sous-secrétaire d'état* for munitions production in the second Briand cabinet, recorded a conversation between Ribot and Freycinet in his *Carnets secrets* for 19 December 1916 in which the latter had asked whether Poincaré continued to intervene as much in cabinet discussions:

Alas, yes! replied Ribot, but recently the President of the Republic referred to such criticism of him and asked me what I thought. I told him: 'As you ask me, I shall tell you respectfully, Monsieur le Président, that you appear to me to be departing from your constitutional role, you should view things from a distance, with greater detachment'.[128]

This had taken place when Ribot was finance minister. But now as premier, according to Ribot, he was able to get Poincaré to confess, 'I overstepped my constitutional role and was aware of it; but I was forced to do so because there was no *Président du Conseil*.'[129]

Though the international position was mixed with the tsar being swept away by revolution in March and the United States coming in on the side of the Allies in April, the domestic picture was bleak. The disastrous failure of the Nivelle offensive in April 1917, which Poincaré had actively and perhaps unconstitutionally supported,[130] and steep rises in domestic prices led to a sagging of national morale in forty-four departments. The Russian Revolution had at first been welcomed by the Allies as likely to reinvigorate the country's tired leadership and the Russian war effort, but its revolutionary fervour soon began to contaminate the French social scene. In the 1917 May Day parade several thousand demonstrators chanted cries of 'Down with war!' In May and June strikes affected 100,000 workers mostly in war industries. On 20 May mutinies broke out at the front not, as the High Command believed, for political reasons, but because of a loss of morale. To combat this, a firm line was taken with 25,000 judgements being passed on mutineers of which 629 were death sentences, though the new supreme commander, Pétain, allowed only 75 to be carried out.[131] It is calculated that some forty thousand soldiers were involved, a relatively small number in relation to the eight million Frenchmen mobilised in the course of the war. However, because of the mutinies' widespread nature it is estimated that some two-thirds of the army was in some way affected. The consequence of this widespread crisis of morale was a demand in many quarters for a compromise peace. Poincaré believed that, in dealing with mutineers and those who sought a compromise peace, 'it was not a time for weakness'. He was severely criticised in parliament in April 1917 for refusing to pardon a number of mutineers. Yet from August 1914 to January 1917 there were on average between twenty-two and twenty-three sentences to death per month for desertion, of which Poincaré reduced 424 to imprisonment, bringing down the average number of executions per month to between seven and eight.[132]

Poincaré had been pointing to Joseph Caillaux since at least 1915 as a ringleader in the peace campaign. He had long held the idea, rightly it would seem, that this campaign was also linked to the Poincaré-la-guerre rumours. Apart from Radical *députés* such as Accambray and Meunier, there were in Caillaux's entourage less reputable figures such as the unscrupulous businessman and journalist, Bolo Pacha, and the anarchist director of *Bonnet Rouge*, Almereyda. They were in contact with Germany through the German legation in Berne, as has already been shown. It would seem that Caillaux genuinely believed that further war could only be to the benefit of revolutionaries or the royalist Action française and was duped by the German authorities into campaigning for a negotiated settlement.[133]

Though Poincaré systematically opposed any negotiated settlement, he did pay much attention to the peace mediation led by Prince Sixtus of Bourbon Parma from December 1916. This can be attributed to Sixtus's personal capacity to inspire trust as a member of an international-minded dynasty now serving as an officer in the Belgian army, while being the brother-in-law of the Austrian Emperor Karl. Poincaré had been impressed by members of the various branches of the French royal family offering to serve in the French forces at the outbreak of war. French anti-monarchist legislation had barred them from doing so, to Poincaré's disappointment in view of the store he set by *union sacrée*. There was perhaps also his long-held fascination with families connected with the Bourbons, whom he willingly acknowledged as having contributed so much in the past to France's greatness and to being a worthy part of the continuum of French history.

Poincaré listened attentively to Sixtus's proposal on behalf of Austria, implying the return of Alsace–Lorraine, and the evacuation of Belgium and Serbia in exchange for Allied support in the maintenance of the Austro-Hungarian empire. In the end, both Poincaré and Ribot grew cynical about this offer on the grounds that Emperor Karl was not sincerely seeking a separate peace. Evidence now shows that they were right, given that at no time did Germany countenance any concessions to France over Alsace–Lorraine.[134] Poincaré was able to dissuade Lloyd George from pursuing this offer, on the pretext that a promise had been made to Italy not to settle with Austria. This increased complaints from pacifists, certain members of the Left, and even the centre, that Poincaré was intransigent. It was only a small step to claim that he had always wanted war, and the Poincaré-la-guerre myth was reinforced. His accusers could also point to his support for the government's refusal, on grounds of morale, to allow a delegation of socialists to accept their Russian comrades' invitation to the Socialist Congress in Stockholm where they would have met their German counterparts.

The mutinies produced a political crisis which began in the secret parliamentary sessions of June and July 1917 and which would continue through the autumn, bringing down Ribot and then the Painlevé cabinet, eventually making way for Clemenceau. On 22 July in the Senate Clemenceau denounced the minister of the interior, Malvy, for his weak attitude in the face of defeatist agitation behind the lines, and forced his resignation on the 31st. *Union sacrée*'s demise in the government was signalled when on 17 August the Catholic Cochin resigned, claiming that his presence gave the cabinet 'an inaccurate appearance'. This was partly motivated by a renewal of anti-clericalism following Pope Benedict XV's offer of mediation on 1 August. No more Catholics agreed to serve in the government.[135] With Malvy's resignation and the government's refusal to allow socialist delegates to take part in the international Socialist Congress, the socialists withdrew their support from the government. The official end of *union sacrée* came a few days later with the collapse of the Ribot ministry on 7 September. Its successor, led by the Radical Painlevé, was formed mainly of Radicals and republican–socialists, even though the Right and the moderates continued to support it. This would be the majority which would support Clemenceau a mere two months later. But the government was quickly weakened by the continuing scandals concerning peace proposals and contacts with the enemy. On 13 November 1917 the Painlevé government was overturned, thereby achieving the dubious record of being the only war ministry to have been defeated.[136]

November 1917 was dismal. Domestic affairs apart, the military position was pessimistic: Russia was in civil war, Romania defeated, Italy routed at Caporetto, and Britain and France nearing exhaustion. The only note of optimism was the American decision to enter the war in April 1917; but even that involved the Allies holding out for some time before the United States could put together, virtually from scratch, an army and transport it across the Atlantic, which in the event would only arrive in March 1918. Poincaré seemed to have exhausted all possible ministerial combinations committed to a victor's peace. According to Poincaré's biographer, Dr Georges Samné, the socialist, Marcel Sembat, encouraged Poincaré to take the unprecedented step of assuming the premiership while retaining the presidency. This extraordinary move had first been suggested to Poincaré in October 1915, when he had declined. It would have conferred considerable power on him. According to Samné, given the gravity of France's position since April 1917, Poincaré now considered the idea very seriously. He told Sembat,

You have just touched the bottom of what have been my thoughts for several months ... The failure of April, the mutinies, the discouragement, have often made me ask what, in the end, would be the solution of despair if everything fell apart. I scoured the text of the Constitution, I searched for precedents, I scrutinised the legality. Nothing says I cannot declare myself *Président du Conseil* tomorrow. It would be a small *coup d'état* in the absence of a precedent, but I would resign myself to it if, all the cards having been played, I only held that one.

But he held one other card, Clemenceau: 'he is our last trump. If he is no good, it will be me'.[137]

Thus Clemenceau seemed the only alternative. As early as 18 October, Poincaré had told Painlevé and Barthou that he was contemplating a Clemenceau ministry because he was popular with public opinion, determined to push ahead the legal cases for treason and because 'I haven't the right . . . to rule him out merely on the basis of his attitude to me'.[138] Clemenceau was popular with the troops and in the country for his commitment to victory, for his colourful denunciation of 'shirkers', 'irresponsible commanders' and incompetent politicians either through his newspaper L'Homme Enchaîné or as president of the Senate army commission. He was in manner all things which Poincaré was not: outspoken, crude, colourful, spontaneous – a bulldozer. He disliked Poincaré, and yet the two men had in common the most important quality – a commitment to victory. But was that enough? With hindsight he appeared the right man. But the political establishment at the time was far from unanimous about calling him. Many socialists saw in him the breaker of strikes, 'le premier flic de France', likely to provoke widespread labour unrest. Others believed that Clemenceau's virtues of tenacity and obstinacy could in certain circumstances prove to be a weakness. Poincaré had always believed, perhaps with a certain malicious pleasure, that a Clemenceau ministry was disqualified because, in senator Jean Dupuy's phrase, it would be to 'gamble France on a throw of the dice', or as Ribot had told him, 'a coin tossed in the air; one doesn't know on what side it will fall'.[139] In short, Clemenceau had seemed a risk. Poincaré was not a man to take risks. Even in November 1917 at the height of the 'difficult year', the soundings he took among senior politicians merely served to underline the ambiguities of a Clemenceau ministry.[140] In the end the final decision rested with Poincaré; it was his most important of the war. Until the last hour he felt the risk: 'I sense more and more the dangers of adventure'.[141] But it was increasingly apparent that the risk lay in not calling Clemenceau. The positive action he finally took was as much for negative reasons: 'the devil of a man has on his side the opinion of patriots and if I do not call him, his legendary strength will ensure the weakness of another cabinet'.[142] Poincaré, who was no gambler, was forced to play one of his last cards.

Clemenceau's reign

Poincaré's decision to ask Clemenceau to form a government was also related to the position of his other political, though infinitely less respected, rival, Joseph Caillaux. Caillaux was increasingly coming to be seen as the leader of the movement gathering in favour of a negotiated settlement with Germany, the continuation of his pre-war policy. Caillaux was seconded in his quest by Briand's negotiations with the diplomat and counsellor to the kaiser, Baron von Lancken, who had first negotiated with Caillaux during the Agadir crisis.

By contrast, Clemenceau symbolised the stubborn and patriotic struggle for a victor's peace. It was already apparent that the two attitudes which alternately would dominate French foreign policy for the rest of the century were taking shape: conciliation and containment of Germany. Poincaré and Clemenceau championed the latter. Hence the former's grave disappointment at the collapse of Russia, the cornerstone of France's policy of maintaining a bulwark against her German rival in the east. It also explained why Poincaré encouraged and supported with such vigour, beyond his constitutional prerogative, the legal proceedings for treason against Caillaux.[143] As he told the radical–socialist Franklin-Bouillon just before summoning Clemenceau, 'They won't be able to criticise me for making a personal choice. What's more, we must choose between Caillaux and Clemenceau. My choice is made.'[144]

Thus on 15 November 1917 Poincaré called the seventy-six-year-old Clemenceau to form his second government; it was in place a day later and was to last for over two years. Contrary to received wisdom, the ministerial team was not composed of second-raters but, rather as he had reproached Poincaré on numerous occasions, of Clemenceau's own 'employees', chosen for their loyalty and their technical competence. Though it relied on the support of the Right, they had no representatives, most of its members being drawn from the Radicals and former members of the Painlevé cabinet. The difference was in the leadership rather than in the team. Clemenceau took on the war ministry, marking his determination, in Daniel Halévy's words, to govern not so much as a statesman but as a warrior, which was soon revealed in his own declaration of 8 March 1918: 'I make war'. His obedient servant, Stephen Pichon, moved into the Quai d'Orsay. The task facing Clemenceau was considerable. One of his principal aims was to put an end to the defeatist campaign, which he did by initiating legal proceedings against Caillaux on 11 December 1917, while a decision was taken on 22 November to bring Malvy to trial before the Senate constituted as a High Court.[145]

Poincaré approved of Clemenceau's actions. When on 15 November the president had offered his rival the premiership, he had done so in the form of a small bargain: 'I shall tell you all I know and all I think. I shall give you my advice freely; you will then make the decisions under your responsibility.' Of course Clemenceau did not have to accept, but he did with the words, 'I shall never take a decision without first coming to talk

with you.'[146] For the first six months relations between the two men
were cordial, indeed collaborative, with Clemenceau often visiting the
Elysée to consult the president, and the latter referring to the premier as
a 'pacified Tiger'. Indeed at the end of January 1918 Poincaré seemed
pleased to record that 'His relations with me are excellent. "We live", he
tells his friends, "like two brothers." There is no doubt that he treats me
like a younger brother, over whom he exercises a paternal authority. But
he apologises with refined politeness.'[147]

Although on many occasions Poincaré tended to take at face value
what was merely Clemenceau's irony, for the moment relations between
the two men were cordial. When alone together before the start of the
first cabinet Clemenceau teased Poincaré sarcastically, 'Now, Raymond
old chum, are we going to fall in love?'[148] The cordiality of their relations
did not imply by any means that Poincaré would regain his former
influence. On forming his government Clemenceau had informed the
president that there would be only one cabinet meeting a week: 'A good
way of keeping me out of things', he noted.[149] Certainly this was a far cry
from the daily meetings of the first year or so of the war, or even the
thrice-weekly regime under Briand. Not surprisingly, Poincaré repeatedly complained in his memoirs that Clemenceau was taking decisions
alone and that there was no collective decision-making in cabinet. There
was even talk of the president of the Republic no longer chairing the war
cabinet, which Poincaré was able to block.[150] But even in his *domaine
réservé* of foreign affairs, over which he had continued to maintain some
influence by dint of his encyclopaedic knowledge and constitutional
prerogatives, Poincaré felt his control slipping away. On 22 January 1918
he noted that before the cabinet meeting 'Pichon comes to apologise
rather vaguely for not talking more often with me. Indeed, he seeks my
advice on nothing, despite our excellent personal relations; he only
confers with Clemenceau'.[151] The honeymoon would soon end and
Poincaré would be reproaching the Tiger for the unstructured nature of
his interviews with him, and for not being kept sufficiently informed.

There is no doubt that Clemenceau preferred to concentrate decision-
making in the conseil de cabinet, chaired by the premier, and to have its
decisions sanctioned by the full cabinet at its weekly meeting, and whose
duration rarely exceeded one hour. At the same time, Clemenceau is
credited with the modern development of the cabinet du ministre
through his use of the *sous-secrétaire d'état à la guerre*, in the person of
Jules Jeanneney and his *chefs de cabinet*, General Mordacq and Georges
Mandel, for military and civil affairs respectively. These artifices shielded
Clemenceau from Poincaré's, and everybody else's, interference.[152]
Though parliamentary control remained, a law of 10 February 1918

gave the government the right to legislate by decree in certain isolated areas. Thus Clemenceau concentrated virtually all power in his own hands, or those of his closest collaborators. He gave life to his own words: 'In the end there are only two useless organs: the prostate and the Presidency of the Republic.'[153] Such remarks apart, Poincaré regarded Clemenceau's decisive control of events and his increasing support in the country with a mixture of admiration and envy.

Poincaré was left with little room for intervention other than chairing the Conseil supérieur de la guerre. It is Clemenceau who offered him the privilege of chairing the Allied conference which resulted in the establishment of a unitary command under Foch from 26 March 1918, though it was Poincaré who managed to get American and British acceptance of Foch. But such ceremonial occasions apart, gone were the days when Poincaré imposed his ideas either by domination of cabinet meetings, or through his 'ferments of ink', as Clemenceau referred to his epistolary pressure. As the president noted painfully, 'In reality decisions are taken by Clemenceau alone without the government being consulted.'[154] What allowed Clemenceau to act so independently and govern so strongly was his popularity in the country and the fact that, for all his authoritarian manner, he operated within the bounds of the constitution and maintained republican legality. As parliament and Poincaré understood, his popularity conferred on him a legitimacy which they dare not contest.[155]

As the near-disastrous second battle of the Chemin des Dames in May 1918 put Paris within forty miles of German troops, relations between the two men deteriorated. Poincaré refused to obey Clemenceau's request that he leave the capital, haunted by the flight to Bordeaux in 1914 and by the prospect of being separated from the government and above all Clemenceau. But the military position improved in August, and relations were patched up. By October 1918, following the constant flow of American troops onto the Allied side, a turnround in the Allies' fortunes and the capitulation of Bulgaria, there was talk of an armistice. Poincaré was adamant that such talk should not sap the Allied forces of their fighting spirit and that Germany should be definitively defeated. He told Clemenceau in a letter dated 5 October that it was impossible to discuss an armistice as long as the enemy occupied any part of French or Belgian territory. Two days later Clemenceau insisted that if Germany made proposals they should at least be listened to, given the exhaustion of Allied troops.[156] On the evening of the 7th Poincaré dashed off another letter to the Tiger warning him that armistice talks would 'hamstring our troops'. Clemenceau's reply threatening resignation revealed the depth of hostility between the two men:

I don't accept that after three years of personal government, which has worked so well, you dare advise me not to 'hamstring our soldiers'.

If you do not withdraw your letter written for the history which you wish to create for yourself, I will have the honour of tendering my resignation.[157]

This exaggerated attack on Poincaré's conduct of the war was more revealing of Clemenceau's nervous tension than a fair picture of the president's wartime role. Peace was only made after the intervention of third parties. But the incident did show Poincaré to be clearly in the camp of those committed to total German surrender. That camp was made up of nearly all of the American press, most of the French Right and a number of Radicals, whereas some 90 per cent of French public opinion, according to analyses of French postal censorship, were divided between those in favour of taking the war into German territory and those who wished for an immediate armistice if Alsace–Lorraine was restored to France, and Germany was unable to recommence hostilities.[158]

Poincaré's views did not carry the day, despite an Allied superiority over the Germans of eighteen divisions and some six hundred artillery pieces. This was apparent on 25 October at the meeting of Allied army commanders at Senlis: Pershing and the Americans favoured a total surrender, but the British were conscious of the exhaustion of their troops and suspected the French of having imperialist designs on the Ruhr, while Foch and Pétain believed that a sufficient sacrifice in human life had been made if a moderate settlement could be reached. On 29 October discussions got underway in Paris between the leaders of the Entente; agreement was reached on 4 November on what should be the conditions of the armistice. Armistices had already been signed with Turkey and Austria on 30 October and 3 November respectively. The Germans were summoned and arrived near Rethondes, in the Compiègne forest, on 8 November by special train – Napoleon III's. In his railway carriage – an old restaurant car – Foch, seconded by a British admiral, communicated the armistice terms to the German delegation on behalf of the Entente. Foch gave them seventy-two hours to accept. The German delegation sought to negotiate, but revolution in Germany on 9 November had led to the kaiser's abdication and the establishment of a social–democratic government. The German delegation was ordered to accept the terms.[159]

The Germans signed the armistice shortly after 5 a.m. on 11 November 1911, with effect from 11 a.m. That day from 4 p.m. Clemenceau was lionised by the Chamber, and though Poincaré had the good grace to admit to himself that he deserved it, he was saddened by the absence of any recognition of his own effort:

For everyone, he is the liberator of the country, the organiser of victory, he alone personifies France. Foch has disappeared, the army has disappeared, as for me, of course, I do not exist. Four years of war during which I presided over the State and which he devoted to a merciless opposition ... are completely forgotten.[160]

Probably prompted by bitterness at Clemenceau's popularity, Poincaré unjustly claimed that Clemenceau had ended the war early to embellish his position for the forthcoming elections. But less than a month later in a generally ecstatic atmosphere in Metz, symbol of a reconquered Lorraine, where Pétain was ceremonially awarded his marshal's baton, Poincaré and Clemenceau publicly embraced. Poincaré was able to bathe in this great manifestation of national pride and glory. He had at last rediscovered the popular adulation that had for so long deserted him, commenting in his memoirs that now he could die. For Clemenceau things were different. When presented with the armistice by Foch, he noted 'If I was preoccupied by my glory, I would die now.'[161] In many ways this was the fundamental difference in the two men's outlook. Poincaré was enslaved by his courting of popular plaudits; Clemenceau, because he took little notice of them, was free to earn them. But the peace still had to be won.

Poincaré's problem during the war was that he remained president of the Republic. The nature of the office was to embody France, to stay above the day-to-day business of government and to act as arbitrator between the competing interests of the French state.[162] But by nature and training much more an advocate than a judge, he found it difficult to remain above the fray. This above all made him ill-suited for the presidency as it operated under the Third Republic, other than under Thiers. And it is to this that must be attributed a partial loss of his reputation as a statesman during the war years: first among the political class who felt that he intervened either too much or too little, and second in the country where there was an affinity for strong leadership and an ignorance of the subtleties of constitutional law. Poincaré understood this, but would have needed either to step back as president from the day-to-day running of affairs, or relinquish the presidency for the premiership. The first demanded abnegation, the second courage; he was temperamentally unprepared for either. What he did achieve during the war years was that France should fight on for a victor's peace. In this his role as president of the Republic was crucial for it enabled him in the end to choose the politician who was as committed to that aim as he was himself – Clemenceau. But whereas his great rival was able to steer France to victory and gain the reputation as Père-la-Victoire, Poincaré was not so fortunate. His obstinacy in avoiding a premature peace was not so readily acknowleged, despite the fact that the 1918 settlement was probably more durable than would have been any compromise peace with Germany in 1917. Unlike Père-la-Victoire, now that peace had been achieved the epithet most closely associated with the president's name would be Poincaré-la-guerre.

8   Poincaré-la-paix

When the armistice was signed and the cease-fire came into operation on the eleventh hour of the eleventh day of the eleventh month of 1918, Poincaré was fifty-eight years of age. This was young in comparison to many senior French politicians of his day: Clemenceau was seventy-eight, Alexandre Ribot seventy-six, Freycinet ninety. Admittedly a new generation of politicians was about to emerge, but despite his youthful age Poincaré tended to be regarded as belonging to that generation alongside which he had always served, albeit rather precociously. He had been the youngest *député* in France at 26, the youngest *rapporteur* of the budget at 30, the youngest education minister ever at 33, had turned down the premiership at 38, and had become the youngest ever president of the Republic at 52. Little surprise, given his comparative youth, that he should think of continuing his political career at the end of his mandate as president, which was to come to a close in a little more than a year on 18 February 1920. Indeed, for a number of years he had even wished that he had not been president of the Republic but *président du conseil*, so few were the powers, in his view, invested in the presidency. When asked on New Year's Day 1919 by Paul Deschanel, president of the Chamber of Deputies, whether he would be willing to stand for re-election as president of the Republic, Poincaré emphatically replied no.[1] But he was seriously thinking about returning to more executive politics. He was spurred on by vanity and the belief that he still had an important role to play 'au service de la France'. The vanity derived from the fact that as president of the Republic his contribution to the war effort had not been sufficiently recognised. His diaries testify to that. At the armistice it was brought home to him far more publicly. On 7 November 1918 he was informed of a proposal recently submitted to parliament that Clemenceau, the French army and Marshal Foch should receive the supreme accolade of having 'bien mérité de la Patrie'. He was clearly disappointed by the absence of his name, remarking, rather spuriously in view of his later acceptance of such a commendation, that constitutionally it would be difficult to include the president of the Republic.[2]

There was no doubt about the magnitude of the task ahead of France in the post-war years. 1,400,000 Frenchmen had died during the war, more than 10 per cent of the working population, proportionally the greatest loss of any of the belligerents, except for Serbia. To that had to be added three million wounded, of whom 750,000 were invalids and 125,000 maimed. The quantitative loss was of itself appalling, but added to the qualitative loss it appeared devastating. France's youth had borne the brunt of the war. As the historian Georges Dupeux has put it, out of ten men aged between twenty and forty-five in 1914 'two had been killed, one became dependent on his fellow citizens, three were weakened for a more or less long time'. For a country whose population had fallen behind the other great powers in the nineteenth century, the demographic consequences of the war were frightening. Though in 1918 politicians such as Poincaré would not have possessed the full demographic statistics and projections, they were aware of France's terrible demographic deficit occasioned by the war. This deficit stood at 1.7 million for the war years, added to which were the 1.4 million killed who would not produce children in the post-war years. All this would have an effect in economic and military terms from 1934 to 1939 when the reduced war generation would be of productive and military age.[3] And then there was the financial cost of the war, let alone reconstruction. Public debt had increased tenfold from 1913 to 1920, of which approximately one-tenth had been supplied by foreign loans, mostly from the United States and Britain.[4] The quantitative dimensions of the problem facing French politicians at the armistice were seriously intertwined with equally pressing, but more subjective, problems of ensuring lasting peace and security. Germany remained a threat: neither her territory nor her industry had been ravaged by the war and her population of sixty-five million still towered above France's forty-one million. As victors who believed they had fought a just war not of their making, it is not surprising that in the immediate post-war period the French should look to the peace settlement as a means of alleviating their problems. This involved an impracticable matrix of keeping the Allies together, while keeping Germany down and making her pay.

Poincaré had the measure of at least the quantitative problems facing France in 1918; he wanted no time to be wasted in working for a solution to them. His mood of frustration and impatience contrasted sharply with the general desire to celebrate victory. He insisted that only military honours had thus far been won and that there should be no relaxation of France's effort to win the peace. When on 11 November Marshal Foch told him that had it not been for the armistice the German army would have been forced into complete capitulation, Poincaré mused gravely in his memoirs, 'Wouldn't this have been more certain?' Eleven days later he noted that Clemenceau's haste in wishing to sign an armistice could sabotage victory: 'How better it would have been to finish beating the enemy on the battle-field!' With typical sobriety he found the numerous victory celebrations premature, for while they were taking place 'the Germans will equivocate and ask for an easing of the armistice'.[5] Still frustrated by the 'yoke' of presidential office, he would all the same seek to impose his conception of a peace best suited to France. Initially that would involve taking a robust line against Germany. But just as in 1912 he had come to power committed to dealing firmly with Germany, only to mellow, with his return to office in 1922 he would undergo the same change.

A mixture of vanity and genuine political motives lay behind Poincaré's desire for a public display of reconciliation with Clemenceau. The vanity stemmed from his desire to bathe in some of his rival's reflected glory; the political motive sprang from his desire to continue the quest for unity of the French nation in the post-war era, a quest which had come so close to success with *union sacrée*. On 8 November 1918 he requested from Clemenceau the favour of being able to accompany him to Alsace: 'I want to embrace you in Metz and Strasbourg'. On 11 November before the cabinet assembled, in the presence of a couple of its members Poincaré embraced Clemenceau. The Tiger's response was probably not what Poincaré had expected: 'Since this morning I have been kissed by more than five hundred young girls'.[6] Unity, and perhaps something even more mystical for Poincaré, surrounded the question of whether the government and president of the Republic should accept the invitation to attend the *Te Deum* to be held at Notre Dame. Poincaré favoured attending, but given Clemenceau's rejection of this idea in cabinet on grounds of respect for separation of church and state, Poincaré decided with Deschanel, president of the Chamber of Deputies, that their wives should attend the *Te Deum* alongside the wives of the diplomatic corps. Ever since early 1915 Poincaré had wished to honour the Catholics' patriotism in the *union sacrée*. He had told the cardinal archbishop of Paris, who had requested his presence at the victory *Te Deum* at the end of the war, that 'After victory, I hope that the government will see no problem in this invitation', but noted sceptically, 'But naturally I promise nothing'.[7]

Such bids to carry the momentum of national unity into the post-war period could occasionally take him on to dangerous ground. The Action française was emerging from the war with a new image. It no longer appeared as an extreme right 'ligue' or as a movement committed to a monarchist restoration. Having won its spurs for its anti-Germanism and patriotic support of the war, and having seemingly put its royalist flag in its pocket, it now commanded more widespread support as the foremost nationalist movement whose ideas for the peace settlement were not notably different from those of eminent republicans such as Clemenceau or Poincaré. Poincaré had himself remarked that 'since the beginning of the war, Léon Daudet and Charles Maurras have forgotten their hatred of the Republic and the republicans, and now they only think of France'. The movement's new-found respectability, its success in the 1919 elections and the convergence of some of Maurras's views on the peace settlement with those of republicans like Poincaré, would draw the latter into wishing to harness its energies to the national cause. Action française was at this time one of the most dynamic and best organised political movements, with considerable influence on intellectuals and the upper middle classes. Maurras's movement would support Poincaré's foreign policy in 1922 and the occupation of the Ruhr. The two men conducted a full correspondence at this time, with Poincaré recognising the important contribution of the monarchy to French history, but always maintaining his republican credentials. He agreed on 7 August 1922 to support Maurras's candidature for the Académie française. There was even the suggestion of royalists participating in the cabinet. Though relations would subsequently sour as Poincaré's foreign policy mellowed towards Germany – Poincaré did not in the end support Maurras for the Academy – it was an example of the lengths to which he would go in his quest for national unity.[8]

Poincaré's other preoccupation at this time was Clemenceau himself. There was more than a little envy of 'Père-la-Victoire'. One senses Poincaré's irritation at the public clamour for Clemenceau to be elevated to the Académie française. It grated all the more for the Tiger's apparent condescension in accepting the honour solely on the grounds that he had accepted an honorary doctorate from Oxford University and could not offend the Academy. It would come as no surprise if the award of a foreign degree to his rival had prompted Poincaré to find time in the winter of 1919 to visit Glasgow University where the students had continuously re-elected him lord rector since 1914. The address he gave on 13 November to the university was certainly a sparkling display of history, erudition, culture and humour. Disingenuously confessing to his ignorance of the English language, he remarked in excellent English that he had read in some newspapers how he was supposed to have learnt English during the war, 'but that was very likely a discreet and roundabout way of letting me know that a Rector of a great Scottish University ought to have, at least, a good British education'. He appealed for closer Franco-British relations through a strengthening of the 'auld alliance' and the Entente Cordiale and quoted Shakespeare: 'If that you will France win/Then with Scotland first begin'. Confessing that as a child Romanticism and history in the works of Sir Walter Scott had inspired his love of Scotland, he did not miss the opportunity of pointing out that his book collection 'was burnt by the Hun shells during the war'. He praised Glasgow University's French Club and noted that the thistle was also the emblem of Nancy 'the cradle of my family'. Adding that the motto of Nancy was 'Qui s'y frotte s'y pique' (Whosoever rubs against it will be pricked), he told his audience, 'During the last war, the Hun rubbed himself against Scotland and Nancy; he pricked himself till he bled'.[9] Poincaré was not going to be outshone by his old rival, Clemenceau.

One might have expected Poincaré to be pleased at news that Clemenceau was thinking of becoming president of the Republic and thus 'prisoner of the Elysée'; but his reaction on 30 November was reminiscent of the dog in the manger: 'I confess that I do not fully understand how a man of action, who holds to his reputation for energy, can think of a post of compulsory inaction and continuous representation'.[10] This was ironical coming from the strong man of 1912. Nevertheless, when it came to the visit to Metz and Strasbourg Poincaré pretended to put behind him his differences with Clemenceau. Several train-loads of senators, députés, ambassadors and ministers attended the ceremony to mark the reunion of France and the 'lost provinces' on 8 December in Metz, capital of Poincaré's beloved Lorraine. There Poincaré ceremonially handed to Pétain his Marshal's baton and embraced him. 'At that moment, Clemenceau was near me. Pushed by an irresistible movement, I said to him: ' "And you also, I must embrace you". – "Willingly", he replied; and we embraced to the frenetic applause from stands and windows.' The spontaneity of the occasion was, of course, simulated; Poincaré was anything but spontaneous and had booked such a display with the Tiger several weeks previously. Nevertheless, for Poincaré the poignancy lay in its association with the unity of a victorious France consecrated in his native Lorraine, finally restored to the fold, and is recorded with the emotion which he reserved for his most private moments. It is on this visit to the regained 'lost provinces' that the final volume of Poincaré's ten volumes of memoirs, published the year before his death, appropriately draws to a close. Given his insistence on union sacrée, his religious funeral and the heavy symbolism of these pages, it is worth noting that before leaving Lorraine for Alsace, Poincaré paid tribute to the Catholic clergy and the faithful in the shadow of Metz cathedral ending his description thus: 'Now, I can die'.[11] The remaining pages concern the American President Wilson's visit to Paris and desultory comments on the dilatory nature of the armistice discussions. His last remark on the last day in the final volume highlighted, with more than a little self-justification, the problems both he and France were to confront in the immediate post-war period: 'For me, the truth is that we would have been better finishing off the defeat of Germany before signing the armistice. But neither Clemenceau nor Foch were of my opinion, the former because he was impatient to preside over the elections, the latter because he wanted, very nobly, to end all the slaughter of battle.'[12]

The peace settlement

French war aims had been remarkably vague since the beginning of the war. This was largely due to the need to preserve *union sacrée*. Until September 1917 socialists sat in the cabinet, and their membership and support of the war governments rested on the premise that France was fighting for defensive purposes. They were particularly sensitive to any policy which in their view smacked of imperialism and thus generally opposed annexationist demands. Given France's experience of living for some forty years in Germany's shadow, the French felt more strongly than other Allied governments that maintaining the coalition was in itself a crucial war aim. Any premature discussion of war aims was thought capable of provoking divisions among the Allies. Thus, even peace initiatives and attempts at mediation had to be rejected on the grounds that they too were potentially divisive, as well as likely to leave France still in a position of inferiority in relation to Germany after hostilities had ceased. Nevertheless for his part Poincaré did everything he could, often well beyond his constitutional prerogative, to focus French attention on war aims from the beginning of the conflict.[13]

Of all French war aims the question of Germany's future status was probably of greater importance for Poincaré than for other politicians. It was influenced by his Lorraine origins which, as he had so often pointed out, always put his homeland in the front line where Germany was concerned; it also derived from an acute sense of history. In quoting the president of the Senate, Antonin Dubost, in November 1914, Poincaré was reflecting his own views of Germany: 'He witnessed 1870. Like for Freycinet, it is for him the same war continuing.'[14] His view of the 'German question' conditioned the need to ensure that there should be no continuation of the Franco-German war. This dictated his view of the peace settlement.

The first public account of French war aims was given by Viviani to the Chamber of Deputies on 22 December 1914. France called for 'indemnities' to rebuild her devastated regions, she would fight on until 'the provinces which have been stolen from her by force' were forever rejoined to her, until Belgium was restored to prosperity and independence and Prussian militarism was smashed. Poincaré had agreed with this statement which had been submitted to the cabinet the previous day. It was sufficiently elastic to fit the most opportune circumstances and Poincaré would ensure that those war aims would retain all of their ambiguity throughout the conflict.[15] This had been clear at the time of Ribot's appointment to the premiership and his ministerial declaration of 21 March 1917 when Poincaré had balked at the new premier's intention to state that France would seek peace 'without a spirit of conquest'. This he believed too categorical and likely to restrict France over, for instance, Alsace–Lorraine by limiting her to reclaiming only the lost provinces of 1870 and not the wider frontiers of 1790. Though he did not mention it at the time, such a formula could also limit France's imperial claims, for example, to certain German colonies or to formalising her influence in Syria and the Lebanon, which had never belonged to France and which strictly would be forms of conquest. In his letter to Ribot he remarked: 'Is it necessary to pronounce openly on the question, which no government has done thus far?'[16] The ambiguity he sought to maintain was politic in not restricting France's bargaining position when it finally came to peace negotiations. Ribot's rejection of Poincaré's point had also been understandable given that at that time the new premier was more interested in securing a large vote for his new government, which entailed using an anti-imperialist language designed to attract the votes of the parliamentary Left.

In early October 1918 Poincaré had been opposed to the signing of what he considered to be a premature armistice, as had Pétain and the American military commander, General Pershing, both of whom wished for a final November offensive to settle definitively the question of German military defeat.[17] But on 5 October the new German government had requested that President Wilson begin peace negotiations on the basis of his Fourteen Points, in the hope of securing better terms. Wilson informed the Allies immediately and negotiations began to decide the armistice conditions. Having failed in his request for a last military push, Poincaré wrote to Clemenceau on 5 October to advise that before any armistice could be contemplated Germany should first evacuate Belgium and Alsace–Lorraine and that certain strategic parts of German territory be occupied by Allied forces. He clarified his position two days later in a meeting with Clemenceau, while the latter underlined the exhaustion of French troops. Poincaré rejected this line of argument and insisted in a letter written on 7 October (which he failed to

reproduce in full in his memoirs) that no one in France expected an
armistice:

Everyone sees the trap which is set for us, everyone has confidence in you to stop
the Allies from falling into it; everyone firmly hopes that our troops will not be
hamstrung by an armistice, however short it may be, and that we will not be
allowed to stop the victorious march of our armies by a German pacifist
manoeuvre. There would be general amazement if we took seriously the
proposals made to us in order to unsettle the morale of the Allies and to make
negotiations possible before the arrival of American forces.

He went on to declare that Britain and Italy had already secured for
themselves militarily a number of guarantees for their interests, unlike
France. 'There is no hiding it, it would be a mock armistice, which
would give us no strength in the negotiations and which would give us
no means of even carrying it out.' This was the crux of the matter for
Poincaré – to be able to negotiate a peace settlement from a position of
strength and ensure that France take advantage of this uniquely
favourable moment to squeeze from Germany guarantees necessary for
France's future safety. In his view that meant fighting on; failure to do so
would allow Germany to recoup her strength by withdrawing into her
own borders.

And we would take no precaution for the event of hostilities beginning again! We
won't even ask for the slightest temporary hold on the enemy, the smallest
bridgehead! How will we then obtain in the peace negotiations guarantees for
demobilisation, for the payment of reparations, for the loyal execution of the
most necessary clauses? We will have disarmed in advance.

Poincaré was anticipating difficulties, correctly, and revealing his future
hard line for the peace and reparations settlement. He was also reflecting
widespread feeling in France, which postal censorship and monthly
police reports revealed as a hatred of Germany and a desire for revenge.
But it was perhaps all too easy for Poincaré to react in this way from a
position of constitutional irresponsibility. Clemenceau's furious reply of
8 October accused Poincaré of personal power, of seeking to create a
name for himself in history, and tendered his resignation. There
followed a fierce 'epistolary duel'. Though the dispute was calmed and
the resignation was withdrawn, it resulted in Clemenceau denying
Poincaré the possibility of communicating with him in writing and only
agreeing to meet him in the presence of one of his collaborators. Though
Poincaré believed that this was only Clemenceau reacting in the heat of
the moment, the incident was a further blow to Poincaré's attempts to
keep control of Clemenceau.[18]

On the substantive issue of ceasing hostilities against Germany or not, historians have continued to differ. Apart from the humanitarian reasons for ending the war, in early October 1918 French leaders did not know how close Germany really was to collapse. There was a fear that continuing the war might lead to further Bolshevik contamination of the continent. There was also the possibility that further delay in accepting an armistice would lead to France losing military dominance of the Allied coalition as American troops flooded the continent. This held out the awesome prospect of a predominantly Anglo-Saxon victory and peace settlement as opposed to a *paix française*. Pre-empting Charles de Gaulle's preoccupations about liberating Paris just a quarter of a century later, Foch's chief of staff, General Weygand, reflected the fears of many: 'French soil would not have been liberated by a pre-eminently French victory: this victory would have been above all Anglo-Saxon, especially American.'[19] Others have disputed this last point and suggest that a final offensive planned by Pétain for 14 November would have sealed German military defeat and have given a decisive role to the French Army in the final stroke of the conflict.[20]

The row with Clemenceau may have been patched over, but it was clear that differences would resurface. It was a victory for Clemenceau; Poincaré was forced to back down and accept his exclusion from decision-making. He was now unable to influence Clemenceau directly, although this did not rule out trying to achieve the same ends by getting Foch to oppose him. This was his only option given that even the cabinet was not consulted on the armistice negotiations.[21]

In the end it was Foch who was able to persuade the Allies that the German army should withdraw from all territories west of the Rhine and that the Left Bank and bridgeheads across the Rhine be occupied by Allied troops. On 5 November Wilson informed the Germans that they could obtain the Allies' armistice conditions from their representative, Foch, and that these were based on the principles of the Fourteen Points. This would allow the Germans later to claim that the armistice was a contract binding the Allies and that the final peace treaty was thus unfair. Meanwhile a revolutionary government was installed in Berlin on 10 November, following the kaiser's abdication the previous day. Of particular importance to those such as Poincaré was the fact that the German army, though almost beaten, was not yet materially defeated. On the day of the armistice not one piece of German territory was occupied by Allied troops, even though the German army was still on French soil and still controlled four-fifths of Belgium, together with enormous areas in Eastern Europe. Thus the German civilian population was not obliged to confront defeat face to face. For the Germans defeat was regrettable, even inevitable, but also unjust and undeserved.

Some, like Poincaré, believed that this augured badly for the forth-coming peace negotiations, though they could not have guessed how explosive would be the use to which it would later be put. For the French in general, 11 November was a mixture of relief and pride in a merited triumph. There was a general belief that it was a victory for France, but also for Right and Justice. There were high hopes that Peace would be just as rewarding and that Germany would be dealt with severely and forced to pay for the devastation caused in human and material terms. 'Germany will pay' was the overriding sentiment which accompanied a blind faith in the remarkably popular Clemenceau.[22]

Of course the armistices were merely technical military documents which set out the conditions for a cease-fire; the Peace Conference proper, at which the twenty-seven coalition countries were represented, was opened by President Poincaré in Paris on the symbolic date of 18 January 1919, anniversary of the first proclamation of the German Empire at Versailles. The organisation of the Conference was through formal plenary sessions, attended by all the Allies, but the real negotiations between the leaders of the great powers took place in the Supreme Council. This was known as the Council of Ten comprising two delegates from each of the victorious powers of Britain, France, Italy, Japan and the USA. But much of the detailed work, particularly on reparations and the League of Nations, was carried out by eight commissions nominally responsible to the plenary Conference. Even so, the important territorial and economic questions were decided in the Supreme Council or in committees appointed by it. Thirty-two countries were represented at the Conference with the American and British delegations alone numbering over 1,000 and 400 personnel respectively; fifty-eight specialist committees dealt with the detailed business. This unwieldy machinery meant that it was not until 7 May 1919 that even provisional terms were submitted to the German delegates. In that time the Conference went through a series of crises over the French, Italian and Japanese claims. Decision-making was made somewhat easier after 24 March when it was decided to reduce the Council of Ten to one of Four comprising, Clemenceau, Lloyd George, Wilson and the Italian prime minister, Orlando. Subsidiary business was dealt with by the foreign ministers of the victorious powers in the Council of Five. Some resistance from the Germans delayed acceptance of the Allied terms, but the Treaty was signed on 28 June 1919. Their work completed, the heads of government left Paris. But there was still plenty of work to be done by the Council of the Heads of Delegations, which now became the supreme body. It worked out the terms of subsidiary treaties, the Versailles treaty being only one, albeit the most important, of five treaties making up the Peace of Paris. But even after the Germans had ratified the Versailles Treaty and the Conference had officially closed on 21 January 1920, a Conference of Ambassadors took over from the Council of Heads of Delegations to finalise treaties with Hungary and Turkey after those with Austria and Bulgaria. It was not until 10 August 1920 that the peacemaking process was at an end.[23]

The peace settlement dominated Poincaré's final year as president of the Republic just as it dominated the political life of the country, and there was scope here for his encyclopaedic knowledge of foreign affairs and his mastery of detail to be usefully employed. By the time the Conference opened, Germany was on the way to ridding itself of its revolutionary experience and was reconstituting itself as a moderate and united state, purged of the centrifugal forces which threatened to see the occupied Rhineland break away. On 10 December the social-democrat president welcomed the returning German armies to Berlin with the words 'I salute you, you whom no enemy has beaten on the battlefield'. General elections by universal suffrage were scheduled for 19 January 1919. Germany was reaffirming her legitimacy and was not going to remain passive on the international scene.[24] Her demobilisation was taking place only slowly; on 1 January 1919 she still had seventy-five divisions compared to France's hundred.[25] On 4 January 1919 Poincaré noted in his personal diary, 'Leygues regrets, like me, that the armistice was signed too early'. The belief that the cessation of hostilities was premature was supplemented by a suspicion that the American position was too pro-German and likely to weaken the peace. Poincaré therefore set up his own monitoring system by asking Foch 'to keep a total of all the violations of the armistice and to think about demanding new guarantees at the next renewal'. At the same time he set in motion his usual self-justification for intervention, this time over economic affairs: 'one feels strongly that nobody is leading the government on economic questions'.[26] The economic and financial picture was indeed dismal as American and British credit, on which France had survived relatively comfortably during the war, ceased. At the same time, serious and growing social unrest was rendered more threatening by contagion from events in Russia.

Relations with Clemenceau remained strained as the Tiger continued to keep Poincaré, Foch, parliament, the foreign affairs commission, the government and public opinion largely in the dark about the peace negotiations.[27] Poincaré was unembarrassed about intervening in cabinet meetings to attempt to ensure that French interests were respected, but such meetings were usually short, infrequent and not strictly about negotiations. Thus when Clemenceau announced with a certain resignation – according to Poincaré – that Wilson and Lloyd George had requested that English be the official language of the Peace Conference, he had spoken out firmly against such a move: 'I point out that after all that she has done, France could not tolerate having the moral benefit of the official language taken away from her.' In the end, French would be given equal status with English. But, Poincaré continued to be kept at arm's length from decision-making, which continued to reside with Clemenceau and a few experts, notably André Tardieu. Poincaré blamed the presidential strait-jacket for his predicament. Thus he rejected a proposal for the presidential mandate to be extended until after the general election; frustration probably also speeded his decision on 17 January 1919 to announce that he would be returning to the Senate on the expiry of his presidential mandate. His intention to return to active parliamentary life was clear.[28]

On the first day of the Conference Poincaré displayed his deep suspicions of Germany, whom he described as having protested about the peace conditions 'in haughty and almost threatening terms'. He concluded that 'it is certain that, already, the enemy is picking herself up and if we do not remain united and firm, everything is to be feared'. Though pleased for France that Clemenceau had been elected chairman of the Peace Conference, envy and cynicism about his rival dominated: was there not an ulterior motive on the part of Wilson and Lloyd George in appointing Clemenceau as chairman? 'They know Clemenceau. They flatter him, they caress his mania for popularity – and will thus obtain perhaps too many concessions from him.' He was obsessive about Clemenceau. Nearly every day of his diary contains some bitter reference to the Tiger. He recorded every complaint made to him about Clemenceau's weakness in pursuing French interests, even though many were from blatant Clemenceau opponents, like Foch. He took a malevolent pleasure in seeing his rival's popularity decline in proportion to delays in the peace negotiations, noting on 10 February that 'the idol is convincingly destroyed, at least for the moment'. He even exaggerated the Tiger's physical deterioration: 'What adds to my worries is that Clemenceau is ageing, he loses his memory and hearing more and more, becomes more and more violent and lightweight. He thinks he is discussing something, gets carried away, doesn't know the question, doesn't listen, is smug'.[29]

An area of particular interest for Poincaré, understandably, was the administering of Alsace. He believed that the French authorities were trying to Gallicise the region far too quickly and that their zealousness on questions such as religious schools was alienating local opinion.[30] He even went so far as to threaten Clemenceau with resignation if this attitude was not moderated.[31] Keeping a close watch over this problem, receiving local journalists and politicians and using their criticisms, he was able to put considerable pressure on the French high commissioner, Maringer, to moderate his desire to impose national legislation as quickly as possible on the reclaimed provinces. In the end he influenced Maringer's replacement by a professional politician, who was eventually to be Millerand. He even used his good relations with the archbishop of Paris, Cardinal Amette, to intercede with the Pope in getting the German bishops of Strasbourg and Metz replaced by French ones.[32] Emotion obviously influenced his attachment to Alsace–Lorraine, but he understood better than most how successful the Germanisation process had been in two generations and how it was necessary gently to win over the local population to the French fold. Doubtless, he was aware of the views of senior French officials like the secretary general of the Quai d'Orsay, Jules Cambon, who had warned that a plebiscite in the area might not show a majority for reunion with France.[33] Perhaps he also feared a re-enactment of the bitter struggles which had followed the 1905 legislation on the Separation of Church and State, given the piety of Alsace–Lorrainers. He was dismissive of the more arrogant French anti-clerical politicians and civil servants who believed that concessions to the local population would mean that 'We are going to have another Vendée on our flank'.[34] It is ironical that the 'laïque' Poincaré should have been instrumental in helping Alsace and parts of Lorraine remain to this day under the pre-1905 regime of the Concordat.

Another issue to which Poincaré paid particular attention was the French economy. It was in a parlous state with massive debt and accelerating inflation. This gave him another stick with which to beat Clemenceau whose lack of interest in financial matters was well known. Poincaré mocked any idea of Clemenceau ever coping with the country's finances and directly pressed the minister of finance, Klotz, to be ruthless in reining in government expenditure. Clemenceau had no problem with that; he later told his former secretary, Jean Martet, 'Klotz was above all Poincaré's man. I took him on so that the Elysée would leave me in peace.' Klotz was unable, or incapable, of controlling expenditure. Clemenceau may have been justifying why, during his premiership, government borrowing increased more dramatically than ever before.[35]

Poincaré's obsession with Clemenceau turned almost to mania following the assassination attempt on the French premier by a young anarchist on 19 February 1919. Despite having been hit by three bullets,

Clemenceau's morale was undented. Having recently been invited to India on a tiger shoot, he leaned across from his bed and with a smile said to his faithful lieutenant, Pichon, 'Well Pichon! I don't think we need to go to India ... It seems the Tiger is shot in the streets of Paris'.[36] Poincaré rushed to his bedside and described his old adversary's levity with a mixture of perplexity and veneration. This soon turned to envy when he realised the effect the attempted assassination was having on the Tiger's popularity: 'If, by misfortune, he were to die, they would make a god of him.' Poincaré seemed almost pleased to hear from the minister of the interior, Pams, that the police believed that such assassinations were contagious and that the president ought to take precautions. It gave him the chance to imitate Clemenceau's courage and cavalier manner and note dismissively, 'I reply to them: professional risk and ineffectual nature of precautions'.[37] But the next day he was green with envy at newspaper accounts of the floral tributes the Tiger had received with inscriptions such as 'saviour of France' and 'Père la-Victoire'. He noted acidly, 'Odd collective madness, strange legend which hide the truth and doubtless distort history'.[38]

Of course, Poincaré's envy was not assuaged by the increasing currency being given to the Poincaré-la-guerre myth. He lapsed into self-pity following an article to this effect in the *Journal du Peuple*: 'And I believe, however, that nobody did more than me, first to stop war, then to help victory'. Of course, he had some justification for resentment at his public image, but this, juxtaposed with the idolatry associated with Clemenceau, seemed to be becoming too much for him. The out-pourings in his diary smacked of paranoia: 'Messianism ... Clemenceau is le père la victoire, the liberator of the country, etc. And it is I who "unleashed war" and "killed millions of French people". The good genie and the bad genie.'[39]

Meanwhile, Poincaré continued to receive 'hate-mail' blaming him for everything from the cause of the war to the cost of living and threatening his life. If his diaries are anything to judge by, things do seem to have got the better of him on 25 February. In a four-page outpouring of self-pity he described his action since the end of 1911 as an example of self-sacrifice and devotion to the country for which, he believed, only Clemenceau had been rewarded. It was a mixture of self-delusion and legitimate grievance and is worth quoting at length as testimony of Poincaré's perception of events. He explained, with not a little disingenuousness, how he had reluctantly agreed to return to power in 1912 out of patriotism, having for so long declined to do so. More accurately, he noted that as *président du conseil* he had attempted two things: to avoid war and to ensure that in the event of France being attacked she should be ready. He explained how he was 'pushed' by colleagues in the ministry to seek election to the Elysée.

I came here, knowing that I would only experience tribulations and that it would be impossible for me to act personally. I wanted, at least, to keep watch on the dual programme which I had set myself: to guard against catastrophe, to ensure victory, if war broke out despite ourselves.

I continued my efforts in that direction. I immediately came up against the double attacks of Caillaux and Clemenceau. I had to put up with cabinets composed of my opponents. I held out, I persevered.

I did everything to prevent war. It came. For more than four years I worked hard. I asked for no reward. I worked in the shadows, without taking a minute's rest.

And then unwittingly confessing his power of influence, if not direct intervention, he explained how he had imposed the Salonika expedition in October 1915, in spite of Clemenceau, Joffre and Delcassé. He was correct in stating how, 'I was faced with the attacks of the defeatists, at the same time as those of Clemenceau. I carried on, I did not waver.' He confessed to having corrected Briand's policy in relation to Greece and again divulged his differences with all the other heads of government: 'I put up with Viviani's nerves, Briand's nonchalance, Ribot's weaknesses, Painlevé's hesitations'. There was, however, genuine self-sacrifice in his final choice of premier, even if by 1917 his freedom to choose was limited: 'I called Clemenceau in spite of his long campaign of calumny. I called him in spite of those who today praise him the most, in spite of Action française which attacked him not without reason, in spite of Sembat and Thomas who threatened me with trouble from the workers.' And he made a virtue out of necessity: 'I stepped aside for him. I had the most serious difficulties with his moods and upswings in his false energy.' While not begrudging Clemenceau his share of credit in the war effort, he understandably wished that his own contribution be recognised:

He rendered incomparable service in stopping the defeatist campaign, but still it was I who instructed him about the Bolo affair, and Caillaux etc.

Similarly, he rendered admirable service in maintaining the country's morale, hope, confidence. But, in that respect, I helped him and I acted like him and before him.

And he was critical of Clemenceau's stance at the end of the war:

On the eve of the armistice, he was intoxicated. He rushed everything to be able to enjoy victory more quickly. He wanted to sign the armistice with ridiculous conditions which would have presaged a disaster. He became annoyed with me, before following my advice. He wrote insulting things to me. I put up with everything. He ended up coming round to my way of thinking while claiming not to have needed my advice.

At the conference he was an incoherent chairman, he ruined everything through his vanity, he upset all the allies.

But the explanation for what was unjust, or at least exaggerated criticism of his rival, was soon revealed:

And he is at his climax. He is the saviour, the country's liberator, the organiser of victory, etc.

He directs nothing, he leaves the liberated departments in complete anarchy, he compromises France in Alsace ... And all Frenchmen believe in him like a new god. And me, I am insulted in the popular press ... I look like I have done nothing for the country; I am hardly talked about other than to be insulted.

Of course, his diatribe was replete with self-pity and jealousy. In the end, he blamed his fate not on his own shortcomings but, as he so often did, on the constitution: 'That is the work of a constitution which makes the President into a mere prompter, an advisor whom one is free not to listen to and who never has the right to be seen.' Or, as he put it more succinctly in his diary: 'Président de la République = zéro'.[40]

As usual, such outpourings on paper, whether in letters or in his diaries, had a cathartic effect. He returned quickly to badgering Clemenceau over the French administration of Alsace which he described as 'a policy of brutal assimilation and an administration wothy of a sub-Prefecture'. He continued to complain that the Peace Conference was getting nowhere, that French policy was disorganised, that the Allies were slipping into an inferior military position, that Germany was getting off the hook.[41] He was proved right in his criticism of Allied leaders for dealing piecemeal with Germany on aspects of the settlement rather than as a whole. The absence of a clear agenda at the Conference did result in delays, an impatient public opinion and a headlong scramble by the Allies to decide most of the German settlement between mid-March and the beginning of May.[42] Even though a number of colleagues insisted to him that article 8 of the constitution stipulated that the president of the Republic negotiated treaties, Poincaré still could not overcome Clemenceau's reluctance to communicate more thoroughly with him, or with the government. With Clemenceau continuing to operate independently of all except his closest advisors, it was not surprising that those who were nervous about his negotiating technique and intentions should meet discreetly and acquire an air of conspiracy. Poincaré himself increasingly received visits from Foch who, as a delegate to the Conference, kept him informed, though he was firmly excluded from the vital secret bargaining with the Allies. For all his claims to Poincaré about Clemenceau's feebleness in the face of the concerted negotiating power of the British and Americans, Foch's activities turned out to be empty gestures of protest which Clemenceau ignored, though the British suggested he be dismissed for insubordination.[43]

Poincaré put a good deal of store by Foch's views. Foch hoped, as did others such as Barthou, Millerand and a stream of journalists, that Poincaré would put pressure on Clemenceau to take a firmer line on the question of French security on the Rhine, which they viewed as vital to the future operation of the peace treaty as a whole. As the moderate Deschanel succinctly put it, 'Without guarantees for France, no guarantees for peace'.[44] But Poincaré could find no means of influencing Clemenceau and was deterred from more forceful action for fear that overt dissent in the French camp could weaken the French position further. Thus he refused to have a show-down over Clemenceau's swapping British and American guarantees for French security in return for French abandonment of an autonomous Rhineland. Poincaré feared that the Tiger might use his popularity to threaten resignation again, and in so doing provoke a serious domestic political crisis, further undermining France's international bargaining position, all of which could backfire against Poincaré. For the moment he switched his attention to putting pressure on Foreign Minister Pichon, whom he knew from experience to be more susceptible to his influence.[45] But this would prove equally ineffectual, given Clemenceau's grip on decision-making. Poincaré had little success with his other policies, notably his predilection for a strong League of Nations with its own army, which in his words would be 'the only form of alliance for us'.[46] But schemes like this and the call for a permanent military command to act as the executive of the League would be rejected by President Wilson in favour of general disarmament.

Poincaré's anxiety over Clemenceau's ability to negotiate favourably on France's behalf was heightened following the Council of Ten's transformation on 24 March into the Council of Four: 'it's terrifying, because Clemenceau is incapable, due to his deafness and ignorance, of defending alone France's interests'.[47] The secrecy of the meetings and Clemenceau's strategy became even more impenetrable. Even when the Tiger agreed to see the president on 27 March, 'with Pichon on a lead', to explain about discussions in the Council of Four, Poincaré was less than satisfied with the visit: 'can one call explanations a few confused, disorganised and truly incomprehensible words? Clemenceau leaves me the impression of being completely "manipulated" by the others'. He referred to Clemenceau as an 'Old, moronic, vain man' completely at the mercy of President Wilson and Lloyd George, exclaiming, 'I am scared stiff'.[48]

The difference between the two rivals increasingly focussed on the question of the occupation of the Left Bank of the Rhine. At the outset, Poincaré and Joffre had favoured an autonomous buffer state in the Rhineland, but this was not to the Allies' liking and the question of an occupation had won the day. Then Poincaré had called for an occupation which would last at least as long as it took Germany to pay France all of the reparations demanded of her, while Clemenceau settled very quickly on a fifteen-year occupation, claiming that Britain and America would agree to no more. The two men's negotiating styles were very different. Poincaré's not very original bargaining technique was to begin by asking for more on the basis of carefully prepared evidence in the expectation of settling for less. The detail of his arguments and his dogged pursuit of his claims made him an exasperating person to negotiate with, as many would testify. But given his legal experience of negotiating settlements for clients, he was probably a more skilled negotiator than Clemenceau. Clemenceau tended to bargain in a more spontaneous, intuitive way, which frightened his rigorous and method-ical rival.[49]

Poincaré was sufficiently dissatisfied with the fifteen-year occupation on which Clemenceau had settled that he attempted to have it over-turned. On 30 March he drafted a letter to Pichon, on whom he continued to put pressure. With hindsight, it is difficult to fault his arguments:

I hope therefore, despite all, that the *Président du Conseil* will obtain for France the right of occupation of the Left Bank as a guarantee for as long as our credit remains outstanding. I fear, I repeat to you, that any other combination will leave us in an impossible situation the day that Germany decides not to pay any more. In that event, England will have the possibility of blocking German ports, but we would have disarmed. Should we then move our troops into the demilitarised zone? That would be a serious step, which would give rise, without doubt, to many difficulties and would risk making us appear the aggressors; we would be blamed for relighting the fire.

He also referred to what had originally been his and Joffre's plan – an autonomous Rhineland: 'I don't believe we need to fear the slightest conflict between the population and our troops. Generals in the occupied zone say that the inhabitants are docile, reassured by the occupation, very defiant towards Berlin, and that petitions have even been handed to General Gérard with a view to autonomy under French protection.' Poincaré still favoured not just an extended occupation of German territory but autonomy for certain areas. On 8 April he noted in his diary that General Gérard had recently returned from Germany with petitions from local dignitaries in the Palatinate showing the desire for the setting up of an autonomous state detached from Germany. Meanwhile, the French army continued to demobilise in the area, drawing his tart comment: 'Anarchy!'[50]

However, none of the Allies was willing to entertain the idea of dismembering Germany, let alone returning her to a pre-Bismarckian decentralised state. Lloyd George in particular retained fears of a resurgence of the old Revolutionary and Napoleonic ambitions of the French in the Rhineland and of a new French hegemony on the continent if a united Germany were to disappear as a counterbalance. After all, France had undisputed military preponderance in Europe due to her formidable land army and airforce, while Britain and America had begun to disarm at the end of hostilities. In particular, British strategists feared French air power's ability to undermine the security once afforded by the English Channel before the advent of the air age. Lloyd George also feared that too harsh a treatment of Germany could see her become prey to Bolshevism. This was the problem confronting Clemenceau who, though initially in favour of Foch's idea of the Rhine being the Allies' common strategic frontier against Germany, was mindful of upsetting the wartime alliance which he strived to maintain in the post-war era. For Poincaré, however, the geostrategic importance of the Rhineland would not abate. Nor were such beliefs in independent German states under some sort of international control the prerogative of the military and nationalists; eminent university professors and certain radical-socialists also campaigned for them.[51]

By the beginning of April Poincaré had become the focus of opposition to Clemenceau's negotiating. On 4 April Ribot came to see him. 'He complains stridently that there is no *Président du Conseil*, that the government is not looking after the financial situation, that the country is being swept onto the perils of the future. He is only too right, but, despite all, I defend Clemenceau.'[52] Poincaré was torn between support for what he saw as French interests and his constitutional duty of support for a still popular head of government. Things came to a head on 6 April when Clemenceau went to the Elysée to complain that Poincaré's friends were constantly attacking him for not defending French interests. In a scene worthy of a boulevard farce, the two men exchanged verbal insults and their respective resignations in front of an astonished Klotz and Pichon. Poincaré's remarks to Clemenceau were more than disingenuous: 'I have never stopped being loyal, which goes without saying; but, I have been, furthermore, devoted and, to say the word, filial; I showed you unfailing deference and confidence.' After this blazing row, relations were again patched up. But there was little sincerity in Poincaré's closing remarks: 'If Briand or Barthou scheme against you, of which I am unaware, and if they invoke my friendship, tell me, help me to destroy the tales.' And he put in an obsequious parting bid for a closer working relationship with Clemenceau: 'I am at your disposal to second you, but help me to do so by hiding nothing from me and by coming to talk to me.' In fact, as soon as they had shaken hands and Clemenceau had left with his ministers, Poincaré put pen to paper in a violent effusion against the person to whom he had just pledged his loyalty: 'And it is this madman of whom the country has made a god'. He poured out his earlier vitriol, stating how Clemenceau had saved the country in 1917, 'because no one in the political world was there to do the task which I felt necessary. He only carried out that burden helped and often pushed by me. He allowed himself to be given all the credit.' And he concluded pessimistically, 'Intoxicated, blinded, he walks in his dream. No one can give him advice, he listens to nobody, and perhaps, alas! he is leading us into the abyss.'[53] Here as elsewhere there was more than a little mutual hypocrisy in relations between Poincaré and Clemenceau. From 1913 to 1917 Clemenceau had ceaselessly attacked Poincaré and attempted to undermine his authority; since that date Poincaré had been returning the favour. Yet deep down there was a strange attraction between these two opposites, albeit stronger on the younger man's side. Strange relationship, then, which evoked more that of feuding father and son – terms which they both used to characterise the relationship – rather than two political rivals.

Poincaré's frustration was broken momentarily the following day, when his vanity was flattered following the reception of a delegation of the Paris city council requesting his choice of a road which could bear his name. Though he at first feigned rejection by suggesting that such a move was contrary to custom, he finally suggested the top of the rue de Babylone where his parents had lived.

From February to April France's battle in the Conference had been for claims to the Rhineland and Saar. But under pressure from Britain and America, by 15 April Clemenceau had been pushed into accepting only demilitarisation and a fifteen-year occupation of the Rhineland in exchange for an Anglo-American guarantee. This, and Poincaré's fears about continued demobilisation of the French army before the peace treaty was signed, further poisoned relations between president and premier. Poincaré described France's general situation as chaotic. Despite the increasing number of representations made to him by critics of Clemenceau's negotiations, of whom Foch was the most vociferous, Poincaré continued to insist that he could not act against the head of government. Foch wanted Poincaré to take over negotiations, claiming that the draft peace treaty was tantamount to treason. Poincaré warned

Marshal Foch that his behaviour might be perceived as insubordination, given that Clemenceau was also minister of war. By 18 April Poincaré was called to arbitrate in the now serious dispute between Clemenceau and Foch over the latter's refusal to summon the German plenipotentiaries to Paris for 25 April because the cabinet had not seen the draft treaty. By 19 April not only Foch, but several delegations, including the president of the Senate, Antonin Dubost, had approached Poincaré to invite him to use article 8 of the constitution, according to which the president of the Republic negotiates treaties, to justify taking over negotiations at the Conference. But Poincaré refused on the grounds that constitutional practice did not permit it.[54]

Public opinion was growing impatient at the duration of negotiations. Clemenceau's strategy from the start had been to reach a quick settlement and to be conciliatory towards Britain and America in the belief that the wartime alliance and friendship would be prolonged beyond hostilities. This now seemed to many not to be paying off. Clemenceau himself seemed to sense this following a visit from Poincaré on 22 April in which he seemed 'all sweetness and light'. He asked for Poincaré's advice on a draft text of the peace proposals. Poincaré despatched by return of post detailed comments which were a reminder of his firm line in dealing with Germany and prophetic in their understanding of the German problem. On the question of the eventuality of France having to reoccupy the Rhineland he noted,

Re-occupation is likely to make us appear the aggressors; it would not be without peril, it would never be equivalent to maintaining the occupation until full payment is made. Anyway, it would be necessary to add carefully: 'Germany agrees not to oppose such a re-occupation in any way and to give orders to all local authorities to facilitate it.'

On the question of the independence of Austria he suggested with equal prescience, 'Recognition of the independence of Austria would doubtless not stop Germany from subsequently incorporating Austria, if she were able to get the latter to suggest this incorporation herself. It would be necessary to add that Germany contracts not to incorporate Austria.' Similarly, he informed Clemenceau that to abandon the Rhineland after fifteen years would be 'a serious danger' because it would mean losing any guarantee of repayment of what was owed to France and it would mean giving up, in Foch's estimation, France's only durable military barrier. The danger, he continued, would be even more 'terrible' if France abandoned this territorial guarantee in the hope of securing alliances and if these alliances were then not ratified by the British parliament or the American Senate. Thus no final date should be placed on the occupation, except when all the conditions had been met by Germany and the alliances with France's partners signed and sealed.[55]

When Clemenceau returned the following day, Poincaré gained the impression that he had not read his comments and wished to ignore his suggestions. But Poincaré was able to get the cabinet to hear Foch's argument on 25 April for a military occupation to continue for as long as reparations were due. However, at that meeting Poincaré refused to speak up for Foch, even though Clemenceau produced counter-arguments. The cabinet approved Clemenceau's position. The whole episode demonstrated the limits of Poincaré's freedom of manoeuvre. He seemed once more to fear provoking a political crisis in which the constitutional impartiality of the president of the Republic would be seriously impugned. Furthermore, just as in 1917 Poincaré had understood the necessity of appointing Clemenceau, now in 1919 he understood how important it was to retain him. Hence his insistence that it would be a disaster if the Clemenceau government were overturned and why, despite the bluster, Poincaré continued to support him as head of government. Complain he might about the Tiger, but the president was haunted by a reluctant admiration for him and a fear that a political crisis following his departure could easily lead to a Caillaux ministry.[56]

By the beginning of May Poincaré was no better disposed towards Clemenceau's negotiations. On 2 May he warned that he would not sign a treaty to which Italy was not a party, Orlando having walked out on the Conference, and he declared to Pichon, whom he found 'spineless and amorphous', that 'I don't understand anything of the method adopted, other than that we are in complete disorder, that everything is run by vanity and casualness and incompetence.' Now he was threatening resignation himself, stating that it was likely to be followed by that of Foch, who indeed threatened his if greater respect was not paid to issues of French security. On 3 May Poincaré was distressed to read the preliminary proposals for reparations, which he considered vital to French interests. He found 'most regrettable' the statement that Germany had insufficient resources to cover the complete payment of reparations and that consequently payment should be delayed. He noted, 'this opens the door to all manner of refusal with which she might wish to oppose us'.[57]

In a cabinet meeting on 4 May, exceptional for its duration and timing – two and a half hours on a Sunday – its members were presented for the first time with the treaty and asked for approval. Poincaré believed that the meeting had been so arranged as to minimise discussion by only asking ministers directly involved in negotiations to report on their area. Clemenceau then spoke on relations with Italy, criticising her demands.

Poincaré found the premier at his most incoherent, 'quite the impulsive and scatterbrain Clemenceau of the worst days'. Poincaré pointed out that the French should be supporting the Italians, their only real friends in the Council of Four. In spite of Poincaré's criticisms, the peace terms were unanimously endorsed.[58]

That evening he dined with his brother and family to seek advice on whether he should resign. 'I ask myself whether I shouldn't hand it in, in any case, in view of the mediocre peace conditions.' Henriette Poincaré and his sister-in-law, Marie-Andrée, believed he should, while his brother Lucien was less categorical, without advising him to stay. In the end Poincaré was saved from a difficult decision by a visit the following day from Pichon, who informed him that the Italians, who had withdrawn from the Conference as a sign of disapproval, had decided to return. He told Pichon: 'I would certainly have resigned if an arrangement had not been reached with Italy. It is still possible that I shall not agree to sign the treaty, because no account has been taken of my observations on the fifteen year occupation.' And he concluded by stating to Pichon that if Marshal Foch resigned he would probably be forced to follow. In the end Freycinet was able to convince him that his resignation would provoke disorder; he was flattered to hear this 'powerful' argument.[59] Whether he would have resigned is doubtful, given his usual procrastination on such important moral issues. It was this kind of episode which led many of his closest friends to conclude that he was lacking in moral courage. Neither would he carry out his threat to resign over the ratification of the treaty, or for that matter refuse to sign it, even though he remained profoundly unhappy with it. On 7 May the Allies hurriedly presented the peace proposals to the Germans with instructions that they were permitted only to make written objections in the following fifteen days rather than enter round-the-table discussions. Even then the Allies would accept no fundamental changes to the treaty, merely 'practical suggestions'.[60]

The Germans found the terms of the draft treaty severe, 'unfulfillable', 'unbearable' and a contravention of the Armistice agreement. They organised their responses around this accusation.[61] But Poincaré continued to believe that France had not won enough guarantees for her security and that the Allies, led by President Wilson, were committing 'a grave psychological error in relation to the Germans' by making concessions to them. Clemenceau himself seemed to be coming round to the idea that force might be necessary and told Poincaré so on 21 May. The reply he received was clear evidence of Poincaré's own long-held psychology of the Germans: 'We are two of a kind, then, because I believe that if we go down the road of concessions to the Germans we are lost.'[62]

While the Allies waited for the main German reply, which came on 29 May, Poincaré continued to lament the handling of the treaty negotiations, noting on that day that 'it appears clearly that Tardieu [commissioner for Franco-American war business], the real author of the treaty, has sacrificed everything to what he believed were the interests of the Franco-American alliance'.[63] At the same time his diaries reveal a number of other preoccupations. He attempted to coach the minister of finance, Klotz, on the intricacies of high finance, knowing that he was one of the few allowed to participate in the next great issue at stake between France and the Allies: reparations. But here again he had little success; Clemenceau, despite his own notorious financial incompetence, had decided to ignore Klotz's suggestions as unrealistic, allegedly commenting, 'Just my luck to get hold of the only Jew who can't count'.[64]

Meanwhile, Poincaré's fascination with the French royal family surfaced again. He was particularly pleased to confer the military cross on the duc de Guise, who in return offered to act as an intermediary with the princes of Germany and Poland. The duc told him that he and his family would be most grateful if Poincaré as president of the Republic could be represented at the funeral of the comtesse de Paris. Poincaré appeared to wish to accept, stating that before her death the countess had been awarded a medal from the 'government of the Republic'. He agreed to discuss it with the government first. However, both Clemenceau and Pichon suggested he refrain from doing so. Disappointed, he remarked, 'I had to be satisfied with sending Pénelon [Elysée's military liaison officer] to the Duc de Vendôme and to the Duc de Guise to express my sympathies'.[65] This recalled Poincaré's earlier flirtations with the various branches of the French royal family, and which singled him out from other senior republican politicians. Rather than constituting a crude monarchism, even less a desire for a restoration, his view of the French monarchy was that it was a missing piece from the enormous mosaic of national unity which he sought for France. He had kind words for the 'patient work of the ancient monarchy' in centralising the French state, claiming that the Republic had inherited the results of that beneficent policy.[66] His old school-friend Paléologue notes a conversation with him in which, while stating that he was republican 'to the bone', Poincaré noted,

That does not stop me from believing 10 August 1792, the invasion of the Tuileries and the arrest of Louis XVI, to be a catastrophic date for our history. Without that horrible day, France would have continued, like England, her normal development under the palladium of monarchist institutions with all the strong discipline which age-old tradition teaches a people and of which we have such a great need.

When Paléologue remarked that Louis-Philippe's declaration to be 'King of the French' was worse because it broke the continuity of the monarchy's legitimacy, Poincaré was said to have replied, 'You have just made me understand why I have always found the Orléanists unsympathetic'.[67] Even allowing for Paléologue's characteristic exaggeration these remarks come as no surprise. But Poincaré was a realist in believing that the Republic was now what best suited the French. That did not stop him appreciating the monarchy and its contribution to the formation of the French nation and French greatness. Just as the Revolution was a *bloc* for Clemenceau, so French greatness was a *bloc* for Poincaré. In that, he was probably no different from many moderate politicians who, in the tradition of French patriotic history, saw French greatness as a seamless robe. But as the playwright, Maurice Donnay, remarked in his reception address for the monarchist writer, Jacques Bainville, elected to Poincaré's seat in the Académie française in 1935, and whom Poincaré had always confessed to admiring, 'Perhaps Raymond Poincaré envied your ability to convey to Frenchmen from your position verities that he was never able to say from his own'.[68]

Poincaré continued to be anxious about his old bugbear, Caillaux, who had recently been questioned in preparation for his forthcoming trial and had made a statement implicating Poincaré in responsibility for the war. He was distressed by Caillaux's claim that in the last days of peace he, Poincaré, had stated that 'France is having difficulty declaring war' (La France ne se laisse pas déclarer la guerre). Poincaré strenuously denied having said anything of the sort.[69] It was a further example of those wishing to propagate the Poincaré-la-guerre myth. As the payment of German reparations came increasingly to dominate international politics, as calls from Germany for a revision of the Versailles Treaty became ever more shrill, and as Poincaré's return to power seemed ever more likely, so the myth gathered momentum.

The peace treaty was finally signed on 28 June 1919 in the Hall of Mirrors of the Palace of Versailles, symbol of French greatness, where almost half a century earlier the German Empire had been proclaimed on the back of a defeated and humiliated France. Poincaré was a mere ten years old when the Treaty of Frankfurt amputated Alsace and part of his native Lorraine and imposed an occupation of French territory until the payment of a huge war indemnity. Now at fifty-eight his legalism and attention to detail would not have missed the reverse symmetry between past and present – he wrote to Pichon on 30 March to remind him that 'The Germans stayed in France until 1873 and were paid before evacuating our territory'.[70] Alsace and Lorraine had been returned to the fold, German territory would be occupied, but there remained the huge question of the amount of reparations Germany would have to pay to France, the most devastated of all the Allies. Reparations would command Poincaré's attention for the next six years.

Reparations

Despite Poincaré's misgivings, the French had largely fulfilled their territorial and financial goals. Though they had compromised more radically than the British on their initial Peace Conference objectives, they had ensured that Germany could not again be a threat to their security – provided the Versailles treaty was faithfully executed.[71] Though the Left Bank of the Rhine remained German sovereign territory, it was demilitarised together with a fifty-kilometre zone on the Right Bank. The Left Bank and the bridgeheads on the Right Bank were to be occupied by the Allies for fifteen years. The Saar, which the French had claimed, was put under League of Nations administration, while its rich coal deposits became French property. After fifteen years a plebiscite would decide its future. In sum, German territory was reduced by one-seventh and its population by one-tenth, while all of its colonies and economic zones of influence were given up. The German army was reduced to 100,000 men, its navy to 15,000, its military academies and High Command suppressed, while at the same time it was denied all heavy artillery, tanks and aviation. Its merchant shipping fleet was largely confiscated and its foreign assets in Allied and associated countries seized. The Allies were also to benefit from 'most favoured nation' status in German trade. Finally, according to article 231, Germany recognised her sole responsibility for the causes and damage of the war and consequently her obligation to pay reparations. These and the method of payment were to be calculated by an Allied reparation commission before 1 May 1921, and in the meantime Germany would make a down payment of 20 billion gold marks. These treaty conditions which dealt with Germany were reinforced by the promise to France of an Anglo-American military alliance in lieu of an autonomous Rhineland. Whatever the deficiencies of the Versailles Treaty, against which Poincaré continued to rail, it contained enough within it to make a new rise of Germany and a second world war impossible, even though it could not hope to win German acceptance. The problem would be one of enforcement, which in itself stemmed from the malfunctioning of coalition diplomacy in the post-war years. No victors' peace conditions are immutable and evolve with the changing balances of power. The problem with the Versailles peace settlement was that it was revised in as little as five years of its being signed, and the remainder overturned within two decades. The peace turned out to be only a truce and in 1939 the war began again, in circumstances far less favourable to the western powers.[72]

Poincaré's dissatisfaction with the Versailles Treaty was arguably overstated; his greater disapproval of its lack of enforcement was not. There was a foretaste of Poincaré's views on the enforcement of the treaty in the speech he made at the grand dinner he hosted for the Conference delegations on the eve of the signing. But he had the good grace to express his discontent in muted terms when he declared that the treaty would be 'a continuous creation'.[73] The treaty was ratified by 372 votes to 53 in the French Chamber on 2 October, unanimously by the Senate on the 12th and was finally prorogued by the president of the Republic on 10 January 1920, whereupon it became operative. It was not for want of trying that Poincaré had been excluded from decision-making in the peace settlement; Clemenceau had seen to that. Whether his hard line would have achieved anything more substantial in the face of the powerful opposition of Great Britain and the United States is doubtful; Poincaré could not ignore the importance of Allied solidarity at this time any more than Clemenceau, as he came to understand when he returned to power in 1922. Of course, Poincaré's tough line may have just been rhetoric; he more than most politicians adopted hard-line positions out of power, which contrasted strikingly with his more conciliatory actions in power. This seriously questions the likelihood of Poincaré achieving a better peace settlement than Clemenceau. But where both men could agree was on the need for the treaty to be effectively executed, which demanded that France maintain her national energy and will-power.[74] Even then, forces beyond French control would quickly undermine the settlement and France's security.

The first step in the undoing of the guarantees to France was the decision by the American Senate on 19 November 1919 not to ratify the Versailles Treaty and the military pact with France. As a consequence the British guarantee also fell. Clemenceau had staked everything on Anglo-American involvement in the international relations of the European continent and thus the security of France. France was again left with no formal allies and thus no psychological, let alone military, security against her German neighbour. The financial and economic consequences of the American withdrawal were no less serious in that the French had hoped to link German reparations to French war debts owed to the United States. Equally disturbing was that, although Britain remained bound by the treaty, her differences with France over its execution were growing. Britain's security was largely catered for by the destruction of the German fleet and her own renovated mastery of the seas. She was therefore inclined to be a good deal more indulgent towards Germany and hostile to French forward action in, for instance, the Rhineland and the Ruhr, which she saw as potentially replacing one continental hegemony with another. Thus France was the only major power left to secure a faithful execution of the treaty from a reluctant Germany. But the Franco-German problem was not limited to bilateral relations. In the inter-war years it extended to the whole of Europe and the newly created states in its central and eastern regions. Here on every issue, from the German–Polish border to the independence of Czechoslovakia, France found herself face to face with Germany: the former representing the *status quo* of 1919, the latter the revisionists. Once again the future of Europe was dependent on Franco-German relations.[75]

The end of 1919 was marked by a cascade of elections not seen since the early days of the Third Republic in 1876. It began with the legislative elections on 16 November under a hybrid system of proportional representation, which met with Poincaré's approval. It ended with the Senate elections on 11 January 1920, in which Poincaré was triumphantly elected for the Meuse, despite his presidential mandate not yet having expired. The general elections were a resounding victory for the Bloc national which, contrary to received opinion, was not the preserve of the Right, but rather a broad coalition of forces grouped around the centre extending to the Left and Right. It was subsequent radical critics who portrayed the new majority as united in reactionary purpose – a reincarnation of the 1871 monarchist assembly or even the 1814 Chambre introuvable, a reactionary surprise in the wake of war. 59 per cent of *députés* were new faces, often having served during the war, thereby conferring on the Chamber its epithet 'Blue Horizon' from the colour of French military uniforms. Though the Chamber had moved to the centre and Right, this tendency was not reflected in the other elections, notably in the Senate, where the Radicals reinforced their position, placing the upper house to the Left of the Chamber and creating a significant problem for future *présidents du conseil*.[76]

With these elections out of the way it was possible to proceed with the elections for president of the Republic. Clemenceau, a long-standing critic of the presidential office, still allowed his name to go forward, while retaining the premiership. At the preliminary meeting of the republican groups from Senate and Chamber on 16 January, Clemenceau was defeated by the moderate and decorative Paul Deschanel (though not a candidate, Poincaré obtained sixteen votes). The next day the old custom – broken by Poincaré – of the president of the Republic being a passive character was restored. On the 18th, mortified by the snub, Clemenceau resigned as *président du conseil*.[77] That evening

Poincaré called on the uncrowned leader of the Bloc national, Millerand, to form a new government.

Millerand's new government combined respect for political tradition and innovation. It contained for the first time since 1877 – Denys Cochin's wartime experience apart – well-known Catholics as well as a significant number of non-parliamentary ministers; it established a minister for hygiene and social security and included a black Senegalese commissioner to oversee black troops. Millerand's belief that the Bloc national were the descendants of the républicains de gauche meant that it rejected extremism, social revolution and clerical reaction. Such views coincided with Poincaré's, as did Millerand's statement that a parliamentary regime and a strong executive were not mutually exclusive.[78] Finally, a large majority of députés were in favour of a strict application of the treaty.

On 17 February 1920 Poincaré's term as president of the Republic ended. His successor, Paul Deschanel, would have his presidential mandate foreshortened by his mental state and tendency to take to the trees in the Elysée gardens. Millerand, who replaced him at the Elysée from 23 September 1920, would attempt to give to the presidency the powers Poincaré had always believed the office should have.

When Poincaré left the Elysée his star was in the ascendant; the Chamber and Senate voted a law declaring, at last, that he had 'well merited la patrie'. In many ways he had not had a 'good war', being at the moment of victory overshadowed by Clemenceau. Now with Clemenceau off touring the United States, he seemed to enjoy newfound recognition. With his appetite for public adulation, his swan-song was a series of official visits to the war-torn areas of the country where he beat the drum of war reparations and Germany's obligation to pay. He ended his tour at Verdun, symbol of France's heroic resistance to Germany, with the following words:

Who would allow the promises, signed by Germany, not to be kept by her? Don't let her believe in any likelihood of weakness. However incomplete it may be, the Treaty itself gives us the means to see it respected ... Let us tear the sword from German hands and not tolerate her picking up the pieces. The right of peoples has been re-established. Don't let us allow the empires which did not respect it to reconstitute themselves secretly, and to threaten it again.[79]

Thus Poincaré sought to have his name associated with a rigorous application of the treaty. It was well taken; on leaving office he succeeded Charles Jonnart on the reparation commission.

When Poincaré took over as the French delegate and president of the reparation commission, Deschanel was still president of the Republic

and Millerand prime minister. Out of office Millerand had had a
reputation for robust views on Germany, but as head of the government
and minister of foreign affairs his policies mellowed, though the public
was never fully aware of the change. This is important for the same
change would affect Poincaré nearly two years later. It is a commonplace of parliamentary democracy that in opposition, or at least out of
power, when freed from the shackles of office and of having to put
words into deeds, politicians are prone to make ambitious statements
designed to seduce public opinion. Once returned to office they may be
deflected from earlier claims by unstable majorities, the momentum of
previous policies and the pressure of events. There can have been few
periods in the history of the Third Republic when such pressures on
political leaders were greater in force and number than in the aftermath
of the Great War. Leaving aside the perennial problem of shifting
parliamentary majorities, there were, for instance, the unparalleled
problems of reconstruction, the restoration of French finances, the
maintenance of France's wartime alliances and relations with Germany,
and all at a time when French public opinion, exceptionally in the
history of the regime, was taking an interest in foreign policy and
international relations, from the treatment of Germany to reparations
and the League of Nations. Co-ordinating and directing such powerful
and often contradictory forces in the direction of one's own policies
was likely to test the fortitude of greater mortals than Millerand and
Poincaré. Political leaders were bound to be pushed off course, as even
the robust and combative Clemenceau discovered at the Peace
Conference. Within weeks of taking office, Millerand was discussing
the economic collaboration with Germany set in train by his predecessors. His finance minister, Frédérique François-Marsal, was a moderate
on reparations who believed in international credit to restore the
economies of Europe, as did Jacques Seydoux, the main foreign
ministry official concerned with economic matters. The two main
French reparations experts from the ministry of finance in the first half
of 1920 roughly agreed with the British economist John Maynard
Keynes's view that it was folly to overload Germany with reparations.
Solely on the issue of establishing a figure for German reparations,
Millerand had been deflected from an earlier tougher stance. He ended
up pursuing a more moderate policy towards Germany. The policy
shifted between maintaining good relations with Britain and trying to
ensure enforcement of the treaty.[80] The Millerand example is instruc-
tive for two reasons: it explains why Poincaré – for the moment still
wedded to a hard-line policy – would resign so quickly from the
reparation commission; more importantly it explains why in moving

into Millerand's shoes in January 1922, Poincaré would act no differently.

Poincaré had hoped that as president of the reparation commission, established by the Versailles Treaty, he would be able to ensure the treaty's strict application. Without believing that it was a good treaty, in the absence of the Anglo-American guarantee of France's security it seemed France's only salvation – and who better than he to ensure respect for a legal text. Characteristically he applied himself to this goal 'au service de la France' with rigour and attention to detail, but he soon found that the commission was merely recording German violations instead of ensuring enforcement of the treaty.[81] It was partly to do with Britain short-circuiting the commission by insisting that all important negotiations should be conducted at cabinet level. Furthermore, Poincaré was increasingly coming into conflict with Millerand's policy of wishing to accommodate Britain over reparations. He informed his old friend that his policy was 'very perilous for our debt' and 'very dangerous for France'.[82] By May, after the Hythe Conference, he had resigned, telling his personal secretary and husband to his niece Lysie, François Guionic, that this had been forced upon him because 'The direction in which we are moving seems to me to be too dangerous for me not to regain my complete freedom of speech and action'.[83]

His new freedom enabled him to publicise his view that the fiction of Allied solidarity should be denounced to allow France to pursue her policy in her own interests. This was more in tune with the desires of French public opinion and the parliamentary majority. Liberated from the constraints of seven years of office he basked in the popularity which his speeches and regular columns for the *Revue des Deux Mondes, Le Temps* and *Le Matin* generated on the need to enforce the treaty. But it was easy to take such a line out of office. As he would learn on his return to power in 1922, unless he was willing to break with Britain, face inter-Allied debt demands and see the franc depreciate, there was little choice but to make concessions.[84] Doubtless there was an element of political expediency and campaigning in the forceful policy he advocated, for he had set his cap at returning to office in the near future, but rather as in 1913, before his election to the presidency, his reputation for anti-Germanism was more rhetorical than real. Jules Cambon, when ambassador to Berlin in 1913, had witnessed a similar change in Poincaré's attitude following his elevation to the Elysée, noting to his brother, 'I am struck to see how aggressive he was about Germany until he was elected, and how benign he has become since his election'.[85] The political situation may have been reversed but Poincaré's tactics had changed very little.

During 1921 Poincaré's political stature continued to grow. Economic, political and foreign affairs gave relief to someone whose image had become tarnished during the war years. As the economy worsened so he was remembered for his pre-war rigour in managing the state's finances; as social unrest grew, he was cited as standing for social order; as the decadence of the 'roaring twenties' shocked, so his austerity and probity were highlighted. It was as if this politician once out of step with his times in the Belle Epoque was now fully in tune. But Poincaré had not changed. Times had come round to suit his qualities. The middle class and its values were under threat. Now the quintessential representative of those values was at his most popular since before the war.

Meanwhile, the German foreign office, through its War Guilt Section, was working to overturn the principle of German responsibility for the war enshrined in article 231 of the treaty. The French authorities were well aware of this campaign from reports from their legations and embassies abroad. As the head of the French legation in Bavaria put it in a dispatch to the Quai d'Orsay on 5 April 1921, 'a violent campaign using the press, posters and meetings is underway in Germany to undermine the legal basis of the Versailles treaty: German guilt in the war'.[86] The French consul in Nuremberg summarised the campaign more tersely: 'the Versailles treaty is based on German guilt. Now Germany is not guilty. Therefore the Versailles treaty must be revised. Immediate consequence: Germany should not be compelled to pay any reparations.'[87] The Quai d'Orsay took this very seriously and compiled a whole archive devoted entirely to German attempts to manipulate the 'war responsibility' debate for its own ends. The French reports show that the campaign was meticulously and openly orchestrated using reputable personalities from the academic world and was directed not only at German public opinion but world opinion, with a particular emphasis on America and neutral powers. The reports also show that, increasingly, German propaganda was attempting to shift the blame on to France and, in particular, Poincaré. As Poincaré's role in the 1920s increased so he became the focus of the propaganda. Certainly the gravity with which the French foreign ministry treated this whole campaign is reflected in the copying of many of the dispatches to France's main embassies.[88] The revisionist thesis would be energetically and relentlessly promoted during these years with as its corollary the development of the Poincaré-la-guerre myth, as has been shown above. It would find a sympathetic audience in the newly elected French Chamber, which contained seventy-two *députés* who formed a group which was in total opposition to the policy of the government over the content and application of the Versailles Treaty. Those such as members of the newly established French Communist party, formed the year before and particularly sensitive to the Soviet desire to discredit their tsarist predecessors, were not averse to encouraging that myth. Not surprisingly, the French secret services became intensely involved in attempting to track down the links between German propaganda and the growing campaign in France. At the end of 1921 a report from the deuxième bureau of the ministry of war was passed to the Quai d'Orsay explaining how German secret services in Switzerland were giving large amounts of money to the Communist party's Librairie de l'Humanité in Paris. The communist publishers had recently produced a damning account by the journalist, Alfred Pevet, of French responsibility in the origins of the war, with particular reference to Poincaré, entitled *Les responsabilités de la guerre*. According to French intelligence reports this was now to be translated into German and distributed throughout neutral countries.[89]

Poincaré was kept informed of the campaign against him. To counter attacks against himself and the treaty in 1921 he embarked on a series of lectures with as their theme the origins of the war. He rebutted the growing theory that French *revanche* had been a major cause of the war. He placed the blame squarely on the kaiser who 'clearly foresaw that the Austrian ultimatum to Serbia had as a probable consequence a general war'.[90] But his efforts stood little chance against the powerful German campaign. He would come into day-to-day contact with the intensified version of it on his return to the foreign ministry in January 1922.

In February 1921 Poincaré secured election to the strategic post of president of the Senate foreign affairs commission. From here he could keep a close watch on Briand's policy, who since 16 January 1921 had formed a centre-left cabinet in which he held the foreign affairs portfolio. Though Millerand, as president of the Republic, was now intervening more directly in foreign affairs, Poincaré kept up his own pressure on Briand's foreign policy. He feared that Briand's track record during the war of being willing to negotiate unofficially with Germany might be detrimental to France's interests.

At first Poincaré must have been pleasantly surprised by Briand's policy of firmness in dealing with Germany. That policy was clearly demonstrated by the Franco-British occupation of three Ruhr towns on 8 March 1921 in order to force Germany into executing the disarmament and reparations clauses of the treaty. It was reflected in Briand's speech to the Senate on 5 April 1921, in which he threatened Germany with 'a firm hand on the scruff of the neck' if reparations were not adhered to. Firmness was also clear from his orders to Foch to prepare a plan for the total occupation of the Ruhr by Britain and France should Germany refuse to pay a total reparations bill of 132 billion gold marks.[91] But by the end of 1921 Britain was of the opinion that German reparations were set too high and Briand, in the interests of the alliance, was inclined to follow. A drift towards conciliation with Germany seemed to be Briand's natural policy. He found support for it on the Left in the person of Edouard Herriot, the president of the Radical party, which had withdrawn from the Bloc national in November 1919; but that policy was not to the liking of the Bloc national or Poincaré, who denounced it. To be fair to Briand, France's weakness and Britain's superiority limited his freedom of manoeuvre. It was only a matter of time before the mismatch between, on the one hand, Briand's parliamentary majority and, on the other, his deference to Britain and conciliation of Germany, would become intolerable. In January 1922, while Briand was attending the Allied conference in Cannes, he received a series of telegrams from President Millerand. These urged him not to concede to a moratorium on German reparations which Britain was demanding in exchange for an Anglo–French guarantee pact. To bolster his position Millerand, in executive style, decided to summon the cabinet in Briand's absence on 10 January and obtain its approval for a rejection of the premier's policy. Briand returned to Paris on 12 January to discover that Millerand's views were in line with parliament's, and resigned that evening. Poincaré was known to be opposed to Briand's policy and to have the support of the Bloc. Millerand called on him to form a government.[92]

With the appointment of Poincaré as premier on 15 January 1922, for the first time in the history of the Republic, though not the last, a former president of the Republic returned to government. No doubt Poincaré's tidy mind took cognisance of the fact that it was ten years almost to the day since he had formed his first ministry. Now, as then, his new cabinet reflected a desire not to break with the Radicals and included four among its number. Poincaré's new government was no different from the others of the Bloc national, which, contrary to received opinion, were centrist governments.[1] Overall the general tone of the government was set by its reliance principally on members of the centre-left Alliance démocratique, such as Barthou and André Maginot. But there was more continuity than change in the new government. Most of Briand's ministers were retained, though occasionally with different portfolios. It would soon be clear that there was almost as much continuity in policy as personnel. A particular characteristic of the new team was the inclusion of political and legal friends direct from the Poincaré stable, like Charles Reibel and Maurice Colrat. This was not inspired by nepotism. Poincaré's experience of government had brought him to the conclusion that too wide a gap often existed between executive decisions and their execution, largely as a result of the independence of senior permanent officials. An inner circle of loyal colleagues could to a certain extent overcome that, as Clemenceau had demonstrated; Colrat was made *sous-secrétaire d'état à la présidence du conseil* to co-ordinate his team. Poincaré, like all heads of government of that legislature, reserved for himself foreign affairs, as indeed would 53 per cent of all premiers from 1919 to 1939, demonstrating foreign affairs' crucial impact on French politics.[2] Paradoxically, though his cabinet included few members of the largest parliamentary grouping, the centrist and right-wing Entente républicaine et sociale, it would provide the mainstay of support for his policy of firmness towards Germany, while dissenting from his domestic policy and desire to keep the Radicals sweet. The Radicals in the Chamber would, however, be split between support and abstention for his policies. But on the question of the occupation of the Ruhr in January 1923 they would vote with him, as would the whole Chamber, except for the extreme Left socialists and Communists. Gradually, as the extreme Right began to raise its head in the country, the Left began to rediscover its unity and the majority of Radicals slid into opposition to the government. This sliding of his parliamentary support towards the centre-right was by default, and was certainly something to which Poincaré was ideologically opposed.[3] Like Millerand, and Briand before him, Poincaré had wished to rely for support on the centre to avoid becoming the prisoner of the Bloc national. This contradicts the subsequent perception of him as the right-wing premier happily leading a right-wing Chamber. Once again it is an example of how, like the Bloc governments themselves, Poincaré has been depicted with hindsight through the eyes of his *future* political adversaries as a political reactionary.

Similar unhistorical processes operated over Poincaré's policy to Germany in the period before the Great War, as has been shown above. The same applies to the 1920s. Because of the currency of the 'Poincaré-la-guerre' myth, fostered by political opponents and by the German authorities, Poincaré's foreign policy of the 1920s has been consistently depicted in a narrowly anti-German light. Recent research has shown this interpretation to be erroneous and that Poincaré's policy towards Germany was markedly more conciliatory, even weak, than has hitherto been believed.

Policy towards Germany

German press reaction to Poincaré's return to power was so hostile that the French ambassador in Berlin was instructed to intercede with the German government.[4] This should have come as no surprise given the massive propaganda exercise underway in Germany designed to undermine German responsibility in the origins of the war by transferring much of the blame on to Poincaré in particular. Nevertheless, part of the German reaction could be attributed to the image which Poincaré had himself fostered since the end of the war – that of ensuring a strict application of the peace treaty and a forceful policy on reparations. This was how he was perceived in France and had never attempted to deny it. It was also the image which Britain had of him. In April 1921 Lloyd George had feared that a flat refusal of Briand's policy for action against Germany, following her default on reparations, would drive France into recalling Poincaré and the adoption of a policy of independent action.[5] This was encapsulated in the famous attempt by Lloyd George to treat

Briand to his first ever round of golf at Cannes in January 1922. According to one member of the party, Jules Laroche, then deputy director of the Quai d'Orsay, Briand got in the way of Sir Edward Grigg's drive, only to be hauled aside by the British prime minister gesticulating at his forehead and warning in elementary French, 'Watch out, if the ball hits here, Briand zap! and then ... Poincaré!' Laroche noted in his memoirs, 'We knew the fear which the Welshman had of a return to power of the Lorrainer, whose juridical mind he detested, a fear which Briand wished to use to get his way.'[6] Following Briand's recall, it was too much for the French nationalist press not to seize on the metaphor of the British prime minister giving a lesson to their leader and presenting the whole episode as the 'coup de Cannes' (punning on the French for golf-club, the name of the coastal resort and the French expression for a caning).

Whatever his public image, there were clear signs in private well before 1922 that Poincaré might adopt a more conciliatory attitude towards Germany. On 16 December 1920, when the French were urging the Germans to reach some sort of programme for economic collaboration with them through a system of reparations in kind, the French delegate to the Brussels Conference, Pierre Cheysson, told his German counterpart that Tardieu, Loucheur and Poincaré 'have now wheeled around and come to the conviction that economic collaboration with Germany is necessary'. The German ambassador in Paris telegraphed to Berlin that later that day Poincaré had approached him at a dinner and had spoken reasonably about reparations.[7] That moderate line was still in evidence on 8 January 1921 when Cheysson reported that Poincaré had told him of his 'readiness to tell Germany that he would examine with "benevolence" her capacity for payment in order to set the sums that the Allies would ask for' and had even approved the plan for a provisional five-year settlement for German reparations.[8]

Thus when Poincaré returned to government at the beginning of 1922 it was with a more open mind than his public persona betrayed; but there was a limited amount of freedom for any politician coming to power at this time. French foreign policy had acquired a general momentum since the peace treaty. The momentum appeared to come more from the French bureaucratic machine than its political masters. Certainly more than at any other time in the history of the Third Republic, foreign affairs actively involved a multitude of interested governmental and unofficial agencies: parliament, the central administration of the foreign ministry, diplomats in the key embassies of London, Washington, Berlin and Rome, the finance and war ministries, the reparation commission, the administration of the occupied terri-

tories, the ministry of commerce and industry, myriad *ad hoc* committees, as well as powerful French pressure groups representing French
industry and commerce. All of these agencies were competing for a say
in foreign policy at one of those rare moments in the history of the Third
Republic when public opinion and parliament were actually taking an
interest in foreign affairs because of their direct impact on daily life from
taxation to retail prices.[9]

Given the enormous growth in bureaucratic activity since 1912, one is
at first surprised to see that Poincaré's cabinet had grown by only two
ministers and two *sous-secrétaires d'état* from a decade earlier. But this
was an attempt to keep a tighter rein on the overall co-ordination of
affairs; Poincaré's 1922 government contained one minister and three to
five *sous-secrétaires d'état* fewer than that of his predecessors.[10] It is a
truism that the situation was radically different from when Poincaré had
formed his first government ten years previously. Even though foreign
affairs and relations with Germany were then also his main preoccupations, there was a major difference of scale. At that time he could take
over the foreign ministry and shape it into a workable tool for his
policies. To produce the same effect in 1922 he would have had to
reorganise virtually the whole of French bureaucracy. This was not an
option even for someone of Poincaré's Herculean capacity for work. The
historian is himself given a measure of the enormously distended nature
of the task of premier and foreign minister since the pre-war years by the
sheer number of documents and archives which it is necessary to consult
to complete the picture. One senses from a reading of these papers that
even Poincaré was not able to dominate policy as he had once done a
decade before: his marginal notes are fewer and his recourse to advisors
greater. His ability to alter the drift of French policy towards Germany
was tightly constrained.

Though unable to reform the Quai d'Orsay machine the way he had
done in 1912, Poincaré was helped by the resignation on 27 December
1921 of its most important permanent official, the long-serving secretary
general, Philippe Berthelot. Poincaré was said to be suspicious of the
Quai d'Orsay's Briandist temperament for concessions and compromise.
Poincaré had crossed swords with Berthelot before the war, and was
only too aware of his power over the foreign ministry. Faced with a
scandal involving Berthelot's brother's nefarious dealings as director of
the Banque Industrielle de Chine, in which Philippe Berthelot had
improperly used his office as secretary general, Berthelot resigned, but
Briand took no sanctions against him. One of Poincaré's acts as foreign
minister was to bring Berthelot before an internal disciplinary committee
which downgraded his position on the foreign ministry reserve list.[11]

The differences between the two men became public and even the subject of the novel *Bella* published in 1926 by the serving diplomat and man of letters, Jean Giraudoux, in which Poincaré was transparently depicted as the austere, callous and dislikeable Rebendart, while Berthelot figured as the sympathetic aesthete Dubardeau.[12] Poincaré's feud with Berthelot would not endear him to a whole clique of diplomats who were part of the secretary general's charmed literary circle, among whom were Alexis Léger (Saint John Perse), Paul Claudel[13] and Paul Morand. Though much has been made of the two men's antipathy to one another, it had less to do with a policy difference, supposedly attributable to Berthelot's predilection for an agreement with Germany and Poincaré's hostility to it, and more to do with Poincaré's desire to run the Quai d'Orsay himself. Indeed, there would be a public reconciliation under Poincaré's fourth ministry with Berthelot returning to his old job. By then Poincaré was more preoccupied with finance and was content to leave Briand in charge of the foreign ministry.[14]

What then was the thrust of the policy which Poincaré inherited? Viewed positively it was a policy of many strands; more negatively it was a cluster of confused and contradictory policies variously grasped at by an anxious and insecure power. It was not a policy of vengeance against Germany by which reparations would be used to break her. Even if that had been the intention, France was prevented from carrying it out by Britain and America, whose goodwill, guarantees and finances she coveted. Indeed, these powers were the key to France's foreign policy in the early 1920s. As in the simplest balance of power equation, when relations with the 'Anglo-Saxons' were strained, given the absence of the Russian counterbalance, relations with Berlin improved. This took the form of overtures on economic and industrial collaboration which Germany had thus far not taken up. Contrary to received opinion, the French authorities understood the problems which Germany faced over the payment of reparations, and economists whom Poincaré had long admired, such as Charles Gide, favoured an 'international solution' whereby the cost of reconstruction would be borne by the international community and not solely Germany. Thus a number of French politicians and newspapers of the centre favoured a 'Financial League of Nations'.[15] American refusal to countenance this scuppered French official efforts in this direction. Though these conciliatory policies were pursued according to circumstance, France had not discarded more coercive action. Theoretically the treaty gave her the right to take direct military action in the event of Germany's refusal to carry out the terms of the treaty, but as Poincaré had pointed out to Clemenceau during the peace conference, whatever the merits of the French case, in the current international climate it was likely to undermine her moral position and lose the support of Britain and America. The same was true of the policy some advocated of subverting German unity and power by encouraging separatist movements in Germany, and in particular in the Rhineland where French occupying troops were stationed. This Rhenish policy was also fraught with danger; if the hand of France was discovered her international credibility would again be threatened.

These then were the avenues which French policy had rather chaotically explored since the signing of the peace treaty. One cannot help feeling some sympathy for France at this time: the only guarantee for her security and economic well-being was a treaty which she and others could not, or would not, enforce. On coming to power Poincaré seemed to have had a number of options open to him; in reality that was not so. Given his lack of taste for risks it was not surprising that French foreign policy did not alter radically following his return to power.[16]

Poincaré's foreign policy towards Germany from 1922 was characterised by a mixture of robustness and conciliation. His experience of dealing with her prior to the war had confirmed him in the belief that Germany only had respect for strength. At that time he had adopted a firm, but unaggressive, attitude when dealing with her. He had told Viviani on 16 July 1914, 'I have never had serious difficulties with Germany, because I have always employed firmness with her'.[17] He believed that this policy had paid off with improved relations between the two countries whose concrete manifestations were the Franco-German treaties over zones of influence in the Ottoman Empire in 1914.

When he returned to power in 1922 Poincaré, and the French in general, could be forgiven for feeling a good deal of resentment at the way the post-war era seemed to be treating France. She was struggling desperately and increasingly in vain to have the Versailles Treaty executed, America had reneged on her guarantees for French security, and Britain was withholding hers. On reparations she felt she had little support from her allies and that any favourable settlement was gradually slipping away from her. Moreover, when Poincaré returned to the Quai in January 1922 there was considerable evidence to show that Germany was stepping up her international campaign to undermine both the Versailles settlement and reparations payments, and that he was increasingly the target on to whom Germany wished the blame to be shifted. He was doubtless aware of the telegram from Charles Laurent, ambassador in Berlin, informing Paris of a recent article in the semi-official *Berliner Tageblatt* which, without excusing Germany for her role in 1914, blamed Poincaré for wanting war and insisting that in the war origins debate there was a 'Poincaré Affair' which needed to be addressed. Laurent was of the belief that the article was inspired by the Wilhelmstrasse and that it and others signalled a new stage in Germany's attempts to liberate herself completely from the 'moral and material burdens accepted with the Versailles treaty'. He went on to explain that the Right wing in Germany believed that prior to 1914 Germany had been encircled by the Entente, while the Left were of Lloyd George's view that all nations were responsible. Even then the socialist *Vorwaerts* newspaper believed that the accidental explanation for war origins did not hold for Berchtold, Isvolsky and Poincaré, the latter being depicted as the 'principal criminal'. Another dispatch from Laurent of 1 January 1922 explained that the *Courrier de la Bourse* had recently stated quite unashamedly that the organisers of this campaign were intent on using it to undermine France's position at the forthcoming Cannes Conference and that 'the Versailles treaty built on the premise of German guilt alone is stamped with M. Poincaré's thinking. Now it is precisely the France of M. Poincaré ... which carries the greatest burden of guilt for the world war.'[18] This was reinforced on 23 January by a dispatch to Poincaré from the French consul general in Hamburg giving detailed evidence that the campaign against German responsibility in the origins of the war was led by German industrialists. He quoted from the annual report of the Norddeutscher Hansa Bund, one of the major economic groupings of the area:

The Norddeutscher Hansa Bund affirms and proclaims that the monstrous and ridiculous stipulations of Versailles, are the sole cause of our economic misery. That is why it has not ceased in the course of the past year to consider as an imperious duty to make known by a ceaseless propaganda the absolute impossibility for Germany to execute the clauses which have been imposed on it by force ...

Furthermore, it considers, and in this declares itself in perfect agreement with all commercial and maritime circles, of supreme importance to free Germany from the odious plot hatched against her concerning responsibility for the war. No, Germany is not and will not be made responsible whatsoever, for the conduct of events which led to the catastrophe. This abominable lie, perfidiously forged and systematically maintained by our enemies, must be denounced energetically and by every means. From all over information comes to the Bund which proves that this infamous manoeuvre delays abroad the work of rebuilding Germany.[19]

Consul General Albéric added that the left-wing press was doing nothing to counter this view in German public opinion. The dispatch was taken seriously by Poincaré's private office at the Quai who immediately communicated it to the Berlin embassy. More reports confirmed Germany's international effort to undermine the idea of her responsibility in the origins of the war. An internal Quai d'Orsay

memorandum summarised a series of dispatches from French diplomatic missions in Scandinavia, Switzerland, Holland and Spain which
described the recent setting up of an international panel of neutral
countries to investigate the origins of the war, '*at the instigation of
German propaganda*', nearly all of whose members were noted Germano-
philes. That committee was now demanding that Poincaré explain the
recent publication of Russian documents dating from before the war in
which Isvolsky attributed hawkishness to Poincaré. Poincaré issued
instructions that such a body should not be given the courtesy of an
official reply, but all the same requested the French minister in Norway
to make it known unofficially to the committee that he had already
refuted the Isvolsky allegations in the Chamber of Deputies on 19
January 1922, following a question from the leading Communist *député*
Marcel Cachin.[20] On the same theme, a dispatch from the French
consul general in Württemberg summarised the recently published
views of the Württemberg government which insisted that it had never
'acquiesced in recognising the fault included in the signature extorted by
the Versailles treaty' and that its efforts to counter it had never ceased.[21]

This flurry of dispatches which greeted Poincaré on assuming office
could only have confirmed him in his suspicions of Germany and her
attempts to wriggle out of the Versailles Treaty's conditions. That was
the view underlined to him at the beginning of March by the French
high commissioner for the Rhine provinces, Paul Tirard, who explained
the powerful effect German propaganda was having in attempting to
disculpate Germany in what was becoming the war origins debate.
Following further publications in the German press of the so-called
Poincaré–Isvolsky documents, Tirard pointed out that ever since the
elections in 1919 the increasingly popular right-wing parties had been
attempting to restore the prestige of the former regime and avoid
reparations. This campaign was gathering momentum so that demo-
crats, centrists and socialists were day by day moving to the same
position: 'The time seems near when the reparations question will cease
to be the preserve of the nationalist parties to become that of the whole
of Germany, and when all parties will proclaim Germany's innocence
and will set about proving it.' And he spelled out the consequences:
'This represents a grave danger for France and for our Rhenish policy in
particular. The question of responsibility, which until now remained in a
background favourable to the calming of minds, is back on the agenda
and will lead to new and strident polemics.'[22] At the end of the month
Tirard forwarded a report to Poincaré warning that German propaganda
was demonstrating to the local population in the occupied territories
that Germany was not responsible for the war and that consequently

'The burdens imposed on her and which weigh so heavily on the population of the occupied territories are due to France's militarist and imperialist spirit, which furthermore, by the worries it inspires, stops Europe from rising from its distress.' Tirard ended, 'I think it must be admitted that the theory of the non-responsibility of Germany, or of her partial responsibility, has gained much ground.'[23]

The success of the German campaign was confirmed in a series of French secret service reports received over the summer, which Poincaré personally scrutinised. These explained that a German propaganda offensive financed by powerful industrialists and subsidies from the Reichstag, and developed over recent months, was using every available means from the press to cinemas, theatres and music-halls to get across its message. It had three aims: a world-wide campaign to rehabilitate Germany and show that she was not responsible for the war; a continuation of the lavishly funded propaganda campaign to bring about a revision of the peace treaties; diplomatic manoeuvres to provoke a definitive break in the entente with Britain.[24] In September the French consul in Königsburg produced evidence from a German newspaper of how Poincaré was becoming the target of much of the propaganda:

> Oh Millerand! Oh Poincaré!
> Par vous la grande guerre fut née
> Les généraux Degoutte et Foch
> Ce sont les véritables Boches
> Oh Poincaré! Oh Millerand
> Vos mains sont pleines de sang.[25]

German documents now available confirm the French contention that Germany was organising a campaign against the Versailles Treaty and reparations.[26] The far-reaching impact of the German propaganda campaign had begun to show in French domestic politics. The French ambassador in Switzerland explained that the secret services of his embassy had discovered that the leading communist *député* Marcel Cachin had recently brought back from the Soviet Union important documents by which the French Communists 'would try to establish French responsibility in the origins of the war. They hope that the emotion produced in France by this publication could make political complications favourable to the development of their influence'.[27] These would eventually be published between 1922 and 1923 as the tendentious three-volume *Livre noir* documents which purported to show Poincaré and Isvolsky's responsibility in the origins of the war.[28] Poincaré attempted to head off the 'venomous and continuous attacks' against him by organising a debate on war responsibility in the Chamber of Deputies on 6 July 1922. As Alexandre Ribot recorded in his diary, it would not put an end 'to the campaign of calumny developed over the last months and which Germany has an interest in encouraging'. Though the debate resulted in a unanimous vote (apart from the socialists) for Poincaré,[29] it did not defuse the tension, especially for those of an unstable disposition. A week later, on Bastille Day, two shots were fired at the prefect of police's car by a would-be assassin in the mistaken belief that Poincaré and Millerand were on board.[30]

Politicians such as Poincaré believed that two things had been vital to France's victory over Germany: *union sacrée* and the support of the Allies. Not surprisingly, in the post-war world they believed in the need to maintain both, domestically by forming the broadest governments possible, and externally by not breaking with Great Britain and the USA. From the moment of his first government statement to the Chamber, Poincaré remained committed to collecting from Germany the full sum of reparations due to France; he also remained committed to maintaining agreement with the Allies. But these two aims would become increasingly contradictory, forcing Poincaré into adopting more flexible policies.

Despite the impact of German propaganda, or perhaps because of it, Poincaré did not abandon the idea of economic collaboration with Germany as an alternative means of obtaining satisfaction for France on reparations. Like his predecessors he still hoped to solve the reparations question by means of a vast credit operation through which reparation bonds would be sold to foreign investors in order to finance German reparations to the Allies, in particular France. However, this needed to be conducted in conjunction with a tight control of German finances by the Allies. Without such a control, loans could not be floated as potential investors would not subscribe to bonds issued on behalf of a potentially bankrupt Germany. Poincaré also believed that Germany would never agree to put her domestic finances in order and that therefore the Allies would have to do it in her stead. This remained his policy right up to the occupation of the Ruhr in January 1923. At the same time he pursued a policy of seeking from Germany reparations in kind which he described as a 'secondary but important' means of payment. Indeed, agreements on this were reached with Germany on 15 March and between 6 and 9 June 1922. Similarly, he endorsed the scheme devised by his minister of public works, Yves Le Trocquer, for large-scale public works programmes to be carried out by Germany in France as a means of paying reparations. During the spring of 1922 he also pursued the schemes developed by his predecessors for Franco-German industrial collaboration.[31]

But despite Poincaré's best efforts it was both the German government and German big business, often blaming each other, which repeatedly sought pretexts for avoiding the completion of any serious Franco-German agreement, including that of insisting every now and then that there could be no negotiation until Allied occupation was ended or until France recognised her share of responsibility in the outbreak of the war.[32] Certainly Poincaré's conciliatory role had not gone unnoticed in elements of the German press who were willing to use it mischievously. The *Hamburgischer Correspondant*, organ of the *Deutsche Volkspartei*, carried an article at the end of March entitled 'A Poincaré crisis', which began by asking 'Is Poincaré worn out?' It explained that there was growing opposition to Poincaré in France because of his conciliatory diplomacy: 'In short, he is not carrying out all the promises contracted during his activity as a writer, and above all he is not bringing to the execution of his programme the desired haste.' This was not untrue; Poincaré had created hostages to fortune by his intemperate public language before his return to power. Sarcasm aside, the article's final remark was evidence of the contradiction between Poincaré's public image and his true policies: 'Poincaré criticised for indulgence towards Germany by French chauvinists? One can hardly believe one's ears.'[33] Though Poincaré received a copy, he needed no reminding that progress on a Franco-German agreement was painfully slow.

By the late summer of 1922 it had become obvious to French officials and Poincaré that Germany was unwilling to respond to this conciliatory approach. Indeed, Germany was encouraged to take a hard line against France in calling for a moratorium on payments by none other than the influential British economist John Maynard Keynes. Keynes was the guest of honour at the Hamburg Overseas Week in August 1922, ostensibly an exercise in civic pomp attended by President Ebert, parliamentarians, diplomats and businessmen, but which doubled as an unofficial conference on German foreign policy. Keynes was introduced by the influential anti-French businessman, soon to become chancellor, Wilhelm Cuno, as 'the man most responsible for the changed attitude of the English-speaking world towards Germany' and was cheered rapturously. His speech of 26 August came five days after Poincaré's Bar-le-Duc speech calling for 'productive pledges' on reparations; Keynes jibed at the French, and Poincaré in particular, claiming that they were 'bluffing' about reoccupying the Ruhr and he advised the Germans to 'keep cool' and not be alarmed. His conclusion was an endorsement of proposals for a moratorium, a loan and reduced reparations. This was telling the Germans what they wanted to hear: Poincaré's 'bluff' should be called. Not long afterwards Cuno would be made chancellor putting

Germany and France on a collision course.[34] In France, too, the belief was hardening that perhaps a more forceful policy was all that Germany would understand.

Poincaré's policy towards Germany had always involved both carrot and stick. This had been the position before the war when he had treated Germany firmly and still negotiated agreements with her. His ideas for a Franco-German entente on reparations went hand in hand with a desire to ensure Allied control of German finances through the reparation commission. He continued to insist that Germany should not be allowed to wriggle out of such controls. But on 7 April 1922 the German government formally rejected the reparation commission's plan. Poincaré was furious. He regularly cabled President Millerand, who had left for an official visit to Africa, to outline steps he was taking on important diplomatic issues. On 12 April he was adamant that if Germany was not able to carry out the decisions of the reparation commission, the latter should 'officially recognise German shortcomings and notify the Governments which will have the respective right to take the necessary sanctions'.[35] Plans for the occupation of the Ruhr were now prepared in detail.[36] This hardened policy towards Germany automatically placed Poincaré on the second horn of the dilemma of French foreign policy in this period: relations with Britain.

Relations with Britain

It is quite clear that Poincaré, like most moderate French politicians, understood the necessity for a Franco-British entente in the post-war period. The ending of the war-time Franco-British alliance was a major loss for France which was not compensated by her new eastern European alliances. The fundamental problem was that Germany's defeat and Russia's collapse made France and Britain rivals again for international influence. After 1918 the age-old mutual suspicion of the hereditary enemies re-surfaced: the French once again suspected the British of wishing to divide and rule on the continent to clear a path for global imperial ambitions; the latter suspected the former of wishing to restore their dominance of the continent and continued to fear their military might. In 1922 British air staff considered war with France 'the greatest menace to this country', while the foreign office opposed construction of the Channel tunnel because relations 'never have been, are not, and probably never will be sufficiently stable and friendly to justify the construction ... it is almost certain that we shall have conflicts with the French in the future'.[37] This climate seriously prejudiced alliance projects. The French felt more in need of Britain than the reverse.

Poincaré had always been sympathetic to Britain and her institutions. Yet she had never been on his foreign travel circuit – paradoxically this man of the north preferred the warmer charms of the Latin countries. Temperamentally and methodologically he was poles apart from his British counterparts. Unlike Clemenceau or Briand, who were suited to the informality and pragmatism of the British negotiating style and policy, Poincaré hated informality and stuck to a rigid and legalistic method of procedure. According to the deputy director of the French foreign ministry, Jules Laroche, he hated conferences, which was unfortunate at this time of conference diplomacy (twenty-four in three years).[38] That hatred probably stemmed from his belief that conference agendas could just as easily be settled through normal diplomatic channels. He hated them even more if he was expected to be present, betraying a shyness and a certain pride at having to concede in public. To be fair, he was not alone in remaining sceptical about the benefits of conferences. They were often ill-prepared and, as the British diplomat Harold Nicolson remarked, their conclusions 'inevitably were inconclusive, intangible, specious, superficial and unreal'.[39]

Just before Briand was replaced by Poincaré in January 1922 a Franco-British pact had been ready for signing. The influential and pro-French H. A. Gwynne, editor of the *Morning Post*, wrote to the British ambassador in Paris lamenting Briand's departure:

... what has distressed me is that he should have gone when, for the first time since the Armistice, we had got the Government to go so far in the direction we wished as to offer a pact.

I always protested against this pact when I saw a copy of it inasmuch as it was too one-sided, and it put France in a position of inferiority to Great Britain. This was really a great political blunder, for anybody who knows the French people – as you and I do – would know that they are extremely sensitive and a very proud people, and this extension of our protection to a nation like the French was particularly galling ...[40]

Lord Derby, the former ambassador in Paris, is credited with having organised a meeting between Poincaré and Lloyd George *en route* from the latter's return from Cannes. Poincaré insisted to him that such a pact should be accompanied by a military convention. Lloyd George, unlike other members of his cabinet, had never favoured a full-scale alliance and replied that a general promise of assistance would be enough.[41] It was a similar clash of diplomatic outlooks to the negotiations over the Grey–Cambon letters of November 1912, when the French faith in legal texts conflicted with the British pragmatic predilection for unwritten agreements.[42]

Poincaré very strongly wanted a Franco-British agreement,[43] and as he told Lloyd George, he was willing to negotiate in a spirit of friendship and cordiality to get one. He told him, rather optimistically, that there were 'differences, but never disagreements' between Britain and France. Despite this, he was not the right man for the job. As Jules Laroche put it, 'his logical mind clashed with Anglo-Saxon empiricism, without ever denting it'.[44] This was not the only explanation for the catalogue of differences and radical disagreements which would characterise Franco-British relations during this period. Despite a fundamental quality of tolerance, which allowed him, according to Laroche, to listen politely to the other point of view and to objections to his own, he was not, as Laroche euphemistically put it, easily convinced. A lack of ability to concede points in a spirit of negotiation was worsened by a complete lack of tact in expressing his own point of view. This made for an explosive concoction when applied to strong personalities such as Clemenceau, Lloyd George or Lord Curzon. Perhaps worst of all, Poincaré rarely lost his temper. He wore away at his interlocutors by a process of attrition characterised by a monotonous and unbending repetition of facts, figures and principles. There is little doubt that issues of personality came to dominate issues of policy and soured relations with Britain. But there was also the fact that whereas the French governing class reluctantly recognised the need for an agreement with Britain, the reverse was not true. Though there was a powerful lobby in London in favour of a Franco-British pact, political leaders such as Lloyd George still needed to be convinced, while men such as the anti-French foreign secretary, Lord Curzon, remained opposed fearing, as had been the case before 1914, that the French would become unrestrained and potentially dangerous with a formal British guarantee of security.[45] Personality differences and divergent views on the need for closer Franco-British relations would eventually come to a head in October 1923 in what Lord Curzon would regard as a French conspiracy to secure his replacement.

In the meantime Poincaré continued his attempts to bring French and British foreign policy more into line and engineer a security pact. On 25 February he and Lloyd George had met at Boulogne to discuss the forthcoming international conference at Genoa. Poincaré, like Mille-rand, disagreed with this conference on the grounds that it was likely to short-circuit decisions taken by the reparation commission, on which France had greater influence, and take decisions concerning the Soviet Union's admission to the international community, which France opposed. He only agreed to France's presence if questions of disarmament and reparations were not discussed. He delayed the conference for as long as he could, and in the end refused to attend personally, dispatching in his stead the French justice minister and deputy premier, Louis Barthou, with a firm mandate not to agree to anything. Poincaré would, according to Jules Laroche, try his best to undermine the conference's proceedings.[46]

At the Genoa conference, further evidence of German bad faith was brought home to Poincaré and the other Allies, by the surprising signing of a Russo-German treaty at nearby Rapallo on 16 April 1922, which re-established diplomatic relations and cancelled mutual financial claims. Poincaré was insistent that Germany should either be excluded from the conference, or abrogate the treaty, but he feared that the Allies might come up with some compromise as Lloyd George favoured bringing Russia back into the international fold. Poincaré informed President Millerand,

The allied note has, moreover, appeared much too weak to French public opinion and its excessive moderation has produced a profound emotion in all parliamentary circles. It would be, in my opinion, extremely dangerous to let pass violations of the Versailles treaty without any precise protest and, if our allies do not wish to join us, we will at least have the advantage of having affirmed and maintained our rights.

He explained a few days later that he had told the French delegate at the Genoa conference, Louis Barthou, that, in 'his personal opinion', if the Soviets and Germans did not renounce their convention, the French delegate should withdraw from the conference to consult with his government. Though Poincaré insisted that such would have been the best course of action, he continued to claim that the Soviet and German replies had not improved the situation 'and that they called for a high level of energy, at the risk of breaking off relations which many people here desire and which everybody would find natural, if any concession were asked of us'.[47]

Poincaré's desire to maintain a firm line against Germany required that the other Allies do the same. But France was the only power with nothing to gain at Genoa. It was increasingly towards Great Britain that he began to direct his censure. Franco-British relations came under strain at Genoa over the question of international disarmament which, according to Poincaré, risked undermining French security still further. The fact that Lloyd George did not support the French point of view caused Poincaré to order the head of the French delegation in Genoa, Barthou, to speak to the British prime minister in private: 'Never, for many years, have England and France taken initiatives of this seriousness separately'. Poincaré insisted to Barthou that he should remind Lloyd George of the Boulogne agreement: 'He is quite the man to give in in the face of an energetic display, especially if it is secret and does not hurt his pride'.[48] But the difference between the two countries about how to deal with German reparations and the Rapallo Treaty showed how stubborn Poincaré could be on what he considered an issue of principle, while revealing something about his rather undiplomatic negotiating style. In an angry speech at Bar-le-Duc on 24 April, Poincaré attempted to put pressure on Britain by making it clear in public that if she did not support France against Germany within the reparation commission France would take her own action, even in defiance of Britain. The episode was beginning to sour relations with his old friend Barthou who, though opposed to further concessions to Germany, was intent on avoiding a break with Britain on the grounds that good relations with her were an imperative for French foreign policy.[49] On 26 April Poincaré informed Millerand that he had told Barthou that there had been considerable indignation at Lloyd George's threats of a rupture in the Franco-British entente and insinuations about French good faith and pacific intentions. Poincaré had insisted to Barthou in his typically imperious manner that if Lloyd George made similar statements then Barthou would be expected to give a cool reply, if necessary leave the room and 'wait for apologies to be expressed to our country'. Barthou defended the British prime minister, explaining that those had not been his words and insisting that if France provoked a split this would block all agreements with Britain and leave France in the kind of isolated position from which the Genoa conference had just extracted her. This last remark incensed Poincaré who, in his habitual desire to cover his actions, took the matter to the cabinet, which dutifully denied any isolation of France. He insisted to Barthou that he did not believe that Lloyd George would have broken up the conference, remarking that

if he spots a relatively good solution for England, he will constantly call for sacrifices from us. I have asked M. Barthou to take advantage of the *détente* which he has noted to make known to Lloyd George how much his words have aggrieved and wounded France and how it would be appropriate that he expunge them by some public statements.

As for Germany he noted that 'Berlin imagines that the Conference will allow her to escape executing the treaty'.[50] To add insult to injury, Germany, so Poincaré informed Millerand, was asking for most favoured nation status, which he claimed was contrary to the Versailles Treaty, and Britain was about to support it. If that were so, it would be necessary for France to put her case clearly and 'if it was ignored to declare that in the face of this breach of undertakings, we are forced to suspend our collaboration'.[51]

Despite unfavourable comments in the British press about Poincaré's Bar-le-Duc speech and criticism from Lloyd George, Barthou was able to calm the British premier. Though Lloyd George agreed on the need to maintain Franco-British collaboration as an essential guarantee of peace, Poincaré increasingly viewed such statements as pious. The Genoa episode had brought home to him that if Rapallo could not convince Britain that France was right about Germany then nothing would. According to Laroche, Lloyd George returned to London all the more annoyed with Poincaré for not having invited him to discussions on his return through Paris.[52] On 23 May 1922 Lloyd George informed the cabinet that he did not think that Poincaré was that interested in concluding a pact. This was certainly not what Laroche understood to be the case. He believed Poincaré did wish to restart negotiations, though he was told, obviously by the Director of the Quai, to draw up instructions for the French ambassador in London, 'by trying to attenuate the fastidious requirements which the *Président du Conseil* would like to accompany reasonable demands'.[53] Lloyd George continued to ignore French overtures for an Anglo-French pact which continued until the end of July.[54] In the end it was the Germans who softened their position and agreed to some measure of control over their finances in exchange for a foreign loan.[55] Poincaré was increasingly of the opinion that Franco-British co-operation could not be counted on to provide a solution to France's diplomatic problems.[56]

Poincaré's view was doubtless reinforced by the fact that the French had been intercepting and deciphering British diplomatic radio traffic for some time. As well as personal remarks by the British foreign secretary, Lord Curzon, referring to that 'horrid little man', Poincaré would have seen at first hand the opposition to closer relations with France, which he knew was led by Curzon. Indeed, suspicion was mutual – as was the reading of each others' diplomatic traffic.[57] This was evident from a secret dispatch of 4 May 1922 from the French ambassador in London, Saint Aulaire, relating information contained in a telegram (probably an intercept) sent from Genoa by the British prime minister's secretary. It revealed the British government's fears about the possibility of a Franco-German entente. Because Germany was not happy with Britain's unwillingness to grant her the advantages she desired at Genoa, the heads of the German delegation 'have begun to ask themselves if it would not be preferable for their country to look for a direct entente with us. They are showing an intention to talk with us, if not at Genoa, at least in Paris, even if we have "heaped insolence and humiliation on them".' Saint Aulaire added that the German ambassador in London had made similar comments to a contact of the French commercial attaché. The French ambassador concluded that Lloyd George's fears showed that France was not 'confronted by a simple German manoeuvre, but really an attempt to take from Britain the direction of European Affairs'.[58] Poincaré would not be averse to exploiting British fears or German opportunities when they arose.

Unofficial hints at German desires for a reconciliation with France continued to reach the Quai d'Orsay from French consulates in Germany, but so too did numerous secret service reports giving evidence of the world-wide German propaganda campaign financed, amongst other sources, by substantial credits voted by the Reichstag in April 1922.[59] This and the fact that the French were also reading German diplomatic traffic seemed to confirm Poincaré in his belief in German bad faith.[60] But cautious as ever, his tactic appears to have been to wait for an opportunity to act, such as an official German default on reparation payments. Poincaré's fear of responsibility, and his lawyer's instinct for presenting a watertight case, explains his wish to cover himself from every angle, rather as he had wanted to ensure that any decision for war in 1914 should be perceived as incontrovertibly defensive. It was not surprising that the more flexible Briand should refer to the stubborn and legalistic Poincaré as 'Raymond de Mon Droit'.[61] France may have had a sound case regarding Germany's refusal to apply the Versailles Treaty, but there was no doubt that she was losing the propaganda war.

The German point of view on war guilt and on her ability to pay reparations was making headway with international opinion and even among France's allies. Poincaré was increasingly being portrayed as bellicose, anti-German, imperialistic or just unreasonable. Perhaps to disprove those attacks, his position over the summer of 1922 became more conciliatory towards British proposals for greater flexibility over German reparations, even though he made clear to the French representative on the reparation commission that he was not happy with this line. He was beginning to distrust Britain as much as Germany. He told the Senate foreign affairs committee on 7 June that he viewed an occupation of the Ruhr as a last resort which in the meantime represented a useful weapon for forcing Britain and America into making financial concessions.[62] Anyway, it would not be possible to put plans for occupation of the Ruhr into operation without a majority decision of the reparation commission declaring a German default.

In mid July 1922, the prospect of the reparation commission granting a moratorium to Germany for two years without future 'guarantees' of payment, such as customs receipts, broke Poincaré's patience. By the end of the month he was threatening independent action. He warned Britain of this on 28 July, and brought things to a head at the Allied conference in London in early August, forcefully pleading the French point of view: 'For three years, the treaty is applied less and less; one could even say that is so with all of its clauses'. In his characteristic legal style he proceeded laboriously to detail point by point where the treaty was being infringed, stressing that Germany's 'bad faith worsens every day' and that on the issue of reparations 'lack of execution is even more striking'. He attacked those who levied criticism against France for being imperialistic and militaristic and for wishing to dismember or crush Germany:

I don't need to repeat once again what my predecessors have, on several occasions, declared: that is to say that there is no more outrageous calumny. France has not had, does not have and will not have the slightest intention of territorial annexation; she respects the will of peoples; she is not thinking of making the slightest conquest, nor of annexing peoples against their will. She respects the freedom and sovereignty of the defeated. What she wants is to escape ruin.

He insisted that France wished to collaborate in European reconstruction, but that her own financial collapse would make that impossible. He made it clear that if Germany could truthfully show that she could not pay, no one would ask for sanctions, but if the Allies judged that this was merely a sham and that Germany was engineering her own ruin to avoid payment 'and that we were obliged to intervene, we would not have the judgement of world opinion to fear'. He ended presciently, 'We are in the presence of a Germany where the spirit of revenge is awaking every day, where reactionary militarism is still possible and where disarmament is insufficiently carried out. If we disarm further, these bad seeds will germinate once more'.[63]

Britain refused to accept French proposals and the London conference collapsed. Thereafter, Germany's attitude to reparations stiffened again. On 16 August Berlin announced that domestic food supply would have priority over reparation payments and by the end of the month, egged on by Keynes, refused to countenance the idea that German state mines and forests should be used as pledges for coal and timber deliveries. Consequently France continued to oppose a two-year moratorium on reparations through the autumn. Germany's financial position continued to deteriorate, and confusion reigned domestically as to the measures she should adopt to improve matters.[64] Poincaré continued to stress into the winter that France was willing to act alone over the reparations issue. On 23 November he personally warned Belgian leaders in Paris that France would occupy the Ruhr if the Allies refused to respect the French point of view. He had now virtually decided that this was the only course of action open to him.[65]

At home, opposition was growing to Poincaré's moderate policy from the right of the Bloc national, who felt that it was getting nowhere, and from the Left, who were beginning to prefer something less 'nationalistic'.[66] Relations with Britain were by now severely strained. For Poincaré, London had added insult to injury by issuing the Balfour Note of 1 August, which called on France to honour her war debts to Britain even if the United States did not remit British debts. France was unable to do so unless Germany paid reparations. The reparation and debt issues were 'inextricably entangled', as Lloyd George's successor as prime minister, Bonar Law, recognised.[67] For his part, Lloyd George had insisted at the end of the London conference in cabinet on 10 August that Britain should not give into 'the tender mercies of M. Poincaré and the French militarists' for that would mean that Britain 'had yielded up the control of Europe not to France, but to M. Poincaré and his chauvinistic friends'.[68] Franco-British differences were at their most personal. Paul Cambon described the London conference as having degenerated into 'a question of pride between two men who detest each other'.[69]

Nor were Franco-British differences restricted to Europe. Over the Chanak crisis in the Middle East in September 1922 Poincaré was said to have reduced the British foreign secretary to tears and a state of nervous collapse. Sir Charles Hardinge, the British ambassador in Paris, denounced Poincaré as a 'dirty dog, a man of very mean character'; Lord Derby, though better disposed towards the French, still thought of Poincaré as 'a very mean, narrow-minded creature ... with a happy knack of saying even the nicest things in the most aggressive way'.[70] Curzon's differences with Poincaré came close to paranoia a year later when, after reading French diplomatic telegrams intercepted by the British security services, the British foreign secretary gained the impression that Poincaré was plotting to have him replaced.[71] This was ironic coming from the British. It would seem that they had themselves been happy to seek Poincaré's downfall by goading him into occupying the Ruhr. As Sir John Bradbury, head of the delegation on the reparation commission told Colonel James Logan, the American observer on the commission, it was the British government's desire 'to let M. Poincaré try out his policy in the face of their sulky disapproval in the hope that, when M. Poincaré had gone a little way on his independent policy, the French people, feeling consequently the weakening of the franc, increased taxation, etc., would rise in their wrath and oust M. Poincaré before too much harm was done'.[72] In a book published in 1930, the well-informed French conservative, Jacques Bardoux, explained how the British intelligence service had spent large amounts of money to oust Poincaré from power:

This action is an historical fact. Definite reality: it will not be enough to deny it to wipe it clean. By the most varied routes, sometimes through the intermediary of more or less official propagandists, sometimes through more or less million-aire patrons, the pound allowed the Cartel to be supplied with files and tracts, with cars and newspapers. Foreign money overflowed. Since the Napoleonic era, the Secret Service excels in these operations after two centuries of experience in India. Its agents of both sexes and of all types have become masters in the art of subsidising kinglets, of bribing soothsayers and of splitting tribes . . . [73]

Poincaré allegedly told the French ambassador to London, just after the Cartel des gauches had won the 1924 elections, that the brother of the proprietor of the left-wing newspaper, Le Quotidien, had confessed that the paper 'was founded and operates with English money, the intelligence service thinking it very clever to pass off its generosity through a relatively rich activist so that nobody suspects that it is the one who is paying'.[74] The veracity of such claims about the intelligence service remains to be proven; not so Poincaré's ability to make enemies. Soon the Germans would be subjected to the full blast of his withering stubbornness.

The occupation of the Ruhr

Plans for the occupation of the Ruhr had been drawn up before Poincaré's return to power. The detailed plan of occupation dated 22 April 1921 was already available for the Allies to execute as a legitimate sanction in the event of a German default on reparations. According to Poincaré, on 1 May 1921 France had for a second time asked the Allies to occupy the Ruhr, only to bow to British opposition. On the day that Germany requested a moratorium, 12 July 1922, Poincaré called for the establishment of an interministerial committee to study the whole question of an occupation of the Ruhr.[75] As has been seen, in 1919 Poincaré had put considerable pressure on Clemenceau to demand that occupation of the Rhineland should not be lifted until Germany had acquitted herself of her reparations payments. First-hand experience as a young boy of similar conditions imposed on France by Germany had not been erased. A serious debate about the nature and modalities of an occupation of the Ruhr took place between civil servants and military planners.[76] Yet Poincaré did not directly participate in the development of the Ruhr doctrine which finally emerged at the end of 1922. The proposals he finally put to the London conference of Allies in

December 1922 were far more moderate than those of the Ruhr working party he had set up. In particular, he was anxious to avoid the thorny question of a Rhenish policy designed to bring about the autonomy of the Rhineland, which many of his senior officials were working for.[77] The reasons were probably his typical caution, but more importantly his reluctance to break with Britain.

The prospect, at last, of improved relations with London loomed after the fall of the Lloyd George government on 19 October and its replacement by that of the avowedly more francophile leader of the Conservative party, Andrew Bonar Law. In early November, before the general election which confirmed the Conservatives in power, francophiles in British governing circles became very active in pushing the new cabinet in favour of a more sympathetic stance towards France over reparations. But the stumbling block continued to be, in the words of Sir William Tyrrell, assistant under-secretary at the foreign office, the 'selfish and treacherous' Curzon, who had been retained as foreign secretary. Keith Wilson has shown how H. A. Gwynne of the conservative *Morning Post* hatched the sophisticated and high-level plot involving the French secret services and the former head of Special Branch to ensure that Curzon's choice for a new ambassador to replace Lord Hardinge in Paris be subverted in favour of a pro-French diplomat. Poincaré was fully informed of the francophiles' machinations, as Gwynne attempted to involve the French ambassador in London, Saint Aulaire, and even Poincaré himself. But, according to Saint Aulaire, Poincaré refused to use against his enemies the kind of tactics they employed against him. Curzon's choice for the Paris embassy, Lord d'Abernon, ambassador in Berlin, was not realised. From these November escapades, Poincaré could at least take heart that forces sympathetic to his policies appeared to be in the ascendant in London.[78]

Britain and France now agreed on a tougher handling of the German request for a moratorium, though they differed on the question of the guarantees she would have to give. With British opinion hostile to an occupation of the Ruhr and French opinion in favour, a break seemed inevitable. Nevertheless, Poincaré, true to form, continued to hesitate about taking the final step. He was willing to be more flexible if Britain and America came to France's financial aid. Though on 27 November the French cabinet approved plans for an occupation of the Ruhr, two days later Poincaré told the Senate foreign affairs commission that no decision to act had been taken and that the threat of occupation was still only a bargaining chip for the forthcoming inter-Allied London conference. Through much of December he gave a demonstration of the kind of hesitation which some reckoned to be his greatest weakness.

French proposals for German pledges as security on a moratorium were further moderated to accommodate Britain.[79] President Millerand telegraphed to him on December 11 to break off talks with Bonar Law on the moratorium and continued to pressure him to do so thereafter. Poincaré refused. On 22 December, ironically for someone with his strong presidential track record, Poincaré wrote to Millerand to complain of this executive use of the presidency and to offer his resignation if it did not stop.[80] By Christmas Eve, Poincaré had actually come round to accepting that security on the moratorium should no longer be a military occupation of the Ruhr, merely a control of its trade. Still Britain refused and came up with counter-proposals at the Paris conference on 2 January 1923, angering Poincaré. That anger seemed increasingly justified given the obstacles Britain unremittingly put in France's path. Ever since the European economic conference at Genoa the British had virtually ceased to work with the French. Lloyd George had even told the cabinet on 15 July 1922:

it might be best the situation reach rock bottom before building up ... The French ... would not come round until the ship was in sight of the reefs ... it would be a mistake to make any proposals to M. Poincaré just at present. It was necessary to leave France to realise all the facts of the situation. Then something might be done.[81]

And that was largely what Britain did for the rest of 1922; she continued to do so in spite of Lloyd George's replacement by Bonar Law, because people like Curzon remained in post. Such brinkmanship was foolhardy for several reasons. First, if the French were intercepting and reading British diplomatic traffic, or being informed by the likes of Gwynne and Tyrrell, they would have been aware of the ploy. Second, it ignored the strong sense of exasperation in French domestic opinion and in the Chamber at the German refusal to honour reparations payments, as well as Britain and the United States' refusal to make any financial concessions to France in exchange for a lighter German reparations burden. All of this was bearing down on Poincaré. The strength of French feeling was apparent when the occupation of the Ruhr was approved in the French Chamber by a massive 452 votes to 72, the dissidents comprising only the extreme Left socialists and Communists. Third, it pricked Poincaré's strong sense of pride and spurred him into action. He was left with little alternative but to demonstrate France's resolve on this issue and put down a marker to show that she could not be treated in such cavalier fashion by either her adversaries or her allies. But even after all this, Poincaré had to be pushed, apparently by President Millerand and the war minister, Maginot. The military urged

that the occupation had to be carried out before the planned reduction
in military service to eighteen months made the expedition impossible,
while certain sectors of the French steel industry saw it as access to Ruhr
coke.[82] Poincaré commented to a friend, 'If I don't carry out the
operation myself, someone else will be asked to do it. And he won't do it
so well.'[83] The diplomat André François-Poncet claims that, just after
the occupation had taken place, Poincaré, worried about German
resistance and adverse comment in the foreign press, told him

> that he had not been a supporter of the operation, the responsibility for which,
> however, he would have to carry in the face of History; he had advised against it,
> so, indeed, had Marshal Foch; but the President of the Republic, Alexandre
> Millerand, and all his ministers, notably André Maginot, his colleague from the
> Meuse, had pushed him with such insistence that he believed he did not have the
> right to go against their feelings.[84]

In the end, Britain was as much to blame as Germany for finally
goading Poincaré into occupying the Ruhr. The German proposal of 22
December was such a calculated decision to force a confrontation that
the German reparations advisor in Paris, Bergmann, did not even
present it to the French foreign ministry. The British attempt to
accommodate it led to a document so complicated that Bergmann said
he would rather pay reparations than try to understand it. If anyone was
going to understand it, it was Poincaré. At the Allied discussions in Paris
on 3 and 4 January, he ridiculed the new British proposal as nothing
more than hollow promises to France, reminiscent of signs outside
French barber shops: 'Free shaves tomorrow.'[85] Since 26 December he
had the support of the reparation commission, which had outvoted
Britain three to one in declaring a German default on timber supplies.
On 9 January it declared a coal default. On the morning of 11 January
1923, French and Belgian troops with a symbolic Italian detachment
entered the industrial heartland of Germany, the Ruhr valley, to escort
the engineers and technicians of the specifically created Mission
Interalliée de Contrôle des Usines et des Mines (MICUM), whose
intention was to determine the true ability of German firms to deliver
reparations. Now that he had come to his decision, albeit reluctantly,
Poincaré would not easily be shifted from it.

What is important about the occupation of the Ruhr is that it was not
a long-term goal of the French government pursued with single-minded
devotion, as many polemicists and historians used to claim. Nor was
Poincaré the tool of French militarists obsessed with the need for a
Rhine frontier, or the instrument of French coal and steel bosses intent
on controlling German coal and steel.[86] As for Poincaré's role in it, he

had abandoned the more extreme plans of his officials for serious economic exploitation of the area, and had nothing to replace them except that of obtaining the coal which France was being denied. Neither was the occupation presented as the great show-down with Germany. The whole operation was almost apologetic, characterised by prudence and moderation, with the French officially announcing to the Germans that it had no military or political character. Poincaré repeated this to the Chamber on 11 January 1923, adding that France had been forced into it by the absence of any acceptable alternative and stressed that she still wished to negotiate with Germany and to help restore her financial stability. On 19 January the Cuno government ordered miners and railway workers to withhold their co-operation in the hope of making the occupation as costly as possible for France, of undermining her finances and the franc on the foreign exchanges and finally in the expectation that British and American diplomatic pressure would be brought to bear on Poincaré.[87] This 'passive resistance' led the French and Belgians to send in more troops and to extend their area of occupation as far east as Dortmund; Germany retaliated by suspending all reparations payments. The number of occupying troops rose to 100,000. The French and Belgians were obliged to exploit the mines and operate the railways themselves. Nevertheless, the French continued to exercise restraint which was criticised in France as a lack of forcefulness.[88] This timidity could be explained largely by the fact that Poincaré had been cornered into the occupation of the Ruhr. To a large extent the threat of occupation had been Poincaré's bluff, which had been called. He had then hoped that occupation would produce rapid results. When that did not happen his pride led him to hold out for a political victory.

For at least the first half of 1923 Poincaré's policy in the Ruhr seemed directionless. He hesitated over, and eventually rejected, a policy of a more extensive exploitation of the Ruhr economy. His only clear aim seemed to be to obtain coal. Yet this was not easy given German resistance and his own reluctance to use more coercion. Only after agreements were negotiated with German mine owners at the end of November 1923 did the total coal deliveries to France reach even five-eighths of the amount Germany was providing before the occupation.[89] It is clearer to state what Poincaré's Ruhr policy tried to avoid. He feared antagonising moderate opinion at home and abroad by too forceful a policy; he did not wish to jeopardise relations with Britain more than was necessary; he wanted to keep the support of the moderate Left at home who were willing to support his Ruhr policy so long as it remained moderate.[90] But neither did he wish to alienate the Germans. He still believed that the long-term salvation and stability of European finances rested on some form of Franco-German economic and financial entente. This is evident from the political correspondence from the French ambassador in Berlin to him.

British reactions to the French occupation of the Ruhr were not as hostile as had been expected. The *Morning Post* of 12 January 1923 carried a leading article entitled 'Good Luck to France', and the paper's editor, Gwynne, told Saint Aulaire that prime minister Bonar Law had congratulated him on this. Keith Wilson has described how by early March 1923 Gwynne and the francophiles were putting together another plan to get the cabinet to adopt a more pro-French foreign policy about which Saint Aulaire, and hence Poincaré, was kept informed.[91] There is little doubt that this influenced Poincaré's diplomatic action. The episode which followed justified to a certain extent Poincaré's long-running frustration in his past dealings with the British foreign secretary, Lord Curzon. It also portrayed him in a better light than the traditional image generated by Curzon's entourage of that 'horrid little man'.

By the spring of 1923 there was a thaw in Anglo-French relations. Optimism was in the air when in May illness forced Bonar Law to relinquish the premiership in favour of Stanley Baldwin in May. Gwynne believed that despite the foreign office remaining with Curzon, who 'hates the French and does not conceal his hatred', prospects for his plan to make 'the Entente the keystone of our foreign policy' were much improved. On 13 June 1923 he wrote to Baldwin to tell him as much. In that letter quoted *in extenso* by Keith Wilson, Gwynne pointed out that 'Curzon is a man who would prefer to score over Poincaré than to agree with him'. He added, 'The relations since November last between England and France have been unnecessarily cold chiefly due to the note-writing propensities of the Foreign Secretary', ironically a charge so often levelled against Poincaré. Gwynne put to the prime minister the arguments which Poincaré had been making for several months on German bad faith, German propaganda and the need for Franco-British solidarity. He told Baldwin that if 'you go and see Poincaré yourself I believe you will find him reasonable and anxious for a settlement'. Above all he exhorted him, once he had decided on a policy, to insist that Curzon carry it out; if he refused, 'you will be rid of a rotten Foreign Secretary and not too loyal a colleague'.[92] Gwynne followed this up two days later with a letter to Poincaré's private secretary, Grignon, explaining the reasons for optimism and suggesting an informal meeting between the two premiers. Intermediaries were used to arrange such a meeting which took the form of an invitation by Poincaré to Curzon to meet him in Paris as the latter returned from his holiday in the south of

France, to which the foreign secretary reluctantly agreed. Keith Wilson describes how the British cabinet then decided to send a fifty-five page note to the French rebutting all their arguments made during the year, apparently as a basis for discussion. This is not how Curzon would interpret it. He was able to restrict his meeting with Poincaré in late August to twenty minutes, before, as he put it, managing to escape. He then told Baldwin that on the basis of the notes exchanged, France and Britain could not possibly agree. But Curzon was thwarted by the meeting between Poincaré and Baldwin on 19 September at the British embassy in Paris which Gwynne's fellow conspirator, Sir William Tyrrell, attended. Though it was not a convergence of points of view, and though Poincaré made known his annoyance and disappointment at Curzon, the press release drafted by Tyrrell did not reflect this. Curzon would not thereafter be on speaking terms with Tyrrell, believing that the communiqué had showed him to be pursuing a different foreign policy to Baldwin. Indeed, differences between the prime minister and his foreign secretary would be pointed up in the following weeks. Baldwin told Saint Aulaire that he hoped that he had exorcised the ghost of Lloyd George; when giving the opening address to the Imperial Conference in London on 1 October he stressed that differences in outlook could not undermine Franco-British co-operation. But four days later, Curzon told the same gathering that France wished to dominate the continent of Europe. On 6 October Poincaré cabled Saint Aulaire about the complete contradiction between this speech and his own cordial conversation with Baldwin in Paris and requested that the French ambassador seek an immediate interview with Baldwin to tell him that the French could not tolerate such a contradiction. Saint Aulaire replied, advising against a procedure likely to provoke a dispute between Baldwin and his foreign secretary which would upset the former's intention to replace the latter. He recommended instead that Poincaré communicate with Baldwin by personal letter. As Keith Wilson shows, these were the telegrams intercepted by the British security services and forwarded to Curzon, and which led him to believe that there was a conspiracy to have him replaced. A plot there may have been, but, as Wilson shows, it was not of French making, rather one concocted by Gwynne and Curzon's own permanent official, Tyrrell, which had wider support.[93] That is not to say that Poincaré did not delight in it, or wish to profit from it if it meant closer Franco-British relations.

Curzon would attempt to extract his revenge, hoping, in his words, 'that we may put Poincaré in a hole', by personally inviting the Americans to attend the forthcoming inter-Allied conference in London on reparations and war debts. This upset a number of British cabinet members. Curzon also ignored American advice that the French should be approached with 'tact and delicacy' about the United States' presence at the conference so that, according to Gwynne, Poincaré only learnt of it through the newspapers. In the meantime Gwynne continued with Saint Aulaire to engineer a reciprocal visit by Poincaré to London in early November. Curzon was again informed of this through more intercepts and complained to Baldwin that Poincaré, Saint Aulaire and Gwynne were reviving their intrigue against him 'in a more perfidious and nefarious form'. He insisted that a visit by Poincaré should receive no encouragement from Baldwin and demanded from the prime minister greater support and loyalty. Baldwin gave this short shrift. A date for Poincaré's visit to London was fixed for the 24 to 26 November. But it was too late. Baldwin dissolved parliament on 13 November 1923 and a Labour government headed by Ramsay MacDonald was returned after the elections.[94] At least Poincaré could take comfort from the fact that Curzon was no longer at the foreign office.

Not knowing where he stood in relations with Britain meant that Poincaré kept open other avenues of foreign policy. Germany was one. This avenue was all the more tantalising for the effect it could have on Britain, which had always, and would always, fear the prospect of an entente between Paris and Berlin. During the summer of 1923 relations with Germany began to thaw and the question of Franco-German collaboration reappeared.

On 3 August the French ambassador in Berlin, de Margerie, Poincaré's loyal pre-war political director of the Quai, reported favourable German press reactions to a speech by the German Chancellor Cuno approving a policy of Franco-German economic co-operation. Nine days later Margerie emphasised that German opinion was ripe for some agreement with France and he suggested that Poincaré should make some direct appeal to the German people: 'Undoubtedly, your Excellency has never stopped ... proclaiming in documents presented to the British Government, that France wants in no way to destroy Germany but asks only for the treaty to be executed and for fair reparations; and that it is only out of necessity that she and Belgium were obliged to secure some pledge.' He went on to remark that France could rightly proclaim that not only did she not want the ruin of Germany but that she considered the latter's financial recovery to be one of the important elements of the world economy and that German recovery was fundamental to the payment of reparations.[95] And Margerie gave further examples of the move in Germany towards an entente with France and Franco-German industrial collaboration. On 12 August 1923 Cuno resigned. His government was replaced by a broad coalition led by Gustav Stresemann, who also took on the foreign affairs portfolio. By 24 August Margerie was insisting on how well disposed the new German chancellor was to France and to a settlement with her. He remarked that Poincaré's latest statements, 'those you authorised me to repeat strongly here at an opportune moment and which I tried to disseminate by means at my disposal in the new Government's circles, have led M. Stresemann to record with satisfaction the declarations by which Your Excellency repudiated once more the supposed annexationist, separatist or destructive tendencies of France towards Germany'.[96] On 27 August he reported an audience with Chancellor Stresemann in which the latter, referring to articles in the French press, had asked whether France wished to destroy Germany, ruin her financially and economically and separate the Rhineland and Bavaria from her simply to be able to dominate her. Margerie replied that the French government, not the press, were what mattered and that he should look for the ideas of the former 'in the numerous speeches in which the responsible Head of French policy had clearly, these last days again, exposed its feelings towards Germany'.[97]

On 4 September, in a highly confidential telegram to Poincaré, Margerie reported the previous day's audience with Stresemann in which the chancellor admitted that the present situation had lasted long enough and that it was time to reach a settlement with France. He confessed to the French ambassador that what he was about to say was for the personal attention of Poincaré and was not known by anyone in the cabinet other than the foreign minister. He wished to know if France was interested in a 'Franco-German economic entente through the establishment of closer relations between certain industrialists of both countries'. Stresemann added that if he could get 'from M Poincaré in a personal capacity' an indication that negotiations could begin on this basis, this would facilitate his action in getting passive resistance lifted.[98]

It was clear that the German government had now moved in favour of economic collaboration with France. This was partly a result of disappointment at not winning British support for their struggle against French occupation,[99] and it was also due to pressure from German industrialists who by September 1923 were experiencing difficulties with exports, the collapse of economic activity and the curtailment of credit resulting from the Ruhr occupation.[100] But Poincaré doggedly refused to take up Berlin's offer until the decrees on passive resistance published by the preceding government had been withdrawn and reparations deliveries had been resumed. This was reiterated to Stresemann. Nevertheless Poincaré did sound out Stresemann unofficially, through Margerie, on the issue of Franco-German industrial collaboration; the

German chancellor replied that such collaboration could not be a means
to a Franco-German settlement, but that he agreed with Poincaré in
believing 'that it should be the crowning achievement'.[101] Stresemann
then stated in the strictest confidence that France and Germany could
begin negotiations to settle reparations and that he would send an
ambassador to Paris.[102] On 26 September the German government,
undermined by a plummeting mark and various revolutionary, reactionary and separatist movements which threatened the survival of the
Reich, officially announced the end of passive resistance and the
resumption of reparations deliveries, though, like the armistice of 1918,
this was still presented as a tactical retreat.[103]

Though the occupation had lasted much longer than anyone had
expected and cost a good deal more, Poincaré had achieved a political
victory. He had calculated correctly that France could hold out longer
than Germany. The technique of firmness in dealing with Germany
since 1912 had triumphed. Since their conference in Brussels on 6 June,
France and Belgium had insisted that no negotiations could begin with
Germany until passive resistance was called off. His obduracy in dealing
with Germany, helped by the collapse of concerted employer and trade
union resistance, had paid off.

The German economy was by now in a parlous state. For months the
Berlin government had continued to print an increasingly debased
currency to pay unemployment benefit to its striking workers in the
Ruhr. On 22 October 1923 Margerie reported to Poincaré that the
American dollar was now worth 43 billion marks.[104] There is some
confusion among historians as to what Poincaré's aim had been in
relation to Germany once he had forced a retraction of passive
resistance. It has been suggested that he moved to a more determined
policy designed to use German financial and political disorder to weaken
her still further and obtain an independent Rhenish buffer state.
Certainly by the autumn of 1923 both left- and right-wing revolts,
including Hitler's attempted *putsch* in Munich, were breaking out across
Germany, leaving France in control of Rhine and Ruhr. But whatever
the zeal among certain of his officials for such a negative policy, Poincaré
did not share their enthusiasm. Jules Laroche, who during the Ruhr
occupation was deputy director of the French foreign ministry, recorded
in his memoirs that Poincaré was opposed to the encouragement of
Rhenish separatism.[105] Most modern historians agree that French policy
over the question of an autonomous Rhenish state was characterised by
confusion and lack of purpose. Even if Poincaré had supported such a
policy he would certainly not have been willing to impose it by force or
commit French resources to the creation of the political and economic

institutions vital to an independent political entity.[106] For someone of Poincaré's native caution such action was fraught with problems. French finances had already suffered badly from the heavy costs of the Ruhr occupation and could not stand further expenditure without increasing taxes less than six months before a general election. A combination of this financial pressure, the unlikely prospect of the virtually bankrupt Germany being able to make any serious payment to France, the need for France to seek British and American financial assistance, the disaffection of Radical party support from his parliamentary majority and the forthcoming French general elections, all pushed Poincaré on 13 November, in a conciliatory gesture, to accept the 'Anglo-Saxon' recommendation to refer the reparations question again to two committees of experts appointed by the reparations commission to inquire into Germany's capacity to pay and methods of stabilising her finances.[107] These would meet in Paris in January 1924, the most important of which became known as the Dawes Committee.

After passive resistance had ended, Poincaré concluded the MICUM agreements with Ruhr industrialists in November 1923, thereby putting an end to the industrialists' opposition to the payment of reparations and obtaining a guarantee for their delivery. However, recent historical interpretations diverge on whether these agreements were actually beneficial to France: some suggest that they provided guaranteed reparations and turned the economy of the Ruhr towards those of France and Belgium; others believe that they made reparations dependent on the goodwill of Ruhr industrialists and on German financial stability and economic recovery.[108] At the same time, spurred on by the declaration on 21 October of a Rhenish republic, Poincaré toyed again with the idea of a strategy for Rhineland independence negotiated with local leaders and sanctioned internationally; but his legalism made him loath to negotiate with unconstitutional separatists, let alone identify French policy with them. By the beginning of December 1923 he had even become disenchanted with constitutional Rhenish patriots like Konrad Adenauer, mayor of Cologne. In the end all this came to nothing. His native caution, fear of overstepping the bounds of legality, distaste for illicit schemes and vacillating temperament, exacerbated by opposition from Britain, led him to discard the separatist strategy. As Charles Maier has written, 'With a keen sense of international constraints, aware that British neutrality had facilitated his victory in the Ruhr, and cautious by temperament, the French premier was not prepared to speculate on windfall gains.'[109] For some, he let an opportunity to capitalise on the Ruhr victory slip from his hands by failing to support either the Rhenish separatists or a general settlement

with Germany and the industrialists. Millerand was said to have wished
for a new treaty bilaterally negotiated with Germany and which would
have drawn together the coal of the Ruhr, the iron ore of Lorraine and
French security on the Rhine. But Poincaré told Charles Reibel, the
minister of liberated regions, 'Discussions with Germany would upset
England. If they wanted to force me into that policy, I would hand in the
resignation of the Cabinet.' Marshal Foch supported Millerand telling
Reibel, 'This is a decisive day. It depends on M. Poincaré whether war
becomes impossible between France and Germany. Mark my words.
The whole of France's victory is in M. Poincaré's hands. If we do not
talk with Germany immediately it is an irretrievably lost opportunity.'
When Poincaré refused, Millerand had thought of getting Poincaré to
relinquish the foreign affairs portfolio in favour of the minister of justice,
Maurice Colrat. But nothing had come of it.[110] Millerand would
harbour a good deal of bitterness against his old friend for not having
grasped this opportunity.[111] Feeling that France was as yet still in a
powerful position after her victory over Germany, Poincaré preferred to
make way for the great settlement which would encompass reparations,
inter-Allied debt and Anglo-American loans to Europe. He was sceptical
of separatist schemes and special Franco-German economic agreements
which would offend Britain. Neither was he willing to court parliamentary isolation which would put him at the mercy of the Right. He
attracted applause from the Left and the Radicals when on 23 November
1923 he told the Chamber that collective action was preferable to
unilateral measures. He wanted to steer a middle path between extremes
in international and domestic politics. He was now of the opinion that
the more unilateral his actions had been the more he had become a
hostage to a narrower and more zealous majority. By keeping to the legal
framework of the treaty, accepting American reparations mediation
while still in a position of strength, he hoped to re-occupy the centre
ground. What could be more natural for a moderate lawyer?[112]

Two committees of experts, led respectively by the American banker,
Dawes, and his British counterpart, MacKenna, worked in Paris from
January until they submitted their reports on 14 April 1924. The Dawes
Committee proposed a five-year reparations settlement funded by an
international loan to Germany and a reduction in her debt. At the same
time, Poincaré's correspondence from January 1924 with the new
British Labour party prime minister, Ramsay MacDonald, gave hope for
a renewal of Franco-British co-operation. But with elections in May it
was too late for Poincaré to draw from the Dawes Plan the political and
financial advantages which may have made the Ruhr occupation appear
a success.

Domestic pressures

The most important plank of Poincaré's overall policy as premier, foreign affairs, had thus far been conducted almost in isolation to domestic politics. However, one principle had remained sacrosanct: the need to maintain a 'republican' parliamentary majority. He was adamant that his government should remain by nature and by its support left-of-centre. Hence the desire not to cut himself off from radical support. They had supported the occupation of the Ruhr, but as time went by they began to distance themselves from Poincaré's Ruhr policy. This was not altogether because they disagreed with it. It had more to do with the forthcoming elections and the Radical party's desire to seek closer relations with the socialists who now seemed natural partners, having lost their majority extreme Left wing to the French Communist party at the Congress of Tours in 1920. A socialist–radical alliance would also ensure that the Radicals did not fall victim to the proportional voting system in the 1924 elections as they had done in 1919. Furthermore, as so often under the Third Republic, the unity of the Left was fostered by the rise of the extreme Right. Ugly demonstrations by the extreme Right *camelots du roi* and their attacks on left-wing *députés* in spring 1923 had encouraged the leader of the Radicals, Edouard Herriot, to criticise Poincaré's government for its inaction, leading communists, radicals and socialists to vote against it on 31 May 1923. As the right-wing of the Bloc national called on the head of the government to choose between it and the Radicals, on 15 June Poincaré again sought to define a 'republican and national' majority along the lines of the *union sacrée* to which he was so idealistically wedded. He was unable to keep any more than twelve Radicals from sliding into opposition, though he did manage to retain three Radical ministers in the cabinet, despite calls from the executive of their party for their resignation. In the Senate Poincaré retained the good will of the Radicals who, like him, still looked to a centre-left coalition with moderate republicans of his ilk. He was no longer in tune with the majority of the Bloc national, which he was said to dislike because it was insufficiently left-leaning.[113] This explains, in part, why he was willing to demur to 'Anglo-Saxon' pressure for France to accept the setting up of another committee of experts, against the will of the French Right and of powerful individuals such as Tardieu and Mandel, but with the support of the Radicals. Though the Bloc national majority had felt bound to support Poincaré, for fear of the alternative, by the beginning of 1924 that support was wearing thin. Thus Poincaré's action in foreign and domestic politics at the end of 1923 and beginning of 1924 contradicts the traditional picture of him as narrowly nationalistic and enthusiastically fulfilling the interests of the Right.

In mid-January 1924 the French franc came under severe attack and panic spread to the French stock exchange, undermining confidence in government securities. Poincaré made it clear to the Chamber on 22 February that it was 'indispensable to balance our budget' as a result of 'the persistent defaulting of Germany'. He was proposing a new instrument of government which would be much used subsequently: a system of decree laws to bring in budgetary savings and a 20 per cent increase in taxes – the 'double décime'. This simple percentage increase enhanced the regressivity of the tax system by taxing predominantly the wealthy while sparing the middle classes. Partly because they did not understand the impact of the new taxes and partly because of the approaching elections, the Radicals attacked new taxes *per se* despite the fact that they largely benefited their middle-class constituents. Thus Poincaré had considerable difficulty getting the legislation through the Chamber on 22 February, but it was expected that he would have no trouble in the Senate – 'It's his back-yard', noted one seasoned observer. However, the government only prevailed on 14 March because the Senate Radicals abstained for fear of bringing down the ministry and having to confront a more militant supporter of the Bloc national, such as Maginot at the interior ministry. He would be likely to encourage the prefectoral corps to be more supportive of Bloc candidates in the election campaign, unlike Poincaré.[114]

While Poincaré struggled to get his tax legislation through parliament, speculation against the franc continued. Poincaré made clear to the Senate on 13 March that the speculation was as much political as financial and had a triple aim: to damage France, to change her foreign policy and to force her to evacuate the Ruhr. He had already publicly named Germany on 26 January in the Chamber and had been informed by other French embassies that the culprit might also be Britain. Indeed, in September 1923 British officials had intimated to Poincaré before he met his British counterpart, Stanley Baldwin, that if differences between the two countries persisted London might not renew the twelve-month French treasury bills she held. As Poincaré had given undertakings to allow the Allies to re-examine reparations once passive resistance was over, no action had been taken, but this could have had serious implications for the value of the franc on the foreign exchanges. In early January 1924 the threat was repeated to the socialist Albert Thomas during a mission to London, on Poincaré's behalf, to make contact with the new Labour government.[115] It brought home to Poincaré just how vulnerable the franc was to foreign governmental pressure. A certain vindictiveness, fired by this attempt to use finance as a diplomatic weapon, would be revisited upon Britain by Poincaré in 1928.

Meanwhile, the run on the franc and Poincaré's successful measures to stabilise it gilded his reputation for sound finances. At the Elysée on 9 March 1924, an emergency meeting of the cabinet, the regents and governor of the Bank of France, the decision was taken to intervene on the capital markets to buy up francs to restore the parity of the French currency. On 8 March there were 123 francs to the pound, by 12 March the franc's value had risen to 105, and the following day passed the important psychological barrier of 100 to the pound.[116] The franc's rate of exchange continued to improve as the speculators realised they had lost the battle and a good deal of money in the process. But on 26 March the government lost an important vote on pensions by seven votes and Poincaré felt obliged to resign. Millerand asked him to form another government, which was duly completed by the 29th, this time with only thirteen ministers and no secrétaires d'état, by way of economy. By the end of April there were fewer than 61 francs to the pound. The financial crisis of 1924 had been overcome.

In his new cabinet Poincaré had retained the foreign ministry, again signalling where he believed France's vital interests lay. Only two ministers remained from the previous cabinet; but Poincaré's fine political balancing was clearly evident. Satisfaction given to the Right was countered by his opening to centre-left Briandist ministers. The Right gave the new cabinet its support, enticed by the awarding of the Liberated Regions portfolio to Louis Marin. But that support was qualified. Everyone had their sights set on the general election of 11 May 1924.

As the elections approached, the division of France into Left and Right appeared to crystallise. The traditional picture is of a Left characterised by the Cartel des gauches and a Right by the rump of the Bloc national. But just as the true nature of the latter at its inception was less politically homogeneous than has often been suggested, so too was that of the former at the 1924 elections. The Cartel was by no means present across the whole of France, but in just over half the constituencies. In some sixteen cases the Radicals formed electoral lists with the Alliance démocratique which had supported Poincaré. Nor were things so clear-cut on the Right, where the extreme Right and hard-line Catholics often preferred to establish their own lists. Thus the former Bloc national, whose lists now went under the heading of 'republican union' or 'concentration', was by no means united in the election campaign.[117]

What then of Poincaré's position in all this? Originally Herriot and the

Radicals had sought to distinguish between Poincaré and the Right in their political attacks, but as the campaign progressed those subtleties disappeared. At the rhetorical level, in a passionate electoral campaign reflected in the exceptionally high turn-out of 83.1 per cent, the Cartel attacked his foreign and financial policy, in particular the new 20 per cent surcharge on all taxes Poincaré had introduced. They also attacked his religious policy as contrary to the secular principles of *laïcité*, but this was more of a rallying cry to unite the Left than a criticism of substance.[118] The socialists were happy to exploit the Poincaré-la-guerre myth during the campaign. A commission of enquiry into the financing of the election campaign subsequently showed that the SFIO rather rashly allowed the Second International to organise collections in Germany, Austria and Britain to fund the French socialists' election campaign on the explicitly stated theme: 'Funds must be collected to combat any continuation of M. Poincaré's policy'.[119] In certain quarters, hostility to Poincaré knew no national bounds.

Poincaré remained remarkably silent during the campaign. Well before the campaign had got underway, President Millerand had badgered him to use his interior ministry to prepare for the elections in the time-honoured tradition of favouring government candidates, but Poincaré would have none of it despite the enthusiasm of certain prefects to support Bloc national candidates.[120] This was partly a reflection of his dislike of the Bloc and partly his legalistic respect for the tradition whereby the incumbent *président du conseil* was expected not to come down in favour of the ruling majority. Most important of all, it was motivated by his desire not to sour relations with the Radicals, for in private he was predicting 'a slight slide to the left';[121] he hoped to govern with the Radicals after the elections in accordance with his belief in republican unity and the importance of non-sectarian governmental majorities. But where Poincaré was reluctant to tread, Millerand stepped zealously. The President of the Republic forsook his impartiality and descended into the electoral arena. He made clear his support for the incumbent parliamentary majority and called for constitutional revision in favour of greater executive power, about which Poincaré had remained remarkably quiet since the end of his presidential mandate.[122]

The elections gave a clear victory to the Cartel in terms of seats, though not votes. The electorate had voted for the Cartel out of weariness and disenchantment at so many apparently vain sacrifices asked of them for so many years. According to prefectoral reports, had the election taken place six months previously Poincaré would have had a resounding centrist victory. The election result was more a protest vote about taxes and the financial situation than an expression of confidence in the Cartel.[123] The Cartel did not even have an overall majority in the Chamber and relied on the support of moderate republicans of Poincaré's persuasion, reluctant to break with the Radicals. Their support for the Cartel would eventually lapse, undermining its parliamentary support and preparing the way for Poincaré's return to power.

In the meantime, Poincaré's government had resigned on 1 June 1924. There was a vain attempt by Millerand to get him to form a new government after Herriot and the Radicals had refused to form any cabinet while Millerand remained in power, so upset were they by his 'unconstitutional' antics. But Poincaré, along with a number of moderate republicans and the rest of the Left, believed that Millerand had departed from his constitutional neutrality and should resign. The constitutional crisis was only settled with the president's resignation on 11 June and the election of the moderate Gaston Doumergue as his successor.[124] A Herriot government was in place by 13 June, led by Radical ministers. Poincaré stepped out of the limelight.

Foreign affairs had dominated Poincaré's eighteen-month-long government; but just as there had been basic continuity between his foreign policy and that of his post-war predecessors on issues such as Franco-German collaboration, so there would be with his successors. Poincaré had hoped to find a solution to the fundamental problems facing French foreign policy in the post-war years. The first was to ensure French security by organising the opponents of German expansion; the second was to ensure the payment of reparations on principle and as a means of restoring stability to French finances. But however clear the pursuit of these objectives might seem while he was in opposition, Poincaré soon found them to be contradictory when in power. Britain, in particular, was loath to side with France if she continued to stick too rigidly to a strict application of the Versailles Treaty, particularly on the question of German reparations. There was always the fear in the back of the minds of many British politicians and civil servants that too great a cowing of Germany could lead to the equally dangerous prospect of French hegemony on the European continent. As relations with Britain cooled, Poincaré came round to the idea of economic collaboration with Germany as an alternative, but German reluctance was to blame for the failure of this attempt and Poincaré felt compelled to occupy the Ruhr. Such shifts in direction justify in part the incoherence which some historians have highlighted in Poincaré's foreign policy.[125] Consequently, although he won a political victory over Germany in the Ruhr, he attained none of the fundamental objectives on security and finance. Domestic political considerations and a desire to maintain Anglo-

American support conditioned his ineffective use of the Ruhr victory. Financial questions and the weakness of the franc were also beginning to affect his decision-making. It brought him to the conclusion that an international reparations settlement was the only feasible means of producing fiscal solvency and monetary stability, and that this demanded agreement with the 'Anglo-Saxons' and an accommodation with the Germans. The international solution to reparations, to which Poincaré was converted by October 1923, meant letting go of the only hold France had on post-war Germany – the Versailles Treaty. However, it did mean that Poincaré was able to retain links with the Radicals and keep the prospect of republican concentration and national unity. In accepting an international reparations settlement, Poincaré was choosing a moderate alternative to the nationalist Right's policy of coercion of Germany and the socialist Left's unilateral abandonment of the Ruhr. As Jacques Seydoux, one of Poincaré's most far-sighted advisors, put it on 27 December 1923, France was moving towards a 'financial reconstruction' of Europe by which it was no longer possible to deal with Germany as 'victor to vanquished'.[126] This is the view of modern historiography which has, in the words of one authority, rescued Poincaré from 'the aggressive and vengeful role which at times has been assigned to him in German, British, and American historiography'.[127] Ironically, the man most committed to upholding the Versailles system at the outset was instrumental in its demise. It was Poincaré who embarked France on the road to Locarno and reconciliation with Germany.[128]

10   Poincaré-le-franc

Poincaré had always had an interest in sound public finance. His reputation before the Great War was largely based on financial rigour, and now in the post-war period financial policy was coming to dominate all other. The need for harmony between finance and diplomacy was becoming as evident to him after the war as had been the need for close co-ordination between military operations and diplomacy in July 1914. This strategic view of French finances in the post-war period was particularly apparent over reparations. Certainly financial threats were more immediate than security threats, as Poincaré explained to the Conseil supérieur de défense nationale on 22 October 1922: 'If for ten or so years we are safe from military adventures, on the other hand for five or six years we are at the mercy of a financial incident.'[1] The potential use of international speculation against the franc as a diplomatic weapon had been made all too clear to Poincaré in early 1924. The outcome of the Ruhr occupation demonstrated the extent to which finance could dictate French diplomacy; it would soon be dictating French domestic politics.

Nor did Poincaré underestimate, the political and social importance of sound finances for what he, and others, considered to be the backbone of the Third Republic – the middle classes. A recent study of material conditions in the Great War concludes that the middle classes were worse affected than the working classes.[2] Some elements of the middle classes had amassed great riches from the wartime economy, whilst others had incurred harsh losses. Poincaré was temperamentally suspicious of the former and sympathetic to the latter. The product of a middle-class family whose success was built on education, not commerce, he was not untypical in viewing 'money' as a subject of vulgarity and the object of suspicion. It was only his wife who had brought order to his personal finances[3] and probably convinced him of the need to open a bank account. Jules Laroche remembered his harsh words in 1922 for French parliamentarians with financial links with the business world and his outburst over the high fee earnings of a barrister colleague:

'One cannot earn that much by only pleading honest causes'.[4] He would have witnessed at first hand among his comfortably off family circle the erosion of their capital and income and would have sympathised with the least fortunate members of the middle classes. In the war and the post-war period the normal mechanisms by which middle-class families sought to minimise the inherent risks of a capitalist economy collapsed. Spectacular losses on Russian bonds apart, capital values and income derived from traditional French 'safe' investments such as government stock, debentures and property were far outstripped by price inflation. Rent freezes during the war and control afterwards through the law of March 1918 were further blows to middle-class incomes. Though the 1920s were characterised by strong growth as French reconstruction moved apace and devaluation of the franc boosted exports, this performance was marred by an inflation rate which took prices in 1928 to six and a half times those of 1914. Inflation was particularly harsh on large sectors of the middle classes. They felt that sacrifices in the war, and now the post-war period, were unequal, and that governments unduly favoured business or labour.[5] Poincaré was well attuned to that feeling. It was Herriot who first coined the term 'Français moyen' in the summer of 1924, reflecting the Radicals' preoccupation with the middle classes, but it was Poincaré who believed something should be done for them. It was Herriot who attacked the 'mur d'argent', but it was Poincaré who understood that that 'wall' was made of more tiny grains of sand than it was of powerful financial blocks.[6] In relative terms, which, after all, is how individuals tended to measure their plight, inflation affected manual workers' salaries less than it did the incomes of a large but heterogeneous collection of middle-class elements from junior clerks and civil servants, to teachers, journalists, artists, widows, *rentiers* and small savers. One measure of this was that personal fortunes in France, calculated according to personal estates at death, show a national decline of 57 per cent in total personal wealth in real terms from 1912–13 to 1925–6, and a dramatic 70 per cent decline for Paris.[7] Equally important to a material loss of wealth for many was the psychological blow of a loss of status, often expressed as 'dignity' or 'respectability'. As the historian Marc Bloch observed, the French middle class in the inter-war years had 'stopped being happy'.[8] Poincaré was not alone in France, or for that matter in Britain or Germany, in believing that if allowed to continue this could undermine features which he saw as fundamental to the stability of the regime – work, thrift, honesty – with the prospect of creating a generation of *déclassés*.[9] Jacques Rueff, future governor of the Bank of France and young *inspecteur des finances* in Poincaré's private office in 1926, described Poincaré as a survivor of the pre-war *époque des notables*: 'He feels that devaluation will impoverish the *rentiers* and those on pensions and will downgrade civil servants and intellectuals to the advantage of shopkeepers, hoarders and speculators of all kinds.'[10] For someone whose early political experiences included the Boulanger years, Poincaré could not have overlooked how such developments could pose a threat to the republican regime from an extreme Right in the ascendant. There were already ample signs of extra-parliamentary activity from political organisations pandering to the discontented lower middle classes, such as Pierre Taittinger's 'Jeunesses Patriotes' founded in 1924, or Georges Valois's 'Faisceau' and Ernest Mercier's 'Redressement Français' established in November and December 1925 respectively.[11]

Price inflation was thus the great evil for people who in the previous century had known remarkable price stability. The rapid inflation of the war years had given way to a period of respite between 1920 and early 1922 when prices actually fell. By December 1922 inflation took off again. With a base of 100 in 1914, retail prices in Paris rose from 294 in March 1922 to 305 in December, then 365 at the end of 1923, 404 at the end of 1924, reaching 463 in 1925. Poincaré believed that inflation was merely a pernicious symptom of an unhealthy economy. Post-war inflation grew out of the war years and governments' predilection for increasing borrowing rather than the more difficult solution of increasing taxes. To finance reconstruction, service the public debt and ensure payment on mature government securities, cabinets preferred to increase borrowing or print more bank-notes, thereby fuelling the inflationary cycle.

Throughout the nineteenth century France had known remarkable currency stability, conferring on the *franc germinal*, created in 1803, an aura of sanctity. However, during the war the franc, like other currencies, came off the Gold Standard only to be artificially supported by Britain and subsequently America. The support which the Allied powers gave to the franc during the war years ceased on 14 March 1919 leading to progressive depreciation against the pound and the dollar. The franc's pre-war parity of 25 to the pound had by the end of 1919 gone to 41 francs to the pound, by the end of 1921 60 francs, by 1923 85 and by the spring of 1924, following the Ruhr episode, 116 francs to the pound, which apart from submitting Paris to an invasion of 'Anglo-Saxon' tourists, seriously threatened the French economy.[12]

Of course, immediate post-war reconstruction in France was bound to produce large budget deficits given the extent of the war-damaged area: twelve French departments had been invaded, equivalent to 8 per cent of France's 1914 territory, and those departments accounted for

30 per cent of her industrial production. Wartime material losses have been calculated at 25 per cent more than France's national income in 1913, while industrial production in 1919 had fallen to 57 per cent of its 1913 level, to which it would return only in 1924.[13] To finance the war France had increased her domestic national debt more than tenfold. This is not surprising given that at the beginning of the war France had one of the least developed systems of direct taxation of a modern state. Income tax would only be introduced in 1917 and then only at a rate of just 2 per cent for all, as against Britain's 6 per cent. Though the rate was increased thereafter, it is calculated that French taxes overall covered just 15 per cent of total government expenditure during the war, which was poor compared to Britain's 30 per cent, if good compared to Germany's 7.3 per cent. The massive French shortfall of 85 per cent had to be met by printing currency and by issuing treasury bonds.[14] The amount of French debt was worsened by its short-term nature, making it unstable and difficult to manage. It was added to after the war by further short-term borrowing and advances from the Bank of France under the misapprehension that reimbursement would soon come via reparations, epitomised in the slogan 'Germany will pay'. The instability of that burden is what would frustrate French governments in the first half of the post-war decade.

Poincaré had made an attempt to tackle the budget deficits during his first post-war government. Unlike his predecessors and successors, rather than increase government borrowing he had attempted to have reconstruction costs included in the budget at the end of 1923, in similar fashion to when, as minister of finance before the war, he had striven to do away with the myriad budgetary annexes and present a unified budget. His aim in 1924 had been to increase taxes to cover the deficit. His determination to solve the financial problem could be measured by his decision to raise taxes substantially only a couple of months away from a general election. But then he had never shied from tax increases for electoral reasons, as witness 1894 and 1914. In 1924 he had raised taxes by 20 per cent across the board – the 'double décime' – and imposed stricter foreign exchange controls. Though such unpopular measures had produced heated debate in both Chamber and Senate, against the background of a run on the franc from January to March he had been able to push his tight budget through on 22 March 1924. Poincaré did not benefit in the short term from these measures, as the elections testified, even though at the beginning of May 1924 speculation against the franc had been reversed. The Cartel was the immediate, though temporary, beneficiary of Poincaré's financial policy. The 1925 budget almost balanced and the balance of payments had improved, but this was counteracted by the psychological climate of mistrust associated with the Cartel's coming to power. The result was a considerable export of capital which outweighed the surplus in the balance of payments. Encumbered by its enormous public debt, France was unable to raise loans on the financial markets; Cartel governments were obliged to resort to loans from the Bank of France and thus to printing money. This culminated in the monetary crisis of July 1926. Prices reached an index of 800 (1913 = 100) and the franc slipped to almost 50 to the dollar as against 5.13 in 1913.[15]

Poincaré's willingness to propose austere financial measures, including higher taxes, did, however, have its bounds. When the franc was under attack in 1925 and the left of the Cartel forced Herriot's government to propose a one-off 10 per cent levy on capital, Poincaré led the Senate on 10 April 1925 in voting against the measure on the grounds that it would lead to a flight of capital and further depreciation of the franc. This brought down Herriot's government – the first time the Senate had brought down a government on a purely financial question. But French financial problems were becoming chronic, and fiscal and monetary issues were becoming the very stuff of politics. From 1923, and especially after 1925, the exchange rate came to be discussed 'more frequently than love used to be and at least as much as the war ever was'.[16] Though Poincaré was active in contesting the Cartel's financial policy, he was a good deal more passive over its foreign policy.

Cartel diplomacy

It was Poincaré's acceptance of the Dawes Plan which had paved the way for the Cartel's policy of reconciliation with Germany. The Plan was based on the idea that American capital should be used to stabilise the German economy and return it to prosperity, thereby allowing the payment of reparations to all concerned, with France first. That Plan did not only reduce the German debt, it fundamentally modified the reparations section of the Versailles Treaty by ending France's legal authority to force Germany to pay through unilateral action. The philosophy was twofold: to safeguard the Reich and integrate Germany into the western liberal bloc.[17] But after Poincaré's policy of firmness towards Germany, Herriot's style was markedly different, characterised by benevolent pacifism and, according to some, incompetence. Though the Cartel had criticised Poincaré's policy towards Germany, socialists and Radicals had not clearly defined an alternative. The socialists were resolutely internationalist, but the Radicals in the jacobin tradition were more circumspect, even suspicious of Germany, as their support for

Poincaré's policy until 1923 had demonstrated. In the Chamber vote which had immediately followed the Franco-Belgian decision to occupy the Ruhr in January 1923, had not most Radical *députés* voted for Poincaré's cabinet, with Herriot abstaining? It was more for reasons of domestic politics than foreign policy that the Radicals had moved into opposition to Poincaré and set up the Cartel. Though the Radicals might criticise Poincaré they had no doctrinal desire to overturn his German policy. But in a bid to win British friendship, Herriot's new government made many concessions in the negotiations at the London Conference in July and August 1924 which saw the official adoption of the Dawes Plan. Without seeking proper guarantees he agreed to an evacuation of the Ruhr by August 1925. At the same time the Cartel placed its full confidence in a reform of the League of Nations to give it more power to arbitrate in the event of conflict between states. Neither British support for such a move nor a Franco-British pact were forthcoming. At the same time Herriot had sought to counterbalance German power by what was becoming a traditional French geo-political reflex in Europe through his recognition of the Soviet Union in October 1924.[18]

Herriot's foreign policy provoked a division in France: the Left believed that only negotiation, whatever the difficulties, could build peace; the Right claimed that victory was being lost and that peace was being compromised. Foreign policy divisions were exacerbated by domestic divisions. Yet Poincaré's comments on the Cartel's foreign policy remained remarkably restrained – particularly in the first few months – to the surprise of some historians,[19] demonstrating the moderate nature of his foreign policy. Criticism of Herriot's policy was more technical than political. Indeed, in May 1924 Poincaré had had a number of meetings with Herriot, with whom he remained on warm personal terms. At those meetings he impressed on his successor the need to link a final settlement of the Ruhr episode with two essential questions: European security and an inter-Allied debt settlement. At the same time he stressed the need to ensure that on the reparations questions any military evacuation of the Ruhr should be proportional to the conversion and commercialisation of German debts. Though Herriot would go armed with these issues to London to negotiate, he would quickly come away with a good deal less.[20]

But it was financial issues which brought Herriot's government down. They were also the cause of the instability of the six Cartel governments which followed in the space of fifteen months.[21] Ministerial instability was at least compensated for by the stability of the longest-serving minister of foreign affairs since Delcassé, Aristide Briand, who would in that capacity continue the process of détente with Germany until he left the Quai d'Orsay in 1932. Poincaré kept him on as foreign minister for as long as he himself stayed in power. As Jules Laroche, political director of the Quai in 1924 and subsequently ambassador to Poland, noted, Poincaré 'showed no urge to block his [Briand's] foreign policy'.[22] Poincaré sanctioned it in the full knowledge of its content and intention, for even when as premier he held the finance portfolio he kept a careful watch on the foreign ministry. He told his friend Léon Bailby, who would engineer the reconciliation with Philippe Berthelot, 'Since I have been premier, I get all dispatches sent to me from the Quai d'Orsay'.[23] Poincaré came to rely on Berthelot as a brake on Briand's more adventurous policies. He told Bailby, 'I understood better what you had told me. Berthelot is not a "civil servant". He is more. He is better. I have read all his memos, his telegrams. They are inspired, I acknowledge, by the most rigorous national feeling.'[24] Thus, as secretary general of the foreign ministry, Berthelot ensured a certain stability and continuity in French foreign policy which suited both Briand and Poincaré: the former because Berthelot's industry compensated for his own leisurely manner; the latter because Berthelot kept a tight rein on the Quai and on ambassadors, whose power Poincaré had always held in suspicion and which diminished considerably during the 1920s.[25] Not surprising that after the Locarno agreements Berthelot noted that Briand was tired and whiled away his days reading detective stories.[26] Overall, though, Poincaré supported Briand's policy of détente with Germany whether in parliament or in public. Indeed, just as in 1914 he had been the first president of the Republic to dine at the German embassy in Paris, so it would be under a Poincaré government that for the first time a German foreign minister would be invited to Paris, for the signing of the Briand–Kellogg pact in 1928 outlawing war as a means of settling international disputes.[27]

Briand's policy began with the agreements which he negotiated with Stresemann, Austen Chamberlain, Mussolini and the Belgian Vandervelde from 5 to 16 October 1925 at Locarno, the Swiss resort on Lake Maggiore. The Locarno agreements were intended to stabilise the frontiers between Germany and her western neighbours. Thus Germany recognised her borders with France and Belgium and accepted the demilitarised left bank of the Rhine established by the Versailles Treaty. Italy and Britain were guarantors of these agreements and were obliged to intervene militarily in the event of their breach. In exchange Germany was to join the League of Nations and was promised a permanent seat on its Council. Berlin also secured the evacuation of Allied troops from the zone around Cologne. Paris reached agreement with Berlin, Brussels, Poland and Czechoslovakia on Germany's eastern frontiers in deference to France's eastern European allies. But those guarantees were far more tenuous than for the western borders. Italy and Britain remained sole judges of what constituted infringements of the agreement and no monitoring system for demilitarisation was put in place. Moreover, Germany was able to reject the notion that, in the event of the League of Nations needing to take military action against an aggressor in eastern Europe, troops could be moved across German territory, thereby denying France the possibility of entering Germany in order to come to the rescue of Poland and Czechoslovakia.[28]

These agreements earned Briand the title of 'pilgrim of peace' on his return to Paris. He presented the Locarno agreements as the beginning of the real peace process whereby Germany at last accepted of her own volition what the Versailles Treaty had imposed on her – the return of Alsace–Lorraine and the demilitarisation of the left bank of the Rhine in perpetuity. The Chamber voted the Locarno agreements by a massive majority, but the agreements were criticised, notably by Poincaré. He did not believe demilitarisation of the Rhineland to be an adequate guarantee. Revealing his suspicion of Germany and some foresight, given the remilitarisation of the Rhineland in 1936, he wrote in a Belgian journal, 'Belgium and France are no longer free to judge the danger in the event of a flagrant breach of the treaty. In exchange for a few concessions, we are obtaining a commitment from the Reich worth only what the reigning mood in Germany is worth.' According to Jules Laroche, he expressed cynicism for promises contracted 'in the abandon of overfamiliar meetings', betraying both his juridical aversion to verbal negotiation and his inability to comprehend the point of informal diplomatic gatherings in which he was incapable of being anything less than formal. It was partly to refute criticism of the inadequate guarantees for Rhineland neutrality that a legal note was added to the Locarno agreements effectively allowing countries such as France the right to intervene, without the League of Nations, to stop any unprovoked aggression, even if France made no use of it to stop Hitler's remilitarisation of the Rhineland in 1936.[29] Nevertheless, Briand had established a momentum in French foreign policy which was widely supported by domestic opinion. Governments might come and go but Briand was sure to stay at foreign affairs.

Poincaré-la-confiance

By June 1926 the financial crisis suffered by the Cartel had provoked a severe political crisis. On 16 July 202 francs would buy just one pound. Memories of the collapse of the German mark in 1922–3 abounded.

Nationwide there was a flood of withdrawals from savings accounts. Herriot led part of the left-wing majority into opposition to Briand's tenth government alongside the Right, splitting the Cartel and giving rise to a new majority. Herriot's own still-born cabinet was overturned on 21 July. With the pound standing at 240 francs the way was open for Poincaré.[30]

Just short of sixty-seven years old, slightly rotund, his goatee beard whitened and his hair well receded, Poincaré more than ever resembled an inscrutable mandarin. He made it a condition of taking the premiership that his government should be one of republican union incorporating the Left. His parliamentary support came from a new solid centre majority based on most of the Radicals and elements of the Right. Though he would have dearly loved to have had a wider majority to form a new *union sacrée* government, he had to settle for one of 'National Union' – two epithets with which his name had always been closely associated. His personality and politics made him the natural leader of this coalition as well as legitimising its very existence. Like Clemenceau in 1917, he was perceived as one of the few remaining French politicians with any credibility among the public; he would not have been displeased with the analogy or with appearing the saviour once again. As at the time of *union sacrée* he embodied the necessary party truce. For the Right he represented social conservatism and financial orthodoxy; for the Left he still commanded respect as a parliamentary republican, a *laïque*, and as someone who had always attempted to work with the Radicals, not least by including them in his post-war ministries. To a certain extent he was also reaping the benefits of his reserve in the 1924 election campaign and in the subsequent presidential crisis.[31] The SFIO abstained. Only the Communists remained in outright opposition; they saw in the crisis facing France an opportunity to end the 'moribund' bourgeois regime and attacked their traditional enemy Poincaré in *L'Humanité* with venom as the 'mediocre *petit bourgeois* who incarnates all that is most sickening in the average Frenchman, all that is most rancid in *l'épargne intellectuelle*'. But the other extremist grouping with an interest in the collapse of the regime, the extreme Right Action française, was disappointed by the prospect of the return of the man in whom the nationalists had placed so much hope over the Ruhr only to have them dashed. Charles Maurras now returned to his original criticism of him in 1913 as being the typical irresponsible centrist parliamentarian who always ended up carrying out the policy of his opponents.[32]

Poincaré put together his fourth government on 23 July 1926 in only two days – he had never taken longer than three.[33] Of the thirteen ministers six were former premiers, symbolising the stand of the old guard of parliamentarianism against its communist and fascist detractors. To reassure the financial community, the victor of the 'financial Verdun' of 1924 took on the finance portfolio for the third time (though this was the first time he had combined it with the premiership), leaving Briand in charge of foreign affairs. Keeping Briand at the Quai showed his desire to continue the policy of détente with Germany, though by now it is doubtful whether any alternative was possible given international and national opinion. To the Chamber he defined his cabinet as 'formed in a spirit of national reconciliation' to save France's finances and financial freedom. He had wished its composition to be even broader by offering a place to the socialist Paul-Boncour, but the SFIO refused any participation in a government which it saw as led by the real leader of the Right. It did include four Radicals, of whom Herriot was given the education and culture portfolio. But fewer members of the centre-right were given a place. Despite the cabinet leaning to the centre-left and excluding any member of the Catholic Right, the latter supported it in the Chamber. It was a subtle dosing which mixed the experience of pre-war personnel with bright new minds; it satisfied the Left on foreign policy and the Right on financial matters; it was characterised by a renewal of the entente between moderate republicans and Radicals. For the first time, according to the seasoned political observer, Charles Seignobos, it achieved 'government by the centres', something which had been the dream of centrists since the beginning of the Republic.[34] At a time when the longevity of Third Republic governments was a contradiction in terms, French public and political opinion would reward this broad cabinet with a remarkable two years and three months of stability. It would take Poincaré's total service as minister of finance since 1894 to 1,311 days, making him the fifth-longest serving holder of that office under the Third Republic and the seventh longest in a line of eighty-eight stretching from 1870 to 1992.[35]

The immediate problem confronting the new cabinet was the monetary crisis. The impressive array of ministers from Herriot to Tardieu and Radical participation signalled to the middle classes that savings were to be protected from taxes on capital or the disguised tax of inflation associated with the Cartel. Hope was placed in a second Poincaré restoration of the franc. Indeed, he had only to be seated at the finance minister's desk for the currency to begin its recovery from a nadir of 243 francs to the pound. On 23 July, the very day Poincaré's government was formed, capital flows were reversed: that morning there had been 218.5 francs to the pound; at 1.30 p.m. Poincaré went to the Elysée to announce his cabinet and that afternoon the franc recovered to 208.25; four days later it stood at 196 to the pound.[36] The ease with which the franc recovered reflected Poincaré's financial reputation, but it also demonstrated the degree to which psychology rather than hard economic facts had been seriously undervaluing the currency. It was not strictly, as the Left would insist, the bankers and so-called 'mur d'argent' who had undermined the Cartel's financial position. Rather it was the millions of small investors each with a clutch of shares and government bonds, fearing measures long associated with the Left, such as income tax and budget deficits, of which the Right's propaganda constantly reminded them, who signalled to the high financiers and the currency markets their lack of confidence in the Cartel's policies.

The history of the next two years is the history of the stabilisation of the franc at a parity broadly in line with France's economic performance.[37] It is also the account of Poincaré's confronting of a dilemma: on the one hand, the need to respect the realities of the French economy; on the other, a personal sense of duty to a host of small savers certain to have their capital slashed should the franc be stabilised at a lower rate than its pre-war value – in other words, devalued. It was not that Poincaré felt a duty to protect the middle classes for purely electoral reasons, as critics would subsequently claim. The picture needs to be far more nuanced than that. First, the nature of the French economy, so different in structure to its British, American or German counterparts, determined that the small-saver be given particular attention, at least according to contemporary economic thought. The eminent committee of experts, assembled by the Cartel government at the end of May that year to suggest the best way out of the crisis, explained in its report, 'In France, a middle-class country of limited industrialisation, a country whose prosperity rests above all on its ability to save, the consequences of monetary instability are particularly serious'. Second, these contemporary economic perceptions blended with contemporary moral issues to make monetary instability seem particularly corrosive. Poincaré was not alone in believing that the middle classes best represented moral values vital to the survival of the Republic. He would have been in full agreement with the experts' assessment of the pernicious moral effects of monetary instability: 'If providence became dupery, if the attraction of speculation and gambling replaced the taste for effort and productive work, we would see, in a short time, the best of our national values collapse. To safeguard the economic life of the country, the franc must have restored to it the fundamental quality of a currency: its stability'.[38] Finally, Poincaré probably believed that large sections of the middle classes had suffered enough during the war and post-war periods; a further blow would be unjust and dangerous.

Poincaré would pilot French monetary stabilisation through three stages over the next eighteen months: measures to halt the run on the franc; *de facto* stabilisation; *de jure* stabilisation. Though few would have disagreed that currency stability was a necessity, the vital question would soon turn on the value at which the franc should be stabilised. During this period a series of partially conflicting, yet intertwined, issues would condition Poincaré's timing in bringing the franc back on to the Gold Standard. Apart from the purely technical, his financial decisions would be influenced by moral, political and international issues, and not a little characteristic hesitation. The moral issue was connected with a legal sense of contractual obligation associated with the value of a currency and would weigh heavily in the balance for Poincaré; politically, he sought to maintain a consensus and avoid being pushed either to the Right or Left; on the diplomatic front he was soon aware of how delaying a return to the Gold Standard could be an effective instrument of foreign policy, if not diplomatic blackmail.

In the short term the vital issue was to effect monetary and financial reform and put the currency on a sound basis. Here, as in other circumstances, Poincaré demonstrated that he was more a manager than an innovator. He would follow all except two of the committee of experts' recommendations (final settlement of France's foreign debt; the need to raise a large loan to back France's currency) submitted before his cabinet was formed. As the Chamber finance commission rather grudgingly put it, Poincaré's measures were nothing more than 'the translation into legislative texts, apart from a few changes in detail, of the fiscal part of the experts' plan'.[39] But he did bring two things to their plan: rapidity of execution (albeit tinged with hesitation) and confidence. The confidence he brought to financial affairs was the essential psychological gel which allowed policies to stick.

Poincaré was helped by broad parliamentary support for his measures, which for once allowed the parliamentary regime to function efficiently. Measures to redeem the financial position were taken rapidly. Only three days after forming his government the Chamber had voted by a majority of 418 to 31 to give the government emergency powers to restore French finances. They became law on 3 August. He pushed further legislation through a panicked parliament in magisterial fashion, mixing humour, irony and that clinching attention to detail which was his hallmark: 'If the measures which we submit to you are not voted without delay, the State will lose 16 millions a day, 660,000 francs an hour, 11,000 francs a minute.'[40] Those measures involved increasing tax receipts by new and higher indirect taxes but lower direct taxes, reducing government expenditure, stabilising Treasury funds and balancing the nation's accounts.

The only opposition came from the Communists, and the socialists led by Vincent Auriol. Indeed, this would be the beginning of some two years of financial jousting with Auriol and Léon Blum; the latter and Poincaré would share a mutual respect, even a surprising affection, which did not go unnoticed in the Chamber.[41] Tax collection was made more efficient and expenditure was reduced by a government economy drive involving the administrative reorganisation and streamlining of several ministries, the first of its kind since the beginning of the Republic. Thus several local law courts were closed, together with over 100 *sous-préfectures*, over 150 tax offices and 700 tax inspector posts.[42] A new unified budget was introduced designed to impress public opinion as much as to balance government expenditure. As a result of these reforms the projected budget deficit for 1926 of 2.5 billion francs was transformed into a surplus of 1.5 billions.[43]

To balance the Treasury's books and absorb the public debt Poincaré decided to create an independent sinking fund, the Caisse autonome d'Amortissement, funded largely from the state tobacco monopoly. It was intended to gain control of the 50 billion francs in short-term debt, principally national defence bonds of three months or less, which were so difficult to manage.[44] Poincaré decided that to give greater solemnity to this measure, the Caisse should be enshrined in the constitution, which involved passing a constitutional amendment to which the Senate was initially hostile, believing any constitutional revision to be question-able republicanism. But playing upon his republican credentials and associating his action with that of his political mentor, Jules Ferry, Poincaré easily convinced the parliament gathered at Versailles on 10 August.[45] This tactical move was a psychological master stroke. Subscriptions for new long-term government stock outweighed redemp-tions, allowing the government progressively to eliminate the unwieldy short-term bonds by 1928 and reduce interest rates on long-term bonds.[46]

The Treasury's current account was in deficit as a result of the massive exports of capital during the run on the franc. By sharply increasing the Bank of France's discount rate on 31 July to 7.5 per cent capital began to flow back into Paris with speculation now beginning to operate in favour of the franc.

The upward pressure on the franc had at first been welcome, but soon began to pose a dilemma for Poincaré which reflected the national debate between those in favour of revaluation and those in favour of stabilisation. On the positive side, the considerable flow of capital into Paris meant that there was no need for France to make use of credit facilities extended by the 'Anglo-Saxons' to shore up the French currency. This was doubly rewarding for Poincaré: national pride was not dented by having to go cap in hand to foreign governments again; and the 'Anglo-Saxons' were denied the opportunity of demanding in exchange that France ratify the unpopular London and Washington agreements on debt repayments negotiated by Poincaré's predecessor at the finance ministry, Joseph Caillaux. Not least of the positive benefits was the fact that small investors could see the currency regaining some of its pre-war value, and for this reason revaluation was supported by conservative newspapers such as *Le Temps*, *Le Figaro* and the *Journal des Débats*, as well as by the influential financier, Baron Rothschild. On the negative side, as the stabilisers like the commerce minister, the Bank of France and many industrialists pointed out, the franc's climb could have adverse effects on the French economy. The increased value of the franc could endanger the recently stabilised public finances by revaluing state and local authority debt. It would make French exports more expensive and imports cheaper, eroding markets, reducing economic output, increasing unemployment, driving down salaries and posing the threat of economic depression and social unrest. Stabilisers pointed to the revaluation of the pound sterling in 1925 and the ensuing economic and social crisis as an example of the dangers of revaluation.[47]

The governor of the Bank of France at this time, Emile Moreau, whose relations with Poincaré were not always cordial, depicts Poincaré as hesitant about what action should be taken.[48] Personally, Poincaré was a revaluer. Despite the Committee of Experts' recommendation, supported by senior Treasury and Bank of France officials, that the franc be stabilised as quickly as possible, Poincaré instinctively hankered after the *franc germinal*. It was suggested that he was congenitally suspicious of bankers and their dealings, something reflected in his reluctance to hold a bank account anywhere other than with the Bank of France. On 9 August the governor of the Bank of France recorded in his diary that 'Monsieur Poincaré tells me that he wants to revalue the franc before stabilising it'.[49] Romantically he hankered after a return to the pre-war value of the franc which he and his parents had known all their lives. Morally he believed that it was unacceptable to dispossess all those patriots who during the war had given up their gold in exchange for bank notes and government bonds, whose gold value he was being told to devalue by some 80 per cent. Legally his juridicism made the contract inherent in any currency sacrosanct. How would anyone ever again have confidence in the honesty of the state of which he was the servant?

Poincaré continued to hold out against pressure from Bank and Treasury officials until the autumn. As with the Quai d'Orsay in 1912, he was suspicious of the independence of permanent officials whose power had increased during the preceding period of diminished political authority. As in 1912 he was intent on imposing his own authority and methods, and, like then, was quite unembarrassed about demonstrating it. On 27 July he and the governor of the Bank of France clashed: 'Monsieur le Gouverneur I remind you that you are a civil servant appointed by the Government. I withdraw your right to speak.'[50] As in 1912 he preferred to work on his own or with a loyal clique of officials. That is why he brought in the *conseiller d'état* Georges Payelle, his close friend since the Law faculty, who had first served as his *chef de cabinet* in the 1890s, to serve as his *chef de cabinet* at the finance ministry.[51]

Poincaré's refusal to stabilise fuelled further rises in the value of the franc in early autumn as speculators gambled on its continued revaluation. Fearing an over-valued currency, industrialists and chambers of commerce called for a quick stabilisation. The governor of the Bank of France warned Poincaré that the motor car manufacturer Citroën was in difficulty. Poincaré countered with a report from the ministry of labour showing that the firm was taking on employees. But small investors with an interest in continued revaluation exerted pressure through the Fédération Républicaine, which was the group of Louis Marin, the minister of liberated regions.[52] Jacques Rueff, a young *inspecteur des finances* in the minister of finance's private office, explained how the governor of the Bank of France was supported in trying to get the premier to halt the franc's rise by the general secretary of the CGT trades union, Léon Jouhaux. Since the beginning of the war, Poincaré had had a number of opportunities to compliment Jouhaux on his patriotism and good judgement; in 1915 he became 'commissaire de la nation' and remained throughout the war a staunch supporter of *union sacrée*, an anti-communist and reformist trade union leader in the 1920s with whom the Poincaré governments were willing to discuss reform even when the *patronat* refused.[53] Jouhaux called on Poincaré several times in October to warn of the risks of unemployment from the franc's rise. Rueff claims this had a decisive effect on Poincaré's thinking, and he was subsequently instructed by Poincaré to carry out a study on the highest value at which the franc could be stabilised. Aware that there was a point at which revaluation would put downward pressure on wage costs, Poincaré specifically asked him to target his study on salaries: 'I want to know, for each industry, what is the minimum exchange rate at which salaries will have to be reduced to maintain markets.'[54] This is what Emile Moreau had pointed out to him on 4 August when he had insisted that stabilisation was not dependent on government will but on economic realities; the rate would have to be set 'between two limits, the rate of the franc resulting from the cost of living index at the time of the operation, and the rate of the franc in the currency markets at the same moment'.[55] Typically Poincaré changed his mind again about stabilisation. On 15 November 1926 Moreau noted in his diary, 'M. Poincaré has become hostile to stabilisation again. Moreover, he believes that there is no hurry and he has delayed a decision on this until the month of February.' Over the next week Moreau records him as changing his mind a further three times.[56]

It was not until 20 December 1926 that the decision was taken to peg the franc at 120 to the pound. Two days later, the Bank of France was granted permission to intervene in the capital markets to peg the franc at that rate. *De facto* stabilisation of the French currency was achieved at almost double its value from when Poincaré had taken over five months previously; but there remained the question of the currency's stabilisation *de jure*, which meant its return to the Gold Standard, as the pound had done in 1925. Again Poincaré would have considerable difficulty in accepting that. Even after December he was still hoping for further gradual revaluation. At the end of January 1927, with a balanced budget[57] and a healthy balance of trade, he told the Chamber finance commission that he remained adamantly opposed to legal stabilisation in the near future.[58] But stabilisation *de facto* would continue for a further eighteen months.

What had been achieved so far was remarkable in terms of France's return to sound finances. Poincaré could be forgiven for indulging in a degree of self-congratulation before the April 1928 elections. In what must rank as one of the longest French parliamentary speeches, stretching over two whole sessions from 2 to 3 February 1928 and filling 212 pages of printed text, Poincaré lambasted his critics with a mixture of good-humoured sarcasm and mounds of statistics. It is this speech (and that of 1929 on inter-Allied debts, calculated to have been twenty-seven hours long) which did so much to create the myth of 'Poincaré-la-mitrailleuse', machine-gunning parliamentarians into submission by a barrage of boring statistics. Cartoonists would subsequently depict him specchifying from the top of a mountain of paper weighing down on the Chamber of Deputies, or towing boat loads of notes ready for another *exposé*.[59] The myth developed of Poincaré the poor orator and boring speaker and was applied retrospectively. As with so many of the myths associated with him, the caricature was overdrawn. Certainly his speeches were remarkably well prepared and did convey substantial amounts of information; in this they were different from the extemporised incantations of the famous orators of the Third Republic such as Gambetta, Jaurès or Briand. But though classed in a different mould, Poincaré was thought of as a fine speaker by fellow parliamentarians;

certainly his speeches were not thought of as boring or uninteresting if the references in the *Journal Officiel* to bouts of laughter or acclamation on various benches of the National Assembly are an indication. His weakness, which seems to have increased in the last years of his political life, lay in a pathological desire to convince, which translated itself into statistical bombardments.

Poincaré began his speech with a quotation from the secretary of the United States Treasury to the effect that the restoration of French finances 'constitutes one of the most astonishing chapters in financial history'. He ridiculed Vincent Auriol for his criticism in 1926 that Poincaré's policies would not work. At that time the wholesale price index had stood at 856, it was now down to 617; wholesale food prices were down from 703 to 551. Castigating Auriol as Doctor Tant-Pis he then set about Léon Blum who had come to the tribune 'to joke with us agreeably'. Returning to the healthy state of the country's finances and economy he explained that the bank rate was down from 7.5 to 3.5 per cent and that he had reimbursed much of the domestic debt before its term. Unemployment was down from a peak of 82,000 in March 1927 to something between 10,000 and 16,000. This was smaller than the pre-1914 figures and less than any other European country, notably Britain's total of just under 1.5 million and Germany's 1.75 million. This justified his opposition for the moment to *de jure* stabilisation of the currency. Demonstrating the continuity of his financial policy, and with an eye to maintaining the support of the Radicals, he repeated his call of 1906 for the 'intelligent and industrious bourgeoisie not to close its ears to the calls of democracy'. He concluded with an appeal to national effort and a pledge that the government would do everything to stimulate 'the love of work' and 'to awaken in every conscience the feeling of duty towards the community, in order to develop general well-being and thus to ensure the relief of all those who suffer'. This action, which he described as 'republican and French, democratic and human', was quintessential Poincarism. It was greeted with considerable acclamation from benches on the centre, the Right and several on the Left, an indication of his broad parliamentary support.[60]

The absence of legal stabilisation of the currency at a time of fixed rate parities had a number of disadvantages. Improved French finances prompted speculators to gamble on a further revaluation of the franc and thus buy francs. To counter further increases the Bank of France was obliged to sell enormous quantities of francs; this meant printing new banknotes to satisfy demand thereby threatening to fuel inflation by increasing the money supply.[61] To ease this position a decree passed on

10 January 1928 lifted exchange controls to enable capital to flow out of Paris.[62]

At the same time anxiety developed as to the unpredictable use which foreign holders of francs might put them to; the currency seemed increasingly at the mercy of foreigners and, more worrying still, foreign governments. Clearly the autumn 1923 run on the franc had forced France to be more conciliatory in foreign affairs. It was felt that speculation against the franc had in no small way been due to a German campaign carried out by banks in Berlin and Amsterdam.[63] Poincaré had evidence of that fact. On 11 March 1924 he had shown two regents of the Bank of France, Edouard de Rothschild and François de Wendel, a translation of secret instructions from the German chancellor, Stresemann, to a special meeting of Berlin bankers which had been held on 4 March. According to Wendel, the document showed precisely 'The plan of offensive against the franc, the methods to be used, the aims to be achieved, the necessity of favouring left-wing parties and of toppling M. Poincaré and his majority'.[64] On 13 March, Poincaré read the same document to the Senate. Though some historians have contested the veracity of the statements made in the document, French intelligence reports appear to corroborate them.[65] But the crucial point is that Poincaré believed that the French currency, and with it French foreign policy, was vulnerable to foreign attack.

In 1928 the anxiety was that at any moment foreign holders of francs could in concert suddenly 'dump' them on the international market and seriously destabilise the French currency. This explains the close watch which French diplomats and the French intelligence services tried to keep on the foreign origins of orders for the purchase of francs. The fear was that Germany might again be orchestrating a campaign to put pressure on France at a moment of Germany's choosing.[66] This would probably have leant Poincaré in favour of a *de jure* stabilisation to anchor the currency against politically motivated speculation.

There was, however, a positive outcome from the speculation in favour of the franc, which would have inclined him against legal stabilisation. Having learnt the hard way in 1923 that foreign currencies could be manipulated to put pressure on a country's foreign policy, Poincaré was acutely aware of the powerful financial weapon in his hands. In selling francs and buying foreign currency to stop the rise of the exchange rate, by the end of 1927 the Bank of France had accumulated massive holdings of sterling. In September 1928, in an after-dinner speech to the French Chamber of Commerce in London, the former financial attaché at the French embassy in London and chief executive of the Anglo-French Banking Corporation explained that France

bought, on the open market, all the pounds and dollars offered to her; world opinion was so optimistic about the restoration of French finances that for months and months foreign currency ceaselessly flowed to the Bank of France, and little by little she found herself holding foreign assets on such a scale that, by the nature of things, she acquired a role of premier importance on the foreign markets, and especially that of London.[67]

This was something of an understatement; what he did not say was that the Bank of France had accumulated enough sterling to buy up all of the Bank of England's gold reserves, which it was legally entitled to do following the pound's return to the Gold Standard in 1925. France had already begun buying gold with her surplus pounds and dollars. Furthermore, her massive holdings in pounds and dollars were tightening credit in these currencies on the international markets and producing a deflationary effect in London and New York. The British authorities were now worried. Discussions were held between the Banks of England and France.[68] This brought home to Poincaré even more forcefully the diplomatic leverage France could apply to Britain by delaying stabilisation. Frustration at finding himself constantly at loggerheads with British diplomacy also came into the equation. He was even more inclined to use the financial weapon against London because, at the time of the speculation against the franc in the spring of 1924, it was suggested that British finance houses, particularly those of German origin, had been part of the German-orchestrated attack on the franc.[69] There is certainly proof that politicians and British Treasury officials had seriously contemplated attacking the franc to modify France's position on reparations. In mid-November 1923 the foreign office asked the Treasury to produce a report to that effect. At the beginning of 1924, the report by Sir Otto Niemeyer, controller of finance at the Treasury, concluded that the only way to put pressure on the present French government would be through a fall in the franc sufficient to undermine the French peasant's confidence in government securities. In London the Labour chancellor of the exchequer, Philip Snowden, told the German minister on 17 February 1924 that 'the franc is our best ally the English and ultimately also the Germans have against Poincaré'.[70] But the decision was taken by the British to hold such a plan in abeyance, to the disappointment of a number of foreign office officials and London bankers. There is little doubt that Poincaré was aware of all this, whether from intercepts of British diplomatic traffic or rumours in financial circles. Indeed, it had been made clear to him face to face, firstly just before his meeting with Baldwin in September 1923, and then by none other than Reginald McKenna, chairman of the second committee of experts, who when he saw Poincaré in mid-February 1924, warned him that the British financial world would not grant France credit unless 'a more reasonable settlement of the reparations question was brought about beforehand'.[71] This would have relieved any scruples he might now have had about brandishing the financial weapon at Britain.

In a long memorandum of 24 February 1928 to Foreign Minister Briand, Poincaré set out his ideas for using finance as an instrument of diplomacy. He described how the Bank of England was obstructing French policy over the reorganisation of Romanian and Greek finances, a traditional area of French financial influence. He had dispatched the governor of the Bank of France to London three days earlier to discuss with his British counterpart, the imperious Montagu Norman, the need for closer collaboration between the two institutions and their governments: 'It is indispensable that each has its sphere of influence, that the gold and currency of the secondary banks of issue should not only be managed by London but also by Paris.' He went on to insist that international loans be realised 'after complete and close agreement between the two institutions, themselves in close liaison with their Governments'. This remarkable demand from France for parity with Britain on international financial policy was predicated on a form of blackmail: Poincaré pointed out that 'M. Moreau is all the more founded in taking a hard line as the London market is in reality at our mercy'. He proceeded to explain that the French Treasury had left on deposit in British banks a large part of the foreign currency acquired at the end of 1926 or transferred to France via the Dawes Plan, and that 'All the funds can be withdrawn almost instantaneously, and such massive withdrawals would without any doubt create deep disturbance on the London market.' For good measure he added that the Bank of France could, if it wished, demand large quantities of gold from London 'in order to provoke the most serious difficulties for the Bank of England'. Of course, he was careful to explain that there was no intention of using 'methods of this kind' to undermine the solidarity which ought to exist between the British and French financial markets, 'but it seemed useful that the Bank of England should be aware of the means we could deploy, if necessary. It is probably the realisation of our strength which will lead it to accept the cordial and close collaboration offered to it by the Bank of France'. Poincaré concluded by noting that Moreau's trip had been most successful, and that it had led to 'an unrestricted entente' with the Bank of England, which now recognised 'that the influence left to the Bank of France abroad in the past had been insufficient and that, to take account of this, its share in new organisations will increase'.[72] Speculation in favour of the franc and the delay in legally stabilising the currency were providing substantial foreign policy benefits which contributed to Poincaré's procrastination in bringing the franc back on to the Gold Standard.

Of course, refusing to give legal status to the stabilisation also meant that Poincaré could avoid, for the moment, putting his name to an 80 per cent devaluation of the currency's pre-war rate. It also enabled him to avoid having to choose between the increasingly well-drawn camps for and against legal stabilisation. For eighteen months he had shunned advice from his officials and the governor of the Bank of France to abandon further revaluation; now he feared the right-wing revaluation campaign, led by his minister, Louis Marin. This came to a head at the beginning of June 1928. Poincaré was faced with a clear threat of resignation by the governor of the Bank of France if he did not stabilise, and that of Louis Marin if he did. This dilemma mirrored that of his conscience. However much he might try his lawyer's respect for the contractual nature of a currency, his genuine distress at not being able to honour the state's promise to its citizens could not be squared with hard economic realities. On 8 June 1928 the senior Treasury official Clément Moret informed the governor of the Bank of France that Poincaré had told him that he, too, was contemplating resignation accompanied by a declaration in favour of legal stabilisation to help his successor. It was the familiar scenario of Poincaré confronted with a serious dilemma: hesitation, threats of resignation and finally resolution. Even though threats of resignation were a common means of proceeding for politicians under the Third Republic, Poincaré must be one of those who most used it. However, whereas a petulant Clemenceau might wield it as a bargaining technique, the solitary Poincaré would, in adolescent fashion, brandish it as a personal test of others' value of him. The governor noted dismissively in his diary, 'So this man without courage does not dare, for fear of losing his popularity, take a step which he knows to be indispensable. This indecision and lack of character mean that, despite all his qualities, he is not a real statesman.'[73] Certainly on issues of principle like this Poincaré went through periods of heart-searching which disappointed his colleagues, but once reassured by others he usually emerged resolute and clear on his action. On 12 June the problem was played out in cabinet. Poincaré threatened his own resignation if Marin resigned. Marin agreed to stay, paving the way for legal stabilisation. On 21 June 1928 Poincaré made an impressive speech to the Chamber in favour of returning the franc to the Gold Standard. Rueff described Poincaré's speech as that of 'an enlightened patriot who, after lengthy struggles with his conscience, has finally decided to submit his feelings to the demands of reason'. And he perfectly encapsulated Poincaré's human condition: 'The scruples over which he has triumphed demonstrate that, in public life, the most difficult and most laudable task is more often than not to acknowledge rather than to do one's duty.'[74] On 23 June 1928 the stabilisation bill was submitted to parliament and passed on the 25th. The franc was stabilised at 124.21 to the pound and once again became freely exchangeable for an amount of gold fixed by law at 65.5 milligrammes – the 'franc poincaré' was born. Though the currency was now worth only one-fifth of the value of the franc *germinal*, France once again had a stable currency and as much as possible of the damage caused by war and its aftermath had been wiped clean. Poincaré's decision to stabilise at such a low rate meant that less national income went to bond-holders and more to the non-*rentier* class who would have lost real income through unemployment during the economic recession.[75] It was a typical Poincarist compromise.

Domestic press reaction was, on the whole, positive, though some like the right-wing Jacques Bainville and Léon Daudet were critical of the consequences for the small investor.[76] However, Poincaré would have savoured the adulatory international press comment the following day. *The New York American* described it as a great work making Poincaré the rightful successor of Thiers, Turgot, Necker, Sully and a long list of brilliant French statesmen. The *New York Times,* while regretting the effective 80 per cent devaluation of the franc for small investors, recognised the impossibility of returning to the pre-1914 rate and concluded that stabilisation restored France to the place she had occupied before the war among the front rank of great economic powers. Other newspapers such as *The Times* noted that Poincaré's success was all the more remarkable for having stabilised the currency without the help of foreign loans, unlike Britain, Italy and Belgium, adding that the Bank of France was now stronger than any other European central bank and that the whole world owed Poincaré a debt of gratitude. The *Daily Mail* attributed the miracle of the franc to Poincaré's courage, authority and knowledge.[77] The Spanish newspaper *Heraldo* made the important point that fortunately the stabilisation had been carried out by a moderate politician who had the confidence of the wealthy classes: 'If it had been done by a cabinet of radical leanings, the conservative classes would be crying spoliation; now they have to resign themselves to the inevitable and to put up with it in silence.'[78] Even John Maynard Keynes, who had been so critical of Poincaré for his firm stance on reparations, expressed praise, albeit ironical. Claiming that Poincaré had always been critical of the idea of a devaluation of the franc, he noted 'we all applaud M. Poincaré for not being hampered by a regard for consistency'. He concluded,

> Since it removes an element of uncertainty from the money markets and stock exchanges of the world, and since French importers and manufacturers need hesitate no longer, a good deal of purchasing power, which has been lying idle, may be returned to active employment. M. Poincaré has therefore done something – perhaps for the first time in his career – to make the rest of us feel more cheerful.[79]

Keynes's carping remarks should not obscure the fact that many observers believed that he had performed an economic miracle. To a large extent, however much more objectively it is viewed today, the 'Poincaré miracle' continues to fascinate modern-day economists. When double digit inflation returned to the industrial economies of the world in the 1970s, economists looked again at the Poincaré experience for solutions, producing studies with titles likely to have tantalised the feminist Lorrainer: 'Stopping moderate inflations: the methods of Poincaré and Thatcher'.[80]

From 1926 to 1928 three things had been accomplished: the return of French finances to a sound footing not seen since before the war; the alignment of the currency with the true state of the economy; the restoration of France's independence and international dignity in the face of pressure from France's 'Anglo-Saxon' creditors. Though it is true that the return of the franc to the Gold Standard was achieved with remarkable skill and probably better managed than that of any other European country, it was not without blemish. Poincaré's delay in stabilising *de jure* did create problems which would surface later. His repeated claims that the Bank of France's purchase of foreign currency to combat upward pressure on the franc would not substantially increase the money supply proved wrong.[81] The issuing of notes by the Bank of France to buy gold and currency to stabilise the exchange rate must be held to account for the rise of money in circulation from 103 billion francs in 1926 to 158 billion francs in 1928.[82]

On a more positive note, the French economy was booming. In 1921 French output had been less than that of 1891. By 1929 her industrial performance had attained a level that would not be reached again until the 1950s.[83] Of course Poincaré was by no means responsible for all that; but, of the eight and a half years between leaving the presidency in January 1920 and leaving the premiership in July 1929, his governments had been in power for nearly five and a half of those years and could at least claim some of the credit for contributing to the strength of the French economy.

Home affairs

Poincaré's desire to delay legal stabilisation of the currency had been supported by the Right, which had wanted to protect the small investor, especially in view of the forthcoming April 1928 general elections. It would have been politically unwise to return the franc to the Gold Standard before the electorate went to the polls. On the other hand, ever since the *de facto* stabilisation in December 1926 consumer demand had picked up, industrial and agricultural production had increased and the recession which some had predicted never materialised. Unemployment had all but been erased and workers' purchasing power had improved substantially. The budgets for 1926, 1927, 1928 and 1929 – the so-called 'Poincaré budgets' – were the only ones since the beginning of the century to register a surplus.[84]

Success on so many fronts did not, of course, silence Poincaré's critics on the Left. Unable to attack him on the economy, or on foreign policy while Briand continued his *détente* with Germany, they criticised him on the social impact of his policies, which they claimed were worsening wealth distribution. Though the Left's criticism remained muted – for which he thanked them in the Chamber on 2 February – they would resort to their old rallying cries of electoral reform and *laïcité*.

Radicals and socialists had won a Pyrrhic victory in having proportional representation (used in 1919 and 1924) replaced by two-round majority voting in July 1927 ready for the April 1928 elections. Respectful of tradition concerning electoral reform, Poincaré's government had feigned not to take sides, but in reality Poincaré had favoured Radical candidates. But the elections were not won by the Cartel, which suffered in part from the Communist party's insistence on maintaining its candidates through to the second round, thereby splitting the Left's vote. The Left obtained some 4.8 million votes against the centre and Right's 4.5 million, but the distribution of scats favoured the latter grouping which dominated the Chamber. During the campaign the majority of Radical candidates claimed to support the Poincaré government and in some thirty-seven cases refused to vote for a socialist candidate at the second round, confirming the slide to the centre-right of part of the Radical party. The 'government of the centres', which Poincaré's cabinet of 1926 represented, won electoral approval. There was general support for the policy of *détente* with Germany and restoration of the franc. Though the elections were a plebiscite for

Poincaré's policies, his desire to continue *union nationale* would soon be made impossible by divisions in the Radical party.[85]

Thus the 1928 election results were not wholly to Poincaré's liking. Moreau noted, 'M. Poincaré is less satisfied with the result of the elections than I expected. He tells me that the new *députés* are an unknown quantity and that he does not know what will be their tendency ... I fear that the reinforcement of the right will lead him to delay monetary reform.'[86] As in 1922–4, Poincaré had wished to retain Radical support to avoid depending on the Right. On 25 March he had stated his desire to govern with the Radicals and to constitute a wide majority which would reflect his government of national union; he had even journeyed down to the Aude department in the south, a bastion of the Radical Sarraut brothers, to give the radicals his imprimatur.[87] Their poor election performance left him more at the mercy of the Right and perhaps delayed a decision to stabilise legally.

Defeat in the elections opened divisions in the Radical party which would signal the end of 'national union'. At the party conference in Angers at the beginning of November 1928 the Left made clear its desire to abandon 'national union'. Its pretext was that old chestnut, *laïcité*: a motion was carried demanding the withdrawal of a clause in the finance bill authorising missionary schools in France. Despite Poincaré's credentials as a *laïque*, the government was accused of being a prisoner of clerical reaction, requiring the resignation of Radical ministers. They resigned on 6 November. Despite the government not having been defeated, Poincaré tendered its resignation. President Doumergue, taking his cue from the election results, insisted that Poincaré form a new government. After some hesitation he agreed and his fifth cabinet was complete by 11 November. It was little different from its predecessor; the Radical party ministers were replaced with members of the 'gauche radicale' or Radical-style senators. However, the right-wing André Tardieu was brought in to the Interior Ministry. Though retaining the premiership, Poincaré passed the finance portfolio to Henri Chéron and retained oversight of affairs relating to Alsace–Lorraine and inter-Allied debt. The government won a convincing vote in the Chamber (330 votes to 139, the Radicals abstaining). The switch of the Radicals into opposition did not convert the 'national union' government straightaway into a right-wing cabinet. That would only occur in January 1929 when the Radicals voted against the government's programme and moved firmly into opposition, harrying the cabinet on every issue. It was a return to the old parliamentary struggles which had so frustrated him in the past. Even so, Poincaré's policy did not alter significantly as international issues came to dominate again.[88] This did not come at a good time, for he was by now beginning to feel the strain of his sixty-nine years and feverish energy. Though he gave no sign of it, he was prey to sharp spasmodic pain from his prostate.

The final struggle

French financial stability was not complete without a settlement of France's debts to her creditors. President Coolidge of the United States was particularly anxious that France should ratify the Mellon–Bérenger agreement negotiated in April 1926 by Caillaux, which set France's total debt and repayment annuities. In Germany there was increasing nationalist agitation against continued occupation of the Rhineland and in favour of a revision of the Dawes Plan. On 27 August 1928 Poincaré warned Chancellor Stresemann that so long as the German government did not complete disarmament there could be no evacuation of Koblenz and Mayence. Stresemann approached the more flexible Briand and on 16 September was able to reach an agreement with France and Belgium whereby negotiations on reparations would be linked to an evacuation of the occupied territories. Despite reservations, Poincaré agreed in the belief that this would fix German payments definitively. The idea was to commercialise the German debt. On 9 February 1929 a committee of experts appointed by the reparation commission met in Paris to work out the details. It was chaired by the American banker, Owen Young, intent on reducing the German debt to a minimum. France was represented by Moreau, the governor of the Bank of France who, supported by Poincaré, did his best to oppose this reduction. But American pressure was such that in June a settlement favourable to Germany was reached. The Young Plan fixed German debt at a reduced level and freed it from the controls imposed by Dawes.[89]

Though Poincaré was not happy with the outcome he hoped to be able to contest it at the Hague Conference scheduled for the beginning of August 1929. He calculated that France would be in a better position to contest the agreement if she had paid off her debts to the United States. The problem was to get the Mellon–Bérenger agreement ratified by the French parliament before the end of July; this would be even more difficult as French public opinion was upset by the concessions in the Young Plan. Repayment of Allied debts was referred to as being to 'Shylocks'. Poincaré would have to muster all his powers of advocacy to pilot the bill through parliament in time, just when his health was deteriorating – doctors had already warned him of the necessity of undergoing a dangerous prostate operation.[90] His determination to secure ratification of the Mellon–Bérenger agreements could be gauged by the apparently massive use of secret funds at his disposal to bribe the French press. Most of the major newspapers, largely under the control or influence of financial and industrial circles, opposed or had reservations about ratification. But in mid-June their position underwent a remarkable transformation. Special assistant Dawson at the American embassy in Paris, in a dispatch to his government, claimed that the change was due to Poincaré distributing secret funds on 12 June to twelve major newspapers from *Le Temps* and *Le Figaro* to *L'Action Française* and *Le Matin*.[91] Though this claim has not been verified, the use of secret funds to bribe the French press was not uncommon and Poincaré, notwithstanding his pristine image, had used secret funds for this purpose in the past.[92] Certainly he regarded ratification as the final plank in his policy of reforming French finances.

For two weeks this sixty-nine year old pleaded his case with banks of statistics every afternoon before the finance and foreign affairs commissions of the Chamber. He was successful but physically drained. But now came the real test: convincing the less reasonable, more passionate Chamber. Right-wing nationalists and the Left were arrayed against him from the outset. On 16 July 1929, in sweltering heat, he presented his case to the Chamber. Next day, as the debate continued on an amendment proposed by Léon Blum, it was noticed that Poincaré's seat on the ministerial bench was empty. There was general commotion. News soon arrived that he had been overcome with fever and his doctors ordered immediate confinement to bed. He was suffering from prostatitis which demanded an urgent operation once his strength had recovered. Nevertheless the next morning he wrote to his *chef-adjoint de cabinet* and friend Marcel Ribière, 'It is indispensable to continue the debate without interruption'. He asked Briand, Barthou and Chéron to deputise for him and insisted that everything should continue as if he were still there.[93]

On 21 July the inter-Allied debts agreement was ratified by a majority of eight. Three days later he wrote to Ribière, 'I am still in the same state. I cannot yet go either to the Chamber or the Ministry ... I would be obliged if you could send me by bag (I have the keys) delayed signatures – private office, *Présidence du Conseil*, Alsace and Lorraine, especially the latter'.[94] It is fitting that one of his last thoughts as premier should have been for Alsace and Lorraine. On 26 July, on the recommendation of his doctor, he addressed a letter to the president of the Republic explaining that it was impossible to go to The Hague and that consequently he was resigning. On 31 July he was admitted to the Paris clinic in the rue de la Chaise where Doctor Marion carried out the first prostate operation. Medical complications ensued. The second phase of the operation further weakened him, and he was confined to a long period of convalescence. Though he recovered some of his strength it was the end of his political career. It was also the end of a period of political stability and the drawing to a close of a generation of politicians associated with power since the end of the previous century; the end of a generation of centrist republican politicians who put national union above party politics. With Poincaré's retirement, the holy grail of *union sacrée* which he had pursued since before 1914 ceased to motivate French politics. The consensual politics which had largely succeeded since 1926 gave way to a Right-Left confrontation which he had tried so hard to combat and which would do so much damage to France in the coming years.[95]

It would have been impossible for someone of Poincaré's temperament to stop all work. He continued to write articles for newspaper publishers in South America, a continent with which he had long had a particular affection. Only much later would he write for the French weekly *L'Illustration*. For the moment he devoted his efforts to writing up the last five volumes of his memoirs for the years 1912 to 1919, appropriately entitled *Au service de la France,* from the daily diary he had kept all his life. The first five volumes concerning the years 1912 and 1913 had been published between 1926 and 1928 following revisions to his secret diaries, while the last volumes, according to Jacques Chastenet, are a more faithful account as his illness prevented him seriously reworking the contemporaneous accounts. His last years were spent convalescing in his apartment in the rue Marbeuf, at his home in Sampigny and at his old friend Gabriel Hanotaux's home at Roquebrune on the Côte d'Azur.[96]

On 23 September 1929 he was re-elected president of the *conseil général* of the Meuse. On 4 December 1929 he spoke in the Senate. He was even offered the possibility of forming a new cabinet, but this was out of the question. He occasionally attended the Académie française. But he was already working too hard. On 13 December 1929 he had a stroke which deprived him of the use of his left arm and restricted his walking, though he continued writing up his *Souvenirs*. One gesture in particular brought him great pleasure: in June 1931 he was made Bâtonnier de l'ordre des avocats, which he described as one of his most precious appointments. His mood was increasingly dispirited and gloomy, exacerbated by the distressing international news which, from the Wall Street Crash to Hitler's coming to power in 1933, seemed to be undoing his life's work. His greatest source of strength was Henriette, who attempted to shelter him from the worst news, but it was impossible for him to be protected from news of the assassination in Marseille on

9 October 1934 of his old friend Barthou and the king of Yugoslavia. He was moved to write a stirring tribute for a newspaper, recalling how in the 1890s he and his friend had been dubbed 'les deux gosses'. The piece never appeared: it was the last thing he wrote. The next day in his Paris apartment in the rue Marbeuf he had another attack, was confined to bed, slowly lost consciousness and on 16 October 1934 at 3.30 a.m. died without speaking. He had not called for a priest, though while he was in a coma one was summoned to administer the last rites.[97]

There followed that mixture of simplicity and pomp which characterises the death of all statesmen. Surprisingly for someone referred to as Poincaré-le-*laïque*, the civil ceremony was constantly shadowed by the religious. At his death he was attended by his close family: Henriette, his brother Lucien, his sister-in-law and his private secretary, Marcel Ribière. He was dressed in tails and laid out in his office for last respects to be paid. André Tardieu saw him and remarked, 'In death M. Poincaré has rediscovered his face of ten years earlier'. On 17 October the body was taken to the church of Saint-Honoré d'Eylau where the nuns of La Sagesse kept vigil over him through the night. The following morning he was transported to the Panthéon for the official civil ceremony where the prime minister, Gaston Doumergue, pronounced a funeral oration which was followed by a military march past.[98] As Jacques Chastenet remarked, 'As 'laïque' as he was, Poincaré was too representative of the whole of France for the Church not to take part in his funeral.' At Notre Dame, whose façade was draped in black crêpe, the pall-bearers were Edouard Herriot, Alexandre Millerand, Gabriel Hanotaux and General Bourgeois, vice-president of the Senate. Cardinal Binet, Archbishop of Besançon, led the ceremony. In driving rain the corpse was transported to his native Lorraine to be interred in a simple grave next to his parents' at Nubécourt. Members of the *conseil municipal* carried his coffin to its final resting place and the bishop of Verdun gave absolution and pronounced the final oration.[99] At whose behest the religious followed on from the civil is not clear. He could have stipulated in his will that there be no religious ceremony, as did Clemenceau, who had died in 1929.[100] Did he allow the religious to figure in deference to his mother and wife in the same way that he had agreed to a religious marriage eight years after his civil union? Was it out of respect for French Catholics, reflecting his earlier statement that a president of the Republic owed it to his Catholic citizens to be married religiously? Or had he rediscovered the faith of his childhood? The co-existence of the civil and the religious was in the end a fitting tribute to one of his greatest virtues – tolerance – and an appropriate symbol of one of his central concerns – to overcome old quarrels in the name of national unity.

Conclusion: Poincaré remembered

Certain French politicians are remembered with a constancy which owes nothing to the efforts of historians. A Gambetta, a Jaurès, a Clemenceau have achieved a place in national history reflected in street names and squares from city to hamlet. Yet the commemoration of such heroes may have more to do with what local politicians believe should be political models than with the memories their constituents actually cherish. Few streets bear the name of Raymond Poincaré. In several Gallup International opinion polls carried out in post-Second World War France on historical personalities, members of the public were asked to give the name of the French person of the past or present with whom they would most wish to converse for an hour. In 1948 Napoleon carried the day, well ahead of Joan of Arc, Henry IV and Louis XIV. Clemenceau came after Louis XVI with twice the score of any other historical personage, including Poincaré. Yet Poincaré always equalled Jaurès's score of between 2 and 5 per cent along with *inter alia* Robespierre, Pasteur, Richelieu and Foch. Gambetta was never cited. In 1967 Gallup found that in response to the question as to which Frenchman, living or dead, had done the most for France since the Revolution, General de Gaulle came out top with Louis Pasteur at just under half his score, Napoleon half of the latter's and Clemenceau just below that. Poincaré now came equal to Léon Blum and Pétain, but had twice the score of Jaurès and General Leclerc, the only other two named personalities.[1] However idiosyncratic such surveys may be, they do suggest that Poincaré has been held in some esteem in the collective memory of the French, even if that has not always been reflected in official signs of tribute.

Why is that? Poincaré seems to have been the victim of an unfavourable historiography which has not found the values he represented either fashionable or to be cherished. French historiography since the 1930s has preferred to concentrate on social forces and trends often associated with socialism and the labour movement, consigning those politicians not closely associated with those movements to the scrapheap of history.

341

René Rémond's comment about historians seeing the Bloc national through the eyes of its opponents[2] applies equally to perceptions of Poincaré. Despite his republican credentials and his unstinting effort to work only with republican majorities of the centre-left, some historians have preferred to classify him as well to the Right. Despite his moderate republican credentials, Poincaré can be said to have represented themes which have since come to be associated with the Right, such as the claim to be above parties, or to reject the traditional Left-Right divide, or the appeals to unity or *rassemblement*. Classification of the politician according to particular ideas is complemented by a definition of the Right according to the politicians it cherishes. Some works on modern French politics define the Right as the idealisation of the father figure, 'which is characterised nowadays by an attraction for those statesmen – Clemenceau, Poincaré, Pétain, de Gaulle – who, are seen to represent the general interest, possessing a brutal frankness linked to a shade of populism'.[3] Unlike other French political leaders of the Right or Left, who with the passage of time have progressively lost their political classification and acquired an apolitical national respect, Poincaré has never been able to rise above his image as a man of the Right.

British and American historians have been no more sympathetic to a politician who, rather like General de Gaulle, was willing to stand up to the Anglo-Saxons when French interests did not coincide with their own. Unlike that of de Gaulle, the Poincaré vintage has not improved with the passage of time. Moreover, until recent monographs on the origins of the First World War and the international history of the 1920s appeared, he was still largely depicted as the bigoted, nationalist Germanophobe. It is to be hoped that his policies might now be regarded as a continuum of firm but open negotiation with Germany.

A question remains with all politicians as to whether personality is the reflection of politics or politics the reflection of personality. Poincaré's politics were, from the beginning to the end of his career, moderate. He never espoused any extreme; unlike Clemenceau, Briand or Millerand he did not slide from Left to Right. He started as a bourgeois republican and ended as one, continuing to cherish the values of patriotism, moderation, economic liberalism and social order. He was the quintessential believer in and practitioner of politics as the art of the possible, and perhaps nowhere more than France under the Third Republic was this pragmatic and centrist approach suitable to keep the extremes of anarchy and despotism at bay. His name is closely associated, rightly, with the Republic; yet he was a republican in the manner of Thiers, whom he admired and whose biography he was preparing, in that he believed that the Republic was legitimate because it was the regime that least divided the French. One is tempted to say that had the monarchy been the regime which least divided the French he would have been a monarchist in the British mould, for the liberal ideals he believed in could as easily have been satisfied through a constitutional monarchy: his overriding aim was to ensure that France remained a liberal–democratic society. Thus his political position was always a corrective one: to ensure that the balance of governmental power favoured the liberal Republic. His contribution to the politics of the Third Republic was to the stability of its institutions and their smooth functioning. By his commitment to making sure that the regime was governed from the Republican centre, trimming to balance the shifting majorities, he contributed to ensuring that the nation retained its unity and the regime survived moments of crisis from Dreyfus to the Great War and the financial disorder of the 1920s. It was Poincaré's characteristic independence of mind – demonstrated by his willingness to associate with political figures at odds with his own ideas, from the duc d'Aumale to Léon Blum – a natural solitude which allowed him to adopt unpopular stances, a mixture of stubbornness and arrogance, which gave him the freedom to adjust his allegiances to safeguard a centre republican majority. This may explain one of his many contradictions. His hesitation and trimming can be construed as an absence of moral courage or as an overweening desire to act as the fulcrum of republican politics – in either case it suited and benefited the shifting political alliances at the heart of the Third Republic. Whether his politics fitted his personality or the reverse is less important than the fact that his action helped to maintain a political balance that ensured that the regime continued to be governed from the centre despite a constant leftwards drift and occasional threats from the Right. Poincaré's politics did not change even if the political landscape did. This, and the fact that his political star was fixed to the middle classes who were the mainstay of the regime, has cast him on the Right.

Despite the manoeuvring necessary to keep power in the centre of the political spectrum, Poincaré does not come across as a political animal in the manner of a Clemenceau or a Briand. He did not seem to enjoy politics, but engaged in it more out of a sense of duty than passion. The rapid ascension of his political career seems less the product of ambition than a rather puerile spirit of competition. Indeed, this seems true of all the strands of his life from lawyer to writer where he reached the top from president of the Bar Council to member of the French Academy but without greatness in any. A remarkable intelligence and success notwithstanding, he comes across as incarnating, arguably more than any other French politician of his day, 'le français moyen'. Given that here lay the bedrock of the Third Republic, it is in that inglorious guise that he was greatest.

Poincaré's contribution to French history is stability in politics, society and finance. Stability is neither exciting nor truly memorable, yet it is essential. Poincaré was never thought of, and has never been remembered as, a hero, as if by definition the moderation and middle-of-the-road qualities he typified precluded him from assuming an extraordinary role in the manner of Gambetta, Jaurès or Clemenceau. If historical rank is dependent on the freedom that the person who acts maintains in the face of circumstances,[4] then Poincaré, unable to take risks, would never free himself sufficiently to be recorded in history as a great man. If anything, Poincaré was the hero of normalcy and moderation, by virtue of which conventional greatness is axiomatically denied. Historically he has been the victim of his finest quality.

Notes

INTRODUCTION

1 Quoted in P. Miquel, *Poincaré* (Paris, 1961), p. 612.
2 On this see René Rémond (ed.), *Pour une histoire politique* (Paris, 1988), and especially P. Levillain, 'Les protagonistes de la biographie', pp. 121–59.
3 J. Chastenet, *Raymond Poincaré* (Paris, 1948); there is also the biographical sketch by Poincaré's friend and political contemporary, Gabriel Hanotaux, *Raymond Poincaré* (Paris, 1934).
4 Miquel, *Poincaré*, (1961 edition), p. 7.
5 *Le Temps*, 17 October 1934.
6 Quoted in Levillain, 'Les protagonistes', p. 123.
7 John Buchan, *Oliver Cromwell* (Reprint society, London, 1941), p. v.

1. THE PRIVATE MAN

1 Archives Nationales, Deschanel MSS, 151 AP 44, p. 391.
2 Pierre Miquel, *Poincaré* (Paris, 1961), p. 26.
3 Poincaré, 'Notes journalières', BN nafr 16024, 10 February 1913.
4 See *JODebPC*, October, November, December 1887. The last time he appears as Poincarré is 12 December 1887, though why is unclear. Did he believe that his new parliamentary position befitted the extra 'r', only to abandon it out of deference to the Poincaré family?
5 *Le Pays Lorrain*, 12 (December 1934), pp. 551–2, 567.
6 See A. Collignon, 'Chez les ancêtres maternels de Raymond Poincaré. Souvenirs de Nubécourt' in *Le Pays Lorrain* 12 (December 1934), pp. 555–67, first published in 1914 in the *Revue Lorraine Illustrée*. The author, professor at Nancy University, was a family friend and a regular visitor to the family home in Nubécourt.
7 *Ibid.*, pp. 560–2.
8 *Ibid.*, pp. 562–6.
9 Fernand Payen, *Raymond Poincaré, chez lui, au parlement, au palais* (Paris, 1936), p. 13. This semi-official biography covering the years up to 1914 is a rich archive as the author was given access to many of Poincaré's private papers by Poincaré and his wife.
10 All quoted in Payen, *Poincaré*, p. 14.
11 Poincaré, 'Notes journalières', BN nafr 16034, 20 August 1919.

12 The graphologist Marthe Desbarolles analysed his handwriting in 1913 with the following results:

'D'abord clarté d'esprit, désir de comprendre et surtout d'être compris ... Impatience, vivacité. Pas agressif, mais défensif, combatif. Indépendance d'idées. Esprit simplificateur. Tout en ayant une possession de soi grande, est un sensitif, impulsif. Simple et pourtant conscient de sa valeur personnelle. Parfois hésitation, suivie bientôt de décision ferme, rapide. Sentiment de devoir assumé, accepté. Fera tout ce qu'il est possible de faire pour mener à bien une chose commencée, mise debout par lui. Ecriture énergique sans rudesse, ferme tout en étant souple. Entêtement. Caractère entier. Froideur un peu distante dans les relations banales.' Quoted in J. Chastenet, *Raymond Poincaré* (Paris, 1948), p. 21.

13 'Manuscrits de jeunesse', *Journal personnel 1871* (juin–octobre), 16 July 1871, Bibliothèque de l'ordre des avocats (Bib. OA), Musée du Barreau de Paris. A few weeks previously he had been given a locket as a present for his future communion which was intended to hold the relics of Mgr. Darbois, Archbishop of Paris, killed in the Paris Commune, and said to be the cousin of his Aunt Magnien. *Ibid.*, 22 June 1871.

14 See Jean Estèbe, *Les ministres de la République, 1871–1914* (Paris, 1982), pp. 99–101.

15 *L'Indépendance de L'Est*, 20 July 1887. Quoted in M. Salviac, 'L'entrée en politique de Raymond Poincaré (1886–1889)' in J. Lanher and N. Cazin (eds.), *Raymond Poincaré, un homme d'état lorrain 1860–1934* (Bar-le-Duc, 1989), p. 29.

16 Quoted in J. Chastenet, *Poincaré* p. 132. His life-long friend Alexandre Millerand, also a *laïque*, would please his wife by completing their marriage by a later religious ceremony (L. Derfler, *Alexandre Millerand. The socialist years* (The Hague, 1977), p. 5).

17 Quoted in Payen, *Poincaré*, p. 406.

18 See F. Roth, 'Poincaré et la République' in Lanher and Cazin (eds.), *Raymond Poincaré, un homme d'état lorrain*, p. 113.

19 R. Rémond, *La Droite en France* vol. I (Paris, 1968), pp. 206–7.

20 Poincaré, 'Notes journalières', 20 August 1919, BN nafr 16034.

21 Jules Laroche, *Au Quai d'Orsay avec Briand et Poincaré, 1913–1926* (Paris, 1957), p. 190.

22 P. Gerbod, 'The baccalaureate and its role in the recruitment and formation of French elites in the nineteenth century' in J. Howarth and P. Cerny (eds.) *Elites in France: origins, reproduction and power* (London, 1981), pp. 45–56.

23 'Bulletin de notes de R. Poincaré', Archives départementales de la Meuse, 848WI, n.d.

24 'Manuscrits de jeunesse', Bib. OA, *Journal personnel 1871* (juin-novembre) 26 September 1871.

25 Collignon, 'Chez les ancêtres'. p. 568.

26 Laroche, *Au Quai*, p. 191.

27 George Samné, *Raymond Poincaré; politique et personnel de la IIIe République* (Paris, 1933), p. 7.

28 Manuscrits de jeunesse, Bib. OA, *Journal personnel 1871* (novembre)–*1872* (mai), 9 February 1872.

29 Poincaré, 'Notes journalières', BN nafr 16035, 30 March 1909. His mourning continued for several days.
30 Quoted in Payen, *Poincaré*, p. 322.
31 Quoted in *ibid.*, p. 321.
32 Sir Maurice de Bunsen (British ambassador to Madrid) to Sir Edward Grey, 13 October 1913, doc. 116, p. 347, in J. F. V. Keiger (ed.), *Spain, 1908–1914* (vol. 28 of Series F, *Europe 1848–1914*) in Kenneth Bourne and D. Cameron Watt (general editors), *British documents on foreign affairs: reports and papers from the foreign office confidential print* (Frederick, Md, 1991), (hereafter *BDFA*).
33 Poincaré, 'Notes journalières', BN nafr 16030, 19 July 1915.
34 Quoted in Payen, *Poincaré*, p. 322.
35 I am extremely grateful to Mr Andrew Booth for allowing me to see and use his fascinating chapter on the philosophical background to the relationship between man and animal in the Victorian era, in his forthcoming Salford University Ph.D., 'The unsettling of boundaries, lines, and divisions in Tennyson's *Idylls of the King*'.
36 Eric Baratay, 'Les controverses contemporaines sur le statut de l'animal: l'exemple de l'Eglise Catholique, France, 1940–1990', *Revue d'Histoire Moderne et Contemporaine*, 41(3), (juillet–septembre 1994), p. 500.
37 On the British and French sides, see Booth and Baratay respectively.
38 *Animal World*, vol. IV, p. 47, quoted in Booth, 'The unsettling of boundaries'.
39 Maurice Agulhon, 'Le sang des bêtes', *Romantismes* 31 (1981), pp. 81–109.
40 Theodore Zeldin, *France 1848–1945* vol. II (Oxford, 1977), pp. 920–1.
41 Payen, *Poincaré*, pp. 211–12, 321–2.
42 Baratay claims that ritualism associated with animals developed in France after 1940 ('Statut de l'animal', pp. 510–11).
43 Laroche, *Au Quai*, p. 186.
44 J. Giraudoux, *Bella*, (Paris, 1926), especially p. 34. Giraudoux was a young attaché in the foreign ministry in 1912 when Poincaré was foreign minister.
45 Gabriel Hanotaux, *Raymond Poincaré* (Paris, 1934), pp. 11–12.
46 'Manuscrits de jeunesse', Bib. OA. 'Récit d'un voyage effectué en Normandie et en Belgique de septembre à novembre 1870' [rewritten in 1874], p. 1.
47 Quoted in Payen, *Poincaré*, p. 17. Payen consulted the 'manuscrits de jeunesse'.
48 Quoted in *ibid.*, p. 17.
49 'Manuscrits de jeunesse', Bib. OA, *Journal 1871* (juin–novembre) [1874], 19 June 1871..
50 On French public opinion in 1870, see S. Audoin-Rouzeau, *1870 La France dans la guerre* (Paris, 1989), pp. 262–6, 268, 270, 272.
51 'Manuscrits de jeunesse', Bib. OA, *Journal 1871* (juin–novembre) [1874],22 July 1871.
52 *Ibid.*, 22 July 1871.
53 *Ibid.*, 25 October 1871.
54 Quoted in Payen, *Poincaré*, p. 18.
55 'Manuscrits de jeunesse', Bib. OA, *Journal 1871* (novembre)–*1872* (mai), 15 December 1871.

56 *Ibid.*, 26 December 1871.
57 Poincaré, Notes journalières, BN nafr 16029, 17 March 1915; *ibid.*, nafr 16030, 6 May 1915; Miquel, *Poincaré*, p. 339; Robert Young, *Power and pleasure. Louis Barthou and the Third French Republic* (Montreal, 1991), p. 80; D. R. Watson, *Georges Clemenceau: a political biography* (London, 1974), p. 278.
58 Quoted in Payen, *Poincaré*, p. 20.
59 'Manuscrits de jeunesse', Bib. OA, *Journal personnel 1871* (juin–novembre) [1874].
60 Payen, *Poincaré*, p. 23. The date must have been either 1875 or 1876 when Wallon was education minister.
61 Probably about 5 feet 4 inches, he does not appear particularly small in relation to others in photographs, especially generals. But then an analysis of twenty-year-old conscripts in 1872 shows some one in eighteen below 4 feet 10 inches (T. Zeldin, *France 1848–1945* vol I: *Ambition, love and politics* (Oxford 1973), p. 304).
62 Albert Guèrard, *Personal equation* (New York, 1948), p. 84, quoted in Derfler, *Millerand*, pp. 5–6.
63 Quoted in Payen, *Poincaré*, p. 27.
64 Anon, *Raymond Poincaré: a sketch* (London, 1914), p. 2. This anonymous work is so remarkably well informed that it can only have been written by someone with an intimate knowledge of the man.
65 *Ibid.*, p. 2.
66 Quoted in Payen, *Poincaré*, p. 31.
67 Gerbod, 'The baccalaureate and French elites'.
68 Payen, *Poincaré*, p. 34.
69 *Ibid.*, pp. 33–4; Anon, *Poincaré: a sketch*, p. 3.
70 Derfler, *Millerand*, pp. 8–9.
71 Payen, *Poincaré*, pp. 34–5.
72 *Ibid.*, pp. 36–7.
73 Millerand papers in the hands of the family, Poincaré to Millerand, 10 March 1880, quoted in Derfler, *Millerand*, p. 9.
74 Payen, *Poincaré*, p. 37; Anon, *Poincaré: a sketch*, p. 3.
75 See R. Girardet, *Le nationalisme français* (Paris, 1983), introduction.
76 Quoted in Miquel, *Poincaré*, p. 62.
77 Quoted in *ibid.*, p. 62.
78 Anon, *Poincaré: a sketch*, p. 4.
79 'Manuscrits de jeunesse', *Essais littéraires*, Bib. OA.
80 See his poems in Payen, *Poincaré*, pp. 42–6.
81 Payen, *Poincaré*, pp. 167–8.
82 Quoted in *ibid.*, p. 424. See also his play about women in 'Manuscrits de jeunesse', Bib. OA, *Journal 12–19*, August 1874, and in his *Essais littéraires*.
83 On this see Robert A. Nye, *Masculinity and male codes of honour in modern France* (Oxford, 1993), p. 56.
84 'Inventaire sommaire des documents concernant Raymond Poincaré', p. 3, Bib. OA. For a brief synopsis of the legal position of women at this time, see James McMillan, *Dreyfus to De Gaulle: politics and society in France 1898–1969* (London, 1985), p. 57.

85 Payen, *Poincaré*, p. 101.
86 McMillan, *Dreyfus to De Gaulle*, pp. 58–9.
87 Quoted in Payen, *Poincaré*, p. 101.
88 *Le Droit des Femmes*, January 1921, p. 469. The president of the organisation was Maria Vérone, a lawyer whose career Poincaré had championed.
89 *Le Droit des Femmes*, January 1921, p. 469; *ibid.*, December 1921, pp. 737–40.
90 McMillan, *Dreyfus to De Gaulle*, pp. 82–3; Christine Bard, 'Les luttes contre le suffrage unisexuel sous la Troisième Ré-mi-publique', *Modern and Contemporary France*, vol. NS3 (2) (1995), pp. 141–8.
91 Nye, *Masculinity*, pp. 155–6; Payen, *Poincaré*, p. 206.
92 Nye, *Masculinity*, p. 156.
93 Barthou's career is remarkably similar to Poincaré's, suggestive of a degree of admiration on the part of the former for the latter. Though Poincaré was two years Barthou's senior, they both moved to Paris to study law, both wrote doctorates on the subject of chattels in Roman Law, with Poincaré introducing Barthou to the Union de la jeunesse républicaine, both pursued successful political and journalistic careers, which led them both to head governments and finally become members of the Académie française. But Poincaré always managed to get there first and stay just that one step ahead. For Barthou's life, see Young, *Barthou*.
94 Derfler, *Millerand*, p. 9.
95 On the *Conférence du stage*, see Derfler, *Millerand*, p. 19; Anon., *Poincaré: a sketch*, p. 8.
96 Anon, *Poincaré: a sketch*, p. 7.
97 Quoted in Payen, *Poincaré*, p. 51.
98 Georges Suarez, *De Poincaré à Poincaré* (Paris, 1928), pp. 104–5, quoted in J-B. Duroselle, *L'Europe de 1815 à nos jours* (Paris, 1970), p. 251.
99 Jean Martet, *Le Tigre* (Paris, 1930), p. 192, quoted in Duroselle, *L'Europe de 1815 à nos jours*, p. 251.
100 Payen, *Poincaré*, p. 56.
101 Derfler, *Millerand*, pp. 19–20.
102 Anon, *Poincaré: a sketch*, p. 6.
103 Samné, *Poincaré*, pp. 73–4.
104 Anon, *Poincaré: a sketch*, p. 6.
105 Stanley Hoffmann, *Sur la France* (Paris, 1976), pp. 39–40.

2. POINCARÉ THE POLITICIAN

1 Jean-Marie Mayeur, *La vie politique sous la Troisième République* (Paris, 1984), p. 208.
2 *Ibid*, pp. 104–5.
3 See, for example, *chef du cabinet du ministre de l'agriculture* to Mme Hacquin, 11 April 1886, and other letters on display in the Musée Raymond Poincaré, Sampigny, Meuse.
4 Quoted in Fernand Payen, *Raymond Poincaré, chez lui, au parlement, au palais* (Paris, 1936), p. 61.
5 Archives de la Meuse, AM 34 M 16, report of 24 June 1886, quoted in

M. Salviac, 'L'entrée en politique de Raymond Poincaré (1886–1889)' in
J. Lanher and N. Cazin (eds.), *Raymond Poincaré, un homme d'état lorrain
1860–1934* (Bar-le-Duc, 1989), p. 26.

6   *Ibid.*, p. 26.
7   AM, J 1378, Papiers Jules Develle, dépôt Bréguet, quoted in *ibid.*, p. 26.
8   Quoted in *ibid.*, pp. 26–7.
9   Quoted in *ibid.*, p. 27.
10 *Ibid.*, p. 27.
11 *Ibid.*, p. 27.
12 *Ibid.*, p. 28.
13 *Ibid.*, p. 28; Payen, *Poincaré*, p. 63.
14 Pierre Avril, *Politics in France* (London, 1969), p. 137.
15 Mayeur, *Vie politique*, pp. 78–9, also P. Guiral and G. Thuillier, *La vie
    quotidienne des députés en France de 1871 à 1914* (Paris, 1980), pp. 31–4.
16 Louis Barthou, *Le politique* (Paris, 1923), p. 17.
17 Guiral and Thuillier, *Vie quotidienne*, p. 47.
18 Quoted in Salviac, 'Entrée en politique', p. 29.
19 *Ibid.*, p. 30.
20 Mayeur, *Vie politique*, pp. 82–3 and Guiral and Thuillier, *Vie quotidienne*,
    pp. 70–3.
21 Jean Estèbe, *Les ministres de la République, 1871–1914* (Paris, 1982), p. 97.
22 Guiral and Thuillier, *Vie quotidienne*, pp. 148–51.
23 Mayeur, *Vie politique*, p. 117.
24 J. P. T. Bury and R. P. Tombs, *Thiers 1797–1877. A political life* (London,
    1986), pp. 219–20.
25 Quoted in Estèbe, *Ministres*, pp. 112–13.
26 Quoted in Payen, *Poincaré*, p. 74.
27 Quoted in Payen, *Poincaré*, p. 68.
28 Mayeur, *Vie politique*, pp. 119–25.
29 See *JODebPC* 1887, 1888, 1889. For his role as *rapporteur* before the nine-
    teenth *commission des pétitions* in 1888, see *ibid.*, pp. 917–18, 1090, 1722–3.
30 Payen, *Poincaré*, pp. 75–6.
31 *Ibid.*, pp. 75–6.
32 *Le journal de la Meuse*, 22 August 1889, quoted in Salviac, 'Entrée en
    politique', p. 32.
33 Robert A. Nye, *Masculinity and male codes of honour in modern France*
    (Oxford, 1993), pp. 184–7, 198.
34 See V. G. Kiernan, *The duel in European history. Honour and the reign of
    aristocracy* (Oxford (paperback edn), 1989), pp. 261–70; Nye, *Masculinity*,
    ch. 9.
35 See C. M. Andrew, *Théophile Delcassé and the making of the Entente Cordiale*
    (London, 1968), pp. 6–7.
36 All quoted in Salviac, 'Entrée en politique', p. 33.
37 *Le patriote de l'est*, 9 October 1889, quoted in *ibid.*, p. 34.
38 *Ibid.*, p. 34.
39 Avril, *Politics in France*, pp. 134–5.
40 On the parliamentary context, see D. R. Watson, *Georges Clemenceau: a
    political biography* (London, 1974), p. 117.

41 Mayeur, *Vie politique*, pp. 106–7, Guiral and Thuillier, *Vie quotidienne*, pp. 221–55.
42 Guiral and Thuillier, *Vie quotidienne*, pp. 235–6.
43 Anon, *Poincaré: a sketch* (London, 1914) p. 8.
44 Jean-Claude Allain, *Joseph Caillaux* vol. I: *Le défi victorieux 1863–1914* (Paris, 1978), p. 214.
45 *Ibid.*, p. 214.
46 T. Kemp, *Economic forces in French history* (London, 1971), p. 217.
47 L. Derfler, *Alexandre Millerand. The socialist years* (The Hague, 1977), p. 10.
48 Quoted in Payen, *Poincaré*, p. 79.
49 Henry de Basty in *Revue d'Histoire Contemporaine* 1 (20 January 1889), p. 10; Jean Dietz, 'Un homme d'état français: M. Alexandre Millerand', *Revue de Belgique* 46 (1 August 1914), pp. 808–9, all quoted in Derfler, *Millerand*, p. 67.
50 *JODebPC*, 24 October 1890, pp. 1769–73. In 1914 and 1924 Poincaré would demonstrate this 'fiscal courage' by voting through taxes just before the elections, which were duly lost.
51 Quoted in Payen, *Poincaré*, p. 81.
52 *JODebPC*, 2 December 1890, p. 2379.
53 See *ibid.*, 22, 24 November 1891, p. 2296.
54 Anon, *Poincaré: a Sketch*, p. 6.
55 Quoted in Payen, *Poincaré*, p. 81.
56 Mayeur, *Vie politique*, p. 108; Guiral and Thuillier, *Vie quotidienne*, pp. 115–20, 130–6.
57 Payen, *Poincaré*, p. 81.
58 Quoted in Pierre Miquel, *Raymond Poincaré* (Paris, 1961), p. 125.
59 *JODebPC*, 28 March 1892, pp. 363, 383–4.
60 Quoted in Payen, *Poincaré*, p. 84.
61 Quoted in *ibid.*, pp. 85–6.
62 *Ibid.*, pp. 85–6.
63 *Ibid.*, pp. 87–8.
64 C. Charle, *Les élites de la République, 1880–1900* (Paris, 1987), p. 408.
65 Estèbe, *Ministres*, pp. 20, 51–3.
66 Guiral and Thuillier, *Vie quotidienne*, pp. 259–70; R. D. Anderson, *France 1870–1914. Politics and society* (London, 1977), p. 58; Estèbe, *Ministres*, pp. 76–8.
67 Estèbe, *Ministres*, p. 24.
68 Quoted in Payen, p. 105.
69 Mayeur, *Vie politique*, pp. 158–60.
70 Quoted in *ibid.*, p. 160.
71 *Ibid.*, pp. 156–60.
72 See Allain, *Joseph Caillaux* vol. I, pp. 125–7.
73 Robert J. Young, *Power and pleasure. Louis Barthou and the Third French Republic* (Montreal, 1991), p. 38.
74 *Ibid.*, p. 38.
75 *Ibid.*, p. 39.
76 Claude Nicolet, *L'idée républicaine en France (1789–1924). Essai d'histoire critique* (Paris, 1982), pp. 163–4.

77 *Ibid.*, p. 183.
78 *Ibid.*, pp. 187–90, 208–9, 212–14, quotation p. 215.
79 *Ibid.*, p. 216.
80 *Ibid.*, p. 217; other militantly positivist politicians cited were Waldeck-Rousseau, Léon Bourgeois, Henri Brisson, Antonin Dubost, Charles Dupuy, Georges Leygues, Stéphen Pichon, Joseph Reinach, Jules Roche and Clemenceau (*ibid.*, p. 249).
81 *Ibid.*, pp. 222–4.
82 *Ibid.*, p. 244.
83 See *ibid.*, pp. 247–8, 261.
84 Quoted in F. Roth, 'Poincaré et la République' in Lanher and Cazin (eds.), *Raymond Poincaré, un homme d'état lorrain*, pp. 103–4.
85 *Ibid.*
86 Quoted in Salviac, 'Entrée en politique', p. 29.
87 Nicolet, *Idée républicaine*, pp. 171, 243–4.
88 *Ibid.*, pp. 168, 251.
89 *Ibid.*, p. 252.
90 John F. Godfrey, *Capitalism at war. Industrial policy and bureaucracy in France, 1914–1918* (Leamington Spa, 1987), p. 33.
91 Quoted in Nicolet, *Idée républicaine*, p. 246.
92 Quoted in Payen, *Poincaré*, p. 155.
93 Nicolet, *Idée républicaine*, p. 246.
94 Quoted in Payen, *Poincaré*, p. 156. Apart from the influence of Ferry on his ideas on education, Poincaré may also have been influenced by the 'guerre scolaire' which had raged in Belgium over religious education from the passing of the Van Humbeeck Law of 1 July 1879 until 1884. This had taken away state subsidies and the clergy's right to teach in state schools, the province or the commune, in order to bring state school teaching exclusively under the power of the civil authorities, resulting in serious divisions. Given Poincaré's sensitivity to consensus, the Belgian example must have been a practical reminder of the need for caution.
95 J-M. Mayeur, 'Louis Barthou et la "question religieuse"' in M. Papy (ed.), *Barthou, un homme, une époque* (Pau, 1986), pp. 139–51.
96 Emile Durkheim, 'Les principes de 1789 et la sociologie', book review of Ferneuil, *Les principes de 1789 et la science sociale* (Paris, 1889), in *Revue Internationale de l'Enseignement* (1890), pp. 450–6, quoted in Nicolet, *Idée républicaine*, p. 314.
97 Quoted in Payen, *Poincaré*, p. 99.
98 Quoted in Anon, *Raymond Poincaré: a sketch*, p. 15.
99 All quoted in Payen, *Poincaré*, pp. 100–3.
100 *Ibid.*, p. 103.
101 Quoted in Anon, *Poincaré: a sketch*, p. 19, no date.
102 Nicolet, *Idée républicaine*, pp. 273–5.
103 On this see chapter 6 above, pp. 147–50.
104 Nicolet, *Idée républicaine*, pp. 273–5.
105 Payen, *Poincaré*, p. 157.
106 *Ibid.*, p. 104.
107 Quoted in G. Krumeich, 'Joan of Arc between right and left' in R. Tombs

(ed.), *Nationhood and Nationalism in France. From Boulangism to the Great War 1889–1918* (London, 1991), pp. 70–1.

108 R. Poincaré, *L'idée de patrie* (Paris, 1910), pp. 8, 20–1.
109 Nicolet, *Idée républicaine*, p. 312.
110 R. Poincaré, *Ce que demande la cité* (Paris, 1912), p. 107.
111 *Ibid.*, p. 30.
112 *Ibid.*, p. 47.
113 *Ibid.*, p. 42.
114 *Ibid.*, p. 66.
115 *Ibid.*, p. 54.

3. POINCARÉ THE OPPORTUNIST

1 Robert J. Young, *Power and pleasure. Louis Barthou and the Third French Republic* (Montreal, 1991), p. 45.
2 For the delay in adopting comprehensive mutualist legislation which eventually came into force in 1898, see André Gueslin, *L'invention de l'économie sociale: le XIXe siècle français* (Paris, 1987), pp. 184–5.
3 *Ibid.*, pp. 308–10.
4 Quoted in *ibid.*, p. 179.
5 *Ibid.*, p. 179.
6 Ministère de l'économie et des finances, *Les ministres des finances de 1870 à nos jours* (Paris, 1992), p. 57.
7 Anon, *Raymond Poincaré: a sketch* (London, 1914), pp. 21–3.
8 Quoted in Fernand Payen, *Raymond Poincaré, chez lui, au parlement, au palais* (Paris, 1936), p. 118.
9 *JODebPC*, 4 December 1894, p. 2131.
10 Quoted in Payen, *Poincaré*, pp. 127–8.
11 For this incident see *JODebPC*, 26 November 1894, p. 2035.
12 Jean-Denis Bredin, *The Affair. The case of Alfred Dreyfus* (London, 1987), pp. 66–7, 76.
13 Quoted in John McManners, *Church and State in France, 1870–1914* (London, 1972), p. 136.
14 *JODebPC*, 11 July 1895, pp. 2141, 2143, 2147, 3148–9.
15 McManners, *Church and State in France*, p. 140.
16 Quoted in Payen, *Poincaré*, p. 170.
17 All quoted in *ibid.*, p. 186.
18 J-M. Mayeur, *La vie politique sous la Troisième République* (Paris, 1984), pp. 167–9.
19 Quoted in Payen, *Poincaré*, p. 188.
20 Quoted in *ibid.*, pp. 190, 191.
21 *Ibid.*, pp. 193–4, 196–9.
22 *Ibid.*, pp. 193–4, 196–9.
23 Mayeur, *Vie politique*, p. 171.
24 Quoted in *ibid.*, p. 171.
25 Mayeur, *Vie politique*, pp. 170–1.
26 Payen, *Poincaré*, p. 203.
27 For his letter to this effect, see *ibid.*, pp. 177–8.

28 Quoted in Anon, *Poincaré: a sketch*, p. 7; see Poincaré's correspondence in the Goncourt case in BN nafr 24544, ff. 448–54.
29 Speech to the Société des Lorrains de Paris, 4 June 1921, quoted in *Le Pays Lorrain*, 12 (December 1934), p. 549.
30 Payen, *Poincaré*, p. 211.
31 *Le Pays Lorrain*, p. 549.
32 For details of the Dreyfus Affair, see Bredin, *The Affair*.
33 *Ibid.*, p. 281.
34 Payen, *Poincaré*, p. 215.
35 Bredin, *The Affair*, pp. 284–5.
36 Payen, *Poincaré*, p. 215.
37 Quotation from *ibid.*, p. 216; Denis Brogan, *The development of modern France 1870–1939* (London, 1940), p. 337; Bredin, *The Affair*, p. 271 and for the list of intellectuals in each camp, pp. 275–85.
38 Payen, *Poincaré*, p. 216.
39 Quoted in *ibid.*, p. 216.
40 Mayeur, *Vie politique*, pp. 175–84.
41 Bredin, *The Affair*, p. 304; J-M. Mayeur, 'Louis Barthou et la "question religieuse"' in M. Papy (ed.), *Barthou, un homme, une époque* (Pau, 1986), pp. 142–3.
42 Payen, *Poincaré*, p. 218.
43 *Ibid.*, p. 218.
44 Bredin, *The Affair*, pp. 309–12, only fifteen socialists abstained.
45 Payen, *Poincaré*, p. 219.
46 *Ibid.*, p. 219.
47 *Ibid.*, p. 220.
48 Quoted in Payen, *Poincaré*, p. 254.
49 *Ibid.*, p. 220.
50 Alexandre Millerand, 'Mes souvenirs', unpublished memoirs in the hands of the family.
51 Quoted in Miquel, *Poincaré*, p. 179.
52 All quoted in Payen, *Poincaré*, pp. 221–2.
53 All quoted in *ibid.*, pp. 221–3.
54 Bredin, *The Affair*, pp. 359–63.
55 *JODebPC*, 28 November 1898, pp. 2305–7.
56 Bredin, *The Affair*, pp. 363–4; Payen, *Poincaré*, pp. 223–4.
57 Bredin, *The Affair*, p. 365.
58 Quoted in Payen, *Poincaré*, p. 225.
59 All quoted in *ibid.*, p. 227.
60 Miquel, *Poincaré*, p. 170.
61 Payen, p. 229; for instance, almost the entire centre and two-thirds of the Radicals voted along with the Right in the Chamber to *désaisir* the criminal section of the Cour de Cassation of its jurisdiction in a re-trial, Bredin, *The Affair*, p. 372, or p. 364 'a very large majority of the Chamber remained fiercely hostile to a revision'.
62 Quoted in Payen, *Poincaré*, p. 229.
63 Quoted in *ibid.*, pp. 427–9.
64 *Ibid.*, p. 232; Raoul Persil, *Alexandre Millerand* (Paris, 1949), p. 19.

65 Quoted in Payen, *Poincaré*, p. 233.
66 Bredin, *The Affair*, pp. 391–2.
67 Quoted in Payen, *Poincaré*, p. 251.
68 Quoted in *ibid.*, p. 254.
69 Paul Cambon to de Fleuriau, 29 December 1913 in Paul Cambon, *Correspondance* (Paris, 1946), vol. III, p. 59.
70 Paul Cambon to Jules Cambon, 6 February 1913, Louis Cambon MSS.
71 Quoted in Payen, *Poincaré*, p. 254.
72 Quoted in *ibid.*, p. 68.
73 Millerand, 'Mes souvenirs'.
74 Paul Cambon to Jules Cambon, 28 November 1912, *Correspondance*, vol. III, pp. 29–30.
75 Quoted in Payen, *Poincaré*, p. 255.
76 Quoted in *ibid.*, p. 269.
77 For other exponents of this theory before F. Goguel's *La politique des partis sous la troisième République* (3rd edn, Paris, 1958), such as Littré and Thibaudet, see Nicolet, *L'idée républicaine en France (1789–1924). Essai d'histoire critique* (Paris, 1982), p. 184.
78 Quoted in Mayeur, *Vie politique*, p. 197.
79 Quoted in George Samné, *Raymond Poincaré; politique et personnel de la IIIe République* (Paris, 1933), p. 46..
80 On the evolution of the north-east and Lorraine to the Right, see Mayeur, *Vie politique*, p. 206.
81 *Ibid.*, pp. 185–6.
82 Quoted in Payen, *Poincaré*, p. 281.
83 Mayeur, *Vie politique*, p. 83.
84 Joseph Caillaux, *Mes mémoires* (Paris, 1947), vol. III, p. 8.
85 Samné, *Poincaré*, pp. 78–9.
86 Quoted in Payen, *Poincaré*, p. 283.
87 J-C. Allain, *Joseph Caillaux*, vol. I: *Le défi victorieux 1863–1914* (Paris, 1978), p. 78. Poincaré maintained an arm's length friendship with Caillaux for whom he provided free legal counsel in 1899 when the latter was a minister. They went on holiday together and Poincaré was a witness at his second marriage in 1911. Caillaux at least regarded Poincaré as a real friend, though relations deteriorated from 1912 onwards. See *ibid.*, pp. 97–8.
88 C. Charle, *Les élites de la République, 1880–1900* (Paris, 1987), pp. 260–1, 263.
89 Pénélope (daughter of one of the Elysée staff?) to Raymond Brugère (son of General Brugère), 29 August 1913, 'Lettres de Poincaré à sa nièce', BN nafr 16827.
90 Raymond Poincaré to Lysie 14 September, 6 October 1908 and passim, Lettres de Poincaré à sa nièce, BN nafr 16827.
91 See the *livret scolaire*, (no date) in *ibid.*
92 Poincaré, 'Notes journalières', BN nafr 16031, 10 August 1915.
93 Payen, *Poincaré*, pp. 410–11; Samné, *Poincaré*, pp. 78–9.
94 Mayeur, *Vie politique*, p. 197.
95 Quoted in Payen, *Poincaré*, p. 286.
96 Mayeur, *Vie politique*, pp. 197–8.

97 On this see Donald G. Wileman, 'Not the Radical republic: liberal ideology and central blandishment in France, 1901–1914', *The Historical Journal* 37(3) (1994).
98 Quoted in Miquel, *Poincaré*, p. 198.
99 See Sir Francis Bertie (British ambassador in Paris) to Sir Edward Grey (foreign secretary), 12 March 1906, doc. 39 in *BDFA*, vol. 12.
100 Quoted in Payen, *Poincaré*, p. 289.
101 Quoted in *ibid.*, p. 289.
102 Quoted in *ibid.*, p. 289.
103 Rumour had it that Poincaré was opposed to the loan but that Foreign Minister Bourgeois pressed for it (*ibid.*, p. 292).
104 Mayeur, *Vie politique*, p. 213.
105 Reginald Lister (chargé d'affaires) to Grey, 22 May 1906; Bertie-Grey, 8 May 1906, docs. 47 and 44 in *BDFA*, vol. 12.
106 Bertie to Grey, 5 June 1906, *ibid.*, doc. 53.
107 See, for instance, Bertie to Grey, 9 July 1906, *ibid.*, doc. 57.
108 Quoted in Miquel, *Poincaré*, p. 206.
109 *Le Temps* claimed that Clemenceau offered the foreign ministry to Poincaré who refused, see British embassy to foreign office, 24 October 1906, doc. 77 in *BDFA*, vol. 12. Payen claims that Clemenceau asked Poincaré to stay at finance or choose another portfolio, but he refused (Payen, *Poincaré*, p. 305). The British embassy in Paris thought this mere manoeuvring to allow Clemenceau to offer foreign affairs to his friend Stephen Pichon, doc. 119 in *BDFA*, vol. 12.
110 General Report on France for 1906, Annex 1, p. 198. doc. 119 in *BDFA*, vol. 12.
111 Payen, *Poincaré*, p. 306.
112 For a similar explanation of Barthou's 'opportunism', see Young, *Barthou*, pp. 67–9.

4. POINCARÉ EN RÉSERVE DE LA RÉPUBLIQUE

1 Quoted in J-M. Mayeur, *La vie politique sous la Troisième République* (Paris, 1984), p. 216 and for much of what follows, pp. 215–20.
2 The rise also applied to senators who had originally requested 16,000 francs, British Embassy General Report on France 1906, Annex 3, p. 211 in doc. 119, *BDFA*, vol. 12.
3 Mayeur, *Vie politique*, pp. 216–17.
4 *Ibid.*, p. 218.
5 P. Miquel, *Poincaré*, (Paris, 1961), p. 223.
6 Quoted in J. P. T. Bury and R. P. Tombs, *Thiers 1797–1877. A political life* (London, 1986), p. 252.
7 See J. Estèbe, 'Barthou écrivain', in M. Papy (ed.), *Barthou, un homme, une époque* (Pau, 1986), pp. 200–1.
8 J. Estèbe, *Les ministres de la République, 1871–1914* (Paris, 1982), p. 185.
9 Another Academician, Paul Hervieu, informed him on 6 August 1906 that he could count on six votes from the dramatists, six from the left-wing parliamentarians and four from the Lorraine group, plus assorted others.

F. Payen, *Raymond Poincaré, chez lui, au parlement, au palais* (Paris, 1936), pp. 295–6.

10 For the Ecole de Nancy's influence on the Meuse, see Christian Debize, '"Art Nouveau" en Meuse: quelques jalons pour baliser un territoire de recherches' in Jean Lanher and Noëlle Cazin (eds.), *Commercy à l'ère industrielle* (Bar-le-Duc, 1994), pp. 23–38.

11 G. Samné, *Raymond Poincaré: politique et personel de la IIIe République* (Paris, 1933), p. 75.

12 *Ibid.*, p. 73.

13 For further examples see Payen, *Poincaré*, pp. 301–2, 342–6.

14 Quoted in Payen, *Poincaré*, p. 346.

15 All quoted in Miquel, *Poincaré*, p. 225.

16 Quoted in Payen, *Poincaré*, p. 303.

17 *Ibid.*, p. 303.

18 Bury and Tombs, *Thiers*. Interestingly, Barthou had also written on Thiers; see Mayeur, 'Barthou et la "question religieuse"'' in Papy (ed.), *Barthou*, p. 144.

19 See J. Estèbe, 'Barthou écrivain' in Papy (ed.), *Barthou*, p. 200.

20 All quoted in Payen, *Poincaré*, pp. 294, 330; for details of Poincaré's campaign, see pp. 323–30.

21 E. Lavisse, *Discours de réception à l'Académie française*, 9 December 1909 (Paris, 1909).

22 Payen, *Poincaré*, pp. 334–6.

23 J-B. Duroselle, *Clemenceau* (Paris, 1988), pp. 509–21.

24 *Ibid.*, p. 516

25 Mayeur, *Vie politique*, p. 221.

26 *Ibid.*, pp. 217–18, 220–2.

27 Quoted in Miquel, *Poincaré*, p. 240.

28 See J. P. T. Bury, *France 1814–1940* (London, 1969), pp. 213–15; Mayeur, *Vie politique*, p. 217.

29 R. Poincaré, *Ce que demande la cité* (Paris, 1912), p. 59.

30 *Ibid.*, p. 66.

31 *Ibid.*, p. 42.

32 Quoted in Miquel, *Poincaré*, p. 241.

33 Quoted in *ibid.*, p. 241.

34 R. Poincaré, *L'idée de patrie* (Paris, 1910), pp. 6–8, 11, 13–16, 18, 20–2.

35 Christian Amalvi, 'Nationalist responses to the Revolution' in R. Tombs (ed.), *Nationhood and nationalism in France. From Boulangism to the Great War 1889–1918* (London, 1991), pp. 39–40.

36 Quoted in Mayeur, *Vie politique*, p. 224.

37 See J. F. V. Keiger, *France and the origins of the First World War* (London, 1983), pp. 25–43.

38 For details of the Agadir crisis, see J-C. Allain, *Agadir 1911* (Paris, 1976), and Keiger, *France and the origins*, pp. 33–7.

39 R. Poincaré, *Au service de la France. Neuf années de Souvenirs* vol. I: *Le lendemain d'Agadir, 1912* (Paris, 1926), pp. 3–4.

40 J-C. Allain, *Joseph Caillaux* vol. I: *Le défi victorieux, 1863–1914* (Paris, 1978), p. 84.

41 Poincaré, *Au service* vol. I, pp. 9–10.

42 Quoted in Payen, *Poincaré*, p. 346.
43 Quoted in Miquel, *Poincaré*, p. 249.
44 Payen, *Poincaré*, p. 365. The five governments which Poincaré would lead were characterised by the speed of their formation. In only one case, that of his last cabinet of 1928, would the difference in time between the preceding cabinet's fall and the establishment of his new one extend to five days; in all other cases there was never more than a three-day gap, which was well under the usual time for ministries under the Third Republic. See J. Jolly (ed.), *Dictionnaire des parlementaires français. Notices biographiques sur les ministres, députés et sénateurs français de 1889 à 1940* (Paris, 1960–72), vol. I.
45 Poincaré, *Ce que demande la cité*, p. 55.
46 J. S. Hayward, *Governing France: the One and Indivisible French Republic* (2nd edn, London 1987), p. 243.
47 Poincaré, *Ce que demande la cité*, p. 55.
48 Bertie-Grey, 14 January 1913, doc. 84 in *BDFA*, vol. 13.
49 Quoted in Gerd Krumeich, 'Poincaré vu de l'Allemagne avant et après la guerre de 1914–1918' in J. Lanher and N. Cazin (eds.), *Raymond Poincaré, un homme d'état lorrain 1860–1934* (Bar-le-Duc, 1989), p. 132.
50 Poincaré, *Au service* vol. I, pp. 25–6, 28.
51 On the myth of the saviour in French political history, see R. Girardet, *Mythes et mythologies politiques* (Paris, 1986), pp. 72–4.

5. POINCARÉ THE DIPLOMAT

1 R. Poincaré, *Au service de la France. Neuf années de souvenirs* vol. I: *Le lendemain d'Agadir, 1912* (Paris, 1926) p. 24.
2 *Ibid.*, pp. 24–5.
3 Gerd Krumeich, *Armaments and politics in France on the eve of the First World War* (Leamington Spa, 1984), p. 31, and for the best account of domestic policy up to the war.
4 Quoted in F. Payen, *Raymond Poincaré, chez lui, au parlement, au palais* (Paris, 1936), pp. 370–1.
5 *JODocPS*, 1911, no. 165, p. 640; Georges Louis, *Les carnets de Georges Louis* vol. II (Paris, 1926), p. 125, and Auguste Gérard, *Mémoires d'Auguste Gérard* (Paris, 1928), p. 449.
6 On this see, J. F. V. Keiger, 'Patriotism, politics and policy in the foreign ministry, 1880–1914' in R. Tombs (ed.), *Nationhood and nationalism. From Boulangism to the Great War 1889–1918* (London, 1991), pp. 255–66; also his, *France and the origins of the First World War* (London, 1983), ch. 2, 'Bureaucrats and diplomats: a period of independence, 1905–11', pp. 25–43.
7 G. Hanotaux, *Raymond Poincaré* (Paris, 1934), p. 11.
8 P. Cambon to J. Cambon, 28 November 1912 in Paul Cambon, *Correspondance, 1870–1924* (ed. H. Cambon, 3 vols., Paris, 1940–6), vol. III, p. 30.
9 P. Cambon to J. Cambon, 4 November 1912, MAE Jules Cambon papers, 25, dos. Paul to Jules.
10 Berthelot to Gérard (ambassador to China), 26 March 1912, AN Gérard MSS, 329 AP 20.
11 Louis, *Carnets* vol. II, p. 212.

12 P. Cambon to J. Cambon, 6 June 1912, *Correspondance* vol. III, p. 17.
13 Viscount Grey of Fallodon, *Twenty-five years, 1892–1916* vol. I (London, 1925), quoted in Poincaré, *Au service* vol. I, pp. 247–8.
14 For what follows on Franco-Italian relations before the war, see Keiger, *France and the origins*, pp. 56–67.
15 D. Brogan, *The development of modern France, 1870–1939* (London, 1940), p. 392.
16 On the cabinet noir, C. M. Andrew, 'Déchiffrement et diplomatie: le cabinet noir du Quai d'Orsay sous la Troisième République', *Relations Internationales* 5 (1976), pp. 37–64.
17 Poincaré, *Au service* vol. I, pp. 236–7, 263, 270; for a full account see Keiger, *France and the origins*, pp. 81–6.
18 For further details of Franco-German relations at this time, see J. F. V. Keiger, 'Jules Cambon and Franco-German *détente*, 1907–14', *The Historical Journal* 26 (3) (1983), pp. 641–59; also his *France and the origins*, pp. 68–81.
19 J. Cambon to Poincaré, 3 March 1912, MAE Jules Cambon papers, 16, dos. Pichon-Z.
20 Poincaré to J. Cambon, 27 March 1912, MAE Jules Cambon papers, 16, dos. Pichon-Z.
21 P. Cambon to J. Cambon, 4 November 1912, MAE Jules Cambon papers, 25, dos. Paul-Jules.
22 For details of France's policy in Syria and the Lebanon from 1912–14, see C. M. Andrew and A. S. Kanya-Forstner, *France overseas, the Great War and the climax of French imperial expansion* (London, 1981), chs. 1 and 2; W. I. Shorrock, *French imperialism in the Middle East* (London, 1976), pp. 83–165; P. Guillen, 'Les questions coloniales dans les relations franco-allemandes à la veille de la première guerre mondiale', *La Revue Historique* 248 (1972), pp. 98–105; J. Thobie, *Intérêts et impérialisme français dans l'empire ottoman (1895–1914)* (Paris, 1977), pp. 647–724.
23 Bompard (ambassador in Constantinople) to minister, 13 January 1912, *DDF*, 3e série, vol. I, no. 465. For details of Franco-Russian relations, see Keiger, *France and the origins*, pp. 88–102.
24 Poincaré to P. Cambon, 13 March 1912, *DDF*, 3e série, vol. II, no. 193.
25 See, for example, G. Louis to P. Loüys, 28 November 1911, 30 January 1912 [?], MAE G. Louis papers (3).
26 Poincaré to Louis, 8 April 1912, *DDF*, 3e série, vol. II, no. 310.
27 Poincaré to Louis, 11 April 1912, MAE NS Russia 41.
28 For details of this complicated affair, see Keiger, *France and the origins*, pp. 93–6.
29 Henri Cambon (on Paléologue and Poincaré's behalf) to J. Cambon, 31 October 1912, letter in hands of the family.
30 Poincaré to P. Cambon, 25 November 1912, *DDF*, 3e série, vol. IV no. 562, for details see Keiger, *France and the origins*, pp. 102–16.

6. POINCARÉ PRESIDENT OF THE REPUBLIC

1 On the importance of the theme of 'unity' in French history, see the chapter in R. Girardet, *Mythes et mythologies politiques* (Paris, 1986), pp. 139–73.

2 The best account of these reforms is G. Krumeich, *Armaments and politics in France on the eve of the First World War* (Leamington Spa, 1984), pp. 32–6.

3 Quoted in *ibid.*, p. 32.

4 Poincaré, 'Notes journalières', BN nafr 16024, 26 and 27 December 1912; F. Payen, *Raymond Poincaré, chez lui, au parlement, au palais* (Paris, 1936), pp. 386–96.

5 Poincaré, 'Notes journalières', BN nafr 16024, 12 January 1912.

6 Quoted in Krumeich, *Armaments and politics*, p. 39.

7 *Ibid.*, pp. 39–40.

8 See *ibid.*, pp 41–2; Clemenceau to Poincaré, 31 December 1912, in Payen, *Poincaré*, pp. 393–5.

9 Quoted in P. Miquel, *Poincaré* (Paris, 1961), pp. 298–9.

10 Poincaré, 'Notes journalières', BN nafr 16024, 14 January 1913.

11 *Ibid.*, 26 December 1912.

12 *Ibid.*, 14 January 1913.

13 Payen, *Poincaré*, p. 396; there is no mention of the duel taking place; neither Duroselle in his *Clemenceau* (Paris, 1988), nor Poincaré in his diaries mention it.

14 J. Estèbe, *Les ministres de la République, 1871–1914* (Paris, 1982), p. 100.

15 For Poincaré's account of the pre-election machinations and his view of Clemenceau, see Poincaré, 'Notes journalières', BN nafr 16024, 14 to 17 January 1913.

16 *Ibid.*, 17 January 1913. There is no mention of this interview in the published version of his diaries, *Au service de la France. Neuf années de souvenirs* (Paris, 1926–33), vol. III, chapter 2.

17 *Ibid.*, 17 January 1913.

18 Quoted in Duroselle, *Clemenceau*, p. 571.

19 *Ibid.*, p. 573.

20 Poincaré, 'Notes journalières', BN nafr 16024, 17 January 1913.

21 J-M. Mayeur, *La vie politique sous la Troisième République* (Paris, 1984), pp. 228–9.

22 On the socialists', and in particular Vaillant's, belief that Poincaré was striving for peace in 1912, see Krumeich, *Armaments and politics*, pp. 40–1, note 98.

23 *Ibid.*, pp. 42–3.

24 Poincaré, 'Notes journalières', BN nafr 16024, 18 January 1913; G. Samné, *Raymond Poincaré; politique et personnel de la IIIe République* (Paris, 1933), p. 80.

25 Jules to Paul Cambon, 19 January 1913, correspondence in the hands of the family.

26 *Ibid.*, 25 January 1913.

27 Payen, *Poincaré*, pp. 397–9.

28 M. Paléologue, *Au Quai d'Orsay à la veille de la tourmente* (Paris, 1947), p. 12. When it was suggested that because he had been a good premier he would be a good president Poincaré noted, 'Hélas!, les qualités utiles à la Présidence du Conseil sont nuisibles – ou inutiles[?] à la Presidence de la République' (Poincaré, 'Notes journalières', BN nafr 16024, 18 January 1913).

29 Quoted in Mayeur, *Vie politique*, p. 229

30 J. F. V. Keiger, *France and the origins of the First World War* (London, 1983), pp. 118–9

31 Samné, *Poincaré*, p. 80.

32 Poincaré was in close contact with the Asian wing of the colonialist movement, was one of the founding members of the Comité de défense des intérêts français en Orient and a member of the Comité de l'Asie française; Jonnart was president of the Comité de l'Afrique française and a 'patron' of the Comité de l'Orient, a colonial association committed to increasing French influence in the Levant; see C. M. Andrew and A. S. Kanya-Forstner, *France overseas, the Great War and the climax of French imperial expansion* (London, 1981), p. 50.

33 Quoted in E. M. Carroll, *French public opinion and foreign affairs, 1870–1914* (London, 1931), p. 258. Poincaré also told the British ambassador that his election to the presidency 'would enable him to give steadiness and "suite" to the foreign policy of France'. Bertie to Grey, 21 January 1913, FO 800/166.

34 Poincaré, 'Notes journalières', BN nafr 16024, 26 January 1913.

35 J. to P. Cambon, 8 February 1913, letter in the possession of the Cambon family.

36 Poincaré, 'Notes journalières', BN nafr 16024, 15 February 1913. On the Three Years' Law, see Krumeich, *Armaments and politics*.

37 Report by Colonel Yarde Buller, military attaché, on the French army, in Annual Report on France for 1912, 1 August 1913, p. 507, doc. 108 in *BDFA*, vol. 13.

38 Poincaré, 'Notes journalières', BN nafr 16024, 18 February 1913.

39 J-J. Becker, *1914 comment les Français sont entrés dans la guerre* (Paris, 1977), pp. 63–4.

40 Poincaré, 'Notes journalières', BN nafr 16024, 14 February 1913.

41 *Ibid.*, 30 and 31 January 1913.

42 *Ibid.*, 21 January 1913.

43 *Ibid.*, 18 February 1913. There were twenty-five francs to the pound.

44 On this see below, chapter 7.

45 G. Hanotaux, *Raymond Poincaré* (Paris, 1934), p. 57.

46 Hippolyte Hamard to Poincaré, no date [October 1913], 31 October 1913, and also 31 January 1915, 3 January 1918, in Papiers Poincaré, vol. XII, 'lettres adressées à Poincaré'. Hamard thanked him for the 400 francs a month which he already received from the interior ministry for his work on the *Courrier du Parlement* commenting, 'J'en suis heureux, car cette faveur le rendra favorable à votre ministère'. Hamard to Poincaré, [October 1913], *ibid.*

47 On Franco-German *détente* and the Ottoman Empire, see Keiger, *France and the origins*, pp. 129–35.

48 J. Cambon to P. Cambon, 5 April 1913, letter in the possession of the Cambon family.

49 See Keiger, *France and the origins*, pp. 125–8.

50 J. Cambon to P. Cambon, 15 November 1913, letter in the possession of the Cambon family.

51 Poincaré, 'Notes journalières', BN nafr 16026, 13 January 1914.

52 Kokovtsov to Nicholas II, 13 December 1913, quoted in A. J. P. Taylor, *Struggle for mastery in Europe, 1848–1918* (Oxford, paperback edn 1973), p. 501.

53 Jules Cambon to de Margerie (political director at Quai), 18 February 1914, MAE Margerie MSS, dos. Jules Cambon.

54 Jules Cambon to Margerie, 13 April 1914, MAE Margerie MSS, dos Jules Cambon.

55 See Payen, *Poincaré*, pp. 406–7.

56 Paléologue, *A la veille de la tourmente*, pp. 100–24; C. M. Andrew, 'Déchiffrements et diplomatie: le cabinet noir du Quai d'Orsay sous la Troisième République', *Relations Internationales* 5 (1976), pp. 37–64.

57 J. Cambon to P. Cambon, 6 June 1913, in the possession of the Cambon family.

58 See L. Bourgeois's remarks in G. Louis, *Les carnets de Georges Louis* (Paris, 1926), vol. II, 5 July 1913, p. 60.

59 Poincaré, 'Notes journalières', BN nafr 16025, 6 December 1913.

60 P. Cambon to de Fleuriau, 29 December 1913, *Correspondance 1870–1924*, (Paris, 1940–6), vol. III, pp. 59–61.

61 Poincaré, 'Notes journalières', BN nafr 16026, 13 January 1914.

62 *Ibid.*, BN nafr 16027, 4 March 1914.

63 *Ibid.*, 16 March 1914.

64 Quoted in Andrew, 'Déchiffrements et diplomatie', pp. 57–8.

65 Poincaré, 'Notes journalières', BN nafr 16027, 29 July 1914.

66 P. Cambon to J. Cambon, 29 April 1914, *Correspondance*, vol. III, pp. 64–5.

67 For what follows, see Becker, *1914*, pp. 68–80.

68 The Socialist party was the real beneficiary of the elections, increasing its seats by thirty to one hundred. The apparent success of the Radicals returning 260 deputies does not imply opposition to the Law; nor does the centre and Right's reduced number of seats. Leaving aside the Radicals' electoral ambiguity over the Law, the elections suggest support for the Law in terms of votes rather than seats. It was the classic anomaly of the two-round majority system exaggerating the victor's number of seats out of proportion to the votes polled. This explains why contemporaries drew erroneous conclusions from the swing in seats and the spectacular progression of the one party clearly opposed to the Law – the socialists. For details of the election results, see Mayeur, *Vie politique*, pp. 230–1.

69 Poincaré, 'Notes journalières', BN nafr 16027, 2–13 June 1914.

70 Keiger, *France and the origins*, chapter 7, pp. 145–64, and also his, 'Britain's "union sacrée" in 1914' in J-J. Becker and S. Audoin-Rouzeau (eds.), *Les sociétés européennes et la guerre de 1914–1918* (Nanterre, 1990), pp. 39–52; Becker, *1914*; D. C. B. Lieven, *Russia and the origins of the First World War* (London, 1983), pp. 140–1.

71 Poincaré, 'Notes journalières', BN nafr 16027, 2 and 11 July.

72 For further details of what follows, see Keiger, *France and the origins*, pp. 145–67.

73 Poincaré, 'Notes journalières', BN nafr 16027, 18 June 1914.

74 Becker, *1914*, p. 140.

75 *Le Temps*, 7 March 1922, in MAE, Europe 1918–1940, sous-série,

Allemagne, vol. 327, Politique intérieure; responsabilité de la guerre Article on Bavarian documents in *Bayerische Dokumentation über den Kriegsausbruch*, edited by Dr Pius Dirr on behalf of the Bavarian Diet.

76 Poincaré, 'Notes journalières', BN nafr 16027, 18 and 16 July 1914.
77 *Ibid.*, 19 July 1914.
78 *Ibid.*, 20 July 1914.
79 The editors of the published French *Documents diplomatiques* made every effort to trace any minutes of these and subsequent discussions, but found none. Indeed the compilers of those documents decided to extend the date-limit of their volumes to 23 July precisely because hitherto there was no sign of any anxiety in the French documents.
80 Poincaré, 'Notes journalières', BN nafr 16027, 19–21 July 1914; R. Poincaré, *Comment fut déclarée la guerre de 1914* (Paris, 1939), p. 32; Lieven, *Russia and the origins*, p. 140.
81 Poincaré, *Comment*, p. 36.
82 *Ibid.*, pp. 49–50.
83 Quoted in *ibid.*, p. 37.
84 See the transcriptions of these telegrams in *ibid.*, pp. 45–6.
85 Poincaré, 'Notes journalières', BN nafr 16032, 28 December 1915.
86 Quoted in Zara Steiner, *Britain and the origins of the First World War* (London, 1977), pp. 221–2; Poincaré, 'Notes journalières', BN nafr 16027, 24 July 1914.
87 Poincaré, 'Notes journalières', BN nafr 16027, 26 July 1914; Poincaré, *Comment*, p. 54; Poincaré, 'Notes journalières', 27 July 1914.
88 Poincaré, 'Notes journalières', 27 July 1914. For the full text of the telegram, see Poincaré, *Comment*, p. 68.
89 L. Albertini, *The origins of the war of 1914* (London, 1965), vol. II, p. 593.
90 Poincaré, 'Notes journalières', BN nafr 16027, 25 July 1914.
91 *Ibid.*, 27 July 1914.
92 *Ibid.*, 29 July 1914.
93 See copies in Poincaré, *Comment*, p. 64.
94 A. Kriegel and J-J. Becker, *1914: la guerre et le mouvement ouvrier français* (Paris, 1964), pp. 63–85, 92–3.
95 Lady Algernon Gordon Lennox (ed.), *The diary of Lord Bertie of Thame, 1914–18* (London, 1931) vol. I, pp. 1–4.
96 On Poincaré's attempts to maintain that fine balance from 1912 to the outbreak of war, see Keiger, *France and the origins*, pp. 88–102.
97 See, for example, Poincaré, 'Notes journalières', BN nafr 16027, 9 March 1914. For a detailed discussion of this, see Keiger, *France and the origins*, pp. 138–9.
98 Quoted in Albertini, *Origins*, vol. II, p. 161.
99 *L'Humanité*, 30 July 1914, quoted in Kriegel and Becker, *La guerre et le mouvement ouvrier*, pp. 88–9.
100 For the details of what was happening across Europe, see Keiger, *France and the origins*, pp. 157–62.
101 Jean Stengers, '1914: The safety of ciphers and the outbreak of the First World War' in C. Andrew and J. Noakes, *Intelligence and international relations* (Exeter, 1987), pp. 29–48.

102 Quoted in Stengers, 'Safety of ciphers', p. 35.

103 See Paléologue's 'Récapitulation des faits qui se sont produits du 23 juillet au 4 août 1914', in MAE Papiers d'agent, Paléologue, 'Correspondance politique', vol. I (1914), f. 81, confirmed by the Marchioness de Laguiche in Stengers, 'Safety of ciphers', p. 35

104 See Laguiche diary, Chambrun's remark to General Laguiche: 'Nous allons le télégraphier au Ministère, le chiffre de l'Ambassade n'étant pas sûr', in Stengers, 'Safety of ciphers', p. 36 and note 40; also Poincaré, *Comment*, p. 94, who explains that it was Basily who insisted that the Russian cipher be used for greater secrecy. This confirms Russia's desire to keep general mobilisation absolutely secret, even by delaying news of it to Paléologue.

105 Quoted in Stengers, 'Safety of ciphers', p. 35.

106 Laguiche in *ibid.*, p. 36; see also the original telegram, Paléologue to Paris, 29 July 1914, no. 304 (23h 45) with the following marginalia in red ink: 'Ce télégramme a été expédié par l'entremise de l'Ambassadeur de Russie à Paris. Suppression au crayon dans le dernier paragraphe de l'indication 1o. et de la phrase: 2o. *à commencer secrètement la mobilisation générale* [underlined in text]', in MAE, Papiers d'agent, Paléologue, 'Correspondance politique', vol. I (1914), f. 44.

107 Stengers, 'Safety of ciphers', p. 36. This corroborates Paléologue's evidence to the commission for the publication of the *Documents diplomatiques français* in which he stated that Chambrun took the initiative to suppress the last sentence of the telegram and then informed his ambassador. *DDF*, 3e série, vol. XI, no. 283.

108 For further details, see Stengers, 'Safety of ciphers', pp. 36–7.

109 Paléologue to Paris, 29 July 1914, no. 306 (24h), MAE, Papiers d'agent, Paléologue, 'Correspondance politique', vol. I (1914), f. 46 (emphasis in original).

110 Poincaré, *Comment*, p. 88.

111 Quoted in Albertini, *Origins*, vol. II, p. 604; Poincaré, *Comment*, p. 89; Poincaré, 'Notes journalières', BN nafr 16027, 30 July 1914.

112 In a telegram to Paris that afternoon, Paléologue explained that he had told Sazonov not to take any military action which could give Germany a pretext for action. Paléologue added that the Russian foreign minister had replied that 'dans le cours de la nuit dernière l'Etat-major russe avait précisément fait surseoir à quelques précautions secrètes, dont la divulgation aurait pu alarmer l'Etat-major allemand'. Certainly Paléologue could have been more explicit about the fact that those measures were total mobilisation. Paléologue to Paris, 30 July 1914, no. 311, (15h 50), MAE, Papiers d'agent, Paléologue, 'Correspondance politique' vol. I (1914), f. 49.

113 Note by Abel Ferry, 30 July 1914, MAE Papiers d'agent, Abel Ferry.

114 Paléologue to Paris, 30 July 1914, no. 315 (19h 50), MAE, Papiers d'agent, Paléologue, 'Correspondance politique' vol. I (1914), f. 51. According to Poincaré this telegram arrived at the Quai that same evening at 11.30 p.m., Poincaré, *Comment*, p. 96.

115 Stengers, 'Safety of ciphers', p. 37; see the excerpt from the hitherto unpublished telegram about the change of cipher in *ibid.*

116 Paléologue to Paris, 31 July 1914, no. 318 (8h 30), MAE, Papiers d'agent, Paléologue, 'Correspondance politique' vol. I (1914), f. 52.
117 Poincaré, *Comment*, p. 119.
118 Viviani to Paléologue, 31 July 1914, nos. 483–4 (21h, 21h 20), MAE, Papiers d'agent, Paléologue, 'Correspondance politique' vol. I (1914), f. 56; Poincaré, *Comment*, pp. 118–19.
119 Poincaré, *Comment*, p. 119.
120 Paléologue to Paris, 1 August 1914, no. 324 (9h 40), 'Réponse à votre télégramme no. 484', MAE, Papiers d'agent, Paléologue, 'Correspondance politique' vol. I (1914), f. 58.
121 Stengers, 'Safety of ciphers', p. 37.
122 'Note rédigée après l'envoi de mon télégramme no. 324', 1 August 1914, MAE, Papiers d'agent, Paléologue, 'Correspondance politique' vol. I (1914), ff. 59–62.
123 Paléologue to Paris, 1 August 1914, no. 333 (19h 30), *ibid.*, f. 68.
124 Poincaré, 'Notes journalières', BN nafr 16027, 31 July 1914.
125 Entry for 31 July 1914 in Guy Rousseau, 'Impressions dans la tourmente. Le journal d'Etienne Clémentel dans l'été 1914', *Guerres Mondiales* 156 (1989), p. 92.
126 See Kriegel and Becker, *La guerre et mouvement ouvrier*, pp. 5–7.
127 Quoted in *ibid.*, pp. 112–13.
128 Poincaré, *Comment*, p. 125.
129 Quoted in Kriegel and Becker, *La guerre et mouvement ouvrier*, p. 117.
130 Poincaré, 'Notes journalières', BN nafr 16027, 1 August 1914.
131 Diary entry 1 August 1914 in Rousseau, 'Impressions dans la tourmente', p. 92.
132 Poincaré, 'Notes journalières', BN nafr 16027, 1 August 1914.
133 Poincaré, *Comment*, pp. 105–6; Poincaré, 'Notes journalières', BN nafr 16027, 3 August 1914, p. 142; A. Ferry note 30 July 1914, MAE, Papiers Abel Ferry.
134 R. Poincaré, *Au service de la France. Neuf années de souvenirs* vol. IV: *L'union sacrée, 1914* (Paris, 1927), p. 458; Poincaré, *Comment*, pp. 119–20.
135 Quoted in Poincaré *Comment*, p. 105; Poincaré, *Au service*, vol. IV, p. 424.
136 Poincaré, *Au service*, vol. IV, p. 479.
137 'Note rédigée de la main d'Abel Ferry', 31 July 1914, MAE, Papiers Abel Ferry, f. 7. The *député*, officer and well-informed *rapporteur* of the Chamber war ministry budget, Paul Bénazet informed Clémentel that the delay was about thirty hours. Diary entry 1 August 1914 in Rousseau, 'Impressions dans la tourmente', p. 92.
138 Poincaré, *Comment*, p. 127; Poincaré, *Au service*, vol. IV, p. 482.
139 Poincaré, *Au service*, vol. IV, pp. 482–3; Poincaré, *Comment*, p. 129.
140 Poincaré, 'Notes journalières', BN nafr 16027, 1 August 1914; Poincaré, *Comment*, pp. 129–30; Poincaré, *Au service*, vol. IV, pp. 483–4.
141 Poincaré, *Comment*, pp. 129–31; Poincaré, *Au service*, vol. IV, pp. 484–6.
142 Poincaré, *Comment*, pp. 116–17, 126–7.
143 Poincaré, 'Notes journalières', BN nafr 16027, 1 August 1914. There is some confusion in the manuscript of the Poincaré diaries regarding the date

of this entry which appears alternately as 1 and 2 August. The latter is correct; Poincaré, *Au service*, vol. IV, pp. 495–6.

144 Two German officers were actually shot on French soil while requisitioning, see Poincaré, 'Notes journalières', BN nafr 16027, 3 [recte 2] August 1914; Poincaré, *Au service*, vol. IV, pp. 500–1.

145 Poincaré, *Comment*, pp. 139–40; Poincaré, *Au service*, vol. IV, p. 502.

146 Poincaré, 'Notes journalières', BN nafr 16027, 2 August 1914.

147 Kriegel and Becker, *La guerre et mouvement ouvrier*, pp. 114–33.

148 Poincaré, 'Notes journalières', BN nafr 16027, 2 August 1914.

149 Poincaré, *Comment*, p. 141.

150 Poincaré, 'Notes journalières', BN nafr 16027, 3 August 1914.

151 *Ibid.*, 1 August 1914; *ibid.*, 3 August 1914, quoted in Keiger, *France and the origins*, p. 162.

152 Poincaré, *Comment*, pp. 142–3.

153 *Ibid.*, p. 155.

154 See, for example, *ibid.*, p. 109.

155 Poincaré, Notes journalières, BN nafr 16027, 3 Aug 1914.

156 *Ibid.*, 3 August 1914.

157 *Ibid.*, 3 August 1914.

158 *Ibid.*, 4 August 1914.

159 *Ibid.*, 4 August 1914.

160 Poincaré, 'Notes journalières', BN nafr 16029, 8 January 1915.

161 *Le Temps*, 7 March 1922, in MAE, Europe 1918–1940, sous-série, Allemagne, vol. 327, f. 113.

162 P. J. Flood, *France 1914–18. Public opinion and the war effort* (London, 1990), p. 15 and note 40.

163 For a full discussion of French public opinion and the *union sacrée*, see Becker, *1914*, pp. 6–9, 99–117, 123–6, 130–1, 190, 249, 367; on the labour movement, Kriegel and Becker, *La guerre et mouvement ouvrier*, pp. 87–105.

164 P. Renouvin, *Le Monde*, 29 July 1964.

165 Poincaré, *Comment*, p. 100.

166 Quoted in S. B. Fay, *The origins of the World War* (New York, 1929), vol. II p. 226.

167 See, for example, Albertini, *Origins*, vol. II, pp 604–7; Jules Isaac, *Un débat historique, 1914: le problème des origines de la guerre* (Paris, 1933), pp. 201–2. For details of Poincaré's role in the July crisis and an overall appraisal of his foreign policy, see Keiger, *France and the origins*, pp. 145–67.

168 K. Robbins, *Sir Edward Grey. A biography of Lord Grey of Fallodon* (London, 1971), pp. 298–9; Steiner, *Britain and the origins*, pp. 240–1.

169 Poincaré, *Comment*, p. 152.

7. POINCARÉ-LA-GUERRE

1 For details of the German effort to combat article 231, see John W. Langdon, *July 1914. The long debate, 1918–1990* (Oxford, 1991), pp. 1–3, 21–4, for the most comprehensive historiographical survey of the war origins debate; also Jacques Droz, *Les causes de la Première Guerre mondiale, essai d'historiographie* (Paris, 1973); also Jean-Baptiste Duroselle, *La Grande*

Guerre des Français, 1914–1918, L'incompréhensible (Paris, 1994), pp. 23–33, for an excellent summary of the war guilt question.

2 *L'Allemagne et les problèmes de la paix pendant la Première Guerre mondiale. Documents extraits des archives de l'office allemand des affaires étrangères* (edited by A Scherer and J Grunewald) vol. I *Des origines à la déclaration de guerre sous-marine (août 1914–31 janvier 1917)* (Paris, 1962); vol. II *De la guerre sous-marine à outrance à la révolution soviétique (1er février 1917–7 novembre 1917)* (Paris, 1966). On this question and what follows, see Droz, *Causes*, pp. 128–34.

3 Duroselle, *Grande Guerre*, p. 32

4 *Ibid.*, pp. 302–3.

5 Poincaré, 'Notes journalières', BN nafr 16028, 13 September 1914.

6 *Ibid.*, 23 October 1914.

7 *Ibid.*, 18 December 1914.

8 *Ibid.*, BN nafr 16029, 15, 31 January, 5 March, 3 July 1915.

9 *Ibid.*, BN nafr 16031, 10, 15 September 1915.

10 *Ibid.*, BN nafr 16032, 13, 14, 28 December 1915.

11 Droz, *Causes*, pp. 27–8 and below.

12 On this see Droz, *Causes*, pp. 128–34, whose conclusions are based on a reading of the German documents edited by Scherer and Grunewald, *L'Allemagne et les problèmes de la paix.*

13 See his entry in J. Jolly (ed.) *Dictionnaire des parlementaires français, Notices biographiques sur les ministres, députés et sénateurs français de 1889 à 1940* (Paris, 1960–72), vol. I, p. 341. In the post-war period he was an influential member of *inter alia* the Chamber Army commission, and may have been a German spy.

14 Entry for 27 September 1916 in the minister of commerce Etienne Clémentel's *Notes aux conseil des ministres*, edited by Guy Rousseau, 'Le conseil des ministres en 1916 d'après les notes d'Etienne Clémentel' in *Guerres Mondiales et Conflits Contemporains* 171 (1993), p. 146. For more names of influential 'pacifists', see Duroselle, *Grande Guerre*, pp. 290–300, 302–3.

15 Droz, *Causes*, pp. 130–1. According to Droz's reading of the documents it was not only French politicians who were targeted but also industrialists, albeit less successfully.

16 For what follows see Droz, *Causes*, pp. 26–32; also Duroselle, *Grande Guerre*, pp. 31–3.

17 The publication of the British documents was also relatively slow, appearing between 1926 and 1938, whereas a very tendentious collection of Soviet documents, critical of Poincaré's relationship with Isvolsky, appeared between 1922 and 1923 in three volumes edited by R. Marchand, *Un livre noir: diplomatie d'avant guerre d'après les documents des archives russes (1910–1917)* (Paris, 1922–3), with a further two volumes edited by F. Stieve. The official Soviet collection appeared between 1931 and 1934. See also Duroselle, *Grande Guerre*, pp. 10–11.

18 Duroselle, *Grande Guerre*, pp. 27–8.

19 Langdon, *Long debate*, p. 51.

20 J-M. Mayeur, *La vie politique sous la Troisième République* (Paris, 1984), pp. 236–7.

21 R. Poincaré, *Au service de la France. Neuf années de souvenirs* vol. V: *L'invasion, 1914* (Paris, 1928), p. 8.
22 Poincaré, 'Notes journalières', BN nafr 16027, 5 August 1914.
23 Poincaré, 'Notes journalières', BN nafr 16027, 6 August 1914. There is no mention of this episode in the published version of Poincaré's memoirs.
24 A few days later in a conversation with the socialist Jules Guesde on the subject of Alsace–Lorraine, Poincaré expressed his opposition to the idea of a plebiscite of the local population in the event of a victory over Germany (*ibid.*, 14 August 1914). This was perhaps because he rightly feared that the Germanisation policy had been successful and that the outcome could not be predicted.
25 Entry for 6 August 1914 in Rousseau, 'Impressions dans la tourmente', *Guerres Mondiales* 156 (1989), p. 97.
26 *Ibid.* According to the Italian ambassador in Paris, Clemenceau had told him that following the meeting their old rivalries had been forgotten and that they were reconciled, quoted in Duroselle, *Clemenceau*, p. 583.
27 Poincaré, 'Notes journalières', BN nafr 16027, 9 August 1914.
28 *Ibid.*, 8 August 1914. A few days later he noted in his typically priggish way one of Doumergue's malapropisms: 'Sir Bertie, comme il dit sans cesse par une ignorance fréquente des choses anglaises.' *Ibid.*, 12 August 1914.
29 See the references to Poincaré in the Italian correspondence in J-B. Duroselle, *Clemenceau* (Paris, 1988), pp. 582–6.
30 Poincaré, 'Notes journalières', BN nafr 16027, 18 August 1914.
31 *Ibid.*, 18 August 1914.
32 *Ibid.*, 19 August 1914.
33 *Ibid.*, 20, 21 August 1914.
34 Duroselle, *Grande Guerre*, pp. 64–7.
35 Poincaré, 'Notes journalières', BN nafr 16027, 22, 23 August 1914.
36 *Ibid.*, 24 August 1914.
37 *Ibid.*, 24 August 1914.
38 Duroselle, *Clemenceau*, p. 583.
39 Poincaré, 'Notes journalières', BN nafr 16027, 25 August 1914. On Clemenceau's refusal to accept a ministry see Duroselle, *Clemenceau*, p. 586.
40 Poincaré, *Au service*, vol. V, p. 92.
41 Mayeur, *Vie politique*, pp. 235–6
42 Poincare, 'Notes journalières', BN nafr 16027, 27 August 1914.
43 A. Fontaine, *French industry during the War* (Newhaven, Conn., 1926), pp. 16–17, cited in Jon Lawrence, 'The transition to war in 1914' in J. M. Winter and Jean-Louis Robert, *Paris, London, Berlin 1914–1919: capital cities at war* (Cambridge, 1996), p. 152.
44 Poincaré, 'Notes journalières', BN nafr 16027, 30 August 1914; on Messimy's replacement by Millerand and Poincaré's role in it, see G. Wormser, *Le septennat de Poincaré* (Paris, 1977), p. 49. According to Raoul Persil, Director of Millerand's *cabinet civil* at the war ministry, it was not until 18 November 1914 that the two old friends would be reconciled (R. Persil, *Alexandre Millerand* (Paris, 1949), p. 88).
45 See Jon Lawrence, Martin Dean, Jean-Louis Robert, 'The outbreak of war and the urban economy: Paris, Berlin, and London in 1914', *Economic*

History Review 45(3) (2nd ser., August 1992), p. 583; Lawrence, 'The transition to war in 1914' in Winter and Robert, *Paris, London, Berlin*, pp. 152–3. The parallels with the Paris of 1870 are striking.

46 Poincaré, 'Notes journalières', BN nafr 16027, 2 September 1914.

47 See the account of the director of Millerand's *cabinet civil* at the war ministry (Persil, *Millerand*, p. 84).

48 Poincaré, 'Notes journalières', BN nafr 16028, 3 September 1914.

49 In early October 1914 the French deciphering service had broken the German code, which the French had lost just before the outbreak of war as a result of indiscretions surrounding the Caillaux trial. *Ibid.*, 9 October 1914.

50 *Ibid.*, 8, 7, 9 September 1914.

51 In March 1915 Henriette Poincaré obtained permission to visit 'Le Clos' and wrote movingly to Poincaré's niece Lysie of the wanton destruction: 'C'est triste, triste!' Henriette-Lisy (Lysie Lannes), 5 March 1915, 'Lettres de Poincaré à sa nièce', BN nafr 16827.

52 Poincaré, 'Notes journalières', BN nafr 16028, 17 October 1914.

53 *Ibid.*, 13, 18 September 1914.

54 *Ibid.*, 9 October 1914.

55 Wormser, *Septennat de Poincaré*, p. 55.

56 Poincaré, 'Notes journalières', BN nafr 16030, 11 June 1915.

57 *Ibid.*, BN nafr 16028, 19 September 1914.

58 *Ibid.*, 22 October 1914. Raoul Persil, in his war diary, refers to Briand as *in partibus* (*Millerand*, pp. 86, 87).

59 Poincaré, 'Notes journalières', BN nafr 16028, 22 October 1914.

60 *Ibid.*, 28 October 1914.

61 *Ibid.*, 8 November 1914.

62 *Ibid.*, 1 December 1914.

63 *Ibid.*, 20 November, 22 October 1914.

64 *Ibid.*, 1 December 1914.

65 *Ibid.*, 4 November [recte 2 December] 1914.

66 *Ibid.*, 5 December 1914.

67 *Ibid.*, 6 December 1914.

68 *Ibid.*, 22 December 1914.

69 *Ibid.*, 10, 12 December 1914.

70 *Ibid.*, 22 December 1914.

71 Clemenceau's newspaper reverted to its original title of *L'Homme Libre* only when he came to power as premier in November 1917 (Duroselle, *Clemenceau*, pp. 587, 601).

72 Poincaré, 'Notes journalières', BN nafr 16028, 31 December 1914.

73 *Ibid.*, BN nafr 16029, 2 January 1915.

74 G. Samné, *Raymond Poincaré; politique et personnel de la IIIe République* (Paris, 1933), p. 75.

75 Duroselle, *Clemenceau*, pp. 602–3. Duroselle, citing Jean-Claude Allain, says that Clemenceau was a better 'collaborateur bénévole de la *Gazette* que Caillaux'. For the constant criticism of Poincaré in the paper see *ibid.*, pp. 617–18.

76 Persil, *Millerand*, p. 86.

77 Quoted in Wormser, *Septennat de Poincaré*, p. 52; Raoul Persil notes the increasing political attacks against Poincaré from 18 November 1914, and from 9 December 1914 the formation of squabbling political clans for and against Foch and for and against Millerand into which Poincaré was dragged (Persil, *Millerand*, pp. 88, 89–92).

78 For the best account of the international aspects of the conflict, see David Stevenson, *The First World War and international politics* (Oxford, 1988).

79 Wormser, *Septennat de Poincaré*, p. 53 and, in the same, Messimy's description of Poincaré's schoolmasterly conduct of cabinet meetings, (*ibid.*, p. 53).

80 Poincaré, 'Notes journalières', BN nafr 16029, 18 February 1915. When approached by a parliamentary delegation appealing to him to curb the independence of the General Staff, he refused on constitutional grounds, noting, 'Je suis donc forcé de m'accommoder d'une constitution qui évidemment fonctionne encore plus mal en temps de guerre qu'en temps de paix'. And he added, 'Mais tout ce que les ministres font de bien même sous mon influence leur appartient en propre et toutes leurs fautes me sont reprochées. Aimable constitution!' (*ibid.*, BN nafr 16030, 21 May 1915).

81 Poincaré, 'Notes journalières', BN nafr 16029, 14 March 1915. For examples of his technical requests to Millerand, see *ibid.*, 2 April 1915.

82 *Ibid.*, 21 March 1915.

83 *Ibid.*, 14 April 1915.

84 *Ibid.*, BN nafr 16030, 27 May 1915.

85 *Ibid.*, 3, 5 July 1915.

86 *Ibid.*, 5, 14 July 1915; Raoul Persil decried the parliamentary intrigue since December 1914, especially the attacks against his boss, Millerand, who told him that a sign ought to be placarded up everywhere reminding everyone: 'On est en temps de guerre depuis le 3 août 1914', Persil, *Millerand*, p. 93.

87 Poincaré, 'Notes journalières', BN nafr 16030, 5, 9 July 1915.

88 *Ibid.*, 27 July 1915.

89 *Ibid.*, BN nafr 16031, 12 August 1915; Raoul Persil describes Viviani at this time as 'plus nerveux que jamais', and 'de plus en plus indécis', (*Millerand*, pp. 103, 104).

90 T. Zeldin, *France 1848–1945*, vol. I: *Ambition, love and politics* (Oxford, 1973), p. 304; I am grateful to Dr Michel Soin for providing me with details of the various stages, symptoms and progression of the disease.

91 Poincaré, 'Notes journalières', BN nafr 16031, 2 October 1915.

92 *Ibid.*, 5 October 1915.

93 *Ibid.*, 9 October 1915.

94 *Ibid.*, 11 October 1915.

95 *Ibid.*, 14 October 1915; *ibid.*, BN nafr 16032, 16, 17 October 1915. Poincaré was not, however, telling the truth when he told Delcassé that he had always been 'scrupulously loyal' to him, as his own diaries testify.

96 *Ibid.*, BN nafr 16031, 13 October 1915.

97 *Ibid.*, BN nafr 16032, 19 October 1915.

98 *Ibid.*, 23 November 1915.

99 *Ibid.*, BN nafr 16031, 13, 14 October 1915.

100 *Ibid.*, BN nafr 16032, 27 October 1915; also Wormser, *Septennat de Poincaré*, p. 64.

101 Raoul Persil describes in some detail what he refers to as the abominable campaign which had been organised against Millerand and Foch by parliament (Persil, *Millerand*, pp. 89–105).

102 Poincaré, 'Notes journalières', BN nafr 16030, 28 July 1915; Poincaré told the *député* Faure that 'prêt à oublier toutes les attaques personnelles, je verrais sans aucun ennui, Clemenceau ministre, apportant dans un conseil son intelligence et son esprit critique, mais que je redouterais, au ministère de la guerre son impulsivité', *ibid.*, BN nafr 16031, 6 August 1915.

103 Mayeur, *Vie politique*, p. 240.

104 See Poincaré, 'Notes journalières', BN nafr 16030, 20 May 1915.

105 *Ibid.*, BN nafr 16032, 19 November 1915. This average of three cabinet meetings a week is confirmed by the minister of commerce Etienne Clémentel's unpublished notes written during cabinet meetings throughout 1916. Rousseau, 'Le conseil des ministres en 1916', p. 140.

106 Quoted in Samné, *Poincaré*, p. 198

107 Poincaré, 'Notes journalières', BN nafr 16032, 17 November 1915.

108 *Ibid.*, 13 December 1915.

109 *Ibid.*, 17 December 1915.

110 *Ibid.*, 17 December 1915.

111 *Ibid.*, 18 October 1915.

112 *Ibid.*, 26 December 1915.

113 Quoted from Galliéni's *Cahiers* in Persil, *Millerand*, p. 104–5.

114 Wormser, *Septennat de Poincaré*, p. 232.

115 See the photograph in his memoirs of the military staff, Poincaré, *Au service de la France*, vol. X: *Victoire et armistice* (Paris, 1933), p. 112 verso.

116 Quoted in Wormser, *Septennat de Poincaré*, p. 68.

117 Quoted in *ibid.*, p. 71.

118 Mayeur, *Vie politique*, p. 240.

119 Poincaré to Reinach, 11 December 1916, Correspondance de J. Reinach, BN nafr 24884, f. 148.

120 Quoted in P. Miquel, *Poincaré* (Paris, 1961), pp. 360–1

121 Mayeur, *Vie politique*, pp. 241–2.

122 Stevenson, *International politics*, p. 113.

123 For details, see Wormser, *Septennat de Poincaré*, pp. 78–81.

124 Wormser, *Septennat de Poincaré*, pp. 84–5.

125 Generally, J-J. Becker, *The Great War and the french people* (Leamington, 1985).

126 Miquel, *Poincaré*, pp. 362–3.

127 Dr Alexandre Ribot, *Journal de Alexandre Ribot et correspondances inédites, 1914–1922* (Paris, 1936), p. 50.

128 Quoted in Wormser, *Septennat de Poincaré*, p. 146.

129 Ribot, *Journal*, pp. 50–1.

130 See Wormser, *Septennat de Poincaré*, pp. 94–7.

131 Mayeur, *Vie politique*, pp. 243–4.

132 Poincaré, *Au service de la France*, vol. IX: *L'année trouble, 1917* (Paris, 1932), pp. 155, 156; Duroselle, *Grande Guerre*, pp. 202, 298.

133 On the mutinies see Guy Pedroncini, *Les Mutineries de 1917* (Paris, 1967); on the politics, Mayeur, *Vie politique*, pp. 242–4.

134 See Duroselle, *Clemenceau*, pp. 611–12; D. R. Watson, *Georges Clemenceau: a political biography* (London, 1974), pp. 267–8; and on the Sixtus affair, Stevenson, *International politics*, pp. 141–4.

135 Mayeur, *Vie politique*, pp. 245–6.

136 *Ibid.*, pp. 246–7.

137 Quoted in Samné, *Poincaré*, p. 228. Earlier suggestions to this effect in October 1915 are referred to in Poincaré's published memoirs, but there is no trace of this in late October or November 1917.

138 Poincaré, *Au service*, vol. IX, p. 321.

139 Poincaré, 'Notes journalières', BN nafr 16031, 19 August 1915; *ibid.*, BN nafr 16032, 14 December 1915.

140 For the soundings Poincaré took of parliamentarians for a Clemenceau ministry from December 1916 until October 1917 and Poincaré's hesitations, see Duroselle, *Clemenceau*, pp. 625–9; also Poincaré's own account, *Au service*, vol. IX, pp. 366–72; generally on the pros and cons of choosing Clemenceau, see Watson, *Clemenceau*, pp. 268–70.

141 Poincaré, *Au service*, vol. IX, p. 367.

142 *Ibid.*, p. 367. On Friday 16 November 1917 Poincaré notes in his memoirs, 'Je connais trop bien le risque ... Je vois les défauts terribles de Clemenceau, son orgueil immense, sa mobilité, sa légèreté; mais ai-je le droit de l'écarter, alors que, en dehors de lui, je ne puis trouver personne qui réponde aux nécessités de la situation?' (*ibid.*, p. 373).

143 On Poincaré's behaviour over Russia and Caillaux, see Wormser, *Septennat de Poincaré*, pp. 104–15 and 116–26 respectively.

144 Poincaré, *Au service*, vol. IX, p. 370.

145 Mayeur, *Vie politique*, pp. 247–9; Watson, *Clemenceau*, pp. 286–90.

146 Poincaré, *Au service*, vol. IX, p. 371.

147 Poincaré, *Au service*, vol. X, p. 30.

148 Quoted in Miquel, *Poincaré*, p. 374.

149 Poincaré, *Au service*, vol. IX, p. 376.

150 *Ibid.*, p. 379.

151 Poincaré, *Au service*, vol. X, p. 18. See also Poincaré's comment of 29 January 1918: 'Le travail collectif du gouvernement est à peu près réduit à néant. Les ministres voient Clemenceau. Il leur dicte ses volontés' (*ibid.*, p. 28).

152 On relations between the two men, see Duroselle, *Clemenceau*, pp. 651–5; on the organisation of Clemenceau's private office and his cabinet meetings, Watson, *Clemenceau*, pp. 278–9, and Wormser, *Septennat de Poincaré*, p. 196; and Clemenceau's predilection for the conseil de cabinet and his intention to govern alone, Poincaré, *Au service*, vol. IX, pp. 376, 378–83, 391.

153 Quoted in Miquel, *Poincaré*, p. 374.

154 Poincaré, *Au service*, vol. X, p. 68.

155 On this see Watson, *Clemenceau*, pp. 276–81.

156 Poincaré, *Au service*, vol. X, pp. 377–9.

157 *Ibid.*, p. 379.

158 Watson, *Clemenceau*, p. 326. For further details on this difference with Poincaré see below, chapter 8. On French public opinion reflected in the

postal censorship archives analysed by Pierre Renouvin, see Duroselle, *Clemenceau*, p. 709.
159 Duroselle, *Grande Guerre*, pp. 414–16.
160 Quoted in Miquel, *Poincaré*, pp. 376–7.
161 Quoted in *ibid.*, p. 381.
162 Poincaré was probably at his most effective cajoling ministers behind the scenes. For instance, it was Poincaré who prodded Briand into setting up the preparatory machinery in early 1917 which would assemble data for the peace conference. Erik Goldstein, *British diplomatic strategy, peace planning, and the Paris peace conference, 1916–1920* (Oxford, 1991), p. 104.

8. POINCARÉ-LA-PAIX

1 Poincaré, 'Notes journalières', BN nafr 16033, 1 January 1919.
2 Poincaré, *Au service de la France*, vol. X: *Victoire et armistice*, pp. 410, 414.
3 Quotation and statistics from Jean Mettas, 'L'entre-deux-guerres. 1919–1939. Des illusions de la Victoire à la 'drôle de guerre''' in G. Dubuy (ed.), *Histoire de la France* (Paris, 1970), p. 524,
4 See the table of economic indicators in Kenneth Mouré, 'La stabilisation Poincaré: situation politique et politique monétaire entre 1926 et 1928' in *Etudes et Documents* (Comité pour l'histoire économique et financière) 7 (1995), p. 231.
5 Poincaré, *Au service*, vol. X, pp. 413, 423, 424.
6 *Ibid.*, p. 413.
7 Poincaré, 'Notes journalières', BN nafr 16029, 1 February 1915.
8 On the Action française at this time and its relations with Poincaré, see Michel Winock, 'L'Action française' in Michel Winock (ed.), *Histoire de l'extrême droite en France* (Paris, 1993), pp. 138–41; quotation from Eugen Weber, *L'Action française* (Paris, 1985), p. 113 (see also p. 161); for Poincaré's correspondence with Maurras from 1909 to 1924, Pierre-Jean Deschodt (ed.), *Cher Maître ... Lettres à Charles Maurras*, Paris, 1995 and pp. 528–9 showing he did not support him for the Académie.
9 'Address delivered by Raymond Poincaré, lord rector of the University of Glasgow', 13 November 1919 (Paris, 1919), pp. 1–13.
10 Poincaré, *Au service*, vol. X, p. 430. One of the arguments against Clemenceau becoming president, circulated by Briand, was that, given the Tiger's atheism and age, and his hostility to the restoration of relations with the Vatican, France might be forced to bury the president in a purely civil ceremony. The Right therefore preferred Deschanel (R. Persil, *Alexandre Millerand* (Paris, 1949), pp. 129–30).
11 Poincaré, *Au service*, vol. X, pp. 440–5.
12 *Ibid.*, p. 461.
13 For this paragraph, D. Stevenson, *The First World War and international politics* (Oxford, 1988), pp. 113–14, and generally on French war aims the same author's *French war aims against Germany, 1914–19* (Oxford, 1982). See also Georges Soutou, *L'or et le sang. Les buts de guerre économiques de la Première Guerre mondiale* (Paris, 1989), who clearly demonstrates Poincaré's

activity from the beginning of the war in attempting to get French war aims clarified, e.g. pp. 171, 174–7.

14 Poincaré, *Au service de la France* vol. V: *L'invasion, 1914* (Paris, 1928), p. 450.
15 Stevenson, *International politics*, p. 114; Poincaré, *Au service*, vol. V, pp. 517, 522.
16 Quoted in G. Wormser, *Le septennat de Poincaré* (Paris, 1977), p. 86.
17 D. R. Watson, *Georges Clemenceau: a political biography* (London, 1974), p. 335, note 17.
18 For the above quotations and the letters see Wormser, *Septennat de Poincaré*, pp. 142–77; Poincaré, *Au service*, vol. X, pp. 379–85. On the state of public opinion, Pierre Miquel, *La Paix de Versailles et l'opinion publique française* (Paris, 1972), p. 426.
19 Quoted in Anthony Adamthwaite, *Grandeur and misery. France's bid for power in Europe 1914–1940* (London, 1995), p. 43.
20 See Watson, *Clemenceau*, p. 335, especially note 17.
21 *Ibid.*, pp. 332–3.
22 For details of the armistice and the psychology of the Germans and French, see R. Poidevin and J. Bariéty, *Les relations franco-allemandes 1815–1975* (Paris, 1977), pp. 224–8.
23 For the best account of the armistice and Peace Conference, see Stevenson, *International politics*, chs. 5, 6.
24 Poidevin and Bariéty, *Relations franco-allemandes*, pp. 226–7.
25 Adamthwaite, *Grandeur and misery*, pp. 43, 46.
26 Poincaré, 'Notes journalières', BN nafr 16033, 4 January 1919.
27 For the remarkable degree to which Clemenceau retained overall control of French policy and sole responsibility for the French contribution to the peace settlement of 1919, see Watson, *Clemenceau*, pp. 338–41.
28 Poincaré, 'Notes journalières', BN nafr 16033, 9, 8, 17, January 1919.
29 *Ibid.*, 10 February 1919.
30 See, for example, *ibid.*, 26, 27 February; 1, 3, 4 March; *ibid.*, BN nafr 16034, 2 April 1919.
31 *Ibid.*, BN nafr 16034, 3 March 1919.
32 Wormser, *Septennat de Poincaré*, pp. 207–11.
33 See D Stevenson, 'French war aims and the American challenge, 1914–1918', *The Historical Journal* 22(4) (1979) p. 884.
34 Poincaré, 'Notes journalières', BN nafr 16033, 31 March [recte 16 March] 1919; see also Poincaré to Jeanneney, 16 February 1919, quoted in Wormser, *Septennat de Poincaré*, p. 212. On this question, see, J-J. Becker and S. Berstein, *Victoire et frustrations, 1914–1929* (Paris, 1990), pp. 200–1.
35 Poincaré, 'Notes journalières', BN nafr 16033, 12, 16, 1, 14, 18 February 1919; Duroselle, *La Grande Guerre des Français, 1914–1918, L'incompréhensible* (Paris, 1994), pp. 156–8 for French debt.
36 G. Samné, *Raymond Poincaré; politique et personnel de la IIIe République* (Paris, 1933), p. 276.
37 Poincaré, 'Notes journalières', BN nafr 16033, 19 February 1919. He seemed almost pleased at the news that in anarchist meetings 'on ne cesse de demander ma mort', *ibid.*, 23 February 1919. For details of the assassination attempt, see Watson, *Clemenceau*, p. 343.

38 Poincaré, 'Notes journalières', BN nafr 16033, 20 February 1919.
39 *Ibid.*, 23 February 1919.
40 *Ibid.*, 25 February and 4 March 1919.
41 *Ibid.*, 1, 2, 3, 4, March 1919.
42 Stevenson, *International politics*, p. 276.
43 Watson, *Clemenceau*, pp. 340–1.
44 Quoted in P. Miquel, *Poincaré* (Paris, 1961), p. 394.
45 Poincaré, 'Notes journalières', BN nafr 16033, 22, 1, 3, 4, 21 March 1919.
46 *Ibid.*, 24, 27 March 1919. The French representative at the peace confer-
    ence, Léon Bourgeois, had advocated this version of the League without
    success in February 1919. Watson, *Clemenceau*, p. 344.
47 Poincaré, 'Notes journalières', BN nafr 16033, 25 March 1919.
48 *Ibid.*, 27 March 1919.
49 Many independent contemporary accounts corroborate Poincaré's impres-
    sion that Clemenceau was more mellow in his negotiations with Britain and
    America, especially in secret session, than his Tiger image suggested; see
    Watson, *Clemenceau*, pp. 342–3.
50 Poincaré, *Au service de la paix, 1919*, (ed. J. Bariéty and P. Miquel Paris,
    1974), p. 295; Poincaré, 'Notes journalières', BN nafr 16033, 30 March
    1919; *ibid.*, BN nafr 16034, 8 April 1919. See also his apparently sympathetic
    record of the remarks by General Fayolle that the Rhineland should have
    been made autonomous (*ibid.*, 20 May 1919). For the wider picture, see
    Alan Sharp, *The Versailles settlement: peacemaking in Paris* (London, 1991),
    pp. 32, 112.
51 On this see Poidevin and Bariéty, *Relations franco-allemandes*, pp. 229–30.
52 Poincaré, 'Notes journalières', BN nafr 16034, 4 April 1919. Barthou, a
    leading member of the Chamber foreign affairs committee and from July
    1918 rapporteur général of the special Commission des Traités de Paix
    responsible for scrutinising the treaty with Germany, was another important
    critic of Clemenceau's negotiations, R. Young, *Power and pleasure. Louis
    Barthou and the Third French Republic* (Montreal, 1991), pp. 151–64.
53 Poincaré, 'Notes journalières', BN nafr 16034, 6 April 1919.
54 *Ibid.*, 7, 8, 16, 17, 18 April 1919.
55 *Ibid.*, 22 April 1919.
56 On the difference between Poincaré and Clemenceau over the Rhineland,
    see Wormser, *Septennat de Poincaré*, pp. 178–94 and Watson, *Clemenceau*,
    pp. 340–1, 347–53. On the consequences of Clemenceau's government
    failing, Poincaré, 'Notes journalières', BN nafr 16033, 31 March 1919; on
    his defence of Clemenceau, *ibid.*, 22 March 1919 and *ibid.*, BN nafr 16034,
    2, 4 April 1919.
57 Poincaré, 'Notes journalières', BN nafr 16034, 2, 3 May 1919.
58 Watson, *Clemenceau*, p. 356; Poincaré, 'Notes journalières', BN nafr 16034,
    4 May 1919.
59 Poincaré, 'Notes journalières', BN nafr 16034, 5 May 1919.
60 Stevenson, *International politics*, pp. 274–5.
61 *Ibid.*, pp. 274–5.
62 Poincaré, 'Notes journalières', BN nafr 16034, 21 May 1919.
63 *Ibid.*, 29 May 1919.

64 Quoted in Watson, *Clemenceau*, p. 354.
65 Poincaré, 'Notes journalières', BN nafr 16034, 27 May 1919.
66 R. Poincaré, *How France is governed* (trans. B. Miall, London, 1913), pp. 93, 130, 181–2, quoted in William R. Keylor, *Jacques Bainville and the renaissance of royalist history in twentieth-century France* (Baton Rouge, 1979), pp. 75–6.
67 Quoted in Miquel, *Poincaré*, pp. 610–11.
68 Quoted in Keylor, *Bainville*, p. 310; for Poincaré's admiration for Bainville, pp. 74–5.
69 Poincaré, 'Notes journalières', BN nafr 16034, 28 May 1919.
70 Poincaré, 'Notes journalières', BN nafr 16033, 30 March 1919.
71 Stevenson, *International politics*, p. 281.
72 For a compelling explanation of the failure of the international system in the inter-war years from which the above is derived, see Stevenson, *International politics*, pp. 308–24, and Watson, *Clemenceau*, pp. 362–5 for an assessment of the Tiger's share in the blame for the unsatisfactory Versailles peace.
73 Quoted in Wormser, *Septennat de Poincaré*, p. 203.
74 For Clemenceau's insistence on this see Watson, *Clemenceau*, pp. 361–3.
75 On this, see Poidevin and Bariéty, *Relations franco-allemandes*, pp. 234–9.
76 For good analysis of the elections, see J-M. Mayeur, *La vie politique sous la Troisième République* (Paris, 1984), pp. 253–9; Becker and Berstein, *Victoire et frustrations*, pp. 179–80, 186–96, analyses the unjustified negative image of the Bloc national and gives a more reliable picture of the elections; Charles Maier, *Recasting bourgeois Europe: stabilisation in France and Italy after World War I*, (Princeton, 1975), p. 108 stresses that the Radicals portrayed the Bloc as the *Chambre introuvable*.
77 Mayeur, *Vie politique*, pp. 258–9; Watson, *Clemenceau*, pp. 385–6.
78 Mayeur, *Vie politique*, pp. 261–3.
79 Quoted in Wormser, *Septennat de Poincaré*, p. 227.
80 On French policy under Millerand, see Marc Trachtenberg, *Reparation in world politics: France and European economic diplomacy, 1916–1923* (New York, 1980), pp. 119–29, and for Millerand's policy of Franco-German economic collaboration and its continuation under his successor, Leygues, pp. 158–91.
81 This was Barthou's criticism of the commission, Young, *Barthou*, p. 161.
82 Draft of letter from Poincaré to président du conseil, no date [3 April 1920], BN nafr 16827, Letters to François Guionic.
83 Poincaré to François Guionic, 18 May 1920, *ibid*.
84 For Poincaré's hard-line articles in the 'Chronique de la Quinzaine' in the *Revue des Deux Mondes* and subsequent constraints on his policy, see Maier, *Recasting bourgeois Europe*, pp. 272–81.
85 Jules to Paul Cambon, 8 February 1913, letters in the hands of the family. The French ambassador to Berlin, who never really liked Poincaré went on to say 'Il suffit que tu lises le Temps pour t'en apercevoir. Il n'est pas possible qu'il n'y ait pas eu là un calcul misérable et antipatriotique après tout, qui a consisté à jouer du nationalisme pour créer le courant de folie et d'amour, ce plébiscite moral, qui à forcé les votes de l'Assemblée Nationale; et maintenant il fait machine en arrière ... '
86 French legation Bavaria to Quai d'Orsay, 5 April 1921, MAE, Série Europe

1918–1929, sous-série Allemagne, vols. 327–8, Politique intérieure· resp~~~· abilité de la guerre.

87 Consul Nuremberg to Paris, 6 Apill 1921, *ibid.*

88 See the whole series which is composed of 12 cartons (vols. 325–36) spanning the years 1918–29.

89 Renseignement SCR2 (Service Central des Renseignements – French security service), 13 December 1921, MAE, Série Europe 1918–1929, sous-série Allemagne, vols. 327–8.

90 Quoted in Miquel, *Poincaré*, p. 422.

91 On Briand's policy see Poidevin and Bariéty, *Relations franco-allemandes*, pp. 247–9.

92 On Briand's policy on reparations and his fall, see Trachtenberg, *Reparation*, pp. 213–36; on the constraints on Briand's freedom of manoeuvre, see Maier, *Recasting bourgeois Europe*, pp. 278–80; on Poincaré's opposition to it, see B. Kent, *The spoils of war. The politics, economics, and diplomacy of reparations 1918–1932* (Oxford, 1989), pp. 166–8.

9. POINCARÉ-LA-RUHR

1 J-J. Becker and S. Berstein, *Victoire et frustrations 1914–1929* (Paris, 1990), p. 198.

2 28 per cent held the offices simultaneously from 1871 to 1918. See Hayward, *Governing France: the One and Indivisible French Republic* (2nd edn, London, 1987), p. 243

3 J-M. Mayeur, *La vie politique sous la Troisième République* (Paris, 1984), pp. 259–69.

4 M. Trachtenberg, *Reparation in World politics: France and European economic diplomacy, 1916–1923* (New York, 1980), p. 237.

5 *Ibid.*, p. 209.

6 J. Laroche, *Au Quai d'Orsay avec Briand et Poincaré, 1913–1926* (Paris, 1957), p. 146.

7 Bergmann to Simons, 17 Dec 1920; Mayer to Auswärtiges Amt, 16 December 1920, both quoted in Trachtenberg, *Reparation*, pp. 174–5. See also the articles in the press by Poincaré and Tardieu to this effect in *ibid.*, p. 174 note 59.

8 R. Poincaré, *A la recherche de la paix 1919* (ed. J. Bariéty and P. Miquel, Paris, 1974), p. 35; Cheysson, 'Conversation avec M. Poincaré, le 8 janvier 1921', MAE, Millerand Papers, vol. 46; both quoted in Trachtenberg, *Reparation*, p. 175.

9 For examples of the institutional incoherence and conflicting advice, see Jon Jacobson, 'Strategies of French foreign policy after World War I', *Journal of Modern History* 55(1) (1983), pp. 86–7. C. Maier, *Recasting bourgeois Europe: stabilisation in France and Italy after World War I* (Princeton, 1975), p. 281 stresses the parliamentary constraints and remarks: 'Poincaré was to discover that the possibilities for firmness were as limited as those of appeasement'.

10 See J. Jolly, *Dictionnaire des parlementaires français. Notices biographiques sur les ministres, députés et sénateurs français de 1889 à 1940* (Paris, 1960), vol. I, pp. 62–91.

11 Laroche, *Au Quai*, p. 189.

12 Jean Giraudoux, *Bella* (Paris, 1926 edn).

13 For Claudel's stinging attack on Poincaré for his hypocritical anti-clericalism in 1912, entitled 'Les plaisirs de M. Poincaré', see Christopher Flood, *Pensée politique et imagination historique dans l'œuvre de Paul Claudel* (Paris, 1991), pp. 70–1, and other accounts of his detestation of Poincaré, links to Berthelot and support for a Franco-German *rapprochement*, pp. 162, 196–8.

14 At Berthelot's death the newspaper *Aux Ecoutes* noted on 1 December 1934: 'On a prétendu qu'il aimait Briand et admirait sa politique. La vérité est qu'avec Aristide au Quai d'Orsay, Berthelot était le maître absolu de la politique étrangère de la France, alors qu'avec Poincaré il devait discuter. Ce fut la seule raison de son attachement à Briand.' Berthelot 'était reconnaissant à Briand de l'avoir tiré de l'abîme où Poincaré l'avait précipité'. MAE, Série dossiers personnel, 2e série, sous-série Philippe Berthelot, vol. 39.

15 On the ideas for an international solution to reparations, see Trachtenberg, *Reparation*, pp. 44–5. On the main thrust of French foreign policy during these years followed here, see *ibid.*, pp. vii–xi.

16 See Trachtenberg, *Reparation*; Maier, *Recasting bougeois Europe*, p. 355; Stephen Schuker, *The end of French predominance in Europe. The financial crisis of 1924 and the adoption of the Dawes Plan* (Chapel Hill, 1976), pp. 18–19; the director of the Quai in 1924, Jules Laroche, remarked of Millerand that he had 'vues plus lointaines que celles de Poincaré, d'avantage le goût du risque'. (Laroche, *Au Quai*, p. 129).

17 Poincaré, 'Notes journalières', BN nafr 16027, 16 July 1914.

18 C. Laurent to foreign minister, 1 January 1922, telegrams 2738–40, 2744, 2746, MAE, Europe 1918–29, sous-série, Allemagne, vols. 327–8, Politique intérieure: responsabilité de la guerre.

19 Albéric Neton to Poincaré, 23 January 1922, MAE, Europe 1918–40, sous-série, Allemagne, vol. 328.

20 Underlined in the original. Note by Direction des affaires politiques, 31 January 1922, with Poincaré's minuted reply. MAE Europe 1918–40, sous-série, Allemagne, vol. 328. Copy of Poincaré's reply in his dispatch to the French minister in Norway, *ibid.*, 2 February 1922.

21 Consul general in Württemberg, 20 January 1922, copied to main embassies, *ibid.*

22 Tirard to Poincaré, 1 March 1922, *ibid.*

23 Tirard to Poincaré, 28 March 1922, forwarding extract of report by the Délégué de la Haute Commission dans le Cercle de Trèves, *ibid.*

24 Bordereau d'envoi, Sous direction Europe, Quai d'Orsay, 22 May 1922, copy of Reichstag budget for propaganda, extract from Reichstag Aktenstück no. 3753, 8 May 1922, MAE Europe 1918–40, sous-série, Allemagne, vol. 408, Propagande allemande 1 April–31 December 1922; Renseignement, SCR 2, 29 June 1922, *ibid.*; German propaganda abroad, 4 July 1922, *ibid.*; Renseignement, SCR2, Subsidies to Pangermanists by major industrialists, 5 July 1922, *ibid.*

25 French consul Königsburg to Poincaré, 12 September 1922, *ibid.*; see also examples of the anti-Poincaré propaganda distributed by the Comité actif des syndicats allemands, Berlin, to factories in the Frankfurt area violently

attacking Poincaré for his pre-war policies entitled 'Un des principaux coupables de Guerre démasqué. L'affaire Poincaré' (translated from the German), Tirard to Poincaré, 20 April 1922, *ibid.*

26 See the German documents referred to in Schuker, *End of French predominance*, p. 22 note 27

27 Henri Allizé to Poincaré, 31 March 1922, MAE Europe 1918–40, Allemagne, vol. 328.

28 R. Marchand (ed.), *Un livre noir: diplomatie d'avant guerre d'après les documents des archives russes (1910–1917)* (Paris, 1922–3).

29 A. Ribot, *Journal de Alexandre Ribot et correspondances inédites, 1914–1922* (Paris, 1936), pp. 298–9, 301.

30 G. Samné, *Poincaré; politique et personnel de la IIIe République* (Paris, 1933), p. 296.

31 See Trachtenberg, *Reparation*, pp. 237–8.

32 See Tirard to Poincaré, 15 March 1922; Laurent to Poincaré, 16 March 1922, Europe 1918–29, Allemagne, vol. 386, Politique Etrangère. Relations avec la France.

33 Newspaper cutting dated 30 March 1922 translation in Albéric Neton (consul general, Hamburg) to Poincaré, 31 March 1922, Europe 1918–29, Allemagne, vol. 386.

34 Niall Ferguson, *Paper and iron. Hamburg business and German politics in the era of inflation, 1897–1927* (Cambridge, 1995), pp. 358–9, and for further details of Keynes's influence on, and support for, German policy, pp. 226, 368–9.

35 Poincaré to Millerand, 12 April 1922, MAE, Papiers d'agent, Archives privées (AP) 118 Millerand, vol. 81.

36 Trachtenberg, *Reparation*, p. 234.

37 Quoted in A. Adamthwaite, *Grandeur and misery. France's bid for power in Europe 1914–1940* (London, 1995), p. 74.

38 Laroche, *Au Quai*, p. 169.

39 Quoted in Adamthwaite, *Grandeur and misery*, p. 71.

40 Gwynne to Derby, 16 January 1922, Gwynne MSS 22, quoted in Keith M. Wilson, *A study in the history and politics of the Morning Post 1905–1926*, Studies in British History vol. 23 (Lampeter, 1990), p. 196. Raoul Persil quotes at length a telegram (7 January 1922?) from Millerand to Briand in Cannes, warning that both he, Millerand, and the cabinet were insisting that 'Une alliance franco-britannique ne peut avoir pour base que l'égalité absolue entre les deux contractants et pour objet que l'exécution intégrale des traités'. Poincaré had had Millerand's view endorsed by the Commission des Affaires Etrangères, of which he was president, and had telegraphed Briand to that effect, R. Persil, *Alexandre Millerand* (Paris, 1949), pp. 143, 147.

41 Wilson, *Morning Post*, pp. 195–7; Laroche, *Au Quai*, pp. 154, 156.

42 J. F. V. Keiger, *France and the origins of the First World War* (London, 1983), p. 110–16.

43 For details of Poincaré's attempts to break the diplomatic deadlock with Britain, Germany and the United States, see Walter A. McDougal, *France's Rhineland diplomacy, 1914–1924. The last bid for a balance of power in Europe* (Princeton, 1978), ch. 5.

44 Laroche, *Au Quai*, p. 169.
45 On the divisions over a pact with the French in the British political establish-ment, see Wilson, *Morning Post*, ch. 7; good examples of the French under-standing of the importance of British friendship are to be found with Barthou, who was no Anglophile, and Clemenceau, in R. Young, *Power and Pleasure. Louis Barthou and the Third French Republic* (Montreal, 1991), pp. 162–4 and D. R. Watson, *Clemenceau: a political biography* (London, 1974), pp. 388–9 respectively. For Lloyd George and Poincaré's mutual provocation, see Maier, *Recasting bourgeois Europe*, p. 281.
46 Maier, *Recasting bourgeois Europe*, p. 281; Laroche, *Au Quai*, pp. 156–7. On Barthou's role see Young, *Barthou*, pp. 168–73.
47 Poincaré to Millerand, 20 and 22 April 1922, AP 118 Millerand, vol. 81.
48 Poincaré to Head of the French delegation, Genoa, 13 April 1922, *ibid.*, vol. 82.
49 For the disagreement between Poincaré and Barthou over Genoa, see Young, *Barthou*, pp. 167–73.
50 Poincaré to Millerand, 26 April 1922, AP 118 Millerand, vol. 81.
51 Peretti de la Rocca (political director at the Quai d'Orsay) to Millerand, 26 April 1922, *ibid.*
52 Laroche, *Au Quai*, pp. 156–7; for a sympathetic interpretation of France's frustration at Genoa, see Maier, *Recasting bourgeois Europe*, p. 285.
53 Laroche, *Au Quai*, p. 157.
54 Wilson, *Morning Post*, p. 197.
55 Trachtenberg, *Reparation*, pp. 243–5.
56 Poincaré continued to believe in the merits of closer Franco-British relations. In early August 1922 at the reparations conference in London, on hearing that the American banker Morgan had stated that a loan to Germany would only be possible if the Franco-British entente remained solid, Poincaré stated his agreement and remarked that 'si l'Entente se trouvait menacée ou affaiblie, la sécurité de l'Europe et du monde entier en serait compromise'. Minutes of 10 Downing Street meeting with Lloyd George, Balfour and Sir Robert Horne, 7 August 1922, MAE, Série AP-PA, AP 118 Millerand, vol. 50, pp. 1, 9.
57 C. M. Andrew, *Secret service. The making of the British intelligence community* (London, 1986), pp. 375, 423–4.
58 Saint Aulaire to Poincaré, 4 May 1922, MAE Europe 1918–29, Allemagne, vol. 386.
59 For reports on German desires for a Franco-German *rapprochement*, see, for example, French Consul Brême to Poincaré, 13 May 1922; French Consul Düsseldorf to Poincaré, 15 May 1922; minute by Quai, 7 June 1922; Laurent (ambassador to Berlin) to Poincaré, 22 June 1922; all in Europe 1918–40, Allemagne, vol. 386. For evidence of the power and financing of German propaganda, see for example Tirard to Poincaré, 20 April 1922; 'Bordereau d'envoi' from the sous-direction d'Europe on Reichstag credits voted for propaganda purposes, 22 May 1922; the many SCR reports for 1922; all in Europe 1918–40, Allemagne, vol. 408, 'Propagande allemande 1/4 – 31/12/1922'.
60 Poincaré explained that the Quai d'Orsay, having 'lost' the German code at

the end of 1911, had broken it again during the war under Clemenceau (R. Poincaré, *Comment fut déclarée la guerre de 1914* (Paris, 1939), pp. 150–1); Christopher Andrew suggests that the French *cabinet noir* was reading German diplomatic traffic in the 1920s, *Secret service*, p. 375.

61 Quoted in Young, *Barthou*, p. 170.
62 On the details of Poincaré's position during this period, see Trachtenberg, *Reparation*, pp. 245–51; B. Kent, *The spoils of war. The politics, economics, and diplomacy of reparations 1918–1932* (Oxford, 1989), pp. 181–2.
63 French embassy in London to French foreign ministry, 8 August 1922, AP 118 Millerand, vol. 50; 'Minutes of meeting 10 Downing Street' between Poincaré, Lloyd George, Balfour and Sir Robert Horne, in AP 118 Millerand, vol. 50, p. 20.
64 For details of Germany's position, see Kent, *Spoils of war*, pp. 191–7; Schuker, *End of French predominance*, p. 23.
65 For details of Poincaré's readiness to proceed with occupation, see Trachtenberg, *Reparation*, pp. 251–4; Young, *Barthou*, p. 174. For the dilemmas confronting Poincaré and other leaders over reparations, Maier, *Recasting bourgeois Europe*, p. 288–90.
66 Maier, *Recasting bourgeois Europe*, pp. 289–90.
67 *Ibid.*, p. 291.
68 Quoted in *ibid.*, pp. 254–5. See also Paul Guinn, 'On throwing ballast in foreign policy: Poincaré, the Entente and the Ruhr', *European History Quarterly* 18 (1988), pp. 430–1; Kent, *Spoils of war*, pp. 186–9.
69 Paul Cambon, *Correspondance, 1870–1924* (ed. H. Cambon, 3 vols., Paris, 1940–6), vol. III, pp. 413–15, quoted in Kent, *Spoils of war*, p. 190.
70 Hardinge to Curzon, 5 May 1922, Derby to Curzon, 16 July 1920, India Office Library, Curzon MSS Eur. F 112/200, 198, quoted in C. Andrew and A. S. Kanya-Forstner, *France overseas, the Great War and the climax of French imperial expansion* (London, 1981), p. 240.
71 Andrew, *Secret service*, pp. 423–4; Wilson, *Morning Post*, pp. 193–4.
72 8 September 1922, 'Secret letters of James A. Logan Jr. The reparation question' (10 vols.; typescript, Hoover Institution, Stanford), cited in Kent, *Spoils of war*, p. 191.
73 Jacques Bardoux, *Le socialisme au pouvoir, l'expérience de 1924* (Firmin-Didiot, 1930), p. 186, quoted in Jean-Noël Jeanneney, *Leçon d'histoire pour une gauche au pouvoir. La faillite du Cartel 1924–1926* (Paris, 1977), p. 115.
74 Comte de Saint Aulaire, *Confession d'un vieux diplomate* (Paris, 1953), p. 698, quoted in Jeanneney, *Leçon d'histoire*, pp. 115–16.
75 Minutes of Allied meeting in London, 7 August 1922, AP 118 Millerand, vol. 50, p. 97; Trachtenberg, *Reparation*, p. 271.
76 For what follows, I have followed the convincing analysis of Trachtenberg, *Reparation*, pp. 259–89.
77 Modern scholarship does not argue that Poincaré went into the Ruhr intent on making it and the Rhineland into an economic and political satellite of France, even though this may have been the desire of a number of his officials. For a concise summary of differing conceptions and motives for a separate Rhineland and Ruhr to be exploited directly by France as an economic bloc isolated from Germany, with a separate currency, all

supported by local leaders, see, Jacobson, 'Strategies of French foreign policy', pp. 87–9.

78 For details of the plot, see Wilson, *Morning Post*, pp. 198–200.

79 According to the minutes of the London conference for 9 December 1922, Poincaré stated that he would accept a moratorium on German reparations for two to three years if Germany were given a loan to ease its financial position. MAE, Série Y, Internationale 1918–40, vol. 687, pp. 49–50.

80 See the letter from Poincaré to Millerand, 22 December 1922, in Michael Carley, 'The shoe on the other foot: a letter from Raymond Poincaré to Alexandre Millerand, December 1922', *Canadian Journal of History* 26(3), (December 1991), pp. 583–7.

81 Cab. 23/26, 15 July 1922, quoted in Guinn, 'On throwing ballast', p. 428. For similar British views see Kent, *Spoils of war*, pp. 190–1; Kent, though agreeing with Trachtenberg about Poincaré's lack of fixity of purpose in wishing to occupy the Ruhr, seems to share the contemporary 'Anglo-American' lack of sympathy for the French cause and its premier in particular, describing Poincaré as 'launching his nation into a self-indulgent act of criminal folly', *ibid.*, pp. 197–202. Young, *Barthou*, pp. 174–5 gives further evidence of Britain's unco-operative attitude and disingenuousness in the international reparations commission.

82 Schuker, *End of French predominance*, pp. 20–1.

83 J. Chastenet, *Raymond Poincaré* (Paris, 1948), p. 245.

84 André François-Poncet, 'Poincaré tel que je l'ai vu', in *Le Figaro Littéraire*, 26 June 1948, quoted in R. Persil, *Alexandre Millerand* (Paris, 1949), p. 149. Persil, though disagreeing that he was pushed into it, believes that he was seriously torn over the decision (see p. 150). Millerand, in his unpublished memoirs, claimed to have pushed Poincaré into the Ruhr (Millerand 'Mes Souvenirs (1859–1941), MS. p. 114 cited in Maier, *Recasting bourgeois Europe*, p. 292, note 136). Barthou, chairman of the international reparations commission, who had not always seen eye to eye with Poincaré, justified the occupation (Young, *Barthou*, pp. 175–6).

85 Schuker, *End of French predominance*, pp. 23–4; quote in Trachtenberg, *Reparation*, p. 288.

86 For a summary of some of the new interpretations of French foreign policy which have emerged since the 1970s, see the review articles by Jon Jacobson, 'Is there a new international history of the 1920s?' in the *American Historical Review* 88 (1983), pp. 617–45 and also his 'Strategies of French Foreign Policy', pp. 78–95; Guinn, 'On throwing ballast', pp. 427–37; Kent, *Spoils of war*, pp. 205–8 provides much support for the modern interpretation, but remains hostile to Poincaré the 'Germanophobic Lorrainer'; J. Bariéty, *Les relations franco-allemandes après la première guerre mondiale, 10 novembre 1918 – 10 janvier 1925: de l'exécution à la négociation* (Paris, 1977), pp. 118–20, 265, 274 depicts the Ruhr episode as a concerted attempt by France to establish a long-term Franco-German coal and steel complex dominated by her, but depicts Poincaré as moderate and flexible over the occupation.

87 N. Ferguson, *Paper and iron. Hamburg business and German politics in the era of inflation, 1897–1927* (Cambridge, 1995), p. 368.

88 Trachtenberg, *Reparation*, pp. 291–5.

89 Trachtenberg, *Reparation*, p. 301 and Maier, *Recasting bourgeois Europe*, pp. 392–3, especially for Poincaré's restraint and hesitation during the Ruhr occupation.

90 Trachtenberg, *Reparation*, pp. 301–5; Mayeur, *Vie politique*, pp. 265–6; Kent, *Spoils of war*, p. 214, mistakenly suggests that Poincaré's policy was dependent on 'a mixed bag of nationalist, militarist, and annexationist supporters'.

91 On this episode, see the fascinating account in Wilson, *Morning Post*, ch. 7, 'Making Germany pay: Gwynne's conspiracy against Lord Curzon'.

92 All quoted in Wilson, *Morning Post*, pp. 200–4; for examples of Curzon's and other British decision-makers' suspicions of France, dating back to 1918, see A. Sharp, *The Versailles settlement: peacemaking in Paris* (London, 1991), p. 191.

93 For details see Wilson, *Morning Post*, pp. 200–8; for the analysis, pp. 208–11.

94 *Ibid.*, pp. 211–16.

95 Margerie to minister, 3 August (telegs. 1141, 1142) and 12 August (telegs. 1014–21) 1923, MAE Papiers de Margerie, PA AP 113, vol. 8, embassy in Germany, political and commercial correspondence July 1923 – December 1924.

96 Margerie to Minister, 24 August 1923 (telegs. 1095–7), *ibid.*

97 Margerie to Minister, 27 August 1923 (telegs. 1057–61), *ibid.*

98 Margerie to Minister, 4 September 1923 (telegs. 1143–53), *ibid.*

99 For further examples of this, see Margerie to Minister, 23 August, 3 and 9 September 1923, *ibid.*

100 Maier, *Recasting bourgeois Europe*, pp. 390–3.

101 Margerie to Poincaré, 10 September 1923, MAE Papiers de Margerie, PA AP 113, vol. 8, embassy in Germany, political and commercial correspondence July 1923 – December 1924.

102 Margerie to Poincaré, 10 September 1923, (très confidentiel), *ibid.*

103 Schuker, *End of French predominance*, p. 26.

104 Margerie to Poincaré, 22 October 1923, MAE Papiers de Margerie, PA AP 113, vol. 8, embassy in Germany, political and commercial correspondence July 1923 – December 1924.

105 Laroche, *Au Quai*, p. 181.

106 Trachtenberg, *Reparation*, pp. 320–6.

107 Guinn, 'On throwing ballast', pp. 432–4.

108 On this Jacobson, 'Strategies of French foreign policy, pp. 89–90.

109 Maier, *Recasting bourgeois Europe*, p. 395; Chastenet, *Poincaré*, p. 249 and Persil, *Millerand*, p. 153, are of the same opinion. For other interpretations of Poincaré's intentions after the end of passive resistance see Jacobson, 'Strategies of French foreign policy', pp. 89–92.

110 Quoted in Chastenet, *Poincaré*, pp. 249–50.

111 He expressed this in his unpublished memoirs; see Jeanneney, *L'argent caché. Milieux d'affaires et pouvoirs politiques dans la France du XXe siècle* (Paris, 1981), p. 198 note 9; for Millerand and Foch's attempts to convince Poincaré of the need to seize this opportunity to impose a Franco-German deal and Poincaré's desire to get back to applying the Versailles Treaty, see Persil, *Millerand*, pp. 152–3. Persil believes, with some hyperbole, that had

Poincaré followed the course of action suggested by Millerand and Foch, the Second World War would have been averted, p. 154. Maier, *Recasting bourgeois Europe*, pp. 406–8 for Poincaré's reluctance to exploit France's advantage.

112 For Poincaré's political calculations, see Maier, *Recasting bourgeois Europe*, pp. 410–13.

113 Mayeur, *Vie politique*, pp. 265–7; Persil, *Millerand*, pp. 140, 157; Maier, *Recasting bourgeois Europe*, pp. 403–6, 411–13, 470–1.

114 For the above, the real impact of the new taxes and the position of the Radicals vis-à-vis Poincaré, see Maier, *Recasting*, pp. 465–72.

115 Jeanneney, *L'argent caché*, pp. 195, 199–201; for details of the international speculation against the franc, see Schuker, *End of French predominance*, pp. 92–108.

116 For details of the operation and the predominantly German, Austrian and Dutch financial institutions which got their fingers burnt during the counter-attack in favour of the franc, see Jeanneney, *L'argent caché*, pp. 223–7; also Maier, *Recasting bourgeois Europe*, pp. 459–62.

117 Mayeur, *Vie politique*, pp. 273–5.

118 *Ibid.*, pp. 273–5.

119 Quoted in Jeanneney, *Leçon d'histoire*, p. 115.

120 Maier, *Recasting bourgeois Europe*, pp. 459, 474–5.

121 François-Marsal quoted in *ibid.*, p. 471.

122 Mayeur, *Vie politique*, pp. 274–5. Not surprisingly, given that he was Millerand's closest collaborator, Raoul Persil suggests that it was an old parliamentary tradition that the head of government should intervene just before elections in favour of the outgoing majority. He says that Poincaré did not do this because 'Il lui répugnait de prendre la responsabilité de défendre devant le pays la Chambre du Bloc National', on the basis that he did not wish to upset Herriot and Léon Blum. This then forced Millerand to speak in favour of the Bloc national; Persil, *Millerand*, pp. 157–8. Since stepping down as president of the Republic, Poincaré's views about a strong presidential role had mollified, as his row with President Millerand in December 1922 demonstrated (see Poincaré to Millerand, 16 December 1922, in Carley, 'The shoe on the other foot', pp. 583–7).

123 Maier, *Recasting bourgeois Europe*, pp. 477–8.

124 Poincaré attempted to dissuade Millerand from addressing a message to parliament which amounted to a vote of confidence in the president and which he lost. Persil presents Poincaré's role in this episode as almost treacherous (*Millerand*, pp. 161–5).

125 On those historians who have recently made this point, see Jacobson, 'Strategies of French foreign policy', pp. 85–93; Trachtenberg, *Reparation*, pp. 331–5. One also begins to wonder whether French interception of other powers' diplomatic traffic had something to do with such swings in direction, especially as Poincaré had, since 1912, a track record for relying heavily on such information.

126 Quoted in Trachtenberg, *Reparation*, p. 335. For criticism of Poincaré's failure to use the Ruhr victory, see Maier, *Recasting bourgeois Europe*, pp. 413–14.

127 Jacobson, 'Strategies of French foreign policy', p. 83.
128 This is, of course, the criticism made of him by the Right, especially in its most extreme guise, the Action française. See in general the virulent criticism by Charles Maurras, Jacques Bainville and in particular Alphonse Daudet, *Le nain de Lorraine*. *Raymond Poincaré* (Paris, 1930), p. 25: 'Poincaré ruhrien de 1923, est devenu locarnien de 1926'.

10. POINCARÉ-LE-FRANC

1 Quoted in Jean Doise and Maurice Vaïsse, *Diplomatie et outil militaire, 1871–1991* (Paris, 1992), p. 337.
2 J-L. Robert and J. M. Winter, 'Conclusions' in J. M. Winter and J-L. Robert (eds.), *Paris, London, Berlin 1914–1919: capital cities at war* (Cambridge, 1997), p. 543.
3 F. Payen, *Raymond Poincaré, chez lui, au parlement, au palais* (Paris, 1936), pp. 410–11; G. Samné, *Raymond Poincaré; politique et personnel de la IIIe République* (Paris, 1933), pp. 74–5.
4 Jules Laroche, *Au Quai d'Orsay avec Briand et Poincaré 1913–1926* (Paris, 1957), p. 166.
5 For the higher proportion of middle-class 'dead, missing and wounded (by occupation)' during the war, see J-J. Becker, *The Great War and the French People* (Leamington, 1985), table C, p. 332.
6 On Herriot's strategic errors regarding *inter alia* the 'mur d'argent', see J-N. Jeanneney, *Leçon d'histoire pour une gauche au pouvoir. La faillite du Cartel 1924–1926* (Paris, 1977), p. 141.
7 Jon Lawrence, 'Material pressures on the middle classes' in Winter and Robert, *Paris, London, Berlin*, p. 251; C. Maier, *Recasting bourgeois Europe: stabilisation in France and Italy after World War I* (Princeton, 1975), p. 43.
8 Quoted in J. Mettas, 'L'entre-deux-guerres 1919–1939. Des illusions de la Victoire à la "drôle de guerre"' in G. Duby (ed.), *Histoire de la France* (Paris, 1970), p. 536.
9 For the war years, see for instance the Professional Classes War Relief Council in Britain, and figures on middle-class incomes in Lawrence, 'Material pressures on the middle classes', p. 246.
10 Preface by Jacques Rueff in Emile Moreau, *Souvenirs d'un gouverneur de la Banque de France. Histoire de la stabilisation du franc (1926–1928)* (Paris, 1954), p. vi.
11 The fall of Herriot's government and Poincaré's return to power in 1926 led to the temporary eclipsing of Taittinger's 'Jeunesses Patriotes'. Poincaré's success in restoring French finances and the franc temporarily diminished the impact of many of the extra-parliamentary extreme Right 'ligues'. See Pierre Milza, 'L'ultra-droite des années trente' in Michel Winock (ed.), *Histoire de l'extrême droite en France* (Paris, 1993), pp. 159, 163–4.
12 Figures from P. Miquel, *Poincaré* (Paris, 1961), pp. 489–505; see also the table of French economic indicators 1920–30 in Kenneth Mouré, 'La stabilisation Poincaré: situation politique et politique monétaire entre 1926

et 1928', in *Etudes et Documents* (Comité pour l'histoire économique et financière) 7, (1995), p. 231.

13 Kenneth Mouré, *Managing the franc Poincaré. Economic understanding and political constraint in French monetary policy, 1928–1936* (Cambridge, 1991), p. 11; B. Kent, *The spoils of war. The politics, economics, and diplomacy of reparations 1918–1932* (Oxford, 1989), pp. 19–20. The best expert on French finance policy at the time wrote in 1919 that 'France's financial policy during the war will always be a model of what not to do' (quoted in François Caron, *An economic history of modern France* (London, 1979), p. 248).

14 Lawrence, 'Material pressures on the middle classes', p. 233.

15 Caron, *Economic history of France*, pp. 250–1; Jeanneney, *Leçon d'histoire*, p. 32; Mettas, 'L'entre-deux-guerres', pp. 525–7.

16 J-M. Mayeur, *La vie politique sous la Troisième République* (Paris, 1984), p. 282; quotation from D. B. Goldey, 'The disintegration of the Cartel des Gauches and the politics of French government finance, 1924–28' (unpublished D.Phil. dissertation, Oxford University, 1962), p. 3, and pp. 1–16 for the political problems associated with French public finance.

17 For details of the Dawes Plan and its philosophy, see R. Poidevin and J. Bariéty, *Les relations franco-allemandes, 1815–1975*, (Paris, 1977), pp. 263–4.

18 *Ibid.*, p. 264; Jeanneney, *Leçon d'histoire*, pp. 44–5 and generally for his condemnation of Herriot, pp. 53–7.

19 Jeanneney, *Leçon d'histoire*, p. 46.

20 *Ibid.*, p. 52.

21 Poidevin and Bariéty, *Relations franco–allemandes*, p. 265.

22 Laroche, *Au Quai*, p. 215. Dr Samné also stresses that Poincaré actively supported Briand's policy of *détente* with Germany (*Poincaré*, p. 337).

23 Press cutting from *Jours Nouveaux*, 'Adieu à mon ami', by Léon Bailby, MAE, Personnel dossiers, 2e série, Philippe Berthelot, vol. 39.

24 *Ibid.*

25 Wladimir d'Ormesson (former French ambassador), *Le Figaro*, 23 November 1934, explained how the Secretary General's powers had increased and that 'Il en est résulté un certain trouble dans le fonctionnement normal du service diplomatique qui n'est pas sans inconvénient' (*ibid.*).

26 Laroche, *Au Quai*, p. 227.

27 Samné, *Poincaré*, pp. 337–8.

28 Poidevin and Bariéty, *Relations franco-allemandes*, pp. 266–9.

29 Quotations from Laroche, *Au Quai*, pp. 214–15.

30 For details of the political and financial collapse of the Cartel, see Maier, *Recasting*, pp. 500–5; on Cartel finance S. Schuker, *The end of French predominance in Europe. The financial crisis of 1924 and the adoption of the Dawes Plan* (Chapel Hill, 1976), pp. 124–68; J-J. Becker, and S. Berstein, *Victoire et frustrations, 1914–1929* (Paris, 1990), pp. 264–77.

31 On the break-up of the Cartel and Poincaré's coming to power, see Goldey, 'Disintegration of the Cartel', pp. ix–x; Mayeur, *Vie politique*, p. 284.

32 Quoted in Miquel, *Poincaré*, pp. 543–4; Maier, *Recasting*, p. 505.

33 J. Jolly (ed.), *Dictionnaire des parlementaires français. Notices biographiques sur les ministres, députés et senateurs français de 1889 à 1940*, vol. I (Paris, 1960).

34 All quoted in Mayeur, *Vie politique*, pp. 284–5; Becker and Berstein, *Victoire et frustrations*, pp. 278–9.

35 Ministère de l'économie et des finances, *Les ministres des finances de 1870 à nos jours* (Paris, 1992), pp. 57, 268.

36 Moreau, *Souvenirs*, 23 July 1926, p. 40 and Rueff preface p. vii.

37 Miquel, *Poincaré*, pp. 542–98 still provides a good account of this period; for the most up to date analysis of all the secondary work on the stabilisation, see the excellent article by Mouré, 'Stabilisation Poincaré', pp. 229–65. I am grateful to Kenneth Mouré for comments on this chapter.

38 Moreau, *Souvenirs*, 3 July 1926, p. 15.

39 *Ibid.*, p. 52.

40 *Ibid.*, p. 57.

41 See, for instance, R. Poincaré, *L'œuvre financière et économique du Gouvernement. Discours prononcé à la Chambre des Députés par Monsieur Raymond Poincaré 2 et 3 février 1928* (Paris, 1928), pp. 22–4, 26; Samné, *Poincaré*, p. 315.

42 Miquel, *Poincaré*, p. 566; see, for instance, the personnel director of the ministry of finance's circular of 18 October 1926 calling for greater productivity and for reductions in internal spending, Archives Economiques et Financières of ministry of finance AEF, Fonds Administration Générale, B 13382; Samné, *Poincaré*, p. 332.

43 J. Chastenet, *Poincaré*, p. 269.

44 On the Caisse, Mouré, *Franc Poincaré*, p. 283.

45 For detailed descriptions of the different pieces of legislation passed and accounts of Poincaré's performance in parliament, see AEF, B 33970, Fonds Administration Générale, Bureau du Cabinet, Dossier 'Projet de loi tendant à la révision des lois constitutionnelles'; B 13382, Fonds Administration Générale, Bureau du Cabinet, Dossier 'Travaux législatifs, vote du Budget: procédure d'urgence, 1926, 1932, 1934'.

46 For the Treasury's account of how this consolidation of the public debt was carried out from 1926 to 1927, see AEF, B 32335, Fonds Trésor, Bulletins mensuels de la DGMF, Bulletin no. 11, 20 January 1928, Annex 2, 'Note sur la dette publique', pp. 1–2.

47 Becker and Berstein, *Victoire et frustrations*, p. 282.

48 Moreau, *Souvenirs*, pp. 57, 70.

49 Quoted in Miquel, *Poincaré*, p. 567.

50 Moreau, *Souvenirs*, 27 July 1928, p. 46.

51 Payelle had been seconded to Poincaré as *chef de cabinet* when Poincaré had been finance minister in 1894 and education minister in 1893. See *Annuaire général des finances* for 1927.

52 Miquel, *Poincaré*, pp. 568–72; Maier, *Recasting bourgeois Europe*, p. 507.

53 See above, chapter 6; André Barjonet, *La CGT. Histoire, structure, doctrine* (Paris, 1968), pp. 21, 25–6; Becker and Berstein, *Victoire et frustrations*, p. 357.

54 Jacques Rueff preface to Moreau, *Souvenirs*, pp. viii–ix. Moreau is not convinced of Jouhaux's influence and believes that pressure from the right of his coalition and industrialists pushed him towards stabilisation (Mouré, 'Stabilisation Poincaré', pp. 251–3).

55 Moreau, *Souvenirs*, p. 60.
56 *Ibid.*, 15, 19, 23 November, pp. 160, 164.
57 In preparation for the 1927 budget debate, Poincaré had the finance ministry prepare a document showing the French budget deficits from 1918 to 1926, corrected to include 'budgets extraordinaires, comptes spéciaux etc.'. These figures give a much truer picture of the real state of France's income and expenditure account than those traditionally used by economic historians:

1918 deficit 49,858 million francs
1919 deficit 42,601 million francs
1920 deficit 25,171 million francs
1921 deficit 16,726 million francs
1922 deficit 13,715 million francs
1923 deficit 10,233 million francs
1924 deficit   3,455 million francs
1925 deficit   1,195 million francs
1926 surplus   362 million francs

AEF, B 33985, Fonds Administration Générale: Cabinet, Budget de 1927.
58 Miquel, *Poincaré*, pp. 576.
59 See the article and cartoons by P. Pagnotta, 'Raymond Poincaré à travers l'iconographie satirique' in J. Lanher and N. Cazin (eds.), *Raymond Poincaré, un homme d'état lorrain, 1860–1934* (Bar-le-Duc, 1989), pp. 69–100, esp. pp. 74, 95–7.
60 Poincaré, *Œuvre financière*, pp. 9–212.
61 See AEF, B 32335, Fonds Trésor, Bulletins mensuels de la Direction Générale du Mouvement des Fonds, no. 6, 10 June 1927, p. 4; no. 11, 20 January 1928, p. 4. These extremely informative secret bulletins on French financial policy were started on 10 January 1927 for internal ministry use and use by France's financial attachés.
62 *Ibid.*, bulletin no. 11, 20 January 1928, p. 6.
63 Jeanneney, *Leçon d'histoire*, pp. 42, 48; J-N. Jeanneney, *L'argent caché. Mileux d'affaires et pouvoirs politiques dans la France du XXe siècle* (Paris, 1981), pp. 199–203; Schuker, *End of French predominance*, pp. 89–108.
64 Cahiers inédits de François de Wendel, C.XIII, 11 March 1924, quoted in Jeanneney, *L'argent caché*, pp. 202–3.
65 On this see Jeanneney, who provides both corroborative evidence for a German strategy and suspicion as to the motives of the supplier of the document, *L'argent caché*, p. 204; Schuker, *End of French predominance*, pp. 95–8; for French intelligence reports on Germany's encouragement of left-wing parties in France, see MAE, Europe 1918–40, Allemagne, vol. 414, 'Propagande et espionnage allemands en France, février 1919 – octobre 1929', ff. 160, 166, 173–4; for French reports on foreign speculative action against the franc, see MAE, Série Y, Internationale 1918–40, vol. 226, Finances publiques françaises.
66 See diplomatic dispatches and intelligence reports by the deuxième bureau of the war ministry in MAE, Série Y, Internationale 1918–40, vol. 226, Finances publiques françaises.

67 H. Pouyanne in *Bulletin de la Chambre de Commerce de Londres*, October 1928, p. 207. I am grateful to Jean-Marc Pennetier for this information.

68 AEF, B 32335, Fonds Trésor, Bulletins mensuels DGMF, no. 6, 10 June 1927, p. 4.

69 On the impression that 'Anglo-Saxon' finance was partly to blame, see Jeanneney, *Leçon d'histoire*, p. 48; Jeanneney, *L'argent caché*, pp. 201, 205–6, 215, 218, though he believes that French speculators were most to blame; Miquel, *Poincaré*, p. 494; Schuker, *End of French predominance*, pp. 98–102 for evidence of British willingness to use the franc as leverage over France.

70 Quoted in Schuker, *End of French predominance*, p. 103; Jeanneney, *L'argent caché*, pp. 205–6.

71 For further examples of British desires to use the franc as a diplomatic weapon, Schuker, *End of French predominance*, pp. 98–104.

72 Poincaré to Briand, 24 February 1928, no. 56, MAE, Série Y, Internationale 1918–40, vol. 226, Finances publiques françaises, ff. 159–71.

73 Moreau, *Souvenirs*, 8 June 1928, p. 581.

74 *Ibid.*, pp. xii–xiii.

75 Maier, *Recasting bourgeois Europe*, p. 506.

76 Miquel, *Poincaré*, pp. 594–6.

77 Analysis of US press reactions to the stabilisation of the franc by the financial attaché of the French embassy in Washington for the president of the council, 28 June 1928; cutting from *L'information financière*, 26 June 1928, all in AEF, B 32315, Fonds Trésor, dossier 'Presse. Questions monétaires: stabilisation du franc: 1928'.

78 Peretti de la Rocca (French ambassador in Spain) to Briand, 26 June 1928, MAE Série Y, Internationale 1918–40, vol. 226, f. 171.

79 J. M. Keynes, 'The stabilization of the franc', *The New Republic* 55 (18 July 1928), p. 218, quoted in Kent, *Spoils of War*, p. 268.

80 Thomas J. Sargent, 'Stopping moderate inflations: the methods of Poincaré and Thatcher' in Rudiger Dornbusch and Mario Henrique Simonsen (eds.), *Inflation, debt and indexation* (Cambridge, Mass., 1983). On the new economic studies on the 'Poincaré miracle', see Mouré, 'Stabilisation Poincaré', pp. 229–45.

81 The French Treasury had worried about the long-term inflationary tendencies of the growth of the money supply resulting from the Bank of France's policy of printing francs to absorb foreign currencies in order to maintain the *de facto* stabilisation of the franc. See AEF, Fonds Trésor, B32335, Bulletin mensuel de la DGMF no. 11, 20 January 1928.

82 Caron, *Economic history of France*, p. 252.

83 Mettas, 'L'entre-deux-guerres', p. 527.

84 Chastenet, *Poincaré*, pp. 273–5.

85 Becker and Berstein, *Victoire et frustrations*, pp. 303–8.

86 Quoted in Miquel, *Poincaré*, p. 586.

87 Becker and Berstein, *Victoire et frustrations*, p. 303

88 *Ibid.*, pp. 309–10.

89 Chastenet, *Poincaré*, pp. 279–81; Miquel, *Poincaré*, pp. 598–9.

90 Chastenet, *Poincaré*, p. 282.

91 Jeanneney, *L'argent caché*, pp. 341–2.

92 See, for instance, the letters to Poincaré when president of the Republic from Hippolyte Hamard regarding 'subventions', apparently at Poincaré's behest, to the *Courrier du Parlement* and *Politique Etrangère*, Papiers Poincaré, BN nafr 16003, Correspondance, 'Lettres adressées à Raymond Poincaré', Hamard to Poincaré, no date [October 1913], 31 October 1913, 3 January 1918.

93 Chastenet, *Poincaré*, p. 283.

94 Quoted in Miquel, *Poincaré*, p. 602.

95 Becker and Berstein, *Victoire et frustrations*, pp. 312–13.

96 Chastenet, *Poincaré*, p. 285.

97 *Ibid.*, pp. 286–91.

98 *Le Temps*, 17, 18 October 1934.

99 Chastenet, *Poincaré*, pp. 292–3; *Le Temps*, 17 October 1934.

100 J-B. Duroselle, *Clemenceau* (Paris, 1988), pp. 951–2.

CONCLUSION: POINCARÉ REMEMBERED

1 G. Gallup (ed.), *The Gallup International opinion polls*, vol. I: *France, 1939, 1944–67* (Westport, Conn., 1976) pp. 116–17, 593.

2 René Rémond, *Notre siècle. 1918–1988* (Paris, 1988), pp. 60–1.

3 Colette Ysmal, *Le comportement électoral des Français* (Paris, 1986), p. 52.

4 See the stimulating prologue to J. C. Fest, *Hitler* (Harmondsworth, 1982), 'Hitler and historical greatness', pp. 3–9.

Select bibliography

This is by necessity a 'select' bibliography, as all modern bibliographies are becoming. It would be unreasonable to cite all works which refer to Poincaré, let alone those dealing with events with which he was involved: the origins of the First World War alone accounts for some 25,000 titles. Works cited are therefore usually those cited in the text.

MANUSCRIPTS

ARCHIVES NATIONALES

Papiers Deschanel, 151 AP 44
Papiers Gérard, 329 AP 20

BIBLIOTHÈQUE NATIONALE (PARIS)

Papiers Raymond Poincaré:
Correspondance (nafr 15992–16023, also 16827, 24544 etc.)
Notes journalières, 1912–15, 1919, 1924, 1929, (nafr 16024–16034)
Œuvres. Varia (nafr 16055).
Registres et carnets (nafr 16056–16063).

Papiers Joseph Reinach:
Correspondance, nafr 24884 etc.

BIBLIOTHÈQUE DE L'INSTITUT DE FRANCE (PARIS)

Papiers Stephen Pichon

MINISTÈRE DES AFFAIRES ETRANGÈRES (MAE)

Country volumes in the Nouvelle série reliée: e.g. Russia.
Série, Europe 1918–1940, e.g. sous-série, Allemagne, vol. 327, Politique
    intérieure: responsabilité de la guerre.
Série Y, Internationale 1918–40, e.g. Finances publiques françaises.

Papiers d'agent, Archives privées (AP):
Jules Cambon
Paul Cambon
Abel Ferry
Auguste Gérard
Georges Louis
Pierre de Margerie
Alexandre Millerand
Maurice Paléologue

Dossiers personnels:
Philippe Berthelot

Paul and Jules Cambon papers in the hands of the family
Alexandre Millerand, 'Mes souvenirs', unpublished memoirs in the hands of the
    family.

PUBLIC RECORD OFFICE (LONDON)

Grey MSS
Bertie MSS

MUSÉE RAYMOND POINCARÉ (SAMPIGNY, MEUSE)(AM)

General Poincaré memorabilia including an audio recording of a speech.
Bulletin de notes de R. Poincaré, school marks on loan from the Archives
    départementales de la Meuse.

BIBLIOTHÈQUE DE L'ORDRE DES AVOCATS (PARIS)

Numerous 'Manuscrits de jeunesse' (diaries, travel notes, catechism lessons,
    school-work, literary essays etc) e.g. *Journal personnel 1871* (novembre) –
    1872 (mai).
Documents et objets concernant Poincaré avocat.
Documents et objets concernant Poincaré homme politique et personnalité
    publique (1905–1919 and no date).

MINISTÈRE DE L'ECONOMIE ET DES FINANCES (PARIS)

Archives Economiques et Financières (AEF)
Fonds Administration Générale, e.g. Bureau du Cabinet B 13382.
Fonds Trésor, e.g. Bulletins mensuels de la DGMF B 32335.

PRINTED DOCUMENTS

Annuaire Général des Finances
Annuaire Diplomatique et Consulaire
Bulletin de la Chambre de Commerce de Londres

Chambre des députés, rapport fait au nom de la commission chargée de réunir et de publier les programmes électoraux des candidats aux élections législatives (Le Barodet)

British documents on foreign affairs: reports and papers from the foreign office confidential print, K. Bourne and D. C. Watt (general eds.), series F, *Europe 1848–1914,* J. F. V. Keiger and D. Stevenson (eds.), vols. 1–35, (Frederick, Md., 1987–92).

L'Allemagne et les problèmes de la paix pendant la Première Guerre mondiale. Documents extraits des archives de l'office allemand des affaires étrangères (edited by A. Scherer and J. Grunewald) vol. I *Des origines à la déclaration de guerre sous-marine (août 1914–31 janvier 1917)* (Paris, 1962); vol. II *De la guerre sous-marine à outrance à la révolution soviétique (1er février 1917–7 novembre 1917)* (Paris, 1966).

Documents diplomatiques français, 1871–1914, Ministère des affaires etrangères, 2e and 3e séries, Paris, 1930–53.

Journal Officiel de la République Française:
Débats Parlementaires (Chambre des Députés), *JODebPC.*
Documents Parlementaires (Sénat), *JODocPS.*

Marchand, R.,(ed.), *Un livre noir: diplomatie d'avant guerre d'après les documents des archives russes (1910–1917)* (Paris, 1922–3).

WORKS BY POINCARÉ CITED IN TEXT

(For an exhaustive list of Poincaré's publications see the bibliography by Pierre Miquel, *Poincaré* (Paris, 1961), pp. 619–24).

Poincaré, R. *Idées contemporaines* (Paris, 1906).
Questions et figures politiques (Paris, 1907).
L'idée de Patrie (Paris, 1910).
Ce que demande la cité (Paris, 1912).
How France is governed (trans. B. Miall, London, 1913).
'Address delivered by Raymond Poincaré, lord rector of the University of Glasgow', 13 November 1919 (Paris, 1919), pp. 1–13.
L'Œuvre financière et économique du Gouvernement. Discours prononcé à la Chambre des Députés par Monsieur Raymond Poincaré 2 et 3 février 1928 (Paris, 1928).
Au service de la France. Neuf années de souvenirs (10 vols., Paris, 1926–33).
  1 *Le lendemain d'Agadir, 1912* (1926)
  2 *Les Balkans en feu, 1912* (1926)
  3 *L'Europe sous les armes, 1913* (1926)
  4 *L'Union sacrée, 1914* (1927)
  5 *L'Invasion, 1914* (1928)
  6 *Les Tranchées, 1915* (1930)
  7 *Guerre de siège, 1915* (1931)
  8 *Verdun, 1916* (1931)
  9 *L'année trouble, 1917* (1932)
  10 *Victoire et Armistice, 1918* (1933)
A la recherche de la paix, 1919 (ed, J. Bariéty and P. Miquel, Paris, 1974).
Comment fut déclarée la guerre de 1914 (Paris, 1939).

394   Select bibliography

MEMOIRS

Alexandre, General, *Avec Joffre d'Agadir à Verdun* (Paris, 1932).

Anon *Raymond Poincaré: a sketch* (London, 1914).

Caillaux, J. *Mes mémoires* (3 vols., Paris, 1942–7).

Cambon, P. *Correspondance, 1870–1924* (3 vols., Paris, 1940–6).

Chastenet, J. *Raymond Poincaré* (Paris, 1948).

Clemenceau, G. *Grandeurs et misères d'une victoire* (Paris, 1930).

Collingnon, A. 'Chez les ancêtres maternels de Raymond Poincaré. Souvenirs de Nubécourt' in *Le Pays Lorrain* 12 (December1934).

Daudet, A. *Le nain de Lorraine. Raymond Poincaré* (Paris, 1930).

Dupin, G. *Les responsabilités de la guerre* (Paris, 1926).

Fabre-Luce, A. *La Victoire* (Paris, 1924).

Foch, F. *Mémoires pour servir à l'histoire de la guerre de 1914–1918* (2 vols., Paris, 1931).

François-Poncet, A. 'Poincaré tel que je l'ai vu', *Le Figaro Littéraire* 16 June 1948.

Gérard, A. *Mémoires d'Auguste Gérard* (Paris, 1928).

Giraudoux, J. *Bella* (Paris, 1926).

Gordon Lennox, Lady Algernon (ed.), *The diary of Lord Bertie of Thame, 1914–18* (London, 1931).

Goutennoire de Toury, F. *Poincaré a-t-il voulu la guerre?* (Paris, 1920).

Grey of Fallodon, Viscount, *Twenty-five years, 1892–1916*, vol. I (London, 1925).

Hanotaux, G. *Raymond Poincaré* (Paris, 1934).

Herriot, E. *Jadis* (2 vols., Paris, 1948).

Hommage à Poincaré (Paris, 1950).

Laroche, J. *Au Quai d'Orsay avec Briand et Poincaré, 1913–1926* (Paris, 1957).

Lavisse, E. *Discours de réception à l'Académie française* 9 December 1909 (Paris, 1909).

Louis, G. *Les carnets de Georges Louis*, vol. II (Paris, 1926).

Messimy, A. *Mes souvenirs* (Paris, 1937).

Moreau, E. *Souvenirs d'un gouverneur de la Banque de France. Histoire de la stabilisation du franc (1926–1928)* (Paris, 1954).

Mordacq, General, *Le Ministère Clemenceau. Journal d'un témoin* (4 vols., Paris, 1930–1).

Paléologue, M. *Au Quai d'Orsay à la veille de la tourmente* (Paris, 1947).

Payen, F. *Raymond Poincaré, chez lui, au parlement, au palais* (Paris, 1936).

de Peretti de la Rocca, E. 'Briand et Poincaré: souvenirs', *Revue de Paris* 15 December 1936, pp. 775–88.

Persil, R. *Alexandre Millerand* (Paris, 1949).

Ribot, A. *Journal de Alexandre Ribot et correspondances inédites, 1914–1922* (Paris, 1936).

Saint Aulaire, Comte de, *Confession d'un vieux diplomate* (Paris, 1953).

Samné, G. *Raymond Poincaré; politique et personnel de la IIIe République* (Paris, 1933).

Suarez, G. *De Poincaré à Poincaré* (Paris, 1928).

Briand (4 vols., Paris, 1940).

Tardieu, A. *La Paix* (Paris, 1921).

Weygand, M. *Mémoires* (2 vols., Paris, 1957).
Wormser, G. *La République de Clemenceau* (Paris, 1961).
Le septennat de Poincaré (Paris, 1977).

PRINCIPAL SECONDARY SOURCES

Adamthwaite, A. *Grandeur and misery. France's bid for power in Europe 1914–1940* (London, 1995).
Agulhon, M. 'Le sang des bêtes', *Romantismes* 31 (1981), pp. 81–109.
Albertini, L. *The origins of the war of 1914* (3 vols., London, 1965).
Allain, J-C. *Agadir 1911* (Paris, 1976).
  Joseph Caillaux vol. I: *Le défi victorieux, 1863–1914* (Paris, 1978); vol. II: *L'oracle, 1914–1944* (Paris, 1981).
Amalvi, C. 'Nationalist responses to the Revolution' in R. Tombs (ed.) *Nationhood and nationalism in France. From Boulangism to the Great War 1889–1918* (London, 1991), pp. 39–49.
Anderson, R. D. *France 1870–1914. Politics and society* (London, 1977).
Andrew, C. M. *Théophile Delcassé and the making of the Entente Cordiale* (London, 1968).
  'Déchiffrement et diplomatie: le cabinet noir du Quai d'Orsay sous la Troisième République', *Relations Internationales* 5 (1976), pp. 37–64.
  Secret service. The making of the British intelligence community (London, 1986).
Andrew, C. M. and Kanya-Forstner, A. S. *France overseas, the Great War and the climax of French imperial expansion* (London, 1981).
Artaud, D. *La question des dettes inter-alliées et la reconstruction de l'Europe 1917–1929* (Paris, 1976).
Audoin-Rouzeau, S. *1870 La France dans la guerre* (Paris, 1989).
Avril, P. *Politics in France* (London, 1969).
Baratay, E. 'Les controverses contemporaines sur le statut de l'animal: l'exemple de l'Eglise Catholique, France, 1940–1990', *Revue d'Histoire Moderne et Contemporaine* 41 (3), (juillet-septembre 1994), pp. 499–514.
Bard, C. 'Les luttes contre le suffrage unisexuel sous la Troisième Ré-mi-publique', *Modern and Contemporary France* vol. NS3 (2) (1995).
Bardoux, J. *Le socialisme au pouvoir, l'expérience de 1924* (Firmin-Didiot, 1930).
Bariéty, J. *Les relations franco-allemandes après la première guerre mondiale, 10 novembre 1918–10 janvier 1925: de l'exécution à la négociation* (Paris, 1977).
Barjonet, A. *La CGT, Histoire, structure, doctrine* (Paris, 1968).
Barnes, H. E. *The genesis of the World War* (New York, 1926).
Barthou, L. *Le politique* (Paris, 1923).
Becker, J-J. *1914 comment les Français sont entrés dans la guerre* (Paris, 1977).
  The Great War and the French people (Leamington Spa, 1985).
Becker, J-J. and Audoin-Rouzeau S. (eds.), *Les sociétés européennes et la guerre de 1914–1918* (Nanterre, 1990).
Becker, J-J. and Berstein, S. *Victoire et frustrations, 1914–1929* (Paris, 1990).
Berstein, S. *Histoire du Parti Radical* (2 vols., Paris, 1980–2).
  Edouard Herriot ou la République en personne (Paris, 1985).
Bonnefous, G. and E. *Histoire politique de la Troisième République* (7 vols., Paris, 1956–67).

Booth, A. 'The unsettling of boundaries, lines, and divisions in Tennyson's *Idylls of the King*' (Ph.D., Salford, forthcoming).

Bridge, F. R. *From Sadowa to Sarajevo: the foreign policy of Austria–Hungary, 1886–1914* (London, 1972).

Bredin, J-D. *The Affair. The case of Alfred Dreyfus* (London, 1987).

Brogan, D. *The development of Modern France, 1870–1939* (London, 1940).

Buchan, J. *Oliver Cromwell* (London, 1941).

Bury, J. P. T. *France 1814–1940* (London, 1969).

Bury, J. P. T. and Tombs, R. P. *Thiers 1797–1877. A political life* (London, 1986).

Carley, M. J. *Revolution and intervention: the French government and the Russian Civil War, 1917–1919* (Kingston, 1983).

'The shoe on the other foot: a letter from Raymond Poincaré to Alexandre Millerand, December 1922', *Canadian Journal of History* 26(3) (December 1991), pp. 583–7.

Caron, F. *An economic history of modern France* (London, 1979).

Carroll, E. M. *French public opinion and foreign affairs, 1870–1914* (London, 1931).

Charle, C. *Les élites de la République, 1880–1900* (Paris, 1987).

Debize, C. ' "Art Nouveau" en Meuse: quelques jalons pour baliser un territoire de recherches' in J. Lanher and N. Cazin (eds.), *Commercy à l'ère industrielle* (Bar-le-Duc, 1994), pp. 23–38.

Derfler, L. *Alexandre Millerand. The socialist years* (The Hague, 1977).

Deschodt, P-J. (ed.), *Cher Maître . . . Lettres à Charles Maurras* (Paris, 1995).

Doise, J. and Vaïse, M. *Diplomatie et outil militaire, 1871–1991* (Paris, 1992).

Droz, J. *Les causes de la Première Guerre mondiale, essai d'historiographie* (Paris, 1973).

Duroselle, J-B., *L'Europe de 1815 à nos jours* (Paris, 1970).

Clemenceau (Paris, 1988).

La Grande Guerre des Français, 1914–1918, L'incompréhensible (Paris, 1994).

Eichengreen, B. *Golden fetters: the Gold Standard and the Great Depression 1919–1939* (Oxford, 1992).

Estèbe, J. *Les ministres de la République, 1871–1914* (Paris, 1982).

'Barthou écrivain' in M. Papy (ed.), *Barthou, un homme, une époque* (Pau, 1986).

Farrar, M. M. *Principled pragmatist: the political career of Alexandre Millerand* (Oxford, 1991).

Fay, S. B. *The origins of the World War* (2 vols., New York, 1928).

Ferguson, N. *Paper and iron. Hamburg business and German politics in the era of inflation, 1897–1927* (Cambridge, 1995).

Fest, J. C. *Hitler* (Harmondsworth, 1982).

Flood, C. *Pensée politique et imagination historique dans l'œuvre de Paul Claudel* (Paris, 1991).

Flood, P. J. *France 1914–18. Public opinion and the war effort* (London, 1990).

Gallup, G. (ed.), *The Gallup International opinion polls* vol. I: *France, 1939, 1944–67* (Westport, Conn., 1976).

Gerbod, P. 'The baccalaureate and its role in the recruitment and formation of French elites in the nineteenth century' in J. Howarth and P. Cerny (eds.) *Elites in France: origins, reproduction and power* (London, 1981), pp. 46–56.

Girardet, R. *Le nationalisme français* (Paris, 1983).

Mythes et mythologies politiques (Paris, 1986).

Godfrey, J. F. *Capitalism at war. Industrial policy and bureaucracy in France, 1914–1918* (Leamington Spa, 1987).

Goguel, F. *La politique des partis sous la troisième République* (3rd edn, Paris, 1958).

Goldey, D. B. 'The disintegration of the Cartel des Gauches and the politics of French government finance, 1924–28' (unpublished D.Phil. dissertation, Oxford University, 1962).

Goldstein, E. *British diplomatic strategy, peace planning, and the Paris peace conference, 1916–1920* (Oxford, 1991).

Guèrard, A. *Personal equation* (New York, 1948).

Gueslin, A. *L'invention de l'économie sociale: le XIXe siècle français* (Paris, 1987).

Guillen, P. 'Les questions coloniales dans les relations franco-allemandes à la veille de la première guerre mondiale', *La Revue Historique* 248 (1972).

Guinn, P. 'On throwing ballast in foreign policy: Poincaré, the Entente and the Ruhr', *European History Quarterly* 18 (1988), pp. 427–37.

Guiral, P. and Thuillier, G. *La vie quotidienne des députés en France de 1871 à 1914* (Paris, 1980).

Hayward, J. *Governing France: the one and indivisible French Republic* (2nd edn, London 1987).

Hoffmann, S. *Sur la France* (Paris, 1976).

Irvine, W. D. *The Boulanger Affair reconsidered: royalism, Boulangism and the origins of the radical right in France* (Oxford, 1988).

Isaac, J. *Un débat historique, 1914: le problème des origines de la guerre* (Paris, 1933).

Jacobson, J. *Locarno diplomacy: Germany and the West, 1925–1929* (Princeton, 1977).

'Is there a new international history of the 1920s?', *American Historical Review* 88 (1983), pp. 617–45.

'Strategies of French foreign policy after World War I', *Journal of Modern History* 55(1) (1983), pp. 78–95.

Jeanneney, J-N. *François de Wendel en République: l'argent et le pouvoir, 1914–1940* (Paris, 1976).

Leçon d'histoire pour une gauche au pouvoir. La faillite du Cartel 1924–1926 (Paris, 1977).

L'argent caché. Milieux d'affaires et pouvoirs politiques dans la France du XXe siècle (Paris, 1981).

Jolly, J. (ed.), *Dictionnaire des parlementaires français. Notices biographiques sur les ministres, députés et sénateurs français de 1889 à 1940* (7 vols., Paris, 1960–72).

Keiger, J. F. V. 'Jules Cambon and Franco-German détente, 1907–14', *The Historical Journal* 26(3) (1983), pp. 641–59.

France and the origins of the First World War (London, 1983).

'Britain's "union sacrée" in 1914' in J-J. Becker and S. Audoin-Rouzeau (eds.), *Les sociétés européennes et la guerre de 1914–1918* (Nanterre, 1990), pp. 39–52.

'Patriotism, politics and policy in the French foreign ministry, 1880–1914' in

R. Tombs (ed.), *Nationhood and nationalism. From Boulangism to the Great War 1889–1918* (London, 1991), pp. 225–66.

'France' in K. Wilson (ed.), *1914: Decisions for war. The management of an international Crisis* (London, 1995), pp. 121–41.

Kemp, T. *Economic forces in French history* (London, 1971).

Kent, B. *The spoils of war. The politics, economics, and diplomacy of reparations 1918–1932* (Oxford, 1989).

Keylor, W. R. *Jacques Bainville and the renaissance of royalist history in twentieth-century France* (Baton Rouge, 1979).

Kiernan, V. G. *The duel in European history. Honour and the reign of aristocracy* (Oxford, (paperback edn), 1989).

Kriegel, A. and Becker, J-J. *1914: la guerre et le mouvement ouvrier français* (Paris, 1964).

Krumeich, G. *Armaments and politics in France on the eve of the First World War* (Leamington Spa, 1984).

'Poincare vu de l'Allemagne avant et après la guerre de 1914–1918' in J. Lanher and N. Cazin (eds.), *Raymond Poincaré, un homme d'état lorrain 1860–1934* (Bar-le-Duc, 1989), pp. 127–37.

'Joan of Arc between right and left' in R. Tombs (ed.), *Nationhood and nationalism in France. From Boulangism to the Great War 1889–1918* (London, 1991), pp. 63–73.

Langdon, J. W. *July 1914. The long debate, 1918–1990* (Oxford, 1991).

Lanher, J. and Cazin, N. (eds.) *Raymond Poincaré, un homme d'état lorrain 1860–1934* (Bar-le-Duc, 1989).

Lawrence, J., Dean, M. and Robert, J-L. 'The outbreak of war and the urban economy: Paris, Berlin, and London in 1914', *Economic History Review* 45(3) (2nd ser., August 1992).

Levillain, P. 'Les protagonistes de la biographie' in R. Rémond (ed.), *Pour une histoire politique* (Paris, 1988), pp. 121–59.

Lieven, D. C. B. *Russia and the origins of the First World War* (London, 1983).

Maier, C. *Recasting bourgeois Europe: stabilisation in France and Italy after World War I* (Princeton, 1975).

Martet, J. *Le Tigre* (Paris, 1930).

May, E. R. (ed.), *Knowing one's enemies: intelligence assessment before the two World Wars* (Harvard, 1984).

Mayeur, J-M. *La vie politique sous la Troisième République* (Paris, 1984).

'Louis Barthou et la "question religieuse"' in M. Papy (ed.), *Barthou, un homme, une époque* (Pau, 1986), pp. 139–51.

McDougal, W. A. *France's Rhineland diplomacy, 1914–1924. The last bid for a balance of power in Europe* (Princeton, 1978).

McManners, J. *Church and State in France, 1870–1914* (London, 1972).

McMillan, J. *Dreyfus to De Gaulle: politics and society in France 1898–1969* (London, 1985).

Mettas, J. 'L'entre-deux-guerres. 1919–1939. Des illusions de la Victoire à la "drôle de guerre"' in G. Duby (ed.), *Histoire de la France* (Paris, 1970), pp. 524–42.

Michel, M. *Galliéni* (Paris, 1989).

Milza, P. 'L'ultra-droite des années trente' in M. Winock (ed.), *Histoire de l'extrême droite en France* (Paris, 1993).

Ministère de l'economic et des finances *Les ministres des finances de 1870 à nos jours* (Paris, 1992).

Miquel, P. *Poincaré* (Paris, 1961).

La Paix de Versailles et l'opinion publique française (Paris, 1972).

Mouré, K. *Managing the franc Poincaré. Economic understanding and political constraint in French monetary policy, 1928–1936* (Cambridge, 1991).

'La stabilisation Poincaré: situation politique et politique monétaire entre 1926 et 1928' in *Etudes et Documents* (Comité pour l'histoire économique et financière) 7 (1995), pp. 229–65.

Nicolet, C. *L'idée républicaine en France (1789–1924). Essai d'histoire critique* (Paris, 1982).

Nye, R. *Masculinity and male codes of honour in modern France* (Oxford, 1993).

Pagnotta, P. 'Raymond Poincaré à travers l'iconographie satirique' in J. Lanher and N. Cazin (eds.), *Raymond Poincaré, un homme d'état lorrain 1860–1934* (Bar-le-Duc, 1989), pp. 69–100.

Pedroncini, G. *Les mutineries de 1917* (Paris, 1967).

Poidevin, R. and Bariéty, J. *Les relations franco-allemandes, 1815–1975* (Paris, 1977).

Prost, A. *Les anciens combattants* (Paris, 1977).

Rémond, R. *La Droite en France* vol. I (Paris, 1968).

Les Droites en France (Paris, 1982).

Notre siècle. 1918–1988 (Paris, 1988).

Rémond, R. (ed.), *Pour une histoire politique* (Paris, 1988).

Robbins, K. *Sir Edward Grey. A biography of Lord Grey of Fallodon* (London, 1971).

Roth, F. 'Poincaré et la République' in J. Lanher and N .Cazin (eds.), *Raymond Poincaré, un homme d'état lorrain, 1860–1934* (Bar-le-Duc, 1989), pp. 101–14.

Rousseau, G. 'Impressions dans la tourmente. Le journal d'Etienne Clémentel dans l'été 1914', *Guerres Mondiales* 156 (1989), pp. 89–103.

'Le Conseil des ministres en 1916 d'après les notes d'Etienne Clémentel', *Guerres Mondiales et Conflits Contemporains* 171 (1993), pp. 139–60.

Salviac, M. 'L'entrée en politique de Raymond Poincaré (1886–1889)' in J. Lanher and N. Cazin (eds.), *Raymond Poincaré, un homme d'état lorrain 1860–1934* (Bar-le-Duc, 1989), pp. 21–36.

Sauvy, A. *Histoire économique de la France entre les guerres* (3 vols., Paris, 1965–72).

Schuker, S. *The end of French predominance in Europe. The financial crisis of 1924 and the adoption of the Dawes Plan* (Chapel Hill, 1976).

Sharp, A. *The Versailles settlement: peacemaking in Paris* (London, 1991).

Shorrock, W. I. *French imperialism in the Middle East* (London, 1976).

Silverman, D. P. *Reconstructing Europe after the Great War* (Cambridge, Mass., 1982).

Sirinelli, J-F. (ed.) *Histoire des droites en France* (3 vols., Paris, 1992).

Soutou, G. *L'or et le sang. Les buts de guerre économiques de la Première Guerre mondiale* (Paris, 1989).

Sorlin, P. *Waldeck-Rousseau* (Paris, 1966).

Steiner, Z. *Britain and the origins of the First World War* (London, 1977).

Stengers, J. '1914: the safety of ciphers and the outbreak of the First World War' in C. Andrew and J. Noakes, *Intelligence and international relations* (Exeter, 1987), pp. 29–48.

Stevenson, D. *French war aims against Germany, 1914–19* (Oxford, 1982).

'French war aims and the American challenge, 1914–1918', *The Historical Journal* 22(4) (1979).

The First World War and international politics (Oxford, 1988).

Taylor, A. J. P. *Struggle for mastery in Europe, 1848–1918* (Oxford, paperback edn, 1973).

Thobie, J. *Intérêts et impérialisme français dans l'empire ottoman (1895–1914)* (Paris, 1977).

Tombs, R. *France, 1814–1914* (London, 1996).

Tombs, R. (ed.), *Nationhood and nationalism in France. From Boulangism to the Great War 1889–1918* (London, 1991).

Trachtenberg, M. *Reparation in world politics: France and European economic diplomacy, 1916–1923* (New York, 1980).

Watson, D. R. *Georges Clemenceau: a political biography* (London, 1974).

Weber, E. *L'Action française* (Paris, 1985).

Wileman, D. G. 'Not the Radical republic: liberal ideology and central blandishment in France 1901–1914', *The Historical Journal* 37(3) 1994.

Wilson, K. *A study in the history and politics of the Morning Post 1905–1926*, Studies in British History vol. 23 (Lampeter, 1990).

Winock, M. 'L'Action française' in M. Winock (ed.), *Histoire de l'extrème droite en France* (Paris, 1993).

Winter, J. and Robert, J-L. *Paris, London, Berlin 1914–1919: capital cities at war* (Cambridge, 1997).

Wright, G. *Raymond Poincaré and the French presidency* (Stanford, 1942).

Young, R. *Power and pleasure. Louis Barthou and the Third French Republic* (Montreal, 1991).

Ysmal, C. *Le comportement électoral des Français* (Paris, 1986).

Zeldin, T. *France 1848–1945* vol. I: *Ambition, love and politics* (2 vols., Oxford, 1973).

Index

401